The Design of Sites

Second Edition

The Design of Sites

Patterns for Creating Winning Web Sites

Second Edition

DOUGLAS K. VAN DUYNE
JAMES A. LANDAY
JASON I. HONG

PRENTICE
HALL

Upper Saddle River, NJ • Boston • Indianapolis • San Francisco
New York • Toronto • Montreal • London • Munich • Paris
Madrid • Capetown • Sydney • Tokyo • Singapore • Mexico City

Many of the designations used by manufacturers and sellers to distinguish their products are claimed as trademarks. Where those designations appear in this book, and the publisher was aware of a trademark claim, the designations have been printed with initial capital letters or in all capitals.

The authors and publisher have taken care in the preparation of this book, but make no expressed or implied warranty of any kind and assume no responsibility for errors or omissions. No liability is assumed for incidental or consequential damages in connection with or arising out of the use of the information or programs contained herein.

The publisher offers excellent discounts on this book when ordered in quantity for bulk purchases or special sales, which may include electronic versions and/or custom covers and content particular to your business, training goals, marketing focus, and branding interests. For more information, please contact:

U.S. Corporate and Government Sales
(800) 382-3419
corpsales@pearsontechgroup.com

For sales outside the United States, please contact:

International Sales
international@pearsoned.com

Visit us on the Web: www.prenhallprofessional.com

Library of Congress Cataloging-in-Publication Data

Van Duyne, Douglas K., 1966–
  The design of sites : patterns for creating winning websites / Douglas K. van Duyne,
James A. Landay, Jason I. Hong.—2nd ed.
    p. cm.
  Includes bibliographical references and index.
  ISBN 0-13-134555-9 (pbk. : alk. paper)
  1. Web sites—Design. I. Landay, James A., 1967- II. Hong, Jason I., 1975- III. Title.

TK5105.888.V36 2006
006.7—dc22

                                            2006026285

ISBN 0-13-134555-9
Text printed in the United States on recycled paper at RR Donnelley in Crawfordsville, Indiana.
First printing, December 2006

Contents at a Glance

Contents

Foreword

In 1979, Christopher Alexander wrote his seminal book, *A Pattern Language*, in which he introduced an innovative yet practical language for architecture, building, and planning. Since then the concept has been applied to other domains, from computer science to user interface design. The fact that what began as an architectural concept has been extended and is still in use today is a testament to its value and validity. Simply put, a design pattern is a generic solution to a commonly recurring problem, whether for software, buildings, landscaping, or Web design.

Design patterns are particularly relevant to Web design because they are so critical to usability. One of the tenets to building a usable product is to support users' mental models for how things should work. Consistency reinforces and helps build ease of use into a product as users learn over time how to navigate the product and build a mental model for how to perform tasks. Design patterns are a means for capturing such best practices and provide a guide for implementing solutions in a consistent manner.

Design patterns can also help an organization scale as it grows. As former vice president of the User Experience and Design group at Yahoo!, I was faced with the challenge of creating effective designs for our ever-expanding suite of products and services with limited budget and head count. With the team growing rapidly and organized along separate product lines, designers increasingly worked independently of each other, and yet I found many to be solving the same design problems. Harvesting and implementing best practices became critical to Yahoo!'s ability to deliver quality design efficiently and consistently. Moreover, with Web design patterns established, the front-end engineers could create reusable, modular code, thereby improving quality and speeding up our development time as well as design time.

The authors of *The Design of Sites* often cite Yahoo! in their examples. These designs were based on extensive usability and ethnographic research, capturing the best practices identified. With Yahoo!'s broad product offering, the team has encountered almost every major consumer product and interface issue. With this book as a reference, you can benefit from what companies like Yahoo! have learned and apply them to your site, even if you don't have a design and research team similarly sized and staffed.

User interactions on the Web are fluid and seamless. With a single click of the mouse, a user can be on a completely different site, which could have its own look and feel and interaction model. Thus, it is more important than ever that the design community understands, applies, and participates in the development of Web design patterns. The more widely common design patterns are used across the Web, the easier the Web will be for users. And that is a good thing for everyone.

To be sure, design patterns are no substitute for thoughtful design, which takes into consideration the constraints and context of its application. But design patterns should be the starting point for anyone designing Web sites and should be followed whenever possible. Designers can start with something known to work and modify or refine it as needed. Time saved from not having to reinvent the wheel frees up designers' time to focus on product-specific issues and innovations. *The Design of Sites* forms the basis of how to think about design problems. It serves as a common language for designers to think about problems, develop solutions, and share ideas.

As vast as the Internet is, many Web design problems are repeated at varying levels. For example, at the architectural level, whether a Web site is content, community, communications, or commerce oriented, design patterns can help guide designers to identify problems and to make decisions critical to the success of the overall execution of the product's strategy. At the user interface level, design patterns help build consistency in the interaction model for completing tasks, thus improving ease of use.

van Duyne, Landay, and Hong, recognizing the various levels at which design patterns can be applied, have captured a wide range of Web design related patterns, and organized them accordingly in this book. The patterns are cross-referenced and many patterns are used in combination with each other. Each pattern is illustrated with examples from a variety of well-known sites with clear descriptions for the rationale, appropriate uses, and pitfalls. As the language of Web design is still evolving, this edition has been updated with patterns that reflect the rapidly changing landscape of Web design. Given the increasing ubiquity of mobile devices and their uses, the authors have also added an entirely new section on mobile design patterns. This unique, comprehensive, and thoughtfully organized book is an invaluable resource for Web design professionals.

—Irene Au
Director of User Experience, Google
Former Vice President of User Experience and Design, Yahoo!

Preface

Four years ago, we began this book with a story of a man who discovers a talking dog. When asked what the dog said, the man replied, "Who cares? It's a talking dog!" For several years after its inception in the early 1990s, the Web was the talking dog, fascinating in its very existence. Then businesspeople discovered that they could sell things using the Web, without paying the huge production and distribution fees that print and television advertising required. Web sites became commercial ventures almost overnight, and a period of rapid evolution began for this new medium. As the Web evolved, the problems faced by its developers were the same ones faced by any industry as it matures: people started to care more about factors like value, convenience, and ease of use than about the novelty of the technology itself. A new term, *customer-centered design,* was coined in an attempt to deal with this change in priorities.

For Douglas van Duyne, James Landay, and Jason Hong, customer-centered design wasn't always a hot topic for e-business. Eight years ago, when we were an entrepreneur with a software design background, a Berkeley computer science professor, and a doctoral graduate student, we had a vision to provide much-needed customer insights to businesses developing for the new medium of the Web. Although the vision eventually resulted in a thriving Web development business and this book, we had many questions to answer along the way. As part of our research into why most Web sites failed to meet customer expectations, we became very interested in how typical design agencies went about their work, and why companies hired outside Web site design firms instead of creating sites themselves.

To help answer these questions, we sent researchers to interview Web designers and their clients. We learned that companies hired design agencies on the basis of their previous work building recognizable brands.

At the time, Web designers distinguished themselves through awards and accolades, not by measured success with real customers. This pattern began to make sense only when we learned that most Web designers got into the business after working in print, film, or television, all non-interactive media. At that time, few tools existed to help designers understand the Web customer experience. In fact, when we studied a new client's site, we could see that the business was suffering, but now we knew it was because of the original designer's blindness to the distinctions of interaction design, along with a tradition that often put form over function.

This scenario became clear in our daily work. We were brought in to assess tough site design problems and fix them. We saw client after client with site designs that were failing, even though all the essentials appeared to be in place. During one such project, when we were testing a client's large-scale e-commerce site, we asked typical site visitors to locate a specific product. Our client had designed the site internally and their designers knew how to find everything, so they were confident that customers could do the same. To the test subjects, however, the product descriptions were cryptic, the navigation controls were unclear, and trying to find a single product resulted in pages and pages of choices. Upon completion of the test, almost all the participants reported success, but in actuality, only a scant few had found the correct product. A site design that was clear to its designers was so confusing to the customers that they did not even know they had failed. As a result of our efforts, the client was able to see that the site had been designed in a vacuum. Only through iterative design and rigorous testing were we able to create a site that was as usable as it was attractive.

Well, a funny thing has happened since those early years. Customer-centered design has risen from obscurity to the forefront of Web site development. During that time, we have used the research tools and methodologies that we developed to iteratively design sites for some of the best-known and best-managed companies in the world. Each in our own way, we've followed our original vision. **Douglas K. van Duyne,** entrepreneur and software designer, is a founder and principal of Naviscent, a Web research and design firm. **James A. Landay** is a professor of computer science at the University of Washington and previously served as the director of Intel Research Seattle, which focuses on the new world of ubiquitous computing. **Jason I. Hong** is a computer science professor at the Human-Computer Interaction Institute of Carnegie Mellon University.

In these roles we have personally met with hundreds of executives to talk about their business models, market strategies, and, of course, Web site development plans. We have found that as Web businesses have matured, organizations have realized the need to focus on improving the customer experience. In fact, we have discovered that the more senior the executive we speak with is, the clearer the mandate for a customer-centered design approach becomes.

This focus on customer-centered design is not limited to our experience. Recently e-business analysts have started evaluating design firms less on their brand design work, concentrating more on the efficacy of their Web customer experience. However, despite the new standards, reviews of top design firms have shown surprising results. Although many of the biggest Web agencies promise to include customer testing as part of their site design services, analysis has concluded their designs do not consistently provide a better customer experience.[1] Much progress is still needed.

Today companies seem to have an almost unquenchable thirst for customer-centered design knowledge, expertise, methodologies, and work practices. The purpose of this book is to help satisfy some of that need, drawing on our years of experience at Naviscent, UC Berkeley, the University of Washington, and Carnegie Mellon, and working on Web research and design projects for more than three hundred clients. We hope that, by keeping the book current with the state of customer-centered Web design as it exists today, we can do our part to ensure that the evolution of the medium continues unabated.

New in the Second Edition

After publication of the first edition, we met and talked with many readers and instructors about their use of the book. A couple of consistent threads of conversation led us to embark on this second edition. One thing people appreciated in the first edition was the breadth of topics in one place. But, it seemed, we managed to miss a couple of important patterns here and there. Readers helped us by suggesting patterns we didn't include in the first edition, like PROGRESS BAR (H13).

Another important factor that influenced the content of this new edition was the development of two important new Web technologies:

---

1 From H. Manning, *The Forrester Wave™: Web Design Agencies Q3, 2005* (Forrester Research, 2005) (www.forrester.com/Research/Document/Excerpt/0,7211,36045,00.html).

AJAX-based interfaces and Mobile Web. With AJAX (Asynchronous JavaScript And XML), interaction techniques previously available only in desktop applications, such as direct manipulation, could now be used to design enhanced Web sites and applications, broadening designer choices. As mobile phone usage has continued to climb, phone browser technology has improved. The Mobile Web creates new opportunities for businesses, and new design challenges. Several new patterns in this edition cover the Mobile Web space.

In addition to the many new patterns in this edition, we've updated other patterns to reflect these technology changes, as well as to provide additional insights that we've learned along the way. In fact, more than one-third of the content of this second edition of the book is either new or updated.

Why Use This Book?

You're probably wondering how this book is any different from the numerous other Web design books out there. This unique book is not about programming or any specific technology. Nor is it a quick fix for all of the problems you and your team will face in developing a Web site. No single book can do that. What this book does offer are principles, processes, and patterns to help you develop successful customer-centered Web sites. With this customer-centered focus, your Web site can be relevant, self-explanatory, and easy to use.

Creating a Web site is easy. Creating a successful Web site that provides a winning experience for your target audience is another story, and that's what this book is about. And when you're finished reading it, it will be a valuable reference tool to keep on your desk. You can turn to it again and again as you design, redesign, and evaluate sites.

Your target customers[2] will differ. Depending on your business, they might be members in a club, students of a university, concerned citizens, or paying shoppers. The goals of each of these audiences will also vary, but the challenge for you is the same: creating an interactive interface that provides tangible value to the people who go to your site.

The patterns in this book provide you and your team with a common language to articulate an infinite variety of Web designs. We developed the language because we saw people solving the same design problems

---

2 We use the term *customers* to mean any person who will use the Web site that you're designing. We use the term *clients* to mean the people for whom you're doing the work, the people providing the funding.

over and over at great time and expense. The patterns examine solutions to these problems. We present the best practices from our consulting experience, our research experience, and our Web development experience—gathered in one place. In *The Design of Sites,* we give you the tools to understand your customers better, help you design sites that your customers will find effective and easy to use, shorten your development schedules, and reduce maintenance costs.

If you do not have "customers," think of *target audiences.* One focus of the book is the design of e-commerce Web sites; however, you can successfully apply the majority of the content to make any Web site better.

Who Should Read This Book?

This book is written for anyone involved in the design and implementation of a Web site. Its focus is tilted more toward Web design professionals, such as interaction designers, usability engineers, information architects, and visual designers. But this book is also written to be a resource for anyone on a Web development team, from business executives to advertising managers to software developers to content editors. The best possible team will understand and buy into the customer-centered design philosophy because every person on the team influences how the Web site is shaped and formed.

Web Design Professionals

Start with Chapters 1 and 2 to understand the motivation for customer-centered design and the patterns approach to Web design. If you already have a strong background in the principles (Chapters 3 and 4) and processes (Chapter 5) of customer-centered design, you can skim these chapters and move quickly to the patterns themselves (Part II of the book). If you have less experience, the three chapters on customer-centered design and development (3 through 5) should prove useful for whatever kind of Web site you're developing.

Business Managers

Read Chapters 1 through 5 to understand the business consequences of ignoring customer-centered design, as well as to learn the principles and processes required to build a customer-centered site. E-commerce sites pose the greatest risk of project failure. These chapters describe techniques that you can use to reduce this risk, decrease feature creep, and minimize implementation and maintenance costs. Customer-centered design will also help you shorten development schedules and increase overall customer satisfaction—and consequently client satisfaction too.

Business Clients

If you are the client who funds development of a Web site, read the first five chapters. Because you're paying, you will be especially interested in why there is such an urgent need for a strong customer focus, and in what steps design teams can take to ensure that your customers' needs are met. You will see why these steps will actually reduce your costs and create happier, more loyal customers.

Benefits of Using *The Design of Sites*

We know that improving your customers' Web experience will take more than reading this book. The principles, processes, and patterns in this book are not a magic solution to your problems. However, by putting them into practice in the design and evaluation of your Web sites, you will improve the overall customer experience. Success requires an extreme focus on customer needs, but one that will pay off in the long run. Your work will result in improved customer satisfaction, a balanced approach to Web design, and incremental improvement of design practices, as described in the sections that follow.

Improved Customer Satisfaction

By focusing on your customers throughout the development process, you will discover their needs, design Web sites for those needs, and evaluate your designs to ensure that those needs are met. You will test your site iteratively with representative customers to make certain that you work out the majority of problems *before* they cause serious problems and *before* they become expensive to fix. Customer-centered design concentrates on making sure that you're building the right features on your Web site, and that you're building those features right!

Balanced Approach to Web Design

Too many books read like ancient scripture, as in, "Thou shalt do this" and "Thou shalt not do that." Such approaches are too dogmatic for Web design, which needs to be flexible and adaptable to a wide range of situations. The Web has led to more customer diversity, as well as a wider range of customer goals and tasks than was common in the past. We acknowledge, however, that customer needs must also be balanced with your business goals, usability requirements, aesthetics, and technological constraints.

That's why we have aimed for general principles, processes, and patterns that can be applied to many Web site genres. We have integrated the three in one book because each is part of a comprehensive solution: The patterns provide a language for building Web sites; the principles and processes provide instructions for how to use the language.

Incremental Improvement of Design Practices

It is unlikely that anyone has time to read and put into practice an entire book about designing customer-centered Web sites in a short period of time. So we have divided this book into many small, digestible parts. The first five chapters describe the key ideas behind customer-centered design. The rest of the book is devoted to Web design patterns that can be applied to practically any Web site. You can skip around, mix and match, skim, and sample what you need. *This is not a book that you must read sequentially from cover to cover.*

The ideas in this book do not require wholesale adoption. You can take small parts at a time and try them out to see what works for you. In fact, we encourage many small steps instead of a few big leaps because it takes time to become practiced in the many ideas presented here. For example, you could improve your design practices by using the design patterns that make up the bulk of this book. Or you could use just some of the techniques described in the first part of the book, such as observing some representative customers using your site. Though often a humbling process, making such observations will help ground your intuitions of the way your customers think, and in the long run improve the overall design of your site.

Conventions Used in This Book

The following typographic conventions are used in this book:

- **Web pages and Web sites** that we reference are set in blue text.
- **Pattern names** are identified as follows:

(A2) PATTERN NAME (A2)

where the letter in parentheses represents the pattern group and the number is the pattern number. In this example, *A2* means the second pattern in pattern group A. Each use of a pattern in the text is also accompanied by a color-coded, circular icon in the margin (as illustrated to the left of the pattern name example above). The color indicates the pattern group. These icons are also shown on each page of the respective pattern.

- **Chapter and pattern group names** are also represented in the book by color-coded icons. The first five chapters are represented by square icons with the chapter number inside the square, and the pattern groups are represented by diamond-shaped icons with the group letter inside the diamond. For example, in the margin here are the icons associated with Chapter 1 and Pattern Group C, respectively. Throughout the book, such icons are shown in the margin of the text wherever a specific chapter or pattern group is mentioned.
- **Code examples** are set in `constant-width type`.
- **HTML tags and attributes** are enclosed in angle brackets (for example, <meta>).

Disclaimer

We use many screen shots of Web sites in this book to illustrate examples of good and not so good design. We offer kudos to the Web teams and companies that made the good designs. However, the examples of not so good design should not be construed as attacks on the Web sites in question or on the companies responsible for those sites. Wrestling the technological, economic, and organizational beasts can be quite an endeavor, and change can be slow, even in Internet time. Besides, we are all still learning. We are all in this together.

We Would Like to Hear from You

Please send us your comments, questions, and any corrections. Although we cannot update your copy, we will organize your feedback at www. designofsites.com/feedback.

We are especially interested in finding out how well particular patterns worked for you and in hearing your suggestions for improving them. We plan to share new patterns that you have discovered with other readers of the book!

You can reach us at doug@naviscent.com, landay@cs.washington.edu, and jasonh@cs.cmu.edu, or through our publisher at AWPro@aw.com.

Douglas K. van Duyne
James A. Landay
Jason I. Hong

October 2006

Acknowledgments

We give thanks to all the designers who have come before us, our spouses, the team of dedicated visionaries at Naviscent, and our colleagues and students at the University of California, Berkeley, Carnegie Mellon University, and the University of Washington, who gave us feedback on this book. We would especially like to thank Mark Newman, whose study of Web designers was the basis for the design process that we describe in Chapter 5. We thank the people who participated in the CHI 2000 Workshop on Design Patterns for their comments on our early ideas. We also thank Christopher Alexander, who originally developed the concept of design patterns in *A Pattern Language: Towns, Buildings, Construction* (Oxford University Press, 1977).

Several people helped with the final production of the book. We would like to thank publisher Mark L. Taub at Prentice Hall. Thanks especially to Dianne Jacob for helping create the proposal and editing many versions of the book. Thanks to Julie Nahil for smoothing the production of the book, which was also much improved by Stephanie Hiebert, who copyedited our manuscript. Special thanks to Colleen Stokes for her initial cover and pattern format designs. Thanks to Sarah Vilaysom for her extensive help with collecting, editing, organizing, and managing the images in the book. And thanks to Matthew Tarpy for his help in collecting several of the screen shots illustrating the patterns and to Kathleen Karcher for obtaining permissions to use these images here. Thanks also to Craig Zacker for drafting assistance. Finally, we appreciate the many reviewers who gave us great feedback on the drafts of this work, including Mitchel Ahern, Linda Brigman, Marc Campbell, Claudia Case, John Cilio, Sunny Consolvo, Sally Fincher, Åsa Granlund, Jeff Johnson, Jef Raskin, Ross Teague, Ken Trant, Maya Venkatraman, Pawan Vora, John Wegis, and Terry Winograd.

Foundations of Web Site Design

Customer-Centered Web Design: More Than a Good Idea

The World Wide Web is no longer a novelty. To many companies and organizations, the Web is a necessity, the foundation of their businesses. As the cost of maintaining a customer service operation increases, the ability of Web site visitors to find information and complete specific tasks themselves can easily mean the difference between profit and loss. Customer-centered Web site design is therefore no longer a luxury adopted only by forward-thinking companies with a special interest in customer satisfaction.

Many of the design elements presented in this book are now the minimum requirements for an effective, professional Web site. As you work your way through the patterns that we discuss, consider how many high-quality sites you've seen that use the techniques described, and how much thought must have gone into their development. Implementing a customer-centered design is relatively easy when you have examples to work from and a wheel that has already been invented.

In this chapter you will discover the thinking behind customer-centered design and learn how to apply it to your projects using the principles, processes, and patterns that we present throughout this book.

1.1 The Evolution of Web Design

First Generation

The mantra was "build it, and they will come." Talented individuals and large teams alike built Web sites. These creative and visionary people managed everything from business planning to graphic design and software development in this new medium. Once having built the site, though, all they could say was that they had a Web site. They could not say how their site was performing from the customer's perspective, or how the site was related to the business's bottom line.

Second Generation

The mantra was "advertise that you sell it online, and they will come." Start-ups invested large amounts of capital in expensive ads to draw visitors to their e-commerce sites. Even established companies put ".com" on their letterhead and ran costly campaigns to let people know they hadn't been left behind.

Unfortunately, this strategy did not work, because Web design was complex and still misunderstood. *For the first time, organizations were building interactive computer interfaces to their products and services.* This task proved to be difficult to execute well. Building a Web site too quickly, in fact, made its probability of being both compelling and easy to use practically zero.

Third Generation

With the first edition of this book we helped shift the mantra to "customer-centered design"—to constructing powerful Web sites that provide real value and deliver a positive customer experience.[1] When visitors consistently give a Web site high marks for content, ease of use, performance, trustworthiness (as well as other indicators of brand value), and overall satisfaction, we call it a **customer-centered Web site.** Consideration of these additional factors is what differentiates customer-centered design from other design approaches (see Figure 1.1).

Fourth Generation

Today new technologies and business models have resulted in more innovative designs, but they also present greater challenges for building

---

[1] We use the term *customer* rather than *user* for three reasons. First, only two types of businesspeople refer to their customers as *users:* drug dealers and computer companies. Second, and more importantly, the term *customer* evokes the idea that successful Web sites account for issues that go beyond ease of use and satisfaction, such as trustworthiness, brand value, and even how well a company's traditional interactions with the customer work, such as telephone-based customer service or the return of merchandise. Finally, taking a cue from Beyer and Holtzblatt's *Contextual Design,* we use *customer* to refer to anyone who uses or *depends* on the site. Customers can be administrators, partners, managers, and producers, among others. To manage the site, many of these individuals will see a completely different interface. We chose the term *customer* because it is more expansive than *user,* referring to all of these individuals and their myriad needs.

Figure 1.1

The key issues driving customer-centered Web design.

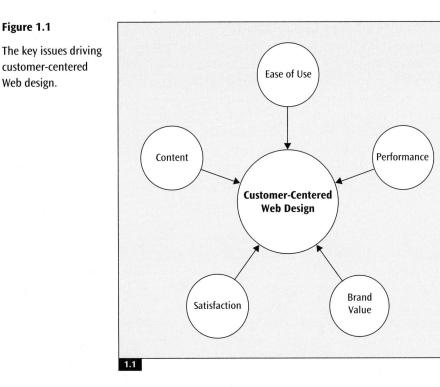

1.1

customer-centered Web sites. With the advent of AJAX (Asynchronous JavaScript And XML), the Mobile Web, and other Web 2.0 capabilities, sites can now provide features that are more compelling, more powerful, easier to access, and easier to use. However, building better interfaces now requires skills that are more specialized and harder than ever to acquire. In this edition of the book, we provide additional design patterns that enable you to build these customer experience–enhancing capabilities into your Web sites.

The challenge to be customer centered exists for all enterprises: large multinationals, government agencies, internal corporate services, small businesses, and nonprofit organizations, to name just a few. General Motors, for example, must manage its customer experience for more than three hundred end-customer, supplier, and distributor Web sites. Government sites, with responsibilities to help the citizenry and other agencies, need to satisfy "customer" requirements as well. Intranet applications that optimize a corporation's workforce must provide positive experiences to employee "customers."

The Importance of Customer-Centered Design

Over the years we have learned that the criteria for building customer-centered Web sites are based on providing a positive experience for all customers, whether those customers are there to find information, to be part of a community, to purchase items, or to be entertained. This focus is called **customer-centered design.** Customer-centered design increases the value of Web sites through better design and evaluation. It is about how you empathize with customers—how well you understand their needs, the tools and technologies they use, and their social and organizational context. It is about how you use this understanding to shape your designs and then test those designs to ensure that the customers' needs are met.

Why go to all this trouble? What will happen if you don't? Suppose your site overruns its budget or schedule. Management could pull the plug before it is completed. Or what if your Web site is finished but turns out to be too hard to learn or use? Customers might visit your site once and never return.

With customer-centered design, you do the work up front to ensure that the Web site has the features customers need, by determining and planning for the most important features and by making certain that those features are built in a way that customers will understand. This method actually takes less time and money to implement in the long run. In short, customer-centered design helps you build the right Web site and build the Web site right!

Here's an example that underscores the importance of customer-centered design. Several years ago, IBM found that its Web site was not working well. Quick analysis revealed that the search feature was the most used function. The site was so confusing that IBM's customers could not figure out how to find what they wanted. IBM also discovered that the help feature was the second most popular function. Because the search feature was ineffective, many people went to the help pages to find assistance. Paying close attention to customer needs, IBM redesigned the site from the ground up to be more consistent in its navigation. A week after launching the redesigned site, customers' reliance on the search and help features dropped dramatically and online sales rose 400 percent.

This is just one of many stories highlighting the increasing importance of good design. But does good Web design really affect the bottom line? You bet! Web sites founded on solid fundamentals and extensive customer research can make the difference between success and failure. A clear, easy-to-use, and customer-centered Web site can help garner better reviews and ratings, reduce the number of mistakes made by customers, trim the time it takes to find things, and increase overall customer satisfaction. Furthermore, customers who really like a Web site's content and quality of service are more likely to tell their family, friends, and coworkers, thereby increasing the number of potential customers. A great example of this result is Google, which has become the dominant search site with little or no advertising. It simply works better than most other search sites, and customers tell their friends about it.

There is also a strong correlation between increased satisfaction and increased profits for commercial Web sites. Underscoring this point, our research shows that increasing customer satisfaction by just 5 percent can lead to a 25 percent or greater increase in revenues. There are two reasons for the revenue increase and the related increase in profits. The first is that customers can find products and services more easily and are thus more likely to return in the future. The second is that support costs are reduced because of a lower number of phone calls, e-mails, and instant messages to help desks, as well as a lower number of product returns.

The stakes are higher now than ever before. Commercial Web sites that are not relevant, fast, trustworthy, satisfying, and easy to use will have a hard time attracting new customers and retaining existing customers, especially if competitors are only a click away.

Providing Tangible Value

Yahoo! is one of the top Web sites today, and it's likely to remain near the top for the foreseeable future. Why? Is it because it has slick graphic design? Hardly. Yahoo!'s homepage uses graphical images sparingly, and most of its other pages have even fewer. Even though Yahoo! was once pointed to as the poster child of boring interfaces, its mostly text interface still is very quick to load because it has so few graphics. So why is Yahoo! so popular? It's pretty simple actually: Yahoo! provides quality services that are useful, fast to download, and easy to use. One of the reasons it is such a popular Web site is that interaction design and usability research are integral parts of Yahoo!'s development process. Yahoo! identifies its customer needs through field studies, interviews, and usability evaluations, and then it tailors its designs to match those needs.

People will leave your Web site if they

- Are frustrated
- Think that navigating the site is too difficult
- Think that you don't have the product or service they want
- Get big surprises that they don't like
- Feel that the site takes too long to load

You cannot afford to abandon a single customer.

Even if your site does not have direct competitors, as is the case with educational institutions and corporate intranets, it can benefit from being customer centered. Simple, clean, and well-designed Web sites can cut down on wasted time for customers, reduce Web site maintenance costs for clients, and improve overall satisfaction.

Our First Steps toward Unifying Design, Usability, and Marketing   1.3

In 1997 we noticed that a few companies had dramatically jumped ahead of the competition and were now leaders on the Web. These companies had publicly stated and acted on making the customer experience their top priority, and they raised the bar for everyone.

While we were actively helping clients develop sites in an ever more competitive environment, we realized we had to move beyond the traditional boundaries of usability, market research, and software design. It was not an easy task, because our clients had committed to these means at varying levels, in different parts of the organization that usually did not talk to one another.

Drawing on our experience in design, consulting, marketing, communications, and human–computer interaction research, we evaluated our clients' Web sites on many levels. We discovered that although a customer focus existed, often it was not reflected on the Web sites. We also discovered that some clients were not improving the customer experience on their Web sites at all. This was not surprising, considering that these companies did not have a clear Web strategy. It was not uncommon for a client's Web design team to have an inadequate budget and little authority to integrate operations with the rest of the company.

Sometimes our clients were simply too busy trying to stay afloat to care about getting a full wind in their sails. One Web business we studied thought that it was doing very well with its health-related news, information, and products. It was receiving thousands of Web-based orders per week. It spent heavily on advertising to draw people to its site, and as advertising spending increased, so did sales. Our team evaluated the ease of use of the site, doing some customer research over a short period of time (later we'll explain how you can run studies like this yourself). We looked at many factors, from first impression, to ease of use, to overall satisfaction.

We found some surprising results that led us to important conclusions. The developers of the site had done a great job of creating a powerful first impression. All the customers in our research panel liked the site, thought it looked easy to use, and said it appeared to have relevant content.

Next, however, we asked the same customers to use the site to carry out a realistic task: finding products for the common cold. Only 30 percent of the customers could find any products at all for colds, or for any other medical condition. This research suggested that about 70 percent of customers who came to the site to solve particular health problems could not find what they were looking for, revealing that, despite the company's perception that its Web site was serving it well, a substantial amount of revenue was being lost to user interface problems. The cost of dissatisfied customers' abandonment of this site could have reached into the millions of dollars over the course of a year.

Our experience with the health site is not uncommon. The bottom line is that poorly designed Web sites frustrate people, fritter away customer loyalty, and waste everyone's time.

1.4 Why We Prefer Customer-Centered Design

One way to explain the value of customer-centered design is to compare it to other design styles. In this section we look at four styles centering in turn on the user, the company, technology, and the designer.

User-Centered Design

Customer-centered design is most closely related to what is known as **user-centered design,** an effort pioneered in the 1980s for engineering useful and usable computer systems. Customer-centered design builds on user-centered design, addressing concerns that go beyond ease of use and satisfaction. In particular, it also focuses on the fusion of marketing issues with usability issues.

On the Web it is much easier to get an audience than by traditional means, but a trickier goal is to convert Web site visitors to customers and keep them coming back. Unlike someone selling shrink-wrapped software to a customer who buys before using it, you want to convince Web site visitors to become customers while at the same time making their first use enjoyable. Pay special attention to business goals, marketing goals, usability goals, and customer experience goals. These goals often conflict with each other, and you will be able to find a balance among them only if you are aware of them all at once. These issues are much more intertwined and harder to design for on the Web than for shrink-wrapped software.

Company-Centered Design

A style that used to be quite popular among Fortune 500 companies is what we call **company-centered design.** Here the needs and interests of the company dominate the structure and content of the Web site. The fatal flaw is that what companies think should be on a Web site is not necessarily what customers need or want. You have probably seen Web sites that are organized by internal corporate structure, with sparse information about the products and services they offer. These kinds of sites are derisively termed **brochureware.** They contain little useful information and completely ignore the unique capabilities of the Web as a medium. Brochureware sites are acceptable only if they are a short-term first step toward more sophisticated and more useful sites.

Another example of company-centered design is the use of jargon known only to those in the business. When one of our friends wanted to buy a digital camera, he turned to the Web for information. As an amateur, he wanted a camera that was easy to use, one that would help him take clear pictures. Most of the sites he found, though, bombarded him with terms like *CCDs, FireWire, PC card slots,* and *uncompressed TIFF mode.* The fact that he didn't know what these terms meant embarrassed him. He was put off and confused. The companies had made the wrong assumption about their customers' knowledge. None of them answered the simple question of which camera was best for amateurs. This is an example of why company-centered design is almost always a bad style.

Technology-Centered Design

Sites constructed on the basis of **technology-centered design** are often built with little up-front research about business needs and customer needs—just a lot of hacking and caffeine. We have all seen Web sites like this—the ones overloaded with animation, audio, video, and streaming banners. The problem with this approach is that it often results in an amateurish Web site that is not useful, usable, or desirable. Technology-centered Web sites were pervasive in the early days of the Web, but thankfully they are becoming less common as the Web matures.

Designer-Centered Design

Designer-centered design (also known as *ego-centered design*) is still popular in certain circles. One designer was quoted in a popular industry rag as saying, "What the client sometimes doesn't understand is the less they talk to us, the better it is. We know what's best." This is exactly what we mean by *designer-centered design.*

Don't get us wrong, though. Some design teams have deep-seated creative urges that are matched only by their incredible technical ability. They can create sites that are cool, edgy, and loaded with the latest technologies. Sometimes this is exactly the image a company wants to project. Unfortunately, such sites can also be slow to download and hard to use, and they may not work in all Web browsers. Designer-centered design is fine for some art Web sites, but not for e-commerce or informational sites whose livelihood depends on a large number of repeat visitors.

The Advantages of Customer-Centered Design

In company-centered design, designers give no thought to why people would visit the company's Web site and what they would want to do there. In technology-centered design, technology is an end rather than a means of accomplishing an end. In designer-centered design, the needs of other people are given less importance than the creative and expressive needs of the design team. Contrast these styles with customer-centered design, which emphasizes customers and their tasks above all, and sees technology as a tool that can empower people.

Company-centered, technology-centered, and designer-centered design styles were understandable in the early days of the Web, when designers were still finding their way. In the old worldview, few people really considered what customers wanted. Now, successful and easy-to-use sites like amazon.com, yahoo.com, flickr.com, and ebay.com are designed from the ground up to meet the needs of their customers. In the new worldview, your careful consideration of customers, as reflected in your Web site, will help you achieve long-lasting success.

Top Ten Signs That Things Are Going Badly

1. "Customers? Our Web site is already intuitive and user-friendly."
2. "We need to start doing some usability tests before our launch next month."
3. "We can use [*XML/SOAP/insert other buzzword technology*] to fix that."
4. "If you stop and think about how the interface works for a second, it makes complete sense."
5. "How can our customers be so stupid? It's so obvious!"
6. "Well, they should read the fantastic manual."
7. "We don't need to do any user testing. I'm a user, and I find it easy to use."
8. "We'll just put an 'Under Construction' sign there."
9. "Shrink the fonts more so that we can put more content at the top."
10. "We need a splash screen."

Nine Myths of Customer-Centered Design   1.5

Why are there so many organizations that do not embrace customer-centered design? In this section we will try to dispel the myths that keep companies from moving forward with customer-centered design.

Myth 1: Good Design Is Just Common Sense

If Web site design is just common sense, why are there so many bad Web sites? Thinking that design is just common sense leads us to think that we know what everyone needs and wants. Time and time again, however, this notion has been shown to be incorrect.

Web design teams always have to keep in mind that they are not the customers. They cannot always predict the way customers will think or act. In addition, they know too much about how the Web site works. They cannot look at it in the same way that customers will. They can avoid this problem by observing and talking to customers and getting feedback from them as often as possible.

Myth 2: Only Experts Create Good Designs

Although experts might apply customer-centered design techniques more quickly or conduct more rigorous analyses, anyone can understand and use these techniques. Anyone devoted to the process can create a good design.

Myth 3: Web Interfaces Can Be Redesigned Right before Launch

Sentiments like "we'll spend a few days working on our site's interface" or "we'll solve the interface problems after all the programming is done" are common. However, these ideas assume that the Web site has the right features and that those features are being built correctly. These are two very risky assumptions that can be costly to fix, especially if the Web site is near completion. Customer-centered design helps minimize these risks by getting constant feedback on designs so that the Web site will be in good shape the day it is launched.

Myth 4: Good Design Takes Too Long and Costs Too Much

Customer-centered design does add some up-front costs because you will be talking to customers, creating prototypes, getting feedback on those prototypes, and so on. However, customer-centered design can considerably reduce **back-end costs**—that is, costs incurred as a result of responding to customer dissatisfaction through help desk calls, returned purchases, general Web site maintenance, and so on. Evaluate the trade-off between spending more time and money at the start of your project and losing revenue over the long run.

Customer-centered design can even reduce the total development time and cost because it focuses on finding problems in the early stages of design when they are still easy to repair, preventing them from ever causing serious problems that are time-consuming and expensive to fix. Of course, your team will not always have the time and budget to do everything possible, so throughout this text we try to identify the trade-offs among the different actions you can take to improve your site. This book discusses many effective approaches that you can use to test your assumptions and to test your Web site, to make sure that it is a winner in the long run.

Myth 5: Good Design Is Just Cool Graphics

An aesthetically pleasing design is an important part of any Web site because it helps communicate how to use a particular interface and it conveys a certain impression. However, graphics are only one part of the larger picture of what to communicate and how. Customer-centered design takes into account what customers want, what they understand, the tasks they perform, and the context in which they do things. Cool graphics by themselves do not address these issues.

Myth 6: Web Interface Guidelines Will Guide You to Good Designs

Web interface guidelines are a good checklist to ensure that the final design has no obvious minor problems. However, guidelines address only how a Web site is implemented. They do not address what features a Web site should have, the overall organization of the Web site, or the flow between individual Web pages. In contrast, the design patterns described in this book are generative. Using them will help you create solutions to your design problems. Furthermore, guidelines do not address the trade-offs of Web site development. Customer-centered principles, processes, and patterns, on the other hand, do take these issues into account.

Myth 7: Customers Can Always Rely on Documentation and Help

Documentation and help are important, but customers are unlikely to be patient enough to sift through a great deal of documentation just to use a Web site. Documentation and help are the last resorts of a frustrated customer.

Think about it this way: When was the last time you read a help page? Did you wish the design team had gone the extra mile in the first place to make using the site straightforward so that you would not need to read the help? Customer-centered design provides tools to see the world from your customers' eyes, to help you understand their worldview, and then to design Web sites to fit their needs.

Myth 8: Market Research Reveals All Customer Needs

Although market research is invaluable for helping to understand customer attitudes and intentions, it does not suffice when it comes to understanding customer behavior. Be careful also about using market research to create lists of customer feature requests. Implementing a laundry list of new features might satisfy customers who have asked for a particular feature, but all these features are more likely to get in the way of offering most of your customers a satisfying and successful customer experience.

What customers say in a market research study can be useful, but when it comes to interfaces, what they *do* is critical. That's why market research must be balanced with direct observation. A customer-centered design team uses a variety of techniques—from observations to interviews—to elicit true customer needs and focus on the areas that will be the most important for most customers.

Myth 9: Quality Assurance Groups Ensure That Web Sites Work Well

Software testing is key to ensuring that you are not launching a buggy, poorly performing site. Although quality assurance is important, its purpose and focus are different from those of customer-centered design. Software testing is often technology driven rather than customer driven. Expert testers try to make sure the product does what the specification says it should. This is different from seeing what happens with real customers working on real problems.

More importantly, Web sites often are tested only *after* being built. At that point it's too late to make major changes. Software testing can help you find and fix only coding mistakes, not major design mistakes. Customer-centered design, in contrast, focuses on quality from the very start—before anyone has written a line of code.

1.6   Applying Customer-Centered Design

Over time we have evaluated the best practices to use when designing powerful, compelling, and useful interactive Web sites. We realize that designers need concepts that they can quickly integrate into their Web site design practices, as well as a process that can be applied universally, from entertainment sites to e-commerce sites, from sites for informal clubs to sites for large corporations. Our experiences, research, and discussions with other Web designers have helped us refine our ideas on customer-centered design into three parts: principles, processes, and patterns.

Principles

Principles are high-level concepts that guide the entire design process and help you stay focused. For example, as we state in one of our key principles, you must acquire a deep understanding of your customers' needs. Another major principle is to design your Web site iteratively, moving from rough cuts to refined prototypes, before creating the production Web site. These principles—described in Chapters 3 (Knowing Your Customers: Principles and Techniques) and 4 (Involving Customers with Iterative Design)—can be applied to any design problem and are the foundation for the patterns that we describe in the second half of the book.

Processes

Processes are how you put the principles into practice. In Chapter 5 (Processes for Developing Customer-Centered Sites), we describe our Web site development process, providing a guide that explains the major steps and milestones for developing a Web site. We also provide a collection of how-to tips, such as how to conduct a focus group, how to run a survey, and how to conduct a usability test (most of these tips are included in the appendixes). If your firm has similar processes, use Chapter 5 to update your process so that the key principles of customer-centered design are supported.

Patterns

Design **patterns** solve recurring design problems, so you can use pattern solutions to design your sites without reinventing the wheel. Patterns are a **language,** a common vocabulary that allows you and your team to articulate an infinite variety of Web designs.

These patterns let you focus your energies on solving new problems, rather than addressing problems that have been worked out hundreds of times before. But design patterns do not make cookie-cutter sites—far from it. Because no two businesses are the same, we created the design patterns for you to tailor to your particular business needs. This book shows you how to create an overall solution that works for your customers and your business.

Using the Principles, Processes, and Patterns

Design is about making informed trade-offs between competing constraints. Customer-centered design tries to make these trade-offs clearer, but only you can solve the problems. The principles help you decide between different process activities at a particular stage of your project. For example, in evaluating whether to iterate on a paper design one more time or to build a high-fidelity version of the design, you might decide to stick with paper because you can easily bring in potential customers to evaluate the design.

You can also use the principles to help you decide among the different design solutions that you developed using the patterns. Say, for example, that you're not sure whether your branding is prominent enough during checkout on your site. You could use online surveys, a common tool of market researchers, to quickly see what potential customers think.

Take-away Ideas   1.7 _____

Your opportunities on the Web are vast, but so are the difficulties of delivering a site that customers will give high marks for content, ease of use, performance, trustworthiness (as well as other indicators of brand value), and overall satisfaction. These problems are not insurmountable if you solve them with the set of principles, processes, and patterns that we describe in this book.

In the rest of this book you will find more reasons to implement customer-centered design, descriptions of techniques to use in your current projects, and over a hundred design patterns proven to enhance your customers' experience. Guidelines for instituting customer-centered design will help you through the process.

This book is meant as the first step in an ongoing conversation to improve the Web. We have not identified all of the useful Web design patterns. New patterns will be found, and the patterns we describe here will evolve as new techniques are invented and customer knowledge and skills change. In fact, this second edition of the book adds 17 new patterns and includes major revisions to 25 of the existing patterns. We encourage you to join in the conversation and keep moving the Web toward the new, raised bar for success.

Making the Most of
Web Design Patterns

1 In Chapter 1 (Customer-Centered Web Design: More Than a Good Idea), we explained why designing for the customer experience is crucial to a Web site's success. We also introduced the notion of Web design patterns, a powerful conceptual framework for building compelling, effective, and easy-to-use Web sites. In this chapter we explain patterns in depth.

We do not expect you to read through all the patterns in this book from start to finish. Instead, we show you ways to explore the patterns so that you can quickly find the right ones for your needs.

2.1 What Are Patterns?

Patterns communicate insights into design problems, capturing the essence of the problems and their solutions in a compact form. They describe the problem in depth, the rationale for the solution, how to apply the solution, and some of the trade-offs in applying the solution.

Patterns were originally developed by the architect Christopher Alexander and his colleagues, in a 1977 groundbreaking book called *A Pattern Language: Towns, Buildings, Construction*. Patterns, Alexander said, can empower people by providing a living and shared language "for building and planning towns, neighborhoods, houses, gardens, and rooms." Alexander intended for everyday people to use patterns to guide the process of creation, whether designing a house for themselves or working with others to design offices and public spaces. By creating a common language, would-be designers could discuss and take part in the design of the spaces in which they worked, lived, and played. Alexander's patterns were also a reaction against contemporary architectural design, which he felt did not take enough of human needs, nature, growth, spirituality, and community into consideration.

Alexander's emphasis was on an entire language for design. He felt that individual, isolated patterns were of marginal value. By connecting related patterns, and by showing how they intertwine and affect one another, he believed he could create an entire pattern language that was greater than the sum of the individual parts.

Likewise, Web design patterns make up a *language* that you can use in your daily work. In fact, though you may not know it, you may already be using some form of pattern language to articulate and communicate your designs. The patterns might reflect your own experiences using the Web. You might have picked them up from another site. They might even come from an insight you learned from a successful design that you developed in the past.

Our Web design pattern language focuses on your customers and their needs. This book is a reaction to the multitude of design patterns implicitly in use that do not take a customer-centered design approach.

Many of our patterns reflect how your customers understand and interact with Web sites. When people go online, they don't start with a blank slate. They take with them all of their experiences, their know-how, and their understanding of how the world works. By now, most visitors to the Web recognize common signposts such as blue links and buttons, and well-known processes such as sign-in and shopping cart checkouts, as powerful ways of making any single site easy to use.

Some patterns reflect abstract qualities that make great Web sites—qualities such as value, trust, and reliability. You will integrate traits like these into the design of the entire Web site, and reaffirm and reinforce them at every point of contact with your customers. These patterns describe the essence of these abstract qualities and how they can be incorporated into the whole Web site.

A Sample Pattern

2.2

Let's start with a pattern that may already be familiar to you: ACTION BUTTONS (K4).[1] Action buttons solve a common problem that customers encounter on Web sites: knowing what can and cannot be clicked on. By adding shading to an otherwise flat button, you make it easier for people to find your links. This visual illusion works because it takes advantage of what people already know about physical buttons (see Figure 2.1).

(K4)

---

1   Patterns in this book are referenced in SMALL CAPITAL LETTERS. The part in parentheses in this case, "K4," means to go to Pattern Group K (Making Navigation Easy) and then to the fourth pattern in that section.

Figure 2.1

People know how to use three-dimensional buttons.

Figure 2.2

Buttons in modern graphical user interfaces appear three-dimensional, to make them look as if you can press them. You can take advantage of this knowledge by making the most important buttons on your Web site look three-dimensional too.

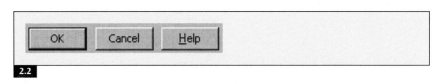

Figure 2.3

The gray **Search** button on the right is an example of an HTML action button. HTML action buttons can be specified in HTML and are created by the Web browser.

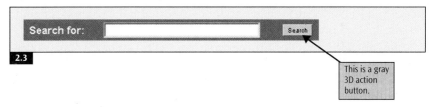

This is a gray 3D action button.

Graphical user interfaces have become another form of transferable knowledge. People who use computers learn that they can press on buttons with a mouse (see Figure 2.2). This becomes a learned behavior that can be transferred to how people perceive and interact with Web sites.

There are two kinds of ACTION BUTTONS (K4): HTML action buttons and graphical action buttons. HTML buttons are specified in HTML, so you have little control over how they're displayed. Figure 2.3 shows an example of an HTML button.

eBay.com and Amazon.com provide two examples of Web sites that use graphical action buttons on their homepages (see Figures 2.4 and 2.5). These buttons are often implemented as a single image that may contain multiple buttons.

Figure 2.4

eBay uses a graphical action button for the **REGISTER NOW** button.

(www.ebay.com, June 28, 2006)

Figure 2.5

Amazon.com uses graphical action buttons for its **Find Gifts** and **Web Search** features.

(www.amazon.com, June 15, 2006)

Making buttons look three-dimensional is not the end of the story, however. What size should these buttons be? Bigger buttons are easier to see and easier to click on, but they take up more space. In addition, if there's an image link, should there also be a redundant text link that goes to the same place? Finally, how does using images as links affect download speed?

These are all examples of **forces** that you will consider when you use the patterns. The forces are the key issues that come into play when you're trying to solve a particular design problem. Within each pattern we include these forces and provide guidance for how to resolve the issues. For example, to improve the download speed of your ACTION BUTTONS (K4), you might use FAST-LOADING IMAGES (L2). You might even consider using AJAX (Asynchronous JavaScript And XML) to display button graphics as they are loaded, as discussed in FAST-LOADING CONTENT (L6).

The preceding explanation of ACTION BUTTONS (K4) has all the essential ingredients of a pattern. It explains the basic problem and describes the general solution. It also points out the forces exerting themselves on a design, and the many decisions and trade-offs that must be made if you use the pattern. Most importantly, it refers to other related patterns that affect how the pattern in question will be used.

As in Christopher Alexander's pattern language, each pattern is connected to certain higher-level patterns and to certain lower-level patterns.

The pattern helps complete the higher-level patterns that are "above" it, and it is completed itself by the lower-level patterns that are "below" it. ACTION BUTTONS (K4), for example, help complete a PROCESS FUNNEL (H1), where moving from step to step requires a clear call to action. Similarly, ACTION BUTTONS (K4) may be completed with FAST-LOADING IMAGES (L2).

The benefit of using patterns is that they embody design experience that all of us as a community have developed and learned. A given pattern may not necessarily be the best solution in every case, but it tends to work in practice.

In the next section we describe the specific format of the patterns presented in this book. If you have ever seen patterns in other domains (such as software design or architecture), you will notice many similarities.

2.3 How to Read a Pattern

The patterns in this book have a more formal format than what you have read up to this point. Each pattern has six parts: name, background, problem, forces, solution, and other patterns to consider. See Figure 2.6 for an example.

The pattern name is the name we have given the solution. It consists of a phrase that you can use in a sentence, such as "What is the name of that PAGE TEMPLATE (D1)?" Each pattern name is written in SMALL CAPITAL LETTERS so that you can quickly identify it on a page. Each pattern also has a pattern number, such as A9. The letter identifies the group to which the pattern belongs. Throughout the book we also flag patterns in the margins with small callouts (such as A9). These callouts are also color-coded to match the corresponding pattern group. In addition, each pattern group is color-coded on the edge of the page so that you can find the group you want by looking at the edge of the book. Following the pattern name is a sensitizing image—a sample implementation of the solution. It shows how the solution might appear on a finished site.

Next comes the background, which provides context for the pattern, describing any other patterns that lead to this pattern and how they are related, as well as the scope of this pattern.

The next part is the problem, a concise statement, in **boldface,** of the specific problem that this pattern addresses.

The forces follow the problem, describing it in more detail, examining how people, their tasks, the technology, and society affect the design problem and its solution.

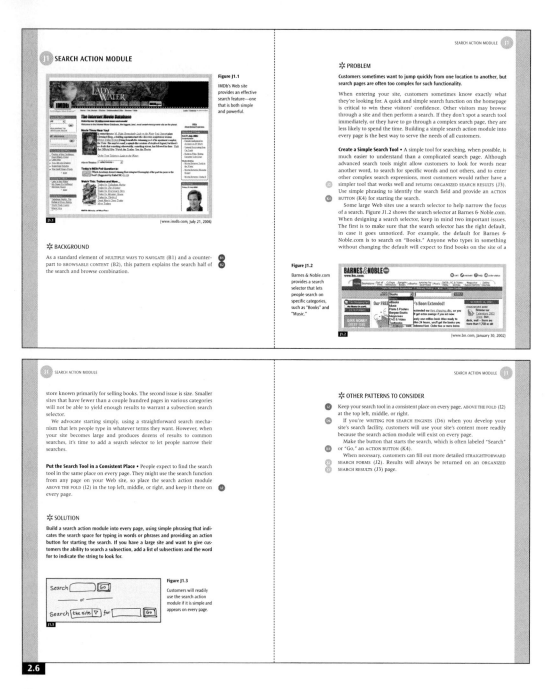

Figure 2.6

Every pattern has the same elements in identical order so that you can quickly find the information you need.

Next is the solution. Also set in **boldface,** the solution is a succinct statement of how to solve the problem. Accompanying the solution is a sketch to help you visualize the solution.

Finally, we discuss other patterns to consider, recommending additional patterns that help complete this one. You should examine and choose these according to your needs.

2.4   How Much Do Patterns Change Over Time?

We are sometimes asked how lasting the patterns in this book are. The World Wide Web has undergone many changes since we published the first edition of *The Design of Sites* in 2002, including the rise of XML and style sheets, the introduction of AJAX Web applications, and the widespread success of blogs and wikis. Are the patterns we describe something ephemeral that will need to be changed next year, or will they stand the test of time?

One way of answering this question is to look at how much specific Web pages have changed since the first edition of this book. Of the roughly four hundred screen shots in this second edition, about 70 are updates of previously included Web pages, and only about 35 are new shots replacing Web pages that either no longer exist or no longer demonstrate the desired design pattern. For example, both Nolo Press and BabyCenter were previously used as exemplars of TAB ROWS (K3), but these sites now use traditional NAVIGATION BARS (K2) instead.

Where screen shots have been updated, we feel that the design of these Web pages has become more professional in terms of cleaner layout, better use of icons and color, and more compelling content. However, *although the visual design of these Web pages has been polished, the underlying principles, structure, and design patterns remain essentially the same*. To underscore this point, Figures 2.7 through 2.9 compare some screen shots that we used in the first edition to what those Web pages look like today.

Figure 2.7 shows how eBay's HOMEPAGE PORTAL (C1) has changed over the past five years. Although there have been a few changes, most notably an increase in the number of elements ABOVE THE FOLD (I2), all of the same essential design patterns are reflected in both designs, including NAVIGATION BAR (K2), SIGN-IN/NEW ACCOUNT (H2), SEARCH ACTION MODULE (J1), and OBVIOUS LINKS (K10). Perhaps the most prominent change in eBay's newer design is to include more FEATURED PRODUCTS (G1) in the main content area in the center, as well as a **Live Help** feature.

2.7a   (www.ebay.com, December 4, 2001)

2.7b   (www.ebay.com, June 28, 2006)

Figure 2.7

Although the information density on eBay's homepage has increased over the years—as these two screen shots, from 2001 (a) and 2006 (b), illustrate—it's clear that eBay has retained all of its core elements and navigation structure.

Figure 2.8

All of the essential design patterns that were featured in Amazon.com's home-page portal in 2001 (a) are still there five years later (b).

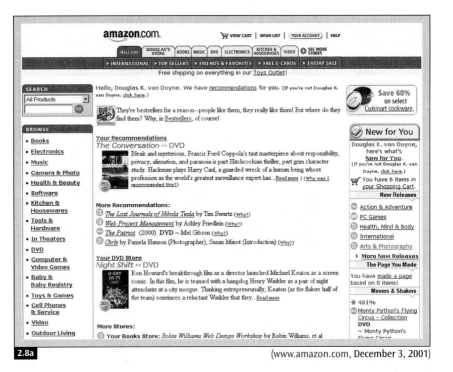

2.8a   (www.amazon.com, December 3, 2001)

2.8b   (www.amazon.com, June 15, 2006)

Figure 2.9

All of the essential design patterns that were featured in Amazon.com's quick-flow checkout in 2001 (a) are still there five years later (b).

(www.amazon.com, December 4, 2001)

Figure 2.9

(Continued)

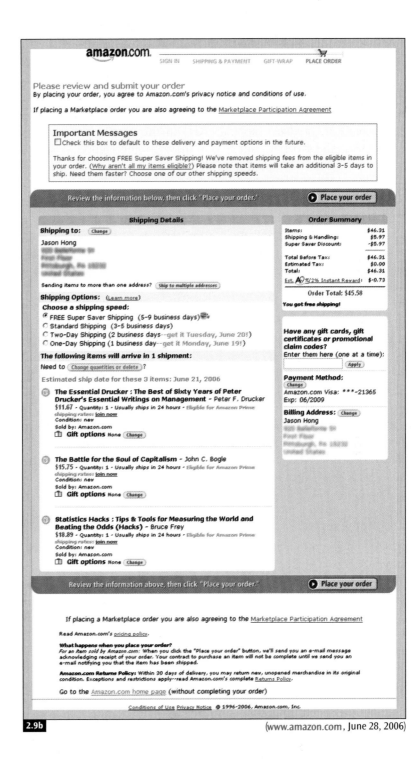

2.9b

(www.amazon.com, June 28, 2006)

Similarly, Figures 2.8 and 2.9 show the evolution of Amazon.com's Web site. As Figure 2.8 illustrates, the underlying structure of Amazon.com's newer HOMEPAGE PORTAL (C1) is still quite similar to its older homepage. Although the number of TAB ROWS (K3) has been decreased and the color scheme is now more colorful, both pages feature the same inverted-L NAVIGATION BAR (K2), FEATURED PRODUCTS (G1) in the center, and ACCOUNT MANAGEMENT (H4) and SHOPPING CART (F3) in the top right. Figure 2.9 shows that the ORDER SUMMARY (F7) portion of the QUICK-FLOW CHECKOUT (F1) has also remained essentially the same.

Figure 2.10 shows how the homepages of some prominent Web sites have changed during the past six years. With the exception of Google, which has always stressed simplicity, it is interesting to note that the only major change has been an increase in the information density of these Web pages. In fact, Web design has already converged on what we call the "common Web look and feel."

Today, the large majority of commercial Web sites have a two- or three-column GRID LAYOUT (I1) with the most important content and navigation  ABOVE THE FOLD (I2), a NAVIGATION BAR (K2) and/or a TAB ROW (K3) along the top, a SEARCH ACTION MODULE (J1) at either the top right or the middle left, a clickable logo to go back to the HOMEPAGE PORTAL (C1), both a PRIVACY POLICY (E4) and an ABOUT US (E5) link at the bottom, SHOPPING CARTS (F3) and QUICK-FLOW CHECKOUTS (F1) for managing purchases, CONTENT MODULES (D2) in the center and along the right side for easily updating content, and so on. Even with AJAX technologies and the Mobile Web, the sheer momentum of billions of existing Web pages makes it unlikely that there will be any tectonic shifts in the way Web pages are designed in the near future.

Returning to the question posed at the start of this section, we argue that all of this means that the design patterns in this book represent the essential foundation of Web design. Though the surface appearance of Web sites might change to accommodate the latest fashion trends, their core underlying structure, as exemplified by our design patterns, is here to stay.

How to Use the Patterns

2.5

Pattern groups are organized by letter and by name, as Table 2.1 shows. Each pattern group contains a collection of thematically related patterns. For example, if you wanted to improve the search feature on your Web site, you would refer to Pattern Group J (Making Site Search Fast and Relevant). Or if your testing showed that customers were having problems navigating your Web site, you would consult Pattern Group K (Making Navigation Easy).

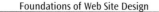

Table 2.1 Pattern Groups

- Ⓐ Site Genres
- Ⓑ Creating a Navigation Framework
- Ⓒ Creating a Powerful Homepage
- Ⓓ Writing and Managing Content
- Ⓔ Building Trust and Credibility
- Ⓕ Basic E-Commerce
- Ⓖ Advanced E-Commerce
- Ⓗ Helping Customers Complete Tasks
- Ⓘ Designing Effective Page Layouts
- Ⓙ Making Site Search Fast and Relevant
- Ⓚ Making Navigation Easy
- Ⓛ Speeding Up Your Site
- Ⓜ The Mobile Web

Generally speaking, the earlier the pattern group appears in this scheme, the earlier it should be used in the design process. For example, Pattern Groups A and B discuss Web site genres and creating a navigation framework for the entire Web site, respectively. Continuing, Pattern Group F looks at basic e-commerce issues, and Pattern Group H contains patterns that help customers complete tasks. These patterns are useful only after you have set the high-level goals and design of your Web site. Moving to the end, Pattern Group K deals with things like links and navigation bars, Pattern Group L looks at speeding up a Web site, and Pattern Group M contains patterns specific to the concerns of Mobile Web interfaces.

Each pattern identifies related patterns in its sections on background, forces, and other patterns to consider. This network of patterns lets you quickly collect the patterns you need to complete your design. You can use the rich pattern vocabulary to articulate an almost infinite number of designs.

2.6 An Example of Using Patterns

This example tells the story of a designer who discovers a costly Web site problem and uses the patterns presented in this book to deploy a customer-centered solution.

Figure 2.10

These screen shots illustrate the evolution of the homepages of CNN, MSN, Yahoo!, and Google from 2001 to 2006. Note that the core structure and the underlying design patterns used by these Web sites have not changed over the years. For the most part, the only major change to these Web sites has been an increase in information density.

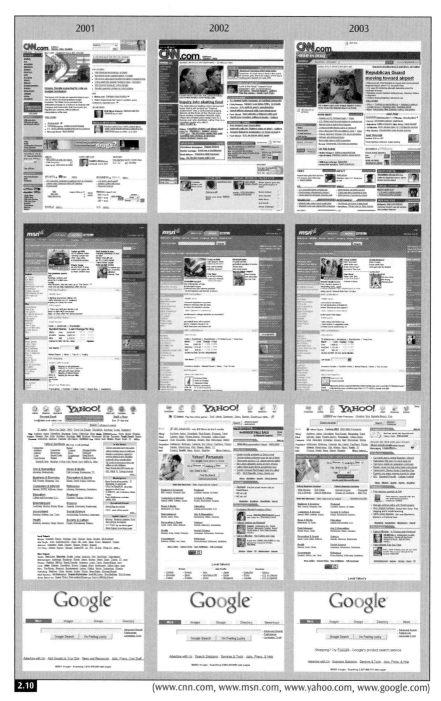

2.10

(www.cnn.com, www.msn.com, www.yahoo.com, www.google.com)

Figure 2.10

(Continued)

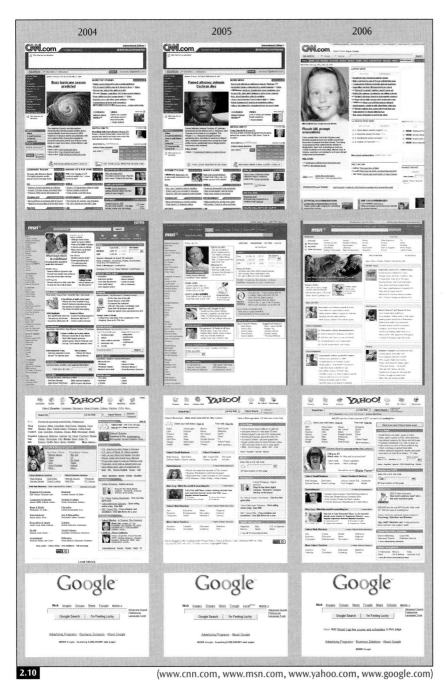

2.10　(www.cnn.com, www.msn.com, www.yahoo.com, www.google.com)

Sarah is part of the design team for an e-commerce Web site. Because the team is small, she has many responsibilities, including designing and evaluating the usability of the site.

While examining the Web site statistics, such as data from server logs, Sarah discovers that most customers are spending a fair amount of time on the site. However, many people appear to be abandoning their shopping carts and leaving the Web site right at checkout, before a sale is successfully closed. This problem is clearly something she needs to fix as quickly as possible.

Sarah brings up the problem at the design team's weekly meeting. It turns out that everyone knows the Web site checkout has numerous problems, but no one has a solution. In a heated discussion, team members voice their opinions, but the meeting ends with no resolution.

After the meeting, Sarah checks whether any design patterns might help. Because this is an e-commerce problem, she starts with Pattern Group F (Basic E-Commerce), quickly skimming through the patterns there.

The first pattern that catches her eye is QUICK-FLOW CHECKOUT (F1). The problem statement seems to match the problem that her Web site faces: "An e-commerce shopping experience will not be enjoyable—or worse, a purchase might not be completed—if the checkout process is cumbersome, confusing, or error prone." This pattern points out several problems with checkouts, including hidden charges, tedious text entries, confusing links, extra buttons, and complicated instructions. The members of Sarah's team took special care to address the issue of hidden charges when they first designed the site because that was something that bothered them on other e-commerce Web sites. She finds, however, that a few links on the site still have confusing names.

Sarah also sees that several other patterns are referenced, including PERSONAL E-COMMERCE (A1). This pattern is in a group that comes before QUICK-FLOW CHECKOUT (F1), indicating that it is a more abstract pattern. Skimming over the PERSONAL E-COMMERCE (A1) pattern, Sarah sees that it describes qualities of e-commerce sites in general, such as privacy, convenience, and returns. Although she finds that the PERSONAL E-COMMERCE (A1) pattern might be useful in the future, she decides that it is at too high a level for what she needs right now.

Another referenced pattern, SHOPPING CART (F3), looks more promising because it describes the features needed to make shopping carts useful. One important design question is how long unpurchased items stay in a shopping cart before they're automatically removed. Premature clearing of shopping carts may lead to lost sales because customers who return to a Web site might be irritated to find that all the time they spent finding the items they wanted to buy was wasted. Sarah makes a mental note to ask the developers on the design team how long items are kept in the Web site's shopping carts. (It turns out to be just one hour.)

(F1)
(H1)   QUICK-FLOW CHECKOUT (F1) also mentions a pattern called PROCESS FUNNEL (H1). Reviewing this pattern, Sarah sees that process funnels are a sequence of pages designed to help people complete extremely specific tasks. Special care is taken to make instructions concise, to minimize extraneous links that might lead customers out of the process funnel, and to shorten the number of steps required for completing the process funnel. Thinking about the current checkout process, Sarah realizes that some of her site's pages are heavy with text instructions. In addition, a few pages have links that could accidentally lead people out of the checkout process.

After studying the patterns, the forces, and the solutions, Sarah understands many of the shortcomings of her team's current checkout design. Using her site's existing design as a starting point, she can now quickly sketch design alternatives for a new checkout process, combining and modifying the solutions that the patterns describe.

After creating three possible solutions, using the patterns as a guide, Sarah asks for informal feedback from the members of her design team. They identify some problems with her proposed designs and point out which changes will be easy to implement and which will not. Sarah uses this feedback to sketch another set of design alternatives, again using the patterns and her team's suggestions.

Sarah knows that a key principle of customer-centered Web design is keeping customers in the loop throughout the design process. She decides to run a quick evaluation with some representative customers. For this round of evaluations, Sarah decides that informally talking to and observing five participants is enough to get a pretty good idea of what the big problems are with the current site. She recruits five people who live nearby, visiting them in their homes. Offering a gift certificate and a free T-shirt makes recruiting pretty easy.

First Sarah asks her recruits to try the old checkout process so that she can get a better feel for the problems they encounter. Then she shows them her sketches for the new checkout process and gets feedback on the early designs.

While observing the participants, she realizes that she has anticipated many of the problems correctly. A customer named Fred, for example, clicks on the wrong link while in the checkout sequence and accidentally exits the process funnel. Although he is momentarily confused, Fred figures out what happened and hits the **Back** button. However, all of the information that he had just typed has disappeared, and he has to enter it all over again. Sarah records this event as a critical error.

Sarah also discovers a few new things that the design team did not realize were problems. Two of the participants have serious problems finding the button that takes them to the third step of the checkout. The correct button is at the bottom of the page. However, these two have fairly old computers, and their monitors are small enough that this button is not visible on their Web browser unless they scroll down. (This is why Fred clicked on the wrong link and fell out of the checkout process funnel.)

Although all five participants successfully complete the checkout sequence, none of them think that it's very easy, and all of them suggest that the process reflects poorly on the Web site. Sarah also realizes that this result is probably affected by testing bias. Given all the problems with the Web site, she doubts that the participants would have finished the task if she had not been sitting beside them.

After the evaluation, Sarah takes out the sketches that she created from the patterns and prior discussion with her team. She shows them to the participants, one at a time, asking them where they think each link will take them if they click on it, and whether the content on the page makes sense.

All five participants like the design sketches and think that each one has more potential than the existing checkout process. However, one of the three design alternatives stands out as the one they like best. Sarah makes a note to explore this design alternative in greater detail.

At the next team meeting, Sarah presents the results of the evaluation. She describes many of the problems that her group of participants experienced and presents ideas on how to fix them. One team member mentions that the HIGH-VISIBILITY ACTION BUTTONS (K5) pattern addresses the (K5) problem of clicking on the wrong links in a process funnel.

Everyone agrees that the existing checkout process is broken and needs to be replaced as quickly as possible. Sarah presents sketches for the design alternative that her recruited participants said was best. The discussion focuses on prioritizing the features. After a brief debate, the team quickly reaches a consensus on the most important features for the next version of the checkout. They start exploring whether any design patterns apply, and they get to work on refining the new design.

2.7 Take-away Ideas

The bulk of this book contains design patterns that you and your team can start using today. With these design patterns you can design a site from scratch, redesign a section of a site, or fix a particular problem on a page. Every design still requires your creativity, intuition, and testing to make the solutions effective. Our patterns simply help direct your creative energies to solving new problems, as opposed to reinventing the wheel. In the words of literary critic Lionel Trilling, "Immature artists imitate. Mature artists steal."

The key is to consider your options in context. If the goal of your site is to challenge your visitors, then many of the design patterns may not apply. But for any business or government site, the goal is to maximize the customers' experience. This means that you'll want to provide valuable, useful, and usable navigation structures and make it easy to find information and complete tasks successfully. For these kinds of sites, our patterns provide design solutions that work.

Knowing Your Customers: Principles and Techniques

A gulf between a design team and the end customers is a fundamental problem inherent in Web site design, whether the Web site is for entertainment, e-commerce, community, or information purposes. To bridge this gulf, you need to focus on customer-centered design. At the heart of customer-centered design are two principles:

1. Know your customers (covered in this chapter).
2. Keep your customers involved throughout the design and implementation process (covered in Chapter 4 [Involving Customers with Iterative Design]).

Knowing Your Customers Helps You Choose Patterns

So far, we have explained why good Web site design is important, and we have presented customer-centered design as the way to create successful Web sites. We have also introduced Web design patterns as one part of customer-centered design, and we have shown how you can use the patterns to create effective Web sites. However, Web design patterns by themselves are not enough. This chapter presents the next part. Knowing your current and prospective customers will help you choose patterns that are relevant to your site design, as well as help you decide between competing trade-offs when you're customizing patterns for your design situation.

To Know Your Customers, You Need Some Special Techniques

In this chapter you will learn the importance of having a deep understanding of your customers, their tasks, the technology available to them, and their social and organizational context before implementing your Web site. Then you will be introduced to the techniques you can use for gaining such understanding, such as task analysis, scenario building, customer interviews, and analysis of existing Web sites.

Take It a Step at a Time

You do not have to adopt these principles all at once. In fact, it's best to take many small steps instead of one big leap. Chapter 5 (Processes for Developing Customer-Centered Sites) explains how to go forward, outlining steps and deliverables for a customer-centered design process. If you're already an expert on customer-centered design and the design process, just skim Chapters 3 through 5 or skip right to the patterns in the second part of the book.

⑤

Principles for Knowing Your Customers

3.1

As you do when you're building any other relationship, you want to become intimate with the lives of your customers. This will not happen overnight. There is no secret formula. Fortunately, though, there are tried-and-true ways to learn about your customers. Before we discuss any of these techniques, let's explore what it means to *know your customers*. This principle really is many principles wrapped into one.

You Are Not Your Customers

One of the most important things that design teams must learn is that *they are not the customers*. Although it might sound obvious, this idea is not always integrated into the way design teams work. Customers do not have the same experiences, do not think the same, do not talk the same, and do not perform things in the same way that design teams do. Therefore, design teams cannot rely exclusively on their own intuition and experience when creating Web sites.

Understand the Elements, Balance the Forces

To understand your customers, consider the competing elements of every design: your customers, their tasks, their technology, and their social context (see Figure 3.1). Each of these elements has certain capabilities and limitations that exert forces on your design. To create a successful site, you must understand and balance these forces so that none of them dominate and each is considered in your final design. The principles and patterns in this book will help you balance your design. Let's begin by examining the elements in more detail.

Figure 3.1

Customer-centered design is about understanding people, their tasks, the technology available, and how these issues are positioned within the social and organizational context of the customer and, potentially, the client who is having the Web site built.

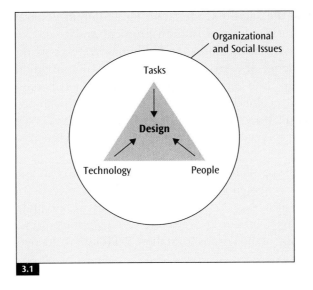

3.1

Understand Your Customers as People

If you understand the needs of your customers, you can use the information about them to shape your Web site design. There are two ways of thinking about this. One way is to understand people as individuals. The other way is to understand the basic characteristics of people in general.

Your Customers Are Different • Understanding people as individuals means having detailed profiles of customers, such as their demographics, attitudes, behaviors, knowledge, skills, and any other characteristics that can have a strong influence on the overall structure, design, and content of a Web site. For example, do the target customers care a lot about aesthetics, or do they prefer a simple and functional Web site? What people will visit the site? Are they children, young adults, seniors, or a combination of these? What level of education do they have? What other Web sites do they currently use? How experienced are they in using computers and the Web?

Understanding people as individuals also means learning the specific skills and language of your customers. If you were building a Web site for medical professionals, for example, you would probably study the terms and idioms in use in the medical profession, and carefully test the wording on the Web site for comprehension and correctness. On the other hand, if you were designing a Web site for pre-med students, you could not make the same assumptions. Instead, you would have to try to use the vocabulary and concepts that they understand, and test for those terms.

Your Customers Are Also the Same • Understanding people in general means knowing the fundamentals of human physical and cognitive abilities—how the human visual, motor, and memory systems work. Factors like these influence the structure and layout of individual Web pages. For example, how many things can an average person remember? What kinds of color deficiency, also known as color blindness, are most common? How well can people click on small Web buttons? What sort of response time is required to support hand–eye coordination?

Knowledge of basic human abilities comes from the fields of cognitive psychology, human factors, ergonomics, and human–computer interaction. Although they are critical to superior design, these disciplines are also quite involved and can take years to master. To accelerate your learning process, we have incorporated many of the lessons from these fields into the design patterns in this book.

For example, the time it takes a person to move a mouse to a target is proportional to the distance to the target divided by the target size (this concept is known as Fitts's Law). In other words, buttons that are small or far away are harder to click on than buttons that are large or nearby. Two patterns influenced by Fitts's Law are DESCRIPTIVE, LONGER LINK NAMES (K9) and ACTION BUTTONS (K4). Fitts's Law will guide you in deciding how large links and buttons should be, ensuring that the ones on your Web site will be large enough to click on quickly.

As another example, sometimes you have to provide MEANINGFUL ERROR MESSAGES (K13) to help customers recover from errors. However, an important design constraint here is that about 8 percent of men and 0.5 percent of women in North America have some form of color vision deficiency. The most severe form, and the one that is most commonly known, is red–green deficiency. If you're designing a site targeted primarily at men, 1 in 12 of them might not be able to easily distinguish between red and green. The example in Figure 3.2 of feedback warning customers that there are problems with data they've entered on a form requires them to discern the difference between red and green. Would customers with color-deficient vision notice this subtle difference? One of our colleagues observed a test participant giving up on a purchase at this stage. It turned out that he had red–green color deficiency and he could not recover from an error because he could not see what he had done wrong. This example demonstrates how good SITE ACCESSIBILITY (B9) can improve the usability of MEANINGFUL ERROR MESSAGES (K13) on your Web site.

Figure 3.2

It might be tempting to use red to highlight an error. Because many people have red–green color deficiency, however, it is not a good idea to depend on their ability to distinguish differences that are communicated through those colors alone.

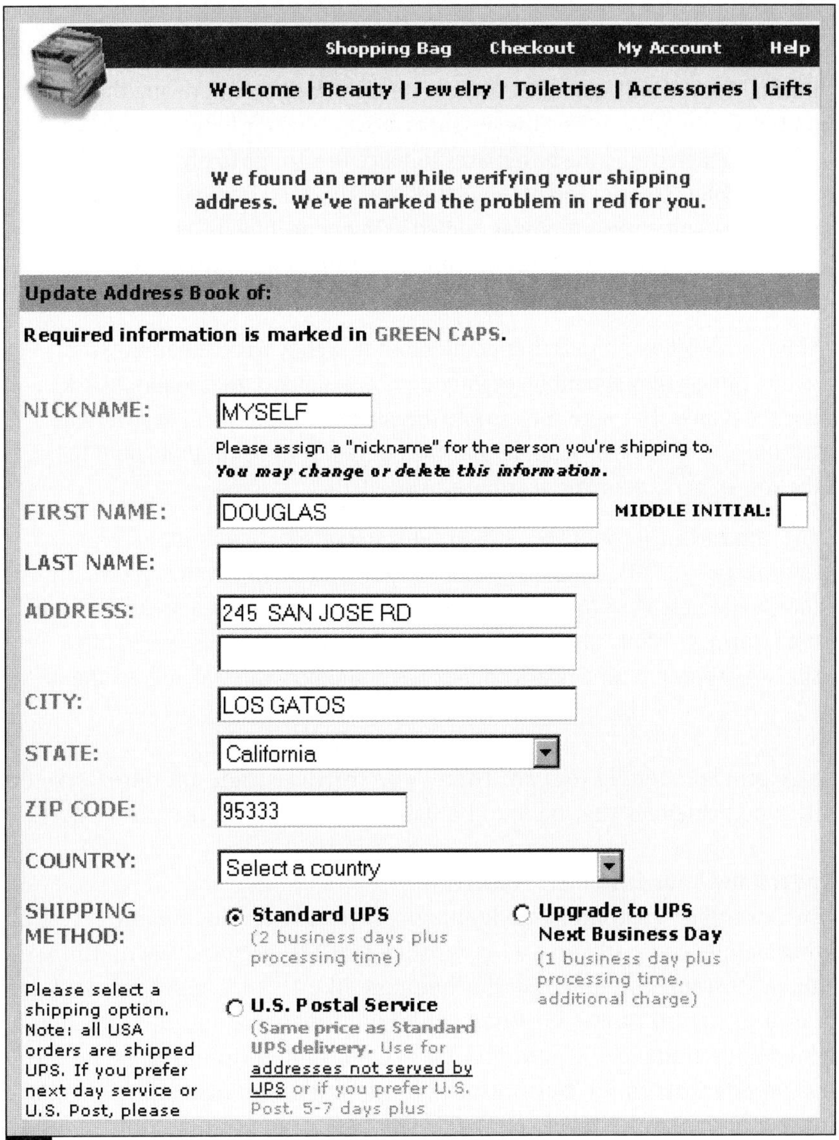
Shopping Bag
Checkout
My Account
Help
Welcome | Beauty | Jewelry | Toiletries | Accessories | Gifts
We found an error while verifying your shipping address. We've marked the problem in red for you.
Update Address Book of:
Required information is marked in GREEN CAPS.
NICKNAME:
MYSELF
Please assign a "nickname" for the person you're shipping to.
You may change or delete this information.
FIRST NAME:
DOUGLAS
MIDDLE INITIAL:
LAST NAME:
ADDRESS:
245 SAN JOSE RD
CITY:
LOS GATOS
STATE:
California
ZIP CODE:
95333
COUNTRY:
Select a country
SHIPPING METHOD:
Standard UPS
(2 business days plus processing time)
Upgrade to UPS Next Business Day
(1 business day plus processing time, additional charge)
Please select a shipping option. Note: all USA orders are shipped UPS. If you prefer next day service or U.S. Post, please
U.S. Postal Service
(Same price as Standard UPS delivery. Use for addresses not served by UPS or if you prefer U.S. Post. 5-7 days plus

3.2

It can be a challenge to balance the information from all the fields we've mentioned with Web design. The design patterns that we present mix theory, research, and practical experience to provide solutions that work. For example, DESCRIPTIVE, LONGER LINK NAMES (K9) will help your customers navigate to the right page, but they also fill up more screen

K9

Customers Who Don't Return

During World War II, some researchers were working on improving the armor on U.S. fighter planes. Because weight is a critical factor for planes, they needed to determine the best places to place the armor to protect the plane and the pilot. They looked at the planes that returned from combat, noting the places where the armor was riddled with enemy bullets. In their report they stated that more armor should be added to these locations because they seemed the most likely to be hit.

Then, however, one researcher pointed out that they were examining the wrong things; they should be examining not the planes that made it back, but the planes that were shot down! The planes that made it back were not the ones hit in critical locations and thus were not the ones that could tell the researchers where more armor was needed.

The same is true for Web sites. It's certainly important to understand your returning customers, but they have already proven willing to cross a certain threshold to use your Web site. What about the customers who are leaving and not returning? What barriers are keeping these people from using your Web site? What concerns and needs do they have, and how can you address them?

space and take longer to read. There is an intrinsic trade-off here between differing principles that have to be balanced to achieve the right effect.

Understand Your Customers' Tasks

Understanding customers' **tasks** means explicitly cataloging and scripting what people currently do and what they want to do when using the Web site. A customer might describe her task like this: "I want to send my grandmother an online birthday card," or "I want to find the best digital camera for under $500 and buy it." The task description says *what* the customer wants to do, but not how he or she might accomplish it.[1] At a more fundamental level, though, understanding tasks also involves thinking critically about how your Web site can help streamline or even augment what people do today.

As a negative example, consider what happened to one of us while looking for a refund form on a company's Web site. The task was to find

---

1 Some authors refer to abstract tasks like this as *goals*. We use the terms *task* and *goal* interchangeably here.

this form online, but the site was so confusing that it was impossible. The company did not understand that this might be a common task that its customers would want to perform. In addition, the company's search engine was relatively useless. Even after the right page was located through an *Internet* search engine, the only information that the site provided was a fax number to request the right form.

If the design team had performed a **task analysis,** they might have discovered this task and streamlined it by letting people download the right forms and print them for themselves. A task analysis would have articulated the things people do, the things they act on, and the things they need to know. Taking their analysis one step further, the team could augment how the task is done today by having an online form for people to fill out and submit electronically.

You might be thinking, "What does it matter? He spent half an hour to find the right Web page, but he still got what he wanted in the end." That's true, but consider these issues: First, how many people do you think he told about this bad experience? Second, do you think he will ever buy something from this company again? We rest our case.

The Importance of Understanding Tasks

Here's a story about why it's important to understand the customer's tasks *before* starting to implement your design. A small dentist's office decided to automate its billing, switching from paper-based forms to electronic versions. Hoping to reduce costs in the long term, the dentist spent a nontrivial amount of money to hire a programming team to develop a new system.

After it was finished and deployed, however, all of the dentist's assistants were extremely dissatisfied with the new system, almost to the point of rejecting it entirely and going back to the paper-based forms. If the programmers had taken a closer look at how the paper forms were used, they would have noticed that many of them had handwritten notes in the margin.

It turns out that the assistants often wrote reminders, such as, "This patient's insurance takes longer than most," on the forms. But the new system simply did not support this kind of flexibility. A careful analysis of the existing tasks could have revealed this use of notes, and the appropriate flexibility could have been designed into the system. Instead, the dentist's office ended up paying a lot of money for an inflexible system that did not please the staff.

Reducing Work • Design teams should consider how they might help reduce the amount of work customers have to do. One way to do this is to use an analogy that people already know. Spreadsheet programs did this by using a metaphor to existing paper spreadsheets. E-commerce sites do this by using metaphors to things in real stores, such as a SHOPPING CART (F3). However, replicating an existing interface is not always the best approach. For example, a design team could create a Web-based telephone directory by taking images of real telephone directory pages, showing one page at a time on the screen, and adding buttons to turn the pages. Now, whether they *should* do this is the real question.

This approach ignores the problems with existing telephone directories and fails to take advantage of the Web medium. It takes time to find a listing in paper-based telephone directories, even if you know the exact spelling. Paper directories are also hard to use if you know only part of a listing. A better approach would be to take advantage of the computer's capabilities to do fast searches and to make partial and close matches.

Task Training • One factor to consider with regard to understanding tasks is how much training is involved. For example, engineers spend many years learning very specific terms and procedures. A Web site targeted at professional engineers may assume a certain level of knowledge. However, a Web site targeted at homeowners interested in maintaining their homes on weekends cannot make the same assumption. It is your job to decide how much hand-holding customers need.

One of the myths of the usability field is that everything needs to be intuitive on first use. Certainly this is true for kiosks at tourist sites or handheld tour guide devices—things a person might use only once. But in many cases, with a little training your customers will become highly effective using the tools that you provide.

There is a real difference between ease of learning and ease of use. For example, kazoos and triangles are walk-up-and-use musical instruments, but they are not all that interesting. With many years of practice, however, people can master playing a difficult instrument such as a violin, and in some cases become creators of music instead of just consumers. Computer pioneer Douglas Engelbart[2] said it best: "If ease of use was the only valid criterion, people would stick to tricycles and never try bicycles." This notion of training the customer or relying on the customer's existing

---

2   Quoted by Howard Rheingold in the online version of his book, *The Virtual Community: Homesteading on the Electronic Frontier,* at www.rheingold.com/vc/book/4.html.

training is one of the key ideas behind the Web design patterns in this book. People become accustomed to operating in a certain way on the Web, and in many cases it makes sense to take advantage of this knowledge.

Design teams have to be careful, though, because it is far too easy to use the bicycle-versus-tricycle argument as an excuse for poor Web design. You should know how much training customers are realistically willing to undergo. Paul Saffo, the noted futurist, writes:

> We do not use tools simply because they are friendly. We use tools to accomplish tasks, and we abandon tools when the effort required to make the tool deliver exceeds our threshold of indignation—the maximal behavioral compromise that we are willing to make to get a task done.[3]

Customers often do not take kindly to having to train to use a product. In this sense Web sites are different from desktop software. With desktop software, customers have already invested a fair amount of time and money purchasing and installing the software, and thus they have a motivation to learn how to use it. With Web sites, it's just the opposite. Customers are not likely to buy something on a Web site or avail themselves of its services if they have to spend lots of time learning to use it, unless they can see that it provides significant benefit. For example, it is highly unlikely that customers will spend more than a few minutes learning how to use an e-commerce Web site. On the other hand, look at how kids attach themselves to video games. They are willing to learn fairly complex controls because they think the game will be a lot of fun.

Helping People Become Experts • You should also consider how your Web site could help people to *become* experts faster. For example, going back to the example of the Web site for homeowners, it's probably not a good idea to scare off newcomers by having lots of complex terms and diagrams on the homepage. However, the Web site could gently introduce a few basic terms, and maybe even have an online dictionary containing all the commonly used terms.

The site could also have a section for beginners, filled with tutorials, basic diagrams, and interesting war stories, all designed to draw people in. Sample home projects could be ranked by difficulty so that homeowners would have some way of knowing what's easy and what's not.

---

3 From "The Consumer Spectrum," p. 87.

The Web site could also support a community, as illustrated by COMMUNITY CONFERENCES (A3) and BLOGS (A12), in which people could ask questions and slowly learn the ropes of taking care of, maintaining, and adding onto their homes. By providing many ways to learn and many places to fall back on, and by making it fun, design teams can "hide" the amount of training required and create a more gentle slope to the learning curve.

Understand the Technology

Do you know which tools your customers have at their disposal, which tools are available to you, and what the capabilities and limitations of these tools are? For example, how many of your customers have fast Internet connections? If most people have slow connections, using a lot of large images is not a good idea. By understanding how the Internet works, you can design Web pages that are faster to download. See Pattern Group L (Speeding Up Your Site) for more information.

Technology is a broad issue, but unfortunately it is often either completely ignored or given too much importance in designs. When Web design teams overlook the fact that many of their customers do not have the latest Web browser and plug-ins, they wind up with customers who are puzzled because they see nothing at all on the Web site. (This is not as uncommon as you might think. Just try surfing the Web with JavaScript turned off or without Flash installed, and you'll see what we mean.) When technology becomes the central factor in Web design, it becomes technology for technology's sake. The customer's needs are certainly not being met on sites like this.

Design teams need to know what's possible with current technologies, as well as the relative advantages and disadvantages of each technology. For example, do you know the differences between a GIF image and a JPEG image? When is it better to use one over the other? [See FAST-LOADING IMAGES (L2) for more information on this topic.] The Web design patterns in this book address some of these issues, but you can get more detail from books that focus on these subjects, such as the sources included in the Resources section of this book.

Here's an example of what happens when human abilities and the technological constraints that affect them are not considered in Web site design. Fast response times help maintain a sense of continuity in a task flow. Generally speaking, response times on the order of 100 milliseconds are needed for things like dragging icons and typing text. Response times on the order of 1 second (1,000 milliseconds) are required to maintain an uninterrupted flow of thought when completing a routine action like clicking on a button. Now, you could read about these response times in a news article or a book on human factors and decide that all the pages on your site must be viewable by customers in less than a second. This notion is well-intentioned, but given the current state of networking and Web technology, it's a completely unrealistic goal. Although they should never be the driving factor, technological constraints should still be considered as part of a Web site's design: people and tasks first, technology second.

Be extremely wary of religious wars. If you talk to enough Web designers, you will meet a few that are slavishly devoted to a specific technology, such as Macromedia Flash. Such viewpoints lead to narrow and severely unbalanced views of the world, putting technology ahead of client goals and customer needs. Remember, if all you have is a hammer, everything looks like a nail. Technology is a tool for helping people get things done—nothing more, nothing less.

Understand Your Customers' Social Issues

Framing how people, tasks, and technology fit within a broader social and organizational context means considering how these social issues broaden the scope of design, putting things into the context of the big picture. Suppose you're designing a Web-based group calendaring system for business use. You will need to know who has an online calendar. You will also ask how groups decide to have meetings. Does a manager decide, or is it a consensual process? These are all organizational questions that will help you design the interface to best meet the needs of your customer.

The importance of looking at organizational issues is illustrated quite nicely by Leysia Palen's 1999 study of online group calendars at two large technology companies. Palen found that it's wise to pay attention to the culture of the company when setting the defaults for enterprise-wide software. For example, should a shared calendar show only that a person is busy, or should it show exactly what the person wrote down for that time slot? This question must take into account personal privacy, company security, and control over the group's personal time. The research found that the preferences for these defaults were vastly different in the two organizations.

Palen's research showed that the success or failure of a group calendaring system lies not only in the functionality it provides, but also in default settings. You could argue that all that's needed to fix the problem is a feature that lets individuals customize this kind of information, but Palen's study showed that over 80 percent of the participants maintained the defaults. This is an important lesson for any user interface design. Even if you build in a lot of flexibility, your customers will probably use the default settings. The choice for your defaults thus will have a major impact on the success or failure of your site. Again, your customers' successful adoption of new software often depends on how the software fits into existing social and organizational contexts.

It is also valuable to understand the flow of work through an organization. Suppose that we wanted to build a new Web-based programming tool. Many enlightened designers might consider just watching software engineers as they program. Although this is a good first step, it actually leaves out quite a bit. We would also want to understand how the programmers interact with quality assurance engineers, designers, technical writers, and marketers. When do these interactions occur? What kinds of things happen during these interactions? Answers to these questions could critically influence our design.

The growing importance of online communities provides another reason to look at social and organizational issues. Before the World Wide Web, the concept of online communities was limited to dial-up bulletin board systems, newsgroups, and e-mail lists. The Web has expanded on these early outposts and proliferated the idea that groups tied together by shared interests or by common values can find a place together in cyberspace. Paying close attention to social and organizational factors can help you see how a Web site will explicitly support a specific group and build a community, cementing a longer-term relationship with customers.

Usually the organizational issues will be about the customer's organization, but sometimes it might be useful to look into the organizational issues of the client. The client might have high-level goals for the Web site that are different from the high-level goals or tasks that you found to be important to customers. Resolving these differences up front might be the difference between success and failure of the project.

Techniques for Knowing Your Customers   3.2

We have described what it means to understand the elements of every design: people, tasks, technology, and social issues. Here we describe specific techniques that you can use to gain this understanding. Techniques such as task and customer analyses, observations, interviews, surveys, focus groups, and Web site evaluations help you characterize target customers and their needs. Some of these techniques are good for qualitative information, others for quantitative. The key is to use a mixture of techniques to get a more complete picture of who your customers are and what they need.

The word *need* here is important. One of the major problems with traditional software engineering methodologies is that they have focused on what clients say they *want*. The difference between what clients ask for and what customers need has led to many project failures in the past. Customers themselves cannot easily express what they need.[4] The methods we present here focus on finding out what these needs are.

One problem that you will repeatedly face is finding your target customers, and getting them to help out. Are they too busy? Perhaps you can buy their time by offering T-shirts, coffee mugs, or gift certificates. Are they still too busy? See if there's an alternative but similar audience. For example, medical doctors are often too occupied to take surveys or to participate in Web site evaluations, but first-year medical students might help out instead. Although students in this case are not the exact target customers, they may be a pretty good approximation.

What if you have no idea who your potential customers are? This is where traditional market research techniques come to bear. Running focus groups and surveys, by telephone or online, with different types of potential customers, can help your team focus on the kinds of people who will be attracted to your Web site. This type of research should be conducted before you start designing the site.

Run a pilot test before showing your site to potential customers. Have some friends first try out your survey, focus group, or Web site evaluation to work out any kinks in the wording or procedure. Analyze the pilot test data to make sure that the data you're collecting is the data you want. This preliminary work will help minimize the problems you will encounter when you collect and analyze information for real.

Start a Task Analysis

One of the first steps in developing a Web site, before any kind of design work or implementation, is **task and customer analysis.**[5] Task analysis will help you understand what your customers do now and how they do it, and it will provide ideas for what your customers could do with your Web site. The key to task analysis is to first identify the target customer

---

4 Customers *are* good at using a Web site and being able to say that it's something they don't need. This is where the iterative design techniques described in Chapter 4 (Involving Customers with Iterative Design) come into play.

5 Our use of the term *task analysis* differs slightly from the traditional definition. We have added customer analysis to this phase. *Task and customer analysis* means that you use task analysis to find out about your customers' tasks, as well as to find out who your customers are—that is, to know your customers.

population, find people representative of that population, and then find out what they do.

When starting a task analysis, use your intuition and experience, as well as informal interviews with task experts, to answer questions that characterize the target audience. Later you can use other techniques, such as observations, surveys, and evaluations of competitors' Web sites, to answer the questions in more detail. If you're revising an existing Web site, you can also evaluate it. Successful design teams often use a combination of these techniques to develop a meaningful understanding of customers and their needs.

The sections that follow describe some sample task analysis questions organized into four familiar categories: people, tasks, technology, and social issues.

People • Who are the customers? What are their interests? What are their ages? Are they children, young adults, adults, senior citizens, or a combination? What level of education do they have? What kind of vocabulary do they use? What kind of computer skills do they have? Are they expert computer users? Are they novices? What is their income range? What is their reading ability? Do they have any physical constraints, such as poor vision or poor hearing? What is important in their lives?

Tasks • What are your customers' current offline tasks? What tasks do they do on other Web sites? What do they come to your current Web site to do? What specific tasks do they want to do there? How are the tasks learned? Will they perform these tasks many times, or just a few times? What tools and information do they need to accomplish their tasks? How often do they perform their tasks? Are there time constraints? Do the tasks need to be done within a certain period of time? What happens if they don't complete a task? What do they do for help if they can't complete a task? In what ways can they recover?

Technology • What kinds of equipment and tools do your customers have? What kinds of Web browsers do they use? What kinds of plug-ins do they have? What other kinds of software do they have and use? What sizes are their monitors? How fast are their network connections?

Social Issues • What kind of social or organizational factors affect your customers? Where will they do their tasks? In what environment will they do their tasks? Is it noisy or quiet? Is it a stressful environment? Is it an office environment? Do they work at home? Do they use a public kiosk or a shared computer? Is security an issue? Do they work late at night? Do they work during peak Internet traffic hours? What is the relationship between the customer and the data? Is it public data? Is it highly sensitive private data? Is the data shared with coworkers? Is it shared with family members?

Experts might ask how you can answer these questions without first doing an in-depth field study, in which you watch customers in action. We think these techniques work best if they're used in tandem. Your task analysis can inform your field observations and interviews, and your interviews and observations can inform your task analysis. You will always have some assumptions going into a field study, and it is advantageous to make those explicit, as the task analysis lets you do. On the other hand, it is unwise to invest too much time in a task analysis before studying real customers. You might become too committed to your initial analysis and have a hard time letting evidence from the field overturn your assumptions.

Quick-and-dirty task analysis before interviewing helps you focus the field investigation. Usually time and resources do not realistically permit an unstructured "let's go in and see what we see" study, so you have to figure out which customers do the tasks that you want to focus on.

Build Scenarios

After your initial task analysis, create scenarios illustrating why people would use your Web site. **Scenarios** are context-rich stories that focus more on *what* people will do than on *how*. (If your background is software engineering, you may be more familiar with the term *use cases*.) Here's an example of a scenario for a hypothetical Web site called ebirthdayz.com that specializes in helping customers shop for gifts:

> Victoria is a bright, young college student looking for a gift for her younger sister, who is turning 16 in two weeks. Like most college students, Victoria is on a tight budget, but she wants to get something memorable and useful for her sister on this important birthday for a young girl. She's heard some of her friends talk about ebirthdayz.com, so she decides to check it out. On the ebirthdayz.com homepage, she sees that the Web site has a gift recommendation feature. Victoria finds the recommendations screen and views gifts based on her sister's age and general interests, as well as her own limited finances. The site shows some suggestions, and Victoria chooses a popular favorite and buys it, including gift wrapping. Total time spent: 20 minutes.

A scenario tells us something about customers and their characteristics, the tasks they want to accomplish, and the context of their use of the site (in this case Victoria's sister's sixteenth birthday, which is important to Victoria).

It is useful to create many different scenarios for each of the several types of customers that you expect to come to your Web site. These detailed illustrative customers are often referred to as **personas.** Get lots of detail about your personas: name, background, what they do, where they live, and so on. Make these details as real as possible. You can put some of these details right in the scenarios, or you might put some only in a document where you describe your personas. Having real people in mind is even better because you can get more details later, when you need them.

Refer to the details when deciding between different ways of carrying out a design. You might ask, "Would Victoria use this feature for sending business gifts to colleagues? No, she's a college student and probably doesn't have a need for business gifts. This feature would be irrelevant to this type of customer." Reuse scenarios throughout the design process as a check, to see whether your design decisions still make sense in relation to the scenarios.

Sometimes scenarios include photographs or sketched storyboards. A **storyboard** is a sequence of Web pages that you create to give a rough idea of how someone might accomplish a given task. The storyboard in Figure 3.3 shows some rough cuts of how people would select different musical genres on a music Web site targeted at the Mobile Web (see Pattern Group M). Although you might be tempted to use software tools to make nice-looking storyboards, there are many good reasons to defer doing that at this stage [see Section 4.4, Rapid Prototyping, in Chapter 4 (Involving Customers with Iterative Design), for more information].

Again, note that scenarios don't say much about how things are accomplished. The preceding scenario does not say where the gift recommendation feature is located, nor does it specify how the gift recommendations are organized. At this early stage it's more important to determine whether the gift recommendation feature is a good idea at all before getting too detailed. Have the design team "walk through" a scenario to see if it makes sense. Is it a compelling story? Does it feel useful? Does it have a good UP-FRONT VALUE PROPOSITION (C2)? Are there any obvious problems with it?

Rich scenarios help you try out design ideas before even building software. They can also provide an idea of which genre patterns and other

Figure 3.3

This sketched story-board shows how a customer would accomplish one task using the design of a music site targeted at mobile device users.

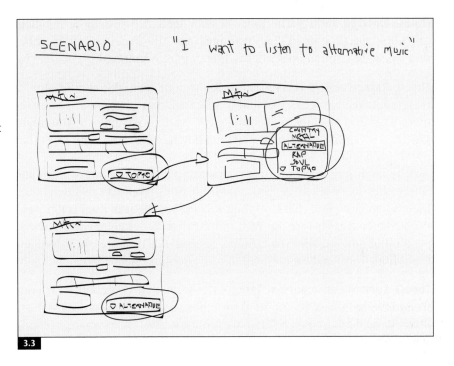

high-level patterns might be appropriate. Our scenario with Victoria, for example, would tell us that we should look at the PERSONALIZED RECOMMENDATIONS (G3) and GIFT GIVING (G6) patterns in Pattern Group G (Advanced E-Commerce). These patterns would be necessary, in addition to the patterns in Pattern Group F (Basic E-Commerce), to support the customer goals in the Victoria birthday scenario. Having several personas and scenarios will help you determine which other patterns might also apply.

Scenarios are also useful for describing to clients and customers what a Web site will offer. They tell us about particular customers, describing their situations and what they're trying to accomplish.

Choose Tasks

We have already mentioned that you can create several scenarios that illustrate your personas accomplishing a variety of goals or tasks. How do you choose these tasks, and what should they look like? These tasks will come from your initial task analysis and will be enriched by later observations and interviews with real customers.

Choose Detailed Tasks • The tasks in your scenarios should be detailed, providing specifics about the customers and the situations. Remember that a task description does not say how it is accomplished.

Choose Representative Tasks • The tasks in your scenarios should also be representative; that is, they should be real tasks that customers or prospective customers currently or eventually will want to accomplish. You might say, "I'm inventing something new; nobody has ever done the tasks that my site will allow!" Your site might allow someone to do things in a new way, but it is quite rare to invent something entirely new. For example, before sites like evite.com, you could not use a Web site to invite your friends to a party and check on their RSVPs, but the task itself is not new. People had parties before the Web was created, and they needed to invite people and find out who was coming. Instead of a Web site, they used letters, phone calls, and even e-mail to accomplish the same task.

Choose Common or Important Tasks • The tasks that you choose for your scenarios should also be common or important. Common tasks are those that will be done frequently. For an invitation site, for example, creating a new invitation and sending it out will be a common task. Important tasks are those that must be done correctly to avoid unfortunate consequences. Again, on our invitation site it is important that customers have the ability to create an account with their name and e-mail address registered correctly so that people they invite will know who is sending the invitation. Getting this wrong would not make the site very useful.

Choose Complete Tasks • Finally, make sure that the tasks you use describe a complete activity—that they are entire tasks, not subtasks or pieces of a task. Thinking about complete activities forces us to consider how features will work together, which is important because the tasks in your scenarios will become the basis for the site design and for the tasks used in future customer tests of the site.

Imagine that you're creating a Web-based banking site. You might decide that there are three different scenarios, each with a different task: (1) checking a savings account balance, (2) checking a checking account balance, and (3) transferring funds between savings and checking accounts. If you develop these three features independently and later test them, they might work just fine. Unfortunately, you might also end up with an awkward design and not know it until the site launches.

A more realistic complete task is a combination of the three subtasks just described to achieve a common customer goal: "Make sure that I have enough money in my checking account to cover the last check I wrote." This task would require first a verification that the checking account had sufficient funds. If not, the customer would next check the balance in savings and then move some money from savings to checking. If your banking site were designed to support only the three subtasks, using them in combination might be tedious. For instance, the design might require going back to a main menu to select a new operation. Only by knowing about complete, realistic tasks in advance would you be able to smoothly support those tasks in your design using, for instance, a TASK-BASED ORGANIZATION (B4) to make it easy to complete those subtasks in order.

The task analysis and sample scenarios generated so far are based on your knowledge and intuition, as well as on any interviews and observations that you might have carried out with prospective customers. In the next section we describe in more detail the techniques that you can use to get feedback from customers. In addition to helping you complete your initial analysis, these techniques can help you determine whether the analysis and scenarios are correct.

Observe and Interview Customers

Techniques for observing and interviewing customers can be quick and informal, consisting of conversations over coffee, or having customers show you what they do now in their homes or at work. We have found that most people are willing to help, especially if you explain that you're using the information to improve your site for them. And paying for coffee or lunch doesn't hurt.

Ethnographic Approaches Can Be Used for Observation • Ethnography is a more formal technique used in sociology and anthropology to observe and interact with people. Ethnographers study people in their normal environments. The advantage that ethnography has over techniques such as interviews and surveys is that you can watch what people actually do, as opposed to what they *say* they do. You can also ask them questions while they show you what they do, to verify your inferences. You can see the people with whom they communicate, the tools they use, and the kinds of things they create—things that may be difficult for participants to remember or explain when taken out of context. Although a rigorous ethnographic observation can be difficult and time-consuming, a more informal and "ethnographically inspired" field study can be fast and still yield valuable information that can drive the design.

For example, if you're building a banking site, your ethnographic research might include visiting a bank for a day and studying all the different types of transactions that customers perform with the teller. Because you're also extending banking capabilities into the home, you might also study the financial activities that people do at home, such as paying bills, checking balances, and transferring money. Ethnographically inspired observation is easier than you might think. First recruit some participants and ask if you can follow them around for a day or two and watch what they do. If they don't mind, use a digital camera to take pictures of their workplace or home. These pictures will make it easier to describe what you learned to your clients and to the rest of your design team.

In addition, see what kinds of Web sites people visit. Ask them to take you through your Web site or through a competitor's Web site. Ask them what they like and dislike about the sites. Observe the kinds of tools they use and note the kinds of information they use to make decisions. Ask questions to make sure you understand what they're doing. Run your interpretations by the customers to see if you're right. Look for any sign of disagreement, even signs as subtle as "Huh?," "Umm," and "Yes, but . . ." Customers will feel uncomfortable until you phrase the question correctly, but they may be hesitant to come right out and say so.

Follow Up with Informal Interviews • Tell any customers you interview what the Web site is supposed to do, and ask them what kinds of things they would like to do on the site. Ask if they have any ideas about how they would organize and structure parts of the Web site. Show them sketches and scenarios and ask what they think about these conceptualizations (do not show these sketches too early in the observation or interview because doing so might bias the customers). Although they cannot develop the design for you, customers can certainly provide a lot of useful information.

When talking to customers, phrase your questions carefully. Do not lead people toward a certain answer. Questions that do not lead to a simple yes or no answer are preferable. For example, questions like, "Would you like this feature?" do not work well because most people will just say, "Yeah, sure, why not?" You want to ask questions that get people talking so that you can hear what they're thinking.

A better way of asking a question is to show two alternatives and ask people what they think. It's difficult to judge something by itself. It's easier to compare the differences between two approaches.

Another way of phrasing the question is to give people a list of features and ask them to state how important each feature is on a scale from 1 to 7, with 1 being "not important" and 7 being "very important."

Recording observations and interviews using an audio recorder can make your job much easier and the data you collect more reliable. It's hard to keep up with taking notes while you're watching someone in action and speaking to them. Use your notes to record only the most important things and remember to write down the time that these events occur. This information will make it easier to find the corresponding place in the audiotape later. Transcribing your audiotapes can be tedious and time-consuming, but having a transcript is valuable for noticing subtle issues that you might have missed and helping you confirm inferences you might have made. Several services transcribe audiotapes for a modest price. We recommend that you take advantage of such a service if you can.

Conducting Interviews

Here are some tips for interviewing people about their work practices.

Avoid Interruptions • Turn off all mobile phones and find a quiet place that will not have any distractions. If possible, conduct your interviews in customers' normal environments, such as at work or at home, so that they can show you things while they're talking. In such cases the interviews are more like ethnographic observations.

Start with Easy Questions First • Wait to pose the harder questions until after the interviewee has talked for a while and is more comfortable speaking with you.

Ask Open-Ended Questions • Avoid asking simple yes or no questions. Ask questions that will get your interviewees to talk about their thoughts and experiences. Short questions that result in long answers are good—for example, "What do you like best about the current site, and why?"

Be Nonjudgmental and Accepting • Try not to be confrontational or condescending. It is not your job to judge what your interviewees are doing; your job is to learn how to make your Web site fit your customers better.

Listen • These are interviews, not conversations, so let the interviewees do the talking. While they're talking, note anything important and write down follow-up questions. Interrupt only if you need a clarification or if they start digressing. Give feedback, such as nodding your head and saying, "Uh-huh," to let your interviewees know you're listening, but note that it's also all right to allow extended periods of silence to let them collect their thoughts.

Organize the Information You Discover • Your observations and interviews will result in a lot of data. Organize and make sense of that information. In **affinity diagramming,** for example, all the individual points and concepts that you've gathered are arranged on a wall-sized, hierarchical diagram (see Figure 3.4). Write each concept on a Post-it note. Group related concepts together, and draw lines between related concepts in different groups. Use different colors to denote groups and even groups of groups, creating a hierarchy. The affinity diagram gives your team a visual explanation of the customer's problems and needs, all in one place. Affinity diagrams can eventually become the basis for your initial **information architecture,** and they are good starting points for scenarios and storyboards.

Card sorting is another easy technique for determining the best site organization. Card sorting helps you understand how to group items so that people will be able to find what they're looking for by recognizing the groups. It also helps you find and fix terminology that would be hard for customers to understand.

Figure 3.4

An affinity diagram organizes the information resulting from your interviews. Over time, this diagram can evolve into a site map representing the site's information architecture.

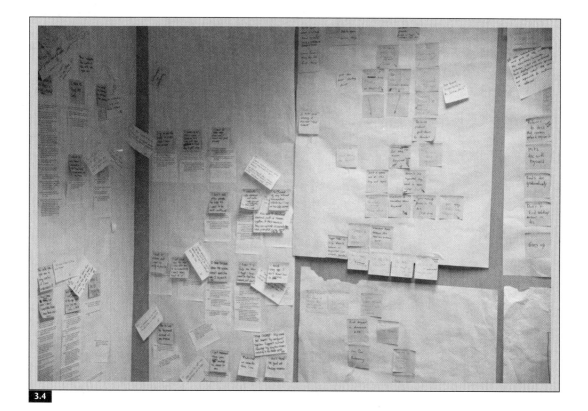

3.4

To understand card sorting, imagine that you want to organize a deck of playing cards. You could organize the cards by suit, separating them into clubs, spades, hearts, and diamonds. You could also validly organize the cards by number—that is, all four kings together, all four queens together, and so on. Alternatively, you could organize the cards by color, separating red cards from black cards. Because the groups in this last case would be relatively large, it might make sense to further subdivide the groups, by suit or by number.

Likewise, there are many ways of organizing Web pages. The point is that there are many valid ways of organizing content, and it all depends on what you need. You group pages in a way that makes sense, and then later you name the resulting categories. Variations of the card-sorting method include sorting the categories into subcategories, or even asking customers to carry out the card sorting.

Card sorting can be a useful exercise if you need to create or validate the organization of a site. For example, suppose your site starts with the following content:

Apples	Oranges	Bananas

Depending on your target customer, your sort might come out differently. If these were categories for a grocery site, you might sort them as follows:

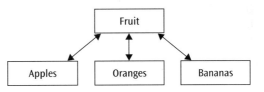

If customers were particularly concerned about freshly picked, locally grown fruit, you might sort the cards like this:

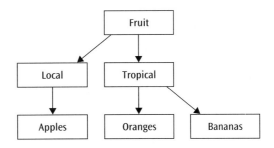

If customers were concerned about pesticide use, you might sort the cards like this:

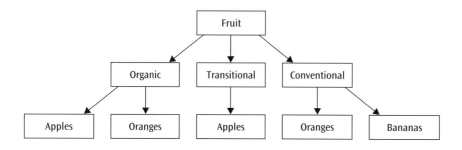

Just for the sake of argument, a botanist would probably sort the cards completely differently, maybe like this:

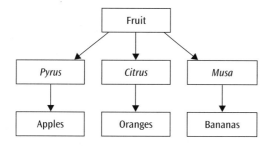

If you carry out a card-sorting activity with several customers or other team members, cluster the resultant groupings to understand where they agree and where they don't. Pay attention to the cases in which consensus could not be reached. Would renaming the item help? Some items might fit into several categories. An easy way to visualize the data is to use SynCaps, CardZort, or the National Institute of Standards and Technology's (NIST's) WebCAT (see the Resources section later in the book for details on downloading these tools). Asking these questions about where to put each content item and what to call the categories will help create the most customer-friendly content structure possible.

Know the Limits of These Techniques • Sometimes it's useful to observe how people work for at least a few days. The amount of information you learn about your customers during this time will be tremendous. However, it is difficult to capture some kinds of information in such a short time. For example, how do the environment or priorities change for families during events such as holiday seasons or childbirth? If you observed a family for just one or two days, you would probably miss subtleties like this.

Unfortunately, few of us have the time to carry out interviews and observations at this level of depth. This is one of the trade-offs you will have to consider, depending on your situation and the type of site you're attempting to design. Extended fieldwork might not be as useful for a site that customers occasionally visit for e-commerce transactions, but it may be crucial to spend lots of time on this type of field study for a Web application that someone will use for much of the day, every day.

Survey Your Customers

Traditionally used in market research, surveys are another useful way of finding out about your customers and helping you confirm who should be your target audience. Surveys are used to gather a great deal of information from lots of people. If you plan to revise your Web site, consider adding a survey on the existing Web site to get feedback from current customers about what they like and don't like. Use a combination of multiple-choice and free-form questions. Multiple-choice questions make your data analysis task easier and allow the respondent to move through your survey faster. Free-form responses let people write at length about what's right (and what's wrong) with the existing Web site.

Surveys can be conducted in several different ways. You can survey people in person. One especially effective technique is to approach people coming into a shopping mall and ask them whether they would like to help improve a Web site. Mailing surveys to your target audience or using a market research firm to ask survey questions over the phone are also common techniques. When mailing surveys, be careful to get responses from a representative sample of customers. This problem largely goes away with telephone sampling. All three of these techniques, however, can be expensive and take a lot of time to yield results.

The Web opens up the opportunity to carry out survey-based research online. Several firms offer this service, or you can have your development team build a simple survey tool for you. Web-based surveys can be delivered via e-mail to research participants (from your customer list or from a list you buy from a market research firm), in FLOATING WINDOWS (H6) to a randomly sampled set of visitors to your site, or as a link on a feedback page. This flexibility offers you a powerful way to get survey results about your customers quickly.

(H6)

Convincing people to participate in a survey usually requires some enticement. Offer potential participants a chance to win a prize in a drawing, a T-shirt, a coffee mug, or cash.[6] The reward you offer will depend on how much time the survey takes to complete. The longer it is, the more you have to "pay." What you pay might range anywhere from $15 to $100 (U.S.). This, along with the fact that people will simply stop participating in a survey that is too long, is one reason to make your survey take less than 15 minutes to complete. This is especially true for Web-based surveys, which people tend to give up on even more quickly. The reward will also depend on the type of participant you're trying to recruit. It is not unusual to offer executive-level participants cash compensation or a donation of $250 or more to their favorite charity in exchange for 45 minutes of their time.

Surveys can be tricky, though. At best, you can get a lot of data and make conclusions that are based on quantitative results. This can be helpful for convincing others in your organization about the usefulness of the results. Unfortunately, when you want to make quantitative conclusions, you need to be sure that those conclusions make sense from a statistical perspective. Surveys have to be designed properly to give you **reliable data**—results that would be found consistently if you ran the survey over and over with the same type of audience under the same conditions. Also make sure you have enough participants, and get a high enough response rate that you achieve **statistical validity**—results that are highly likely to be right.

A lot of the survey work that we've seen on the Web simply falls down on one or both of these issues. We recommend that you work with a firm that has expertise in this area, as well as read a good book on survey design to understand the full impact of drawing conclusions on poorly collected data.

Also keep in mind that surveys report on what people *say*, not on what people *do*. A lot of research has found that what people say does not always correspond to what they do. This is especially true when people have to reconstruct specific details about what they do on the Web. People can remember things at a high level, but they tend to quickly forget the details. Despite these shortcomings, surveys have repeatedly proved effective for determining the target market, product and concept feasibility, price elasticity, attitudinal and brand image, general opinions, and preferences.

---

6 It is amazing what well-paid people will do for a free T-shirt or coffee mug that would ordinarily cost them maybe ten U.S. dollars.

Ultimately, however, if you want to know what people really do, or are going to do, you should watch them in action.

Run Focus Groups

Focus groups are commonly used by market researchers to find out about customers and their opinions. In a **focus group,** a handful of people (6–12) who are representative of target customers are brought into a meeting as a group. They may or may not know each other beforehand. As in the interviewing process already described, people are asked questions about competitors' Web sites and about the proposed Web site. If you're revising your Web site, you might ask members of the focus group what they like and dislike about the site. If you're creating a new Web site, ask them the same questions about your competitors' Web sites. Get their feedback on the proposed Web site by showing them sketches or pictures of how it will work. It is also common to present scenarios of future use to see how these ideas resonate with the group.

Just like the Boy Scouts, you should have the motto "Be prepared!" when it comes to focus groups. Do not go in blindly and hope you will find useful information. Identify what you want to find out. Have an idea of what you're looking for, and make sure that all of the questions you ask will help you learn whether you're going in the right direction. Also be ready for criticism. Although it may sting a little in the short run, it will result in higher-quality designs in the end. Other members of the development team or management can sit in on these meetings. Hearing comments directly from customers is much more convincing than reading reports. Be sure to keep the number of these insiders low, though, so that you don't overwhelm the focus group.

Focus groups are difficult to run well. Often the moderator can be too controlling and drive the group to conclusions that he or she would like to see. Another common problem is that an individual in the group dominates and causes groupthink to emerge as the other members defer. To draw out these other members, you'll need to quiet the dominating person. Find moderators who have experience running a focus group, because they will be familiar with these problems and know how to handle them gracefully.

Note also that you may get different results, depending on the chemistry of the people in the group. Sometimes your results will be positive, sometimes negative, and sometimes very negative—all in response to the same questions and the same examples. For this reason it is usually a good idea to run a focus group several times, with different types of people, in different geographic locations. Also be careful in your recruiting to avoid **professional respondents,** focus group members who make money on the side by going from group to group. You want to get people who are representative of your customers, not people who are just conveniently available.

One caveat about focus groups is that, like surveys, they let you learn only what people *say,* but not necessarily what they actually *do.* In other words, you can learn a lot about people's attitudes and perceptions, but not much about what they might do in practice. This is why focus groups are more useful for the early stages of design, when you're more interested in finding out about your customers than in trying to evaluate what they will do with a Web interface that you have not yet built or even prototyped. This kind of information is still valuable, but it should be supplemented with the other techniques described here.

Analyze Existing Web Sites

Another way of getting information about potential customers and their needs is to ask them to evaluate existing Web sites. Use your existing Web site or a competitor's Web site to get a feel for what works and what doesn't. Recruit some representative customers, and observe what they say they want to do on the Web site, what they actually do, and what steps they take to do it. Make note of the kinds of mistakes they make, and pay special attention to what they say they like and don't like. You might also want to have a questionnaire that they can fill out, to learn more about their demographic information and their interests and subjective ratings. In Chapter 4 (Involving Customers with Iterative Design), we discuss in more detail how to do this.

Start your analysis by finding all the people who sent you e-mail about your Web site. Whether they suggested a new feature or criticized a feature that did not make sense, these are the customers who cared enough to make a comment about your site in the first place. If they live close enough, consider asking if you can visit them for an interview, or if they can come to your office to help evaluate the Web site.

Don't rely only on this type of customer, though. Because they have voluntarily sent a complaint or suggestion, such customers have already been self-selected as having a certain type of personality or level of expertise that may differ from that of the majority of your customers. Make an effort to find a wide range of people who are representative of your overall customer base.

3.3   Take-away Ideas

A customer-centered design process involves first knowing who your customers are and then keeping them involved throughout the design process. In knowing your customers, you will learn their skills and knowledge (people), what they want to do on your site (tasks), the equipment and software they use (technology), and the larger social and organizational context in which they work, play, and live (social issues).

The potential customers visiting a Web site, the things they want to accomplish, the technologies available to them, and their social and organizational contexts are all highly variable. This is why you need a good understanding of these variables before starting implementation. The methods we have described in this chapter may seem too time-consuming if you haven't used them before. Start with one at a time. Run a few informal surveys or interviews of your customers early in the design process for a new project. As you become more comfortable with the process and its benefits, add more.

If you don't know your customers, it is easy to build features that customers consider only marginally useful or even useless. It is also easy to overlook features that customers deem important. And even if the selected features are right, it's just as easy to build them incorrectly, by organizing the information in a confusing manner, using unfamiliar terms, or having an error-prone navigation scheme that makes the features impossible to find. Chapter 4 (Involving Customers with Iterative Design) and the pattern group chapters will help you build the features right.

Involving Customers with Iterative Design

The primary principle of customer-centered design is *know your customers,* as discussed in Chapter 3 (Knowing Your Customers: Principles and Techniques). Now you will learn three related principles: (1) keep the customers involved, (2) conduct rapid prototyping, and (3) evaluate your designs. Omitting any of these principles from your design processes is a major risk. Studies by the Standish Group International have attributed many of information technology's frequent project failures to a lack of end-customer input.

Iterative design addresses this problem by calling for setting measurable goals and repeatedly refining and testing design prototypes with customers until the final design meets or surpasses those goals. Your goals can be high-level and strategic, such as increased customer satisfaction or increased sales. They can also be short-term and tactical, such as reduced time to find items or fewer mouse clicks to check out and complete a purchase.

4.1 The Iterative Design Process

In **iterative design,** a new or existing design is reworked until it fits the needs of customers. This process is widely considered to be a valuable technique for designing interfaces, but at a more fundamental level iterative design acknowledges that *no design team is perfect.*

Teams are made of people, and people do not always know the right answers. It is difficult to have complete information about the needs of customers and clients. Iterative design compensates for these shortcomings, letting you continually improve a design. The key to iterative design is to quickly create design prototypes that are good enough to provide feedback but flexible enough for significant changes to be made

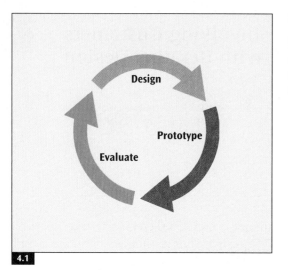

4.1

Figure 4.1

Iterative design is an ongoing cycle composed of three steps: design, prototype, and evaluate.

down the line. The goal is to conduct as much iteration as possible to solve as many problems as possible early, when they are inexpensive to fix.

The iterative design process has three steps (see Figure 4.1):

1. **Design.** In this step, teams consider business goals and customer needs, setting measurable goals and developing design concepts.
2. **Prototype.** In this step, teams develop artifacts as basic as scenarios and storyboards, and as complex as running Web sites, that illustrate how the site will accomplish the goals outlined in step 1.
3. **Evaluate.** In this step, teams assess the prototypes developed in step 2 to see if they meet the desired goals.

The results of this process are used to inform design in the next iteration, and the entire process repeats until the goals have been met. Sometimes, however, scheduling and budgeting constraints force work to begin on the final production site before all the goals have been met.

Use design patterns to help you move quickly through each step of iterative design. During the initial design stage, use the information you learned about your customers, the genre patterns, and other high-level patterns to rough out the basic features that your site will need. Use the more detailed, low-level patterns to help you storyboard and prototype Web pages for specific scenarios. After evaluating your prototypes with customers, clients, and other team members, use the patterns again to find solutions to the particular problems they encountered. Use these solutions in the next design iteration.

Before working on the final production site, go through this iterative cycle several times in the early stages of design and *make simple prototypes instead of full-fledged sites*. Real Web sites can take several weeks or months to implement, and by the time a site is completed and ready for evaluation, it might already be too expensive and time-consuming to fix any problems.

In contrast, prototypes can be created in just a few hours or days. The prototypes will not have all the features of a finished site, and many features will be faked, but they will be real enough to give customers a flavor of what the final site will be like. In this way you can get a lot of feedback about what works and what doesn't. (We talk more about how to create prototypes in Section 4.4, Rapid Prototyping.)

4.2   Reasons to Use Iterative Design

There are three main reasons to use an iterative design process:

1. It will help you find problems while they're still inexpensive and easy to fix.
2. It ensures that the site you're building will have the features that your customers need.
3. It ensures that you're building those features in a way that your customers can use.

Fixing Errors While They're Still Inexpensive and Easy to Fix

Why is it important to fix errors as early as possible? It has been well documented in many disciplines that fixing errors in the later phases of design can be expensive. The famous architect Frank Lloyd Wright[1] said it best: "An architect's most useful tools are an eraser at the drafting board, and a wrecking bar at the site." Clearly, using the wrecking bar and rebuilding is far more expensive than simply erasing and redesigning. In the realm of software development, a general rule of thumb is that errors cost about *ten times* more effort and money to fix late in the process than if they are caught in an earlier phase. Watts Humphrey and others in the

---

1   Quoted in D. A. Aaker, *Brand Portfolio Strategy: Creating Relevance, Differentiation, Energy, Leverage, and Clarity* (New York: Free Press, 2004).

field of software engineering have even documented costs on the order of a hundred to a thousand times more effort and money to fix problems after deployment.

Why does it cost so much to make downstream changes? There are three reasons: (1) All the deliverables generated in later phases of design have to be made consistent with the proposed changes. (2) Sometimes one change forces other changes to be made so that everything will work correctly. (3) Most importantly, anything that causes a change in the software source code and HTML is expensive. Think about the time it takes to change a simple sketch versus the time it takes to rewrite the code that implements the ideas in the sketch.

Suppose that you already have a Web site but want to add LOCATION BREAD CRUMBS (K6), tiny markers like **Home > About > History,** at the top of each page so that your customers always know where they are in the site. Not only does this change have to be made on every page, but you also have to redesign the overall page layout to accommodate that change. Style sheets and other template mechanisms may make the technical part of this change much easier, but you will still have to make significant design and layout changes so that it all makes sense.

Now this is just a trivial change. Imagine the kind of effort it would take to make more involved changes, such as altering the way information is organized on the site or adding a significant feature that requires new code. Add these costs to what was spent in the first place, and you'll see why downstream changes are expensive.

K6

Building the Right Site, and Building the Site Right

What kinds of mistakes are made on Web sites? Figure 4.2 categorizes the problems by feature and implementation. The top right-hand quadrant shows the right feature but the wrong implementation. For example, a SHOPPING CART (F3) is definitely the right feature for an e-commerce site, but it could have implementation problems that make it hard for customers to check out and finalize purchases. Iterative design and testing will help you discover these types of problems.

F3

The bottom left-hand quadrant of Figure 4.2 shows the wrong feature but the right implementation. For example, providing extremely sophisticated search features for power users is not very useful if most of your customers cannot even understand the basic search capabilities.

The bottom right-hand quadrant shows the wrong feature and the wrong implementation—a design that is not useful *and* does not work correctly.

Figure 4.2

Iterative design helps design teams find the features that customers need (the "right" features) and make sure that those features are implemented correctly (the "right" implementation).

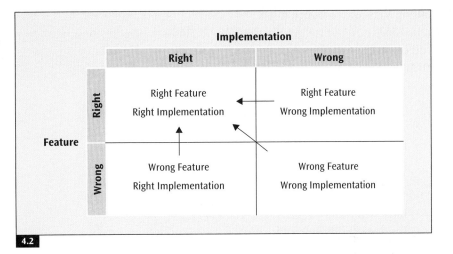

A good design process, like the one presented in Chapter 5 (Processes for Developing Customer-Centered Sites), should filter out most of these sorts of problems.

Ultimately, you want to be in the top left-hand quadrant, with the right features and the right implementations of those features. Iterative design helps push you toward the top left by getting constant feedback from customers about features and their implementation.

To summarize, design mistakes are costly, and it pays off in the long run to find them as early as possible in the development cycle. This is why rapid iterative design is so important in the early phases: it helps teams find and root out as many problems as possible *before* the site is deployed.

4.3 Designing with Goals and Principles in Mind

The design process is driven by both goals and principles. Goals come directly from analyzing your business and customer needs [see Chapter 3 (Knowing Your Customers: Principles and Techniques)]. Design principles come from research in human–computer interaction, as well as graphic design. Following these principles as you iterate on your design will help you reach your goals. Most of these goals and principles will apply whether you're working on your site's information architecture, navigation design, or graphic design.

Setting Measurable Design Goals

What does it mean to "get the site right"? This is where business, usability, and customer experience goals come into play. Some possible design goals include the following:

- Faster task completion
- Successful completion of more tasks
- Greater ease of learning
- Commission of fewer errors
- Abandonment of fewer shopping carts
- Greater pleasure or satisfaction
- More fun
- Increased visitor-to-customer conversion rate
- Increased customer repeat visits
- Increased revenue

Studies that we've conducted show that achieving many of the usability and customer experience goals, such as giving a more satisfying experience, have a direct impact on achieving business-related goals such as increased customer repeat visits.

The key to achieving all of these goals is testing and measuring. The rest of this section outlines examples of tests and measures that you can undertake to assess your progress toward your design goals.

For example, suppose that you want to know how long it takes to complete common tasks, such as checking out and finalizing a purchase. In this case, task completion time is an important metric. You could recruit representative customers to try out the site to measure the time it takes to complete these tasks, time how long it takes them to finish each task, see if they complete their tasks successfully, observe where they have problems, and determine whether there's any commonality among the problems. Are the problems occurring in the same places? Are they navigation errors? Are they problems with the search feature? See if an existing design pattern from this book can help. Implement the necessary changes and retest to see if you solved the problems.

Suppose your server logs indicate that customers who start to post messages in the community section of your site have a low rate of completing the postings. A follow-on usability study confirms that customers are distracted in the middle of the posting process and tend to follow some tangential links, never to return. This finding might indicate a good place to apply a PROCESS FUNNEL (H1), which will help your customers go through the steps of completing their initial task: posting a message.

Another approach to achieving your design goals is to compare two different prototypes to see which one works best. You might find that with one of the designs, customers are 20 percent faster on average than with the other design. A similar approach is to compare the new site design to the existing design or the design of one of your competitors' sites.

Alternatively, you might want to know how quickly customers get up to speed using the sites. Obtaining this information can be harder than it sounds. You could measure how many hours of use customers need on average to complete a particular set of tasks successfully. Or you could measure how many tasks customers complete in a certain amount of time. Both of these forms of ease-of-learning measures can be used to compare your site designs to one another and to the competition.

Another option is to measure and compare the average number of errors made on each site. If your customers make errors and become confused, they will not be able to achieve their goals on the site. For example, they will not be able to buy your products. To measure errors, first define them. Does clicking on the browser's **Back** button indicate an error? For example, suppose a customer is purchasing five cartridges of printer toner online. As he finishes the checkout process and fills out a form with his credit card number and address, he notices that he forgot to change the quantity on the order form on the previous page. The customer has to go back to correct the mistake. Is simply going back an error? When he goes forward again, the billing information might be lost. Is losing the billing information an error? Probably, but you have to define what you're measuring first.

Sometimes you can find issues with specific pieces of your site that do not necessarily indicate an interface problem but might indicate a general problem with your content or policies. For example, many sites measure the rate of shopping cart abandonment before checkout. The checkout process might be too long [this interface problem is addressed (F1) in QUICK-FLOW CHECKOUT (F1)], but there are several alternative explanations that may be based on your content. Customers might abandon their shopping carts if they cannot find all the products that they want to purchase. Another explanation is that your prices are higher than a competitor's, and people are just there to comparison-shop. A fourth explanation could be that customers are surprised at how high the sales tax or shipping and handling costs are and decide to leave. At any rate, the metric of shopping cart abandonment is certainly tied to your business's revenue numbers.

The key to any of the numerical measurements discussed so far is to make sure that you're looking at numbers that make sense. This is where statistics and research design come into play. As we mentioned in Chapter 3 (Knowing Your Customers: Principles and Techniques), when designing surveys and usability studies you want to ensure that your numerical results are both reliable and valid. Be certain you have enough research participants to get statistically significant results. Often 20 to 50 participants might be required, depending on the variability in their background and performance.

You might also want to look at more subjective metrics. Do your customers find your site more pleasing or satisfying than the last version of the site, or your competitors' sites? Is your site fun? You can measure responses to questions such as these on an ongoing basis to understand how your site and your customers' opinions change over time. This information will help you know when you need to conduct more in-depth research. Again, these numbers can be tied directly to your bottom-line revenue or profit.

You can measure these subjective issues with surveys. Online surveys are easy to create and can be sent to a representative sample of your customers, or they can be made available on one of your Web pages. Target additional surveys for specific pages, or for times when customers take specific actions. Would you like to ask visitors why they abandoned their shopping carts? You can ask them with a survey, right when it happens!

The design goals that we've talked about so far are only an approximation of the higher-level client and business goals you might have. For example, shorter task completion time and less shopping cart abandonment are important metrics to work toward, but the business goal for an e-commerce site is to increase revenue. The problem is that you simply cannot gather this kind of metric using prototypes. Still, prototypes are good enough to provide useful feedback that will bring you closer to the overall goals.

Adhering to Design Principles

Design goals represent the destination you want to reach when you're finished building a Web site. Design *principles* guide you to that destination. The patterns in this book were guided by design principles, as well as by observation of what has worked well for customers. Here we present some basic design principles that you can use to tailor the patterns to your particular situation. Entire books could be written about these principles. The seven that we present are based on those from some of the most respected sources, specifically Ben Shneiderman's eight golden rules of interface design, Jakob Nielsen's ten heuristics, and Edward Tufte's musings on information presentation:

1. **Be consistent throughout.** Consistency applies across several dimensions. Use a consistent sequence of actions to carry out similar tasks. Pages should have consistent color, layout, and fonts, implemented manually or by the use of STYLE SHEETS (D11). For example, your NAVIGATION BAR (K2) should be in the same place on every page, and ACTION BUTTONS (K4) that do the same thing should appear in the same general location across different parts of the site. Use identical terms in different places across the site. Make your site consistent with the real world: follow real-world conventions, and use FAMILIAR LANGUAGE (K11), sticking to terms that your customers will understand rather than technical jargon.

2. **Offer informative feedback.** Make the status of the system visible, and keep your customers informed about what's going on. For example, this is the principle behind SECURE CONNECTIONS (E6), which lets customers know whether the information that they're about to send over the Internet will be safe, and the PROGRESS BAR (H13), which indicates to the customer that a Web site is still functioning.

3. **Rely on recognition over recall.** Short-term memory is the key limitation in human cognition. Reducing the short-term memory load is easy if people can *recognize* what they need to know from visible objects, actions, options, and directions. The memory load is much higher if they need to *recall* this information from memory with no visual aids. This is why a visual user interface like that of the Macintosh or Windows is easier to learn than a command language–based interface like DOS. This is also why ACTION BUTTONS (K4) should always have a textual label to go along with the graphical icon.

4. **Help customers avoid and recover from errors.** Errors cause frustration, poor performance, and a lack of trust in your site. PREVENTING ERRORS (K12) will help avoid many of these problems. Unfortunately, no matter how well you design the site, humans will make occasional errors. Help people recover from errors by presenting MEANINGFUL ERROR MESSAGES (K13). Tell them what happened and how to recover, or better yet, offer to automatically carry out the steps that would help them recover from the error.

5. Support customer control and freedom. Customers should sense that their actions determine the site's responses, and that they're not being forced down a fixed path. Providing MULTIPLE WAYS TO NAVIGATE (B1) is one example of how to support this impression on your site. It also means that the customer is given easy exits, such as undo and redo options, for mistaken choices. The browser's built-in **Back** and **Forward** buttons and LOCATION BREAD CRUMBS (K6) are mechanisms that give customers easy exits on the Web.

(B1)

(K6)

6. Help frequent customers use accelerators. Keyboard shortcuts are important for expert customers. Your site can support frequent actions automatically. For example, your site can store information, such as shipping addresses, and use PREDICTIVE INPUT (H11) so that your customers do not have to retype this information every time they come back to a page. Design an ACCOUNT MANAGEMENT (H4) interface that makes it easy for your customer to see and change this stored information.

(H11)

(H4)

7. Strive for aesthetic and minimalist design. Clean aesthetics make using your site a pleasing experience. A GRID LAYOUT (I1) is one common technique you can use to ensure that your site has a clean, understandable look. Well-designed type, images, and graphical elements communicate how the site works. Often visual elements are overused. If removal does no harm to the site, take out irrelevant information and graphics from all pages. Every extra element draws attention away from the ones that matter.[2]

(I1)

These principles sometimes conflict. Use your best judgment to resolve these conflicts. For example, supporting individual control and freedom may conflict with helping customers avoid errors. Sometimes, as in the case of a PROCESS FUNNEL (H1), restricting control and freedom can help customers complete their tasks. Use these restrictions judiciously, though. We have tried to make these conflicts apparent when discussing the forces that come to bear on each pattern in Part II of the book.

(H1)

Information Architecture, Navigation Design, and Graphic Design

No matter what form of design you're carrying out—information architecture, navigation design, or graphic design—use the design goals and

---

2   As Edward Tufte says, "Graphical excellence is that which gives the viewer the greatest number of ideas in the shortest time, with the least ink in the smallest space" [from *The Visual Display of Quantitative Information* (1983), p. 51].

Figure 4.3

The spaces of information architecture, navigation design, graphic design, and usability evaluation overlap. Traditional user interface design is primarily navigation design and usability evaluation, with a touch of information architecture and graphic design.

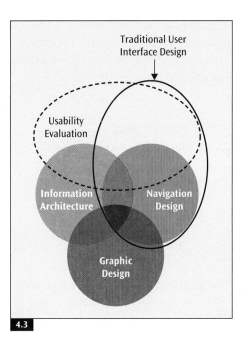

4.3

principles that we have described to guide your work. **Information architecture** means identifying, structuring, and presenting groups of related content in a logical and coherent manner.[3] **Navigation design** means designing methods so that customers can find their way around the information structure. **Graphic design** means developing the visual communication of information, using elements such as color, images, typography, and layout. Information architecture and navigation design are typically carried out before graphic design.

Figure 4.3 shows how these three types of design relate to one another, as well as how usability evaluation and traditional user interface design fit into the picture. All three approaches to design are necessary.

---

3 There is an ongoing (and sometimes heated) debate in the design community about the delineation of *information architecture* versus *information design*. In general, information architecture focuses more on things like structure and language, while information design concentrates on presentation and perception. However, distinctions between these two fields are still very blurry. Information architecture and information design represent a convergence of multiple disciplines with different backgrounds, vocabularies, and cultures. The key here is to go beyond these superficial differences and to focus on what they all have in common: helping customers find, understand, and manage complex information.

A graphic design that is rich with images cannot compensate for a poor information architecture. Likewise, a clean information architecture cannot make up for a navigation design that hides the location of all the navigation elements.

Rapid Prototyping

As we said earlier, a key principle of iterative design is rapid prototyping— quickly creating rough-and-ready mock-ups that provide useful feedback. These prototypes can help reduce risk, lead to smaller and less complex systems, and nail down what customers really need. In the sections that follow we describe how to do rapid prototyping, beginning with a description of the different design artifacts that are created during iterative Web site design.

Site Maps, Storyboards, and Schematics

Typically, early in the design and prototyping phases three kinds of design artifacts are developed: site maps, storyboards, and schematics. A **site map** is a high-level diagram showing the overall structure of a site (see Figures 4.4 and 4.5). It is used primarily to reflect an understanding of the information structure, or architecture, of the site as it is being built and, to a limited extent, the navigation structure, or **flow** through the site.

A **storyboard** is a sequence of Web pages depicting how a customer would accomplish a given task (see Figures 4.6 and 3.3). Use storyboards to illustrate important interaction sequences, or flows through a site. When showing ideas to a client, you can accompany storyboards with a narrative about the task that the customer is trying to accomplish. That is, you might show the client the complete **scenario** you developed, or at least a small piece of it.

Schematics are representations of the layout and content that will appear on individual pages (see Figure 4.7). They are usually devoid of images, though they may indicate, with a label, where to place an image. The fonts, colors, and layout are often quite preliminary, not indicating a final decision, but instead giving the graphic designer hints about which information needs to be highlighted or grouped together.

You probably noticed that the illustrations of site maps, storyboards, and schematics here look pretty basic. At this stage they are just abstract representations, not to be taken literally. Their purpose is to get the big ideas across, without the irrelevant details that distract reviewers.

Figure 4.4

A site map is a high-level diagram that depicts the overall organization of a site. This site map shows the structure of a Web site that helps people find online deals and electronic coupons. The set of pages on the right represents a naviga-tion bar that is avail-able on every page.

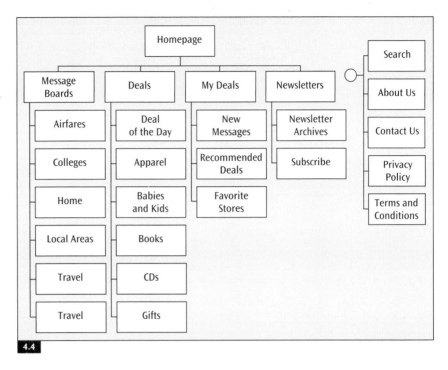

4.4

Figure 4.5

This site map shows part of the structure and flow of a person-alized news site. [This design has a problem: it forces people to sign in before they see any content. See the SIGN-IN/NEW ACCOUNT (H2) pattern for more details.]

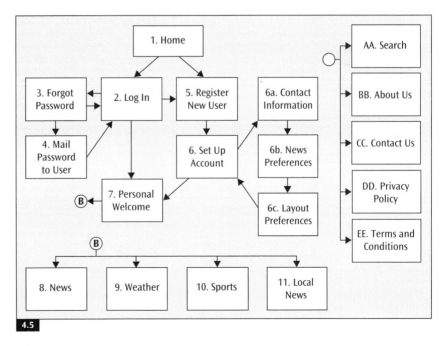

4.5

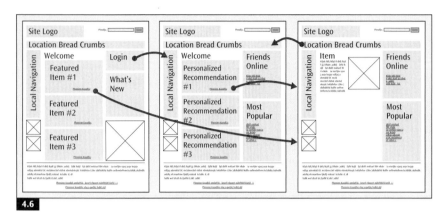

Figure 4.6

Storyboards show the steps that a customer would take to accomplish a task. This storyboard shows how a customer interacts with a site that lets groups of friends find, recommend, and share things with each other.

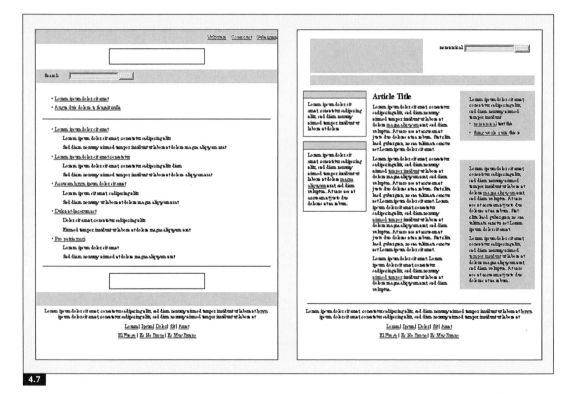

Figure 4.7

These two examples of schematics have the feel of complete individual Web pages.

Research that we carried out with Mark Newman, a human–computer interaction researcher, found that often designers first sketch out all three of these representations on paper (see Figures 4.8, 3.3, and 4.9). Before showing these representations to clients or customers, many designers like to clean them up by creating electronic versions. Others are comfortable showing the informal, sketched representations to get validation earlier in the process and keep the discussion focused on the important issues. Cleaning things up too much may cause your reviewers to improperly focus on the colors, fonts, and visual alignment. It really depends on your clients and their expectations. If you manage their expectations well, your clients will understand why you're showing them rough sketches.

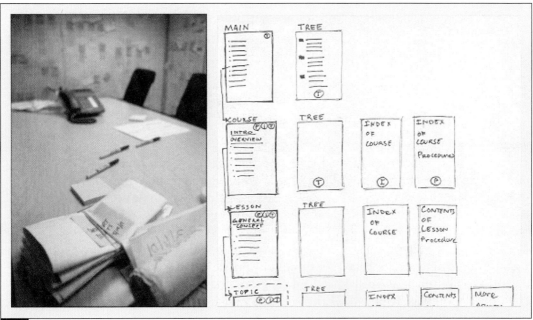

4.8a, b

Figure 4.8

Create site maps on walls, using pens, papers, and Post-it notes (a). This technique, known as *affinity diagramming*, lets multiple team members brainstorm simultaneously and provides a large, immersive display for working on large sites. When you're finished brainstorming, copy the site map to paper (b) or take a digital photo to capture the design.

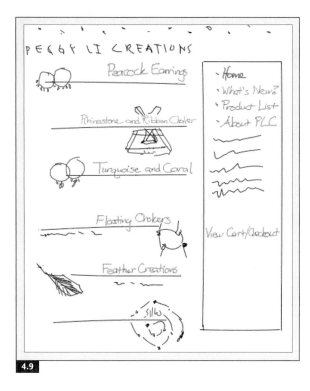

4.9

Figure 4.9

A low-fidelity prototype is a quickly created, rough sketch that gives an overall feeling of what's needed on the page, without going into unnecessary detail. This sketched schematic illustrates the main functionality available at a Web-based custom jewelry store.

Progressive Refinement, from Low Fidelity to High Fidelity

The great thing about prototypes is that they can be created quickly and used to get feedback from customers. Low-fidelity prototyping is one technique that many designers use to accomplish this task. In **low-fidelity prototyping,** you use paper, whiteboards, Post-it notes, and markers to create rough cuts of a Web site. That's it. Sketches are low-fidelity ("low-fi") when they are far from the final design in both their visual and their interactive details. For example, Figure 4.9 shows hand-drawn graphics and handwritten text, much of it represented by squiggly lines. In addition to sketching, you can use cut, copy, and paste techniques with scissors, glue, and photocopying machines.

Using a set of low-fidelity pages, you can test a design with representative customers. Sit them down in front of your sketches and ask how they would complete a particular task. On the basis of the customer's verbal responses or pointing, one of your teammates can "play computer" and flip to a new page to show the designed output of the site. Observing what customers do with these low-fi designs will give you valuable information

Figure 4.10

A high-fidelity proto-type, such as this one, is detailed and rich with typography, color, and graphics.

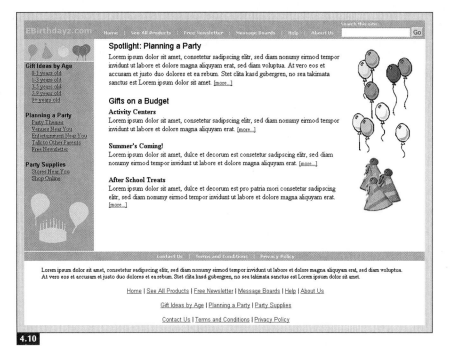

about how to refine your early design ideas. This type of prototyping and testing can let you go through an entire iterative design cycle—design, prototype, evaluate—in less than a day.[4]

Our personal experience has shown that it is *at least* ten to twenty times easier and faster to create a low-fidelity prototype than an equivalent high-fidelity ("hi-fi") prototype. By **high-fidelity prototype,** we mean one that looks polished and complete, created with computer-based tools such as Macromedia Dreamweaver or Adobe Photoshop or Illustrator (see Figure 4.10). We're not saying that you don't need hi-fi prototypes—just that you don't need them in the *early stages of design*. It's not worth the effort of focusing on colors, fonts, and alignment when there are more important issues, like organization and overall site structure, to worry about.

---

4   Read Mark Rettig's article, "Prototyping for Tiny Fingers" (see the Resources section later in the book), for a great how-to on creating low-fidelity prototypes and testing them with customers. Another, more in-depth resource in this area is Carolyn Snyder's book titled *Paper Prototyping*.

Another advantage of low-fi prototypes is that, because specific programming or graphic design skills are not required, the contributions and insights of each team member can be easily integrated into the design. Even CEOs have been observed creating low-fi prototypes! Creating low-fi prototypes and evaluating them with customers is a good team-building experience, even for people whose roles traditionally do not include interaction with customers. Going through this process will get everyone on the same page about what customers really need. You will find that it is a lot more effective and fun to create low-fi prototypes than to argue endlessly about what customers *might* want.

Avoid Computer-Based Tools in the Early Design Stages • Research shows that designers who work out conceptual ideas on paper tend to iterate more and explore the design space more broadly, whereas designers using computer-based tools tend to take only one idea and work it out in detail.

Nearly every one of the designers we have talked to has observed that *the discussion is qualitatively different when people are presented with a high-fidelity prototype*. Clients often respond with comments like, "I do

What's in a Paper Prototyping Kit?

It's a good idea to create a paper prototyping kit, a small box of goodies for making paper prototypes that everyone on your team can access. Here's a shopping list of supplies that every kit needs to be complete:

Lots of paper (both white and colored construction paper)
Lots of index cards
Lots of Post-its
Transparencies
Scotch tape
Scissors
An X-ACTO knife
Paste
Markers (with lots of colors)
Pens
Rulers
Duct tape (hey, you never know when it will come in handy)

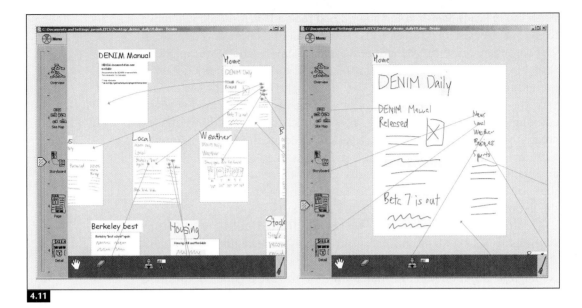

4.11

Figure 4.11

These two screen shots illustrate how DENIM, a sketch-based Web site design tool for the early stages of design, allows you to quickly sketch Web pages, create links among them, and interact with them in a run mode. You can use zooming to integrate the different ways of viewing a site, from site map to storyboard to individual pages.

not like your color scheme," or "These two buttons need to be aligned correctly." When presented with a low-fidelity prototype, however, clients are more likely to say something like, "These labels on the navigation bar do not make sense to me," or "You're missing a link to the shopping cart here on this page." In other words, with low-fidelity prototypes, which lack irrelevant details like color, font, and alignment to distract the eye, people focus on the interaction and on the overall site structure.

All of the tools used in Web design today focus on creating finished products. Tools like Microsoft FrontPage, Adobe GoLive, and Macromedia Dreamweaver help you create production Web sites, not early prototypes. Other tools used by designers, such as Microsoft Visio, Macromedia Director, Adobe Illustrator, and Adobe Photoshop, have the same problem. Until tools that support the progression from low-fidelity to high-fidelity prototypes become widely available, we advocate that you delay using computer-based tools. Incidentally, we have developed a research-quality tool called DENIM that allows you to "sketch" low-fidelity prototypes on a computer (see Figure 4.11).[5]

5 If you are ambitious, try out DENIM at dub.washington.edu/denim.

When You're Ready, Switch to Computer-Based Tools • When should you move to computer-based tools? It depends on your work practices. If you find that you absolutely must save designs and e-mail them to others, you might be ready. Design teams often want to switch to using a computer when they're presenting to clients. In our interviews, the general consensus was that you should not show low-fidelity sketches to clients, because they are perceived as unprofessional. However, high-fidelity mock-ups take a long time to create, and again they have the drawback of directing the discussion toward extremely fine details too soon. One solution is to go ahead with sketches and, as we mentioned before, manage clients' expectations by explaining that you're using sketches instead of computer-based designs to speed up the iteration process and to focus on the right issues at this stage.

Another solution is to use what we call **medium-fidelity prototypes** (see Figure 4.12). Medium-fidelity prototypes have many more details about content, but they do not distract clients or customers with fonts, colors, and graphics. Medium-fidelity prototypes are a good compromise if you need to present mock-ups.

At some point your team will have most of the major structural and interaction issues hammered out and satisfactorily tested with customers.

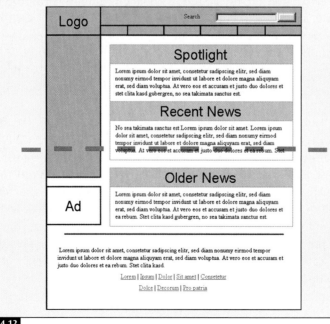

Figure 4.12

A medium-fidelity prototype is a cleaned-up illustration that shows more detail about content, without specifying typography, color, or graphics. This kind of prototype is often shown to clients in lieu of low-fidelity or high-fidelity prototypes.

This is a good time to create high-fidelity prototypes—ones that are richer and closer to what the final site will look and feel like. You will probably create these hi-fi prototypes with HTML-based tools such as Dreamweaver and graphic design tools such as Illustrator and Photoshop.

Again, the key here is to fake it! For example, suppose your site lets people view stock prices. You do not have to show the real prices, or even real graphs. Just create one or two sample images and use them for all of the graphs. You will show enough to give people the feel of the final site. As another example, if you're building a site that uses personalization technology to improve the customer experience, when applying PERSONALIZED **(D4)** CONTENT (D4) you might mock up the customization at this stage and make it look the same for all of your test participants.

Horizontal and Vertical Prototypes

In the very early stages of design, you often want to create prototypes that show a broad swath of what the eventual Web site will support. These **horizontal prototypes** might show the top-level pages, but without much depth behind them. The homepage might have all the links you expect to have, and each will take you somewhere, but any links from those second-level pages that implement specific features will not exist yet. These prototypes are good for making sure the basic features of the site are present and organized logically.

In contrast, sometimes you will want to flesh out and test the steps that a customer will go through to complete a particular task, such as SIGN-IN/NEW **(H2)** ACCOUNT (H2). A **vertical prototype** implements only the key pages along the path for completing a particular task. This step is appropriate when a complex feature is poorly understood or needs to be explored further. You will not yet support any links that connect to other tasks or to other parts of the site.

Often you will want to combine these two techniques, as in Figure 4.13. Prototype the entire top level of the site with a horizontal prototype to give a flavor of what will be on the site. Then focus on one particular feature, and use the vertical approach to prototype the pages illustrating that feature in detail.

Limits of Prototyping

There are some downsides to using prototypes. Many people believe that creating prototypes takes time away from building the actual site. Take care to explain the value of creating and testing *rapid* prototypes. In addition, although prototypes are useful for getting some kinds of information, they

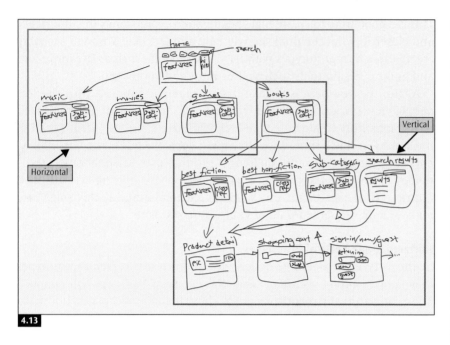

4.13

Figure 4.13

This figure shows a combination of the horizontal and vertical prototypes. Whereas horizontal prototypes illustrate the broad functionality of a design at a high level, vertical prototypes take one feature and detail it in depth. A combination makes a useful demonstration of the broad features in a site (horizontal) and the detailed functionality (vertical) as exemplified by one section.

are not as effective for others, such as estimating download speeds and quality of customer service. Finally, when using medium- and high-fidelity prototypes, you need to manage expectations. Seeing something that looks and feels as if it's working can make customers and clients think that the site is almost done. Take the time to explain that the prototypes still represent early stages of design, and that things are still open to change.

Evaluating Your Web Site   4.5

Web site evaluation is the third (and most often overlooked) part of iterative design. Without evaluation you cannot know if you have met your target goals. You can evaluate your Web site by having it reviewed by experts, by informally testing it with a few participants, or by conducting a more formal study with customers. Each of these methods has its pros and cons, as described in the sections that follow.

Expert Reviews

Expert reviews are an effective technique for evaluating sites without involving customers. The most common type of expert review is a **heuristic evaluation,** which was developed by noted Web guru Jakob Nielsen.

The basic idea is have three to five expert judges independently evaluate a site, using a list of usability heuristics or principles. Nielsen's site, useit.com, lists ten such heuristics, though the seven design principles that we listed earlier in this chapter would work just as well.

In a heuristic evaluation, the judges go through the site, often with a set of sample tasks as a guide, looking for violations of the heuristics. They note each violation and make a suggestion for fixing it. For example, if a site were found to use different terminology for the same concept on two different pages, the judges would note a "consistency" violation and suggest using one of the terms on both pages.

The judges also rate each violation with a level of severity. Severity levels are usually assessed on the basis of the expected customer impact and frequency of the violation.

After each judge has independently evaluated the site, all the judges compare their lists of violations. The point of this step is to merge the lists into one and find agreement on the severity levels. Nielsen's research shows that multiple experts will find different problems, and only by using multiple judges will you have a high probability of finding most of the problems on the site. The more expertise your judges have on user interface design, usability, and heuristic evaluation, the fewer judges you will need. If you can get true experts, we recommend you use three judges. If you're using any team member you can get your hands on, we recommend you involve five or six.

Heuristic evaluation can be an especially effective technique for finding potential usability catastrophes. It also works well for identifying subtle problems that most usability studies might not reveal, such as a poor choice of colors. We have found that heuristic evaluations do not work as well on low-fidelity prototypes as on high-fidelity prototypes. Inexperienced judges tend to focus on the pieces that are missing. We recommend not carrying out a heuristic evaluation until you have a high-fidelity HTML prototype of your site.

With any heuristic evaluation, keep in mind the following caveats: Often experts know too much or not enough. They might be much more sophisticated than your customers and overlook things that will trip up real customers. On the other hand, your site might be designed for customers who have a lot of domain knowledge, such as doctors, and the judges might not have the background necessary to understand the site.

More importantly, heuristic evaluations have a tendency to reveal lots of false positives. **False positives** are violations that are identified by the heuristic evaluation but never found in a usability study of the same interface. In other words, experts often find problems that do not turn out to be problems in practice. Fixing these false positives could end up wasting lots of critical design and engineering resources. Still, a heuristic evaluation is inexpensive, can be carried out in a few hours, and is good for revealing possible usability problems. We suggest that you review Nielsen's site and papers for details on carrying out a heuristic evaluation, and use this technique in tandem with informal and formal usability tests.

Informal Evaluations

Informal evaluations are a natural outgrowth of rapid iteration and low-fidelity prototyping. The idea is quite straightforward: recruit five to ten people who are representative of your target customers, show them your Web site prototype, ask them to do some of the tasks from your task analysis, and take good notes. Your goal is to obtain qualitative feedback from customers about what works and what doesn't, both from what they say and from what they actually do.

The prototype does not have to be computer based. It can be as simple as a paper prototype. In this case, have people point and click with their fingers, just as they would do with a mouse.

You might recruit several representative customers to come to your offices and ask them to complete the tasks with the prototype. Alternatively, you might visit customers in their homes or offices and ask them to do the same.

Before you begin, ask participants to "think aloud," to say what's going on in their minds. This is known as a **think-aloud, or verbal, protocol.** They will probably find this a little strange at first, but they'll get used to it quickly. You may have to prompt them every so often by asking a question like, "So, what are you looking for now?"

The data collected in informal evaluations is qualitative **process data.** This kind of data gives an overall feeling of what works and what doesn't. While participants are testing, keep an eye out for instances in which they seem confused, say something negative, or even swear. These are called **critical incidents.** Use them as a starting point for places you will redesign. Look for positive incidents, cases in which the customer liked your site or things appeared to be going smoothly. Positive incidents give you a hint about which parts of your design work well, and you might be able to take advantage of some of the same ideas elsewhere.

We do not recommend that you use informal evaluation techniques to show that one site design is better than another, or to say how long certain actions will take. Instead, use the results to identify potential problem areas that need to be improved. After you think you have solved the problems, rerun the tests with a new set of representative customers and see if the problems have been addressed properly.

See the appendixes for more information on how to set up and run usability tests. They lay out the roles the testers assume, scripts for what to do and say during the evaluation, and tips for how to analyze the information you collect.

Formal Usability Studies

As soon as you have a running prototype of your Web site, you can start getting hard numbers on whether the site meets the goals that your team has set. For example, one of your goals might be that customers be able to register and create an account in less than two minutes. You can run this study with as few as ten participants, though it generally takes more participants when you want to test numerical goals.

The type of information to collect in this situation is quantitative **bottom-line data.** Bottom-line data consists of hard numerical metrics where you're looking for statistical significance—a serious and reliable difference instead of one due to chance.

Bottom-line data is especially important for simple, repetitive interactions; for example, "Are customers completing the task faster when this button is placed on the left or right side of the page?" This type of data is also useful for comparing two different interfaces; for example, "Can more people successfully make purchases and check out using shopping cart interface A or B?"

Online testing makes it easy to test a variety of similar issues. It lets you recruit and test many participants to achieve statistical accuracy quickly. Several companies offer products to set up and run online tests. These sites can recruit research participants for you, or allow you to enter a list of e-mail addresses from current customers or your own participant pool. The sites then automatically e-mail research participants, lead them to a test site, and ask them to complete tasks that you have defined in advance. Most systems allow you to track the pages the participants go through, as well as ask survey questions.

Some practitioners have developed creative—and potentially controversial—ways to measure usability. One Web site study used "returns to the homepage" as an indication of an error. The inference was that people got lost and had to go back to the homepage. This might be a big assumption without further data to back it up. What if customers want to return to the homepage simply because they're done with a particular section?

If you want to measure the number of errors, make sure that you define errors beforehand and that everyone agrees on the definitions.

See the appendixes for more details on running formal usability evaluations, both offline and online.

Choosing an Evaluation Technique

When do you use expert reviews, informal evaluations, and formal evaluations? The answer is to use multiple techniques. The techniques should be balanced by your cost constraints, as well as by how early in the process the evaluation is taking place. For example, testing low-fi prototypes is especially effective in very early stages of design. In later stages, because you have defined more of the site details, you might want to create HTML prototypes instead so that you can evaluate these details.

Always run expert reviews and informal evaluations as you iterate, to work out basic design flaws. To help you figure out where the problems are, focus especially on qualitative process data in the early stages of design. Use the patterns to find solutions to these problems and then iterate. Do a few formal evaluations as your Web site matures, as it gets closer to deployment, or even after it has been deployed. This strategy will help you refine and polish your site.

Sometimes using five to ten test participants will be good enough to convince you and your teammates that the problems found during testing are legitimate design issues that must be resolved. However, it will often be harder to convince management or the marketing organization that you need to make changes, especially on a high-traffic page like the homepage. In that case, use more formal usability studies and techniques, such as online usability testing, which makes it easy to test the site quickly with fifty to two hundred customers.

A small number of test participants uncover only a small number of the potential problems, according to research by the consulting firm User Interface Engineering.[6] This firm's theory is that many Web sites attract a varied set of customers who have a wide range of goals that they're trying to accomplish, so a small number of participants cannot accurately reflect the diversity of customers. Again, this problem can be overcome by testing with a larger number of customers, on a larger variety of tasks. We believe that online usability testing is a necessity because traditional usability testing with fifty to two hundred participants would take too long.

---

6 Cited in C. Perfetti and L. Landesman, "Eight Is Not Enough" (2001) (www.uie.com/articles/eight_is_not_enough).

4.6 Take-away Ideas

The key to designing successful Web sites is to follow a customer-centered, iterative process that first identifies the expected customers and their tasks. Following the principles of (1) keeping the customers involved, (2) conducting rapid prototyping, and (3) evaluating designs leads to design ideas and prototypes that you evaluate with real customers. The evaluation leads to redesign, and then you iteratively repeat this process until you achieve your usability and business goals. Involving your customers throughout this process will keep your design on track.

Set your team's usability goals early in the design process, and continually evaluate your progress toward these goals. The iterative design process is the least costly way to improve the site design. When the site launches, continue to monitor ongoing customer metrics to see how you're doing, to inform changes, and to help set your goals for the next version of the site.

Processes for Developing Customer-Centered Sites

This chapter takes the patterns, principles, and techniques of customer-centered design as described in Chapters 2 through 4 and places them in the context of a complete Web site design process. Think of this chapter as a rough guide to designing, implementing, and maintaining a Web site. You probably have a design process that you use today, and you might say that it's good enough. What we offer is not a quick fix, but a program that will make any Web site you design more useful, usable, reliable, and satisfying for customers.[1]

Our goal is to provide a general process that you can use when creating or updating a Web site—something that will help you focus your time and energy on clear goals. A well-defined process is also useful for your clients. It lets them know what they can expect from you and what you need from them to build a Web site that meets their expectations and the needs of their customers.

The design process will not always go as smoothly as described here. It is *iterative;* that is, it repeats and jumps back and forth when necessary. Nor will this process solve all your problems. Tailor it to your team, your project, and your organization. Formal procedures that are necessary for large teams may be overkill for small teams. Techniques that work for art-centered design firms are unlikely to work for e-commerce–centered design firms. At a minimum, however, include in your process the major activities discussed in this chapter—that is, the first four phases of development, as defined next.

---

1 Again, we use the term *customer* to mean any person who will use the Web site that you're designing, whether it's a business or a government site, and whether the person is an end customer, employee, site administrator, or partner. We use the term *clients* to refer to the people for whom you're doing the work, the people providing the funding.

Development Process Overview

Generally speaking, development of a Web site can be broken down into seven phases (see Figure 5.1):

1. **Discovery.** Understanding the target customers and their needs, and conceptualizing the business and customer goals for the Web site.
2. **Exploration.** Generating several rough initial Web site designs, of which one or more will be chosen for further development.
3. **Refinement.** Polishing the navigation, layout, and flow of the selected design.
4. **Production.** Developing a fully interactive prototype and a design specification.[2]
5. **Implementation.** Developing the code, content, and images for the Web site.
6. **Launch.** Deploying the Web site for actual use.
7. **Maintenance.** Supporting the existing site, gathering and analyzing metrics of success, and preparing for the next redesign.

The first four steps, Discovery through Production, focus on the overall design of a Web site, clarifying what customers can do on the site and how they do it. You might describe these four steps as *the* design process. Each is characterized by rapid iteration with progressive refinement, moving the design from high-level and general to increasingly specific and detailed. During these stages we have found that the more time you spend up front in the tight iterations, the more likely it is that the Web site will meet customer expectations. In the Discovery phase a team might iterate five to ten times or more on paper. As the team moves into the electronic representations used in the Refinement stage, it might iterate much less, perhaps only three or four times. The exact number of iterations depends on how well the design performs when evaluated.

Punctuate each of the first four steps with a presentation to the client. Hand over any other agreed-upon deliverables at this time, such as a site map, a high-level diagram of a Web site, or a specification document detailing what the Web site will do when it is completed. The main point

---

2 Note that *production* in this case does not mean creating the site but refers instead to creating the "blueprint" for the site so that someone can build it. Some design firms use the term *production* to mean the actual creation of the Web site—that is, what we have termed *implementation*. However, most designers from our interviews used *production* in the same sense that we have defined it here, so we have kept the term.

Figure 5.1

The Web site development process, both as a whole and at each individual phase, uses iterative design.

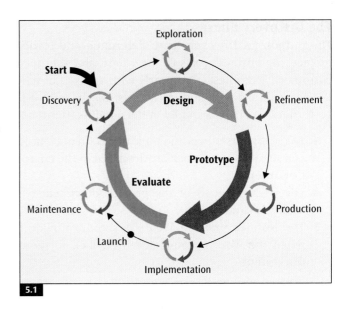

of the presentation, though, is to obtain approval about the work you performed during that phase.

These presentations should be only one part of what will now have become an ongoing dialogue with the client. Several parties have a stake in the design process, including the client and the intended customers. At many points in the process the design team can and should report back to the client to ensure that it's on the right track. For many design consultancies, the client calls the shots, so the client's needs and requirements are considered on a regular basis.

The last three phases—Implementation, Launch, and Maintenance—may not be part of your development process. In fact, many design firms stop at Production, handing off all documentation and interactive prototypes to another team, often in the client's organization but sometimes in a third firm, which goes on to do the rest of the work.

We do not include detailed planning at this stage for two reasons: First, each organization has its own way of handling issues such as scheduling, budgets, and risk management. Second, *the process is by no means linear.* A team may be in the Exploration stage and discover that it needs to do more Discovery activities. Another team may be in Production and realize that it needs to go back to Refinement or Exploration to hammer out some details. Such is the nature of design. Although going backward may seem like a defeat of sorts, take heart in the knowledge that time and money are actually being saved if changes are made sooner rather than later.

The Discovery Phase

The purpose of Discovery is to determine and clarify the scope of the project, the business goals of the client, and the needs of the intended customers. This phase often starts with analysis of whether a Web site is the best solution for the client's goals. By the end of Discovery, you and your client will have a shared understanding of three things:

1. The target customers and their needs (people, tasks, technology, and social issues), which are described in the **customer analysis document**
2. The business goals of the project, described in the **business analysis document**
3. The features that the Web site should provide for customers when the work is completed, described in the **specification document**

You will deliver these three documents to the client by the end of this phase. The process of creating these three documents is also known as **requirements gathering**. The sections that follow look in more detail at each of the steps of Discovery and the documents that result from this process.

The Discovery Process

Step 1: Determine the Overall Goals of the Web Site • You and your client will work together to answer questions before creating a new Web site or redesigning an existing site. These questions might include the following: What value will the Web site provide to customers? What will the site accomplish? Is the goal of the site to sell products online, promote products, educate, inform, provoke, communicate, or provide a community? What will be the focus of the site? *Why should the site be built at all?*

Other crucial questions that must be asked are these: What value will the Web site provide to the client? What role does the site play in relation to the rest of the company? How will the site further the client's overall goals? The design team often starts this phase by defining the site together with the client, focusing on the client's goals, the high-level services the client wishes to offer, and preliminary customer categories. These decisions form the basis for the rest of the Discovery process.

Some techniques that might be applied at this phase include interviewing or corresponding with clients to clarify what they expect. Discover the needs of the site's target customers by interviewing, running focus groups

with, and surveying target customers online and offline. These techniques
3 are described in greater detail in Chapter 3 (Knowing Your Customers:
Principles and Techniques).

This is also a good time to evaluate the existing Web site, as well as to
review and evaluate competitors' Web sites for opportunities to improve
and differentiate your site from theirs. Techniques for these evaluations
4 are described in Chapter 4 (Involving Customers with Iterative Design).

Step 2: Decide on the Web Site's Value Proposition • One of the most impor-
C2 tant patterns that come into play here is the UP-FRONT VALUE PROPOSITION (C2).
The value proposition states what the Web site offers to the target customers.
The goal is to explain the Web site's value convincingly to someone on
the street, in one sentence. Everything you will put on the Web site
draws on this single idea; it is the theme that unifies the site. Figure 5.2
shows compelling value propositions from some actual Web sites.

If you're creating a new Web site, think through the value proposition
carefully, making many drafts before you decide on the best one. If you're
updating or redesigning an existing Web site, you may need to reconsider the
C2 existing value proposition. In either case the UP-FRONT VALUE PROPOSITION (C2)
pattern provides steps for hammering out the right one.

You will also consider initial branding ideas at this early design phase.
What do you want people to think of when they think of your Web site?
What kinds of feelings do you want people to have after visiting your
site? Do you want to be thought of as reliable and trustworthy, or maybe

Figure 5.2

Many Web sites make their value propositions
clear from their taglines. The goal of the value
proposition is to provide a single, powerful idea
of what the Web site is all about.

5.2

(www.shutterfly.com, www.slashdot.org, www.firstgov.gov, 2001)

exciting and fun? The SITE BRANDING (E1) pattern provides exercises to help you decide what kind of impressions to give customers.

At this stage, start thinking about whether personalization is useful for individual customers. The PERSONALIZED CONTENT (D4) pattern provides some starting points. For example, if you're working on an e-commerce site, consider how personalization can help your customers find interesting and useful products. Maybe your Web site can recommend products, or maybe it can let people see a list of the most popular items. If you're developing a news site, perhaps your visitors can specify zip codes to get local news and weather.

Speaking of zip codes, this is a good time to bring up the issue of internationalization, because some countries outside of the United States do not use zip codes. Again, it comes back to the question of defining your customers. Do you expect people from other countries to use your Web site? If so, there are a host of issues to consider, including currency, color, icons, and layout. We discuss many of these issues in more detail in the INTERNATIONALIZED AND LOCALIZED CONTENT (D10) pattern.

Be Firm about Not Skipping Discovery • Some clients may insist on skipping the Discovery phase and jumping straight to Web site development. Unless the scope of the project and the needs of the customers have already been defined, this is usually a bad idea and a likely prescription for failure. It is your job to explain the importance of this phase. [We can help. See Chapter 3 (Knowing Your Customers: Principles and Techniques) for some convincing arguments.]

Avoid Gold-Plating the Web Site • The term **gold-plating** means trying to get the Web site absolutely perfect before deploying it. You have probably visited other Web sites, seen something cool, and have kept saying to yourself, "We should have this on our Web site too!" Usually that cool thing is technically complex (and fun) to design and implement but, frankly, may not be all that helpful to customers.

You can avoid the problem of investing a lot in something that has little gain for the customer by getting continuous feedback from customers about what's useful and what's not, and prioritizing the features on the basis of that feedback. This strategy will help you cut through the morass of features and keep you focused on what needs to be done. You do not have to develop and deploy all the features simultaneously. Deploy the features in stages, in many small steps instead of one big leap. Plan for future growth, but also plan for the next deployment.

Get the Web Site Fundamentals Right First • The last thing to watch out for is not taking care of the fundamentals first. This becomes an issue when you design things out of order. For example, for e-commerce sites it does not make sense to design and implement PERSONALIZED RECOMMENDATIONS (G3) or a RECOMMENDATION COMMUNITY (G4) if there are still problems with the SHOPPING CART (F3) and the QUICK-FLOW CHECKOUT (F1). Take care of the things that the Web site absolutely must have before adding the icing that makes it more attractive.

Discovery Deliverables

Design teams produce three main documents as an outcome of the Discovery phase: the customer analysis document, the business analysis document, and the specification document. Let's look at each one in turn.

Customer Analysis Document • This document gives the design team and the client a deep understanding of and empathy for the Web site's intended customers. It fleshes out the intended customers, describing their characteristics, their needs, and their tasks. It includes the following details:

- The motivation of customers to visit the Web site, or the UP-FRONT VALUE PROPOSITION (C2).
- A **task analysis** of the intended customers, describing the people, their tasks, the technologies they use, and their social and organizational issues. One increasingly popular way to do this is by creating personas, or highly detailed fictional people, who are representative of the customers. Giving the customers names makes it easier to talk about them.

We provide more details about customer analysis in Section 3.2, Techniques for Knowing Your Customers, in Chapter 3 (Knowing Your Customers: Principles and Techniques).

Business Analysis Document • This document spells out the business needs of the client and the business goals of the Web site. It explores how the goals of the client map to the tasks and customers discovered during the task analysis. For example, suppose the client's goal for an intranet site is to be the primary source of company information. What does this goal mean to an administrative assistant who is just trying to find the information he needs to get his job done?

If you're revising an existing Web site, a new business analysis is probably not necessary, but it is still a good idea to check every so often that the business goals are the right goals, and that the Web site works toward those goals. A business analysis document usually includes the following:

- **Business plan.** This plan describes the business goals of the Web site and the client's needs. Some goals might be to support existing customers, to bring in new customers by providing information about products, and to increase sales by enabling purchases online.
- **Competitive analysis.** This analysis determines the features that competitors have on their Web sites, and it identifies which features are important to customers and which are not. It also discusses the competitive advantages that the proposed Web site will have over others, and it expresses these advantages as high-level goals.
- **Metrics for success.** How will success be measured for both the business and the competitive goals? For example, how many customers does the site need to draw to stay in business? But just as important as attracting customers is retaining them, keeping them coming back for more. How many are repeat customers? What is the conversion rate; that is, how many visitors become paying customers? How many become community members?

Specification Document • Also known as a *requirements document,* the specification document identifies what the Web site should provide when the work is complete. It describes any functionality that the Web site needs, as well as any constraints on the system. At this point you do not have to start thinking about how you'll achieve the needed functionality. Focus instead on what you'll accomplish. A specification document contains the following:

- **Project description,** describing the common purpose and ultimate goals of the project, from both client and customer perspectives.
- **List of tasks, scenarios, and storyboards,** fleshing out the features [see Chapters 3 (Knowing Your Customers: Principles and Techniques) and 4 (Involving Customers with Iterative Design) for more information]. These tasks will form the basis of the Web site evaluations. The number of tasks depends on the complexity of the proposed work. Simple projects can make do with ten to twenty complete tasks, but larger projects will need enough to cover all the proposed features. Label tasks as *easy, moderate,* or *difficult.* Customers should be able to complete all of the easy and moderate tasks and many of the difficult ones.
- **Comprehensive list of proposed features,** classified in importance as "must have," "should have," or "could have." Use competitive comparisons, as well as surveys and other market research techniques, to

3 4

obtain this type of information. Decompose features into subfeatures. For example, a Web site that helps manage personal information will likely have a contact manager, which lets people add new contacts, edit existing ones, and search for contacts by name. Each feature also includes a short statement on how it will be evaluated or tested in the final Web site.

- **Overall design goals,** such as reducing the number of mistakes that customers make on the existing site, decreasing the time it takes to make purchases and check out from the shopping cart, or making the site faster to use.

- **Metrics** to measure whether the team has reached these goals and requirements, such as keeping download time to less than five seconds for 90 percent of the target customers. State how each feature will be measured in the final Web site. (A more precise test specification will be developed later, spelling out more of the details.)

Not writing a specification document is the biggest risk you can take, yet this is the most often skipped step. A specification document does not have to be long or formal, but it is useful because it forces you to think through important details and make sure that they make sense and are realistic. A specification document also makes it easier to communicate with clients and with other team members so that everyone has a shared vision of what the Web site will be like when completed.

Specification documents are often tedious to read. Be brief and concise, and use lots of diagrams to illustrate what you mean. Make it interesting enough that you would take the time to read it yourself.

5.3   The Exploration Phase

During the Exploration phase you will generate and explore several designs. These initial designs often do not reflect ideas about color, imagery, and typography. However, they do reflect ideas about site structure and navigation. By the end of Exploration, you will have several prototypes to present to the client, who will select one for further development and sign off on the work done. Sometimes a client will want to fund continued development of two sites for further refinement before making a final choice. In either case, the selected design is supported by evaluation results that show it is the best at meeting the business, client, and customer goals.

The Exploration Process

Typically you will generate medium-fidelity site maps, storyboards, and schematics [see Chapter 4 (Involving Customers with Iterative Design) for details about medium-fidelity prototypes, and about the differences among site maps, storyboards, and schematics]. Test all your designs quickly with target customers to ensure usefulness and usability.

More design patterns come into play here too. The HOMEPAGE PORTAL (C1) pattern describes some of the ways to structure your homepage, as well as what you'll want on your homepage, such as a PRIVACY POLICY (E4) and a SEARCH ACTION MODULE (J1).

Begin initial work on the information architecture—the overall organization of the Web site's content—at this phase as well. The BROWSABLE CONTENT (B2) pattern provides more details on how to design and implement your architecture.

Exploration Deliverables

Medium-Fidelity Site Maps, Storyboards, and Schematics • At the end of the Exploration phase you will present several sets of medium-fidelity site maps, storyboards, and schematics to your client. Each set represents a design alternative that addresses the issues described by the customer analysis document, the business analysis document, and the specification document. In particular, the storyboards will show the initial ideas for how the scenarios in the specification document will be carried out. However, at this phase none of the deliverables will have much detail; rather they will have just enough detail to represent the general idea. Figure 5.3 shows an example of a medium-fidelity site map.

The Refinement Phase   5.4

After you have chosen a design idea from the variations presented in the Exploration phase, you need to develop the selected idea further. Polish the navigation, layout, and flow of the selected design more, providing a clearer understanding of how the Web site will look and feel. By the end of Refinement, you will have a highly detailed prototype to present to your client, and you'll probably expect the client to sign off on the work.

The Refinement Process

During the Refinement phase, iteratively refine, detail, and informally test the design. Determine aspects such as the precise typeface of labels and body text, the exact sizes and appearances of images, and color schemes and palettes. For most sites you will not find it necessary to design every page at this stage, because you will break down the site into

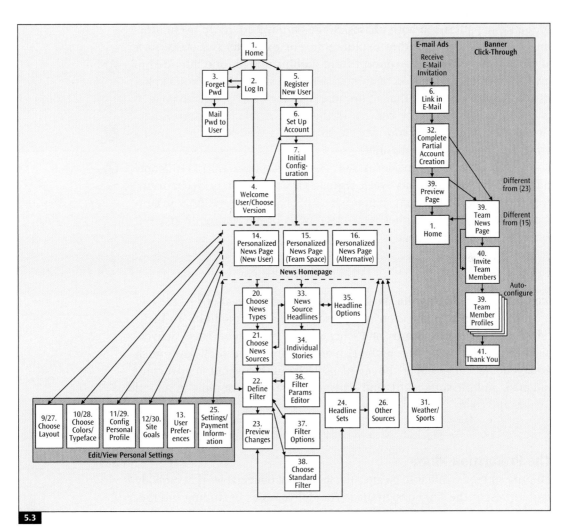

Figure 5.3

Medium-fidelity site maps such as this one can quickly communicate the flow of a site in an easy-to-read format.

classes of pages (such as homepage, second-level pages, and pages for specific types of content). An example, or **template,** can represent each of these classes of pages.

In this phase, site maps are still abstract representations of the entire Web site. On the other hand, storyboards and schematics are no longer drab and dull; instead they are now rich with images, icons, typography, and sophisticated color schemes.

The main difference between Refinement and Exploration is that the design you create in the Refinement phase has more detail than the designs you generated during the Exploration phase. You can apply many of the same patterns in both phases. Some patterns are more useful during Refinement than during Exploration. For example, the CLEAR FIRST READS (I3) pattern takes a concept from graphic design, one intended to give a quick first impression of a visual design. It suggests that you explicitly design the first thing that a potential customer sees on a Web page to give an overall feel for the content of the page. A related pattern is GRID LAYOUT (I1), which gives you ways of structuring Web pages in a consistent and understandable manner.

Another pattern to consider is MULTIPLE WAYS TO NAVIGATE (B1). People navigate Web sites in many ways, using a variety of search mechanisms, text links, buttons, and navigation bars. This pattern shows how to provide multiple and sometimes redundant ways of navigating, to make it easier to find the right page.

Refinement Deliverables

Medium- to High-Fidelity Site Maps, Storyboards, and Schematics • At the end of the Refinement phase, you will present one set of medium- to high-fidelity site maps, storyboards, and schematics to your client. These deliverables are similar to the ones in the Exploration phase, but they have much greater detail. For example, the site maps flesh out the overall site structure in detail, and the storyboards and schematics make use of more graphical images and color.

The Production Phase   5.5

The goal of Production is to create a detailed set of deliverables that embody and represent the final design idea. The deliverables, including interactive prototypes, written design descriptions, design guidelines, and technical specifications, are high-fidelity and contain as much detail as possible about the layout, navigation, visuals, and content for each Web page. Exactly what is delivered at the end of this phase depends on whether you will continue to the next phase (Implementation) or hand off the design to someone else.

If you will be handing off the design, make the interactive prototypes and specifications precise and highly detailed so that there's no ambiguity about what the next team will implement. You may want to call for more evaluation during Implementation to ensure that the specification is being implemented correctly. The client should review the ongoing development to catch any problems before the new team does too much work.

Ideally, though, the design team will work hand in hand with the engineering, art, marketing, editorial, and management teams so that the site is implemented as designed and tested, and so that the inevitable questions that arise can be answered.

The Production Process

During the Production phase, continue evaluating the product with real customers. Because this will be the first time that the entire design comes together, often with more complexity than existed in earlier prototypes, new interaction issues may arise.

During Production the patterns become more low-level as the problems become increasingly technical. For example, one pattern that will be used here is ACTION BUTTONS (K4), which explains how to make buttons that look like they can be pressed. Another useful pattern at this stage is OBVIOUS LINKS (K10), which discusses why links must be easy to see and explains how to make them that way.

Production Deliverables

The deliverables of the Production phase vary. Here we list the most common ways of describing the design in detail.

Design Document • In contrast to the specification document, the **design document** describes in great detail how the Web site works. It takes all of the features from the specification document and uses site maps, storyboards, and schematics to describe the flow of interaction.

If your work stops here and you hand the project off to another team, the design document needs to be detailed, descriptive, and unambiguous. If the same design team continues to do Implementation, the design document does not need to be so detailed. Provide just enough information that the client and the team understand precisely how customers will interact with the Web site, and how and when the site is complete.

Interactive Prototypes • Often delivered along with the design document, an **interactive prototype** gives you and your client a better grounding for how the finished Web site will look and behave. Create interactive prototypes using standard Web site production tools, such as Adobe GoLive or Dreamweaver, as well as prototyping tools such as Macromedia Director. The idea is to provide enough detail that everyone can see how the final Web site will look and feel. (For example, not all of the links have to work correctly, as long as it's clear what they're intended to do.)

Some firms deliver interactive prototypes in lieu of a design document but embed many of the details as annotation to the prototype. For example, moving the mouse over certain sections of the prototype might pop up a specification of the font family and size.

Technical Specifications • Technical details are explained in this document, which includes things like the kind of Web server, the kind of programming and scripting languages, the kind of database, and the version of HTML that will be used. Performance metrics can also be included, such as the number of customers who can be supported simultaneously. Optionally, the technical specifications might include some engineering prototypes as a proof-of-concept demonstrating that the difficult parts of the proposed design are technically feasible and can realistically be built.

Design Guidelines • These guidelines are the general rules to be followed on every Web page to minimize inconsistencies between pages. A design guideline could describe which fonts should be used, what color the links should be, when the logo should be used and where it should be positioned, what color scheme to use, what the maximum file size of each Web page is, and so on. The person who will implement and/or maintain the Web site should be able to understand and use the guidelines. Optionally, the guidelines might also include a style guide to ensure that the writing is consistent throughout the Web site, for example, using the term *e-mail* instead of *email*.

Web Page Templates • Web page templates are the HTML files that represent typical Web pages on the site. The goal of using these templates is to avoid inconsistencies between pages. With a minimum of effort you can copy and modify these templates with content specific for a particular page. Six patterns that are useful to consider when you're developing Web page templates are PAGE TEMPLATES (D1), GRID LAYOUT (I1), ABOVE THE FOLD (I2), CLEAR FIRST READS (I3), EXPANDING SCREEN WIDTH (I4), and SITE ACCESSIBILITY (B9).

(D1) (I1)
(I2) (I3) (I4)
(B9)

The Implementation Phase   5.6

The aim of Implementation is to create the HTML, images, database tables, and software necessary for a polished and fully functional Web site that can be rolled out and used by its target customers. Making sure that you've reached this goal requires running formal usability tests to ensure that customers can complete the tasks they want to do. The quality assurance group, both individually and as a whole, will test all the code, graphics, and HTML thoroughly so that the Web site works as intended and downloads quickly. [See the LOW NUMBER OF FILES (L1), FAST-LOADING IMAGES (L2), and FAST-LOADING CONTENT (L6) patterns in Pattern Group L (Speeding Up Your Site).] Check all the content for accuracy at this stage.

The Implementation Process

Devote more effort to content in the Implementation phase. Two patterns that come in handy here are WRITING FOR SEARCH ENGINES (D6) and DISTINCTIVE HTML TITLES (D9), which look at how to improve the internal structure of Web pages for search engines and for customers. Another useful pattern is INVERTED-PYRAMID WRITING STYLE (D7), which describes techniques for making text content easier to skim and faster to read. On sites with content that changes frequently, a useful pattern for building a content management system is CONTENT MODULES (D2), which put content in a database to keep production costs low and site reliability high.

Tools useful at this stage include a revision control system for storing and sharing files among a group of people, and a bug database for tracking problems. Choose tools that you already know how to use and that have been proven to work. The Implementation phase of development is a bad time to try out an unknown product. (However, do try out new tools between projects, to keep your skills sharp and up-to-date.)

You also need to determine naming conventions for folders and files. For example, which folder will contain the images? Will there be just one folder or many? If you're selling products, what will be the name of each product's CLEAN PRODUCT DETAILS (F2) page? Is the naming set up to make it easy to add new product pages in the future?

If you're using SECURE CONNECTIONS (E6), you may need to apply for digital certificates at this time. **Digital certificates** are a way for Web servers to prove that they really are who they say they are, and they are issued by a variety of trusted third-party vendors known as **certification authorities.** Keep in mind that digital certificates are often bound to a specific server name, so you may encounter problems if you try to move a digital certificate from a test server to the actual Web server. In this situation, it might not be a bad idea to get multiple certificates, for all the Web servers that you will be using.

The Web site also needs to be rigorously tested in this phase to ensure that it is high-quality and professional. This testing consists of performing

more usability tests, doing some editorial spot-checking, and running automated test suites. The following checklist identifies some of the tests that need to be done during Implementation:

- Check that the Web site has all of the features stipulated in the specification document, and that the features are implemented correctly.
- Check that the developed Web pages are compatible with various Web browsers, including text-only browsers used by the blind.
- Test that the developed Web pages can be viewed on monitors of different sizes.
- See if the Web pages can be downloaded in a reasonable amount of time over slower Internet connections.
- Stress-test the Web site, by simulating simultaneous use by hundreds or even thousands of people, to ensure that it still performs reasonably.
- Check for grammar and spelling errors.

These tests will produce bug reports, which your team will use to guide any necessary redesign, code changes, and simple fixes for the problems found during testing.

Implementation Deliverables

Completed Web Site • The completed Web site includes all of the HTML Web pages, all of the software, and all of the database tables required for the Web site to work.

Maintenance Document • The maintenance document describes in detail how to maintain the completed Web site. It explains which parts of the Web site will be periodically updated, how often they need to be updated, and who should update them. It should also describe the database tables, showing how they fit together.

Test Plan Document • The test plan spells out what steps will be taken to ensure that the Web site works as intended. At a minimum, it should include checking for performance, spelling, broken links, and the like. It should also explain how the site will be tested for usability, as well as how each of the features described in the specification document will be tested to ensure that they simply work.

Updates • Any documents that are out-of-date should be updated at this time (if they have not been already). These include the specification document, the design document, design guidelines, and Web page templates.

5.7 The Launch Phase

The Launch phase deals with the live deployment of the Web site. At this point, there is time to do only minor polishing on the Web site, such as checking for misspellings, grammatical errors, broken links, and broken images. All of the major checks should have been done in the previous phase, Implementation.

Some design teams choose to roll out the Web site in stages. Instead of developing the entire Web site at once and waiting until the very end to deploy it, selected parts of the Web site are created and deployed incrementally. Develop the most important functions and subsites first, and post them on a beta Web site for early adopters. Use the resulting feedback to drive the immediate design and development of the rest of the Web site. Handle staged deployment carefully because if the Web site is rolled out too early and shows a lack of content and polish, potential customers may avoid the site later.

Many design teams find a postmortem a useful exercise after launch, to assess what things went right, what did not, why, and how to avoid these problems in the future.

5.8 The Maintenance Phase

Maintenance is perhaps the most neglected aspect of Web site design. The objective of the Maintenance phase is to perform all of the activities needed to sustain a Web site. Beyond basic tasks such as updating the site with new content and promptly answering customer e-mail, Maintenance includes the following:

- Changing code and fixing bugs
- Collecting usability and satisfaction metrics
- Verifying that all links point to valid pages
- Checking that there are no spelling or grammatical errors
- Ensuring that pages in the Web site follow the design guidelines
- Periodically backing up the entire Web site (to a safe, distant computer)
- **(H7)** Updating the FREQUENTLY ASKED QUESTIONS (H7) pages
- **(D6)** Checking that your team is WRITING FOR SEARCH ENGINES (D6)
- **(J3)** Maintaining server logs that show where people come from, what search terms they use [see ORGANIZED SEARCH RESULTS (J3)], and what they're doing on the site

Maintenance includes assessing the Web site, collecting measurements on how customers use the Web site, analyzing and summarizing the metrics you collect, and making the metrics available to the rest of the team and the company. Metrics are one of the most important parts of maintaining a Web site. They are the heartbeat of a Web site, measuring its overall health. Without them, you cannot tell which aspects are working and which are not.

The Maintenance Process

The Maintenance phase is the longest part of the design cycle. Consequently, it is also the most expensive—an often overlooked factor that must be considered when the budget is being developed. The most important decision in this phase, though, is determining when a revision to the Web site is necessary. A revision can be anything from a minor change to a complete overhaul. In any case, use all of the metrics, wisdom, and experience you have gained from developing and maintaining the old Web site to help ensure that the new Web site will succeed.

Small redesigns or additions to the existing site can go through an accelerated development process. In these cases you do not have to revisit such things as the business analysis document. However, pay attention to the specification document, the design document, and the design guidelines, with the goal of keeping the Web site's look and feel the same throughout. (Some design teams insist on making their work look different from the rest of the Web site. Unless there is an extremely compelling reason to the contrary, however, insist on maintaining a consistent look and feel for the entire Web site to make it easier for customers.)

On the other hand, complete overhauls mean going through the entire Web site development process again. Complete redesigns take place when major changes are needed, such as when customer expectations change, when customer behavior changes, when there are new technology considerations, when fresh content and functionality are necessary, or when the Web site starts looking outdated.

Get customer feedback before making the final switch to a new Web site. The best way is to run usability tests on your new site to verify that customers can complete the essential tasks. Another way is to provide a link on the homepage to let customers try out the new site and to ask them what they do and don't like. If you have a list of e-mail addresses, you can contact your customers to let them know that the Web site will be updated soon.

A third way of getting feedback is through virtual testing. In this case a few select customers will see the updated Web site instead of the regular Web site. You can compare what these customers do on the new Web site to what customers do on the regular Web site to see if any interesting new strengths or weaknesses are evident with the new site. Amazon.com and Google use this method quite successfully. You can use online surveys for this purpose as well.

Maintenance Deliverables

Periodic Web Site Metrics • Most of your metrics will come from the business analysis document produced in the Discovery phase. They can include such things as the total number of hits, the conversion rate (the number of people who become paying customers), satisfaction metrics, and usability evaluations.

Bug Reports • Customer e-mails, Web site evaluations, and server log file analyses are good ways to find bugs. Rate each of these in terms of severity (such as "must fix," "should fix," and "could fix"), and estimate how long it will take to fix the problem.

Periodic Backups • Back up the entire Web site periodically as protection in case some files are accidentally erased, the Web servers are damaged, or hackers break into the site. Store the backups far away from the building that houses the Web server, in case of an environmental disaster like flood or fire.

5.9 Take-away Ideas

The process described in this chapter gives you a structure to make sure your Web site will meet the needs of your clients and the needs of their customers. The principles and techniques of customer-centered design and iterative prototyping are embedded in every stage. Many Web site design firms and internal design groups in companies have similar processes, though the stages and deliverables might have slightly different names. The names are not what's important here. The key is to make sure you have a customer-centered process that is documented, is reproducible, and can be improved by your organization over time.

PART II

Patterns

We have organized the patterns conceptually and divided them into groups, starting with site genres and moving progressively toward particular page elements. This structure gives you a way to navigate the patterns quickly.

You may wish to read each pattern group as a whole or skim from group to group. Each pattern connects to related patterns in other groups. Once you have chosen one pattern, refer to the related patterns you need to fill out your design. You may also want to read the related material that we reference in the Resources section of the book.

If you read about patterns outside your core site needs, you may find that at first the patterns don't seem to make sense for your Web site. But you may end up using patterns that you didn't plan to use, because they embody principles or features necessary to complete your vision. We are presenting what we see as the essential elements of customer-centered Web site design.

Keep in mind that this collection of patterns is by no means complete. Patterns are a constantly evolving language that changes as our tools, technologies, practices, and culture change.

Pattern Group A
Site Genres

In this pattern group we have categorized Web sites into types that we refer to as *genres*. Each genre has its own content, needs, and audience.

Pattern Group A provides the framework that you need to construct many different kinds of sites. Each site pattern gives you concrete ways to differentiate your site and explains how to deliver the best experience to your customers. The site genre patterns are high-level and fairly abstract, describing general properties and characteristics of various types of Web sites.[1] Throughout the text of each pattern are many references to other, lower-level patterns, which contain more details for designing and implementing the ideas presented, as well as references to other related patterns.

Not all Web sites have the same customer requirements. STIMULATING ARTS AND ENTERTAINMENT (A9) sites and EDUCATIONAL FORUMS (A8), for example, differ as much in design as they do in content. Arts and entertainment sites engage people by immersing them in new worlds and ideas; educational forums build dialogues around the concerns of the educational community.

That said, you might pull ideas from one genre to another so that each can benefit from elements of the other. Educational forums may benefit from clearly defined areas that purposely break the rules of navigation to encourage exploration and discovery. Stimulating arts and entertainment sites may include educational forums on related topics, to promote a depth of understanding.

Just as there are differences between genres, though, there are also strong similarities. For instance, both types of sites in the previous example need good navigation cues and searchable pages.

---

1 It is the more abstract nature of the Group A patterns that singles out the group for this expanded introduction that Pattern Groups B through M do not get.

Site Genres

This pattern group is about building sites in general. It explains the unique aspect of each site genre and helps you choose more detailed patterns. The rest of the book contains patterns that may be specific to a type of site or general to all sites.

A1.1

(www.llbean.com, February 2, 2002)

Figure A1.1

L. L. Bean gives customers a sense of familiarity because the categories on the site (left) are similar to what they find in L. L. Bean's physical stores and catalogs. The bright colors, clean layout and navigation, and picture in the center work together to draw people in.

✳ BACKGROUND

This pattern forms the core that makes online shopping possible. Start by using it in its most basic form, then expand and extend it as needed. Use it separately or in conjunction with other site genre patterns, such as NEWS MOSAICS (A2), VALUABLE COMPANY SITES (A7), and STIMULATING ARTS AND ENTERTAINMENT (A9).

✳ PROBLEM

Customers appreciate the convenience of ordering online, but if a site is cumbersome, is veiled about its pricing and policies, or does not seem to provide a personal benefit, they leave.

E-commerce holds the promise of making customers' lives easier and more enjoyable. They can find things that they otherwise would never come across, and they can order anywhere, anytime, with only a few button clicks (see Figure A1.2). People enjoy the pleasure of the discovery, the simplicity of the process, and the convenience of the delivery. But on many e-commerce sites, customers do not always understand what's being offered and whether it will be of any personal benefit.

Make It Clear Why People Should Purchase from You • It's important to make clear from the outset what value you're providing to customers. Why should they purchase anything from your Web site? Do you offer low prices? Fast shipments? Unbiased, high-quality product reviews? A wide selection of products? A specialized set of products that are hard to find?

Figure A1.2

Amazon.com offers all of the basic features that an e-commerce site needs, and many of the advanced features as well. It adds value by showing customers items they might want on a homepage customized for them.

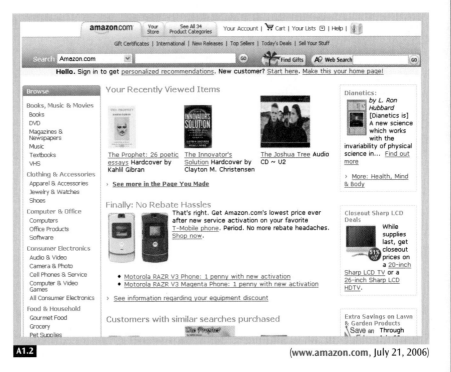

(www.amazon.com, July 21, 2006)

Ease of use? This is your UP-FRONT VALUE PROPOSITION (C2), the core value that is woven into the design and organization of the entire Web site.

Provide Many Ways to Find Products • Web sites must provide MULTIPLE WAYS TO NAVIGATE (B1) because customers look for products in many different ways. Some customers know exactly what they're looking for and want to type the name of the product into a SEARCH ACTION MODULE (J1) and jump straight to that product's page. PREDICTIVE INPUT (H11) can help streamline the product selection process further. Other customers have only a vague notion of what they're looking for and want to explore lots of BROWSABLE CONTENT (B2) to get a better sense of what's available.

Searching and browsing are two basic approaches to navigating through Web sites. However, they are often not very effective for revealing the interesting products—the ones that everyone else is buying, the ones that are on sale, or the ones that are just plain cool. Once you have the basics of e-commerce down, find new ways to help your customers scratch itches they didn't even know they had. Tell your customers what new and interesting products you have by showcasing FEATURED PRODUCTS (G1) on your HOMEPAGE PORTAL (C1). Help them find related or more expensive versions of products by CROSS-SELLING AND UP-SELLING (G2). Drive more sales by providing PERSONALIZED RECOMMENDATIONS (G3) specially tailored to their individual interests and needs. Finally, offer a RECOMMENDATION COMMUNITY (G4) in which customers can provide feedback and comments on products. By fostering a thriving community, you are partnering with your customers, having them create new content for your Web site, and, in effect, providing everyone with yet another reason to visit your Web site again in the future.

Keep It Convenient • Customers love to be able to search vast stores of information, see many CLEAN PRODUCT DETAIL (F2) pages that provide thorough descriptions, and compare products. In doing so, they can make more educated decisions about the products and services they need. On the flip side, if the information you provide is not easy to find, your customers will become frustrated and perhaps even leave.

Finding one thing they like may motivate customers to look for other things they like. A site that facilitates collecting multiple items in a SHOPPING CART (F3) can greatly simplify the shopping process.

Keep customers focused on their tasks so that they don't become distracted when they go through the QUICK-FLOW CHECKOUT (F1) process. Customers might abandon the entire order if checkout doesn't seem

Figure A1.3

Half.com's checkout interface is simple and straightforward: It lets customers purchase items by taking them through a logical sequence of steps. It always shows customers where they are in the process and what they have to do to finish.

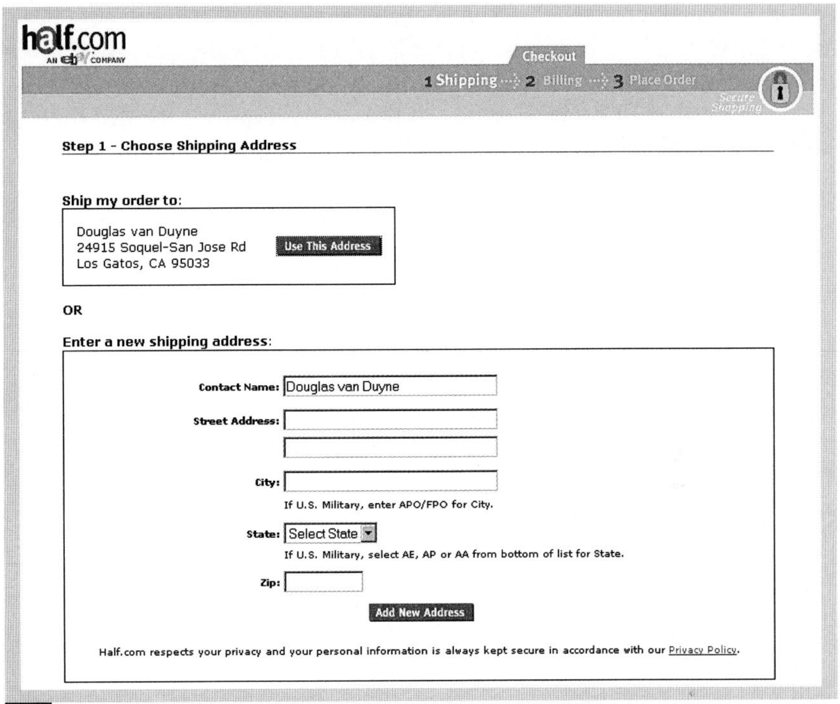

half.com
AN ebY COMPANY

Checkout

1 Shipping ···⁀ **2** Billing ···⁀ **3** Place Order

Secure Shopping

Step 1 - Choose Shipping Address

Ship my order to:

Douglas van Duyne
24915 Soquel-San Jose Rd   Use This Address
Los Gatos, CA 95033

OR

Enter a new shipping address:

Contact Name: Douglas van Duyne

Street Address:

City:
If U.S. Military, enter APO/FPO for City.

State: Select State
If U.S. Military, select AE, AP or AA from bottom of list for State.

Zip:

Add New Address

Half.com respects your privacy and your personal information is always kept secure in accordance with our Privacy Policy.

A1.3

(www.half.com, October 1, 2001)

simple and straightforward. Remember, at this point their goal is to finish shopping, and your goal should be to close the sale as smoothly and as quickly as possible (see Figure A1.3).

For an e-commerce business that might benefit greatly from impulse buying, it's a good idea to create a site that supports as many computing platforms as possible so that customers can act on their impulses whenever and wherever they are. The MOBILE SCREEN SIZING (M1), MOBILE INPUT CONTROLS (M2), and LOCATION-BASED SERVICES (M3) patterns can help you incorporate mobile Web capabilities into your sites.

One common problem of many early Web sites was that they forced potential customers to create a new account through the SIGN-IN/NEW ACCOUNT (H2) process even before the customers could see what the Web site had to offer. Needless to say, many visitors balked. Some e-commerce sites still require customers to sign in or create a new account before going through QUICK-FLOW CHECKOUT (F1). You can avoid the problem by letting customers use a GUEST ACCOUNT (H3) and then create an account after the purchase is completed.

Consider Including Some Advanced Features • After you've solved the basic mechanics of shopping and purchasing, you might want to look at some more advanced issues. For example, many people purchase products as gifts for other people. GIFT GIVING (G6) involves numerous details, such as wrapping, receipts, personalized notes, returns, and buying multiple gifts and sending them to MULTIPLE DESTINATIONS (G5). As another example, some people may be interested in seeing their ORDER TRACKING AND HISTORY (G7) to check the status of their purchases or see what they've bought in the past.

G6

G5

G7

Avoid Surprises • Customers want to know what to expect when they start shopping because it will take at least a few minutes to complete the transaction, and they don't want to have a surprise toward the end. Full disclosure about site policies up front is important to shoppers. They generally have three areas of concern:

1. **Privacy and security.** Customers value their anonymity because it provides them with a sense of privacy and security from being defrauded or abused by people who gain access to their personal information. Many want to shop in total anonymity and complete their transactions while revealing only what they have to. Build trust by establishing a set of FAIR INFORMATION PRACTICES (E3) that will be followed throughout your company, and make these practices clear in your PRIVACY POLICY (E4). Furthermore, you can give customers the ability to select PRIVACY PREFERENCES (E8). Also be sure to use a SECURE CONNECTION (E6) whenever personal or financial information is being transmitted.

E3

E4

E8

E6

2. **Additional charges.** Sometimes, given economies of scale, customers find products at a lower price when shopping online, only to discover that the shipping and handling charges erase the savings. Granted, if people factor in the time saved because they're not personally traveling to and from the store, shipping and handling costs can sometimes be justified. However, if the costs of shipping and handling are surprisingly high, shoppers become discouraged. They think the online merchant is trying to trick them, and they become distrustful. Providing information about all the costs involved with a purchase early in the shopping experience will build trust and keep customers from experiencing "sticker shock," one of the reasons that people abandon shopping carts (see Figure A1.4).

Figure A1.4

Netmarket avoids surprises by showing its customers shipping and handling costs, as well as taxes, as soon as they add items to their shopping cart.

A1.4   (www.netmarket.com, August 24, 2001)

3. **Returns.** Many shoppers prefer to see, hear, touch, smell, or taste some products in person before buying. This is one of the major reasons that as many as 45 percent of consumers are researching gift purchases in stores and catalogs and then purchasing them online, and 50 percent of consumers are using the Web to research products and then buy them either in a store or through a catalog.[2] Although some people may never shop online, more will shop on a site that provides EASY RETURNS (F9) because they know that, if what they buy doesn't work for them, they can return it for a full refund.

✳ SOLUTION

Differentiate your site so that customers know why it's compelling and valuable. Give shoppers browsing and searching tools, and provide rich, detailed information about your products and services. Make your site accessible to everyone. On every page include clear links to your privacy and security policy, shipping and handling policies, return policy, and frequently asked questions. Let customers collect items in one place and check out quickly, with minimal distraction.

2 From the *2003 eHoliday Moody Study,* conducted by Shop.org and BizRate.com (www.shop.org/press/03/120903.asp).

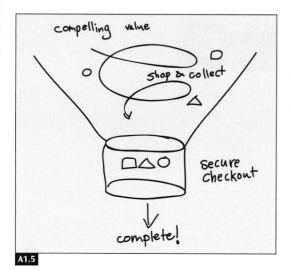

A1.5

Figure A1.5

E-commerce sites should offer value, allowing customers to shop, collect multiple items, and then quickly check out in a secure manner.

❊ OTHER PATTERNS TO CONSIDER

All E-Commerce Sites

Apply the solutions in Pattern Group F (Basic E-Commerce). Create an UP-FRONT VALUE PROPOSITION (C2) on your HOMEPAGE PORTAL (C1), and provide clear links for everyone for SITE ACCESSIBILITY (B9). Give customers MULTIPLE WAYS TO NAVIGATE (B1), make sure you have BROWSABLE CONTENT (B2), and provide CLEAN PRODUCT DETAILS (F2) so that people can compare different offers, pick the products or services they want by putting them in their SHOPPING CART (F3), move through your QUICK-FLOW CHECKOUT (F1) using CLEAR FORMS (H10), and, if necessary, take advantage of EASY RETURNS (F9).

Provide a FREQUENTLY ASKED QUESTIONS (H7) page that answers common questions about security, privacy, shipping, and returns. Build trust by making your PRIVACY POLICY (E4) always available and using FAIR INFORMATION PRACTICES (E3) throughout your company.

Advanced E-Commerce Sites

Choose options from Pattern Group G (Advanced E-Commerce). You may want to add daily FEATURED PRODUCTS (G1) to keep customers coming back for a glimpse of what your reviewers recommend, and to show them something that they may not have seen before.

Customers don't want to waste time, and sometimes they buy more than one thing. Help people save time, and perhaps show them something they might want but haven't seen, by CROSS-SELLING AND UP-SELLING (G2). Shoppers like to hear recommendations from others they trust, but they don't want to be pigeonholed as a particular kind of person. By using PERSONALIZED RECOMMENDATIONS (G3), you can offer ideas based on what you know someone might be looking for, without resorting to a formulaic recommendation. Customers like helping others too. By offering a RECOMMENDATION COMMUNITY (G4), you allow customers on your site to make their own recommendations.

Sometimes customers who are GIFT GIVING (G6) need to send gifts to people in many places. With the MULTIPLE DESTINATIONS (G5) feature, they can buy and send all the gifts in one order. Sometimes customers need to review their orders to make sure that the products they ordered arrived. And if a product that has shipped does not arrive when it should, the ORDER TRACKING AND HISTORY (G7) feature helps customers solve shipping problems.

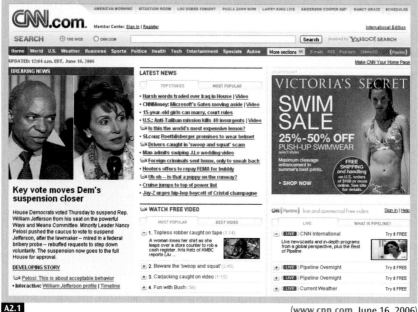

A2.1

(www.cnn.com, June 16, 2006)

Figure A2.1

On its Web site, CNN provides not only the top news of the day, but also archives of reporting from years gone by. It varies the content with diverse topics, in short form and in depth. The site encourages readers to use cnn.com as a resource, and it provides a quick guide to what's important today.

✳ BACKGROUND

This pattern forms the core that makes news sites useful. Use it separately or in conjunction with any other site genre pattern, such as PERSONAL E-COMMERCE (A1) if you sell products or services, GRASSROOTS INFORMATION SITES (A6) for expert analysis or content and links to the best sources of information on the Web, or COMMUNITY CONFERENCES (A3) and BLOGS (A12) for discussion of the day's topics. No matter what type of news site you create, it must have this basic capability of news mosaics.

A1

A6

A3 A12

✳ PROBLEM

Many readers come to Web sites to learn about their world through news and history. These sites must deliver the news that their readers want, with the depth and breadth of coverage necessary to engage them, and make the historical record available online so that customers can search for older stories.

News on the Web borrows heavily from what has been learned by offline news organizations, but it also poses new problems unique to the online medium. In terms of time and access, form, and audience, there are key differences between the way news is presented in television, radio, and print, and the way news is presented on the Web.

Time and Access • News stories on television, on radio, and in print last only the moment, the day, or sometimes the week, and then they're banished to a library archive. In other words, they appear today and become mostly inaccessible tomorrow. Web-based news is different in that any kind of news—up-to-the-second news, two-week-old news, or five-year-old news—can be accessed online. The information in your database remains both newsworthy and historical in value (see Figure A2.2).

Because the Web can deliver the "scoop" faster than other media can, it can create many time pressures. One time pressure comes from the need to publish new content in a timely way. You do not want to be re-creating the page layout and manually copying and pasting in text every time you need to add a new story. Use PAGE TEMPLATES (D1) that contain one or more CONTENT MODULES (D2). The content modules can be linked to a database, making publication as simple as adding a new story to the database and adding the associated HEADLINES AND BLURBS (D3) to other pages.

Another time pressure comes from the need to check sources. As with many other businesses, the long-term value of a news organization is based on the continuing quality of its product. This is especially true on the Web, where trust and reputation are closely tied to quality. Make sure you go the distance and properly check the sources of the stories on your site. The Web makes it easy to offer links to attributions and references, further encouraging the trust of your readers. In fact, studies have shown that people perceive news articles as more credible if there are references and EXTERNAL LINKS (K8) to other Web sites.

Form • News stories on television have the impact of motion and sound but are usually limited in duration, and therefore depth. Radio has the

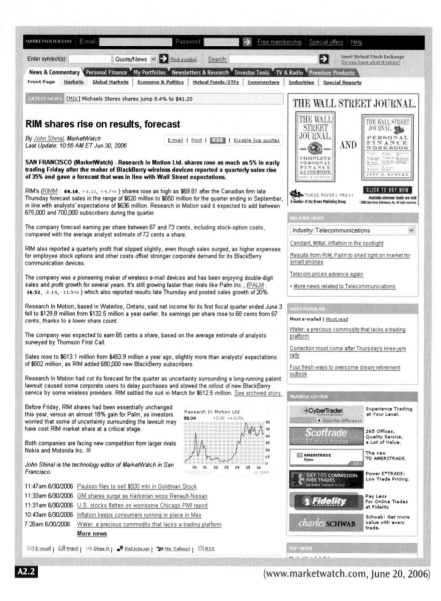

Figure A2.2

MarketWatch uses embedded links and sidebars to link to stock prices, further research, and stories related to the current article.

(www.marketwatch.com, June 20, 2006)

storytelling and music advantages of audio but is also usually limited in duration and depth. Unlike TV, however, radio travels well and does not consume precious eye time. Print has the benefit of more space, more depth, and mobility. The Web has some of the advantages of all three offline media, but it has other limitations.

One limitation is how people read online. Many people skim Web pages instead of reading them closely. If something isn't interesting, people hit the **Back** button pretty quickly. Draw people in by using a CLEAR FIRST READ (I3) that sets and unifies the visual and writing style for the article, and by using an INVERTED-PYRAMID WRITING STYLE (D7) that gives the most important information first.

Another limitation is that online news lacks the portability, large format, and legibility of print. It is true that online news can include video, audio, print, hyperlinked text, and historical access to stories. Unfortunately, it is often difficult to search on these kinds of media or to make them accessible to people with physical impairments unless a transcript is provided.

Take advantage of the Web's strengths. Provide short and long forms of your news using hyperlinks. Break up the text into manageable chunks to make it easier to read, thereby giving your readers the benefits of both TV's brevity and print's depth (see Figure A2.3). In addition, use EMBEDDED LINKS (K7) or CONSISTENT SIDEBARS OF RELATED CONTENT (I6) to add depth to a story. A text-based news article can link to video footage, audio interviews, or a richer set of images. That way you don't have to fit the different media on a single Web page. Finally, consider porting the entire site to a Mobile Web format, using MOBILE SCREEN SIZING (M1) and MOBILE INPUT CONTROLS (M2) to accommodate the small screens on handheld devices.

Audience • Whereas television, radio, and print are limited to targeted demographic groups, Web-based news can be tailored to each person. The Web creates opportunities, as well as possible limitations. Although readers can specify exactly the kinds of news they would like to read or receive, they also might be limiting their exposure to news outside their immediate areas of interest. As Andrew Shapiro observed in a review of online news, the result can be a further Balkanization of information, wherein we no longer have communities that share common experiences and sources of information, and we splinter off into small communities that do not fruitfully interact with one another.

Your challenge is to select not only the information that your readers want, but also the high-quality information that they don't know about that you want them to read. Your decisions are critical because your customers are looking for a guide when they come to a site with lots of information. With virtually unlimited "rack space," the volume of news can be overwhelming. Traditional media provide stories in a hierarchical manner. You need to make similar decisions about how you display the news,

Figure A2.3

CNN's news articles mix text with photo essays, audio, and video clips.

(www.cnn.com, June 16, 2006)

on the basis of what you know about your readers and their interests. One way to prioritize the information on a page is by screen placement and type size, as illustrated by cnn.com (see Figures A2.1 and A2.3).

When readers come to your site, they want to browse for articles on subjects that are important to them. Your challenge is not to bury everything but the most popular news, thereby making it harder for readers to find the more personal topics they seek. Give readers MULTIPLE WAYS TO NAVIGATE (B1). Let them look for topics by category, by keyword, or by historical reference. Also make it easy for people to search for specific content by WRITING FOR SEARCH ENGINES (D6), providing ORGANIZED SEARCH RESULTS (J3), and using PREDICTIVE INPUT (H11).

Some news sites, such as cnn.com, nytimes.com, and washingtonpost.com, provide archives, but only one of these examples archives the news in files and directories with PERMALINKS (K15) (permanent addresses): cnn.com. An EXTERNAL LINK (K8) on your site to a CNN news story today will always be an unbroken link. Most other news sites do not provide this capability.

Getting news right on the Web is also important for societal reasons. A study by the Pew Research Center for the People & the Press found that 75 million Americans used the Internet during the 2004 election to get news, discuss candidates in e-mail, and participate directly in the political process.[3] This finding shows that the quality of your news site can have a major impact.

❋ SOLUTION

Build a mosaic of news by providing breadth and depth of coverage through a diversity of categories and further refinement through subcategories. Within each category, highlight the most important article and lead text, while also identifying articles that might otherwise be missed. Within each article, provide a high-level summary first, for people who are looking for a quick read, but include more in-depth information in the rest of the article. Link together related news items, whether they are articles, radio stories, or video clips. Archive this information in the same place on your servers for historical reference.

---

3   From a Pew Internet & American Life Project report titled *The Internet and Campaign 2004* (www.pewinternet.org/PPF/r/150/report_display.asp).

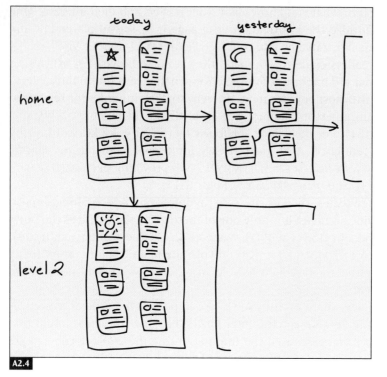

A2.4

Figure A2.4

Provide a mosaic of news in your article arrangement. Your site organization should give readers quick access to the most important news on various subjects, but it should also allow people to drill down for other articles on a subject, as well as back in time to earlier related articles.

❊ OTHER PATTERNS TO CONSIDER

Basic News Mosaics

Make this information easily accessible by providing top-level navigation to the various topic regions and to historical content through MULTIPLE WAYS TO NAVIGATE (B1). Start every page with a CLEAR FIRST READ (I3) of the main article. Make links to subcategories available on a NAVIGATION BAR (K2), as well as through article HEADLINES AND BLURBS (D3). Using the INVERTED-PYRAMID WRITING STYLE (D7), write content both for quick reads and for more in-depth reads.

Improve your search capabilities by supporting PREDICTIVE INPUT (H11) in your SEARCH ACTION MODULES (J1), WRITING FOR SEARCH ENGINES (D6) and displaying ORGANIZED SEARCH RESULTS (J3). Lay out topic sections using PAGE TEMPLATES (D1), with each article in CONTENT MODULES (D2) so that they can be created quickly and updated frequently through a database.

Advanced News Mosaics

Provide ways for readers to subscribe to news updates in particular topics with E-MAIL SUBSCRIPTIONS (E2).

News Mosaics Available by Subscription Only

Create accounts and provide sign-in capability using the SIGN-IN/NEW ACCOUNT (H2) pattern, and give people the ability to subscribe using QUICK-FLOW CHECKOUT (F1).

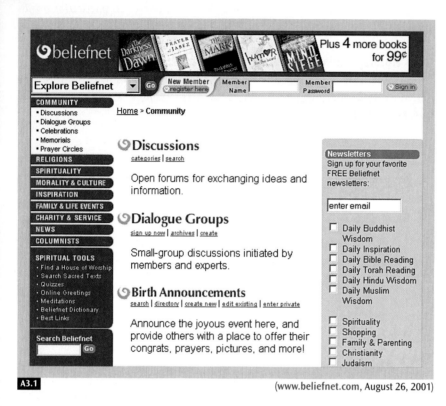

A3.1

(www.beliefnet.com, August 26, 2001)

Figure A3.1

Beliefnet's community section offers many ways for people to come together: large open discussions, smaller closed groups, and personal groups used on special occasions for families and close friends.

✳ BACKGROUND

MESSAGE BOARDS (D5) are only one part in creating an ongoing and thriving community. This pattern endorses responsibility and open discourse. As a place where people can trust one another to speak honestly and intelligently without fear of hooliganism, community conferences can be used in conjunction with and integrated into VALUABLE COMPANY SITES (A7), PERSONAL E-COMMERCE (A1), EDUCATIONAL FORUMS (A8), BLOGS (A12), and other site genre patterns.

✳ PROBLEM

Community members want to share ideas, views, and opinions with other like-minded individuals, whether they live across the street or across the planet. However, a host of issues must be resolved, such as community usage policies, moderation of forums, anonymity, archives, interaction, trust, sociability, growth, and sustainability. The challenge is to strike a balance within the online community.

The ability to have ongoing conversations with anyone, anywhere, any-time, is one of the most powerful aspects of the Web. However, many issues that are intrinsic to online communities are very different from our everyday experiences in the real world. In this section we discuss many of the policy issues that have to be resolved for all community conferences.

Community Usage Policies • Managing online communities is not easy. It is far easier to set up MESSAGE BOARDS (D5) and let things just happen. Developing a community conference takes time and effort to organize, invite, give access, monitor, and facilitate. Which rules are important to the community? Should you remove off-topic comments from a discussion thread, or should you archive them to a separate location? What kinds of things are acceptable for people to post? What happens if a member breaks the rules?

Every community must declare its own standards and enforce those standards (see Figure A3.2). Every community must also establish a set of FAIR INFORMATION PRACTICES (E3) that dictate how personal data will be used, and communicate these practices through a clear PRIVACY POLICY (E4). Getting the members of your community to agree on rules, such as by using PRIVACY PREFERENCES (E8), can be time-consuming, but once agreement is reached, our experience shows that their discussion will be more thoughtful and enlightening.

Synchronous or Asynchronous Communication • One immediate question with respect to community conferences is whether people must interact with one another now or can respond later. The former is an example of **synchronous communication,** meaning that all parties have to be online simultaneously and interaction takes place in real time. Examples of synchronous communication include chat rooms, video conferencing, and shared drawing spaces. The latter is an example of **asynchronous communication,** meaning that members can leave messages that others can respond to later. Examples of asynchronous communication include e-mail, MESSAGE BOARDS (D5), BLOGS (A12), and community-created Web pages.

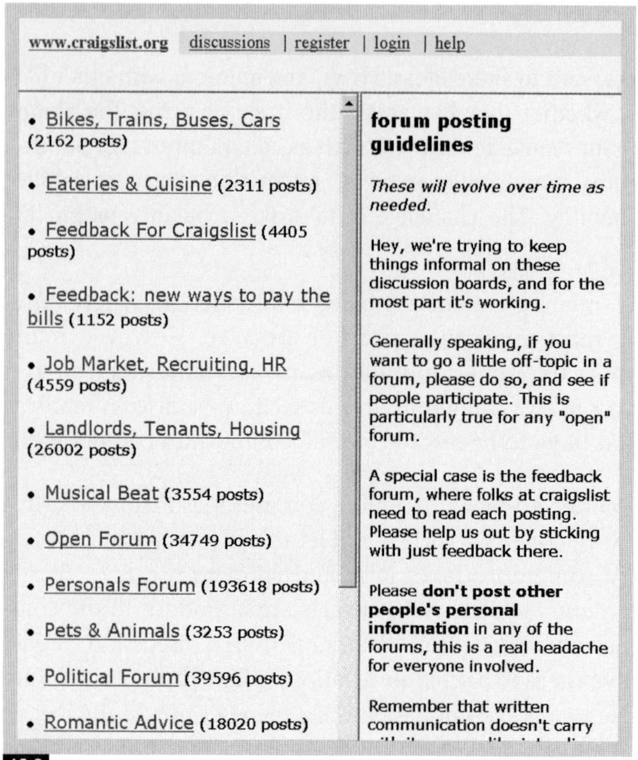

Figure A3.2

The online community craigslist sets the ground rules for posting as soon as customers go to the list of forums.

www.craigslist.org   discussions | register | login | help

- Bikes, Trains, Buses, Cars (2162 posts)
- Eateries & Cuisine (2311 posts)
- Feedback For Craigslist (4405 posts)
- Feedback: new ways to pay the bills (1152 posts)
- Job Market, Recruiting, HR (4559 posts)
- Landlords, Tenants, Housing (26002 posts)
- Musical Beat (3554 posts)
- Open Forum (34749 posts)
- Personals Forum (193618 posts)
- Pets & Animals (3253 posts)
- Political Forum (39596 posts)
- Romantic Advice (18020 posts)

forum posting guidelines

These will evolve over time as needed.

Hey, we're trying to keep things informal on these discussion boards, and for the most part it's working.

Generally speaking, if you want to go a little off-topic in a forum, please do so, and see if people participate. This is particularly true for any "open" forum.

A special case is the feedback forum, where folks at craigslist need to read each posting. Please help us out by sticking with just feedback there.

Please **don't post other people's personal information** in any of the forums, this is a real headache for everyone involved.

Remember that written communication doesn't carry

A3.2

(www.craigslist.org, August 25, 2001)

Each approach has pros and cons. Synchronous communication is more spontaneous and often leads to faster decision making. However, people with slow Internet connections suffer enormously, and sometimes it's hard to keep track of who's saying what. Asynchronous communication can be more thoughtful (though not always!), and participants can reply to posted messages at any later time. Because of slow turnaround, however, it is sometimes difficult to come to a consensus on issues, and it can be difficult to manage and take part in the many continuing conversations.

You can support both synchronous and asynchronous forums, depending on the interests and needs of your customers. For example, it is not uncommon for Web sites to host both MESSAGE BOARDS (D5) and chat rooms. Also note that there is not always a strict separation between synchronous and asynchronous communication. A synchronous chat can be archived for other people to see later, at which point it becomes an asynchronous resource.

Moderation • Another question that you'll need to answer up front is whether your forums are moderated, and if so, to what degree. On **moderated forums,** messages are filtered and processed by one or more moderators who must approve all messages to make sure that they follow the established rules and norms. An example of a moderated forum is a message board for people coping with cancer. The moderator in this case would probably approve all messages except for blatant advertisements and trolls (messages intended to inflame and infuriate others).

Unmoderated forums are free-for-all discussions in which anything goes. People can say whatever they want, and it is up to the members of the community to enforce any rules and social norms. An example of an unmoderated forum is an ad hoc chat room set up by a high school student where she and her friends can talk about whatever they want. The only thing keeping people from being viciously rude to one another in this case is the fact that they know each other and have an ongoing relationship, seeing each other in school.

There are many options between these two extremes. For example, an e-mail list could be moderated to the extent that the first few messages by each participant would have to be approved by a moderator, but unmoderated in the sense that after someone had three messages approved, her messages would no longer require approval to be posted. As another example, a message board could be unmoderated except for occasional spot checks to make sure that no one was posting copyrighted material. Furthermore, people could send complaints or notifications of usage violations to the owner of the message board, who could then act reasonably in handling the complaint.

The upshot is that there are many options with respect to moderation. Your choice of the level of moderation depends on what kind of community and discussion you want.

Anonymous, Pseudonymous, or Identified by Real Name • Anonymity is an extremely important and sometimes contentious issue that you will have to deal with on community conference sites. The online world's capabilities for anonymity can be liberating, freeing people from social norms and pressures (see Figure A3.3). However, they are also highly prone to abuse, as potential sources of false and libelous information. Because anyone can create an anonymous identity, your customers can pretend to be someone they're not.

In a positive sense, anonymity means that community members can veil their identity or playact, giving them the opportunity to "try on"

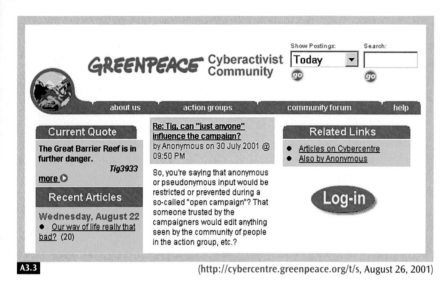

A3.3

(http://cybercentre.greenpeace.org/t/s, August 26, 2001)

Figure A3.3

Anonymous postings can be important on the Greenpeace Cyberactivist Community site, where visitors might want to participate in environmental activism without alerting their employers.

being a different person, similar to acting in theater or playing make-believe. This freedom is critical for people who need to hide their true identities, such as victims of abuse, who, with anonymity, can participate in online discussions without fear of reprisal from their abusers.

On the negative side, because it's difficult to trace activities that are completely anonymous online, people abuse complete anonymity for hostile and sometimes illegal purposes. At the annoying but benign level, being completely anonymous is a consequence-free way to digress and ruin an otherwise enlightening conversation. At hostile but not illegal levels, some people use complete anonymity to abuse others with angry comments. Tragically, when adults prey on children in complete anonymity, or commit other crimes online, the whole online community suffers. If you cannot restrict access by requiring participants to verify their true identities, abusive activities can go unchecked.

There is a fair balance between no anonymity—that is, real names (see Figure A3.4)—and complete anonymity. When your customers inform you of their true identity and then assume a different name in the community, they can realize the benefits of partial anonymity. The assumed name is known as a **pseudonym.** By restricting access to only those individuals who are willing to divulge their true identities *to the site operators,* an online community fosters more responsible behavior.

Figure A3.4

In The WELL's community, like-minded individuals can share ideas, develop a rapport, and build strong, trusting relationships. Requiring real names and confirmed identities helps build this trust.

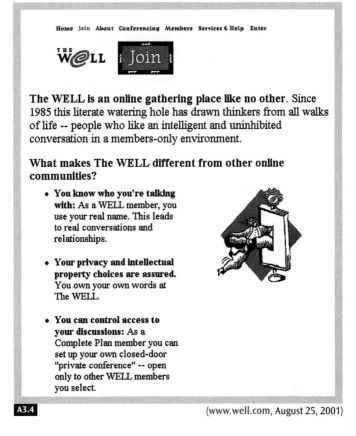

Home Join About Conferencing Members Services & Help Enter

W@LL Join

The WELL is an online gathering place like no other. Since 1985 this literate watering hole has drawn thinkers from all walks of life -- people who like an intelligent and uninhibited conversation in a members-only environment.

What makes The WELL different from other online communities?

- **You know who you're talking with:** As a WELL member, you use your real name. This leads to real conversations and relationships.

- **Your privacy and intellectual property choices are assured.** You own your own words at The WELL.

- **You can control access to your discussions:** As a Complete Plan member you can set up your own closed-door "private conference" -- open only to other WELL members you select.

A3.4

(www.well.com, August 25, 2001)

Table A3.1 shows the levels of anonymity that are reasonable in different online contexts.

Archives • There are three basic questions to answer here. (1) Will messages be stored? (2) If so, for how long? (3) Who has access to see and possibly delete old messages? For example, messages in chat rooms are usually not stored, but message boards often save all posts and make them permanently available for all people to see. On the other hand, it's not unheard of for chat sessions to be archived, or for message board posts older than one month to be automatically deleted.

There are many pros and cons to storing archives of past messages. Some messages represent useful knowledge, and searching for that information can be easier and faster than having someone repeat it over and over. For team projects, a message archive can be a record of design rationale, helping someone who later joins the team understand why a

Conference Type	Level of Anonymity Required	Information Disclosed to Community	Information Disclosed to Site Operator
Adult educational conference	None	Name and contact	Name and contact
New-parent support group	None	Name and contact	Name and contact
K–12 class discussions	Partial	Anonymous or student-created user name	Name and contact
Abuse victim discussions	Partial	Nothing	Name and contact
Government or corporate whistle-blower site	Complete	Nothing	Nothing

Table A3.1

Reasonable Levels of Anonymity in Community Conferences

certain design decision was made. These archives are also useful to researchers, letting them see patterns of communication among community members and changes in those patterns over time.

There are also some potentially serious disadvantages of archiving past messages. Some messages just aren't that valuable. There's not much point in archiving informal chats about computer games or gossip, for example. Also there is the danger that things people write in haste will come back and haunt them many years later. It does seem somewhat unfair that people can search on someone's name and see something that he thoughtlessly posted 12 years earlier. As a result, long-term archives might cripple open discussion and lead to potentially embarrassing situations in the future. In fact, it's not unheard of for a company's e-mail archives to be subpoenaed in a legal dispute.

These considerations lead into the next question: How long should archives be kept? Short-lived archives can help people remember recent messages and avoid problems with those messages being taken out of context in the future. Long-lived archives are useful for finding important messages in the past. There is no single answer, unfortunately, and decisions have to be made on a case-by-case basis.

The last question about archives has to do with access. Who should be able to access the archives, and should those who have access be able to delete old messages? For example, one possible policy is to let only the person who posted a message see his or her own old messages. Another is to let anyone in the community search for and see all old messages, and allow posters to delete their old messages. This decision should be part of your PRIVACY POLICY (E4), as well as your community's usage policy.

Trust and Sociability • Although some of the benefits and social cues of in-person contact are lost online, online conferences do have many benefits: Your readers can be geographically dispersed; they do not have to be together at the same time; conversations can last weeks, months, or longer; and newcomers can join and read the history of the conversation so far.

Once involved, moderators must keep conversations on track and turn major digressions into their own discussion threads. Creating an online community is time intensive but well worth the effort when responsibility, respect, and a shared commitment to intelligent conversation are the standards.

Publish and follow these basic rules:

- We seek thoughtful and intelligent people to enrich each conference.
- Newcomers are allowed to visit and listen, and to join in when they're ready.
- Each member's view will be respected.
- Personal attacks are not allowed.
- People who are not respectful and thoughtful will be ejected.
- If you ever feel harassed, you can e-mail the moderator and express your concern.
- No single person will run the whole conversation, because the community is not a personal soapbox.

Growth and Sustainability • Creating an ongoing and thriving community is a difficult task. The greatest obstacles are attracting people to your community and then getting them to participate. When first starting out, you will probably have to nurture and lead some discussions to get things going.

Ideally, you want your community to exhibit a positive network effect, in which newcomers will join your community because it already has a lot of members, all without much effort on your part. Most communities have a critical mass—that is, a minimum number of participating community members for the community to become self-sustaining. Reaching this critical mass is much more important than it may seem at first because it marks the beginning of a fairly successful online community. This milestone has significant benefits for recruiting new community members because new people will come to see what all the hubbub is about, attracting more visitors to the community and encouraging them to stay longer.

Moderating Message Boards

Teresa Nielsen-Hayden is an editor and writer of science fiction, as well as a popular blogger. In a panel on handling trolls and spammers, she came up with a list of things that must be done to moderate message boards. She also popularized the term *disemvowelling,* which means "removing the vowels from annoying posts" rather than simply deleting those posts.

The original list, at nielsenhayden.com/makinglight/archives/006036.html, is reproduced here.

1. There can be no ongoing discourse without some degree of moderation, if only to kill off the hardcore trolls. It takes rather more moderation than that to create a complex, nuanced, civil discourse. If you want that to happen, you have to give of yourself. Providing the space but not tending the conversation is like expecting that your front yard will automatically turn itself into a garden.

2. Once you have a well-established online conversation space, with enough regulars to explain the local mores to newcomers, they'll do a lot of the policing themselves.

3. You own the space. You host the conversation. You don't own the community. Respect their needs. For instance, if you're going away for a while, don't shut down your comment area. Give them an open thread to play with, so they'll still be there when you get back.

4. Message persistence rewards people who write good comments.

5. Over-specific rules are an invitation to people who get off on gaming the system.

6. Civil speech and impassioned speech are not opposed and mutually exclusive sets. Being interesting trumps any amount of conventional politeness.

7. Things to cherish: Your regulars. A sense of community. Real expertise. Genuine engagement with the subject under discussion. Outstanding performances. Helping others. Cooperation in maintenance of a good conversation. Taking the time to teach newbies the ropes.

    All these things should be rewarded with your attention and praise. And if you get a particularly good comment, consider adding it to the original post.

8. Grant more lenience to participants who are only part-time jerks, as long as they're valuable the rest of the time.

Moderating Message Boards (*Continued*)

9. If you judge that a post is offensive, upsetting, or just plain unpleasant, it's important to get rid of it, or at least make it hard to read. Do it as quickly as possible. There's no more useless advice than to tell people to just ignore such things. We can't. We automatically read what falls under our eyes.

10. Another important rule: You can let one jeering, unpleasant jerk hang around for a while, but the minute you get two or more of them egging each other on, they both have to go, and all their recent messages with them. There are others like them prowling the net, looking for just that kind of situation. More of them will turn up, and they'll encourage each other to behave more and more outrageously. Kill them quickly and have no regrets.

11. You can't automate intelligence. In theory, systems like Slashdot's ought to work better than they do. Maintaining a conversation is a task for human beings.

12. Disemvowelling works. Consider it.

13. If someone you've disemvowelled comes back and behaves, forgive and forget their earlier gaffes. You're acting in the service of civility, not abstract justice.

The longer people try out a community conference, the more they will become accustomed to the forums, discussions, customs, social norms, and people in the community. And most importantly, whereas it's easy for people to switch to a competing e-commerce site and buy something there, it's much more difficult for people to switch to a competing community conference. They simply can't switch their friends and chat partners as easily.

Additional Information • A great deal of high-quality information about creating, managing, and sustaining an online community is available. Use the sources listed in the Resources section later in the book to find more information about nurturing a community, running a large online community, hosting conversations, free speech, and many, many other issues.

✳ SOLUTION

To make a community conference site work, establish a clear community usage policy that specifies acceptable behaviors, as well as sanctions that will be imposed on anyone who breaks the rules. Set up a variety of synchronous and asynchronous forums to suit you and your customers. Determine if the community will be moderated, and if so, to what degree. Agree on the level of anonymity that your community will support. Decide whether messages will be archived, and if so, how they will be archived and who will have access to them. Increase trust and sociability by keeping discussions on track and establishing social norms of behavior. Promote growth by leading discussions and attracting new community members.

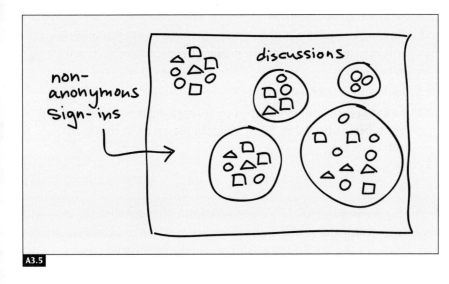

A3.5

Figure A3.5

When you require nonanonymous sign-ins for access to community conferences, your community members will act more respectfully and responsibly. Managed discussions keep conversations on target.

✳ OTHER PATTERNS TO CONSIDER

Basic Community Conference

BLOGS (A12) can be used to quickly set up simple community conferences. Make your FAIR INFORMATION PRACTICES (E3) clear to your customers through an understandable PRIVACY POLICY (E4) available on all pages. Ask all potential participants to create nonanonymous accounts using SIGN-IN/NEW ACCOUNT (H2). Verify the addresses of the individuals by sending an e-mail message to which they must respond, and if security needs dictate (and the privacy policy allows), call them on the phone as well.

A12
E3
E4

H2

Place BROWSABLE CONTENT (B2) in the MESSAGE BOARDS (D5). Manage these message boards on a daily basis, creating new threads for major digressions.

Advanced Community Conference

Give members a way to understand how their values are being perceived. If you have hundreds or thousands of members, use a RECOMMENDATION COMMUNITY (G4) to let people rate each other on how insightful and helpful their assessments and views really are to others. This feedback will help newcomers better judge each person and give them the goal of earning respect.

A4 SELF-SERVICE GOVERNMENT

(www.cityofsydney.nsw.gov.au, June 16, 2006)

Figure A4.1

The official site of Sydney, Australia, provides access to government information and services from the convenience of each citizen's desk, eliminating bureaucracy and frustration.

✳ BACKGROUND

This pattern describes how to build an environment that makes government services more available and accessible. You can add other site genre patterns, such as PERSONAL E-COMMERCE (A1) and COMMUNITY CONFERENCE (A3).

✳ PROBLEM

Making a government agency's information available on the Web can be helpful, but if the agency is too large and centrally controlled, its Web site can seem unresponsive, bureaucratic, and impersonal to its customers.

A September 2000 study by Hart and Teeter found that the U.S. public believes that online interaction between citizens and their government, or e-government, means better government, and that investing tax dollars in e-government should be a medium to high priority. According to Hart and Teeter, 61 percent of Americans believe that the Internet should be used to make it easier for citizens to interact with government to find the information and services they need, when they need them. If your job is to make e-government a reality, your local, state, or federal government Web site needs to provide this capability while avoiding the problems that citizens currently face in their offline interactions with government agencies: red tape and a faceless bureaucracy.

Red Tape • A preponderance of evidence shows that red tape is a result of government agencies growing too large. Whether wasting time waiting in line or battling red tape as they're bounced from one bureaucrat to another, citizens must fight their way through centrally controlled government processes. This red tape can come in many forms. People must submit formal requests and wait until their requests are processed. This process can take a day, a week, or months, and there is little or no feedback about where the request is in the process or what the estimated time to complete it is. In the case of a problem, generalized regulations and centralized control prevent low-level government agents from having the autonomy to make decisions on their own. To a large, centrally controlled agency, local community issues are unmanageable.

Faceless Bureaucracy • When customers come to use many Web-based government services, there are more problems. They find that online government agencies are usually even less personable than offline: They are nameless, faceless, and generic, and they provide no feedback. Site visitors might find a government form, but usually the form must be printed and submitted offline. Even if they're submitted online, such forms are processed as offline forms. If individuals are named on a Web site at all, they are usually so far removed from individual services (such as the mayor) that they're of no help.

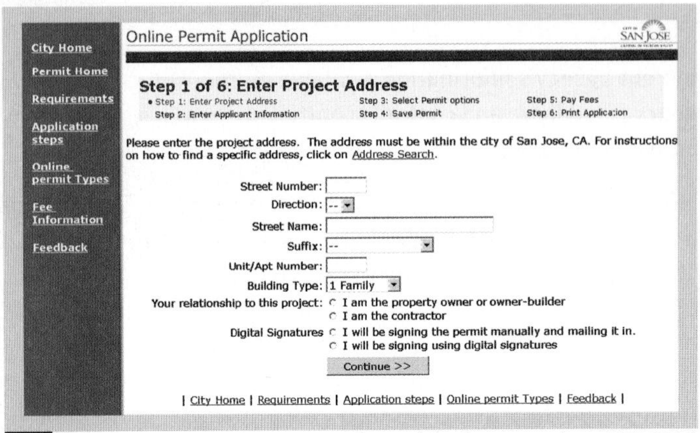

Figure A4.2

The city of San Jose's Web site shows how e-government can be done. It has taken much of the hassle out of getting a construction permit by allowing citizens to complete the entire process online.

(www.ci.san-jose.ca.us, August 24, 2001)

Given these issues, we conclude that your government agency Web site can provide better levels of service than offline services alone can if you do the following:

- Provide small, autonomous self-service applications that give feedback as requests are being processed (see Figure A4.2).
- Deliver comprehensive and personalized answers to general and local community questions.
- Connect people to local agents who have the autonomy to solve problems and answer questions (see Figure A4.3).

To make a government Web site work most effectively, you must also address the issues of universal access and of privacy and trust.

Universal Access • Any government that attempts to take advantage of the Web to provide government services online needs to give everyone access to the Web, whether this means subsidizing purchases of Internet appliances (à la Minitel in France), low-cost PCs, or making Web access devices ubiquitous in public spaces, such as libraries and post offices. Web sites should also be built so that people with slow Internet connections, older computers, and older software can still use them. Finally, be sure to build your site for SITE ACCESSIBILITY (B9), to serve citizens who require special assistance in reading, hearing, or navigating Web sites.

B9

Privacy and Trust • When it comes to online services, the government must respect the privacy of each citizen. The entire agency behind the

Figure A4.3

The state of California's Web site offers several useful self-service applications. This page allows citizens to make appointments at the Department of Motor Vehicles.

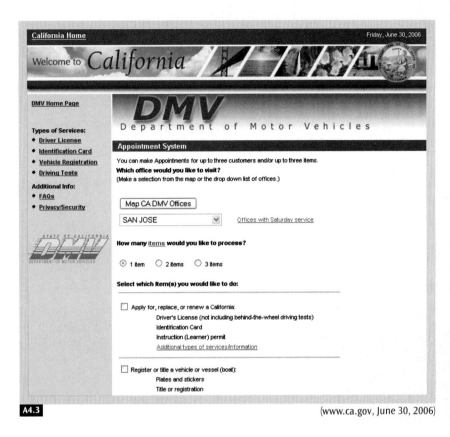

A4.3   (www.ca.gov, June 30, 2006)

E3 Web site must establish FAIR INFORMATION PRACTICES (E3) that will be respected and followed by everyone involved. These practices must
E4 also be clearly explained in a prominently displayed PRIVACY POLICY (E4). In general, avoid the use of IP tracking and cookie-based PERSISTENT
H5 CUSTOMER SESSIONS (H5) unless absolutely needed because these can inadvertently create an image of abuse of government power and infringement on the rights of the citizenry. On the other hand, do provide
E6 H2 SECURE CONNECTIONS (E6) and a SIGN-IN/NEW ACCOUNT (H2) process for any transactions that contain personal and trusted information. Government
E9 sites should also contain mechanisms for PREVENTING PHISHING SCAMS (E9), to prevent unscrupulous individuals from creating sites that masquerade as government sites.

✳ SOLUTION

Provide secure, autonomous self-service applications that report current process status through your site and e-mail after the initial request submission. Give your customers the estimated time to completion, on the basis of the kind of request made. Personalize site information for each citizen by giving direct access to that citizen's agency representative and providing answers to questions posted by local community members.

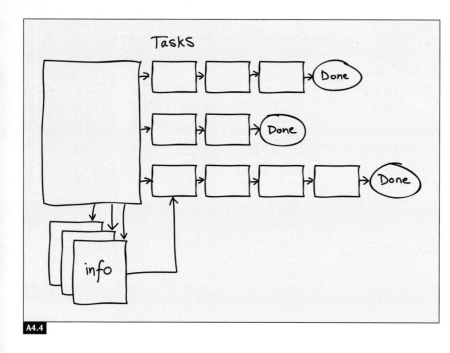

A4.4

Figure A4.4

Secure, autonomous applications eliminate the need for people to wait in line, and personalized pages give people direct access to local agents and information.

✳ OTHER PATTERNS TO CONSIDER

Develop a site organization using MULTIPLE WAYS TO NAVIGATE (B1) so that citizens can easily find the information and services they need. Determine your FAIR INFORMATION PRACTICES (E3) and state them clearly in your PRIVACY POLICY (E4) so that people know how their private information will be used. Using SECURE CONNECTIONS (E6) and PREVENTING PHISHING SCAMS (E9) will also build trust. Provide SITE ACCESSIBILITY (B9) to all.

B1
E3
E4
E6
E9 **B9**

Develop secure, autonomous applications by creating PROCESS FUNNELS (H1) that require SIGN-IN/NEW ACCOUNT (H2) creation and use noncookie PERSISTENT CUSTOMER SESSIONS (H5).

Provide local-agent contact information and local-issue question and answer information, as well as general information through PERSONALIZED CONTENT (D4) and CONTENT MODULES (D2). Keep citizens informed about their pending requests using weekly E-MAIL SUBSCRIPTIONS (E2).

Figure A5.1

VolunteerMatch uses the Web to help volunteers and non-profit organizations find each other.

A5.1   (www.volunteermatch.org, June 16, 2006)

❋ BACKGROUND

This pattern forms the core of all nonprofit sites. Integrate other site genre patterns into a nonprofit site to expand its capabilities or use this pattern to add a charitable service to a VALUABLE COMPANY SITE (A7), PERSONAL E-COMMERCE (A1) site, NEWS MOSAIC (A2), GRASSROOTS INFORMATION SITE (A6), or EDUCATIONAL FORUM (A8).

A7

A1 A2 A6

A8

❄ PROBLEM

Nonprofits rely on financial sponsors, volunteers, and staff members to benefit the needs of a client cause. If these groups are not brought together in a network, a major benefit of the Web is neglected.

A nonprofit's financial sponsors, volunteers, and staff members all want to help its beneficiaries, but each group has its own needs and criteria for participation. Addressing these needs is the first and most basic step of developing a nonprofit Web site. Such a design may provide access to information anytime anywhere and start to build an individual relationship between the nonprofit and each visitor to its site.

A True Network of Help • Providing only "the basics" keeps each visitor isolated and does not leverage the tremendous power of the Web as a network. A Web site can be the nexus of communications that allow people to connect directly to one another.

There are many reasons to connect everyone involved in a nonprofit. Most nonprofits are organized around projects and schedules that bring together volunteers, beneficiaries, and sponsorships from financial contributors—all organized and coordinated by staff members.

Coordinating these projects requires effort and precious staff time, as well as continual updates to the entire team about the project status. Invariably, issues arise that you must address with employees, volunteers, sponsors, beneficiaries, or the entire project team. Individual volunteers and beneficiaries can benefit others by sharing what they've learned. Financial sponsors benefit from seeing the project process in action. Staff members seek to learn and help their systems evolve from one project to the next. Each project becomes a success story to document and publish. Everyone involved becomes a key part of the success story.

Connecting people on a nonprofit Web site reduces management costs, while improving communication between the players. Tools such as MESSAGE BOARDS (D5), BLOGS (A12), online schedules, and content management tools[4] facilitate the coordination of teams and the sharing of information without costly overhead and administration. By providing these tools on a central project management server, you can create a system in which people communicate more frequently because the tools eliminate time and location constraints. Such a benefit is called a **network effect** because everyone gains more benefit as more individuals use this network of connections.

---

4   Druple (druple.org) is a popular open source content management tool.

Providing Specific Solutions • Financial sponsors, volunteers, staff members, and beneficiaries will have different questions, and they will carry out different tasks. These needs form the basis of the solutions shown in Table A5.1. A basic nonprofit site must entice each group to participate by

Group	Question or Task	What to Provide as a Solution
Financial sponsors (see Figure A5.2)	Why do I want to fund this nonprofit?	The benefits of funding this nonprofit
	What does this nonprofit do?	ABOUT US (E5), an overview of the program
	Who are the beneficiaries?	An overview of beneficiaries and some of their stories
	How will my money be used?	Statistics on how much of each dollar is used for the cause and how much covers administrative overhead
	How do I make a donation?	Instructions for making donations offline or online, with the online version providing a SECURE CONNECTION (E6) through a PROCESS FUNNEL (H1)
Volunteers (see Figures A5.3 and A5.4)	Why is this a worthy cause?	ABOUT US (E5), an overview of the program
	What do volunteers do?	The benefits for volunteers, volunteer stories
	How do I become involved?	A schedule of events, a volunteer sign-up form, E-MAIL SUBSCRIPTIONS (E2) for newsletters and nearby events
Staff	Who are the current volunteers, financiers, and beneficiaries?	Secure page listing volunteers, financial sponsors, and beneficiaries
Beneficiaries	Who are the people helping me?	Statements of gratitude directed to all the financiers, volunteers, and staff members, that identify (in general) what they contributed
Everyone	What are the latest developments with current projects?	MESSAGE BOARDS (D5) and BLOGS (A12) with current topics open for discussion, HEADLINES AND BLURBS (D3) about new events

Table A5.1

Sample Questions, Tasks, and Solutions for Nonprofits

(E5)

(E6)
(H1)

(E5)

(E2)

(D5)
(A12)

(D3)

Figure A5.2

The Rotary Foundation, a division of Rotary International, is the charitable-works arm of Rotary clubs. Its site allows visitors to make gifts to the foundation, manage their gifts, find local sponsors for initiatives, and see what their district has donated.

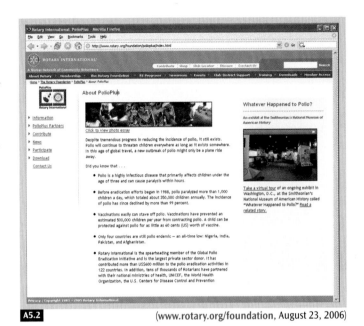

(www.rotary.org/foundation, August 23, 2006)

Figure A5.3

Kiwanis International is dedicated to serving its community and promoting the needs of children worldwide. Its Web site features relevant news headlines and makes it easy for members to join events and discuss issues.

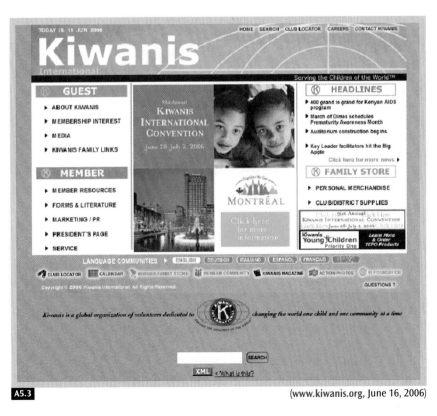

(www.kiwanis.org, June 16, 2006)

Figure A5.4

Network for Good promotes civic participation and philanthropy. Its Web site aggregates content and resources from over twenty nonprofit organizations, making them conveniently available all in one place.

A5.4 (www.networkforgood.org, June 16, 2006)

answering these key questions. An advanced nonprofit network of help provides the means for entire projects to be coordinated online. In such a case the Web site becomes the primary vehicle for connecting groups in a coordinated activity and shared dialogue.

✳ SOLUTION

At a minimum, provide information that addresses the questions posed by financial sponsors, volunteers, staff members, and beneficiaries. To harness the power of the Web as a network, give people the ability to sign up for projects in a place where all team members can coordinate, participate, and record project developments for future reference.

Figure A5.5

Basic nonprofit sites provide compelling reasons for people to become financial sponsors, volunteers, staff members, and beneficiaries. To make the most of the network, a nonprofit site must help coordinate people around specific projects.

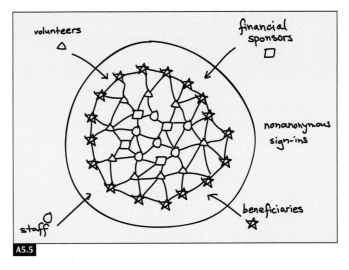

A5.5

❋ OTHER PATTERNS TO CONSIDER

Basic Nonprofit Networks of Help

Build a site that provides program information targeted to your distinct audiences: financial sponsors, volunteers, staff, and beneficiaries. Provide MULTIPLE WAYS TO NAVIGATE (B1) to a CATEGORY PAGE (B8) for each audience, where you publish success stories and past accomplishments in CONTENT MODULES (D2) for easy updating. Keep your project calendar up-to-date.

Give volunteers a CLEAR FORM (H10) and a PROCESS FUNNEL (H1) for signing up. Also place an E-MAIL SUBSCRIPTION (E2) form on or just off of the HOMEPAGE PORTAL (C1) to make it easy for visitors to remain informed about events.

Make your FAIR INFORMATION PRACTICES (E3) clear through a simple and understandable PRIVACY POLICY (E4).

Advanced Nonprofit Networks of Help

Make it easy for people to contribute by giving visitors the opportunity to make donations online through a QUICK-FLOW CHECKOUT (F1) process.

To take advantage of the Web's network effect, use your project calendar to help volunteers choose a particular project by qualifying their participation online using a PROCESS FUNNEL (H1). Provide a SECURE CONNECTION (E6) and create CLEAR FORMS (H10) for them to use on a

SIGN-IN/NEW ACCOUNT (H2) page. After they have signed in, let them
access a PERSONALIZED CONTENT (D4) area of the site specifically for the
project team.

In addition, publish progress reports through CONTENT MODULES (D2)
and provide MESSAGE BOARDS (D5) so that otherwise disconnected volunteers and financial sponsors can talk with other volunteers and
financial sponsors, as well as with staff members and beneficiaries. On
the public site, excerpt and publish the results of each project using
CONTENT MODULES (D2).

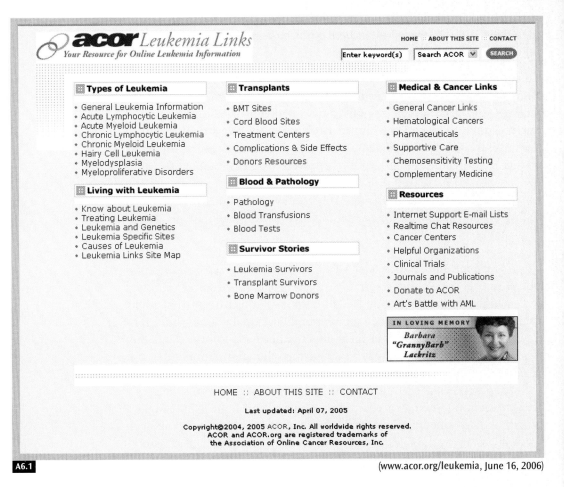

(www.acor.org/leukemia, June 16, 2006)

Figure A6.1

The Leukemia Links grassroots information site is one of the best resources on the Web for information about leukemia, consistently ranking in the top ten on Google in searches on *leukemia*. Although a modest site, it is valuable because it provides not only basic information about leukemia, but also a well-organized, comprehensive, prequalified list of links to the best leukemia sites on the Web.

❈ BACKGROUND

This pattern forms the core of all information reference sites. You can integrate other site genre patterns to build a resource site, including

VALUABLE COMPANY SITES (A7), COMMUNITY CONFERENCES (A3), BLOGS (A12), and EDUCATIONAL FORUMS (A8).

✳ PROBLEM

Sorting through hundreds of search results about a particular topic is time-consuming. Without a guide, visitors become discouraged and give up, or possibly act on only partial information.

Customers often search for topical information on the Web, but any complete topic overview is usually buried so deeply that it takes a long time to uncover. Search engines do a good job of finding reams of results sorted by each site's **value ranking.**[5] But even highly ranked sites usually provide only one point of reference, or a piece of the overall picture. Directories like Yahoo! work well to an extent, but the number of librarians required to build comprehensive catalogs for all categories of information on the Web would bankrupt the directories. As a result of seeing only a partial picture, some people act on partial information.

Why a Grassroots Information Site? • People who build grassroots information sites have a deep interest in a particular topic (see Figure A6.2) and have scoured the Web to build a comprehensive picture of that topic. Initially they might want a Web site for purely personal reasons, but eventually, realizing the value that their site could provide to others in need, the authors post their pages and let others read the information, reference it, and act on it.

  Readers appreciate site authors who answer tough questions, and they respect them for their expertise, commitment, and honesty. To build a grassroots site—one that builds traffic through word of mouth—you need to create value and establish trust and credibility. Building a grassroots site takes time and commitment because the site must be continually updated to address new issues and provide better resources.

Answering Questions • When people go to an information site, they hope to have their questions answered quickly and easily. Answers can come in the form of an extensive Web site of self-created or collected knowledge, as an extensive directory to the best resources on the Web, or as a combination of the two (see Figure A6.3).

---

5 Google is such a search engine. Its value rankings are guided by the idea that the best Web sites have the most links pointed to them from other sites. In other words, if many other Web site publishers think a site is worth referencing, it must be a good site.

Figure A6.2

Grassroots sites can be one person's attempt to help others. This site publicizes the plight of victims of the 2004 tsunami, as well as victims of other natural disasters worldwide.

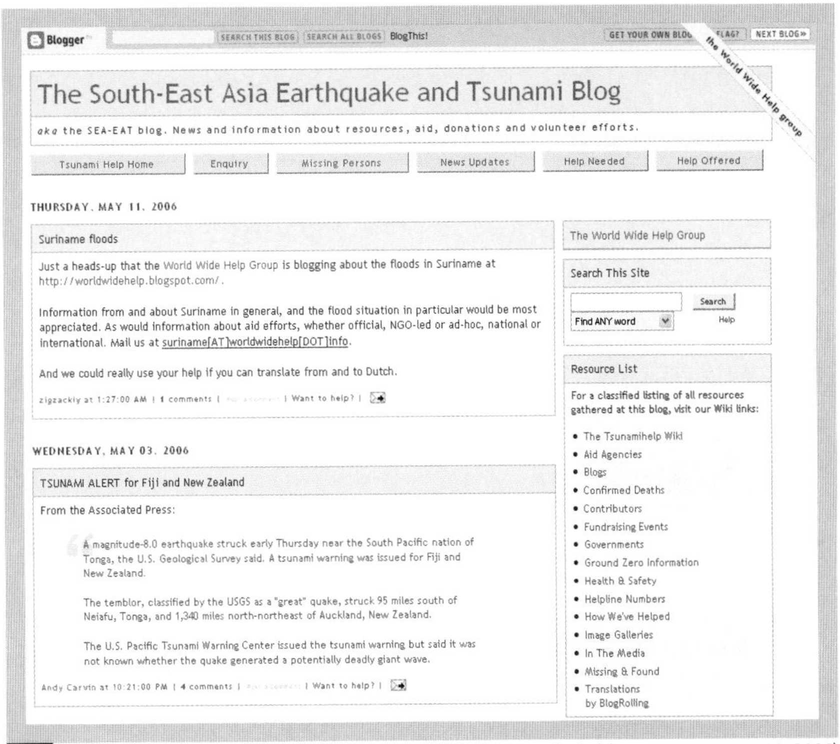

A6.2   (tsunamihelp.blogspot.com, June 16, 2006)

Credibility and Trust • When people trust a site, they trust that the information is accurate. When they trust a site on a particular topic, they believe it will answer most questions that they pose. To establish trust and build credibility, provide information that is both accurate and comprehensive. Also date all of your Web pages so that people will be able to assess how old the information is and whether it is still relevant to them.

Writing Style • The most basic rule of writing applies here: know your audience. In this case there are two audiences to keep in mind. The first is search engines because presumably many people will find your Web site through one of these. [See WRITING FOR SEARCH ENGINES (D6) for more details.]

The other audience is your readers. If your site is fact based and aims to be an authoritative news site, use an INVERTED-PYRAMID WRITING STYLE (D7). Keep in mind, though, that this style of writing does not work

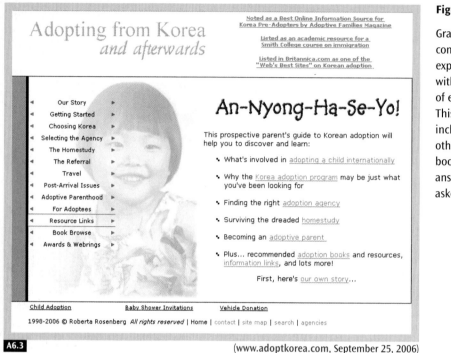

A6.3

(www.adoptkorea.com, September 25, 2006)

Figure A6.3

Grassroots sites often combine personal expertise on a topic with a good selection of external resources. This adoption site includes links to other relevant sites, book reviews, and answers to frequently asked questions.

well for some grassroots information sites, such as those with a sarcastic or storytelling bent.

External Resources • When building a grassroots information site, use basic organization and navigation principles. Avoid long lists of EXTERNAL LINKS (K8) because visitors have no way of knowing which of these are interesting and which are not. Editorialize by adding a few comments about each link, describing what kind of content the site has and what you thought of the site. This information helps visitors find what interests them and lets them know more about your personality, outlook, and standards.

If you have an especially large number of links, organize them by grouping similar content together and then labeling the group with a high-level name. Try to make the list of external links fit on a single Web page that can be viewed without excessive scrolling. If the list becomes unwieldy, break it up into separate pages with fifteen to twenty links per page, and provide a top-level directory of categories so that readers can find the particular information they're looking for quickly, or jump to one of the recommended sites. Keep the number of top-level links leading to categories or external sites to less than twenty. Break all lists of twenty or greater into subcategories. See HIERARCHICAL ORGANIZATION (B3) for more information on creating categories.

We chose fifteen to twenty as a list limit because long lists are difficult for people to read, and they make it hard to locate a particular item. The high-traffic directory sites that we reviewed, such as Yahoo! Directory (dir.yahoo.com) and Google Directory (directory.google.com), did not exceed this number at any level in their organization. These sites have put a lot of effort into researching how to present this type of information. Take advantage of their findings.

Growing the Site • Grassroots information sites often start out small, with just a few pages of highly focused, interesting content. Over time they grow, with new pages and resources added every so often, but this goes only so far. To take the site to the next level, the site maintainer will need to add some way for visitors to participate, turning it into both an information site and a COMMUNITY CONFERENCE (A3) site. This step represents a fundamental shift in how the Web site operates. The site will change from a place where only a few site maintainers collect and disseminate information, to a self-sustaining and ongoing conversation where many people contribute, interact with one another, and create new content about the core topic that brings everyone to the site in the first place.

✳ SOLUTION

Establish value by answering potential questions, either by providing content that you author yourself or by directing people to Web sites that can answer their questions. On your homepage, create a topic directory of up to twenty categories or external links. Provide contact information if customers have new questions or suggestions, or if they find new sources of information.

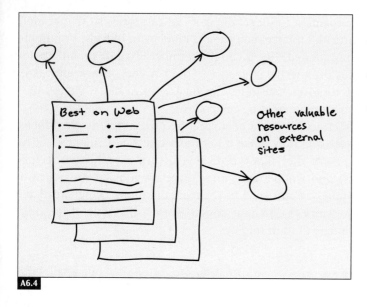

Figure A6.4

Grassroots information sites provide background or specialized information on a topic and organize other valuable resources by offering links to external sites.

❋ OTHER PATTERNS TO CONSIDER

Set up your homepage with BROWSABLE CONTENT (B2). Provide EXTERNAL LINKS (K8) so that customers know when they're leaving your site. If you have many links, try using a HIERARCHICAL ORGANIZATION (B3) to break them into categories. Use the WRITING FOR SEARCH ENGINES (D6) pattern, and tell your story and research methodology using the INVERTED-PYRAMID WRITING STYLE (D7) if that matches the style of your site.

B2
K8
B3
D6
D7

Figure A7.1

IBM's homepage prominently displays links to its products and services, as well as links for specific customer groups (for example, home, small business, and government). Links for less important visitors, such as developers, partners, and investors, are displayed in a less prominent position and in a lighter font at the lower left side of the page.

A7.1

(www.ibm.com, February 5, 2002)

✳ BACKGROUND

This pattern forms the core of all company sites. Combine it with one or more of the other site genre patterns, especially PERSONAL E-COMMERCE (A1), EDUCATIONAL FORUMS (A8), and WEB APPS THAT WORK (A10).

✳ PROBLEM

Company sites must address the needs of many audiences, but a site that does not balance its attention to these different audiences in proportion to their size will not succeed.

Company sites engage, sell to, and support customers and partners. They also promote to media, inform investors, and recruit employees. These audiences have varying needs. If you want your company site to be valuable to its primary visitors, focus on that primary audience and take care of its needs first. Other audiences can be served as well, but in a less directly accessible way.

The visible space on the homepage is a constraint of site design. Because this is the page that customers usually visit first, it must direct them to the information they need (see Figure A7.2). To allocate this precious space, classify your site visitors to give the largest groups priority over all others.

Potential customers, current customers, partners, members of the press, investors, and potential employees need basic information about a company, from an overview of the company and its policies to details about its products and services. Although these groups ask and need different things, a valuable company site must provide answers to all. The solutions that we derive from these questions and tasks are listed in Table A7.1.

Balance Space for Brand against Space for Navigation • Balance the homepage trade-off between space used for communicating the company's value and

Figure A7.2

This site has everything that customers might want to see about HP (Hewlett-Packard). They can look up product information, purchase products, get the latest software drivers, or access support information.

(www.hp.com, June 16, 2006)

Table A7.1

Sample Questions, Tasks, and Solutions for Company Sites

(C2) (D8) (E5) (D3) (E2) (B8) (F2) (K8) (G4) (F2) (F3) (F1) (H7) (D5) (A12) (C2) (E5) (E5) (E5)

Group	Question or Task	What to Provide as a Solution
Everyone	What does this company offer?	An UP-FRONT VALUE PROPOSITION (C2), a set of PRINTABLE PAGES (D8) of product and service overviews and details, ABOUT US (E5) to describe company background and establish credibility
	What's new?	HEADLINES AND BLURBS (D3), latest product and service announcements, press releases, E-MAIL SUBSCRIPTIONS (E2) to a free company newsletter
	What products and services does the company offer?	Listings on CATEGORY PAGES (B8) and CLEAN PRODUCT DETAILS (F2) of all products and services, both current and past, organized in multiple ways based on customer needs
Current and potential customers	Who uses this company's products and services?	Typical customer profiles and a list of existing customers
	How do people use the products and services?	Case studies and white papers, EXTERNAL LINKS (K8) to reviews, testimonials, RECOMMENDATION COMMUNITY (G4)
	How do I buy the products and services?	Ordering information, CLEAN PRODUCT DETAILS (F2), SHOPPING CART (F3), QUICK-FLOW CHECKOUT (F1)
	What are the support options?	Customer service, training, product specifications, online manuals and support guides, FREQUENTLY ASKED QUESTIONS (H7), MESSAGE BOARDS (D5), BLOGS (A12)
Current and potential partners	What would a partnership offer my company?	An UP-FRONT VALUE PROPOSITION (C2) for partners, including partner benefits and partnership details
	How do I become a partner?	Partnership application form
Press	Who can provide more information?	ABOUT US (E5), press contacts page
Current and potential investors	What's the background of this company, including past financial performance?	ABOUT US (E5), company background, management, current investors, current customers, ticker symbol, quarterly and annual reports
Potential employees	Do you have a job for me?	Open job listings, online job applications
	Why would I want to work for this company?	ABOUT US (E5), company background, leadership, corporate culture, benefits

differentiation, and space used for giving customers the navigation tools to find what they seek. We have made three observations that provide solutions:

1. Because the CLEAR FIRST READ (I3) on the homepage is often the company's brand in the top left corner (see Figure A7.1), and the second read is often the UP-FRONT VALUE PROPOSITION (C2), most of the company's value and differentiation should be clear from the outset. If they are not, the value proposition and SITE BRANDING (E1) are not executed well enough yet. Have your team focus on improving these two aspects rather than on using more space on the homepage for branding.

2. People scan when they read on the Web, and they scan the homepage for succinct phrases and for links that they recognize and deem potentially valuable (see Figure A7.3). Focus your design on finding the proper wording for these phrases, and on making them easy for your customers to scan.

Figure A7.3

The Microsoft homepage provides quick links to all the major parts of its site but emphasizes the product and support areas. Links to information for partners and journalists either are less prominent or are positioned below the fold.[6]

A7.3 (www.microsoft.com, June 16, 2006)

6 The **fold** is an imaginary line on a Web page that delineates what's visible in a browser without making the visitor scroll down. See ABOVE THE FOLD (I2) for more information.

3. Every primary Web site audience is really composed of many subgroups, and each subgroup needs answers to its specific questions. For example, if the primary audience consists of investors, you might answer the questions of both institutional investors and direct investors. If the primary audience is a buyer of products and services, you might answer the questions of the decision maker, recommender, and technical reviewer. When you're offering an online service or account, you can often take existing **H4** customers directly to their ACCOUNT MANAGEMENT (H4) page from the homepage while still answering questions for potential customers using the rest of the page (see Figure A7.4). Use the techniques described in **3** Chapter 3 (Knowing Your Customers: Principles and Techniques) to understand what these roles are for your customers and your site.

Figure A7.4

SurveyMonkey's homepage persuades people to try its service by having a clean layout, providing a good overview of features and pricing, and being easy to use.

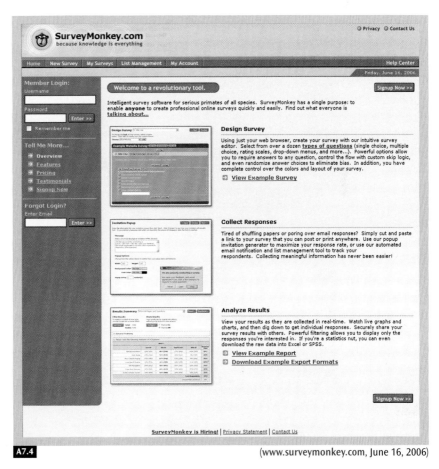

A7.4

(www.surveymonkey.com, June 16, 2006)

From this previous analysis we conclude that a **splash screen**—that is, an opening screen, often heavy with multimedia, that is shown before the homepage—cannot help build a valuable company site. There are places for product and service overview animations and presentations, but they should be self-selected destinations by customers, not automatic commercials on the very first page of a site.

Organize for Customers' Convenience • A company's internal organization does not make good Web site organization. This is a common mistake in the designs of company sites. What makes sense to people internal to a company may not make sense to its customers. Williams-Sonoma's Web site is organized with its customers' needs in mind (see Figure A7.5).

A7.5

(www.williams-sonoma.com, June 16, 2006)

Figure A7.5

Williams-Sonoma's homepage provides quick links to all the major parts of its site. It also provides highlights to special features, such as cooking for kids, barbecues, and wedding and gift registries.

✳ SOLUTION

On the company homepage, above the fold, dedicate 95 percent of the area and links to the visitor groups that account for 95 percent of the total visitor population, and keep the remaining area and links for the visitor groups that account for the remaining 5 percent. Use the space below the fold of the homepage to provide explicit links for each group, including those in the 5 percent category. Balance space for your branding against the navigation needs of your target audience. Throughout the site, focus attention on the specific roles of your customers, and use value propositions that they'll understand. Include in-depth presentations and lists of information to keep visitors engaged if they want to know more.

Figure A7.6

A company homepage must focus on its primary audience without forgetting about secondary audiences or company branding.

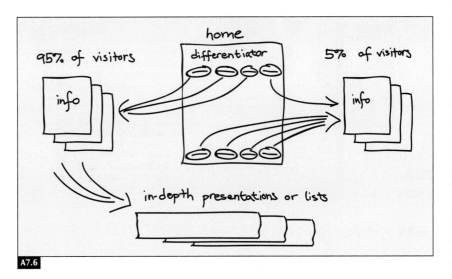

✳ OTHER PATTERNS TO CONSIDER

For valuable company sites, using the 95 percent–5 percent solution, create a HOMEPAGE PORTAL (C1) that gives people an UP-FRONT VALUE PROPOSITION (C2) and MULTIPLE WAYS TO NAVIGATE (B1). Use FAMILIAR LANGUAGE (K11) targeted to the role and kind of visitor, including customer, partner, press, investor, or potential employee. Make use of online marketing by offering E-MAIL SUBSCRIPTIONS (E2) to a free company newsletter, to maintain ongoing contact with previous site visitors. Post job openings to recruit potential employees.

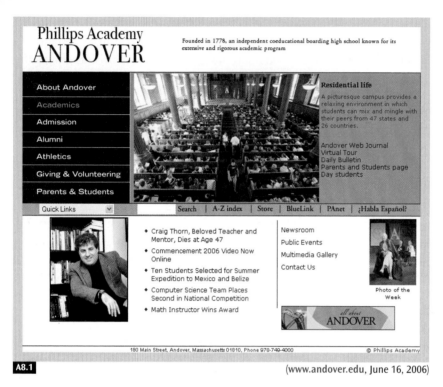

Figure A8.1

Phillips Academy's Web site provides resources that bring together parents, teachers, and alumni mentors to support student education.

A8.1

(www.andover.edu, June 16, 2006)

✳ BACKGROUND

Educational sites promote learning by providing schools, universities, and online institutions with a way to publicize using NEWS MOSAICS (A2), to build COMMUNITY CONFERENCES (A3) for student development, to deliver online learning and research tools, and to offer courses online. This pattern describes the keys to making these types of sites succeed.

A2

A3

✳ PROBLEM

Bringing together students, parents, mentors, alumni, and educators is essential to educational sites. If no forum among these groups is created, the students' education suffers, and so does the institution.

The primary goal of any educational institution is student development. But students do not learn just from reading and solving problems. They require interaction with other students, teachers, parents, and mentors. The physical classroom provides student–teacher interaction, but depending on class size, geography, and transportation issues, this interaction can be limited. Furthermore, parents and teachers have limited opportunity to interact, usually only through in-person meetings or phone calls.

An educational site can bring together these groups, across geographic and economic boundaries, for the benefit of students. In NONPROFITS AS NETWORKS OF HELP (A5), we argued that a network effect[7] cannot occur unless certain tools and capabilities are part of a site. The same is true for educational forums. An educational forum functions as a valuable resource and support system for students by providing a network for student development through student–teacher, student–student, parent–teacher, student–mentor, and parent–parent relationships.

When an educational site focuses on improving the efficiency of school administration, it leaves the effectiveness of the education behind. *Educational forums can be the conduits, the networks that bring together and help build school communities.* In a primary school, parents, teachers, and classmates need to communicate on an ongoing basis. In a university setting, professors, students, and teaching assistants need ongoing forums of discussion. If the educational forum is the central communication tool, all students benefit from sharing ideas, questions, and problems with classmates, parents, and teachers. Such forums enhance intellectual and social life at school, thereby enhancing students' complete education. An educational forum establishes tight connections that extend beyond the school grounds, where social pressures to conform sometimes outweigh students' genuine desire to learn.

Different Visitors Have Different Needs • Students, parents, and mentors need basic information about an educational institution—from an overview

---

7 Person-to-person connections increase as a result of a communication network. The value of a network grows in proportion to the square of the number of people connected.

of the institution's policies, to details about its curriculum and schedules. The same might be true for potential students, potential and current teachers, potential and current employees, and researchers and students at other institutions. In addition, educational institutions need to maintain a lifelong relationship with their alumni. The needs of these groups vary, and an educational site must provide answers (see Figure A8.2). The solutions that we derive from the questions and tasks relevant to each of these groups are listed in Table A8.1.

Taken to an advanced level, an educational forum can provide course material online, including teacher- and student-developed training materials, quizzes, exercises, complete courses, and archived or live video (see Figure A8.3).

A8.2

(www.cmu.edu, December 7, 2001)

Figure A8.2

The designers of Carnegie Mellon University's site did a good job of identifying its customers, including prospective students, researchers, alumni, and current students. The designers created clear links to information targeted for these different groups.

Table A8.1

Sample Questions, Tasks, and Solutions for Educational Forums

Group	Question or Task	What to Provide as a Solution
Students and prospective students	When are classes?	A searchable, printable table of class schedules with links to teachers, syllabi, and course materials
	Who are the teachers, and how do I contact them?	Teacher profiles and ratings, links to classes
	What am I going to learn in class?	Class profiles and syllabi
	What are the school's policies?	A series of documents showing the school's policies
Parents and mentors	How do I contact someone in charge, such as the principal, president, or dean?	A page with administration contact information, including e-mail addresses
	How do I contact a teacher?	A page with teacher contact information, including e-mail addresses
E2 What is taking place at the school this week?		An E-MAIL SUBSCRIPTION (E2) detailing the highlights of the upcoming school week and any special information that parents might need to act on
Teachers	How do I contact a parent?	A secure page with student and parent contact information
Potential teachers and employees	Why do I want to work for this school?	School overview, leadership, employment benefits
D3 Alumni	What's new at the school?	HEADLINES AND BLURBS (D3) to press releases detailing new programs, new buildings, important research, and other activities of interest, and an E-MAIL SUBSCRIPTION (E2) for **E2** newsletters about alumni updates
E6	How do I make a donation?	SECURE CONNECTIONS (E6) to pages where gifts can be given to the institution or where alumni can leave contact information for follow-up
Researchers	What research is a particular professor or department working on?	Easy access to faculty and department directories that link directly to their own Web sites
D5 Everyone	What does the community think about any particular new program?	MESSAGE BOARDS (D5) with current topics open for discussion

Figure A8.3

A8.3

(http://mathforum.org, June 16, 2006)

The Math Forum is a valuable resource for both students and educators. The Teacher2Teacher community allows parents and teachers to ask questions, discuss problems, and find ideas for new problems and exercises. At the Student Center, students can ask Dr. Math questions about solving math problems, and they can find fun challenges in mathematics.

Raising the Bar • The education reformer John Holt was once quoted as saying, "I suspect that many children would learn arithmetic—and learn it better—if it were illegal."[8] This sentiment captures many of the problems with education as it exists today. Advanced educational forums need to draw students in, challenging them with real-world problems that everyday people face, not artificial problems commonly found in classroom textbooks. They need to stimulate students' natural interests and foster a social norm of educational excellence and lifelong learning. Internet access alone is not enough. There needs to be an ongoing and thriving community—both online and offline—of enthusiastic experts, programmers, designers, alumni, parents, teachers, and students to make it happen.

---

[8]   From J. Holt, *Learning All the Time* (Reading, MA: Addison-Wesley, 1989, p. 45).

Many attempts at introducing educational technologies into the curricula have failed. Numerous issues are involved with costs of procuring the hardware and developing the software, with making these tools fit into existing work practices, and with training teachers to use these tools effectively. In fact, it is not uncommon for students to be more comfortable and experienced with using computers than the teachers are.

Basic educational forums need to support all of the routine and ordinary tasks that students, teachers, alumni, and parents face. Advanced educational forums need to look even further, seeking new ways of creating a sustainable and inclusive community of learning and scholarship.

✳ SOLUTION

Provide news and information for students, potential students, former students, parents, mentors, and teachers. Help coordinate offline activities by supplying class schedules, reading lists, exam schedules, and contact and office hour information for teachers and administrators. As a part of student registration, gather parent and student e-mail and phone information for direct updates. Optionally publish curricula and research for site visitors from other schools and universities.

To create a forum for online student–parent–teacher–mentor support of student development, create a secure area on the site that provides the following:

- Direct communication between parents and teachers, students and teachers, and students and mentors
- Public communication between students in the same class and the teacher
- Parent–teacher conferences
- Online writing, exhibits, experiments, exercises, projects, and other activities
- Online course material
- Online examinations

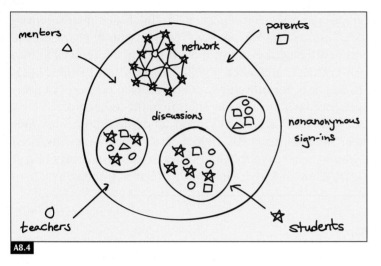

Figure A8.4

An educational forum is a secure area where students, parents, teachers, and mentors can share concerns, present ideas, and codevelop and share activities.

A8.4

✳ OTHER PATTERNS TO CONSIDER

Basic Educational Forums

To address the needs of the different audiences using the site, use a HOMEPAGE PORTAL (C1) with MULTIPLE WAYS TO NAVIGATE (B1) to the class information, teacher backgrounds and contact information, department information, and school background. Provide news on the homepage and CATEGORY PAGES (B8), each with CONTENT MODULES (D2) containing stories about accomplishments, events, and plans.

    C1 **B1**

    B8 **D2**

If you create an online student application and registration system, use a PROCESS FUNNEL (H1) to facilitate a smooth process.

    H1

Update entire classes, the entire school, and alumni with E-MAIL SUBSCRIPTIONS (E2) to school announcements and weekly schedules. As an option, use CONTENT MODULES (D2) to publish class curricula and research on the site.

    E2
    D2

Advanced Educational Forums

To create a forum for online student–parent–teacher–mentor support of student development, create a secure area using SECURE CONNECTIONS (E6) and have people create nonanonymous accounts using SIGN-IN/NEW ACCOUNT (H2).

    E6

    H2

Once a person has signed in, show PERSONALIZED CONTENT (D4) on the homepage for each visitor, with class news and links. Within the class information for students, provide a directory of teacher contact information,

    D4

and e-mail addresses for student–student and student–mentor communication. Within the class information for parents and mentors, provide only the teacher and mentee contact information.

D5 For each class, create a MESSAGE BOARD (D5) for student–teacher–mentor–parent discussions, as well as a separate message board for teacher–parent discussions.

Provide students with Web publishing tools and a directory to upload class projects.

Publish course materials online and keep the material engaging by **A9** using the STIMULATING ARTS AND ENTERTAINMENT (A9) pattern.

H1 To conduct online examinations, bring students into a PROCESS FUNNEL (H1) **D2** to complete questions dynamically generated in CONTENT MODULES (D2). Alternatively, link to an existing courseware system, such as WebCT or Blackboard, for online exams, grading, and course management.

A9 STIMULATING ARTS AND ENTERTAINMENT

A9.1

(www.pbs.org, June 16, 2006)

Figure A9.1

PBS.org provides a straightforward interface to audio clips, video clips, and games on the site, as well as guides to the many offline programs that PBS produces. If visitors play the games on the site, though, they find that new interface metaphors abound.

BACKGROUND

This pattern forms the core of any site specializing in engaging content. Combine this pattern with other site genre patterns—including PERSONAL E-COMMERCE (A1), VALUABLE COMPANY SITES (A7), and EDUCATIONAL FORUMS (A8)—to create a hybrid.

A1 A7 A8

✳ PROBLEM

Arts and entertainment sites evoke new feelings and thoughts by challenging customers or by offering them an escape. But presenting visitors with a hard-to-use interface too early in their exposure to your site will turn them away.

People do not enjoy being forced to sit through something they're not prepared for. Sites that display animated movies on the first page can be frustrating for this reason; nothing can warn customers before they arrive at a site. Similarly, sites that require complex navigation schemes from the very first page, as part of the "artistic experience," tend to lose visitors who cannot appreciate why the experience is important. Customers like to be challenged with thoughtful, well-executed arts and entertainment, but they want to choose for themselves (see Figures A9.2 and A9.3). If they're not given the choice of where to go on a straightforward introductory homepage and they're immediately dropped into an animation or strange interface, they will probably choose to leave.

Figure A9.2

Sports fans can go to espn.com to read the latest headlines; find information about players, teams, and game schedules; and even enjoy seeing some of the action through links to video clips.

(www.espn.com, September 19, 2006)

Figure A9.3

Random Art show-cases a variety of computer-generated art, and even lets people submit their own as well as vote for their favorites.

A9.3

(www.random-art.org, June 16, 2006)

People enjoy arts and entertainment because they are moved and challenged by the experience. Whether a movie that evokes strong emotions of fear, sadness, excitement, or romance, or an exhibit of paintings that stimulates thoughts of an era gone by, these are powerful cultural experiences. Online arts and entertainment sites are no different.

Online Exhibits Come in Many Forms • When art or entertainment is exhibited online, it can range from pictures of a gallery installation to an online-only animation (see Figure A9.4). The Web provides a low-cost, widely accessible medium for delivering these different "exhibits."

Set Expectations before Breaking the Rules • Site designers who break design rules with a purpose, in places where people know to expect it,

Figure A9.4

Apartment is an interactive exhibit that starts by asking the visitor to select a city. As the visitor types, rooms start to take shape in the form of a blueprint. The layout is based on a semantic analysis of the visitor's words. The apartments are then clustered into buildings and cities according to their linguistic relationships. The site sets clear visitor expectations for large page loads and the potential need to download an additional plug-in.

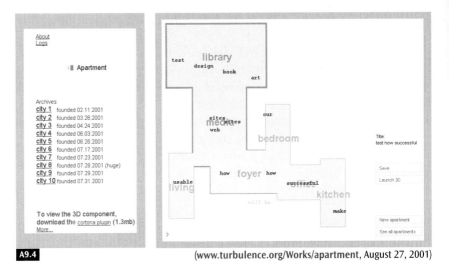

(www.turbulence.org/Works/apartment, August 27, 2001)

can use the medium to provoke and challenge in positive ways. In an experimental interface, many of the design patterns in this book may not make sense. Perhaps links should not be obvious, and things should not have descriptive names. This kind of interface has its place on arts and entertainment sites.

Setting customer expectations about what they will experience is key. Table A9.1 shows some examples of how to include a few words in exhibit descriptions to set expectations before launching an exhibit.

Often online content augments offline content. In addition to using your introductory pages to set people's expectations, you can use it to provide information about accessing offline exhibits, such as exhibit hours, addresses, and driving directions.

Table A9.1

Sample Exhibit Descriptions for Setting Customer Expectations

Exhibit	Text Included in the Description
Guided tour	Fifteen screens (30 seconds on 1 Mbps DSL)
Movie	2 minutes on 1 Mbps DSL
Music	John Cage's 433 seconds (20 seconds on 1 Mbps DSL)
Gallery exhibit	17 images, each 1MB (2.5 minutes on 1 Mbps DSL)
Interactive exhibit	Experimental interface

✷ SOLUTION

On the first page or pages of the Web site, provide a straightforward interface that describes the exhibits on your site and provides links directly to them. Link from the introduction pages to background information pages that expand on the exhibits. In a separate area provide the actual exhibits and entertainment in whatever formats are required. Once a customer has chosen an art exhibit to view or a movie to play, the interface should conform to whatever is required by the artist or work of art. This is where it is permissible to break the usual rules in order to challenge or entertain your customers.

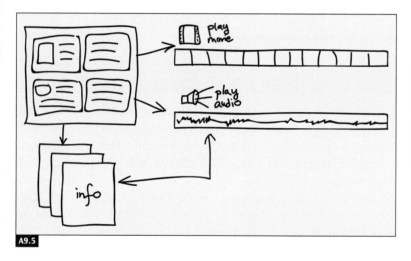

A9.5

Figure A9.5

Easy-to-use homepage and background pages provide familiar navigation cues so that people don't get lost. The actual art exhibits, movies, audio clips, games, or other entertainment are in well-defined areas.

✷ OTHER PATTERNS TO CONSIDER

Use your HOMEPAGE PORTAL (C1) to provide basic navigation elements that will be familiar to customers immediately, by giving them MULTIPLE WAYS TO NAVIGATE (B1). Within the homepage and the additional background pages, use CONTENT MODULES (D2) to highlight recent additions, and to provide links to archived content through CONSISTENT SIDEBARS OF RELATED CONTENT (I6).

C1

B1

D2

I6

Figure A10.1

Salesforce.com offers a Web application for automating sales functions. With this application, salespeople can see tracking, forecasting, and editing capabilities after they create a customer account.

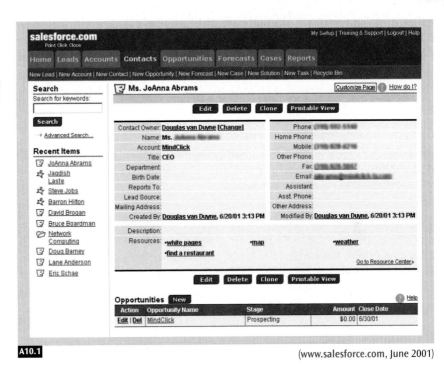

A10.1

(www.salesforce.com, June 2001)

✳ BACKGROUND

Like other site genre patterns, this pattern is flexible enough to add to almost any other, including VALUABLE COMPANY SITES (A7), EDUCATIONAL FORUMS (A8), COMMUNITY CONFERENCES (A3), and STIMULATING ARTS AND ENTERTAINMENT (A9). PERSONAL E-COMMERCE SITES (A1) can also place a Web application at the focus of a business. This pattern shows what's at the core of a Web application.

✳ PROBLEM

Web applications are not like software applications that come in a shrink-wrapped box. Web applications are services that are sold online rather than in a store, that sometimes offer a form of online collaboration, and that often do not have printed documentation. Customers use Web applications differently from traditional Web sites as well: they use them for real work, often for hours every day.

Web applications get customers up and running without time-consuming and costly software installation, configuration, and maintenance. Because Web applications run on the Internet, they can immediately take advantage of a connected network of customers.

Customers Want to Try before They Buy • Providing a Web application requires a special approach. When customers arrive at a site that sells a Web application, they expect to learn about it, see it in action, try it out, buy access to it if they like it, use it from any location at any time, and get quick online support and training. If the application cannot meet even one of these expectations, customers will be much less likely to buy and use it.

Help your customers by providing lots of information about your service. Make the UP-FRONT VALUE PROPOSITION (C2) clear on the HOMEPAGE PORTAL (C1), letting customers know what your service does and how it can help them get their work done faster or better. Take customers through a sample task by showing them static or animated screen shots of someone using the Web application. If it's feasible to do so, let customers go through the SIGN-IN/NEW ACCOUNT (H2) process and create a temporary account so that they can try your service and see if they like it. Finally, help convince customers that you offer a high-quality service by providing testimonials from real customers and EXTERNAL LINKS (K8) to positive reviews.

Web applications must also have an extremely strong focus on usability. People buy shrink-wrapped software first, often before trying it out. Because they have already made a large financial commitment, they have more motivation to spend the time to learn how to use it. With Web applications, however, it's just the opposite. People try a Web application first, and if they don't like it they just go somewhere else. Draw people in by establishing MULTIPLE WAYS TO NAVIGATE (B1) to the various applications and options. For critical tasks, take customers through a PROCESS FUNNEL (H1), and provide a FREQUENTLY ASKED QUESTIONS (H7) page and CONTEXT-SENSITIVE HELP (H8) to assist customers whenever they encounter problems.

C2
C1

H2

K8

B1
H1
H7
H8

Web Apps Rely on Web Principles • If you work for a traditional software company that wants to sell a Web application, be aware that installable software does not quickly convert into a Web application. Nor can it always be converted into a successful Web application. Your company must adopt Web principles for design, development, testing, security, IT, marketing, sales, billing, documentation, support, and training.

From an application design perspective, a Web application can provide either a relatively simple interface using standard HTML, or an enhanced interface that uses AJAX (Asynchronous JavaScript And XML). Standard HTML provides the best cross-platform, cross-browser compatibility (see Figure A10.2). But if you use standard HTML, each page may be limited to only a few atomic actions (see Figure A10.3), and you cannot offer DIRECT MANIPULATION (H9) of objects in a page.

If you use AJAX, you can add DIRECT MANIPULATION (H9), PREDICTIVE INPUT (H11), DRILL-DOWN OPTIONS (H12), and FAST-LOADING CONTENT (L6),

Figure A10.2

The First Internet Bank site lets customers easily transfer funds between accounts, view canceled checks, and manage bill payments. The site follows Web principles: home banking customers often arrive over slow network connections, so the site is light on graphics and performs just fine with a 56K modem.

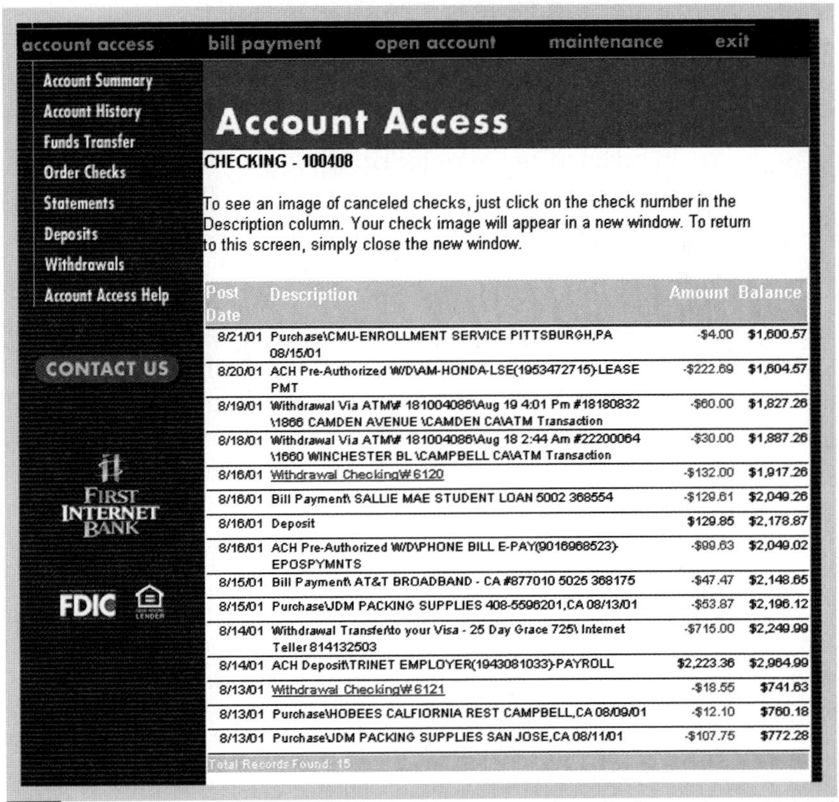

(www.firstib.com, August 21, 2001)

A10.3

(www.hotmail.com, June 16, 2006)

Figure A10.3

MSN Hotmail offers much of the same functionality that a basic, desktop-based e-mail client offers, such as an address book, folders, and filtering. The site has a clean design, and although it has many tabs and buttons, it has a decidedly Web-based look and feel, evident in the link to the homepage at the top left and in the Web search action module at the top right.

and create applications that look and feel very similar to installable desktop software. In addition to desktop-like interaction techniques and a feeling of direct control, these capabilities support heavy file processing and many other customer-side computation-intensive or disk-based activities (see Figure A10.4).

Powerful design tools now make building some AJAX-based interfaces easier to implement, eliminating cross-browser issues at the same time. Although no tool can do everything you might wish to do, you can always resort to custom code. Only when a single standard implementation of AJAX exists, or when better tools are developed, will the extra effort required to make pages work across browsers be eliminated.

Offer Informative Feedback • Another difference between HTML-based Web applications and installable desktop software is that the Web has inherent **latency** limitations, even within intranets. Unless you're using AJAX, your Web application will not be able to respond to customer actions immediately. Your customers will become impatient and will often commit errors, such as executing the same command multiple times or inadvertently interrupting a command.

Although you might want to give your customers more room for their work in your Web application, eliminating the standard browser buttons

Figure A10.4

Writely provides a desktop word-processing application experience in a Web browser. By using AJAX, Writely's creators are able to dynamically change the screen layout, autosave the current document, and provide direct manipulation of on-screen objects like text blocks, all without reloading the page.

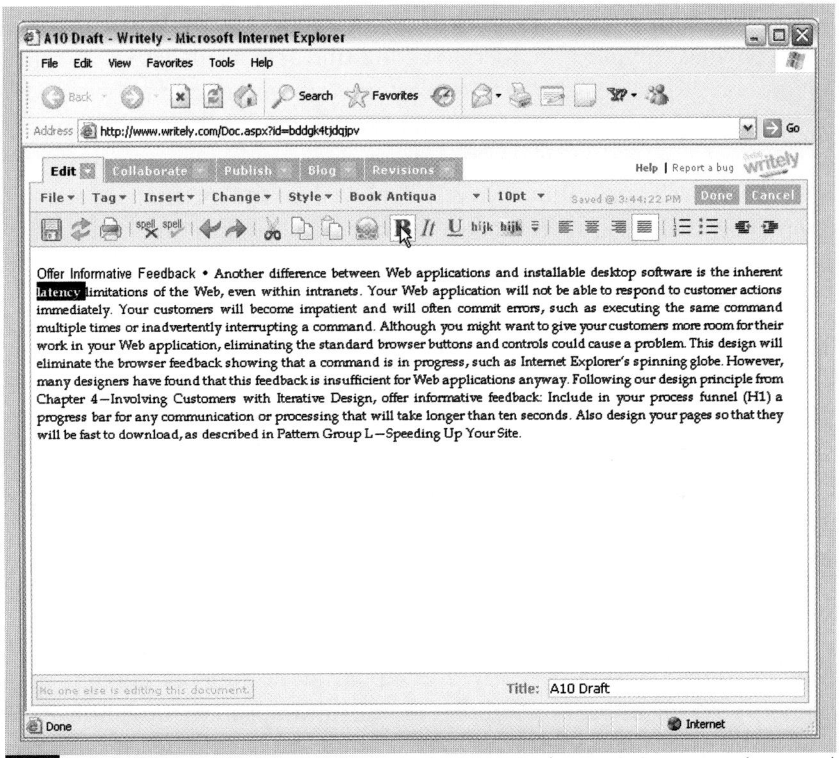

A10.4

(www.writely.com, March 29, 2006)

and controls could cause a problem. This design will eliminate the browser feedback showing that a command is in progress, such as Internet Explorer's waving flag. However, many designers have found that this feedback is insufficient for Web applications anyway. Following our design principle from Chapter 4 (Involving Customers with Iterative Design), offer informative feedback: include a PROGRESS BAR (H13) in your PROCESS FUNNEL (H1) for any communication or processing that will take longer than ten seconds. Also design your pages so that they will be fast to download, as described in Pattern Group L (Speeding Up Your Site).

Provide Abundant Help • Most Web applications are tools that your customers will use for several hours every day. They do not have the same walk-up-and-use requirements—that is, immediate usability—that a general consumer-oriented Web site has. Sometimes you have to trade efficiency for learning time. CONTEXT-SENSITIVE HELP (H8) becomes important because at least some tasks in every Web application won't be immediately obvious to your customers. Making this help available via FLOATING WINDOWS (H6) will ensure that the customer doesn't lose important work.

If you're designing your Web application for an intranet, you can minimize employees' learning time by making the application consistent with other Web applications already deployed on the intranet. As a result, employees will get up to speed on the new application much more quickly.

Make Security and Privacy Tight • Because Web applications host confidential information for multiple customers, you need to reassure customers of the security and privacy of their data. Use SECURE CONNECTIONS (E6), and inform customers of the security precautions and FAIR INFORMATION PRACTICES (E3) that you've employed. Also make it easy for customers to set their PRIVACY PREFERENCES (E8) from the ACCOUNT MANAGEMENT (H4) page. A reviewer considering the purchase of a Web application will use this information to help make an informed decision.

Support Different Roles • Many Web applications support different customer roles, including application administrator, primary operator of the application, and management. These customers have different views of the applications and varying access to their capabilities. Your Web application must provide the ability to set up and manage these roles, as part of regular application maintenance.

✳ SOLUTION

Provide a public site where potential customers can preview the application, see how it will work, and sign up to try it. Once they have signed up, give them access to their application home through a secure sign-in, and provide a menu of options for their roles. Use standard Web interface widgets for complete cross-platform, cross-browser compatibility, or an enhanced AJAX-based interface that gives more direct control. Give effective feedback about communication and processing delays. Provide online documentation, training, and support.

Figure A10.5

A Web application can be sold over the Web through detailed information pages and demonstrations. Once customers have signed up and received secure access to their application home, they see a menu of tasks and associated online help.

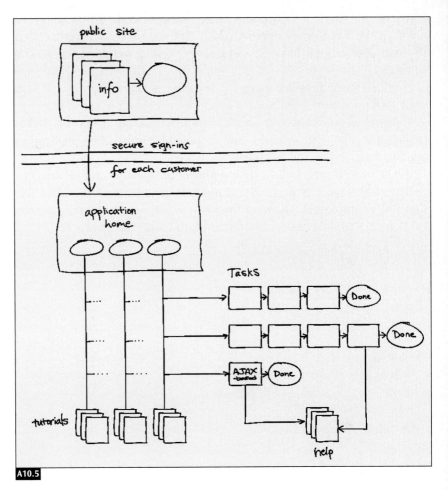

A10.5

✳ OTHER PATTERNS TO CONSIDER

On your public homepage, provide MULTIPLE WAYS TO NAVIGATE (B1) to information and demonstrations of the various Web applications that you sell. If visitors decide to buy, you can ask them to pay online with QUICK-FLOW CHECKOUT (F1). Create a SECURE CONNECTION (E6) and ask customers to use SIGN-IN/NEW ACCOUNT (H2). Build an application home with PERSONALIZED CONTENT (D4) for each customer's role. Again, establish MULTIPLE WAYS TO NAVIGATE (B1) to the various applications and options, where each discrete task that a customer may perform is a PROCESS FUNNEL (H1) and has CONTEXT-SENSITIVE HELP (H8).

If you use AJAX, you can add DIRECT MANIPULATION (H9), PREDICTIVE INPUT (H11), DRILL-DOWN OPTIONS (H12), and FAST-LOADING CONTENT (L6) to create applications that look and feel very similar to traditional desktop software.

Provide informative feedback by showing a PROGRESS BAR (H13) in your PROCESS FUNNEL (H1) for any delays longer than ten seconds.

If you're designing a Web application for ENABLING INTRANETS (A11), make sure that it is as consistent as possible with other applications already deployed on the intranet.

Use SECURE CONNECTIONS (E6), and inform prospective and existing customers of the security precautions and FAIR INFORMATION PRACTICES (E3) that you've employed. Also make it easy for customers to set their PRIVACY PREFERENCES (E8) from the ACCOUNT MANAGEMENT (H4) page.

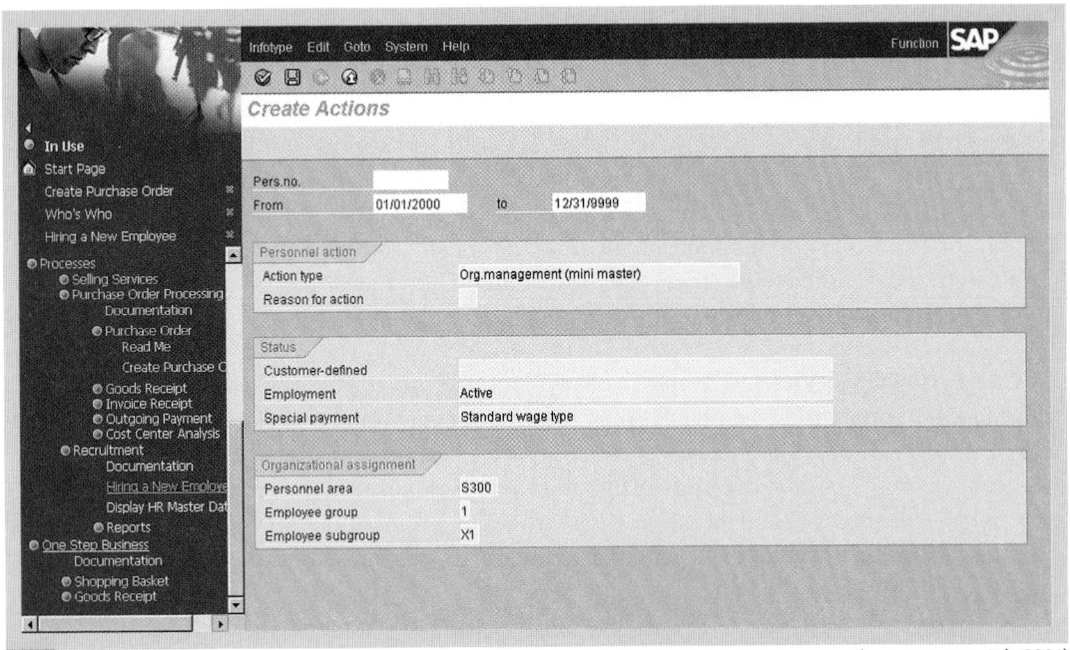

(www.sap.com, July 2001)

Figure A11.1

This "intranet in a box" from SAP provides many of the basic applications that a business needs for sales, human resources management, and finance. Customers can find these applications immediately on the left-hand navigation bar.

✳ BACKGROUND

Unlike the other site genre patterns, which cater to external customers, intranets support the internal work of an organization. You may employ entire site genre patterns, like NEWS MOSAICS (A2) and WEB APPS THAT WORK (A10), within the intranet. This pattern forms the core of what makes an intranet work.

✳ PROBLEM

Companies need employees to be more productive, but each employee's responsibilities change over time. Employees should not have to constantly learn entirely new computing systems to carry out their new responsibilities.

Developing a corporate intranet has many benefits, from improving internal communications to streamlining processes and reducing costs. To realize the benefits, you will need to build a site or use intranet software that provides the kinds of information and applications that will make employees more productive and satisfied with their jobs. In addition, you will need to update, maintain, and administer your intranet content and applications.

Provide Personalized Views • Employees will not use all the company information or applications. Probably some information and applications—such as salary information or financial management applications—will be off-limits to some employees but available to others. So an intranet needs to provide capabilities that depend on each employee's roles and responsibilities. These will change over time if an employee is promoted, quits, or changes jobs within the company.

An intranet can provide many pieces of information that employees need. The solutions that we derive from some sample questions and tasks are listed in Table A11.1.

Support Workflows • Because an intranet connects all employees, intranet Web applications can help manage the flow of work through an organization. As Table A11.1 illustrates, when employees fill out expense reports in the expense report Web application (see Figure A11.2), those reports will automatically be submitted to their managers online, thereby reducing the time spent on this regular administrative task. These kinds of automatic workflow management features can be built into any Web application that facilitates work among employees, and even with partners and customers.

You may already have legacy applications to facilitate workflow. The problem is that these applications may not be accessible from the Web. If you think it's worth the time, money, and effort, seriously consider creating bridges between these legacy applications and your intranet, to make it easier for employees to access these applications.

Be Consistent Throughout • This key design principle, discussed in Chapter 4 (Involving Customers with Iterative Design), becomes all the more important for intranets. Create a consistent interface in terms of the

Table A11.1

Sample Questions,
Tasks, and Solutions
for Intranets

Group	Question or Task	What to Provide as a Solution
All employees	Who is my HR contact?	Custom resources profile per employee
	What is Mary's phone number?	Database of employees
	When are the company holidays?	Holiday information page
	How do I submit an expense report?	Expense report WEB APPS THAT WORK (A10)
	What's the latest company news?	Updated news page with HEADLINES AND BLURBS (D3) and EXTERNAL LINKS (K8)
Team manager	How do I write a review?	Employee review WEB APPS THAT WORK (A10) with tips and pointers for what to write about
	How do I hire someone?	Job requisition and interview WEB APPS THAT WORK (A10)
	What are my employees' expenses this month?	Team manager side of expense report WEB APPS THAT WORK (A10) to approve or reject each report
	How do I become a partner?	Partnership application form
Financial manager	What are the accounts receivable amounts?	Report over a SECURE CONNECTION (E6) from accounting data
	What's the sales forecast for this quarter?	Report over a SECURE CONNECTION (E6) from sales data
	What are the current month's expense reports?	Financial manager side of expense report WEB APPS THAT WORK (A10) to review approved reports
Salesperson	Is this product available right now?	Report over a SECURE CONNECTION (E6) from inventory database
	Can we customize this product for our customer right now?	WEB APPS THAT WORK (A10) for product customization
	What's the status of this purchase?	Report over a SECURE CONNECTION (E6) about product fulfillment
Sales manager	How much business does each sales representative forecast for this month?	Forecast report roll-up from sales database over a SECURE CONNECTION (E6)
CEO	What are our production capacity, inventory, and sell-through numbers?	Reports over a SECURE CONNECTION (E6) pulled from production, warehousing, and sales channel data

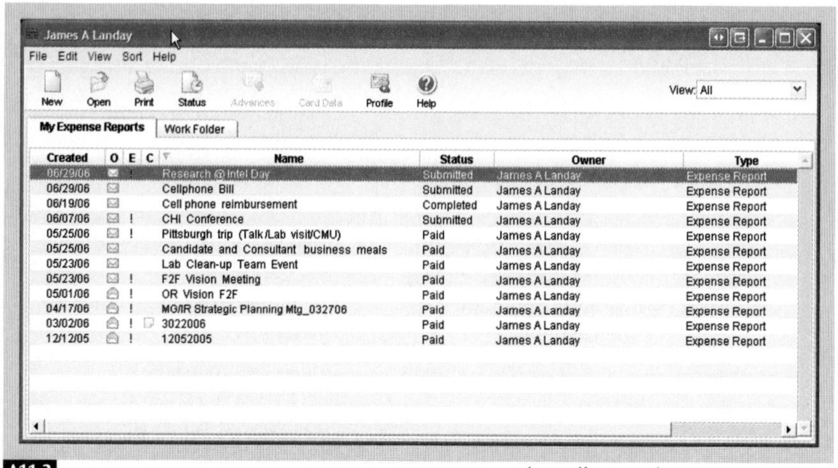

A11.2

(www.ibm.com/notes, June 20, 2006)

Figure A11.2

This expense report application shows the current status of each submission, what's been paid and what's pending, while supporting the workflow through the organization.

terminology you use and the interfaces that you design for each Web application. Consistency is the best way to keep employee skills and knowledge up-to-date as employees' roles change in your organization. It will also save money for the company because employees will be able to get up to speed quickly on new applications.

Establish Policies on New Content • Who will maintain the intranet? Will all employees be allowed to add new pages, or will there be a dedicated team for this purpose? Do project teams own a Web space where they can publish proposals, designs, and status reports? How will new pages be added? Are there any checks on the content that is published internally, to make sure that no confidential information is being published? Are there any guidelines on the design of new pages, to make sure that the interfaces are consistent? These are just some of the questions about content that need to be addressed, ideally before the intranet is deployed.

Provide Simple Ways to Add New Content • One way of simplifying the addition of new pages is to use PAGE TEMPLATES (D1) that contain one or more CONTENT MODULES (D2). The content modules can be connected to a database, making it easy to add new pages, serve up new content in existing pages, and search for old information. Also consider creating a special administrator page that makes it easy to add new content, as described in CONTENT MODULES (D2).

D1

D2

D2

Start Simple but Plan for Growth • You don't want to build an entire intranet all at once. It's best to start simple and take many small steps forward. For example, you could begin by focusing on making forms, documents, and news about the company accessible to employees. At the same time, you could devote effort to making sure that security is being maintained properly. Then you could start looking at administrator pages that make it easy to add new content and WEB APPS THAT WORK (A10) for handling workflows (eliminating the need for many of the forms).

✳ SOLUTION

Provide a secure area, customized for each employee, where the employee can go to see a list of applications and information. List employees' current pending requests of others and any pending requests made of them. Automatically trigger new requests via an application workflow. Support employee learning by using consistent terminology across the intranet, and by designing consistent interfaces for your Web applications.

Figure A11.3

If provided with customized lists of applications and information, employees need not wade through unnecessary items that they'll never use. Applications that trigger requests forward a request automatically to the next person in the workflow.

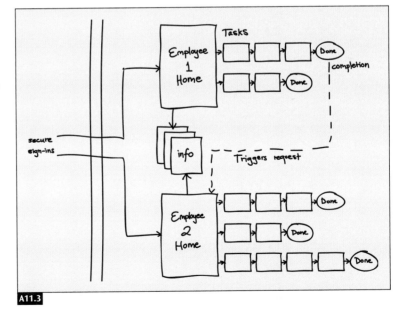

❊ OTHER PATTERNS TO CONSIDER

All employees must use a SECURE CONNECTION (E6) and go through a
secure SIGN-IN/NEW ACCOUNT (H2) page to access the intranet from outside
the firewall.

    Once on their HOMEPAGE PORTAL (C1), employees will see PERSONALIZED
CONTENT (D4) and company news. Requests that are pending and requests
that require action from the various WEB APPS THAT WORK (A10) are displayed
in CONTENT MODULES (D2). Employees can find information about human
resources issues, company product and service issues, and project status
through MULTIPLE WAYS TO NAVIGATE (B1). Each employee's WEB APPS THAT
WORK (A10) are accessible as well.

E6
H2

C1
D4
A10
D2

B1
A10

Figure A12.1

Blogs can be a powerful medium for getting your message out. Richard Marcello, a senior vice president at HP, uses his blog to communicate with employees, customers, and industry analysts. The **XML FEEDS** button underneath the calendar also lets readers subscribe to Marcello's blog via RSS (Really Simple Syndication) or even syndicate the content for reproduction on their own site.

A12.1

(www.hp.com/blogs/marcello, January 31, 2006)

✳ BACKGROUND

Web logs (**blogs**) can be a popular and simple way of communicating with people, as well as an important part of a VALUABLE COMPANY SITE (A7), a STIMULATING ARTS AND ENTERTAINMENT (A9) site, a NEWS MOSAIC (A2) site, an ENABLING INTRANET (A11), or a GRASSROOTS INFORMATION SITE (A6). Depending on how they're used, blogs can also be the basis of a COMMUNITY CONFERENCE (A3) site.

A7
A9 **A2**
A11 **A6**

A3

✳ PROBLEM

Blogs cannot be an effective medium of communication if they don't attract a regular readership.

Blogs are becoming a powerful medium for communication, with the total estimated number of blogs in late 2005 to be about a hundred million. In its simplest form, a blog is a Web page with dated entries, but it has already rapidly evolved to fit many genres, supporting VALUABLE COMPANY SITES (A7), COMMUNITY CONFERENCES (A3), NEWS MOSAICS (A2), and ENABLING INTRANETS (A11), to name just a few. The key to a successful blog is attracting an audience that reads it on a regular basis. What's the best way of using a blog to match your needs? In this pattern we provide some tips.

Establish Credibility • Why would someone want to read anything you have to say? More importantly, why would anyone care what you have to say? The first thing you need to do is to establish your credibility in a way that is appropriate to your target audience. Many of the ideas from Pattern Group E (Building Trust and Credibility), which often are couched in terms of PERSONAL E-COMMERCE SITES (A1), also apply to building trust and credibility for blogs. For example, if you are a corporate executive, then you might have an ABOUT US (E5) page that contains relevant background information, successes, and possibly news articles about you. If you're blogging for a GRASSROOTS INFORMATION SITE (A6), you might want to share personal stories about why you're committed to your cause. If you're blogging for a company, consider ways of leveraging the company's SITE BRANDING (E1).

Keep in mind, though, that these are just some surface issues in establishing your credibility. Other important factors include having sharp and unique insights that other blogs don't offer, providing fresh content, being honest (which can be quite difficult for corporate blogs or product blogs), responding well to criticism of your blog entries, having compelling content, and most importantly, bringing passion to your topic area.

Determine Your Blog Genre • There are as many kinds of blogs as there are reasons for publishing on the Web, as Table A12.1 illustrates. The kind of blog you want depends primarily on your goals and what content you have to offer.

For example, you might want to create a blog promoting a certain product. An example is the *Freakonomics* blog (freakonomics.com/blog),

What Makes a Good Blog?

Most of the content in this pattern deals with the mechanics of running a blog, but not much is said about what actually makes a good blog that keeps readers interested and coming back for more. There is no consistent recipe for success, but the following recommendations are based on observations of some of the most popular blogs out there today.

1. **Publish unique content with a focus that separates you from the crowd.** What special perspective do you have that will make people want to read what you write? For example, people read Lawrence Lessig's blog (lessig.org/blog) because he is one of the lead lawyers in the fight for reforming intellectual property law. People read Bruce Schneier's blog (schneier.com/blog) because he is a well-known expert in computer security. People read Wonkette (wonkette.com) because it provides a sharp and sarcastic insider's view of all the juicy gossip going around Washington, DC.

2. **Have a distinct writing style.** Your writing doesn't have to be consistent, nor does it need to follow the INVERTED-PYRAMID WRITING STYLE (D7) used in journalism, but it needs to be sharp and distinctive rather than simply a stream of consciousness (also known as *bloghorrea*). For example, Fafblog (fafblog.blogspot.com) is highly satirical ("the whole world's only source for Fafblog"), economist Brad DeLong's blog (delong.typepad.com) is authoritative and intentionally controversial (often running contests for the "world's stupidest person"), and Boing Boing (boingboing.net) is wisecracking, playful, and a little geeky, with headlines like "Disney Main Street Built from Legos" and "Toilet-Seat Guitar."

3. **Foster a community of readers.** Ultimately, a community of readers is what makes a blog successful. One way of fostering your community is to respond to comments from your readers. Another way is to ask your readers who they are and how they think you can make your blog better. A third way is to hold a contest in which you ask readers to submit some content (such as the best photo they've ever taken).

Site Type	Examples
Product blog	*Freakonomics* (book): freakonomics.com/blog
	Battlestar Galactica (television show): scifi.com/battlestar/blogs
	Ford Mustang (car): blog.ford.com
VALUABLE COMPANY SITE (A7)	General Motors: fastlane.gmblogs.com
	Fast Company: blog.fastcompany.com
	Flickr: blog.flickr.com
	Google: googleblog.blogspot.com
NEWS MOSAIC (A2)	*The New York Times* (movie): carpetbagger.nytimes.com
	The Washington Post: blogs.washingtonpost.com/washpostblog
	Digg: digg.com
STIMULATING ARTS AND ENTERTAINMENT (A9) site	PostSecret: postsecret.blogspot.com
	Fark: fark.com
GRASSROOTS INFORMATION SITE (A6)	Daily Kos: dailykos.com
ENABLING INTRANET (A11)	An internal project with entries from team members
	Internal memos describing marketing strategy and industry forecasts

Table A12.1

Examples of How Blogs Can Be Used for a Variety of Site Genres

A7

A2

A9

A6

A11

which markets the book by that name. The book looks at applying economic analyses to everyday phenomena, such as cheating, housing prices, and naming your children. The blog is used as a way to describe new findings, publicize events, and generally help publicize the book.

Product blogs can also be useful as products are being developed, to generate marketing buzz, as well as to get feedback before a product is actually released. For example, many game companies maintain developer diaries that show screen shots and provide previews of what that game will be like. As another example, Ford Motor Company maintained a blog during the development of its new Mustang car (blog.ford.com), featuring entries from some of the lead designers and engineers about their thoughts and the memories they were trying to recapture in the new design.

The SCI FI channel also maintains several blogs for its most prominent shows, such as *Battlestar Galactica* (see Figure A12.2) and *Stargate,* giving viewers a behind-the-scenes perspective on episodes, answering questions from fans, and dropping hints about upcoming episodes. Many of these kinds of blogs also provide a separate MESSAGE BOARD (D5) for fans to discuss topics, adding to the marketing buzz and helping to foster a community of people that will keep coming back.

Alternatively, you might want your blog to be part of a SITE BRANDING (E1) strategy for a VALUABLE COMPANY SITE (A7). For example, Work in Progress (weblogs.macromedia.com/mc) is run by Adobe and features tips on how to use certain products, as well as relevant news about the Web. The photo-sharing site Flickr has a blog (blog.flickr.com) that showcases exceptional photos and is also used to make people aware of new features that Flickr offers. Sometimes there is no clear distinction between a company blog and a product blog, especially for Web-based companies. For example, Google's blog (googleblog.blogspot.com) describes updates

Figure A12.2

Blogs can be used to discuss products as they're being made. For example, Ron Moore is the current executive producer for the television show *Battlestar Galactica.* In his blog, he answers questions from fans about the series, drops hints about what might happen in future episodes, and also describes what it's like writing and producing a television show.

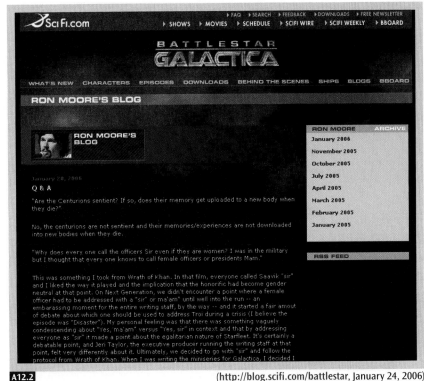

(http://blog.scifi.com/battlestar, January 24, 2006)

to existing services in a way that reinforces its image as a hip and fun-loving company.

Some NEWS MOSAICS (A2) have their own blogs, sometimes as an official part of the site, sometimes as an unofficial part written by journalists hired by that site. For example, *The New York Times* online has journalists maintain blogs about the movie industry (carpetbagger.nytimes.com), technology (nytimes.com/technology/pogueposts), and real estate in New York City (walkthrough.nytimes.com). *The New York Times* online also creates blogs for current events—for example, on U.S. Supreme Court confirmation hearings, on auto shows in Detroit, and on the annual World Economic Forum at Davos. Another newspaper, *The Washington Post,* also maintains a blog (blogs.washingtonpost.com/washpostblog) in which the newspaper editors discuss their site policies, new features, and goals for the Web site.

A2

Some blogs also act as NEWS MOSAICS (A2) by aggregating news sources across the Internet. Digg (digg.com) features news about topics like science, gadgets, and software development (see Figure A12.3). What's interesting about digg is that it uses a simple community-based voting system to determine which posts should go on the front page.

A2

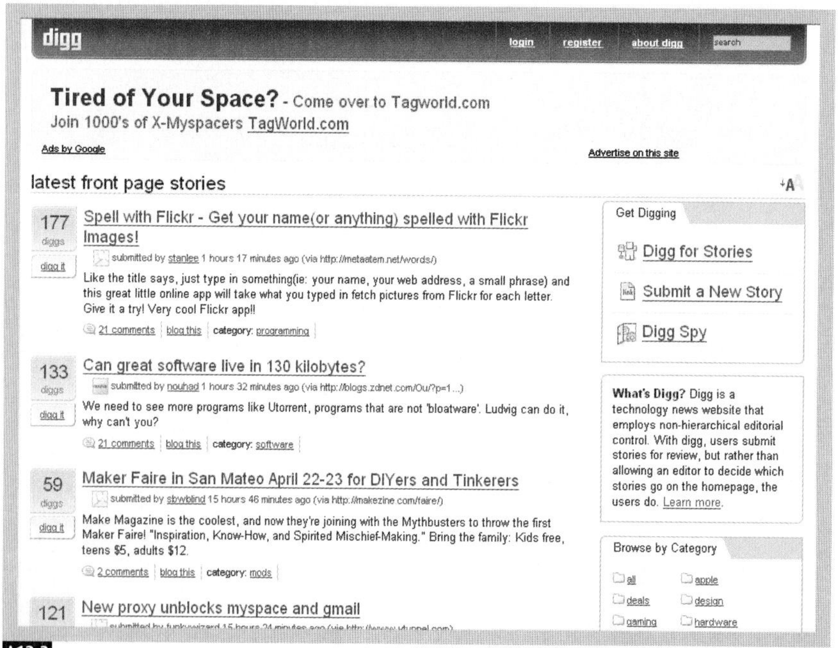

A12.3

(www.digg.com, January 31, 2006)

Figure A12.3

Some blogs act as news mosaics by making it easy to aggregate articles from all over the Web. Digg does this by letting community members vote on which articles they want to see on the front page.

A9   Blogs are also created for STIMULATING ARTS AND ENTERTAINMENT (A7) sites. According to Technorati (technorati.com), for example, PostSecret (postsecret.blogspot.com) is one of the most highly ranked blogs. PostSecret features scanned-in postcards from readers who want to share a secret that no one else knows, ranging from their deepest desires, to things they got away with at work, to their struggles with depression. Although the concept itself is simple, the effect can be quite powerful. As another example, Fark (fark.com) headlines news of the weird and other humorous odds and ends found on the Internet. Readers submit short headlines, and editors decide what goes on the front page.

A6
A5   Blogs can also be used to support GRASSROOTS INFORMATION SITES (A6) and NONPROFITS AS NETWORKS OF HELP (A5). Such blogs might include political commentary sites, disaster relief diaries, repositories of information about charities and volunteering opportunities like those at Grassroots.org (grassroots.org), and local community sites, such as the blog for the town of Northfield, Minnesota (northfield.org; see Figure A12.4).

A11   Finally, blogs can be used internally as part of an ENABLING INTRANET (A11). For example, some product teams use intranet blogs to maintain awareness

Figure A12.4

Blogs can be used as grassroots informa-tion sites, providing political commen-tary, organizing peo-ple for disaster relief, or giving people a view of what's going on in a local commu-nity. This blog for Northfield, Minnesota, contains entries about events in the town.

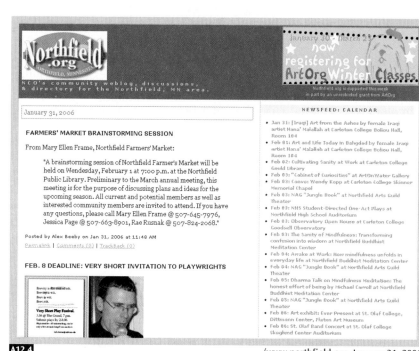

(www.northfield.org, January 31, 2006)

of the current status of a project, with team members writing brief daily entries about what they're working on. Blogs have also been used by upper management at large companies to outline their forecasts of where the industry is going and to lay out their business strategy. Intel CEO Paul Otellini maintains an internal blog in which he discusses challenges that the company is facing, new opportunities, upcoming product lines, and the competition. A very important thing to be aware of, however, is that even though a blog may be internal, it is likely to be leaked. For example, the *San Jose Mercury News* has published portions of Otellini's blog.

Decide How the Blog Will Be Run • In addition to the kind of blog you want, you need to consider how the blog will be run, whether by a single individual, by a small group of people, or by an entire community of people. Table A12.2 gives examples of blogs run in each of these different ways.

Individual blogs are perhaps the best known and most numerous type of blog on the Internet. For example, Wonkette (wonkette.com) is a popular blog run by Ana Marie Cox. Wonkette is well known for juicy gossip about goings on in Washington, DC, as well as sharp wit and sarcasm. In another example, Seth Godin, an author of books on business and marketing, keeps a blog at sethgodin.typepad.com, where he writes about topics like branding, creativity, and product life cycles. These kinds of blogs are easy to set up and good for advocating a position, as in a GRASSROOTS INFORMATION SITE (A6), as well as for promoting oneself.

A6

Many blogs are run by a small group of people. For example, Boing Boing (boingboing.net) is a highly popular blog featuring posts about technology, politics, and culture. Boing Boing is currently managed by

Blog Type	Examples
Individual	Wonkette: wonkette.com
	Seth Godin: sethgodin.typepad.com
Group	Boing Boing: boingboing.net
	The Huffington Post: huffingtonpost.com
	Engadget: engadget.com
Community	MetaFilter: metafilter.com
	Daily Kos: dailykos.com
	Lifehacker: lifehacker.com

Table A12.2

Examples of How to Run Blogs

four editors, each of whom can add or edit posts. The Huffington Post (huffingtonpost.com) is a political blog that features daily columns from its namesake, as well as timely entries by many guest bloggers on such topics as politics, entertainment, culture, and business. Maintained by a few bloggers, Engadget (engadget.com) features interviews and news articles about high-tech electronics. One nice feature of Engadget is that its weekly roundup summarizes the posts for that week, so you don't have to check it every day to get value from the site.

Some of the most popular sites on the Internet are blogs run in a decentralized manner by a large community of people. The key difference between community blogs and both individual and group blogs is that, in community blogs, community members are the primary creators of content. As with **D5** MESSAGE BOARDS (D5), community blogs must deal with issues such as keeping the community coherent, making it easy for community members to author posts, and policing troublemakers who love to cause grief for others. In addition, because community sites tend to generate a great deal of traffic, the costs of bandwidth and a Web server are no small matter.

MetaFilter (metafilter.com) is a community blog centered around popular culture, current events, online games, and other odds and ends on the Internet (see Figure A12.5). Each member can make one post per day on the site's front page, and community members provide comments on front-page posts, helping to foster a certain kind of writing style. MetaFilter offsets the cost of running its Web server by having new community members pay a small onetime fee (about five U.S. dollars) to join. This fee also helps ensure the quality of discussion because miscreants are not likely to pay a fee just to cause trouble.

Another well-known example of a community blog is Daily Kos (dailykos.com), a politically oriented blog for progressives. Although a few primary members manage the blog, Daily Kos also features diary entries from members about such topics as the environment, campaign finance, and public policy. The costs for Daily Kos are offset by targeted advertising, as well as by subscribers (who, once having paid for a subscription, no longer see any ads).

Lifehacker (lifehacker.com) is a community blog where members make posts about how to improve personal productivity, ranging from time management to do-it-yourself projects to software hacks. Currently, Lifehacker uses an invitation-only system, to prevent spammers from posting advertisements and to keep the quality of posts high. Lifehacker is supported by banner ads.

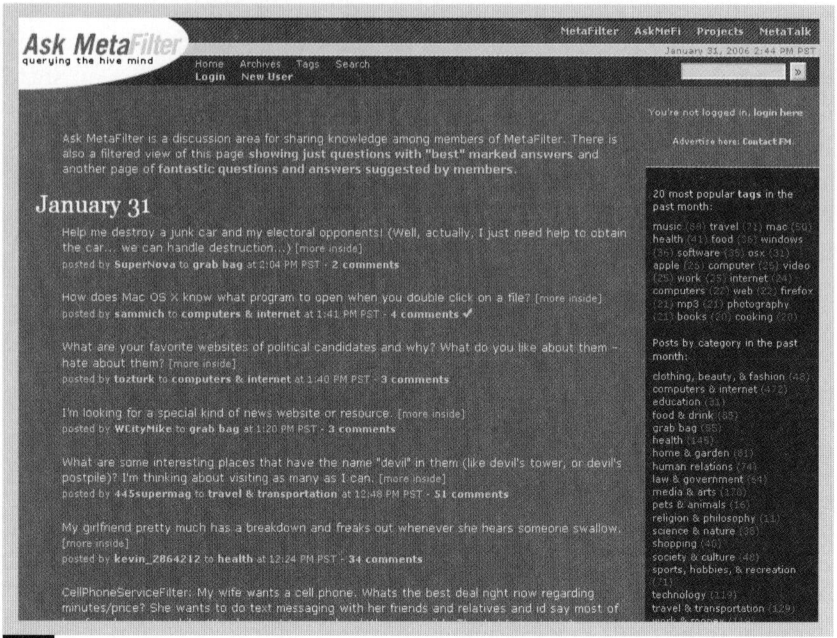

A12.5

(http://ask.metafilter.com, January 31, 2006)

Figure A12.5

Blogs can be run by an entire community of people. Although it can be difficult to maintain coherence on community blogs, these kinds of blogs are among the most popular sites on the Internet. Members of the MetaFilter community blog can post new blog entries and make comments. Shown here is a section of MetaFilter where people can ask questions and get tips and advice from other community members.

Consider Whether to Allow Comments from Readers • An important question to consider for blogs is whether to allow readers to post comments about a blog entry in a MESSAGE BOARD (D5). This is an issue only for individual or group blogs, since it is pretty much expected that members can post comments in community blogs.

The pros of allowing comments are that members may then feel like they're part of a community, you can get useful insights and feedback, and people have another reason to come back to your site. However, there are also two cons to allowing people to post comments. The first is spam messages that try to advertise something. Sometimes these messages are posted by people; sometimes they're posted by software programs known as **bots.** Either way, you will need to either moderate your MESSAGE BOARDS (D5) or install software to prevent these bots from posting to your message boards in the first place. The second, arguably more important con is that allowing comments potentially exposes you to criticism. This is especially true for politically oriented blogs, as well as company- and product-oriented blogs. For example, in January 2006 the *Washington Post* news site closed down its message boards for its blogs because of profanity, vitriol, and hate mail directed toward some of its journalists.

To give you a feel for how many blogs allow comments and how many do not, we did a quick analysis on Technorati (technorati.com), a Web site that measures the popularity of blogs, looking at how many allow comments. Of these, 6 of the top 10 blogs allowed comments, 12 of the top 20, and 35 of the top 50. So again, whether you want to allow comments or not depends on the goals that you're trying to achieve, the kind of community that you want to foster, and the amount of time and resources that you're willing to devote to managing spam posts and messages from angry visitors. The tips in COMMUNITY CONFERENCE (A3) can help you deal with these issues.

Make It Personal • Rather than being dry and completely "professional," consider adding a more personal touch to your blog. For example, Randy Baseler, vice president of marketing at Boeing, presents in his blog (boeing.com/randy) an insider's view of the airline industry, Boeing's market strategy, and events going on in Seattle, the site of Boeing's main manufacturing plants and their former corporate headquarters. Baseler adds some of his personal humor and warmth in his posts, as well as some of his personal views on living in Seattle and highlights of his trips around the world.

Similarly, General Motors runs a blog (fastlane.gmblogs.com) featuring posts and podcasts from corporate executives talking about what products are coming out, where GM is heading, and the industry in general. These posts are written more on a one-on-one fashion, with the executives speaking directly to you, rather than in the style you might typically expect from corporate executives.

These kinds of blogs are useful for getting the right message out and creating a new kind of dialogue with industry analysts, your employees, and, most importantly, your customers.

Make It Easy to Find Information on Your Blog • The fact that there are literally millions of blogs makes it hard for any single person to find yours. Furthermore, even after locating your blog, a person is unlikely to read entries beyond what's posted on the front page, limiting your blog's utility. One way of addressing this problem is to WRITE FOR SEARCH ENGINES (D6), using a combination of DISTINCTIVE HTML TITLES (D9), a simple writing style, and clean layout [see Pattern Group I (Designing Effective Page Layouts)] that is easy for search engine crawlers to understand.

Another way of helping visitors after they have found your blog is to use tags. Tags are simple textual descriptions that you can attach to blog entries—for example, *funny, public policy,* or even *Pittsburgh.* The right-hand side of Figure A12.5 shows an example of how tags are used on MetaFilter to organize posts. Most blogging software supports tags, making it easy for visitors to find more posts pertaining to a common topic. Tags are easy to use for individual and group blogs; the real difficulty comes with community blogs, where people might use different spacings or spellings—for example, *public-policy* versus *public policy, economics* versus *econ,* or *Web layout* versus *Web design.* It can take a great deal of community effort and coordination to agree on common tags.

You should also help your visitors find new content by providing an RSS feed on your blog. **RSS (Really Simple Syndication)** provides two benefits. First, RSS makes it easy for you to syndicate your content on other Web sites. This means that people can show summaries of your content on their Web sites, helping to broadcast your content and increasing traffic to your Web site. Second, RSS makes it easy for people to track updates on your Web site. For blogs, this is a simple way for people to see what new blog entries you have without going explicitly to your blog. Instead, people can subscribe to multiple RSS feeds and then view all of their RSS feeds in a single aggregator, making it easy to see what's new with all their favorite blogs and Web sites. Many of the latest Web browsers support the aggregation of RSS feeds, as do many personalized Web portals, including My Yahoo!, Google, NewsGator, Bloglines, Pluck, and Rojo. Most good blogging tools will create an RSS feed for you automatically.

✳ SOLUTION

Establish credibility and a strong community of readers through a combination of unique and fresh content, passion, and responsiveness to community members. Determine what blog genre you want, how the blog will be run (by individuals, small groups, or an entire community), and whether you will allow comments. Finally, write your content so that it will be easy to find on search engines.

Figure A12.6

Good blogs are a combination of credibility, unique content, compelling writing style, and a strong community of readers.

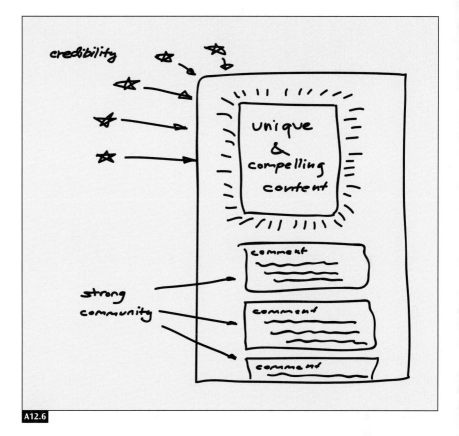

A12.6

✳ OTHER PATTERNS TO CONSIDER

E5 Establish credibility by having an ABOUT US (E5) page that contains relevant background information about yourself. If you're blogging for a **E1** company, consider ways of leveraging the company's SITE BRANDING (E1).

D5 Most blogs support MESSAGE BOARDS (D5), but if you have one on your blog, be prepared for tough criticism and occasional spammers and trolls **A3** (people who like to cause grief). The tips in COMMUNITY CONFERENCE (A3) can help you deal with these issues.

D6 Be sure to WRITE FOR SEARCH ENGINES (D6), using a combination of DIS-**D9** TINCTIVE HTML TITLES (D9), a simple writing style, and clean layout [see **I** Pattern Group I (Designing Effective Page Layouts)] that's easy for search engine crawlers to understand.

Creating a Navigation Framework ◆ B

One of the challenges of designing for the Web is that customers can come to a site in many different ways. They may not enter at your homepage, and their goals and tasks often vary widely. One of the keys to a satisfying customer experience is a Web site's ability to support these differences. This pattern group will help you maximize your site's flexibility to accommodate customers' different navigation, browsing, and search habits.

B1 MULTIPLE WAYS TO NAVIGATE

B2 BROWSABLE CONTENT

B3 HIERARCHICAL ORGANIZATION

B4 TASK-BASED ORGANIZATION

B5 ALPHABETICAL ORGANIZATION

B6 CHRONOLOGICAL ORGANIZATION

B7 POPULARITY-BASED ORGANIZATION

B8 CATEGORY PAGES

B9 SITE ACCESSIBILITY

B1 MULTIPLE WAYS TO NAVIGATE

B1.1

(www.amazon.com, July 21, 2006)

Figure B1.1

Amazon.com understands that both intention and impulse are navigation motivators. Customers can look for what they *intend* to buy, using browsing and searching tools. The site also provides links to *impulse* items that customers might not have intended to buy but end up purchasing anyway.

✳ BACKGROUND

Used by all the patterns in Pattern Group A (Site Genres), from PERSONAL E-COMMERCE (A1) to BLOGS (A12), this pattern provides techniques that support how customers navigate sites.

✳ PROBLEM

Customers navigate Web sites in many ways. If any of the key navigation tools are hard to find or missing, visitors will find the site tedious to use.

Customers navigate through a site to gather information and to accomplish goals. They may look for information, activities, or products in any number of ways. One customer may have something specific in mind and use the search tool to find it. Another customer may also have something in mind but may prefer to browse the site by following hyperlinks. A third customer may only vaguely know what she or he wants and may wish to look around and see what catches the eye. Because customers want to move through Web sites in different ways of their choosing, your site needs to offer them multiple ways to navigate.

Intention and Impulse Drive Customers to Act • Before you design a navigation framework, it helps to understand what drives customers to take action online. Customers come to a site with a goal: to accomplish a specific task (for example, to find someone's phone number); to do something more general (such as to buy the best ski jacket); or just to look around, perhaps because someone else recommended the site. Once on a site, however, customers also navigate on the basis of things that grab their attention, whether targeted promotions or simply related items of interest.

From these observations we have identified two things that drive customers to action: intention and impulse (these can also be thought of as goal and trigger, or need and desire). Neither intentional nor impulsive behavior is inherently good or bad, but a site that omits intention-based navigation might feel shallow and quirky, and one that omits impulse-based navigation might seem boring. You can take advantage of both intention- and impulse-based behavior to help your customers have a satisfying experience. Figure B1.2 diagrams the feedback loop among customer attitudes, intentions, impulses, and behavior.

Different Motivations Lead to Different Styles of Navigation • Familiar navigation helps customers the most, regardless of whether they have a clear idea of how to move forward. Navigation options include the familiar *search* and *browse* styles (see Figure B1.3), as well as the *next-step*, or *wizard*, style. The *relate* and *promote* navigation styles work best with impulsive behavior. Table B1.1 shows how motivations and navigation styles are supported through specific navigation tools.

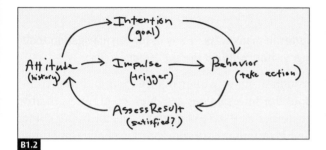

Figure B1.2

Two kinds of motivation drive customers to act: intention and impulse. Your customers' histories and attitudes form their goals and triggers, from which they take action and assess their satisfaction. This experience feeds back into their histories to start the loop all over again.

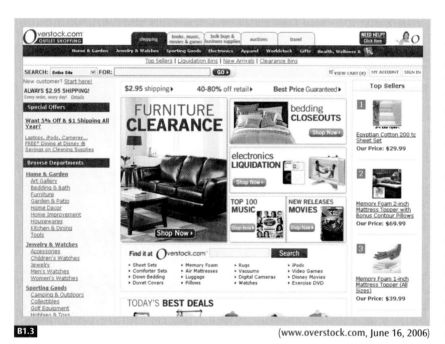

(www.overstock.com, June 16, 2006)

Figure B1.3

The navigation options at the top of this page provide customers multiple ways to search. The navigation options on the left let customers choose from and browse through multiple shopping categories. The main content area showcases the hottest sellers, providing images and links for more details, as well as links to buy the items right on the spot.

Put Tools Where Customers Will Find and Use Them • Not only does it make sense for each navigation tool to appear consistently in a specific place so that customers can find it, but on the basis of past experience on the Web, customers have come to expect these tools to be in certain places. Consistent placement of navigation tools is one of the most important ways of making navigation easy. One thing you can do to help ensure that your Web site has a consistent navigation scheme is to use PAGE TEMPLATES (D1) that have a strong GRID LAYOUT (I1).

D1

I1

Table B1.1

Motivators, Styles, and the Tools That Support Them

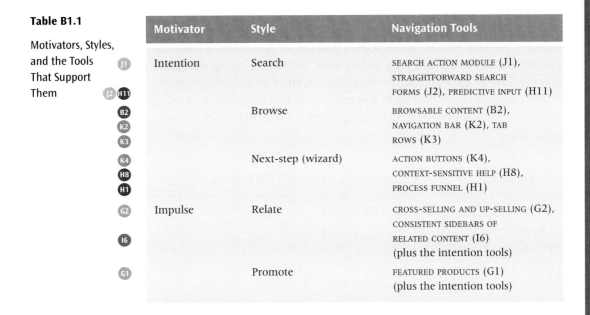

Motivator	Style	Navigation Tools
Intention	Search	SEARCH ACTION MODULE (J1), STRAIGHTFORWARD SEARCH FORMS (J2), PREDICTIVE INPUT (H11)
	Browse	BROWSABLE CONTENT (B2), NAVIGATION BAR (K2), TAB ROWS (K3)
	Next-step (wizard)	ACTION BUTTONS (K4), CONTEXT-SENSITIVE HELP (H8), PROCESS FUNNEL (H1)
Impulse	Relate	CROSS-SELLING AND UP-SELLING (G2), CONSISTENT SIDEBARS OF RELATED CONTENT (I6) (plus the intention tools)
	Promote	FEATURED PRODUCTS (G1) (plus the intention tools)

After opening a Web page, customers must find the links that will enable them to complete their goals and intentions. Put the tools that start visitors on the path toward their goals near the point at which they'll begin reading. This location ensures that the tools will be found and used. The tools that help customers continue or complete their goals also need to be near the top of the page so that customers can see them without scrolling. These tools work best when placed on the opposite side of the page (top right) from where customers start reading. Customers tend to scan from start to finish, so they also expect the continuation links to lie toward the finish (bottom).

Because you cannot guarantee that your customers will have an impulsive reaction, the impulse navigation tool's screen space is less valuable. You can push it down or to the side of the page opposite where customers start reading (right).

❊ SOLUTION

To ensure that your visitors complete their goals, place search and browse navigation tools at the top and start of the page. Position next-step navigation tools toward the top, but opposite the start, as well as at the bottom. Always include navigation tools that relate and promote so that customers find things that they might otherwise miss, but position these tools farther down the page.

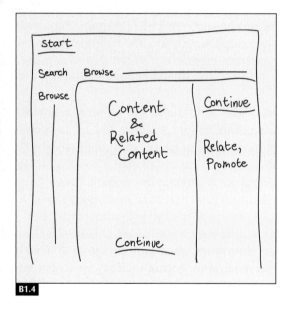

B1.4

Figure B1.4

By giving your visitors multiple ways to navigate on your site, depending on their goals and desires, you can keep them engaged.

❊ OTHER PATTERNS TO CONSIDER

Give customers multiple ways to navigate by consistently using intention-based navigation: Place a SEARCH ACTION MODULE (J1) or a link to your STRAIGHT-FORWARD SEARCH FORMS (J2) at the top of every page, include a consistent NAVIGATION BAR (K2) on every page, and provide BROWSABLE CONTENT (B2). Make it easier for everyone to navigate your site with SITE ACCESSIBILITY (B9). Place all of these elements in a PAGE TEMPLATE (D1) that has a strong GRID LAYOUT (I1), to help enforce consistency across your entire Web site.

Help customers complete their tasks by using ACTION BUTTONS (K4) and links to CONTEXT-SENSITIVE HELP (H8) located at the top right of the page. Use a PROCESS FUNNEL (H1) for tasks that absolutely must be completed.

Provide impulse-driven navigation capability by including CONSISTENT SIDEBARS OF RELATED CONTENT (I6) and promotions that use DESCRIPTIVE, LONGER LINK NAMES (K9).

Figure B2.1

Wal-Mart's site provides customers with easy navigation and clear signals for finding their way back. They can click on the Wal-Mart logo to return to the homepage, on the tab row at the top or the navigation bar on the left to go to another section, or on the location bread crumbs near the top to backtrack.

B2.1

(www.walmart.com, February 12, 2002)

✳ BACKGROUND

A Used in any pattern of Pattern Group A (Site Genres) that allows customers to navigate by browsing, and as a requisite element of MULTIPLE **B1** WAYS TO NAVIGATE (B1), this pattern makes content browsable through a combination of organization and navigation cues.

✳ PROBLEM

Browsing content on a site can be difficult if the information is not organized, or if there are no clear and consistent navigation cues for finding content and returning to it later.

Customers group and organize information in many ways. Just go to a local library and take a look at how things are organized. In the United States, every library uses either the Dewey decimal system or the Library of Congress system for organizing books. These methods work fairly well for a wide variety of libraries—from small libraries of just thousands of books to national libraries of millions of books. Libraries are organized for searching. If patrons know the system, they can find anything.

Now think about how a bookstore is organized. In contrast to a library, magazines are usually grouped together in the front of the store, recent novels are in another section nearby, children's books are in yet another section, and so on. Often books are organized alphabetically by author within each group, but sometimes a series is so successful and numerous that it warrants its own subsection. Bookstores are organized for browsing as well as searching. Customers of bookstores and patrons of libraries have slightly different needs. The same is true for content on the Web.

Use an Organizational Scheme • Web sites need architectures that are tailored to the types of information involved, to the amount of information, and to customer tasks. Finding the best organization schemes for a particular site requires analysis. We have included patterns on HIERARCHICAL ORGANIZATION (B3), TASK-BASED ORGANIZATION (B4), ALPHABETICAL ORGANIZATION (B5), CHRONOLOGICAL ORGANIZATION (B6), and POPULARITY-BASED ORGANIZATION (B7). Other organizational schemes that might make sense for your site include spatial (for example, geographic) or numerical organization. Use CATEGORY PAGES (B8) as directories to content in subcategories.

B3
B4 **B5**
B6 **B7**

B8

Structure Content with Customers in Mind • Use card sorting [see Chapter 3 (Knowing Your Customers: Principles and Techniques)] to group items so that people will be able to find what they're looking for by recognizing the group names. It is best to do this with several customers to see if there is a consensus. If there isn't, try to change the names of the items or groups that are causing confusion. Asking these questions about where to put each item and what to call the categories will make it easier for customers to browse your content, picking the right links each step of the way.

3

Provide Information Scent • The text labels you use should also provide information scent indicating whether people are nearing the content they're looking for. *Information scent* is a term coined by researchers at the famed Xerox PARC research lab. At a conceptual level, **information scent** is the perceived proximity to desired information, delivered by cues such as text, link names, images, headings, grouping, page layout, and previous pages seen.

For example, suppose that an e-commerce site displayed the following options:

- Clothes
- Computers
- Electronics
- Movies
- Music

If you were looking for DVDs, you would probably click on **Movies.** This is an example of good information scent because it would take you closer to your goal. On the other hand, if you were looking for a digital music player like the iPod, would you click on **Computers, Electronics,** or **Music?** This is an example of poor information scent. Overall, a set of labels (or more broadly, an information architecture) is good if it supports the large majority of expected tasks.

One way of improving information scent is to provide a few examples of the kinds of things customers would see if they clicked on the link. The best-known example of this is Yahoo!'s hierarchical Web directory (see Figure B3.1). Another way of improving information scent is to provide redundancy. For example, digital music players could be listed under both **Computers** and **Electronics,** improving the chances that a customer would find them. You can also use card sorting, as described in Chapter 3 (Knowing Your Customers: Principles and Techniques), to have customers help you organize the content on your site.

Help Customers Find Their Way Back • While navigating from page to page, customers can follow a path on purpose to explore or follow a path accidentally and find themselves lost. If they can't find their way back to a place they remember, they'll feel less adventurous. Leaving links on TAB ROWS (K3) or as LOCATION BREAD CRUMBS (K6) gives customers the reassurance they need to explore freely and to find their way back (see Figure B2.1). Most customers expect to be able to return to a site's homepage by clicking on the site logo in the upper left-hand corner of any page, as described in SITE BRANDING (E1).

When Does Content on a Page Become Too Much? • Customers can be over-loaded with too much information, and the overload might shut down their ability to read, even though your page could be jam-packed with valuable information. Many factors contribute to the feeling of being overwhelmed—from fonts that are too small, to sections on a page that are indistinguishable, to an unclear hierarchy of content. You don't want customers to concentrate too much on figuring out what's important and what's not. You can mitigate information overload by using techniques that allow customers to scan a page and find what they seek. Lay out each page with a clear GRID LAYOUT (I1), a strong visual hierarchy, consis-tent content areas, consistent NAVIGATION BAR (K2) and link areas, and a font that customers can read easily, even if it means that they'll need to scroll (see Figure B2.2).

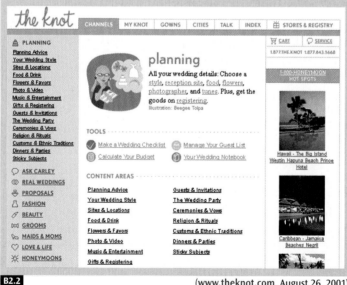

Figure B2.2

The information on The Knot's Web site is organized clearly and aligned in a clean grid layout. The navigation bar consists of a tab row along the top and links along the left-hand side, making it easy to move through the site.

(www.theknot.com, August 26, 2001)

✳ SOLUTION

Organize your content in several ways, in categories that make sense to your customers and in the intuitive ways that they think about doing their tasks. Build navigation tools and cues that let customers know where they are, where they can go, and how to get back. Build each page with its own reading hierarchy so that customers can scan it quickly.

Figure B2.3

Present content in a simple, scannable format that leads browsing readers from one page to the next, while giving them clear naviga-tion markers to make their way back.

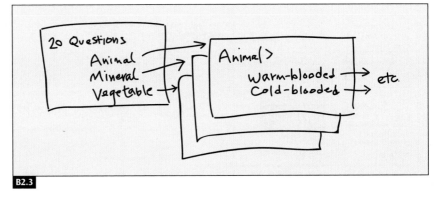

B2.3

✳ OTHER PATTERNS TO CONSIDER

Determine the best organizational schemes for your content by using HIERARCHICAL ORGANIZATION (B3), TASK-BASED ORGANIZATION (B4), ALPHABETICAL ORGANIZATION (B5), CHRONOLOGICAL ORGANIZATION (B6), and POPULARITY-BASED ORGANIZATION (B7) separately or in combination. Use CATEGORY PAGES (B8) as directories to content in subcategories. Using SITE ACCESSIBILITY (B9), make it easier for everyone to navigate your site.

Give customers ample opportunity to find their way back, by employ-ing NAVIGATION BARS (K2), TAB ROWS (K3), SITE BRANDING (E1), and LOCATION BREAD CRUMBS (K6).

On every page, make the content browsable by building a hierarchy of content with a clean GRID LAYOUT (I1), CLEAR FIRST READS (I3), and clearly defined areas with CONTENT MODULES (D2).

Figure B3.1

Yahoo! uses hierarchies to categorize thousands of Web sites (left). Categories range from "Arts & Humanities" to "Society & Culture."

B3.1

(www.yahoo.com, April 16, 2006)

✳ BACKGROUND

Used as part of MULTIPLE WAYS TO NAVIGATE (B1) and BROWSABLE CONTENT (B2), **B1** **B2** this pattern provides a way to organize large amounts of content when the content can be structured in a hierarchy.

✳ PROBLEM

Organizing information in a hierarchy of categories can help customers find things, but building an effective hierarchy is not easy.

Hierarchies are a common way of breaking long lists into smaller chunks, but customers think in different ways and may not group the same smaller chunks together in the same categories. What makes good organization depends on your audience, on the language that the audience uses to describe the subjects that you'll categorize, and on the amount of information that you present at a given time.

The best-known example of a hierarchy on the Web is the one created by Yahoo!, which contains several thousand Web sites (see Figure B3.1). Despite the enormous number of categories, customers find things easily because the items are grouped according to a logical scheme. Yahoo! built its directory over time, through serious and thoughtful debate among the information architects and content experts working for the company.

Building a smaller hierarchy is not as daunting but requires the same dedication to understanding the way your customers think and talk about the topics.

Organize Your Hierarchy to Match the Way Customers Think • This task can be quite a challenge because customers do not all think alike, and because a designer may not think like customers do. For example, would most customers expect to find "organic apples" under "groceries," "produce," "fruits," or "organic fruits"? Should you cover your bases and create all the categories? Or should you create just one category? An important term that information architects use to describe this problem is *information scent* [see BROWSABLE CONTENT (B2)]. Categories with strong information scent will help your customers choose the right path.

To make this decision requires interviewing customers about where they would expect to find things. Use card sorting, as described in Chapter 3 (Knowing Your Customers: Principles and Techniques), to have customers help you organize the content on your site. You can relate the resulting categories by creating links between them. It is also useful to provide a few redundant links to the same information, especially if different customers consistently give different names for the same thing.

Alternatively, if you can't afford to interview customers, be sure to engage a domain expert who is able to create the categories that customers are most likely to use. This will help ensure that you don't use words that make sense only to your company, and not to customers.

Use Descriptive and Distinctive Category Names • Customers may choose unexpected names for categories. It's not that customers won't understand the names that a designer chooses, but words that a designer thinks best describe a category may not be the same as those that most customers choose.

One example comes from a health and nutrition site we tested that used the generic label *information* as the link name for a category that included nutrient characteristics and disease information. Although the term *information* made perfect sense to the site designers and to a few of the customers, 70 percent of customers could not find where "disease information" was located when starting at the top of the hierarchy. This seemingly simple name choice had huge consequences when customers could not purchase products because they couldn't find them.

Category labels need to be descriptive of what the categories contain. Avoid labels such as *miscellaneous* and *other*—names that are so ambiguous that customers will not know what they mean. Category labels also need to be distinctive from one another. For example, having the label *nutrition information* by itself is fine. Having both *nutrition information* and *diet information* as labels makes things confusing because they sound too similar. Which link would have information about vitamins? What about vegetarianism?

The key here is to test the categories and category labels. You can use card sorting with one group of customers to help you come up with potential categories and category labels. Then you can test the effectiveness of these names by using category identification and category description with another set of customers. The basic idea behind **category identification** is to give people a list of category names and a list of tasks, and ask them to choose the category that they think would help them complete each task. In **category description,** people are asked to describe what they think a given category contains. Both of these techniques are described in greater detail in FAMILIAR LANGUAGE (K11). (K11)

Provide Examples in Each Category • FindLaw's Web site (see Figure B3.2) has 14 top-level categories, including "Bankruptcy & Debt" and "Estate Planning." FindLaw also provides some second-level links, describing a few of the items found inside each category. Because customers can thus

Figure B3.2

FindLaw uses a hierarchy to categorize legal information, providing links to top-level categories, as well as examples within each category.

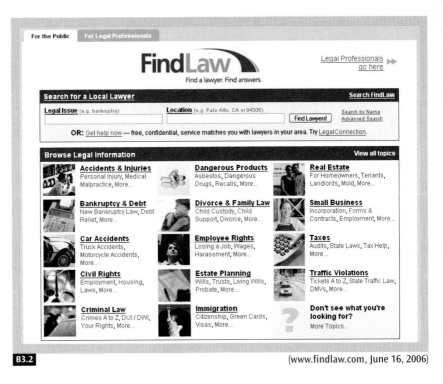

(www.findlaw.com, June 16, 2006)

more easily understand what a category contains, they are more likely to pick the right one. Yahoo! does the same thing with its well-known hierarchy (see Figure B3.1).

Use Fewer Than Fifty Subcategories • When subcategory lists are too long, they become cumbersome to read because there is so much information to process on one page. Keeping the number of subcategories to 50 or fewer (two columns of 25) will make your pages easier to read and faster to navigate. If you have more than 50 items, try to make sub-subcategories or to combine similar categories.

✳ SOLUTION

Build a hierarchy of categories with input from customers or from experts known for good communication skills in the subject area. Use descriptive category names that are distinctive from one another. Use techniques such as card sorting to develop the categories and labels, and use techniques like category identification and category description to test. Repeat items in multiple categories where it makes sense. Keep the maximum number of subcategories per category below 50, and avoid generic terms like *miscellaneous*.

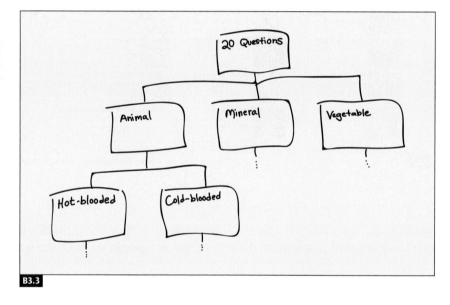

B3.3

Figure B3.3

Use words that are familiar to your customers without overloading a single category with too many subcategories.

✳ OTHER PATTERNS TO CONSIDER

Use card sorting, category identification, category description, and the techniques in FAMILIAR LANGUAGE (K11) to find the names of your top-level and second-level categories. Use CATEGORY PAGES (B8) as directories to content in subcategories. This pattern can be combined with other organizational patterns, including TASK-BASED ORGANIZATION (B4), ALPHABETICAL ORGANIZATION (B5), CHRONOLOGICAL ORGANIZATION (B6), and POPULARITY-BASED ORGANIZATION (B7).

K11
B8

B4
B5 B6
B7

Figure B4.1

This page from
Yahoo! illustrates
how stringing tasks
together can make
a site faster and
more useful. Here,
coffee houses and
theaters are only
a click away from
a restaurant listing,
making planning
a night out on the
town easier.

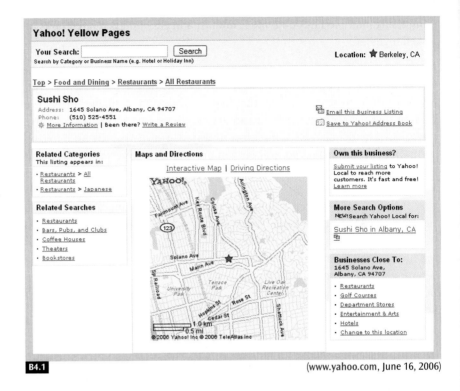

B4.1

(www.yahoo.com, June 16, 2006)

✳ BACKGROUND

B1 B2 Used as part of MULTIPLE WAYS TO NAVIGATE (B1) and BROWSABLE CONTENT (B2),
this pattern deals with organizing content according to the way customers
use it.

✳ PROBLEM

Completing multiple tasks on a site is not fast and easy unless related tasks are linked together.

When customers perform tasks on a site—whether they're searching for information, shopping for a product, or performing a process in a Web application—the task is often the first of many in a bigger project. If related tasks are not linked, customers are forced to return to a central page to start the next task, making repeated use of the site tedious. By grouping related tasks—so that customers complete one task and immediately link to the next—the site simplifies and speeds the flow of work.

Organize content and processes by how customers are likely to use them. For example, if customers search for a restaurant using Yahoo!'s map service, Yahoo! provides not only a map and directions, but also task-related links that make it easy to find nearby movie theaters and coffee houses (see Figure B4.1). Similarly, on Salesforce.com's site, salespeople set meeting reminders in their calendars, and while they're recording notes, the site provides links to create follow-up meetings (see Figure B4.2). These shortcuts save customers time.

Figure B4.2

Clicking on a task subject on Salesforce.com's site provides you with space to enter update information and schedule a follow-up task.

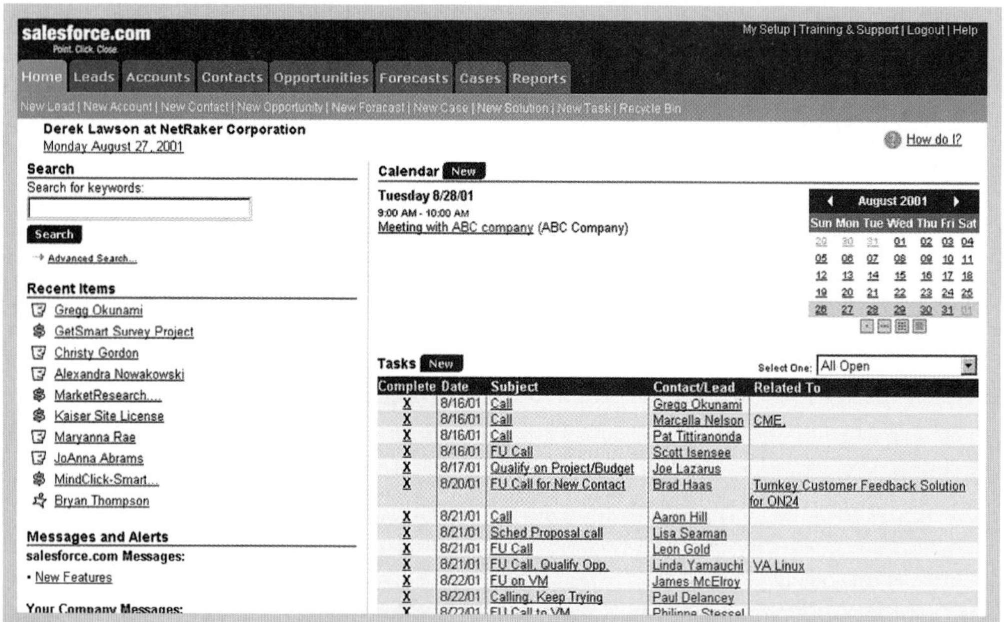

B4.2

(www.salesforce.com, August 27, 2001)

Study What Your Customers Do • What do your customers do online, offline, and on your Web site? In creating the map example of the preceding section, you could have asked your customers, "What kinds of places do you look up on Web sites that provide maps?" Or you could look at the Web server log files to see which destinations customers are typing in. Or you could use ethnographic methods and visit customers to observe what they actually do. When you observe your customers, they will reveal things they might not even realize they're doing. [See Chapter 3 (Knowing Your Customers: Principles and Techniques) for an overview of techniques to help you understand customer needs, including interviews, ethnographic observations, and surveys.]

Build Scenarios of Related Tasks • Once you understand how customers might use your site, you can build scenarios of related tasks, modeling the flow between tasks. From one task, the next available tasks should be the ones that regularly follow the first. For example, if for task A the next logical step is task B, C, or D, but not E or F, then the available options should be B, C, and D (see Figure B4.3).

Once you have built a description of related tasks, create links on task completion pages that will take customers directly into the next task or tasks. As a result, your customers will be able to move more quickly through your application, and their overall experience will be enhanced.

Let's consider a hypothetical site, called BasementFares.com, that lets customers search for and book airplane tickets. Figure B4.4 shows what the Web site looks like after a visitor selects a round-trip ticket. At this point the tasks include buying the ticket, holding the ticket for later purchase, searching for other flights, or canceling the entire transaction and starting over. The Web site supports many other tasks, such as renting a car and booking a hotel, but they are not emphasized on this page because they do not make sense in the context of the current task, which is purchasing an airplane ticket.

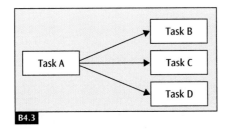

B4.3

Figure B4.3

Link logically related tasks together. For example, if task A can be followed by task B, C, or D, add links to those tasks on completion of task A.

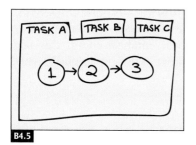

B4.4

Figure B4.4

This fictitious Web site, which we created, is representative of several actual major travel sites. On BasementFares.com, customers search for flights and selected itineraries by schedule or price. Once they have chosen the flight they want, the site takes them directly to the purchasing options. Customers can also search for other flights, which is another common task at this stage of the process.

☀ SOLUTION

Study customers, the tasks they do, and the sequence in which they do them. Then build relationships between tasks and link them so that the completion of one task can immediately precede the start of the next.

Figure B4.5

Link the completion of one group of tasks to the beginning of the next related task or tasks.

B4.5

☀ OTHER PATTERNS TO CONSIDER

PROCESS FUNNELS (H1) are similar to task-based organization but are focused on completing extremely specific tasks, with few choices at each step. If you have a HIERARCHICAL ORGANIZATION (B3) of different types of tasks, use CATEGORY PAGES (B8) as directories to content in subcategories.

H1
B3
B8

Figure B5.1

An alphabetically organized list works well when the list is fairly short and the pieces of information are unrelated, or when their names are well known.

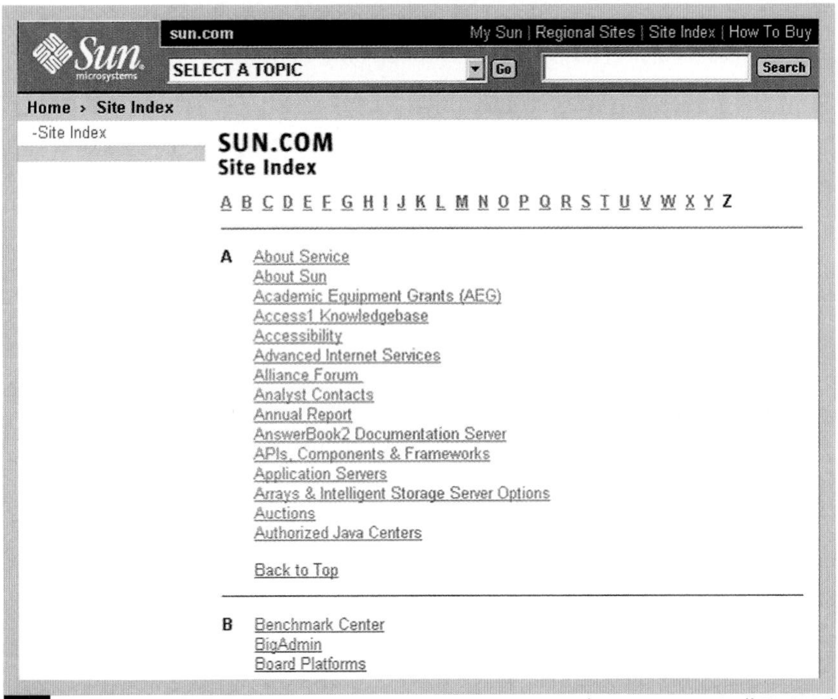

(www.sun.com, April 13, 2001)

✳ BACKGROUND

B1 B2 Used as part of MULTIPLE WAYS TO NAVIGATE (B1) and BROWSABLE CONTENT (B2), this pattern provides a way to organize a relatively small amount of content when the content is unrelated or is made up of items with well-known names.

✳ PROBLEM

Alphabetizing a list seems like an obvious way to organize content. Long alphabetical lists on a site, however, are cumbersome to use.

Alphabetical organization is ingrained in the way people remember things. It is effective when the individual pieces of information are known by name more than by what they represent.

When Does an Alphabetical List Work? • As long as customers know the precise word or phrase they're seeking, they can quickly find the items they want in an alphabetical list. Alphabetical lists can be useful for organizing information such as the following:

- Desired items, if known by name
- All documents on a Web site, if the document names are well known
- All of a company's customers
- All products that a company offers

Try to Keep the List on One Page • If an alphabetical list is split into multiple Web pages, customers must click on the first letter of the first word and wait for that letter's page to download. Long waits like this can be frustrating when the desired link is not guaranteed to be on the next page. Imagine looking for a video. Is it listed under *T* for *The Last Tango in Paris* or under *L* for just *Last Tango in Paris?* Neither order is right or wrong, but if the entire movie list appears on one page, it is easy to find it in either place. You can create an index at the top of the page that links to each letter group, as illustrated in Figure B5.1. You can also use a TAB ROW (K3) **K3** to do the same thing. Both techniques let your customers find the section they want without a lot of scrolling.

Alphabetical organization may not work well for people who grew up with nonalphabetical languages, such as Japanese and Chinese.

✳ SOLUTION

Provide links to each letter group at the top of your single alphabetical list page of well-known items.

B5.2

Figure B5.2

A page with the entire alphabetical list works best when it has links at the top to jump to each individual letter group.

❊ OTHER PATTERNS TO CONSIDER

Create an alphabetical TAB ROW (K3) at the top of your page that links to each letter's group farther down on the page, or use PREDICTIVE INPUT (H11) to load specific sections of the alphabetical list.

B6 CHRONOLOGICAL ORGANIZATION

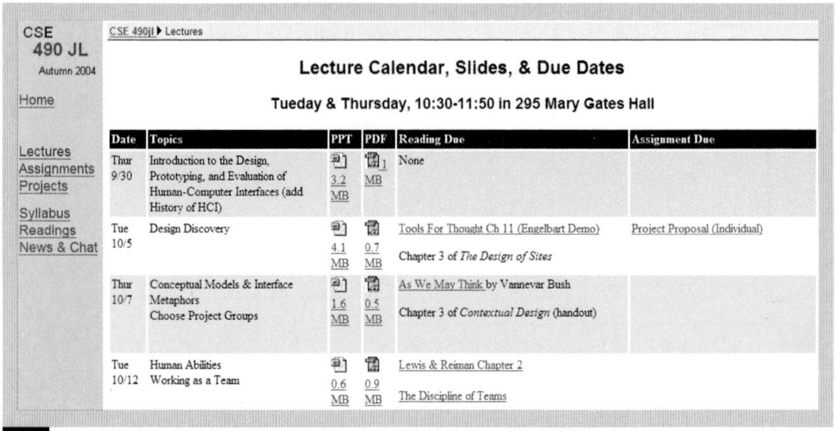

Figure B6.1

This course Web page offers information about an interface design and evaluation class taught by one of the coauthors of this book. It uses chronological ordering to organize the class assignments and materials as they were presented.

(www.cs.washington.edu/education/courses/cse490jl/04au/lectures.html, July 11, 2006)

✳ BACKGROUND

Used as part of MULTIPLE WAYS TO NAVIGATE (B1) and BROWSABLE CONTENT (B2), this pattern provides a way to organize content related by time.

B1 B2

✳ PROBLEM

Chronologically organizing content on a site helps visitors understand the order of content in time, whether past or future, but very long lists of events are difficult to read and use.

Chronological structure makes sense for things that have a strong notion of time, such as historical events, plane tickets, and changes on a Web page. But if a list is too long, with no hierarchical breakdown into eras, types, or milestones, reading and scrolling through it will take too long, and thus it will become less useful.

Display Chronological Information in Lists or Time Lines • One way of displaying time-related content is to show it as a vertical list in which the sorted column shows the time. This is the simplest solution because it can be implemented quickly, but it is not as intuitive as a time line, where

Table B6.1

Some Useful
Groupings for
Dividing Large
Chronological Lists

Content	Suggested Group for Breakdown
Musical events this month	Day
The history of the Christian Church	Century
What drives economic boom-and-bust cycles	Decade
The major milestones of World War II	Topic—for example, Nazi invasion of Poland, Pearl Harbor, D-day

content appears horizontally from left to right. The latter is how most people visualize time, but its implementation on the Web is more difficult because text is not laid out with much precision. Lists and time lines are useful when you want to display content in relation to well-known dates (such as the 1960s, '70s, or '80s) or in chronological relation to other content (such as "event X came before event Y").

You could also use a calendar to group information, showing events on a daily, monthly, or yearly basis. But this method does not work as well when you have to display large lists, because each day, week, or month can show only a fixed number of items.

Limit Chronological Lists to Fewer Than Fifty Items • When sorting items in chronological order, keep the lists short and easy to use. Chronological lists do not work well when they're long, because there are too many items to read. If you have to, organize your events into hierarchies based on spans of time, or use another kind of organization. For example, if you had more than 50 items in your chronology, you could break them out as shown in Table B6.1.

✳ SOLUTION

Display chronological lists in a vertical, horizontal, or calendar format, keeping the total number of items in each list under 50 by dividing the list into smaller groups of time.

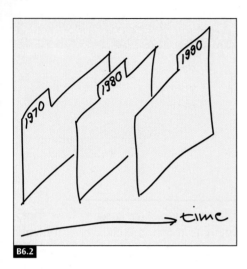

Figure B6.2

Organizing chronological content into smaller groups of time makes reading about each era that much easier.

✳ OTHER PATTERNS TO CONSIDER

Use a PAGE TEMPLATE (D1) to publish your vertical, horizontal, or calendar display in a CONTENT MODULE (D2) to keep it in a well-known place. Use HIERARCHICAL ORGANIZATION (B3) to keep lists of chronological items manageable. Use a CATEGORY PAGE (B8) as a directory for each group in the hierarchy.

D1
D2
B3
B8

Figure B7.1

Billboard shows customers the top music hits, from top-selling CDs to singles and airplays. Customers can also view top hits grouped by music genre, as well as by number of hits on the Web.

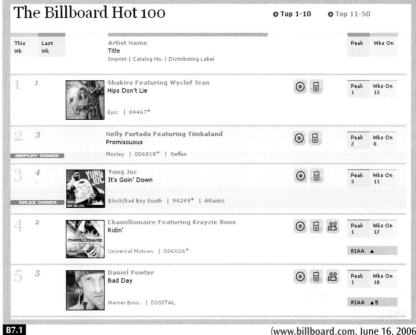

B7.1

(www.billboard.com, June 16, 2006)

✳ BACKGROUND

B1 B2 Used as part of MULTIPLE WAYS TO NAVIGATE (B1) and BROWSABLE CONTENT (B2), this pattern provides a way to organize content related by popularity.

✳ PROBLEM

Some customers want to see which content or products are the most popular. But without clear labels indicating how the content was rated and over what period, popularity lists are useless.

Some customers enjoy seeing what other customers think is popular. Whether they reflect the most-purchased products, a controlled democratic tally, or a popularity contest, these lists are intriguing, no matter how they're displayed. But if the list of rated items does not clearly indicate how the content was rated, it becomes suspicious and ineffective.

How to Create a List • Identifying the most popular items on your site can be a fairly straightforward matter, or it can be devilishly complex. Should you buy the list of content ratings from a provider (such as the *New York Times* "Best Sellers" lists)? Should you use a RECOMMENDATION COMMUNITY (G4), where you ask customers to rate your content? For example, both IFILM and YouTube ask visitors to rank short films on a scale from 1 to 5. Or should you automatically extract the information from customers' page views or purchases? In the example in Figure B7.2, Yahoo! provides a page where customers can view the most e-mailed news photographs and news stories of the previous six hours.

G4

How to Determine the Time Period for Taking Measurements • Customers expect the content in a list to be interesting news or to have historical value. The most popular content from three months ago will not be interesting, unless three months ago coincided with an important event. The most popular information from this week, compared to last week, might be interesting if enough movement has occurred.

From the information you've gathered, build a rating that changes frequently enough that visitors coming back on a regular basis will see movement. If customers come back daily, you should have enough information to show a daily best. If customers come back every month, monthly or quarterly scores might be more appropriate.

Figure B7.2

Yahoo! has a popularity-based news Web page that shows the most popular stories and photographs, according to the number of times they were e-mailed by customers.

(www.yahoo.com, August 26, 2001)

Flickr is a photo-sharing site that lets people upload photos and tag them with words like *birthday* or *cute*. Figure B7.3 shows Flickr's **tag cloud,** a visualization of the most popular tags currently used, with larger fonts indicating more popular terms. The "Lycos 50 Daily Report" shows the 50 most popular search terms for that week (see Figure B7.4). Sometimes, just for fun, Lycos features special categories, such as the most popular teen singers or the most popular actors.

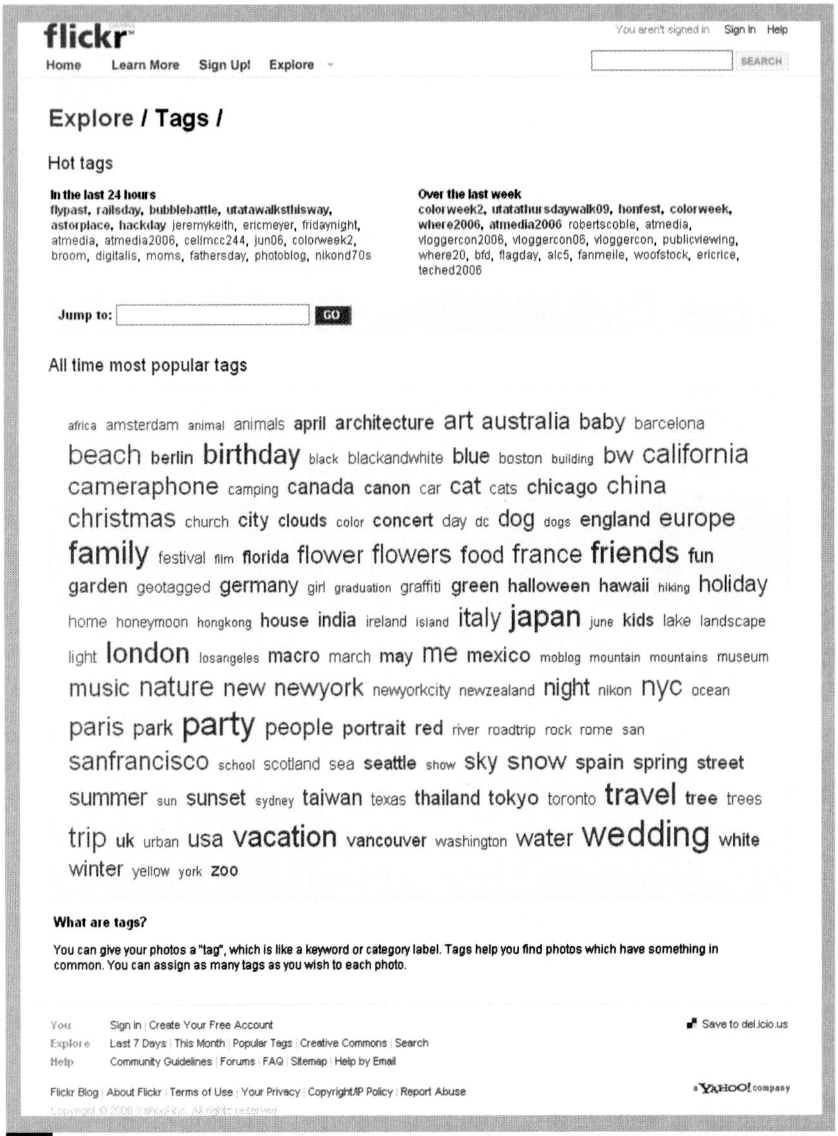

(www.flickr.com, June 16, 2006)

Figure B7.3

Flickr lets people upload photos and tag them with any words they want, making it easy to find specific photos later. This screen shot shows Flickr's tag cloud, a simple visualization that lets you see what the most popular tags are.

Figure B7.4

The "Lycos 50 Daily Report" shows visitors the 50 most popular customer search subjects on the Lycos search engine.

B7.4

(http://50.lycos.com, June 16, 2006)

✳ SOLUTION

Build your lists of popular content from customer usage, customer ratings, or acquired outside lists. Label each list with a descriptive title that indicates what was rated and over what period.

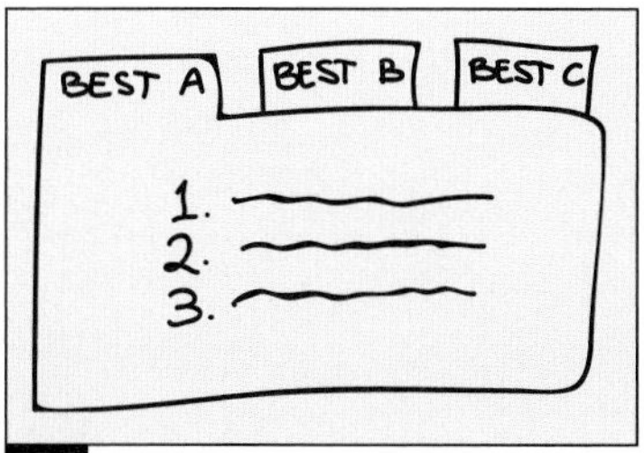

Figure B7.5

Show the most popular content, but be sure to descriptively label how it was rated, and to show the time period that the ratings cover.

B7.5

✳ OTHER PATTERNS TO CONSIDER

Integrate multiple popularity-based organization lists into levels of a HIERARCHICAL ORGANIZATION (B3). Use CATEGORY PAGES (B8) as directories to content in subcategories. Employ customer usage meters, a RECOMMENDATION COMMUNITY (G4), or acquired data to generate your lists. Also, if relevant, show your customers the time period during which you acquired the data.

Figure B8.1

Categories are labeled well and laid out consistently throughout Martha Stewart's Web site. When visitors travel deeper through the levels, they know where they are by the color scheme, the navigation elements, and the content.

(www.marthastewart.com, February 1, 2002)

✳ BACKGROUND

This pattern shows how to design different sections of a Web site so that they are distinct but still obviously part of the larger overall site. Category pages are often reached through one of the MULTIPLE WAYS TO NAVIGATE (B1) including any of the organization schemes for BROWSABLE CONTENT (B2), such as HIERARCHICAL ORGANIZATION (B3), TASK-BASED ORGANIZATION (B4), CHRONOLOGICAL ORGANIZATION (B6), and POPULARITY-BASED ORGANIZATION (B7).

✳ PROBLEM

As customers navigate through a site, if category sections are not introduced with a consistent layout, each section may seem like a new site.

Whether navigating through sections of content, products, or applications, when customers come across a new area, it must be consistent with the rest of the site or they might think that they've gone to a new site. Category sections that are consistent in layout and navigation elements reinforce a sense of location (see Figure B8.2). This does not mean that all categories must look exactly alike, but the basic structure must be the same. With a consistent structure, customers can recognize not only their location, but also the main elements of the section.

Use a Consistent Layout • Customers may become confused if they expect to find a section title in a certain location and it's not there. They might go to another page even if they're actually in the right place. Keep all the content and navigation elements in the same locations on each page so that people recognize the layout and feel secure that they're still on the right site. Keep the name of the section in a consistent place as well so that you can maintain a strong sense of location while introducing customers

B8.2

(www.rei.com, August 21, 2006)

Figure B8.2

Consistently colored categories and banner titles show REI.com customers, no matter which section they're in, that they're still on the same site.

to a new section. You can do this by using the same or similar PAGE TEMPLATES (D1) and GRID LAYOUTS (I1) throughout your Web site and positioning these key elements consistently in the same place.

Maintain Consistent Navigation • Make your navigation system the same throughout your site. You can change the color of a TAB ROW (K3), for example, and the subsection search element of a SEARCH ACTION MODULE (J1), to give it a sense of place, but avoid radical changes to other elements.

Provide Strong Feedback That Visitors Have "Arrived" • When you drive into a new town, it helps to see a big sign that says, "Welcome to Woebegone"; you know you've arrived. The same is true on the Web and within sections of your site. Provide a large sign or just a page title that indicates the category page section name the way it appears in navigation elements throughout the site.

Provide Cues for Strong Information Scent • As explained in BROWSABLE CONTENT (B2), information scent is the perceived proximity to desired information. For example, if you were looking to purchase toys, a page with strong information scent would provide text labels, images, and navigation that suggest either you're getting closer or you're on the right page. The cues to this information scent might include an organization that breaks down toys into smaller subcategories, pictures of featured or the most popular toys, and a color scheme that reflects a sense of play.

✳ SOLUTION

Use a section category layout consistently throughout your site, with the same navigation elements, giving customers a strong sense that they have "arrived" at a new section and a clear idea of how to get back.

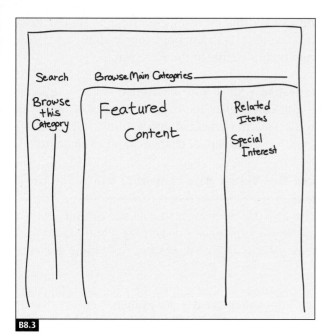

Figure B8.3

Focus category pages on the featured content, while using consistent navigation.

B8.3

☀ OTHER PATTERNS TO CONSIDER

Build a consistent category page layout using a PAGE TEMPLATE (D1) and CONTENT MODULES (D2), with consistent GRID LAYOUT (I1), NAVIGATION BARS (K2), and LOCATION BREAD CRUMBS (K6) to indicate where the customer is on the site. Use BROWSABLE CONTENT (B2) to provide strong information scent that customers either are getting closer or are on the right page. If you're using TAB ROWS (K3), you might change the color of the tab for each category section. If you're using a subsection element in a SEARCH ACTION MODULE (J1), make the default the current section. Use the CLEAR FIRST READ (I3) to indicate the section name so that visitors know that they've "arrived" at a new category.

D1
D2 I1 K2
K6
B2
K3
J1
I3

Figure B9.1

Web sites need to be designed for access and use by everyone, regardless of physical ability or computer capability. This example shows a screen shot from the text-based Lynx Web browser, which gives a flavor of what the Web is like for people who are blind.

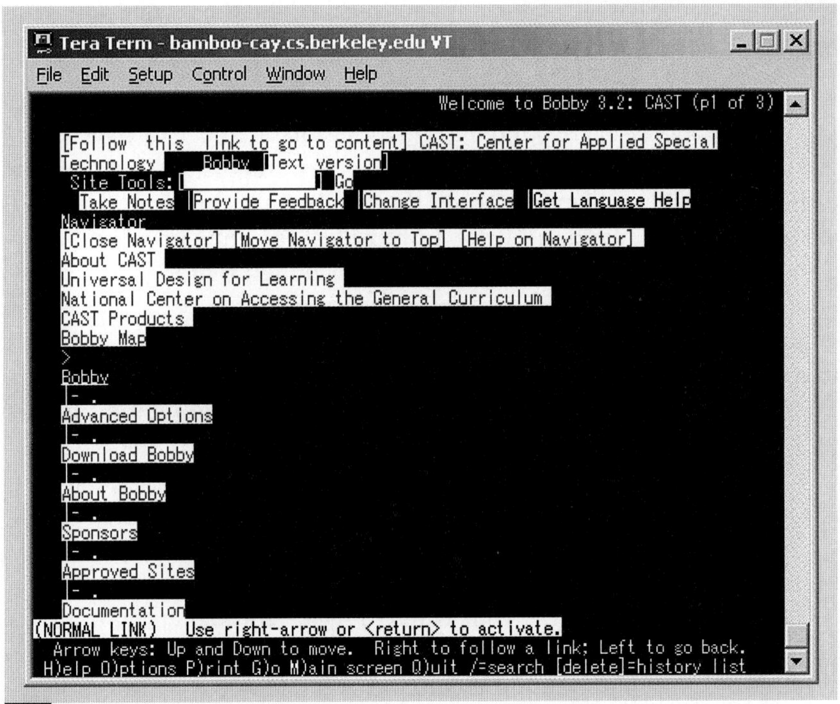

B9.1

(www.cast.org, October 31, 2001)

✳ BACKGROUND

People with disabilities find it difficult to use many Web sites. By law, SELF-SERVICE GOVERNMENT (A4) and other sites that are provided by, purchased by, or used by the U.S. government must be universally accessible. There are also regulations in Canada, the United Kingdom, and the European Union mandating minimum levels of accessibility for government Web sites based in those countries. Used in any pattern of Pattern Group A (Site Genres), this pattern describes how to structure your Web site to improve navigation accessibility for people with disabilities.

✳ PROBLEM

People with audio, visual, motor, or cognitive disabilities find it difficult to use Web sites that are not explicitly designed with their accessibility in mind.

A significant portion of the population has difficulty accessing and using the Web. People who are blind, have poor vision, are deaf, or have physical disabilities find it difficult—sometimes even impossible—to navigate through Web sites designed without their accessibility in mind.

Age is also an important factor to consider. On one end of the spectrum, young children have not fully developed their motor skills. On the other end, senior citizens may also have poor motor skills, as well as impaired vision and hearing. These are two potential customer segments to consider when designing your Web sites.

More and more mobile Internet devices, from mobile phones to personal digital assistants (PDAs), are Internet enabled. Clearly these devices do not have the same screen sizing options [see MOBILE SCREEN SIZING (M1)], **(M1)** input capabilities, and processing power of desktop computers. People who use these kinds of devices form another potential customer segment to consider when you're creating your Web site.

If the U.S. government is your client, a legal requirement also affects your accessibility design. Section 508 of the Rehabilitation Act requires all electronic and information technologies purchased by the U.S. government to be accessible. This stipulation explicitly includes services such as Web sites used by the federal government. Many other world governments have similar regulations.

Accessibility helps more than just its intended audience. *Accessibility helps everyone,* just as it does outside of the Internet. Curb cuts meant to help people with wheelchairs also make things easier for people traveling on roller blades, pushing baby strollers, and pulling luggage on wheels. Closed captions on television programs help not only people with hearing deficiencies but also people in loud sports bars, people in exercise centers, people trying to learn English, and spouses quietly watching television in bed at night.

The same is true for Web site accessibility. Offering captions and transcripts of audio and video, using clearer link names, and providing alternative text for images will improve the usefulness and usability not just for customers with disabilities, but for everyone else as well. It's a win–win situation. One general theme for Web accessibility is *text equivalence.*

The idea is to try to accompany as much of your Web content—including images, audio, and movies—with plain text, since text is highly accessible.

Note that much of Web accessibility is work in progress. A good source for keeping up-to-date on how to use HTML and CSS to improve accessibility is the World Wide Web Consortium's (W3C) Web Accessibility Initiative (WAI), available at w3.org/WAI.

Whether you're designing a new Web site or revising an existing site, here are some issues to think about. The ideas outlined in the sections that follow are not meant to be exhaustive, but they should give you an idea of the range of possibilities, as well as some of the simpler things you can do to improve accessibility.

People with Physical Difficulties Use the Web • Although there's a wide range of physical difficulties, focus your efforts on keyboard and mouse input because these are the primary input modes of computers for the near future. A customer with a physical disability might not be able to use a keyboard effectively, or even at all. The same is true for use of a mouse. Here's how to address these problems:

- Test whether your Web site can be used without a mouse. Determine whether a visitor could use just the keyboard to navigate through your Web pages.
- Minimize the amount of typing a visitor has to do. For example, a common technique in QUICK-FLOW CHECKOUT (F1) is to have customers enter their shipping address and then be able to indicate that this is also the billing address just by clicking a button with the mouse. This is much simpler than having a customer type in the same thing twice. Another way to minimize the input required of customers is to save the information that they typed in on a previous visit to the site, providing them with a QUICK ADDRESS SELECTION (F4), a QUICK SHIPPING METHOD SELECTION (F5), and a streamlined PAYMENT METHOD (F6) the next time they purchase something. Similarly, utilizing PREDICTIVE INPUT (H11) can help you reduce the amount of typing required by your customers.
- Make sure that your navigation elements are large enough to see clearly. Avoid links that are in small fonts and links that use small images. These elements are just too difficult to click on with a mouse. This caution applies to NAVIGATION BARS (K2), ACTION BUTTONS (K4), and OBVIOUS LINKS (K10).

People with Auditory Disabilities Use the Web • Most Web sites do not make heavy use of audio and video, but this is changing rapidly as more and more customers have broadband connections at home and as podcasting has taken off. If your site relies heavily on audio, provide text descriptions of audio sound files. For sites that include video, provide text transcripts and video captioning so that customers with auditory disabilities will know what's being said.

People with Visual Disabilities Use the Web • This segment of the population includes people who are blind, have impaired vision, or have color deficiencies. The relevant issues are basic readability of text and links. Here are some tips for ensuring the readability of your Web site for people with visual disabilities:

- **Provide sufficient contrast between the text and the background.** Use either dark text on a light background or light text on a dark background. Also avoid complex background patterns because they can make reading text extremely difficult. Use simple patterns or solid background colors instead.
- **Use a sufficiently large font.** Cramming in more information by shrinking the font merely forces customers to move closer to the monitor and squint. Web browsers have a default font size, and people with visual disabilities often increase this default size, so if you use relative font sizes, the text will usually be the right size. Do not override the end user's font choices, and make sure that your page layout still looks right when the font sizes change.
- **Avoid using ALL CAPS for text,** because the letter forms of capitals are more difficult to read. It's OK to use this technique sparingly to bring attention to something, such as "NEW" features or a "SALE." Capitalizing whole words is a good way of bringing attention, but doing it excessively can slow down reading.
- **Avoid animations and blinking text.** These kinds of distractions can make reading difficult.
- **Avoid creating text that runs all the way from the left of the page to the right.** This format makes it difficult for people's eyes to pick up the start of the next line. It also makes the text feel tight, as if it were being crammed in. A little white space on both sides of a Web page will make text easier to read. Using a FIXED SCREEN WIDTH (I5) will help you easily achieve this effect.

I5

- **Stay away from link color combinations that people with color deficiencies will not be able to differentiate.** In particular, avoid green for unvisited links and red for visited links because those colors are hard for people with red–green color deficiency to distinguish.
- **Consider adding an audio track.** If you have multimedia information that is purely visual, such as a graph, consider having a concurrent audio track that explains the information.

All of these tips notwithstanding, note that good readability by itself is not sufficient. People with visual disabilities must also be able to navigate your Web site. One way to ensure navigation capability is to underline links and use a distinct color, as described in the OBVIOUS LINKS (K10) pattern. Pattern K10 also describes how to use the <title> attribute in hyperlinks to describe where the link goes.

So far in this section we have talked just about issues affecting people with poor vision. What about people who can't see at all? People who are blind access Web sites by using a special hardware device or software program, called a **screen reader,** that takes all the text on a page and uses computer-based speech synthesis to read it out.

You can help blind customers by making sure your links make sense when taken out of context. People who are blind often skip text and go straight to the links (on most Web browsers they can do so by hitting the **Tab** button). Pressing **Tab** causes the screen reader to jump over most of the surrounding text and just read out the text of the link, making short link names like "click here" useless. Using DESCRIPTIVE, LONGER LINK NAMES (K9) will help significantly.

People who are blind will not want to use images as the only way to navigate your Web site. You could have both a regular Web page and a text-only copy of the Web page to remedy this situation, or you could create redundant navigation links—that is, text and image links that go to the same place.

Provide text descriptions for images by using the <alt> attribute to describe them. Here's an example of how to use the <alt> attribute:

```
<img src="img.jpg" alt="Text describing the image">
```

Here's how <alt> attributes are used on the Weather Channel's Web site:

```
<img src="http://image.weather.com/pics/banners/banner_general.jpg"
     border=0 alt="click on banner to return to Home Page">
```

B9.2

(www.weather.com, July 17, 2000)

Figure B9.2

The <alt> attribute
on the Weather
Channel's site is dis-
played as a tool tip
when a customer
moves the mouse over
the image. It is also
useful for people who
are blind, because
their screen readers
can read out the
description of the
image.

Screen readers read out the <alt> attribute to describe an image. And there are other advantages to using <alt> attributes. Figure B9.2 shows how visitors with normal vision can get text descriptions of images in the form of tool tips.

The <alt> attribute is also useful if you have a broken link to an image. Figure B9.3 shows what a person with normal vision would see if the Weather Channel's banner were missing. Interestingly, this is also what a person sees *before* the image is loaded, making it a FAST-LOADING IMAGE (L2). Thus, <alt> attributes let customers with slow network connections navigate through a Web page without waiting for all its content to load!

> click on banner to return to Home Page

B9.3

(www.weather.com, July 17, 2000)

Figure B9.3

Another advantage of the <alt> attribute is that it is shown if the image cannot be displayed.

People with Color Deficiencies Use the Web • A fair number of people with color deficiencies will use your Web site. Roughly 8 percent of males and 0.5 percent of females have difficulty distinguishing certain kinds of colors, most commonly red and green. People who suffer from red–green color deficiency cannot easily see differences between these two colors. Other rarer forms of color deficiency include the inability to distinguish between blue and yellow, and **monochromatism,** meaning that a person cannot see any colors at all.

Here are some simple things you can do to help these customers:

- **Avoid using highly saturated colors.** The left half of Figure B9.4 shows a palette of pure, highly saturated colors. You should avoid using these kinds of colors for two reasons: First, looking at highly saturated colors for a long period of time can tire a person out because it causes people's eyes to refocus more than less saturated colors do. Second, people with color

Figure B9.4

People with color deficiencies will have a hard time seeing the differences between certain pure, highly saturated colors like those on the left. These highly saturated colors can also make people feel tired if they look at them for a long time. Instead, use desaturated colors that, like those on the right, mix in some gray to reduce the purity of the color.

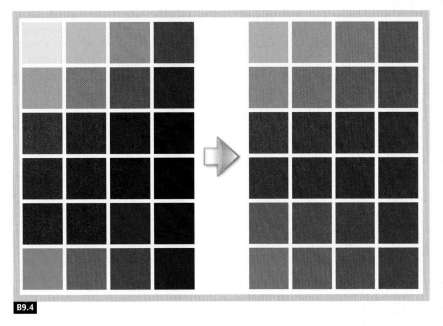

B9.4

deficiencies may have a hard time distinguishing between highly saturated, pure colors. Instead, use desaturated, pastel colors that are a mixture of colors, like those in the right half of Figure B9.4. It is also a good idea to have a strong contrast in the brightness or intensity of a color, because intensity is easier for people to see than the hue of a color is.

- **Don't rely solely on color for cues on important Web pages.** Figure B9.5 shows a Web page that, in user testing, people with color deficiencies had a hard time comprehending because it mixes the use of red and green. For this reason, it is good to have redundant **affordances,** or visual cues, such as texture and shape, that do not rely on color at all. For example, Figure B9.6 shows how traffic signs use a combination of color, shape, and text to communicate to drivers.

People with Cognitive Disabilities Use the Web • A cognitive disability can make it hard for people to read, write, and navigate. Here are four ways that you can make these tasks easier:

1. **Provide a consistent navigation scheme throughout your Web site.** Place navigation elements in a standard GRID LAYOUT (I1), and place the most important content ABOVE THE FOLD (I2).
2. **Use OBVIOUS LINKS (K10) and ACTION BUTTONS (K4) to ensure clarity** (see Figure B9.7).
3. **Avoid distracting elements,** such as animations and blinking text.

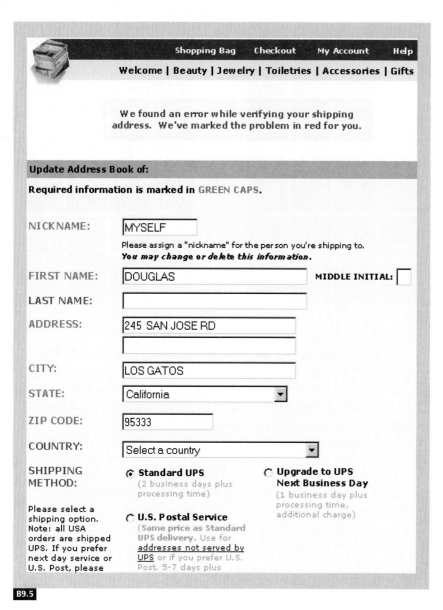

B9.5

Figure B9.5

People with color deficiencies may have problems distinguishing visual cues in your Web pages. This example highlights errors in the text input fields that user tests showed were difficult for people with red–green color deficiencies to see.

4. **Use recognition over recall.** In other words, minimize the amount of information that visitors have to remember to use your Web site. Search engines, for example, display not only search results, but also the search terms that the visitor typed in, making it easier for a visitor to remember a past action.

Figure B9.6

Use redundant cues to help people with color deficiencies. Designers of visual cues in the physical world have learned this lesson. These two traffic signs use three different cues to signify their meaning: color, shape, and text.

B9.6

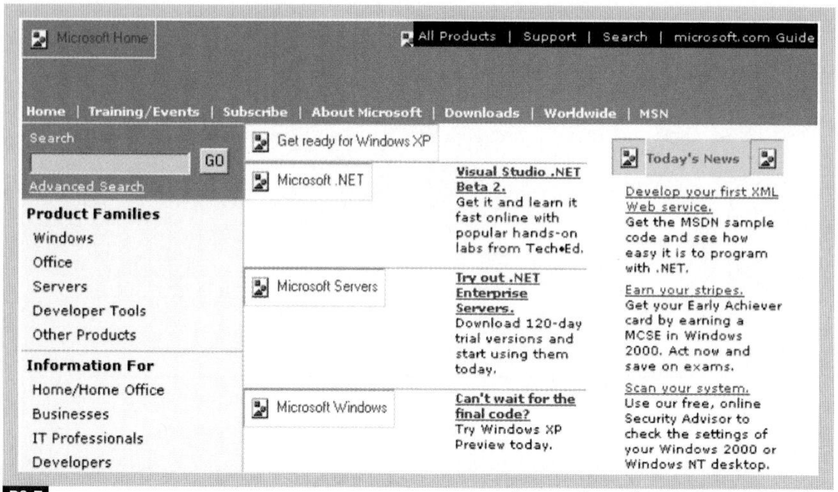

B9.7

(www.microsoft.com, August 26, 2001)

Figure B9.7

Microsoft uses a simple organizational scheme, good link labels, and clear text labels for all of its images, making it easier for customers with disabilities to access its Web pages.

People May Use the Web with Mobile Internet Devices • Although more and more mobile Internet devices are coming out on the market, there are still significant challenges in making Web sites that can be used on them. These challenges are important for you to solve, since most mobile phones now include Web browsers. The mobile device is the primary Internet browsing device in much of Asia, and this trend is soon likely to be true for the rest of the world. Compared to desktop computers, mobile devices are poor in terms of screen sizing, processing power, battery life, and input [see MOBILE SCREEN SIZING (M1) and MOBILE INPUT CONTROLS (M2) for details].

M1 **M2**

Currently only a few standards are in place for small devices, including the Handheld Device Markup Language (HDML), the Wireless Application Protocol (WAP), Compact HTML (CHTML), and XHTML Basic. The field is young and is still subject to rapid changes. For now, though, here are a few suggestions for how to improve your Web pages for small devices today:

- **Minimize the amount of text input required of customers.** Text input is quite difficult on small devices, even if they include a keyboard. You could help people by letting them enter personal information on a desktop computer, for example, and then associate that information with the device they're using. Make sure your site offers PREDICTIVE INPUT (H11) to minimize typing.

H11

Web Content Accessibility Guidelines

The World Wide Web Consortium (W3C) has developed a set of ten simple tips for improving the accessibility of your Web site. Keep in mind that these are simply stepping stones toward accessibility, and following all of these does not guarantee complete accessibility. The full Web page is available at w3.org/WAI/References/QuickTips.

1. **Images and animations.** Use the <alt> attribute to describe the function of each visual element.

2. **Image maps.** Use the client-side map and text for hot spots.

3. **Multimedia.** Provide captioning and transcripts of audio, and descriptions of video.

4. **Hypertext links.** Use text that makes sense when read out of context. For example, avoid saying simply, "Click here."

5. **Page organization.** Use headings, lists, and consistent structure. Use CSS for layout and style where possible.

6. **Graphs and charts.** Summarize or use the <longdesc> attribute.

7. **Scripts, applets, and plug-ins.** Provide alternative content in case active features are inaccessible or unsupported.

8. **Frames.** Use the <noframes> element and meaningful titles.

9. **Tables.** Make line-by-line reading sensible. Summarize.

10. **Check your work.** Validate. Use the tools, checklists, and guidelines at w3.org/TR/WCAG.

- **Do not rely exclusively on images for navigation.** When you do use images, include the <alt> attribute for them.

- **Use the <title> attribute for links,** as discussed in OBVIOUS LINKS (K10). Doing so provides an alternative name for links that some devices and browsers can use.

- **Use DISTINCTIVE HTML TITLES (D9) on each Web page.** These titles are likely to be at the top of the device, describing the page. They need to be short enough to fit on a small display, but descriptive.

- **Put the most important information at the top of each page.** Because portable-device screens are so small, important information should be placed ABOVE THE FOLD (I2), and in this case the fold is quite limiting.

- **Provide alternatives for scripts, applets, and plug-ins.** Not all devices and Web browsers will be able to run Java applets, play sound files, and show Macromedia Flash content. Providing alternative but similar content will let more customers use your Web site.

Use Style Sheets to Separate Content from Presentation • When HTML was first created, it mixed content with presentation. For example, HTML files would contain information about which text should be bold, what size fonts should be, and so on. Furthermore, to achieve a desired layout, Web designers often resorted to (mis)using tables or using hacks like transparent images.

Although this approach allowed designers to create pixel-perfect Web sites, it also adversely affected accessibility. Screen readers for people who were blind would often read out much of this hidden markup, leading to confusion. For people with poor eyesight, this approach made it hard to adjust the fonts and colors to make things easier to read.

Rather than mixing this kind of presentation information with your content, we advocate using STYLE SHEETS (D11) to separate the two. With style sheets, all of your content is kept in regular HTML files, and all of the information about layout, sizing, fonts, and background colors is specified in a separate style sheet file. Using style sheets is perhaps the single most useful thing you can do to make your Web site more accessible to people with visual disabilities.

Style sheets can help you improve accessibility in other ways as well. See STYLE SHEETS (D11) for more information.

Usability Testing Targeted at Customers Who Are Blind

In 2005, Mankoff, Fait, and Tran ran a study to understand the relative effectiveness of automated tools, expert reviews by designers with and without a screen reader, and remote usability testing with blind users. By comparing these four approaches to an actual laboratory study, they found that having multiple developers do an expert review with a screen reader was the most successful technique for finding usability problems, discovering roughly 50 percent of the problems identified by the laboratory study. Surprisingly, the remote study with blind users was fairly ineffective. However, the researchers note that the best approach is to use a combination of techniques, since only 50 percent of the usability problems were found with any single technique.

Accessibility Tools

There are a great number of online tools for improving the accessibility of your Web site. The Web Accessibility Initiative, part of the World Wide Web Consortium, maintains a comprehensive list of tools at w3.org/WAI/ER/existingtools.html. Here's a short list of some useful tools:

- WebXACT (webxact.watchfire.com) is an online tool that can help assess basic quality, accessibility, and privacy issues. You simply provide a Web address, and WebXACT will scan that page looking for common problems. It also contains a tool called *Bobby* that provides a large number of basic tips for improving accessibility.
- The Colorblind Web Page Filter (colorfilter.wickline.org) and Vischeck (vischeck.com) are two sites that let you see your Web pages the same way an individual with color deficiency would view them.
- Fangs (standards-schmandards.com/index.php?show/fangs) is a plug-in for the Mozilla Web browser that lets you emulate a screen reader, a tool used by people with visual impairments for reading out what is being displayed. Although it does not synthesize speech, Fangs will reorder the text and show you how much text a person with visual impairments would hear while browsing through your Web pages.

✳ SOLUTION

In designing your Web site, keep in mind accessibility for people with audio, visual, motor, and cognitive disabilities. Make the navigation and content both understandable and usable by employing good layout, clean visual design, straightforward text descriptions for all images and links, and alternative text-based formats for rich multimedia. Use features built into HTML that simplify accessibility.

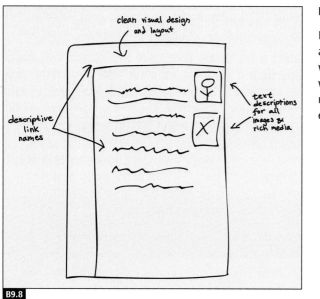

B9.8

Figure B9.8

Making your site accessible to people with disabilities will make your site more accessible to everyone.

❄ OTHER PATTERNS TO CONSIDER

C1 **F1** Focus first on making accessible the most important pages, including the HOMEPAGE PORTAL (C1) and QUICK-FLOW CHECKOUT (F1). In terms of naviga-

K2 **K10** tion, concentrate first on improving the accessibility of key navigation elements, including NAVIGATION BARS (K2), OBVIOUS LINKS (K10), and ACTION

K4 **K9** BUTTONS (K4). Use DESCRIPTIVE, LONGER LINK NAMES (K9) and FAMILIAR

K11 **D9** LANGUAGE (K11) for all links. Also use DISTINCTIVE HTML TITLES (D9) for every page.

Using the <alt> attribute for all images also improves responsiveness because people can click on linked images even before the image has

L2 downloaded. This feature is emphasized in FAST-LOADING IMAGES (L2).

I1 Align the content and navigation in a consistent GRID LAYOUT (I1). The

I2 most important content should always be near the top, ABOVE THE FOLD (I2).

I5 For pages with lots of text, use a FIXED SCREEN WIDTH (I5) to make it easier for customers to read and skim.

Making your site accessible also helps customers on mobile devices, but

M1 be sure to specifically address issues of MOBILE SCREEN SIZING (M1) and

M2 MOBILE INPUT CONTROLS (M2) to create even better interfaces for these important devices.

Creating a Powerful Homepage

The homepage is the most visited page on any Web site, and its design deserves serious attention so that it can accommodate the rich diversity of customers and their needs. This pattern group describes how to design a powerful homepage to fit the needs of your customers.

C1   HOMEPAGE PORTAL

C2   UP-FRONT VALUE PROPOSITION

C1 HOMEPAGE PORTAL

C1.1

(www.msnbc.com, June 16, 2006)

Figure C1.1

MSNBC gives readers a broad selection of topics to explore, while highlighting news of general interest. With its clearly distinguished links, customers need only a quick glance to see how to navigate the site. Subsections highlighted in the navigation bar show more detailed areas of interest. Readers can customize the news by entering a zip code to get local news.

❊ BACKGROUND

Used by almost every site and site genre [see Pattern Group A (Site Genres)], a homepage must satisfy the needs of all potential and current customers by establishing the company's identity while providing MULTIPLE WAYS TO NAVIGATE (B1). This pattern forms the core for homepage designs.

🔺 A

🔵 B1

❋ PROBLEM

The homepage of a Web site is the portal through which most visitors pass. A homepage must seduce visitors while simultaneously balancing many issues, including branding, navigation, content, and the ability to download quickly.

The homepage is usually the first thing that customers see on your site. This page is critical because, not only is it seen ten to over a thousand times more than any other page, but also it must provide an exceptional customer experience to seduce visitors to continue.

The space on the page, however, especially ABOVE THE FOLD (I2), is limited. It must be divided among the following goals: creating the right look and feel, building SITE BRAND (E1) and identity, providing valuable content, making navigation easy to use, establishing a cohesive and logical page layout, and delivering high performance. Creating a seductive page while striking a balance among all of these elements requires iterating and refining your page through testing. It also requires that you focus on building trust and providing value and options to your customer population.

Build Site Identity and Brand • Customers need to know that your site holds a valuable promise. They also need to know that it's a promise they can trust you to fulfill. And if the site is valuable, they will want to remember it for later, to use for themselves or to recommend to friends. This is what it means to build a positive identity and a valuable brand. Building a site brand requires presenting a promise of what your site offers, with the goal of attracting customers to come in, and earning their trust and respect by continually fulfilling that promise.

Attaining this goal means focusing on the company's UP-FRONT VALUE PROPOSITION (C2), SITE BRANDING (E1), and PRIVACY POLICIES (E4) using text, logos, photos, and illustrations to convey that you are trustworthy and professional. But the site itself must reinforce the brand by fulfilling the promise and building trust on every page.

Make a Positive First Impression with the Right Look and Feel • Visitors can be turned off by style alone, or by a homepage look and feel that says, "This site is not for me." Whether a site uses inappropriate colors and graphics, or the writing is unfamiliar or grating, customers respond negatively to a style that is not targeted to them. Neon green, screaming graphics and a skateboarding illustration might appeal to teens, but if you use a similar approach to represent a serious family issue or a conservative business, visitors will immediately question if they've come to the right place.

When you design for your target customers, you will get a positive response to your look and feel. Tune the site's style by showing it repeatedly to a dozen or more members of your intended audience. Conduct further testing to determine how *useful* your customers perceive it to be, as well as how *usable* it is. Although it takes time to conduct tests, avoiding early feedback will cost more in the long run when you have to redesign the site because it's not working.

Seduce with Content • Each customer makes a judgment within just a few seconds of entering a site. This is the amount of time you have to get the visitor's attention and keep it. Lively writing and visuals are essential, as is bringing compelling and timely content to the front page. This content can be news, enticing imagery, seductive navigation text, and/or personalization.

Organize content into headlines, summaries, and body. Entice visitors with a catchy HEADLINE AND BLURB (D3) or a CLEAR FIRST READ (I3), and follow through on the target page with the content body text. To make your design cost-effective, establishing a publishing system can help you update and rotate CONTENT MODULES (D2) automatically. Several commercial and open-source tools make this easier to do for larger Web sites.

Personalize Content If Possible • Visitors appreciate coming to a site tailored to their needs because it makes the site feel more useful, faster, and more personal. As a result, customers feel more important. However, a personalized site requires additional effort for visitors to use. This is especially true if customers are required to enter personalization information to use the site at all. Personalized sites, also known as *customized sites,* are also more difficult to design and develop, and they require more Web server and database resources, not to mention support for logins or cookies. But if the content is varied enough, personalization can help customers find what interests them and use the site more effectively.

A personalized homepage will contain CONTENT MODULES (D2) and use PERSONALIZED CONTENT (D4) to tailor the homepage to individual customers (see Figures C1.2 and C1.3). To be willing to provide this personal information, visitors need to trust you enough to tell you, directly or indirectly, about their desires and requests. You must use the information they provide ethically, for their benefit only, and they must trust that you will do so. To help gain their trust, be sure to follow the FAIR INFORMATION PRACTICES (E3) and to have a clear PRIVACY POLICY (E4) in place.

Figure C1.2

My Yahoo! shows how to build customer loyalty by personalizing everything from news and stock quotes to calendars.

(my.yahoo.com, November 14, 2001)

Balance Space for Brand against Space for Navigation • There is a trade-off between space used to communicate the site's value and differentiation, and space used to give customers navigation tools to find what they seek. We have made three observations that provide solutions:

E1

C2

1. Because the first read on the homepage is often the SITE BRANDING (E1) in the top left corner, and the second read is the UP-FRONT VALUE PROPOSITION (C2), both parts must be instantly clear to customers. If they aren't, customers may become doubtful, confused, or irritated enough to go elsewhere. Have your team focus on designing these two parts well, rather than on using more space on the homepage for branding.

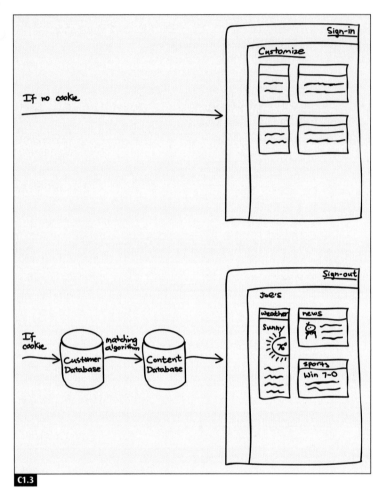

Figure C1.3

Personalized homepages are customized for each customer. This sketch shows how to return a default page for a new customer (top), and a personalized page for a returning customer (bottom).

2. Customers skim when they read on the Web, and they will skim your homepage as well, looking for succinct phrases and links they recognize and deem potentially valuable. Focus your design on finding the proper wording for these phrases, and on making them easy to skim. Be sure to use DESCRIPTIVE, LONGER LINK NAMES (K9).   **K9**

3. Every primary audience is really composed of many subgroups, and each subgroup needs answers to its specific questions. For example, if the primary audience consists of investors, you must answer the questions of both institutional investors and direct investors. Dedicate 95 percent of the area and links above the fold to the primary audience. Keep the remaining area and links for secondary groups.

3 If the primary audience is a products and services buyer, answer the questions of the decision maker, recommender, and technical reviewer. You can often take these customers to a subsidiary page where they can select their role to obtain more targeted information. Use the techniques described in Chapter 3 (Knowing Your Customers: Principles and Practices) to understand these roles for your customers and your site.

Make Navigation Easy to Use • The only way people can find their way around a site is by understanding the navigation. This means that all levels of visitors—with varying degrees of computer skills, domain expertise, and experience with your Web site—must quickly comprehend how to **B1** get around. Give your customers MULTIPLE WAYS TO NAVIGATE (B1) so that each customer has a way that fits his or her previous Web experience.

There are two essential rules to navigation. First, people know that some things on a Web page can be clicked on. *Do not make them guess what's clickable and what's not.* Second, people know that when they click on something, an action will take place. *Make those actions clear and predictable.*

Provide Strong Information Scent • **Information scent** is the perceived proximity to desired information. A good homepage provides multiple cues to improve information scent, such as meaningful text, seductive **K9 B2** images, DESCRIPTIVE, LONGER LINK NAMES (K9), BROWSABLE CONTENT (B2), and **B1** MULTIPLE WAYS TO NAVIGATE (B1). Strong information scent will help your customers easily understand how the information on your site is organized and bring them closer to the content they seek. See BROWSABLE **B2** CONTENT (B2) for more tips on improving information scent.

Provide a Cohesive and Logical Page Layout • A disorganized page layout can confuse site visitors. They need to be able to identify the most important objects to view immediately so that they know they're in the right place.

Create a homepage that makes it easy to understand what the Web site **I1** is about and where things are located. Implement a clean GRID LAYOUT (I1) **D1** in a PAGE TEMPLATE (D1) that organizes the entire page cohesively. Apply **I3** the CLEAR FIRST READS (I3) pattern. The **first read,** a concept from graphic design, is the single element that draws their attention first and pulls the Web page together. Having a clear first read on your homepage helps customers quickly and easily identify the most important information, and it provides a design focus for the page.

Place the most important navigation tools and content ABOVE THE FOLD (I2), making them visible so that the customer will not have to scroll down. People don't always realize that they can scroll down for more information, and they might miss out on things you want them to see right away, if those things are below the fold.

I2

Make the Homepage Download Quickly • You know all about this. If the homepage of a new site that you're visiting takes a very long time to load, you're likely to back out to another site.

Test your site to ensure that the homepage takes no more than a few seconds to download and appear in a browser. Here are some strategies for faster downloads:

- The images on your homepage are guaranteed to be the slowest the first time a visitor comes to your site because at that point the images are not cached yet. To combat this problem, take advantage of HTML POWER (L4) and use text as much as possible instead of graphics. HTML text is the first thing that downloads, so the visitor gets all the necessary text information without waiting for image downloads.

L4

- Some people will tell you that HTML text is ugly. Make the best of it by working with a Web-savvy graphic artist who can move your site to the next design level. This professional can choose the right complementary font colors, background colors, and font styles and make an exciting and dynamic homepage design.
- Use FAST-LOADING IMAGES (L2) to improve the speed of your site. Crop, shrink, reduce colors, and increase compression to make images smaller and faster to download.

L2

- For legacy designs, but not for new sites that can use STYLE SHEETS (D11) exclusively, use SEPARATE TABLES (L3) for page layout instead of one large HTML table. The problem with using a single large table is that it forces customers to wait until all of the images are loaded before they can see anything. If you separate your Web page into multiple tables, people can see some parts of the page as it is loading.

D11
L3

- On the main homepage, avoid slow-loading content such as sounds, splash screens, animations, and Java applets. If you include features such as these, not only will you make your main homepage slower to load, but you will risk having it look like Figure C1.4 to visitors who do not have the latest technologies installed on their computers.

Figure C1.4

Don't let this be your homepage. Unless there is an extremely compelling reason, keep Java applets, browser plug-ins, and other "bleeding-edge" technologies off of your main homepage.

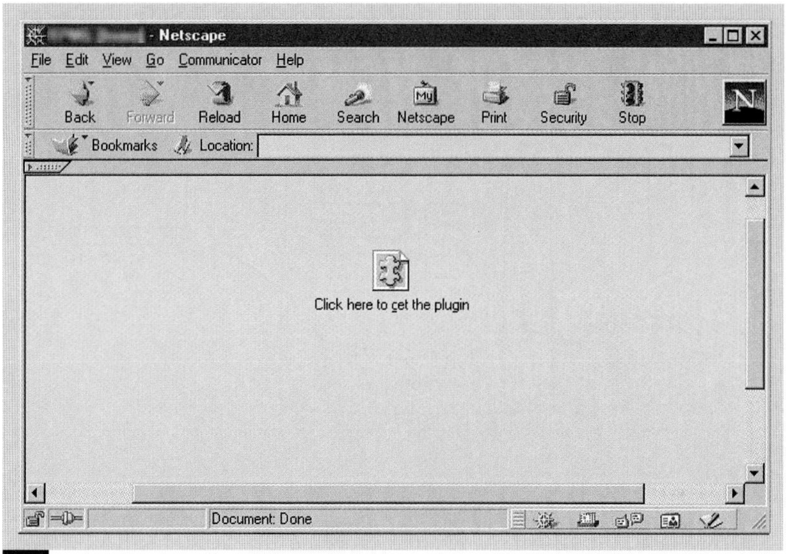

C1.4

☀ SOLUTION

On your homepage portal, establish and reinforce the value of your site with a strong, clearly stated promise that is fulfilled on every page of the site. Dedicate 95 percent of the area and links above the fold to the visitor groups that comprise 95 percent of the total visitor population. Keep the remaining area and links for visitor groups that make up the remaining 5 percent. Use additional links in the footer of the homepage to make explicit links for each group, including those in the 5 percent category. Build a homepage layout that provides strong cues to define navigation and content, and that downloads quickly. Test your homepage design to ensure that you have created the right look and feel—one that seduces visitors with content, regardless of whether it is personalized.

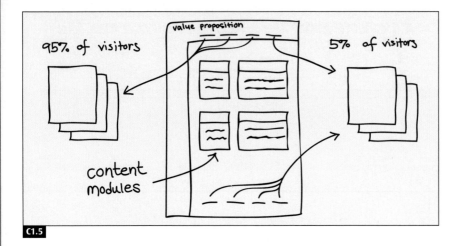

C1.5

Figure C1.5

Sketch out strong first impressions of your homepage with compelling titles and logos, and simple navigation.

✳ OTHER PATTERNS TO CONSIDER

On the homepage, clearly state the site's UP-FRONT VALUE PROPOSITION (C2), show the SITE BRANDING (E1), and provide links to the site's PRIVACY POLICY (E4).

Use a publishing system to automatically update and rotate CONTENT MODULES (D2) on the homepage. A personalized homepage will contain CONTENT MODULES (D2) and use PERSONALIZED CONTENT (D4) to tailor the homepage to individuals.

Make navigation easier and provide stronger information scent by creating consistent MULTIPLE WAYS TO NAVIGATE (B1) and by establishing your navigation design on the homepage. Create BROWSABLE CONTENT (B2) and use NAVIGATION BARS (K2), OBVIOUS LINKS (K10), ACTION BUTTONS (K4), DESCRIPTIVE, LONGER LINK NAMES (K9), and EMBEDDED LINKS (K7).

Create an easy-to-read homepage using a PAGE TEMPLATE (D1) and GRID LAYOUT (I1) with CLEAR FIRST READS (I3). Put the most important navigation tools and content ABOVE THE FOLD (I2).

Have a LOW NUMBER OF FILES (L1) on your homepage, and use FAST-LOADING IMAGES (L2) and HTML POWER (L4) to increase both its actual and its perceived performance.

Figure C2.1

Epicurious's value proposition—"for people who love to eat"—is reinforced by the images, navigation, and text on its homepage.

C2.1

(www.epicurious.com, June 16, 2006)

✳ BACKGROUND

The HOMEPAGE PORTAL (C1) must communicate the purpose of the site immediately and clearly. This pattern describes how to come up with that message.

✳ PROBLEM

On many Web sites, people often cannot tell upon arrival what the company or site offers.

If first-time visitors to your Web site don't see a clear, persuasive promise about what your company or site has to offer, they must figure it out on their own. Sometimes they leave the site right then and there because they cannot be bothered or they don't have time. Sometimes they surf around your site to find the answer, and sometimes they never do understand the site or company's full value, even if you have stated it on the homepage. This miscommunication can lead customers to undervalue your site or, worse, your entire company in their critical first moments of using your site. Changing a customer's initial impression later can cost you substantial money and time because you will have to earn their trust in order to reeducate them.

Even if you get it right, a value proposition alone will not make a site valuable. You must fulfill your promise on every page and reinforce it offline through your business practices. A compelling value proposition, along with these other elements, will create a positive impression with customers. This in turn will build trust and goodwill that you can enhance and expand over time. This pattern focuses on offering you a proven way to articulate a powerful promise.

To get there, you will need to work through many ideas and iterations until you create the strongest statement possible. Our solution provides a framework to make this development easier.

Requirements • The homepage is an advertisement for the rest of the site. It must sell customers on continuing their journey to explore, use, possibly purchase, and return again and again. As David Ogilvy reveals in his book *Ogilvy on Advertising,* an advertisement is much more effective when it persuasively promises a unique benefit. Not only are customers more likely to read it, but they are also more likely to purchase the product. For a Web site, that means visitors are more likely to explore and use your site.

Here's what you need (see Figure C2.2):

- A persuasive promise
- A unique offering
- Descriptive wording and images that are easily and quickly understood

Figure C2.2

These value propositions quickly communicate the types of services that the companies behind them offer. They speak broadly to the overall benefit, instead of one particular benefit, and they are easy to understand and quick to read. Read each and rate for yourself how persuasive and unique they are.

C2.2 (www.snapfish.com, February 11, 2002; www.techbargains.com, www.culturefinder.com, February 5, 2002)

Creating a persuasive and unique statement about what your company provides can be difficult without the right processes, people, and tools. To write and select the best promise, use creativity and brainstorming exercises to pull together an initial list of candidates. Customer research, which has been proven to help identify the most persuasive offer, can also help you shape your promise.

Exercise 1: Articulate the Value

Develop an initial list of value propositions. Invite everyone on the site design team to a brainstorming session, especially the most visionary, imaginative, and vocal members of the team. Seat everyone in a comfortable space that has a whiteboard on the wall. Ask this question: In ten words or less, what do we promise to our visitors that is persuasive and unique?

In a brainstorming session, no one passes judgment. Every statement is equally valuable, and no statement is wrong. Everything goes. Write down all suggestions, even if you don't like them, they're longer than your target number of words, or they're not unique or as persuasive as you would like. Continue for half an hour or more, if time permits. Then copy all the ideas onto a piece of paper or a computer for later review (this is not the final step).

Exercise 2: Select the Strongest Candidates

Distribute the list developed in the brainstorming session to a core group of marketing and business visionaries on the site design team. Ask them to identify the ten most persuasively articulated value propositions that make a unique offer. Tell them to be prepared to defend their choices. Convene a meeting to choose the ten best promises. To determine the best, ask these questions: Is this promise consistent with our strategic direction? Is it persuasive? Is it unique? If not, why not? Can it be improved? This meeting could easily take longer than the initial brainstorming session, so limit the time to a couple of hours to make the process manageable.

Research Project 1: Have Customers Nominate the Best

Now turn to your customer base and ask a sample of 100 customers to participate in a research survey to rate each of the team's ten chosen value propositions [for an overview of customer research methods, see Appendix A (Running Usability Evaluations)]. Ask customers to rate the promises for *importance*, from "not important at all" (0) to "very important" (10); and for *uniqueness*, from "not unique at all" (0) to "very unique" (10). From the results, identify the value propositions that averaged a 7 or higher in both importance and uniqueness. If none of the value propositions rates this high, go back to Exercise 1 and start over.

Research Project 2: Have Customers Select the Top Value Proposition

Turn to your customer base one more time (coordinate this test with other research to reduce time and costs) and ask a sample of 100 customers to choose their top choice from the highly rated value propositions found in the previous test, again based on its importance and uniqueness. The winner is the one that most appeals to your customers. Congratulations! You've got your value proposition.

Integrate Your Value Proposition into the Site • Now develop some sample designs that emphasize this new value proposition. Think about the different ways you can get your message across to customers in a quick, simple fashion (see Figure C2.3). Other patterns that will help include SITE BRANDING (E1) and CLEAR FIRST READS (I3).

C2.3   (www.ciena.com, July 2001)

Figure C2.3

Ciena's value propositions are integrated directly into the main logo and are some of the first things visitors will read.

✳ SOLUTION

Your value proposition is a site advertisement that must persuasively articulate your company's uniqueness. Use team brainstorming to develop ideas, and refine the best ideas into a list of the top ten candidates. To determine the best value proposition, ask your customers to rate each promise on importance and uniqueness. Place the value proposition next to your logo on the homepage for quick scanning and maximum exposure.

Figure C2.4

A customer's positive impression starts with a clear value proposition in the form of a persuasive and unique promise. By fulfilling the promise through a valuable Web site and trustworthy business practices, you can continue to build customer loyalty and a strong reputation through word of mouth.

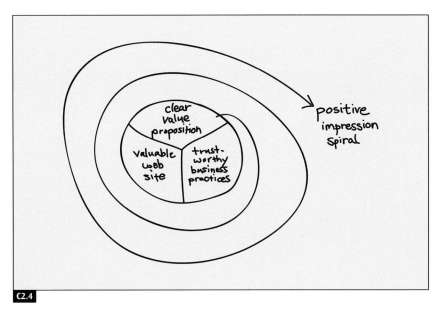

C2.4

✳ OTHER PATTERNS TO CONSIDER

 Integrate your value proposition with your SITE BRANDING (E1), making it a CLEAR FIRST READ (I3).

Writing and Managing Content D

In your Web site design, two of the big issues to sort out are how to manage large amounts of content, and how to make it presentable to all kinds of visitors. This pattern group presents an overview to help you create and manage your content effectively.

(http://news.yahoo.com, October 29, 2001)

Figure D1.1

This page template from the Yahoo! News homepage targets its database content to specific locations on the page.

❋ BACKGROUND

Many of the patterns in Pattern Group A (Site Genres) are based on database content, which allows information to be published dynamically to the site without individual files having to be moved to the server. The result is a streamlined publishing process and enhanced productivity. Even if a site is not database driven, customers come to expect images and text to be in the same place when they're moving around a site or returning to a particular page. You can organize your information into BROWSABLE CONTENT (B2), with CATEGORY PAGES (B8) and content pages. Each of these pages requires a template to describe its content. This pattern provides the solution.

A

B2 B8

✳ PROBLEM

A site that is not consistent from page to page is difficult for customers to navigate and hard for site managers to maintain. However, it is challenging to design Web pages to be consistent because not all pages are the same, and many will need some way to be updated.

Your homepage implicitly establishes a pattern for layout and design of your entire Web site, and from then on, customers expect to find key elements of the page in the same places on other pages. You can build a system that takes advantage of the HOMEPAGE PORTAL (C1) design by creating a family of page templates that all relate to one another but have their own variations.

Designing, editing, and publishing unique pages can be time-consuming and tedious. Even if content does not come from a database, a standard design benefits the site team by giving everyone a system to work within, and therefore less work. Often page designers are not the same people who write the content. Separating the design from the writing helps the process by letting each team focus on its strong suit, but it makes a consistent approach across the board all the more important. This pattern provides the solution that addresses the needs of the site team and the customers.

Build a Page Template by Using Grids • People read along vertical and horizontal lines. If you use implied lines on your page designs, as described in GRID LAYOUT (I1), customers can skim and read more quickly than when objects and text are not aligned. Help your visitors read more easily by using grids as the backbone of every template you build.

Define Global and Individual Page Templates • Keep the basic graphic design structure the same throughout your site. Customers remember where navigation tools and content appear from page to page, so keeping these places consistent will make the site easier to use. Create a page template by setting aside areas of every page for navigation, content, and CONSISTENT SIDEBARS OF RELATED CONTENT (I6) (see Figure D1.2). Each area needs rules about what to put in that space. The template becomes especially important when multiple teams are updating different parts of a site.

Global page templates describe the overall page structure and layout of every page on a Web site. Included are navigation elements at the top of the page template, like SITE BRANDING (E1), NAVIGATION BARS (K2), and SEARCH ACTION MODULES (J1), as well as supplementary elements often found at the bottom, like ABOUT US (E5), PRIVACY POLICY (E4),

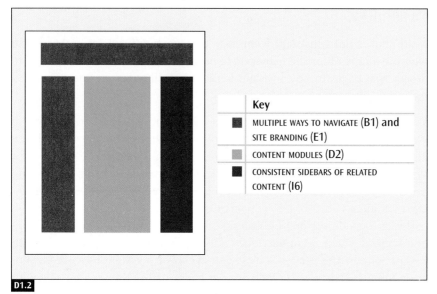

D1.2

Figure D1.2

Page templates
define areas for navi-
gation, branding,
content, and related
links on every page.

FREQUENTLY ASKED QUESTIONS (H7), and CONTEXT-SENSITIVE HELP (H8). Depending
on the site genre, you might have other elements as well, such as a SHOPPING
CART (F3) or an ACCOUNT MANAGEMENT (H4) link.

Individual page templates build on global page templates, describing
specific types of pages. For example, you might have individual page
templates for your CATEGORY PAGES (B8) (see Figure D1.3), CLEAN PRODUCT
DETAIL (F2) pages, and news articles.

Be consistent with how you adjust your layout to browser window
resizing, using either EXPANDING SCREEN WIDTH (I4) or FIXED SCREEN WIDTH (I5).
Key items must be ABOVE THE FOLD (I2), just as in the HOMEPAGE PORTAL (C1)
pattern.

CONTENT MODULES (D2) contain the live content that turns templates into
actual pages. Either new content will appear as you publish it, or more
sophisticated personalization will target special content to each customer.
The page template is the skeleton that holds everything together, and the
content modules are the muscles and flesh that bring life to a page.

CONTENT MODULES (D2) also need to be part of the basic graphic design of
the page. However, the length of a content module can range from a few
lines to several pages because content modules can be retrieved dynamically from files or from a database. Because of the way HTML works, if
one content module has too much information, it will become extremely
long and lead to an unbalanced visual design.

Figure D1.3

Amazon.com uses a global page template to maintain consistency across the entire site, and individual page templates to maintain consistency for categories of pages. The global page template is first designed to have the site branding, tab row, search action module, and sidebars appear in the same locations. Individual page templates are then created from the global page template. Both of these screen shots show examples of category pages created from the same individual page template.

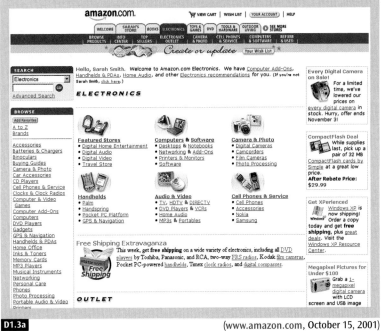

D1.3a   (www.amazon.com, October 15, 2001)

D1.3b   (www.amazon.com, October 15, 2001)

Set standards for the length of the content or the length of every page. For text-based articles you can use multiple pages, which let you break up a long piece of writing into more readable chunks. If your site is supported by advertising, readable chunks of text broken into pieces across several pages will also provide more ad impressions. Customers also need a way to view the entire article in a single PRINTABLE PAGE (D8) so that they can easily print it if they want.

Use Other Patterns to Build Templates • Different global and individual page templates will show some variation. The goal is to design for small multiples of differences, by creating templates that are basically the same but with small differences, to suit particular customer and business needs.

For example, Figure D1.4 shows two different pages from Banana Republic's Web site. The pages are essentially the same in terms of color, layout, and navigation structure, but they are slightly different in terms of the NAVIGATION BAR (K2) and REUSABLE IMAGES (L5).

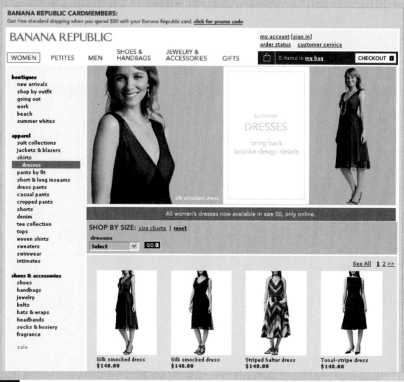

Figure D1.4a, b

On Banana Republic's site, the basic template remains the same in each section. Small variations address particular visitor needs, yet reinforce the overall design.

(www.bananarepublic.com, June 16, 2006)

Figure D1.4a, b

(*Continued*)

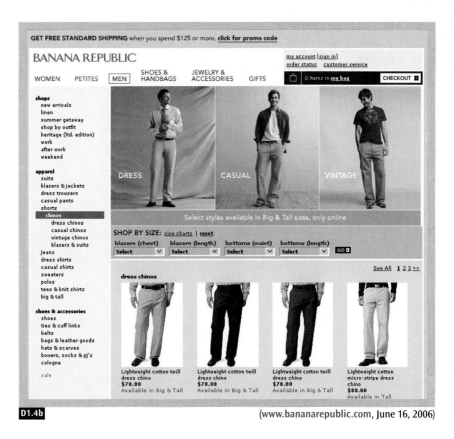

D1.4b

(www.bananarepublic.com, June 16, 2006)

✳ SOLUTION

Use a grid layout to help define a global template that includes the basic navigation elements, major content areas, and any areas for related content. For each kind of page, define an individual template that specifies content size limits for images and text. Each individual template should use the global template as part of its structure.

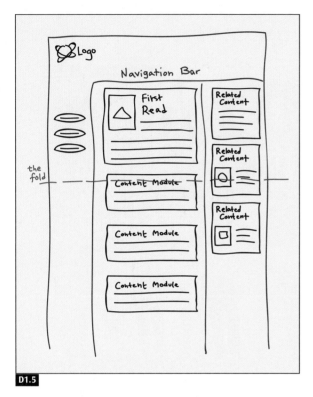

Figure D1.5

Use a grid layout to align content modules in your templates.

`D1.5`

✳️ OTHER PATTERNS TO CONSIDER

In the global page template, make the GRID LAYOUT (I1), as well as CLEAR FIRST READS (I3) and the NAVIGATION BAR (K2), consistent. Also consider including an ABOUT US (E5) page, a PRIVACY POLICY (E4), FREQUENTLY ASKED QUESTIONS (H7), and CONTEXT-SENSITIVE HELP (H8) at the bottom of the page template. Choose between EXPANDING SCREEN WIDTH (I4) and FIXED SCREEN WIDTH (I5). Employ templates that use REUSABLE IMAGES (L5) and a LOW NUMBER OF FILES (L1).

Within each individual page template file, create section-specific CONTENT MODULES (D2), and use CONSISTENT SIDEBARS OF RELATED CONTENT (I6) and FAST-LOADING IMAGES (L2). Separate templates that incorporate MOBILE SCREEN SIZING (M1), MOBILE INPUT CONTROLS (M2), and LOCATION-BASED SERVICES (M3) will be needed if you choose to support your site on Mobile Web platforms.

Figure D2.1

Content modules make it easy to update and display content. On the **My Monster** homepage, visitors can select which content modules they wish to display. Not all sites will need this level of personalization, though.

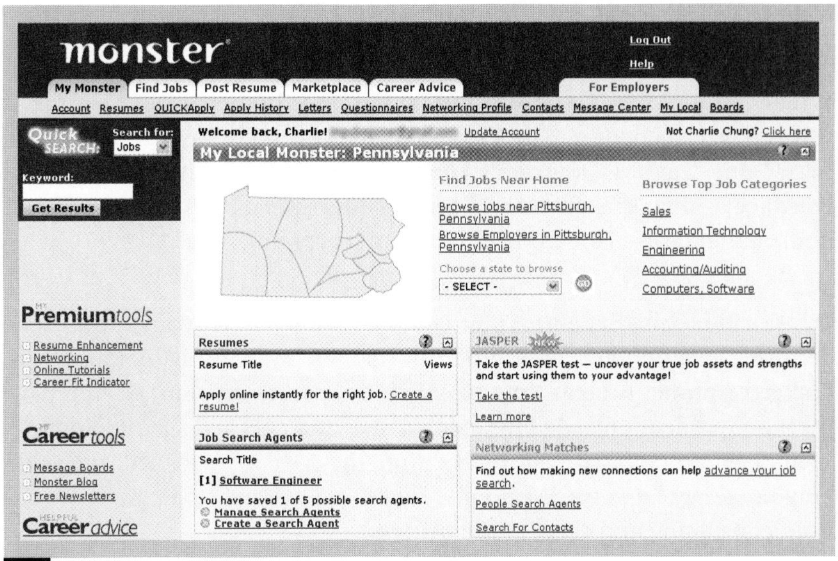

`D2.1`

(my.monster.com, June 16, 2006)

✳ BACKGROUND

In BROWSABLE CONTENT (B2) we provided a solution for finding content on a site, and in PAGE TEMPLATES (D1) we described how to present page elements in a consistent and easy-to-use manner. This pattern describes content modules, a key component of every page template and a way of managing the publishing process.

✳ PROBLEM

Without a good system, publishing and managing large volumes of content are time-consuming and error-prone processes.

When customers visit your site and find that the homepage is the same as it was a week ago, or maybe a month ago, they might say, "Nothing new here!" and leave. If you don't keep the site updated, it's probably not worth revisiting. Customers will find a better site, one that has the latest information. Fresh content keeps customers coming back.

Create a Publishing System • You might be tempted to let your site go stale because updating and publishing information by hand is tedious, slow, and error prone. It takes time to create or acquire content. A Web page must be recoded, uploaded, tested, revised, and checked again before the final page can be published. By the time the page is published, the news may no longer be news. Without a publishing system, updating a site is a time-consuming and error-prone process.

A publishing system can simplify the process if you're willing to plan ahead. These systems use a content database to hold and publish content. This way you can avoid recoding each page that has content when the content changes. The publishing system can use the file system or a real database. Different levels of engineering are required for each, but the net effect is the same. It all depends on the amount of content on your site and the kinds of features you want to provide to your customers. Whereas small sites can use files to store articles, more sophisticated and larger sites should use a database, especially if PERSONALIZED CONTENT (D4) is provided. A sophisticated system might store content in a database, have the data (such as the date) automatically trigger updates, and then push new content through. Either way, a publishing system can save large amounts of time.

When you create a publishing system, you will want to include content modules. These are the active areas on a page that change whenever new content comes online. Designing content modules into a site's pages makes updates quick and easy. Content modules and their component pieces deliver the power to integrate new content pages into an existing browsing structure. They can also be used to promote new related content, as well as to provide highly PERSONALIZED CONTENT (D4) tailored for each individual site visitor.

To create an article for a content module, define its content HEADLINES AND BLURBS (D3), body copy, reference information, byline, related content, related products, and related links (see Figures D2.2 and D2.3). These pieces can then be connected to a specific content module in a specific page that reassembles the content on demand (see Figure D2.4).

Define Where You Want to Position Content on a Page • Creating a PAGE TEMPLATE (D1) with content modules makes it easy to add new pages and plug in new content, saving you the trouble of trying to figure out how to lay out the document every time.

To give customers potentially useful information that is related to the current item, make space on the side for CONSISTENT SIDEBARS OF RELATED CONTENT (I6). These items can be directly related to the current article, or indirectly related through the current content category. Related links can also help keep customers engaged longer, clicking on related articles or products.

To hook visitors into related articles, use the headline from the related content and perhaps a short description or blurb to explain the content of the related article. These HEADLINES AND BLURBS (D3) entice customers to click through to the full article. Related links can be grouped by subject or by whether they are EXTERNAL LINKS (K8) to other Web sites. Or if there are only a few of them, related links can just be thrown together in no particular order.

Figure D2.2

Store this information in all your content files or content database records. Program your publication system to use the information to publish content pages and related links on other content pages.

Figure D2.3

Here's how information might look in a content file or record.

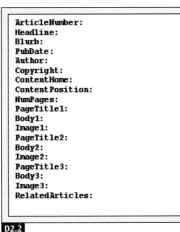

```
ArticleNumber:
Headline:
Blurb:
PubDate:
Author:
Copyright:
ContentHome:
ContentPosition:
NumPages:
PageTitle1:
Body1:
Image1:
PageTitle2:
Body2:
Image2:
PageTitle3:
Body3:
Image3:
RelatedArticles:
```

D2.2

```
ArticleNumber: 12345
Headline: For Whom Pacific Bell
Tolls
Blurb: Long derided for poor serv…
PubDate: 20010511
Author: Alexander Graham
Copyright: 2001 NewArch Media, Inc.
ContentHome: Utilities
ContentPosition: Middle
NumPages: 3
PageTitle1: Once for the Money
Body1: Ipso facto decorum unum…
Image1: http://www.newarch.com/img…
PageTitle2: Two for the Show
Body2: Ipso facto decorum unum…
Image2: http://www.newarch.com/img…
PageTitle3: Three to Get Ready
Body3: Ipso facto decorum unum…
Image3: http://www.newarch.com/img…
RelatedArticles: 56789, 98765
```

D2.3

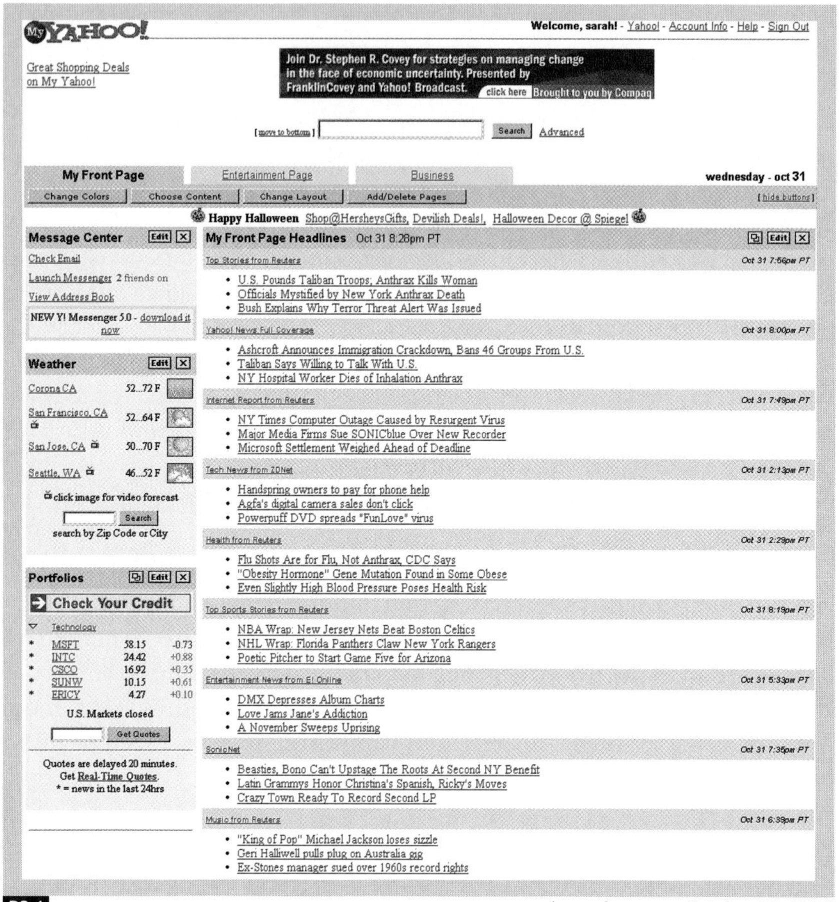

Figure D2.4

My Yahoo! provides many types of content modules, including news, stocks, and weather. Weather always appears in a content module on the left, and news appears in the middle. Short headlines entice customers to click through to read more.

D2.4

(my.yahoo.com, October 31, 2001)

Create an Administration Page • Building a content module publishing tool reduces the time and effort it takes to publish content. All you need is a Web-based form that includes all the content fields plus publication date and their location in the site. This form lets you publish faster and more often (see Figure D2.5).

Figure D2.5

eDealFinder.com helps people find special deals and coupons. These two administration pages show how new advertisements are added to the site (a) and how affiliate Web pages, logos, descriptions, search keywords, and so on are managed (b).

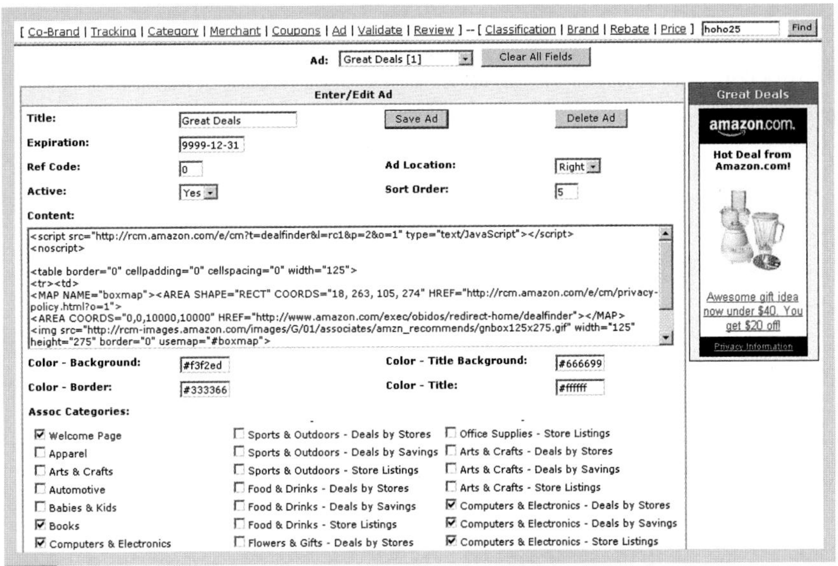

D2.5a

(www.edealfinder.com, November 28, 2001)

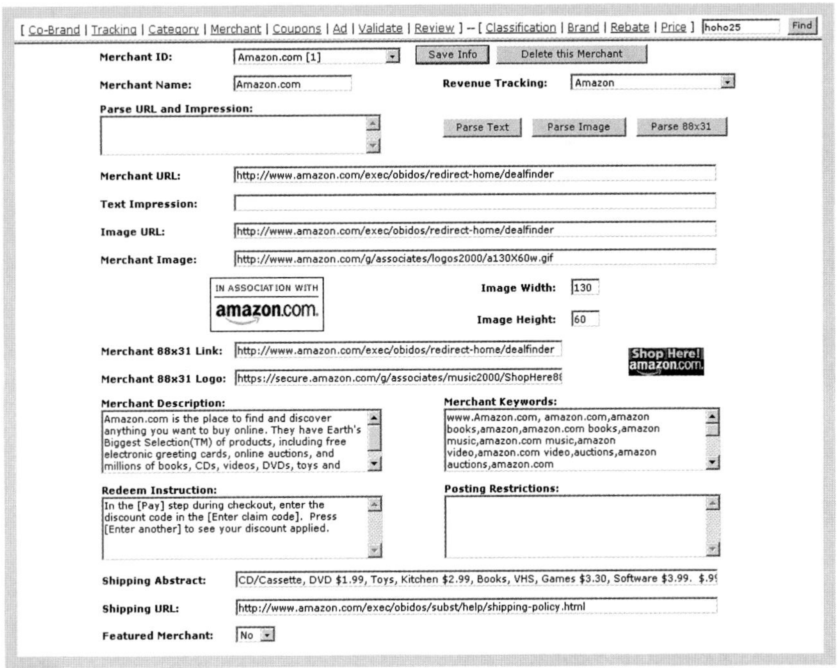

D2.5b

(www.edealfinder.com, November 28, 2001)

✳ SOLUTION

Define content locations in page templates. Organize all content into the file system or into a content database. Manage content from an administration page.

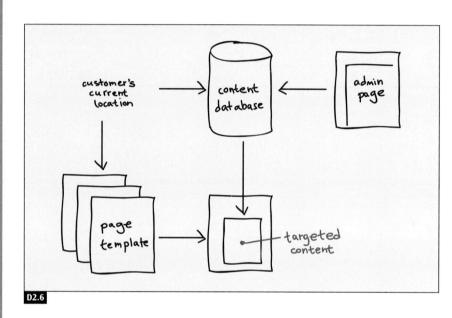

Figure D2.6

The customer's location in a site is used to target content to content modules in a page template.

✳ OTHER PATTERNS TO CONSIDER

Define locations where content is targeted on each PAGE TEMPLATE (D1). These content modules can be articles, CONSISTENT SIDEBARS OF RELATED CONTENT (I6), or EXTERNAL LINKS (K8). Give visitors a hook into related articles by defining HEADLINES AND BLURBS (D3) for each piece of content, and put those headlines and blurbs on related pages. Organize content in a content database, and use it to publish general visitor content, as well as PERSONALIZED CONTENT (D4) if personalization is part of the site. Sites with personalization can also offer visitors DIRECT MANIPULATION (H9) capability to define which content modules they want to see and where the modules should appear on the page.

Figure D3.1

The World News site uses database-driven headlines and blurbs to draw readers' attention to the full article on a page deeper in the site.

D3.1

(www.worldnews.com, June 16, 2006)

❊ BACKGROUND

For NEWS MOSAICS (A2), headlines and blurbs are critical ways to drive reader interest. COMMUNITY CONFERENCE (A3) sites can take excerpts from MESSAGE BOARDS (D5) and BLOGS (A12) and make them blurbs on the HOMEPAGE PORTAL (C1) to highlight what's taking place in the discussion forums. ENABLING INTRANETS (A11) can highlight new events, services, or places where the company is mentioned in the media.

In PAGE TEMPLATES (D1), we defined the structure of each page and how CONTENT MODULES (D2) can be used to publish new content. To draw people into these detailed pages, though, each piece of content needs a hook in the form of a headline. This pattern forms the core of the content hook.

✳ PROBLEM

Content pages need short, descriptive headlines and blurbs to hook customers into clicking for more content deeper on a site. These hooks also need to be published elsewhere on a site so that visitors will be able to see them.

On most sites, visible content is only the tip of the iceberg. A site's content cannot be revealed in its entirety on just one page. Finding all the content that is buried in a site is a challenge. Customers need MULTIPLE WAYS TO NAVIGATE (B1) to find their way around. In addition, from their experience with newspapers and magazines, people are accustomed to seeing headlines and blurbs to introduce every story when they scan for content.

B1

In fact, headlines and introductory paragraphs provide tantalizing leads to pull visitors into the text. According to the INVERTED-PYRAMID WRITING STYLE (D7), when an article's conclusion is put in its headline, and the main conclusions are put in the beginning paragraphs, the reader is pulled in to read more.

D7

The style of writing a headline and a short introduction, with each piece hooking the reader further into the story, is what we call *headlines and blurbs.* Use blurbs to give customers a quick grasp of the content. These blurbs can consist of the first few lines of an article, placed on an opening page to tantalize readers about what lies ahead. Or they can be sentences that stand on their own and provide a complete thought.

The sections that follow present some guidelines for writing headlines and blurbs.

Write a Hook • For both headline and blurb, think about what makes the content *important, unique,* and *valuable* to the reader. Think about why visitors would want to read your content. Will they learn something new? Get a bargain? Have a good laugh? Meet people with the same hobbies? Look at your subject matter from the reader's perspective, and then write directly to the reader, with a promise of value.

Headlines and blurbs have a particular structure on Web pages. **Headlines** are typically a sentence fragment, roughly ten words or less so that they can appear in large type in a small space. A headline articulates the hook in the shortest form possible. The **blurb** is a continuation of the headline, providing details of the customer benefit, reinforcing what is important and unique about the content. Blurbs have to be short and precise, not more than one or two sentences.

Using a DISTINCTIVE HTML TITLE (D9) as the headline is possible if the title is descriptive enough. By employing the INVERTED-PYRAMID WRITING STYLE (D7)

D9
D7

when writing articles, you can pull a blurb from the first paragraph of the article that is also the conclusion.

Try the following exercise: Write out three to five sets of headlines and blurbs and test them with your team and, if possible, with real customers. They will tell you if you have hit upon what's valuable to them. Continue shaping your message until you can succinctly articulate what customers find important and unique. Now you've created a reason for visitors to click through and experience more of your Web site. The final step is to formulate the hook as a finished headline and blurb.

Put Headlines and Blurbs in the Content Database • Writing one headline and blurb for each longer piece of text gives you the capability to place a reference to the text anywhere on your site, especially on the HOMEPAGE **C1** **D1** PORTAL (C1) and other key PAGE TEMPLATES (D1). Referencing content on other pages becomes as simple as referencing the article number. The code on related pages looks up the article number and places the headline, blurb, and content link in the page. Figure D3.2 shows an example of how the content for a piece of text might be broken up into a database-compatible form.

Put Headlines and Blurbs into Various Content Modules throughout the Site • To bring content to the fore, you must highlight it throughout the site, as headlines and as sidebars. Promote content pages using headlines and blurbs **D2** **C1** in CONTENT MODULES (D2) on the HOMEPAGE PORTAL (C1) (see Figure D3.3), and **I6** in CONSISTENT SIDEBARS OF RELATED CONTENT (I6) (see Figure D3.4).

If there are only a few headlines and blurbs, just use CHRONOLOGICAL **B6** ORGANIZATION (B6). A chronological structure makes it easier to find what's new, on the basis of the date.

Figure D3.2

A content file or record might show information in this way in a database.

```
ArticleNumber: 12345
Headline: For Whom Pacific Bell
Tolls
Blurb: Long derided for poor
customer service by its DSL
subscribers, Pacific Bell has
continued to over-commit on DSL
installations as it tries to beat
the cable industry in the broadband
Internet services business. So why
is Pacific Bell still a good
investment?
PubDate: 20010511
Author: Alexander Graham
Copyright: 2001 NewArch Media, Inc.
ContentHome: Utilities
...
```

D3.2

D3.3

Figure D3.3

The Pew Internet & American Life Project highlights recent research results in a series of headlines and blurbs. In fact, this whole page is an enticement to go deeper into the site.

(www.pewinternet.org, June 16, 2006)

If there are lots of headlines, organize them by related topic. Newspapers, for example, have categories such as national news, local news, sports, and entertainment. Some companies have categories such as new products, company information, and a contact section. Within each section, use a CHRONOLOGICAL ORGANIZATION (B6).

B6

Figure D3.4

The Children's Place promotes products on its Web site with headlines and blurbs in content modules, providing a way to highlight new products easily.

✳ SOLUTION

Write a hook, in the form of a headline and blurb, that articulates why the content is important and unique to the visitor. Store these headlines and blurbs in the content database, along with the longer article, so that they can be targeted to content modules on different pages.

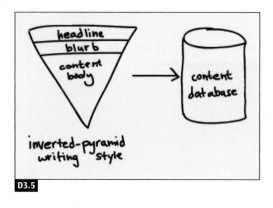

Figure D3.5

Use the inverted-pyramid writing style to write your headlines and blurbs.

D3.5

✳ OTHER PATTERNS TO CONSIDER

Use the headline you create for the content as the DISTINCTIVE HTML TITLE (D9) for the target page containing the longer article. You might also use the blurb as the first paragraph in an article, as part of the INVERTED-PYRAMID WRITING STYLE (D7). Put related headlines and blurbs in CONSISTENT SIDEBARS OF RELATED CONTENT (I6).

D9

D7

I6

Figure D4.1

One of the first sites to personalize content for each visitor, My Yahoo! provides news, weather, stock quotes, e-mail, and many other customizable options.

D4.1

(my.yahoo.com, October 31, 2001)

❈ BACKGROUND

 PERSONAL E-COMMERCE (A1), NEWS MOSAICS (A2), and all the other site genres can benefit from personalized content. PAGE TEMPLATES (D1) provide the framework for CONTENT MODULES (D2) and HEADLINES AND BLURBS (D3), two of several mechanisms for displaying personalized content. This pattern provides the solution for personalizing content to individual visitors.

✳ PROBLEM

Personalized information can be more useful to people than generic information. However, engineering a dynamic site can produce less-than-satisfactory results if the basic structures and designs are not in place first.

Dynamic content targeting is a powerful way to provide individualized content. In contrast to a one-size-fits-all approach, dynamic content targeting gives customers a site tailored specifically to their needs. However, designing and implementing a system to manage all the content types for all customers can be daunting, requiring significant database and algorithm development. Yet it can also be of great value to customers, giving them another reason to return to your Web site. If done well, a dynamic, personalized site can be a significant competitive advantage. The framework that we provide here, used in conjunction with other patterns in the book, makes personalization a more manageable development process.

This pattern describes two forms of dynamic content targeting. The first form uses information explicitly entered by customers to dynamically create targeted content. We call this **intentional personalization.** The second form uses information about where visitors go and what they do on a site to target content to their needs. We call this **automatic personalization.** These approaches can be used separately or together.

By targeting content using the methods we describe, in conjunction with other content management techniques, like PAGE TEMPLATES (D1) and CONTENT MODULES (D2), you can make personalized content an integral part of your site.

Create a Site with Intentional Personalization

Personalization gives customers the power and satisfaction of building their own environment. To make this possible, a site needs categorized and scored content. Using a targeting engine, you can target relevant content to each customer profile. See Figures D4.2 and D4.3 for examples before and after targeting is applied.

Require Minimal Personalization Up Front • Visitors often do not know that they can personalize a site (or that they might want to) until after they have spent some time on it. If you require visitors to your site to enter personal information before they're comfortable with the site, they'll shy away altogether. Before you find out anything about your visitors, give them a sampling of what the site has to offer. For example, many e-commerce sites list top-selling FEATURED PRODUCTS (G1), thereby letting visitors know what other customers are purchasing.

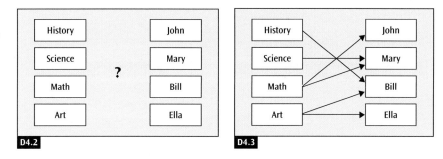

Figure D4.2

Before targeting your content to people, categorize it and decide which profile format you will use for each customer. If visitors say they're interested in art, for example, the system will show them content that is categorized under the heading *Art*.

Figure D4.3

Once customers have completed their profiles, you can target content to each person, creating a personalized site.

Figure D4.4 shows a more sophisticated example. My Yahoo! provides newcomers with basic content, such as stock prices and headline news. It also places a large notice in the center that tells people they can create personalized content whenever they want to.

The upshot of all that we've said here is this: Don't force people to personalize your site before they're ready, because they may not want to spend the time if they can't see what's in it for them.

Invite Visitors to Personalize • People need a simple and enticing offer that invites them to click through to the personalization menu. The invitation must be obvious and clear so that they can't miss it. Entice them by providing an idea of what they'll be able to do once they personalize the site. For example, Figure D4.5 shows how Monster takes a different approach from that of Yahoo! The site has little value for individual visitors until they go

Figure D4.4

First-time visitors to My Yahoo! see a simple page that offers basic content, as well as a note to let them know that they can personalize what they see.

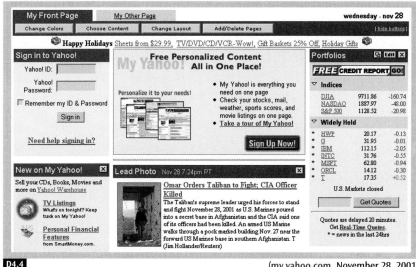

(my.yahoo.com, November 28, 2001)

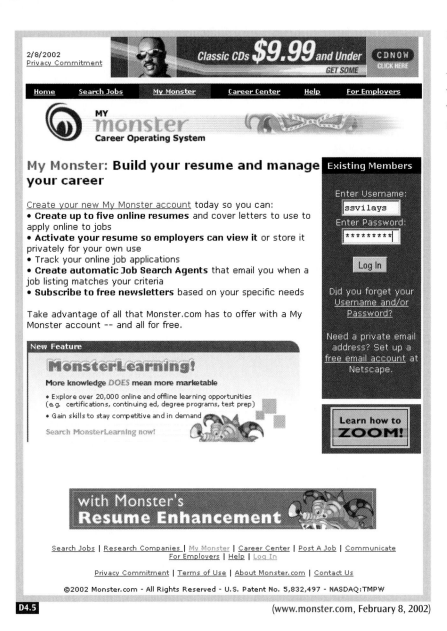

(www.monster.com, February 8, 2002)

Figure D4.5

Monster makes clear the benefits people will get if they do what it takes to personalize the site.

through the personalization process, so it tells them up front what the benefits will be. Lands' End invites people to personalize its site by creating a fun and interactive experience with a virtual model (see Figure D4.6).

Categorize Content • Let customers choose the content they want to see on their personalized pages so that there's no ambiguity about what

Figure D4.6

Customers are invited to create a virtual model at this fun part of the Lands' End site. The model gives visitors a sophisticated and personalized shopping experience.

D4.6

(www.landsend.com, February 18, 2002)

information interests them. Arrange content by subject, date, or task, depending on how it's organized. Use the same information architecture designed for BROWSABLE CONTENT (B2) to lay out the options because this structure will make sense to customers and provide consistency with the information structure of the site. Keep in mind that not all content needs to be strictly related to one category in a site. For example, news about technology could be categorized under either "news" or "technology."

Use People's Background Information • If customers are willing to identify who they are, where they live, how old they are, what they've done in life, and/or what type of business they're in, you can use this information to make inferences about their interests. This level of detail can be much more enlightening and useful to you than the information gathered from surfing habits. For example, you can provide a great deal of local information for site visitors in the United States—such as weather, news, and traffic conditions—just on the basis of their zip codes (see Figure D4.7).

D4.7

Figure D4.7

After customers fill out a very short form about their backgrounds, MSNBC's Web site offers local news, weather, and personalized stock quotes.

(www.msnbc.com, June 16, 2006)

Map Content to Each Visitor • Establish the fundamental selection criteria for how people receive personalized content. To map people's interests to content, devise a schema showing the relationships between the two. The schema can be as simple as a map between areas of a site and areas of expressed interest (see Figure D4.3). Or the schema can use a map of content zones and personality profile vectors (see Figure D4.8).

Create a Site with Automatic Personalization

With automatic personalization, people's interests are inferred on the basis of the actions they take, such as pages they visit, links they click on, and products they buy. Such inferences can lead to erroneous assumptions about visitors' interests, however, because people's intentions may be different from the actions they perform. For example, if a visitor looking for recipes mistakenly navigates to an area of a site focused on cooking classes instead of recipes, her profile will indicate an interest in cooking classes, which may not be true.

Create a Scoring System • Devise a system that automatically matches the needs of the audience to the content you have available. The basic idea is to divide customers into groups, on the basis of a shared characteristic, and to look for trends within those groups. It is assumed that, because customers within a group are similar in one way, they may be similar in other ways. For example, if Victoria is placed in a group with 20 other people, 15 of whom really like the novel *The Scarlet Letter,* the odds are that she will like it too.

Figure D4.8

A schema designed to show the relationship between people's interests and site content may be based on a mapping algorithm that uses personality vectors and content regions. This example shows that Bill is a beginner with computers, but more advanced in finance.

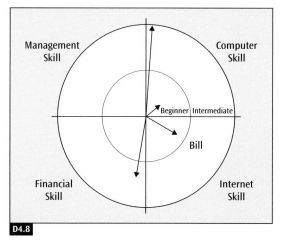

Use one or more of the following scoring methods to automatically divide customers into groups:

- **Rank.** An ordered list of how the students in a class ranked on an exam, for example.
- **Top rank.** A list of the top three scores only.
- **Threshold score.** A list of only those students who scored over a particular percentage on the exam.
- **Required attributes.** A list of all students who answered a particular question correctly.

Here's how a scoring system would work. Suppose that you offer 500 products on your site. Instead of making visitors sort through all 500 products to determine which one is best for them, you want to present only those that best fit their needs. If you have initially rated each product for speed, power, ease of use, and price, you can now have visitors score or rate the same criteria through a quick online interview. Store each customer's scores in a database. To determine which products to present to visitors, reference each customer profile by looking up the person's account using the account ID that you stored in that customer's cookie (cookies will be discussed shortly), and show only those products that meet the guest profile threshold scores.

Use Personalized Content-Matching Schemes

You can create personalized pages by matching a customer to the highest-rated content in an area and by pushing the content to CONTENT MODULES (D2) in PAGE TEMPLATES (D1). Include a list of all the related content by publishing links to CONSISTENT SIDEBARS OF RELATED CONTENT (I6) so that visitors can browse and make their own selections.

Here are four techniques for gathering information: edit, interview, deduce, and filter. The first two are forms of intentional personalization, and the last two are forms of automatic personalization.

1. **Edit.** Visitors click on buttons to make selections. They edit and configure each CONTENT MODULE (D2) area, choosing which modules they most desire. For an example, see the top of Figure D4.4, which shows My Yahoo!'s editing options. Also consider letting visitors use DIRECT MANIPULATION (H9) to put the content modules exactly where they want on the page.
2. **Interview.** Visitors answer questions by clicking on multiple choices in an interview. For an example, see Figure D4.6, a screen shot from the

virtual model at landsend.com. Store information in each customer's database profile, and offer visitors the option to continue the personalization process over time.

3. **Deduce.** Observe visitors' behavior preferences, record them, and offer them personalized results later. Amazon.com tracks the products that visitors order, for example, and later offers them a list of PERSONALIZED RECOMMENDATIONS (G3) of similar or related products, selected by Amazon merchandisers, that they might like to buy. Store this kind of information in each customer's database profile.

4. **Filter.** Build a list of customer preferences and display the recommended items to visitors. Amazon.com does this when it tracks the books that all its readers buy most and displays them as FEATURED PRODUCTS (G1). Provide CONTENT MODULES (D2) based on similar customer profiles. To determine areas of interest, analyze the correlation of all the guest profiles. This is also known as *collaborative filtering*.

Employ these techniques singly or in combination. By providing initial personalization from filtering, customers do not need to enter any special information up front. Over time, implicit and explicit information voluntarily offered by a customer can be added, allowing you to target customer needs more directly.

Use Predefined Content Locations • Follow the pattern of CONTENT MODULES (D2) to display content in predefined areas on each page. This way you can code each page in a uniform template.

Track Customer Visits and History with Cookies • Use cookies to track and remember what visitors found valuable on your site. A **cookie** is a way of storing uniquely identifying information in a customer's computer. A site can store anything in a visitor's cookie: an account ID, user name, even historical information, like the number of times each customer visits a different area of the site. For security reasons, the cookie is accessible only by the site that created it. What makes cookies especially useful is that they enable a site to remember visitors automatically when they come back. Cookies are discussed in greater detail in PERSISTENT CUSTOMER SESSIONS (H5).

If you want to use cookies, make sure you offer a way to let people move from machine to machine, such as from home to office. Create a personalization recovery scheme, in case the cookie is deleted, by providing ACCOUNT MANAGEMENT (H4) tools for customers to create and manage their user name and password.

There are also several legal and privacy issues with respect to cookies and to the kinds of information that may and may not be collected about minors under a certain age. See FAIR INFORMATION PRACTICES (E3), PRIVACY POLICY (E4), and PRIVACY PREFERENCES (E8) for more details.

E3
E4 **E8**

✳ SOLUTION

It is best not to force people to personalize your site before they can use it. Draw customers in by providing basic but valuable content to new customers that, later, can be personalized. Next, invite customers to personalize the site from a menu of options, using information that can be gathered quickly, such as their backgrounds and areas of interest. Gather this information by conducting interviews or by giving people the ability to edit their interests. Deduce what other things might interest your customers by tracking the areas of your site that they visit and scoring the information. Categorize the content and map it to the people who might find such content useful. Structure the site into page templates and content modules that receive content from the targeting engine.

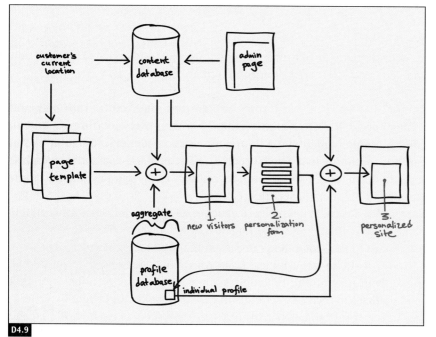

D4.9

Figure D4.9

A personalized site uses page templates and customer information to target content modules.

✳ OTHER PATTERNS TO CONSIDER

D1 D2
I6
Target content to PAGE TEMPLATES (D1), CONTENT MODULES (D2), and CONSISTENT SIDEBARS OF RELATED CONTENT (I6) on the basis of information in each customer's profile. Use the same information architecture designed

B2
for BROWSABLE CONTENT (B2) to lay out the options consistently with other

H4
pages. Provide ACCOUNT MANAGEMENT (H4) tools to let people see and edit their profile data.

E3 E4
E8
FAIR INFORMATION PRACTICES (E3), PRIVACY POLICY (E4), and PRIVACY PREFERENCES (E8) describe several legal issues that must be addressed when data about individuals is collected and stored.

G3
PERSONALIZED RECOMMENDATIONS (G3) are one form of personalized content tailored specifically for e-commerce.

D5 MESSAGE BOARDS

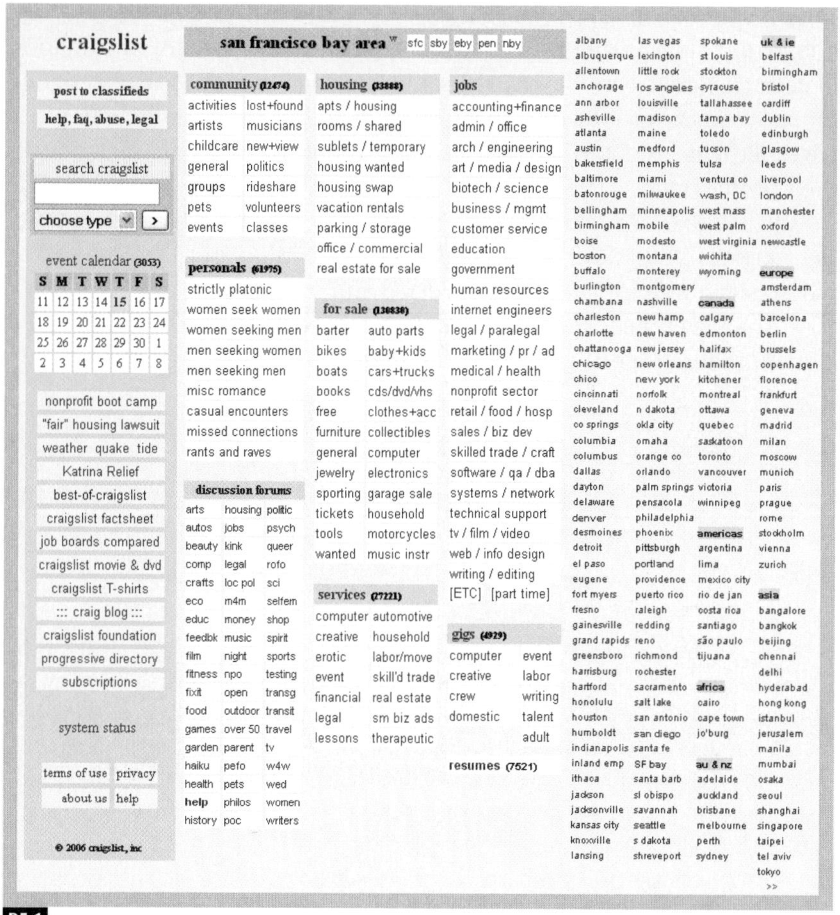

D5.1

(www.craigslist.org, June 16, 2006)

Figure D5.1

Craigslist provides a broad spectrum of message board topics and organizes them into hierarchical categories.

BACKGROUND

Used by COMMUNITY CONFERENCES (A3), NONPROFITS AS NETWORKS OF HELP (A5), EDUCATIONAL FORUMS (A8), and BLOGS (A12), message boards are a tested way for people to communicate with one another. Whereas these site genres provide the framework for building respectful communities, this pattern forms the core of posting, searching for, and reading messages on message boards. This pattern can also be applied to e-commerce through RECOMMENDATION COMMUNITIES (G4).

A3 A5 A8 A12

G4

✳ PROBLEM

Message boards can engage customers if they're easy to find and use. But managing boards to keep them from becoming unruly requires administrative tools and manual labor.

The ability to communicate directly with other people is one of the great benefits of online communication. People can carry on conversations with communities around the clock and around the world. If customers can find their favorite boards time and again, and use them with ease, the communities that form around these message boards can grow. *The challenge here is to foster high-quality and meaningful discussions.*

We suggest starting with one or two message boards and adding more as your community grows. It's best to start simple, but keep the potential for expansion in mind when you're designing message boards.

Decide Whether to Allow Anonymous Posts • One of the first issues you'll have to address is whether to allow community members to post anonymously. If your target visitors want anonymity, you can choose to let them use your message board without revealing their complete names and personal information. Even without complete anonymity, however, some people might act irresponsibly. To prepare for such cases, you must build in systems to ensure that your boards do not become overrun with off-topic, off-color, and perhaps even illegal conversations.

Some communities allow no anonymity because administrators know that if a name is attached to a message, the person is likely to act more responsibly when posting. Other communities make it a rule that visitors may not have complete anonymity, though a visitor's identity might be known only by the site administrators. These kinds of rules are important because, in cases of criminal activity such as fraud, libel, or corruption, law enforcement officials must be able to investigate. This requirement forces site administrators to track more information about people who **(E4)** post, and it potentially changes the site's PRIVACY POLICY (E4).

Decide Whether to Moderate Your Board • On moderated message boards, a site administrator reviews messages before they're posted to make sure that everyone is conforming to the rules of the community. On unmoderated message boards, if one person posts a message and another visitor complains, the administrator can choose to remove the message, but otherwise it's a no-holds-barred, free-for-all forum where anything goes.

Some message boards use a hybrid approach in which first-time posters are moderated but, once approved, can post as much as they want.

Moderated boards can be kept organized and on topic, but they require more administrative work and they can slow down conversations. Although unmoderated boards offer freedom and speed, they are also more unruly, and certain individuals can sidetrack or dominate conversations.

Both kinds of boards must be monitored at some level, either by customers who challenge other customers on their behavior, or by site management. Both kinds of boards require tools to delete messages, but only moderated boards require tools to review posts before they appear on the site.

Make It Easy to Find Your Message Boards • People need to find your message boards to take advantage of them. If you put the boards in a separate area from the rest of the related content on the site, they become harder to find. Also, people want to return to the boards that interest them most and see replies to posts that they've written.

Build a UNIFIED BROWSING HIERARCHY (K1) to include content, commerce, and community message boards, and link content through CONSISTENT SIDEBARS OF RELATED CONTENT (I6) to give customers MULTIPLE WAYS TO NAVIGATE (B1).

K1
I6
B1

Store your visitors' lists of favorite boards, and let them edit those lists through an ACCOUNT MANAGEMENT (H4) page so that it's easier for them to find the message boards that they've visited before (see Figure D5.2). This feature requires customers to sign in with SIGN-IN/NEW ACCOUNT (H2) before saving a favorites list. At a minimum, add LOCATION BREAD CRUMBS (K6) on pages and give them DISTINCTIVE HTML TITLES (D9) so that people can bookmark message boards in their list of favorites.

H4
H2
K6
D9

Once inside a message board, customers might want to search by keywords, scan the latest messages, follow the thread of one conversation, or scan posts by authors they like. A SEARCH ACTION MODULE (J1) that searches the posts gives customers consistent access to keyword search capability, and a filter that provides CHRONOLOGICAL ORGANIZATION (B6) makes it easy to look for the latest messages. A POPULARITY-BASED ORGANIZATION (B7) scheme can also be used to let visitors know which posts were most read or most highly rated by other visitors.

J1
B6
B7

Unlike an unthreaded view (see Figure D5.3), a threaded view lets people follow conversations very quickly (see Figure D5.4). On the other hand, a column sort that provides ALPHABETICAL ORGANIZATION (B5) of messages provides quick access by author.

B5

Figure D5.2

The Motley Fool gives customers the ability to save a list of favorite message boards for the next time they sign in.

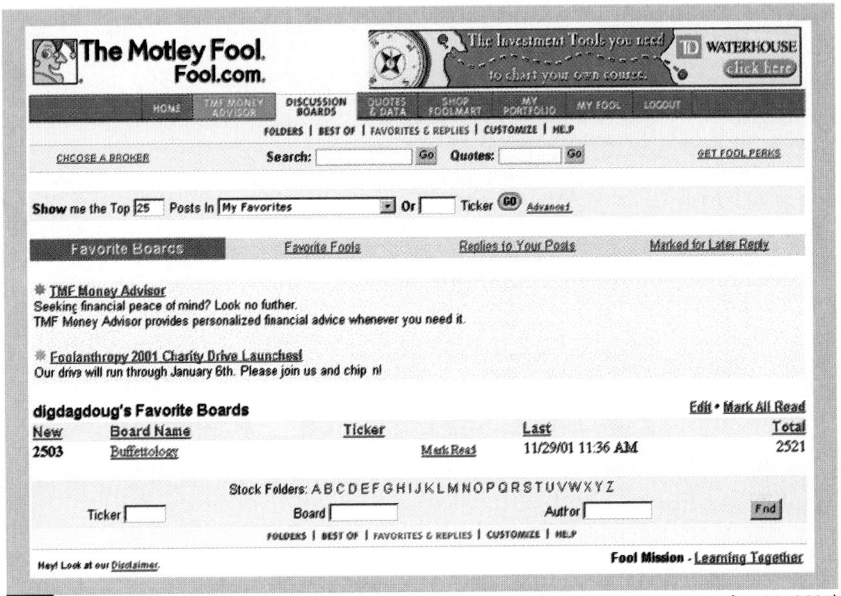

D5.2
(www.fool.com, November 29, 2001)

Figure D5.3

The Motley Fool site provides the ability to search, filter by date, view each thread, and sort alphabetically. This screen shot shows an unthreaded view.

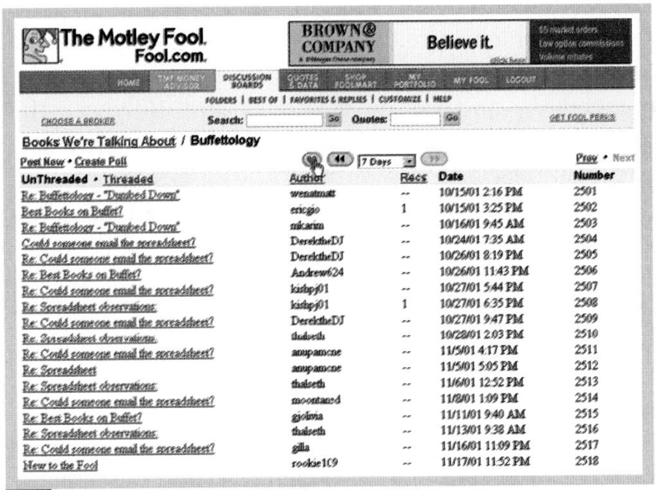

D5.3
(www.fool.com, November 28, 2001)

Require Newcomers to Sign In after Reading Posts • Some sites let newcomers read message boards without going through SIGN-IN/NEW ACCOUNT (H2) but do not let them post until they have registered. This approach lets people "lurk" and see what a community is like before joining it. Once a

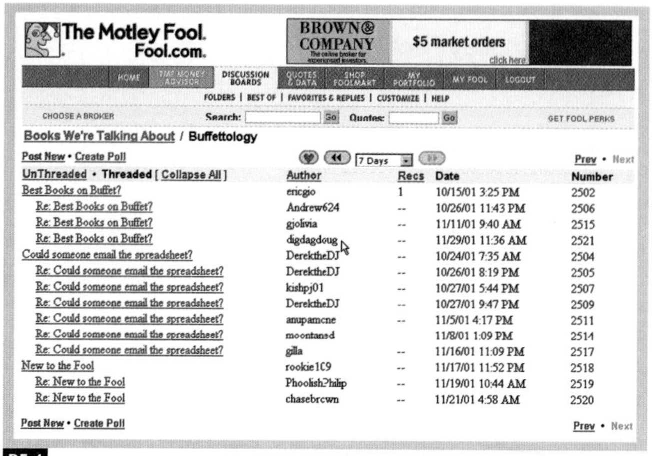

Figure D5.4

This screen shot shows a threaded view of the same message board that is shown in Figure D5.3.

D5.4 (www.fool.com, November 28, 2001)

visitor has decided to become a community member, you can offer PERSONALIZED CONTENT (D4), in the form of favorite message boards and favorite community members.

Other sites require newcomers to go through SIGN-IN/NEW ACCOUNT (H2) before they can even read any posts, thereby ensuring that only registered community members can read and post messages. However, this approach may irritate people who do not like to create an account before they can see what the message boards offer.

In stricter communities where true identity is important, or where content is of an adult nature, you may want to ask for a credit card number to validate a customer's identity and age.

Present Clear Rules • Each site must establish rules of behavior for its message boards. Customers will not want to waste their time writing posts that won't be accepted or must be removed. If customers are malicious, the rules might dissuade them from posting at all, making site management easier.

The first area to address is a site's FAIR INFORMATION PRACTICES (E3). What kind of information is collected about community members? For what purposes? For how long? And are there any legal requirements, such as content that cannot be viewed by international audiences or by minors? This kind of information needs to be made clear through the site's PRIVACY POLICY (E4) and PRIVACY PREFERENCES (E8).

To help visitors remember specific rules, present the rules before they **H6** post a message. Use a FLOATING WINDOW (H6) or put the rules directly on the page (see Figure D5.5). Specifically, message board rules must address the following:

- Whether the site is moderated
- The fact that you will terminate site privileges and possibly pursue legal action against people who post copyrighted, hateful, threatening, illegal, racist, or other undesirable information (such as spam) on your site
- Whether hyperlinks are allowed in messages
- Whether images are allowed in messages
- How long posts are retained
- Whether people can delete their posts

Figure D5.5

Yahoo! News makes its message board rules clear right on the posting page.

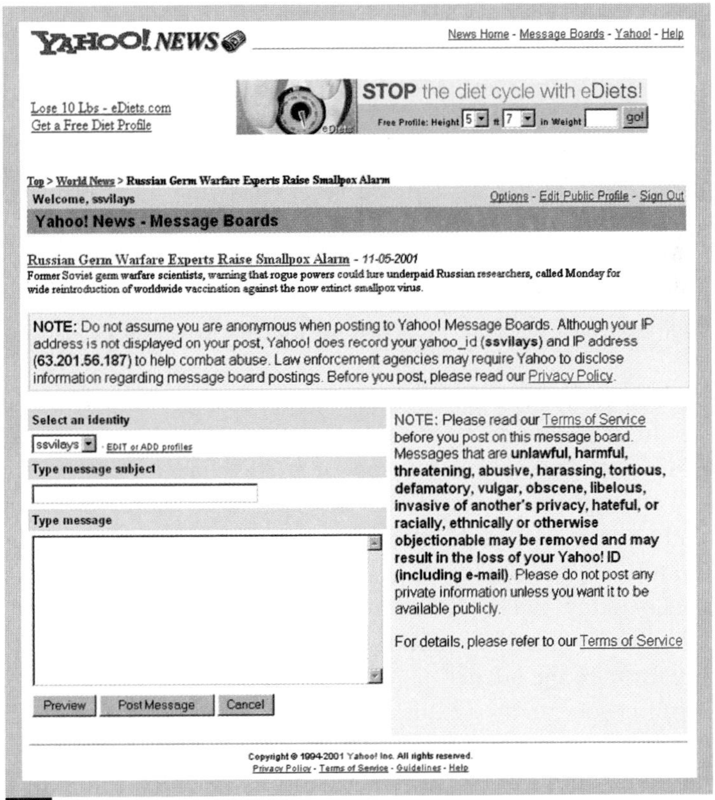

D5.5

(www.yahoo.com, November 28, 2001)

Make Posting Painless • People can create new messages or reply to a current message. Place ACTION BUTTONS (K4) that lead customers to these two options on every message, to let them continue conversations. Also provide just the **New Message** ACTION BUTTON (K4) in strategically placed locations to let community members start new conversations.

Place the message to which visitors are replying on the same page where they're composing a new message because they may be responding to one or several points that they want to refer to. Create a form so that customers can edit their messages. Customers creating new messages need fields—one for the title and one for the body. When replying to a message, automatically create the title on the basis of the original message by using the term *re,* as in "Re: What is the best book to buy on cooking pasta?" Community members can change the title if they want to. Also be sure to have a **Submit Message** ACTION BUTTON (K4) at the bottom of the form.

A preview capability helps customers visualize how their messages will look to others. If the site allows images or HTML in posts, the preview capability is an essential function to help people verify the links and look of their posts. Create a **Preview Message** or a **Preview Reply** ACTION BUTTON (K4) below the form (see Figure D5.6).

Help New Community Members Make Good Posts • Anyone who has been part of any COMMUNITY CONFERENCE (A3) long enough is familiar with the situation of a "newbie" posting a question or comment that veterans find annoying, either because the newbie is not familiar with the social norms of that message board or because he is intentionally interested in annoying people.

You can do two things to avoid this problem. First, you can create a higher barrier to entry for first-time posters. For example, you could require a small fee for a new account (as MetaFilter does), or impose a 24-hour delay after an account is created before that account is allowed to post (as Daily Kos does). On the one hand, these preventive measures are likely to increase the quality of posts and decrease the number of newcomers deliberately making inflammatory posts. On the other hand, these measures are also likely to reduce the total number of people participating on your message boards.

The second thing you can do is explain the social norms of your message boards. For example, many message boards let you create "sticky" posts that are always at the top of the list of message threads. Many communities use these sticky posts to highlight FREQUENTLY ASKED QUESTIONS (H7),

Figure D5.6

The Motley Fool has a straightforward interface for entering new posts and replies, and it lets customers e-mail replies directly to the original poster, making it much easier for the original poster to respond.

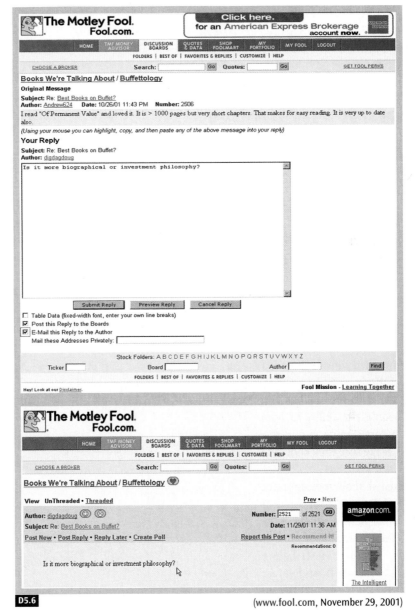

D5.6 (www.fool.com, November 29, 2001)

making it easy for newcomers to know which topics are well worn. Another technique that some message boards use is to provide tips on making good posts—for example, "introduce yourself before asking questions," "be sure to stay on topic," and "have a good, concise title."

Create an Administrative Back End • On moderated boards, an administrator must review all new posts. This interface provides the ability to preview each post and accept or reject it. Create a CHRONOLOGICAL ORGANIZATION (B6) of posts that takes an administrator to a preview page, with ACTION BUTTONS (K4) for accepting posts that follow community standards and rejecting posts that violate any rules.

For all boards, administrators need the ability to remove posts, and to remove access for customers who violate the rules. The administrator's view of the message boards, accessed through a special SIGN-IN/NEW ACCOUNT (H2) form, provides the capability to click a **Remove Post** ACTION BUTTON (K4) on the post pages and remove undesirable content.

✳ SOLUTION

To make message boards easy to find and use, build them into your navigation hierarchy and link to the boards from related content. Provide the means for people to save their favorite boards in their customer profile, and save board links in the browser favorites. Let visitors search for keywords in posts, filter posts by date, view threaded and unthreaded conversations, and sort posts by the name of the person posting. Give people the ability to read posts before signing in or registering. Make sure they know the board rules so that they're not surprised if their messages are removed. Provide a simple form to post a new message or a reply. Enable administrators to approve or reject posts before posting, if the site is moderated, and give them the ability to remove messages on both moderated and unmoderated boards.

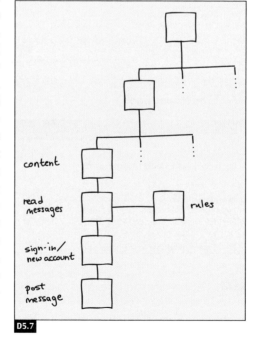

D5.7

Figure D5.7

Build message boards into your navigation hierarchy, and provide a simple way for people to reply to posts.

✳ OTHER PATTERNS TO CONSIDER

Build message boards into your UNIFIED BROWSING HIERARCHY (K1) and link to content through CONSISTENT SIDEBARS OF RELATED CONTENT (I6), giving customers MULTIPLE WAYS TO NAVIGATE (B1). Message boards can also form the basis for RECOMMENDATION COMMUNITIES (G4) on e-commerce sites.

Store customers' lists of favorite boards in their profiles, and let them edit their profiles through ACCOUNT MANAGEMENT (H4). These features require customers to go through the SIGN-IN/NEW ACCOUNT (H2) process. At a minimum, provide LOCATION BREAD CRUMBS (K6) on pages and give pages DISTINCTIVE HTML TITLES (D9) so that people can save them in their browser favorites.

Provide a SEARCH ACTION MODULE (J1) on every page so that people can search for keywords in posts. Allow people to filter posts by CHRONOLOGICAL ORGANIZATION (B6) so that they can see the latest messages. Provide an ALPHABETICAL ORGANIZATION (B5) of page contents to give people quick access to authors they like, and a POPULARITY-BASED ORGANIZATION (B7) to see what others liked.

Require people to sign in with SIGN-IN/NEW ACCOUNT (H2) before posting new messages. Verifying that people are signed in requires checking before each post, and before the selection of any PERSONALIZED CONTENT (D4), such as favorite message boards.

Address message board FAIR INFORMATION PRACTICES (E3) and community rules in a site's PRIVACY POLICY (E4), in a FLOATING WINDOW (H6), or directly on the message-posting page.

Give people **Reply to Message** and **New Message** ACTION BUTTONS (K4) on existing posts, and a **New Message** ACTION BUTTON (K4) on every page. Create a **Submit Message** ACTION BUTTON (K4) at the bottom of the message-posting form.

For moderated message boards, give board administrators a CHRONOLOGICAL ORGANIZATION (B6) of posts that takes them to a post preview page with ACTION BUTTONS (K4) for accepting and rejecting posts.

For all board administrators, provide a view of the message boards, accessed through a special SIGN-IN/NEW ACCOUNT (H2) form, that gives administrators the capability to remove undesirable content by clicking a **Remove Post** ACTION BUTTON (K4) on the post pages.

See COMMUNITY CONFERENCE (A3) for more tips on fostering a strong community.

D6 WRITING FOR SEARCH ENGINES

D6.1

(www.eloan.com, November 2001)

Figure D6.1

E-LOAN keeps most of its keyword-filled content high on the homepage, which helps it score high on search engine rankings.

✳ BACKGROUND

When searching the Internet, or an intranet, people will not be able to find your site if it appears too many pages away from the front of the search results list. Your site needs as high a ranking as possible on the list so that customers can find it quickly and regularly. The writing on a site becomes critical for a high listing because most search engines index words to build a database of search results. This pattern provides the solution for writing pages that will be highly ranked by search engines.

✳ PROBLEM

It is difficult to find a site on a list of search engine results if it is too far down the list. Making a site appear toward the top of any search requires writing site content in customized ways.

Search engines are one of the primary tools that people use to find sites,[1] just as they are one of the most popular ways that people find pages within a site. But one of the biggest problems people face on search engines is that they have to wade through page after page of results to find a site that meets their needs. Because your potential visitors start at the top of the first page and read down, your site needs to be near the top of the first page of search results, before readers lose interest or find your competitors.

Some search engines rank sites purely on their relevance to searchers' keywords, and each search engine has its own way of calculating relevance. Other search engines rank sites that have paid for top listings first, but they also list all other sites with relevant results. Understanding how relevance is ranked on various search engines is the key to building a site that returns high rankings because rankings are built from the content of sites. This pattern provides the solution for writing content that ranks sites higher and is clicked on more frequently in search result pages.

Remember That Search Engines Crawl and Index Web Sites • Search engines have such a vast and widespread index of the Internet (or an intranet) because half of their job is to crawl every page they can find and index every distinctive word. These programs, called **crawlers** or **spiders,** start from a list of a few sites and go from link to link, opening pages and indexing the words on those pages. The other half of a search engine's job is to generate results for every search query, whether a query consists of one word or many.

Some search engines calculate relevance scores from the frequency of word occurrences in a page or site; others rank sites according to their importance, as estimated by the number of Web pages that link to that site. Either way, the words and content on your site (see Figure D6.2) must match the keywords that searchers use when they type in the search form. And the results that search engines display depend on the words and content of your pages as well.

---

1 According to information gathered from comScore Media Metrix's "Top 50 Properties" table (www.comscore.com/press/release.asp?press=906) and from Alexa's Global Top 500 (www.alexa.com/site/ds/top_500), search engines consistently ranked as some of the most popular sites on the Web in 2006.

Figure D6.2

The National Cancer Institute uses keywords in the body of its **Cancer Topics** page to help improve its search engine rankings.

D6.2

(www.cancernet.nci.nih.gov/cancertopics, June 16, 2006)

Strategies That Work

Here are the content-writing strategies that we use to improve site rankings and make search results easier to use overall.

Write Distinctive Titles for Every Page • DISTINCTIVE HTML TITLES (D9) are important to search engines for two reasons. First, many search engines rank Web pages higher if one of the search terms is in the title. Second, search engine designers often make HTML titles the leading description for each search hit in the ORGANIZED SEARCH RESULTS (J3) page. If a page does not have an HTML title, the search engine will have to fall back on the **anchor text** for a link—namely, the hypertext label used to link to the page—or, in the worst case, the URL of the Web page, as the title of a search result.

D9

J3

Write Keyword-Filled Descriptive Text Near the Top of Each Page • Some search engines give text near the top of a page more weight than text near the bottom. If you place your site's most often used keywords ABOVE THE FOLD (I2), search engines are sure to include those words as part of a site's index. Simply put, **keywords** are significant and descriptive words that describe the content and services offered by a site. For example, a site designed for parents might have keywords like *parents, parenting, children, baby, babies, adoption, family,* and *marriage.*

Write keyword-filled descriptive text so that the customer's search results include the keywords in context and so that the links from the search engine to the site will make sense to the customer (see Figure D6.3).

Use <meta> Tags • Most search engines recognize keyword **<meta> tags,** which are markers in files that indicate to software applications, including search engine crawlers, what a site and page contain. Use keyword <meta> tags on all pages to provide additional keywords not included in

Figure D6.3

To help customers scan for the most relevant site, Yahoo!'s search results include each keyword as it is used in context on each site. Including keywords in context is one of the most important strategies for improving site rankings and click-through.

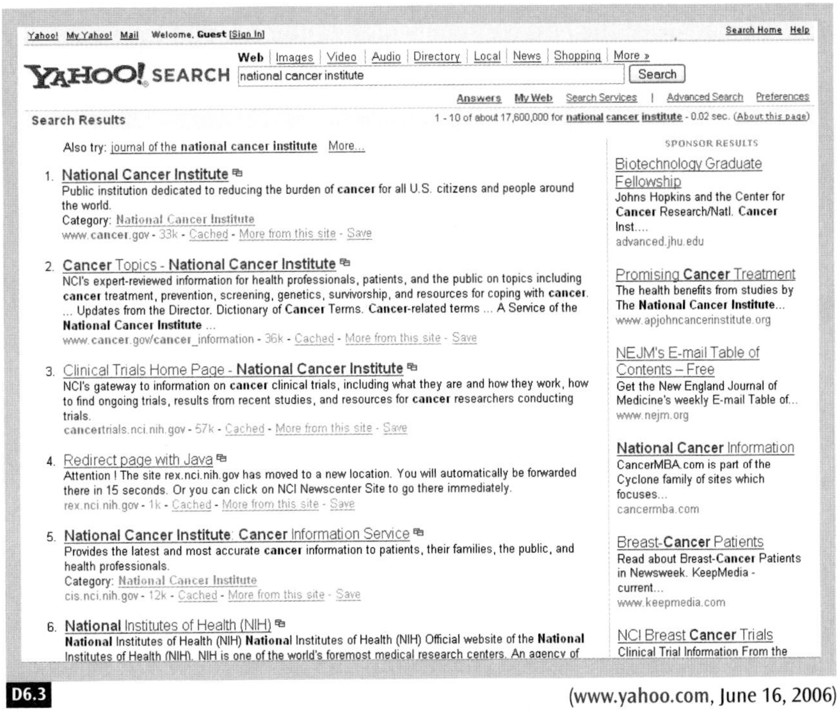

(www.yahoo.com, June 16, 2006)

the text, including synonyms, phrases, and language translations. A keyword <meta> tag looks like this:

```
<html>
<head>
    <title>Acme Corporation - Homepage</title>
    <meta name="keywords" content="best widgets available,
    gadgets, electronics, machinery">
</head>
```

Strong content for <meta> tags includes the following:

- Terms that customers use most frequently (found in the log of a site's own search engine requests)
- Main site themes
- Synonyms
- Common misspellings
- Foreign-language translations of keywords if your site's audience is international

Make Your Site Accessible to Web Crawlers • People who have impaired vision are some of the best customers of the Internet, and they often use text-only browsers and text-to-speech converters to navigate through Web sites. However, many SITE ACCESSIBILITY (B9) barriers make it difficult for them to enjoy a Web site as much as people with normal vision do.   **B9**

Interestingly, the same kinds of barriers that stop people with impaired vision also stop Web crawlers. You can address both issues at the same time by making sure that there is always at least one full version of content in a form that people with visual impairments can read. Label pictures clearly with **<alt> text** (text that takes the place of an image that's not being displayed) to explain what a person with normal vision would see. Also be sure to have text versions of multimedia files, such as images, image maps, movie files, sound files, and Flash presentations. Examples of these techniques are given in SITE ACCESSIBILITY (B9).   **B9**

Finally, be judicious with frames. Many Web crawlers are easily confused by frames, and some crawlers avoid framed pages altogether. Having a PRINTABLE PAGE (D8) version of content helps here.   **D8**

Specify in a Robots File the Content That You Don't Want Crawled • The robots exclusion standard is a convention used by search engines, telling a crawler what it can and cannot crawl. It is a file called *robots.txt* that can be found off the root of a site. For example, the robots file for *The New York Times* can be found at nytimes.com/robots.txt.

The robots file is a convenient way of telling crawlers to avoid database-backed pages, pages that are likely to change quickly, pages that require sign-in through SIGN-IN/NEW ACCOUNT (H2), and multimedia files. Do not use the *robots.txt* file to specify the location of confidential information, because anybody can look at this file. For a humorous example, check out sun.com/robots.txt.

Counterproductive Strategies

Writing for search engines is a black art. Most search engines closely guard the secret of their relevance-ranking algorithm because of competition from other search engines and because of deceptive tricks used by some site developers. One such trick is to add popular but nonrepresentative search keywords, such as *sex* and *MP3,* to drive traffic to the site. The logic is that such a Web site will be more likely to appear in search results because so many people search for these keywords, even though the Web site has nothing to do with sex or MP3s. Another trick is to present one set of fake pages for search engines while presenting another for site visitors.

We consider many of these schemes for improving rankings in search engines unethical. Furthermore, the managers who run search engine services are constantly watching out for these kinds of behavior. In fact, some of these strategies may decrease a site's ranking because the search engine algorithms may think that the site is cheating. In February 2006, for example, Google gave the German BMW site a "death penalty," removing all search references to BMW's Web site because of purported cheating by BMW to improve its ranking on Google.[2]

Here's a list of search engine strategies to avoid:

- Repeated keywords
- Keywords that do not describe the content of the site
- Trademarks owned by other sites
- Colored text that is the same color as the background, used to hide words that are not really content on the site or to repeat keywords
- Repeated URL submissions to search engines
- Use of **search engine optimization (SEO)** sites
- Fake pages for search engines

---

2 As reported by BBC News (news.bbc.co.uk/1/hi/technology/4685750.stm).

Even some nonmalicious design choices may adversely affect search engine ratings. Here are some examples:

- Slow connections that take too long to download pages.
- Pages with the same HTML title.
- Pages with the same content but different URLs.
- A <meta> refresh tag that repeatedly loads a page.
- Use of JavaScript for all navigation. If you use JavaScript for menus and navigation, make sure there are hard links elsewhere on your pages.
- Numerous instances of spam hyperlinks—for example, advertisements posted in your BLOGS (A12) or COMMUNITY CONFERENCES (A3).
- Content hidden in CGI (Common Gateway Interface), Java, or JavaScript.
- Content hidden behind SIGN-IN/NEW ACCOUNT (H2) forms.
- Content hidden within databases, behind SEARCH ACTION MODULES (J1).
- Content from disreputable Internet service providers (ISPs) known to host pornographic Web sites or to send unwanted spam.

✳ SOLUTION

Begin by writing distinctive HTML titles for every page because they are used as the page title in search results and sometimes search engines rank pages higher if search terms are contained in titles. Use keywords, those you would use most frequently to describe the site's purpose and offering to customers, at the top of each page and in the body of the text. Include descriptive <meta> tags representative of the content contained in each page. Make your site accessible to people with impaired vision because doing so also helps search engines. Avoid rigging the system with bogus keywords and text—an approach that is often counterproductive.

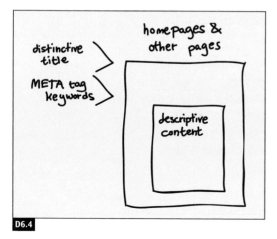

Figure D6.4

Use the page title, keywords, and descriptive text in your Web pages to help ensure high rankings in Web search results.

❋ OTHER PATTERNS TO CONSIDER

D9 DISTINCTIVE HTML TITLES (D9) are important to search engines because programmers often use HTML titles as the leading description for each search **J3** hit in the ORGANIZED SEARCH RESULTS (J3) page, and because they are often favorably weighted if they contain search keywords. If you position the most often used keywords about the category of service that your site **I2** provides ABOVE THE FOLD (I2), search engines are sure to include those **B9** words. Make your site accessible. SITE ACCESSIBILITY (B9) also helps search engines by making the nontextual content textual, such as by giving images <alt> text descriptions. When these descriptions contain keywords, they become part of a search engine's index.

D7 INVERTED-PYRAMID WRITING STYLE

Figure D7.1

A concise yet descriptive headline, an engaging blurb, and simple, clear writing make the first paragraphs on the CNET News.com site a prime example of the inverted-pyramid writing style.

D7.1

(www.news.com.com, June 16, 2006)

✳ BACKGROUND

Whether you write text to accommodate MULTIPLE WAYS TO NAVIGATE (B1), for HIERARCHICAL ORGANIZATION (B3), as BROWSABLE CONTENT (B2), or for better SITE ACCESSIBILITY (B9), there is no escaping the written word on the Web. This pattern forms the core for all site writing.

B1
B3 B2
B9

✳ PROBLEM

People move about quickly on the Web, skimming for information or keywords. If a site's writing is not quick and easy to grasp, it is usually not read.

Your customers want Web pages to be fast to download, easy to use, and quick to skim. They don't want to wade through self-promoting propaganda or scroll through pages of text to get to the point. Although customers will be more tolerant if they know of no alternative site, you can't count on their good nature. If a page doesn't deliver, your visitors will be gone in a single click.

Often customers find a lot to read on sites, but all this text can be tedious for people who are skimming or looking for specific pieces of information. To help them, you can employ a common journalistic style called **inverted-pyramid writing.** Newspapers and magazines excel at this style because they know that readers tend to scan and skim until they reach a particular item of interest, and even then they may not read past the headline or first paragraph. This pattern explains how to write in this style.

Create a Concise but Descriptive Headline • A descriptive headline tells readers what to expect in the following text. People can read a concise title quickly. As we said in HEADLINES AND BLURBS (D3), you must articulate in the headline why the content is *important* and *unique*. Implicit in the headline is a promise about what the content offers.

The headline is typically a sentence fragment, roughly ten words or less so that it can appear in large type in a small space. A good headline does all of the following:

- It contains keywords, most importantly subject and verb. The best headlines indicate action, such as "Buy or Sell Anything Here."
- It confirms the information that follows in the blurb.
- It does not reveal the whole story, so the reader is compelled to continue.
- If it is news based, it states the most important aspect of the relevant news.
- It is clean, simple, and specific. The headline "Social networks poised to shape Net's future" in Figure D7.1 is a good example.
- It is not a boring label, such as "Blue Slacks."
- It is humorous without annoying or perplexing its readers.

A powerful headline is important for many reasons. When implementing a page, take care to put the title in two places: (1) in the HTML <title> tag, as described in DISTINCTIVE HTML TITLES (D9); and (2) in the body of the text itself. HTML titles are used by search engines [see WRITING FOR SEARCH ENGINES (D6)], and in favorites, bookmarks, and desktop shortcuts. Also, a descriptive title makes it easy to create a DESCRIPTIVE, LONGER LINK NAME (K9).

Continue with the Most Important Points in the Blurb or Lead • If you're writing a short list of blurbs, focus on the point you want to make. Keep your target customer in mind at all times.

It is difficult to write short, succinct blurbs, so write something longer first and edit it down to its essence. If you want your page to show a list of blurbs, place the most important ones ABOVE THE FOLD (I2) so that readers can quickly determine whether they're on the right page. The blurb in Figure D7.1 begins like this: "Social networks, mobile video and 'Googlism' will continue to transform the Net in years ahead."

The term **lead** refers to the first few paragraphs of a story or longer text. It reinforces the headline and entices the visitor to read more (see Figure D7.2). Following the inverted-pyramid style, state the most important idea first and continue to the least important.

Use Less Text • Text on computer monitors is harder to read than on paper, so people read less online than they do on paper. This means that online articles must be shorter than those in print (see Figure D7.3). Instructions for using a Web application must be kept especially short to keep reader attention on the navigation items and the other application objects.

Write Short Sentences and Check Your Work • Write in a straightforward manner, avoiding complex sentences. Use simpler words and FAMILIAR LANGUAGE (K11) to ensure that readers can understand what you're communicating.

Just like short sentences, short blocks of text are easier to read than long blocks. If you break up long paragraphs into shorter ones, readers can skim more quickly. Finally, to avoid confusion and mistakes, run the text through a spell checker and a grammar checker, and then completely proofread it before publishing. These kinds of errors are the easiest to correct, but they are embarrassing if they actually appear on the site.

Avoid Hype • Do not underestimate your customers. They can easily become frustrated and annoyed when presented with self-promoting hype and blatant advertising. By avoiding hype, you raise your site's credibility.

Figure D7.2

The most important paragraph in this news article is at the top and in boldface. The following paragraphs continue the story and draw readers in.

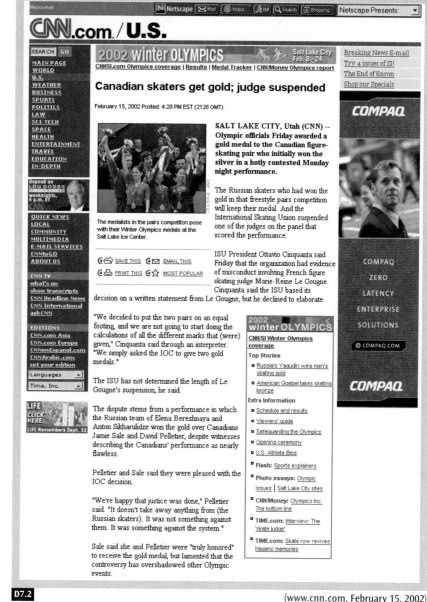

D7.2

(www.cnn.com, February 15, 2002)

Concise Title

Short Summary Paragraph

Short, Easy-to-Read Bulleted List

Simple Follow-up Paragraphs

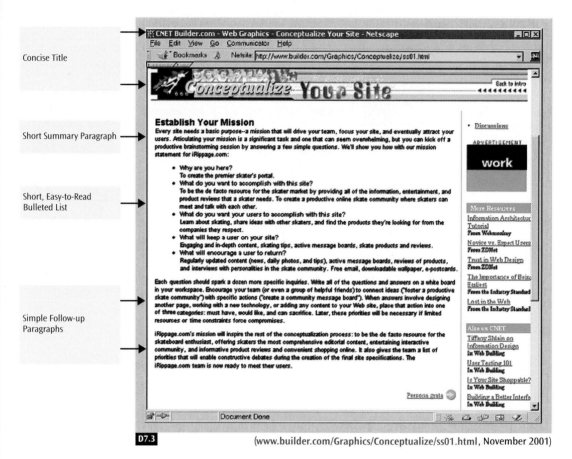

D7.3

(www.builder.com/Graphics/Conceptualize/ss01.html, November 2001)

Figure D7.3

This Web page uses an inverted-pyramid style. It has a concise title, a short summary paragraph, and supporting paragraphs. However, it's not necessary to read the supporting paragraphs to understand what the page is about.

Present facts clearly and concisely, without sounding self-promoting. Hype can backfire if you say that your product is the best. Visitors might have found your site in a search engine list, so they can research your competitors' sites as easily as they found yours, just by clicking the **Back** button.

Use Bullets and Numbered Lists • Readers appreciate bulleted lists for the following reasons:

- They draw people's attention.
- They are conducive to rapid skimming.
- They highlight information quickly.
- They identify the most important information.

However, follow these guidelines when you use bulleted lists:

- Use them when the order of the items is not important. Use numbered lists if the ordering matters.
- Use HTML bullets, instead of fancy images, to improve download time.
- Apply bullets sparingly, or they will lose their effectiveness.
- Avoid having too many bullets in the list. Seven is usually the most you should have.

Use Embedded Links • EMBEDDED LINKS (K7) help visitors find more information about a topic that is mentioned in an article. **Embedded links** are contained in the body of a text (as opposed to being listed at the end of an article; see Figure D7.4 for an example). Embedded links make text easier to skim because people can scan for them, but they may also distract readers.

Experiment with Different Writing Styles for Entertainment Purposes • If your Web site centers on fun over usability, figure out how to use humor, but carefully. Stories and humor do not need to be written in the inverted-pyramid style. Tailor your presentation to your specific audience.

Figure D7.4

This article from MarketWatch uses an embedded link (Read the full government report) to give readers immediate access to another article mentioned in the text of this article.

(www.marketwatch.com, June 16, 2006)

✳ SOLUTION

Start with a concise but descriptive headline, and continue with the most important points. Use less text than you would for print, in a simple writing style that uses bullets and numbered lists to call out information. Place embedded links in your text to help visitors find more information about a related topic. Experiment with different writing styles for entertainment purposes.

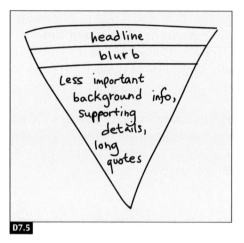

D7.5

Figure D7.5

For inverted pyramids, start with a good title, continue with a few blurbs, and follow up with supporting information.

✳ OTHER PATTERNS TO CONSIDER

Articulate in HEADLINES AND BLURBS (D3) why each page is *important, unique,* and *valuable* to visitors. Write DISTINCTIVE HTML TITLES (D9) and integrate them with WRITING FOR SEARCH ENGINES (D6) to improve search engine results. Use FAMILIAR LANGUAGE (K11) that your target visitors will understand. Provide DESCRIPTIVE, LONGER LINK NAMES (K9) for other articles to reference. Place the most important information ABOVE THE FOLD (I2) so that readers can quickly determine whether this is a page they want. Because they're easy to spot, EMBEDDED LINKS (K7) make text easier to skim.

D3
D9
D6
K11
K9
I2
K7

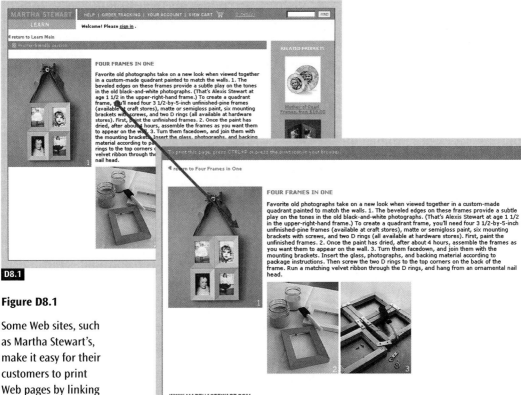

Figure D8.1

Some Web sites, such as Martha Stewart's, make it easy for their customers to print Web pages by linking them to a special printable format that strips out navigation elements, frames, and advertising, leaving only the logo and the content.

(www.marthastewart.com, February 20, 2002)

✳ BACKGROUND

Every site genre has pages that could be useful to print, especially the HOMEPAGE PORTAL (C1), CATEGORY PAGES (B8), CLEAN PRODUCT DETAIL (F2) pages, and ORDER CONFIRMATION AND THANK-YOU (F8) page. This pattern describes how to print any Web page.

❋ PROBLEM

Sometimes customers want to print what's on their screen. They become frustrated if a printed Web page chops off content, goes on and on with pages of irrelevant data, or does not offer a "printer-friendly" version.

To print a page on a Web site, a customer might hit the **Print** button on the browser and see what comes out. Sometimes the result is too short, with chopped-off key content, such as the last lines of text or important images. Or it might be too long, with pages and pages of irrelevant data. Visitors with advanced knowledge of computers might be able to save the HTML and edit it, or take a screen shot. But novice computer users are more likely to abandon the process, and perhaps abandon the site. This is unfortunate because creating a separate printer-friendly version of most pages is easy.

Modifying any existing page to make a printer-friendly version requires numerous changes that restrict your design options for images and layout. For this reason it's better to create an alternate page with the same content that is more appropriate for printing. You can do this by creating a printer-friendly PAGE TEMPLATE (D1) and then loading the content from the original page into the template.

D1

Remove Extraneous Navigation and Content from the Printable Template • To convert a PAGE TEMPLATE (D1) to a printer-friendly version, remove all frames, CONSISTENT SIDEBARS OF RELATED CONTENT (I6), and side-running NAVIGATION BARS (K2) that run vertically down a page, because these are not very useful in a printed form. STYLE SHEETS (D11) can be used to make this task much easier.

D1
I6
K2
D11

Sometimes articles are split across multiple Web pages, making it difficult to print them in their entirety. For your printer-friendly version, join split-page articles into one page each (see Figure D8.2).

Add Labels to Help People Find the Article Online Again • Creating a printer-friendly version of your Web page gives you a chance to pass on useful information to customers. List the title, the author, the date, and the URL of the page. Some Web sites sneak in an advertisement or two here as well.

Take the Main Content Out of Any HTML Tables • Tables and GRID LAYOUTS (I1) are one of the main sources of problems in printing. Unless it needs to be formatted as such, make sure that the main content is not placed within a table in the printer-friendly PAGE TEMPLATE (D1).

I1

D1

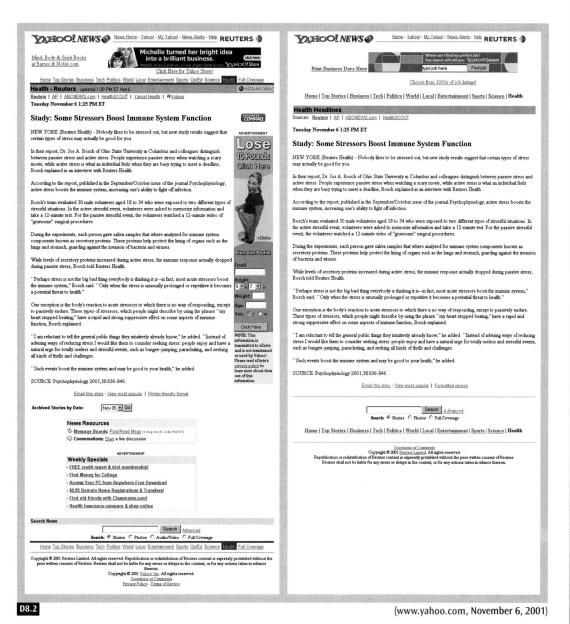

Figure D8.2

The printer-friendly version of Yahoo! News (right) is formatted in a single column and omits the sidebar of related content at the bottom of the page.

✳ SOLUTION

Create a printer-friendly page template by using a style sheet that removes frames, additional columns, navigation bars, and sidebars. Join content split across multiple pages, and label the printable page with the page title, author, and URL. Finally, be sure that the main content is not placed within an HTML table, because tables can cause serious printing problems.

D8.3

Figure D8.3

To make your pages more printable, simplify them by removing extraneous columns and navigation and by combining content split across multiple pages.

✳ OTHER PATTERNS TO CONSIDER

Create a printer-friendly page template by removing frames, CONSISTENT SIDEBARS OF RELATED CONTENT (I6), and NAVIGATION BARS (K2) that run next to the content going down a page. If the HTML in your Web pages is structured well, printable pages can be easily created with STYLE SHEETS (D11).

Creating printable versions of your content can help with SITE ACCESSIBILITY (B9), as well as with WRITING FOR SEARCH ENGINES (D6).

I6 **K2**

D11

B9 **D6**

Figure D9.1

In this screen shot of an MSNBC article about a Harry Potter book, note the exceptional title in the Web browser window title bar (top arrow). The bottom window shows how to create the HTML title (bottom arrow). You need good, distinctive HTML titles for bookmarks and favorites, shortcuts, search engines, and mobile Internet devices.

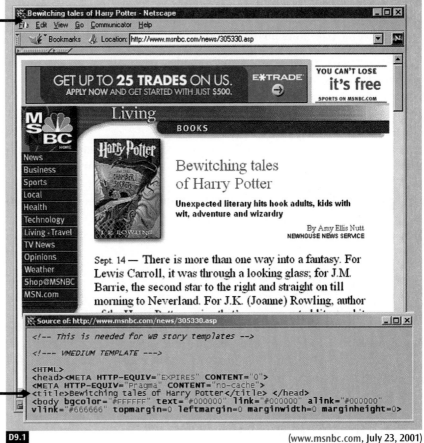

D9.1

(www.msnbc.com, July 23, 2001)

✳ BACKGROUND

In HEADLINES AND BLURBS (D3), WRITING FOR SEARCH ENGINES (D6), and INVERTED-PYRAMID WRITING STYLE (D7) we maintained that well-written HTML titles add to a site's value. This pattern provides the foundation of a distinctive HTML title.

✳ PROBLEM

HTML page titles are used as browser bookmarks or favorites and as desktop shortcuts. They are also used by search engines when displaying search results. Often, however, page titles do not provide useful clues to page contents.

Word-processing documents and spreadsheets with ambiguous file names are confusing. People are forced to open up documents with names like *foo.doc* and *misc-calculations.xls* just to see what they actually contain, and they are justifiably annoyed if there are dozens of poorly named files.

The same is true for Web pages. Customers need to remember the content of a page, whether on or off the Web. HTML titles are used as the default names for Web pages if they are saved to a local drive or stored as bookmarks or favorites in the Web browser. In addition, some search engines use HTML titles to index site pages and present search results. In this case, people use the HTML title to make an educated guess about whether this is the page they want. However, vague titles make it difficult for people to distinguish one Web page from another. You can address all of these issues at once by writing distinctive HTML titles.

HTML Titles Are Used for Headlines and Blurbs • The key here is to understand how HTML titles are seen by customers. Figure D9.1 shows how such titles are displayed by Web browsers. It also demonstrates that good headlines are resources for well-written HTML titles. Figure D9.2 shows that an HTML title can be reused as the name of a link to a page. See HEADLINES AND BLURBS (D3) for hints on writing good headlines that are also good HTML titles.

D3

HTML Titles Are Used by Search Engines • Search engines use HTML titles when presenting ORGANIZED SEARCH RESULTS (J3). Figure D9.3 shows the results of MSNBC's site search. The first hit looks like an automatically generated title, which is not very useful when customers are trying to understand the search results. The fourth search hit, however, uses the HTML title to display the name of the page. Figure D9.4 shows what the same search result looks like in an Internet-wide search engine.

J3

HTML Titles Are Used by Desktop Computers • HTML titles are also used as desktop shortcuts (see Figure D9.5), as well as bookmarks and favorites in Web browsers (see Figure D9.6).

Figure D9.2

These headlines and blurbs come from an MSNBC page.

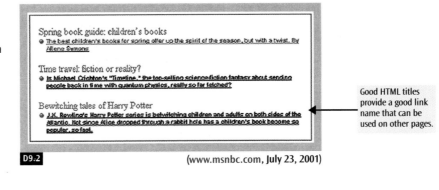

Good HTML titles provide a good link name that can be used on other pages.

D9.2   (www.msnbc.com, July 23, 2001)

Figure D9.3

This result comes from an MSNBC search on the term *Harry Potter*.

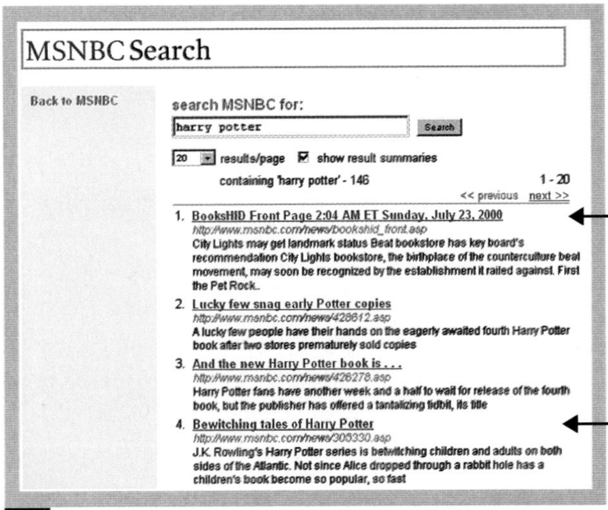

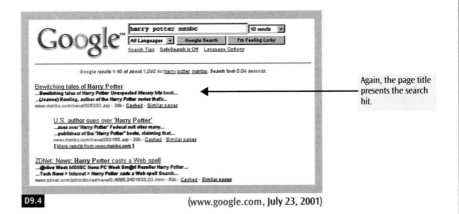

This is what happens when HTML titles are not set correctly.

Here the HTML title is used as the name of the search hit.

D9.3   (www.msnbc.com, July 23, 2001)

Figure D9.4

This sample result from Google, based on a search for the term *Harry Potter,* uses the HTML title of the page as the name of the hit.

Again, the page title presents the search hit.

D9.4   (www.google.com, July 23, 2001)

Figure D9.5

Desktop shortcuts use HTML titles as names.

D9.5

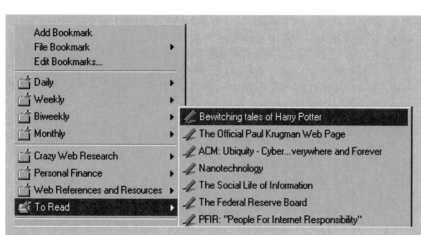

D9.6

Figure D9.6

Web browsers use HTML titles as the names of bookmarks.

Distinctive HTML titles make it easier for customers to find the right page. They also provide useful link names that can be used on other pages. A poorly chosen title—or worse yet, no title—can be confusing, and it looks unprofessional. Figure D9.7 shows some examples of bad HTML titles.

Vary Titles from Page to Page • It would be easy to make all the titles on a site the same, but then visitors would not know which page to choose, or which page they were on. You might do this accidentally if you use a PAGE TEMPLATE (D1) and forget to change the title for each page.

D1

Use Titles and Bread Crumbs • When you add a new page to your site, you need to write a new title. Using a system similar to LOCATION BREAD CRUMBS (K6), base the title of the page on the path that a customer would

K6

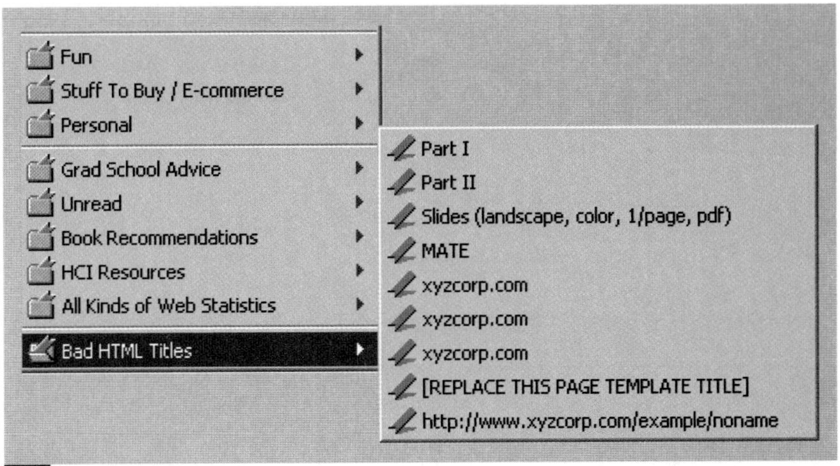

Figure D9.7

These examples illustrate bad HTML titles. Titles like "Part I" and "Part II" are vague. One bookmark, for the fictional Web site xyzcorp.com, is listed three times because all of the page titles on its site are the same. The last bookmark, the URL, is listed that way because the page has no HTML title.

take to get there. A path-based title helps customers locate the page again later, while providing some important context about the page.

CNN takes an approach like this on its site, by using its Web site name, the article type, the article name, and the date to title its Web pages. Here are two page title samples:

- CNN.com—Technology—Study Retail sites fall short on customer service—December 13 2000
- Technology—Global Web sites prove challenging—August 22 2000

CNET uses a similar approach, with titles such as the following:

- CNET.com—News—E-Business—How to build that elusive customer loyalty
- CNET Builder.com—Web Graphics—Conceptualize Your Site

✳ SOLUTION

Create distinct names for each page, even if the pages are generated from page templates. Consider using the site's organizational hierarchy as the basis for titles that describe the categories and subcategories of each page.

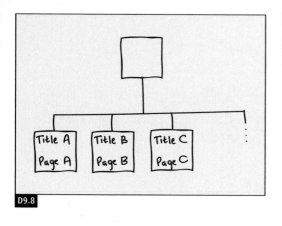

Figure D9.8

Use a different name for each page on your site.

D9.8

✳ OTHER PATTERNS TO CONSIDER

The titles of pages can be the same as the paths created for LOCATION BREAD CRUMBS (K6). It is easier to create an ORGANIZED SEARCH RESULTS (J3) page if each Web page has a distinctive HTML title because titles are displayed as the name for each page. A distinctive HTML title also makes it easier to create DESCRIPTIVE, LONGER LINK NAMES (K9) to a page because the title of the page can often be used as the link itself. Having good HTML titles also improves SITE ACCESSIBILITY (B9) for people using mobile Internet devices to access your Web site.

D10.1

Figure D10.1

Web sites need to be internationalized and localized for a world-wide audience. These screen shots compare Yahoo!'s U.S. Web site (background) to its Taiwan Web site (foreground).

(www.yahoo.com and tw.yahoo.com, June 16, 2006)

✳ BACKGROUND

All site genres can be created for an international audience. This pattern provides the foundation for building sites that are localized to different audiences around the world.

✳ PROBLEM

The Web is a global medium, but many sites do nothing for international and nonnative audiences. People from all over the world can visit a site, but they will find the experience frustrating if language, cultural, and economic transactional issues are not handled well.

Internationalization and localization are becoming increasingly important factors as more Web sites cross national borders.[3] Internationalization and localization range from simple issues, such as how information like a phone number is represented, to extremely complex issues, such as political and religious beliefs. **Internationalization** refers to the software changes required to support different languages, dates and times, currencies, weights and measures, and number formats. **Localization** is the process of redesigning the user interface and translating content to support a local culture.

The best solution calls for designing internationalization into a site during initial site design, and then localizing for specific audiences on the basis of need. Because most sites are not originally designed with a global audience in mind, it is often difficult to localize them when the time comes.

Store Strings Separately from Code • A Web site's flexibility for localization depends on how well the underlying code is designed to support internationalization. For easier translation and a simpler process when text changes are necessary, store strings of text as separate resources from site code. A modular approach to page layout allows for flexibility and substitution of elements. Many commercial localization tools exist to help manage the external assets for sites. However, you must decide how you intend to manage locale-specific assets internally.

Do Not Rely Exclusively on Machine Translation • Although software programs for translating from one language to another have come a long way in recent years, a lot of research still needs to be done before text can be automatically translated in a meaningful way. Computers simply do not understand context.[4] For example, if you use the word *cook* as a navigation element in your Web site, which form of the word do you mean? Do you mean the verb *to cook,* the noun *cook* (as in *chef*), or someone who

---

3 Note that the terms *internationalization* and *localization* are often abbreviated *I18N* and *L10N,* respectively, because of the large number of letters in each word.

4 A researcher at Microsoft once commented that computers are idiots—just really fast idiots.

has the name *Cook,* as in *Captain Cook?* A machine will translate the word only one way, and that may not be the way it was intended. Without an experienced human translator distinguishing the many meanings of various words, the result will be a shoddy translation.

Hire Competent Translators • The common adage "you get what you pay for" holds true for translators. Although most translators have the best intentions, if they do not devote significant time during translation to understanding the specific needs and cultural differences of your customers, as well as the specific requirements of your particular domain and application, they may make embarrassing mistakes. No one wants to appear amateurish with poor word choices, bad grammar, or nonsense statements.

Choose Centralized or Decentralized Localization Management • There is much to be said for both approaches. *Centralized* localization management provides translation services to the entire site team but does not usually have the domain expertise of each of the areas. *Decentralized* localization management takes advantage of domain expertise spread throughout the organization, but it lacks the localization organization to help manage the process most effectively. It is also more difficult to achieve consistency with decentralized teams because they may not know what other teams around the world are doing. Evaluate the capabilities of the organization's resources and financial investment to decide what approach works best. In many cases, a hybrid approach, using some aspects of centralized management together with local expertise, is the best solution.

Be Aware of Terms and Concepts That May Not Be Widely Known • Terms like *IRS* and *MLB* may be familiar to people in the United States, but they are not as recognizable in other nations. In fact, most acronyms, except the most international ones, such as *SCUBA,* will not be known. Things like government agencies, government policies, and local laws and practices often have different names and responsibilities in other countries. Consider whether more universal concepts can convey the same point.

Recognize Holidays, Customs, and Nonverbal Communication • Because not every holiday in one country is a holiday abroad, you will need staff for vital services like customer support on holidays or staff who reside in the regions that you support.

Another important localization issue to be aware of is color. For example, whereas black is the color of mourning in western countries, white is the color of mourning in China and Taiwan. Colors, images, and icons that have one meaning in one cultural context may be offensive in another. Take the time to understand the value of specific color choices and icons. In some cases those colors and icons contribute a great deal to brand identity and add a local feel. There is a fine balance between global structure and local appeal.

Transform Your Representation of Dates, Currencies, Weights, and Measures •
A great deal of confusion can arise if special care is not taken here. For example, the date format 1/3/01 can mean either March 1, 2001, or January 3, 2001, depending on whether dates are represented as day/month/year or month/day/year. In cases like this, it is better to spell out the name of the month so that there is no room for ambiguity.

Time zones add more complexity to sites if you're executing time-sensitive functions and updates. Most contact databases do not track the time zone of the resident. If a site allows people to schedule appointments with someone in another time zone, the invitation should account for both participants' time zones.

Currencies represent a unique challenge. In the simplest case, a site must support the representation of the local currency. In more complex cases, when you're selling across national borders, your site must handle representation of the currency and the exchange rate fluctuation.

Table D10.1 lists the types of information that must be represented differently in different locales.

Table D10.1

Information That Must Be Represented Differently in Different Locales

Type of Information	Global Format Examples
Number	100,000.00 or 100.000,00
Date	March 3, 2005, or 3 Mar 2005
Time	6:04 PM, 18:04, or 18.04
Time zone	GMT −08:00 or FMT +02:00
Currency	$1, ¥1, £1, €1, or ₣1
Unit of measure	lb or kg
Phone number	(415) 555-1212 or 098-88-1234
Address	two lines or four lines
Postal code	90210 or BYT 123
Punctuation	Hello?, ¿Hola?, "Hello," or <<Hallo>>
Character set	Hello! or Привет!

Prepare for the Varying Devices That People Use to Surf Web Sites • In many countries, mobile devices for accessing the Internet are very popular—sometimes more popular than desktop computers. You might need to make your site accessible from mobile devices as they become popular in new locales. Pay attention to MOBILE SCREEN SIZING (M1) and using the appropriate MOBILE INPUT CONTROLS (M2) to make your content remain valuable on these devices. The page description format for mobile devices also varies from region to region. Where one country might have mostly WAP (Wireless Application Protocol) devices, another country might use mostly HDML (Handheld Device Markup Language). In addition, instant-messaging protocols are sometimes popular. You might need gateways to these protocols to enhance your site's value in local markets. Some of the issues involved in designing for mobile devices are discussed in more detail in SITE ACCESSIBILITY (B9).

Understand the Local Legal Issues • Legal issues may become important when customers start accessing your site from abroad. If your site sells products, foreign trade laws and customs might apply. These factors can affect what you can sell, what you can send, when it is sent, and how long it will take to get there. Tax laws change from country to country as well, and when products are sold overseas, international sales tax may also apply.

Your site may also need to support different privacy laws and offer more ACCOUNT MANAGEMENT (H4) tools to manage customer profiles. For example, the privacy laws in the European Union are more comprehensive than those in the United States, stating that, where reasonable, individuals must be able to access and manage all information stored about them. Privacy issues are discussed in depth in FAIR INFORMATION PRACTICES (E3), PRIVACY POLICY (E4), and PRIVACY PREFERENCES (E8).

Finally, there may be issues with the legality of content. Some countries restrict content that might be on your site. For example, France restricts the sale of any Nazi-related material within its borders. Research each country before opening for business, and avoid having to remove content. If you're starting an auction site, for instance, these restrictions can be important to how you structure your service to make sure postings comply with the local laws.

Provide Tailored Services • Translation is not always enough; sometimes you must personalize a service to the desires and tastes of your audience. What are the local food preferences? What do customers there do for fun? How many times a week do your customers go shopping? These questions might have different answers, depending on where customers live. Do the research to find out. Online marketing and usability research can help, providing concrete answers without the expense and time of travel [for more information about how to do this, see Appendix E (Online Research)].

✳ SOLUTION

Store strings separately from code so that text can be sent to your translation team easily. Do not rely on machine translation. Hire competent translators. Manage internationalization and localization processes through either a centralized or a decentralized system. Understand that certain local terms and concepts may not be widely known, and that holidays, customs, and nonverbal communication in other cultures can affect a site's design and staffing. Transform how you represent certain information, such as dates and currencies. Be aware of the devices that people use to surf Web sites because mobile customers may be a large audience for your services. Understand which legal issues might affect your business. Consider providing tailored services to locales that do not have the same practices as those you're addressing domestically.

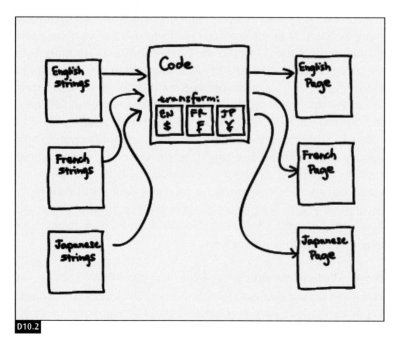

Figure D10.2

Store strings for different languages in separate files.

❋ OTHER PATTERNS TO CONSIDER

Local representations of dates, times, currencies, taxes, addresses, and

shipping requirements should be reflected in the site's SHOPPING CART (F3)
and QUICK-FLOW CHECKOUT (F1). Certain countries may have stricter
privacy laws, which should be reflected in the site's FAIR INFORMATION

PRACTICES (E3) and PRIVACY POLICY (E4).

D11.1a

Figure D11.1

The New York Times uses a style sheet called *global.css* for displaying pages on a desktop screen (a), and one called *print.css* for displaying pages for a printer (b).

(www.nytimes.com, May 6, 2006)

Figure D11.1

(Continued)

D11.1b

(www.nytimes.com, May 6, 2006)

✳ BACKGROUND

 On every site, from PERSONAL E-COMMERCE (A1) sites to BLOGS (A12), style sheets can simplify changes, and make pages more accessible.

✳ PROBLEM

Page-by-page update of a site design—including layout, colors, and fonts—is a time-consuming and error-prone process.

As customers visit your site, you can learn something about what they like and what they don't like in terms of content and look and feel. You can also learn what works and what doesn't work in terms of navigation. You might glean this feedback from informal conversations with customers, from server logs indicating that people don't click on certain links, or from more formal usability and market research. But once you have some information about what could be improved, fixing it on your site can be daunting unless you've planned ahead.

If you have a design problem to fix on all your pages, it will be hard to justify the changes if you must edit every page. It takes time to open, edit, and save every file; then test every file; and possibly open and edit the file again if you find more problems. Only when you have severe problems might you decide to change the look and feel of your entire site, changing the color scheme, updating the page layout, and rearranging where different kinds of navigation and content appear on your pages. One reason such wholesale change can be difficult is that HTML pages mix content with presentation. That is, Web pages contain information about what content should be shown to visitors, as well as markup that describes *how* that content should be shown.

You can avoid the problem of mixed content and presentation and make it easy to modify the presentation of all of your Web pages by using **Cascading Style Sheets** (**CSS**). Figure D11.2 shows one way you might structure your HTML without CSS.

Although it is not difficult to make changes to HTML structured without CSS, such changes become problematic if you have to make them for

Figure D11.2

One way of creating a Web page is to mix content and presentation. Here the content is the word *Example*, and the presentation is all of the markup specifying alignment, font, color, and size.

```
<html>
    <h2 align="center">
        <font color="green" size="+4" face="Times New Roman, serif">
            <em>Example</em>
        </font>
    </h2>
</html>
```

D11.2

entire sections of a Web site. *CSS offers a way of separating presentation from content.* With CSS, you specify all of your content in standard HTML files, and specify how that content should be displayed in a CSS file. Here's how the example in Figure D11.2 would be simplified by using CSS. In one file, you would have the content (Figure D11.3). In a separate CSS file, in this case named *example.css,* you would specify how various markup should be shown on the screen (Figure D11.4).

CSS offers flexible and powerful control over the layout and appearance of Web pages. In fact, whole books and Web sites are devoted to CSS, detailing all the minutiae so that you can have a pixel-perfect site. See the Resources section for references to good Web sites and books on CSS. Our goal with this pattern, however, is to focus on how CSS fits into the bigger picture of Web site design and how it influences the usability of your site. In the paragraphs that follow, we will discuss some other advantages to using CSS, as well as some site-level design issues that you will face if you're using CSS.

Define a Standard Style Sheet as Part of Your Sitewide Page Template • Style sheets can be used as part of your PAGE TEMPLATES (D1) to create flexible and attractive Web pages. You might define one default style sheet that all Web pages on your site will use—one that defines the basic look and feel of your site. Some areas where style sheets can help include creating

D1

Figure D11.3

Another way of creating a Web page is to separate content from presentation. In this HTML file, only the content is specified. A separate style sheet (see Figure D11.4) contains all the information about presentation.

```
<html>
    <head>
        <link rel="stylesheet" href="example.css" type="text/css" />
    </head>
    <h2>Example</h2>
</html>
```
D11.3

Figure D11.4

This is an example of a Cascading Style Sheet. CSS makes it easy to update the look—layout, color, fonts—and feel of your Web site.

```
h2 {
    text-align: center;
    color: green;
    font: italic large "Times New Roman", serif;
}
```
D11.4

flexible GRID LAYOUTS (I1), NAVIGATION BARS (K2), TAB ROWS (K3), and OBVIOUS LINKS (K10). You can also use style sheets to specify background images, as well as the color schemes for individual CONTENT MODULES (D2).

Define a Separate Style Sheet for Printable Pages • It's a good idea to have a separate style sheet for creating PRINTABLE PAGES (D8). This style sheet can be a much simpler version of your PAGE TEMPLATE (D1) style sheet because printed Web pages will not display navigation elements such as TAB ROWS (K3) and NAVIGATION BARS (K2), extra CONTENT MODULES (D2) such as CONSISTENT SIDEBARS OF RELATED CONTENT (I6) or EXTERNAL LINKS (K8), or advertising. Figure D11.1 shows how the same content can be displayed in two different ways, one for the screen and one for printing.

Define a Separate Style Sheet for Mobile Content and Mobile Input • Creating a separate style sheet for mobile content and input can make it easy to adapt your site for MOBILE SCREEN SIZING (M1). Figure D11.5 shows how the same page appears on a standard computer screen and on a small screen. To reduce the amount of content on a page, you will need to reevaluate your PAGE TEMPLATE (D1) style sheet and probably remove some CONTENT MODULES (D2), such as CONSISTENT SIDEBARS OF RELATED CONTENT (I6), as well as advertising. Because MOBILE INPUT CONTROLS (M2) are not fluid cursor controls, we recommend moving essential navigation elements, such as NAVIGATION BARS (K2), to the very top of the page, perhaps reducing their size as well. For more information on creating mobile CSS, go to w3.org/TR/css-mobile.

Use Style Sheets to Make Your Site More Accessible • Style sheets are an effective way of improving SITE ACCESSIBILITY (B9) for people with visual impairments. Before style sheets were introduced, the visually impaired had to wade through some of the markup in a Web page, including formatting and layout information that was often meaningless to them. HTML tables and the <blockquote> tags were also commonly abused to achieve a desired layout, but these workarounds only made things worse for the visually impaired.

Style sheets can also make things easier for people with poor eyesight. Custom style sheets can be specified in the Web browser by the customer, and they are cascaded (combined) with any style sheets that you've defined for your Web pages. This makes it easier for people with visual impairments to control things like font size, background, and contrast.

Figure D11.5

The Opera desktop browser makes it easy to see what your pages will look like on a small screen. A **Small Screen** setting transforms the desktop version (a) into one that works on mobile devices (b). In the small-screen version, notice that the navigation options stack, the large graphic at the top disappears, and the two-column format becomes a single column.

D11.5a

There are several things you can do with respect to style sheets that will improve the accessibility of your site. The first is to use HTML tags and style sheets instead of images where possible, because screen readers can more easily process normal HTML markup than images. The second is to ensure that all information conveyed with color is also available without color—for example, through context or markup. The third is to

Figure D11.5

(Continued)

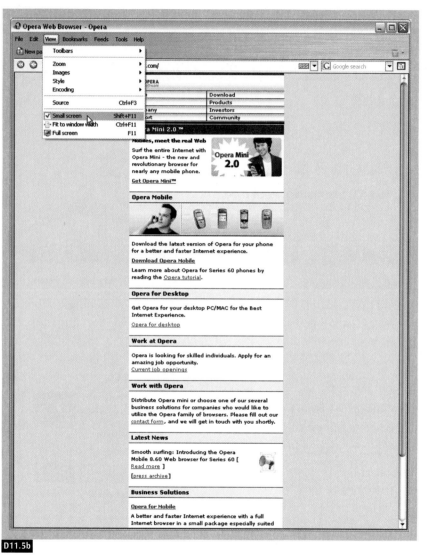

D11.5b

use style sheets to control all aspects of layout, rather than transparent images, tables, or the <blockquote> tag.

In addition, a special workaround allows you to improve the Web experience for visitors who are visually impaired. In CSS, HTML pages are often divided into separate sections by a <div> tag. For example, one <div> tag might specify the navigation on your Web page, and another might specify the content. What's important here is that most screen readers read out this content in the order that it's specified in your HTML pages rather than in the way it appears on screen. Therefore, if the <div> tag containing navigation comes before the <div> tag containing content, visitors who are visually impaired will hear all of the navigation information first. The workaround is to put <div> tags containing content at the top of the HTML files so that they don't affect the actual appearance of your Web pages but they improve the usability of your Web pages for customers who are visually impaired.

Much of Web accessibility is a work in progress. A good source for keeping up-to-date on how to use HTML and CSS to improve accessibility is the World Wide Web Consortium's (W3C) Web Accessibility Initiative (WAI), available at w3.org/WAI.

Be Aware of Browser Incompatibilities with Style Sheets • Currently, the W3C has specified two standard levels of Cascading Style Sheets—*CSS1* and *CSS2*—and is developing a working draft of a third level, *CSS3*. Each level specifies a certain set of features and represents a superset of the previous level. For example, CSS2 includes all the features of CSS1, as well as some additional features.

As of this writing, no Web browser has full support for CSS1 or CSS2, although the most common Web browsers support the large majority of the CSS1 feature set. Furthermore, some browsers have known bugs in how they handle certain CSS features.

The upshot here is that, when using CSS, you will need to test your site with multiple browsers, and you should avoid features that are not yet fully supported across the most popular browsers. This is especially important if your target visitors are using older browsers, some of which support a minimal set of CSS features.

✳ SOLUTION

Start your site design using a style sheet so that changes will be easier to make later. Separate content and navigation from design and layout so that you can build different designs from your content and navigation. If your site pages are likely to be printed, create a print style sheet. If customers will want to use your site from a mobile device, create a mobile style sheet. If you build pages in this way, your site will be more accessible to everyone.

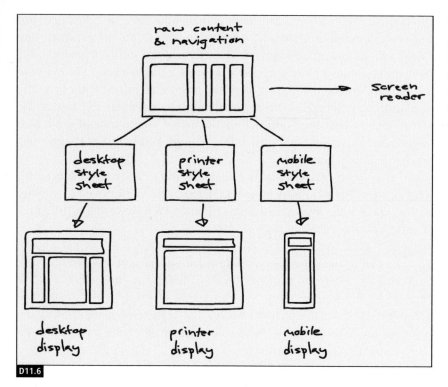

Figure D11.6

Style sheets let you separate content from look and feel so that you can change each independently of the other.

✳ OTHER PATTERNS TO CONSIDER

Make a default style sheet part of your standard PAGE TEMPLATE (D1) to help foster a standard look and feel for your entire Web site. You can also define custom style sheets to help with SITE ACCESSIBILITY (B9) and PRINTABLE PAGES (D8). In addition, style sheets are a convenient way of specifying the appearance and layout of navigation and content, letting you control how and where things like TAB ROWS (K3), NAVIGATION BARS (K2), CONSISTENT SIDEBARS OF RELATED CONTENT (I6), and EXTERNAL LINKS (K8) appear on your Web pages. You can also define GRID LAYOUTS (I1) and OBVIOUS LINKS (K10) in your style sheets. Finally, style sheets can be used to define the font and color scheme for individual CONTENT MODULES (D2).

Style sheets are another way of using HTML POWER (L4).

D1

B9
D8

K3 **K2**
I6 **K8**
I1 **K10**

D2
L4

Building Trust and Credibility

Trust and credibility are essential to establishing a relationship with customers. Without them, people have no reason to believe (or purchase) anything on your Web site. This pattern group gives an overview of issues related to trust and credibility.

E1 SITE BRANDING

E2 E-MAIL SUBSCRIPTIONS

E3 FAIR INFORMATION PRACTICES

E4 PRIVACY POLICY

E5 ABOUT US

E6 SECURE CONNECTIONS

E7 E-MAIL NOTIFICATIONS

E8 PRIVACY PREFERENCES

E9 PREVENTING PHISHING SCAMS

E1 SITE BRANDING

E1.1

(www.msn.com, February 12, 2002)

Figure E1.1

MSN uses color, layout, fonts, and its logo consistently throughout its site to reinforce its brand.

✳ BACKGROUND

In all site genres (see Pattern Group A), it is important to build a site brand to help visitors identify where they are on the Web, and to help build an identity for the company. In the HOMEPAGE PORTAL (C1) pattern we showed how to balance the various elements on that page and how to provide a strong UP-FRONT VALUE PROPOSITION (C2). This pattern describes how to establish successful branding throughout a site.

A

C1

C2

✳ PROBLEM

Brand is more than just a logo and a tagline. Customers need to know where they are and whether they can trust that place to provide something important and unique.

The identity created on a Web site, through advertising and in interactions with people at a company, persists even after customers leave their computers, close their magazines, or hang up their phones. Some may suggest that **brand** is the image, the graphic look, or even the logo of a company. But it's more than that; it's what people remember. And like the cattle brand of cowboys, a company brand can't be removed once it has been created with customers.

People are bombarded with facts and opinions suggesting what's important for them to think, feel, and do. These messages permeate almost every aspect of our lives, from print and television ads to endorsements by famous people, traveling even by word of mouth through friends and peers. People respond to these suggestions in different ways, depending on their background and what they value. Some people may value getting the best price on a purchase; others may value getting the highest-quality product. The brand that a company builds depends on the audience it hopes to reach and the values that that audience deems important.

Our research has shown that a Web site is assessed according to five criteria:

1. **Content quality.** Does the site have what I want?
2. **Ease of use.** Can I find what I want simply and efficiently?
3. **Performance.** Is the site fast?
4. **Satisfaction.** Is the overall experience satisfactory?
5. **Brand value.** Does the site provide something important and unique?

To build a trusted brand requires creating a positive assessment for all five criteria. The rest of the book helps with the first four. This pattern provides insight into building brand value through differentiation and a Web brand identity program.

Differentiating a Brand • Customers will try to discern the differences between one company and its competitors, particularly the promises they make and their abilities to fulfill promises. Figure E1.2 illustrates many of the factors that will have an impact on your brand. A company can

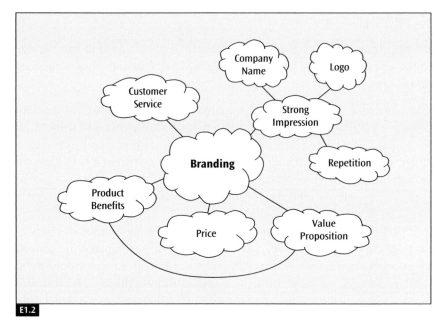

E1.2

Figure E1.2

Many factors must intertwine to create a good branding statement.

dominate only one area of business: price, access, product, service, or experience (as many well-respected businesspeople have said). A company may excel at one or more other areas, but because of market and business limitations, it cannot dominate all the areas. If you establish an important and unique brand value, customers are more likely to remember that value when they need it.

What assessment does the company want to trigger? The first thing customers will do is evaluate your purpose. Perhaps the company offers something less expensive or more entertaining than what its competitors offer. Whatever the differentiation, it must translate into a message people will remember. What branding message do you want visitors to your site to remember? As you would when "dressing for success," consider the kind of impression you wish to make. By carrying out the exercises that follow, you can find out more about your audience's likes and dislikes and hone a brand identity plan.

Exercise 1: Write a Narrative Distinguishing Your Site

Write a one-page narrative about why your Web site is different. Specifically, explain how the idea for the Web site came about, and what problems the site solves. Take about half an hour for this task, and write at least 350 words.

Exercise 2: Use Descriptive Terms to Create an Identity

Pick from the following list of adjectives, or from your own list, the words that best describe the identity that you plan to create:

- Sincere
- Trustworthy
- Reliable
- Competent
- Accessible
- Friendly
- Functional
- Smart
- Expensive
- Inexpensive
- Fun
- Techno-savvy
- Fashionable

Now sort your list by picking the top three adjectives that describe your site.

Exercise 3: Write Customer Scenarios

Write site **scenarios,** one-page narratives about what it feels like for different customers to use the Web site. Put yourself in the shoes of at least three kinds of customers. Write at least 250 words about each. For an example of a scenario, see the discussion on building scenarios in Section 3.2, Techniques for Knowing Your Customers, in Chapter 3 (Knowing Your Customers: Principles and Techniques).

3

Exercise 4: Write Brief Purpose Statements

Write ten short "what we do" sentences that accurately describe the purpose of your Web site. If you like, use the same list that you created in Exercise 1 of the UP-FRONT VALUE PROPOSITION (C2) pattern. Test these statements with customers to identify the single most powerful description. These purpose statements can also become the basis of a tagline for your Web site. For example, Flickr's tagline is simple and concise: "The best way to store, search, sort and share your photos."[1]

C2

---

1 www.flickr.com.

Exercise 5: Test Logo and Color Use

It's not all about words. If you have a logo and color treatments in place for your homepage, test them through research. Customer research is the best way to identify which treatment best matches the identity you wish to create. Survey your customers or run focus groups, as described in Section 3.2, Techniques for Knowing Your Customers, in Chapter 3 **3** (Knowing Your Customers: Principles and Techniques). You can also do this type of research online [for details, see Appendix E (Online Research)].

Establishing Brand Identity • Customers need to be able to identify a Web site by its brand image. If visitors arrive at a Web site and don't know where they are, this means that the color scheme, fonts, page layout, images, and logo that make up the brand image are not prominent enough on the homepage, perhaps being overwhelmed by other elements. A weak brand image can also confuse customers as to which Web site they're on when they go to other pages on the same site. Site designers must quickly convey the brand. If too dominating, however, the brand can adversely minimize the many other important things on the site.

Here are the four main graphic design considerations for every Web brand treatment:

1. **Consistency.** Studies show that repetition helps customers recall information. So, use the same fonts, graphics, relative positions, and proportions for each Web page on your site. A uniform navigation scheme coupled with a good color scheme can also help reinforce your brand image. You can make it easier to achieve this kind of consistency by using PAGE TEMPLATES (D1) that have a strong GRID LAYOUT (I1). **D1 I1**

2. **Size.** Make the logo large enough to be the second or third item that will be read on the page. See CLEAR FIRST READS (I3) for some examples of how to do this. **I3**

3. **Position.** The established location for the logo is the upper left; people already know to look there to identify the site and they expect that clicking on the logo will take them back to the HOMEPAGE PORTAL (C1). **C1**

4. **Reuse of graphics for speed.** REUSABLE IMAGES (L5) help ensure that each page is displayed quickly. You may also want to use a logo that is integrated into the NAVIGATION BAR (K2) and maintain a LOW NUMBER OF FILES (L1). **L5** **K2 L1**

Involve your team in the branding design process. Consider hiring a consultant with expertise in strategic marketing. Once the branding process is complete, the editorial and graphic design teams will have a clear understanding of the identity to convey and reinforce.

✳ SOLUTION

Build a strong site brand by differentiating your company from other companies through the promise you make and through the actions your company takes to satisfy customers. Reinforce the brand image across your Web pages by (1) being consistent in style, (2) having a moderately sized logo, (3) positioning the logo in the upper left corner, and (4) including reusable images optimized for speed.

Figure E1.3

Make the brand the first read in the upper left corner of every page on your site.

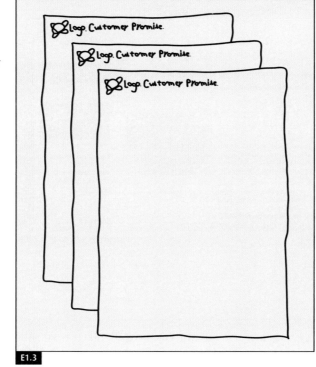

✳ OTHER PATTERNS TO CONSIDER

Take advantage of CLEAR FIRST READS (I3) to quickly convey your brand. A logo that is integrated into the NAVIGATION BAR (K2) will load faster and help you keep a LOW NUMBER OF FILES (L1).

Figure E2.1

Big Brothers Big Sisters has a text entry field in the middle left portion of its homepage that makes it easy for people to subscribe to news about upcoming events and new Web site features.

E2.1

(www.bbbs.org, July 7, 2006)

✳ BACKGROUND

Maintaining contact with visitors to your site can be difficult. E-mail subscriptions are one way of informing interested and self-selected visitors of new and interesting content, such as upcoming events, sales, or news. This pattern looks at different kinds of e-mail subscriptions and ways that e-mail newsletters should be written for greatest impact. This pattern complements E-MAIL NOTIFICATIONS (E7).

E7

✳ PROBLEM

Companies need a way of maintaining contact with customers who are interested in what their Web site has to offer.

E-mail subscriptions are an inexpensive way of maintaining a connection with customers, and they are especially effective if customers are interested in what a Web site can offer. Providing customers with fresh, timely, and relevant information is a great way of giving them another reason to visit your Web site again.

There are three basic kinds of e-mail subscriptions:

1. **Newsletters** are periodic bulletins that provide useful information, such as interesting tidbits and links, tips and tricks, press releases, and descriptions of new services and content.
2. **Focused advertisements** draw attention to new promotions, special offers, and new products.
3. **Periodic reminders**—for example, reminding people about your PRIVACY POLICY (E4) or about the steps they can take to PREVENT PHISHING SCAMS (E9).

Make It Easy to Sign Up for an E-Mail Subscription • Offering a subscription on your HOMEPAGE PORTAL (C1) is a simple way of getting site visitors to give you their e-mail addresses. Big Brothers Big Sisters has a text entry field directly on its homepage that lets visitors easily subscribe to its newsletter (see Figure E2.1). Figure E2.2 shows part of the women.com Web site, which lets people sign up to be notified when the site redesign is deployed.

Another good place to set up a subscription is the SIGN-IN/NEW ACCOUNT (H2) page, when a customer is creating a new account. One Web site that does this is yahoo.com, as Figure E2.3 shows. A third place is the ORGANIZED SEARCH RESULTS (J3) page, notifying customers when new information matching their search criteria is found. Figure E2.4 shows how Amazon.com does this with product searches.

Figure E2.2

Many Web sites let people sign up to be notified when major new features or site redesigns are deployed.

(www.women.com, September 22, 2001)

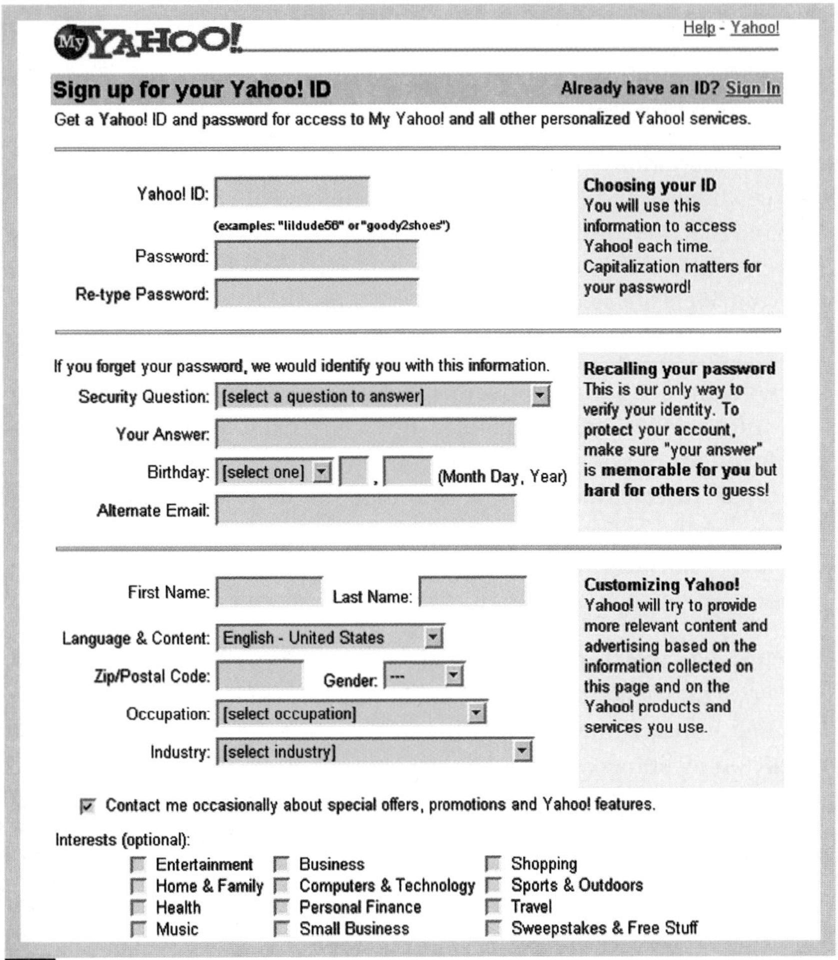

E2.3

(www.yahoo.com, October 6, 2001)

Figure E2.3

Yahoo! lets people sign up to receive special offers and promotions when they create an account.

E2.4

(www.amazon.com, September 23, 2001)

Figure E2.4

Amazon.com has a feature on its search results page that notifies customers when new products matching their search criteria come out.

Figure E2.5

TVEyes uses e-mail subscriptions to notify customers when any of the keywords they have selected are spoken on television.

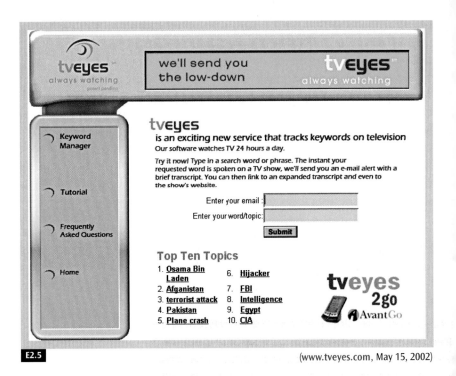

E2.5

(www.tveyes.com, May 15, 2002)

Some Web sites use e-mail subscriptions in very novel ways. For example, TVEyes alerts people whenever a preset keyword is spoken on television. Figure E2.5 shows how easy TVEyes makes it to start an e-mail subscription.

H10 The fewer barriers there are to creating a subscription, the more subscribers you will have. Make it easy to find the subscription request, use CLEAR FORMS (H10), and make what you're offering obvious. If it's a newsletter, provide a few samples to help set expectations. Finally, keep the information you need from your customers short. The more information you require, the less likely it is that people will bother subscribing.

Write Newsletters, Advertisements, and Reminders in Inverted-Pyramid Style •
D7 Using an INVERTED-PYRAMID WRITING STYLE (D7) for your e-mail subscriptions will make it easier to get your message across, especially to people who receive 70 or more e-mails every day. Have specific e-mail subject lines, and use short, concise paragraphs. Put the most important information or a summary at the top of the e-mail, and use headings and bulleted lists to call out information.

Use Text E-Mail Messages • Unless you have a compelling need for graphics, avoid HTML e-mail and use text messages only. Some people cannot read HTML e-mail, and they end up seeing a lot of junk. This is not the impression of your Web site that you want to convey.[2] At the very least, offer your subscribers the option of which version they prefer.

Text e-mail messages should be at most 70 characters wide and word-wrapped. Long lines do not always appear correctly in some e-mail readers, and they make e-mails look amateurish. Be careful of smart curly quotes. Some word processors will automatically convert straight quotes (") to curly quotes (" "). However, curly quotes sometimes appear as numbers. It's best to avoid word processors and use text editors when composing e-mail subscription messages. Finally, be sure to run all e-mail messages through a spell checker and a grammar checker to avoid simple typos.

Indicate How to Subscribe and Unsubscribe in Each E-Mail • Each e-mail message that you send should contain information about how to subscribe and unsubscribe. The subscribing information is included in case your customers forward the message to their friends. You want their friends to be able to sign up easily too! The unsubscribing information is included in case the customer is simply not interested and does not want to receive any more messages. Generally customers unsubscribe by sending an e-mail to a certain address or by clicking a link in the e-mail. Clicking a link is usually easier for the customer, so support this option if you can. The same information should also be included on your FREQUENTLY ASKED QUESTIONS (H7) page.

(H7)

Use Your Customers' E-Mail Addresses Only for What You Say You Will • One of the FAIR INFORMATION PRACTICES (E3) is *choice.* Your customers' e-mail addresses should be used only for the e-mail subscriptions they signed up for, and nothing more. Remember, the way you treat your customers will affect their perception of your brand. If you develop a new feature for your customers, give them a choice of opting in rather than having to opt out.

(E3)

Write Your E-mails to Help Prevent Phishing Scams • Phishing scams are fake e-mails and Web sites that masquerade as legitimate ones, and they are a major source of online fraud today. One reason phishing scams work is that Web sites teach their customers bad habits, like clicking on hyperlinks in e-mails and not using e-mail addresses that sound like they're from the actual company. See PREVENTING PHISHING SCAMS (E9) for more information on protecting both your customers and your company.

(E9)

---

2 This caveat may not be necessary in the future as the programs and devices that we rely on begin to use HTML e-mail exclusively.

❊ SOLUTION

Make it easy for people to set up an e-mail subscription. Write newsletters, focused advertisements, and periodic reminders in an inverted-pyramid style. Use text e-mail messages unless you know that the recipients can read HTML e-mail. Include information about how to subscribe and unsubscribe in each e-mail message. Be sure to use your customers' e-mail addresses only for what you say you will.

Figure E2.6

E-mail subscriptions can be used to send newsletters, focused advertisements, and periodic reminders to interested and self-selected customers.

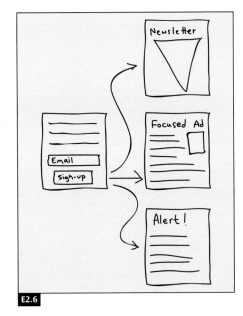

❊ OTHER PATTERNS TO CONSIDER

 Three places to offer e-mail subscriptions are the HOMEPAGE PORTAL (C1), the SIGN-IN/NEW ACCOUNT (H2) page, and the ORGANIZED SEARCH RESULTS (J3) page.

Write newsletters, focused advertisements, and periodic reminders in INVERTED-PYRAMID WRITING STYLE (D7). Include information about subscribing and unsubscribing in each message, as well as on a FREQUENTLY ASKED QUESTIONS (H7) page.

Collect and handle your customers' e-mail addresses according to FAIR INFORMATION PRACTICES (E3). Furthermore, communicate these policies to your customers through a PRIVACY POLICY (E4) and modify them using PRIVACY PREFERENCES (E8). E-mail subscriptions should also be written to PREVENT PHISHING SCAMS (E9).

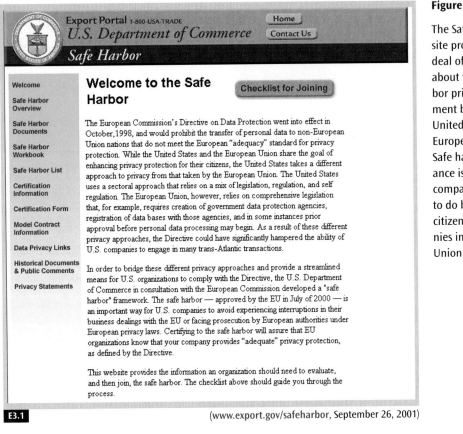

Figure E3.1

The Safe Harbor Web site provides a great deal of information about the safe harbor privacy agreement between the United States and the European Union. Safe harbor compliance is crucial for companies wishing to do business with citizens and companies in the European Union.

(www.export.gov/safeharbor, September 26, 2001)

✳ BACKGROUND

It's not always clear how a company should handle and manage the personal information of its customers. Web companies often collect this information on SIGN-IN/NEW ACCOUNT (H2) and E-MAIL SUBSCRIPTION (E2) pages. This pattern describes fair information practices, which provide guidelines for the kinds of policies and procedures that Web sites should have to ensure that customers' personal information is collected and handled equitably and securely.

✳ PROBLEM

Privacy is a serious concern for many people using the Web. However, it is not always clear what policies and procedures a Web site should have to collect and handle personal information in a fair and secure manner.

Privacy is becoming an increasingly critical design issue as more people come online. A myriad of complex issues must be addressed, such as what information can be collected, as well as how and from whom. This pattern gives an overview of the privacy landscape. We also advise you to consult legal experts in determining how your Web site will help manage your customers' personal information.

The U.S. Privacy Act of 1974 created the notion of fair information practices. Although this act applies only to U.S. government agencies, it has significantly influenced privacy policies worldwide. So far, the most important of these has been the European Union's Directive 95/46/EC (commonly shortened to *the Directive*) on the protection of individuals with regard to the processing of personal data and on the free movement of such data. This directive became effective in October 1998 and has served as a framework to help European Union (EU) nations create legislation that enforces fair information practices.

The Directive has already had a significant impact on e-commerce because one of its articles stipulates that EU countries may prohibit data transfers from EU citizens or companies to non-EU countries that do not ensure "an adequate level of protection." Currently the United States has no national laws guaranteeing such protection. To address this issue, the U.S. Department of Commerce and the European Commission have drawn up a safe harbor framework as a means of having companies based in the United States regulate themselves. Companies can be certified as being compliant with safe harbor, which in turn makes them compliant with the Directive.

The seven safe harbor principles are as follows:[3]

1. **Notice:** Organizations must notify individuals about the purposes for which they collect and use information about them. They must provide information about how individuals can contact the organization with any inquiries or complaints, the types of third parties to which it discloses the information and the choices and means the organization offers for limiting its use and disclosure.

---

3 These descriptions of the safe harbor principles come directly from www.export.gov/safeharbor/sh_overview.html.

2. **Choice:** Organizations must give individuals the opportunity to choose (opt out) whether their personal information will be disclosed to a third party or used for a purpose incompatible with the purpose for which it was originally collected or subsequently authorized by the individual. For sensitive information, affirmative or explicit (opt in) choice must be given if the information is to be disclosed to a third party or used for a purpose other than its original purpose or the purpose authorized subsequently by the individual.

3. **Onward Transfer** (Transfers to Third Parties): To disclose information to a third party, organizations must apply the notice and choice principles. Where an organization wishes to transfer information to a third party that is acting as an agent, it may do so if it makes sure that the third party subscribes to the safe harbor principles or is subject to the Directive or another adequacy finding. As an alternative, the organization can enter into a written agreement with such third party requiring that the third party provide at least the same level of privacy protection as is required by the relevant principles.

4. **Access:** Individuals must have access to personal information about them that an organization holds and be able to correct, amend, or delete that information where it is inaccurate, except where the burden or expense of providing access would be disproportionate to the risks to the individual's privacy in the case in question, or where the rights of persons other than the individual would be violated.

5. **Security:** Organizations must take reasonable precautions to protect personal information from loss, misuse and unauthorized access, disclosure, alteration and destruction.

6. **Data Integrity:** Personal information must be relevant for the purposes for which it is to be used. An organization should take reasonable steps to ensure that data is reliable for its intended use, accurate, complete, and current.

7. **Enforcement:** In order to ensure compliance with the safe harbor principles, there must be (a) readily available and affordable independent recourse mechanisms so that each individual's complaints and disputes can be investigated and resolved and damages awarded where the applicable law or private sector initiatives so provide; (b) procedures for verifying that the commitments companies make to adhere to the safe harbor principles have been implemented; and (c) obligations to remedy problems arising out of a failure to comply with the principles. Sanctions must be sufficiently rigorous to ensure compliance by the organization. Organizations that fail to provide annual self certification letters will no longer appear in the list of participants and safe harbor benefits will no longer be assured.

The safe harbor principles apply only for U.S. companies that want to do business with citizens and companies in the European Union. The landscape for Web sites that operate entirely in the United States is much more chaotic. There has not been a lot of legislation in this regard, but the safe harbor principles still provide a good starting point. In fact, in May 2000 the U.S. Federal Trade Commission (FTC) issued a report on privacy online. This report recommended legislation of four practices that Web sites should have for collecting and handling personal information. Although these practices are currently not legally required in the United States, they offer a reasonable guideline for Web sites. The practices are as follows:

(E4)

1. **Have a clear and conspicuous privacy policy.** Provide a clear and understandable PRIVACY POLICY (E4). Typically, the link to a Web site's privacy policy is posted in the footer of each Web page. However, this link should be made especially conspicuous on key Web pages, such as the HOMEPAGE PORTAL (C1), QUICK-FLOW CHECKOUT (F1), and SIGN-IN/NEW ACCOUNT (H2) Web pages. The privacy policy should describe what information is collected, how it is used, and how it is shared with others. See PRIVACY POLICY (E4) for more details.

(C1)(F1)
(H2)

(E4)

2. **Let people choose how their personal information is used.** If personal information is to be used for purposes beyond the primary intent, let people choose how it will be used. For example, e-commerce sites need mailing addresses to ship products. However, this information can also be used for marketing back to consumers. This is an example of a secondary intent. In these cases, offer customers a choice of PRIVACY PREFERENCES (E8) so that they can specify whether their personal information may be used in this manner.

(E8)

(E2)

Choice is especially important for E-MAIL SUBSCRIPTIONS (E2). Some Web sites ask for a valid e-mail address and then start sending people unwanted e-mail advertisements. When customers create a new account with your Web site, make it clear up front how their e-mail addresses will be used. As an alternative, make it possible for customers to use a one-time GUEST ACCOUNT (H3) on your Web site.

(H3)

(H4)

3. **Tell people what information the Web site has about them.** Web sites should provide an ACCOUNT MANAGEMENT (H4) facility to let people review and in some cases change the information that the Web site has collected about them. The information that a Web site has about a person may be inaccurate or simply outdated, making an account management system a practical necessity.

4. Take reasonable precautions to protect personal information. Web sites should take reasonable steps to protect all of the information about their customers. Such steps include using SECURE CONNECTIONS (E6), testing any custom software for potential security flaws, keeping up-to-date with security-related software updates, having clear policies on how customer information is to be handled internally, and period- ically auditing the entire process to ensure that procedures are being . followed properly.

✳ SOLUTION

Have a clear privacy policy, and make it conspicuous on key Web pages. Let your customers choose how their information is used. Provide account management tools to let them review and correct their information. Pro- tect your customers' personal information. Be certified as a safe harbor Web site if you're doing business with customers or companies in European Union nations.

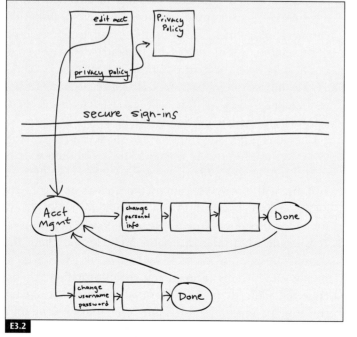

Figure E3.2

Make your privacy policy clear, keep your customers' information secure, and make it easy for customers to manage and update their information.

✳ OTHER PATTERNS TO CONSIDER

One way of maintaining openness and transparency is by stating a PRIVACY POLICY (E4) on all Web pages. At a minimum, post privacy policies on key Web pages, such as the HOMEPAGE PORTAL (C1) and other major entry points, the QUICK-FLOW CHECKOUT (F1) page, and any Web page where substantial personal information is collected, such as SIGN-IN/NEW ACCOUNT (H2).

Give people the choice of specifying PRIVACY PREFERENCES (E8) stating how their e-mail addresses are used, especially for E-MAIL SUBSCRIPTIONS (E2). An alternative is to let customers use one-time GUEST ACCOUNTS (H3).

Use SECURE CONNECTIONS (E6) for any transactions involving sensitive information, including passwords, personal finances, and e-commerce purchases.

Provide an ACCOUNT MANAGEMENT (H4) facility, letting people see what information your Web site currently has about them.

PRIVACY POLICY

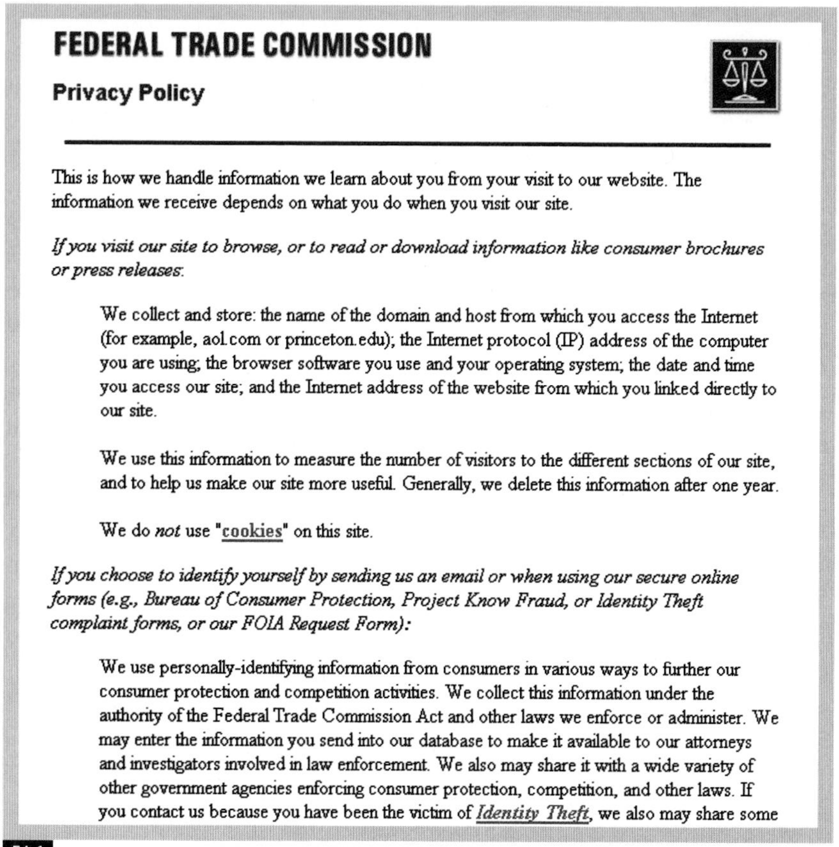

FEDERAL TRADE COMMISSION
Privacy Policy

This is how we handle information we learn about you from your visit to our website. The information we receive depends on what you do when you visit our site.

If you visit our site to browse, or to read or download information like consumer brochures or press releases:

> We collect and store: the name of the domain and host from which you access the Internet (for example, aol.com or princeton.edu); the Internet protocol (IP) address of the computer you are using; the browser software you use and your operating system; the date and time you access our site; and the Internet address of the website from which you linked directly to our site.

> We use this information to measure the number of visitors to the different sections of our site, and to help us make our site more useful. Generally, we delete this information after one year.

> We do *not* use "cookies" on this site.

If you choose to identify yourself by sending us an email or when using our secure online forms (e.g., Bureau of Consumer Protection, Project Know Fraud, or Identity Theft complaint forms, or our FOIA Request Form):

> We use personally-identifying information from consumers in various ways to further our consumer protection and competition activities. We collect this information under the authority of the Federal Trade Commission Act and other laws we enforce or administer. We may enter the information you send into our database to make it available to our attorneys and investigators involved in law enforcement. We also may share it with a wide variety of other government agencies enforcing consumer protection, competition, and other laws. If you contact us because you have been the victim of *Identity Theft*, we also may share some

E4.1

(www.ftc.gov, September 22, 2001)

Figure E4.1

Web sites need to provide privacy policies that make it clear what kind of information is being collected and how that information will be used.

✳ BACKGROUND

The FAIR INFORMATION PRACTICES (E3) pattern described the kinds of policies and procedures that Web sites should have when dealing with customers' personal information. This pattern describes how to communicate these policies and procedures to your customers through a privacy policy.

E3

✳ PROBLEM

Many customers are concerned about their privacy online. Web sites need a way to tell their customers what kinds of information they're collecting and how that information is used to provide value, as well as the conditions under which that information is disclosed to others.

Surveys and interviews have repeatedly shown that most people are concerned about their privacy online. According to a 2000 study by the Pew Internet & American Life Project, privacy concerns are especially high among Internet novices, parents, older Americans, and women. One way of directly addressing these concerns is to have a clear and reasonable privacy policy.

   Privacy is a complex and rapidly changing issue. Legislation, regulation, and self-regulation will certainly change while the issues are worked out. The best thing to do is to get legal expertise to help guide you through this rapidly changing area. This pattern is meant simply to give you a flavor of what's required.

Make the Privacy Policy Available on Each Web Page • Good Web sites place their privacy policy in the footer of each page and make it more conspicuous on key pages, such as the SIGN-IN/NEW ACCOUNT (H2) and QUICK-FLOW CHECKOUT (F1) pages.

(H2)
(F1)

Address Fair Information Practices in the Privacy Policy • The privacy policy should address how the FAIR INFORMATION PRACTICES (E3) are implemented. It should include an explanation of what information is collected, how it is collected [for example, with cookies for PERSISTENT CUSTOMER SESSIONS (H5)], how the information is used, and with whom the information is shared. The policy should also identify the security precautions used, such as SECURE CONNECTIONS (E6). For example, Procter & Gamble, Kodak, and Netflix have simple and easy-to-understand privacy policies that make it easy to see how their sites address each of the issues raised by these practices (see Figures E4.2 and E4.3).

(E3)
(H5)
(E6)

Consider Having a Multilayered Privacy Policy • In early 2005, the European Union's committee of data privacy commissioners, also known as the Article 29 Working Party, published a plan calling for EU member states to adopt common rules for privacy policies that are easy for consumers to understand.

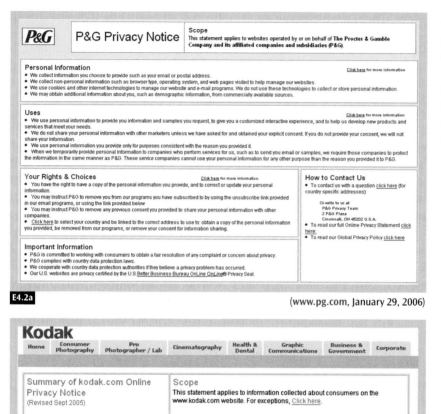

Figure E4.2

Both Procter & Gamble (a) and Kodak (b) use condensed privacy notices that are clear and simple to understand.

E4.2a

(www.pg.com, January 29, 2006)

E4.2b

(www.kodak.com, January 29, 2006)

Figure E4.3

This sample privacy policy comes from Netflix, a Web site that offers DVD rentals. Note that it is clear and readable, and it provides a good overview of the topics covered by the policy.

E4.3

(www.netflix.com, July 21, 2006)

This plan also called for displaying privacy policies in three layers: short, condensed, and complete. The *short privacy policy* is only a few sentences at most, and is something that can be printed on a warranty card or sent via a mobile phone message. It might also contain a link to the condensed privacy notice. The *condensed privacy policy* is a half-page summary of the *complete privacy policy*. The condensed privacy policy only summarizes the most important points, whereas the complete privacy policy might span multiple pages and be comprehensive.

Procter & Gamble has an example of a condensed privacy policy on its Web site, which uses simple language and has a clear visual layout to make it easy to understand (see Figure E4.2a).

Be Aware of Special Privacy Policies for Children • On April 21, 2000, the Children's Online Privacy Protection Act (COPPA) was put into effect in the United States, limiting the information that Web sites can collect about children. The key provisions stipulate that sites must do the following:

- Provide parents with notice of the site's information practices.
- Obtain verifiable parental consent before collecting a child's personal information (see Figure E4.4).

- Give parents a choice of whether their child's information will be disclosed to third parties.
- Provide parents access to their child's personal information and allow them to review it and/or have it deleted.
- Give parents the opportunity to prevent further use or collection of information.
- Do not require a child to provide more information than is reasonably necessary to participate in an activity.
- Maintain the confidentiality, security, and integrity of information collected from children.

Web sites must support these special privacy policies if they have content targeted specifically for children. Such sites must assume that the majority of their visitors will be children and hence must comply with the privacy policies outlined here. For general Web sites, however, the standard is less strict, and site operators can simply ask visitors their age and assume that these visitors are stating their age correctly. For example, PBS Kids (at pbskids.org) features games, stories, and music from television shows on the Public Broadcasting System. Because this site is targeted at children, it has a very strict privacy policy. On the other hand, the main PBS site (pbs.org) is targeted more at adults, so when collecting personal information, it needs to ask only if a person is over the age of 13.

The FTC provides additional details and resources at the following Web sites:

- ftc.gov/bcp/conline/edcams/kidzprivacy
- ftc.gov/bcp/conline/pubs/ buspubs/coppa.htm

Keep in Mind the Privacy Policy Requirements of U.S. Government Web Sites • All federal SELF-SERVICE GOVERNMENT (A4) Web sites in the United States are required by law and policy to establish clear privacy policies and to comply with those policies. In June 1999, the Office of Management and Budget published a memorandum directing every U.S. federal agency to post a PRIVACY POLICY (E4) on all major entry points of its Web site, as well as on Web pages where substantial personal information is collected.[4] The memorandum also stated that the privacy policy must inform Web site visitors of three things: (1) what information the agency collects about individuals, (2) why it is collected, and (3) how it is used.

Consider Special Exceptions for Valid Legal Procedures • Figure E4.4 shows part of the Exploratorium's privacy policy, describing how its Web site will

---

4 OMB Memorandum 99-18, June 1999.

Figure E4.4

The Exploratorium is a hands-on children's science and art museum in San Francisco. Its Web site has a short and simple privacy policy, explaining the kind of information that is collected, how that information is used, the exception conditions, and the fact that personally identifiable information from children is not requested.

Exception

One exception to this policy is that we will release specific information about you or your account to comply with any valid legal process such as a search warrant, subpoena, statute or court order.

Privacy of Minors

The Exploratorium does not solicit personal information from minors. Consistent with the Children's Online Privacy Protection Act of 1998, we will never knowingly request personally identifiable information from anyone under the age of thirteen (13) without prior verifiable parental consent.

If we become aware that a subscriber is under the age of thirteen (13) and has registered without prior verifiable parental consent, we will remove his or her personally identifiable registration information from our files. Please note: we may nevertheless maintain a record of that person's name and address in a "do not register" file to avoid subsequent registration by a child under the age of thirteen (13).

E4.4

(www.exploratorium.edu, September 22, 2001)

comply with well-established and valid legal procedures, such as search warrants or court orders. Detailing these kinds of exception conditions will help smooth out any potential problems with criminal investigations.

Offer Tangible Value for Providing Personal Information • One of the missteps that many early Web sites made was collecting too much information about people. Like a nosy neighbor, these Web sites intrusively asked for information that had no bearing on the customer's current task. Many people simply balked and left those Web sites, perhaps for good. To avoid this problem, request only the information you really need. For example, ask for a customer's postal code only if you need it for billing or to PERSONALIZE CONTENT (D4) (such as weather reports).

Note, however, that people are willing to trade some privacy for convenience and value. For example, credit card companies keep a record of purchases, providing a trail of what purchases are made, and when and where they are made. Likewise, mobile phones provide a rough level of location tracking, providing information about where a person is. It is precisely the high value that these products offer that keeps people using credit cards and mobile phones in spite of the privacy issues.

When collecting personal information, state why you're collecting it and how it benefits the consumer. For example, if your Web site requires a visitor to create an account, make it clear that the reason is to provide

PERSONALIZED CONTENT (D4), PERSONALIZED RECOMMENDATIONS (G3), or  E-MAIL SUBSCRIPTIONS (E2). If your Web site keeps track of people's addresses, let them know that the reason is to streamline the checkout with QUICK ADDRESS SELECTION (F4) and QUICK SHIPPING METHOD SELECTION (F5).

✳ SOLUTION

Make the privacy policy available on each Web page. Address the fair information practices in the privacy policy. Be aware of special privacy policies for children. Keep in mind that U.S. government Web sites must have a clear and conspicuous privacy policy. Communicate special exceptions for valid legal procedures in your privacy policies. Provide tangible value for personal information.

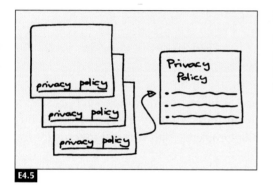

E4.5

Figure E4.5

Make a bulleted, easy-to-read privacy policy available on each page of your Web site.

✳ OTHER PATTERNS TO CONSIDER

The privacy policy is part of the FAIR INFORMATION PRACTICES (E3) pattern, which describes reasonable rules to follow when you're collecting and handling personal information. Make the privacy policy available on most pages on your Web site, and especially prominent on key pages like SIGN-IN/NEW ACCOUNT (H2) and QUICK-FLOW CHECKOUT (F1). Consider adding a link to your privacy policy on your PAGE TEMPLATE (D1) as well.

SECURE CONNECTIONS (E6) are one way of helping to provide security for personal information transmitted over the Web. Personal information can be used for such things as PERSONALIZED CONTENT (D4), PERSONALIZED RECOMMENDATIONS (G3), E-MAIL SUBSCRIPTIONS (E2), QUICK ADDRESS SELECTION (F4), QUICK SHIPPING METHOD SELECTION (F5), and PERSISTENT CUSTOMER SESSIONS (H5).

Figure E5.1

Google's **About Us** Web page targets several customer groups, including people interested in learning more about search engines, site owners interested in advertising and improving their ranking in search results, and prospective employees.

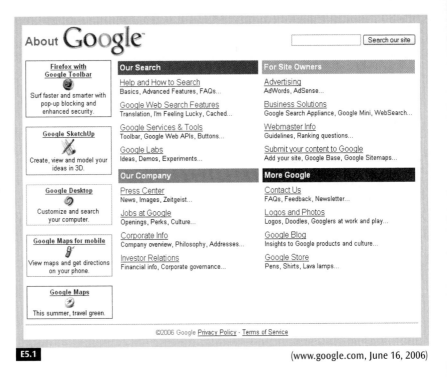

E5.1

✳ BACKGROUND

Another way of building trust is to provide information about the company or the people behind the Web site, including basic real-world information, such as a mailing address, phone number, and fax number, as well as background information on the company and the people in the company. This pattern describes how to organize this information in the **About Us** pages of your Web site.

✳ PROBLEM

Many Web sites have a great deal of useful background information that is distinct from the main focus of the Web site, such as contact information and public relations. You need a way of organizing all of this information.

When people encounter your Web site for the first time, they have three questions in mind:

1. Who are you?
2. What do you do?
3. Why should I trust you?

The **About Us** pages are one way that a Web site can help answer these questions. **About Us** pages collect assorted background information about a Web site, providing information about the people, the organization, and/or the company behind the HTML. **About Us** pages are also important for establishing trust because they let customers know that there are real people and a real organization behind an otherwise virtual world.

The **About Us** pages should provide information tailored to customer demographics, interests, and needs. The list that follows identifies some of the things often found on **About Us** pages, and the discussion following the list elaborates on each of these items.

1. Organizational profile
2. Contact information
3. Disclaimers and legal information
4. Customers and partners
5. Employment opportunities
6. Public relations
7. Investor relations
8. Community relations
9. Site credits
10. FREQUENTLY ASKED QUESTIONS (H7)   **H7**

This list is by no means definitive, and you will have to tailor it for your specific Web site genre, but it should give you a flavor of what to include.

1. Organizational Profile • The profile describes who you are and what you do. It might include a description of the team behind the Web site, a brief history of the company, an overview of products and services, and a mission statement that communicates your UP-FRONT VALUE PROPOSITION (C2).   **C2** However, the profile should be written from a customer-centered perspective (see Figure E5.2). Although you know what your company does, visitors

Figure E5.2

Craigslist has a simple, down-to-earth About Us page. The "mission" section describes the values and history of the site. The "press" section provides links to where the site is mentioned in mainstream media, as well as a public relations kit for journalists. The "using the site" section describes what is acceptable behavior in the community forums. The "team" section describes the people behind the site and includes a charming minibiography about the founder by his mother.

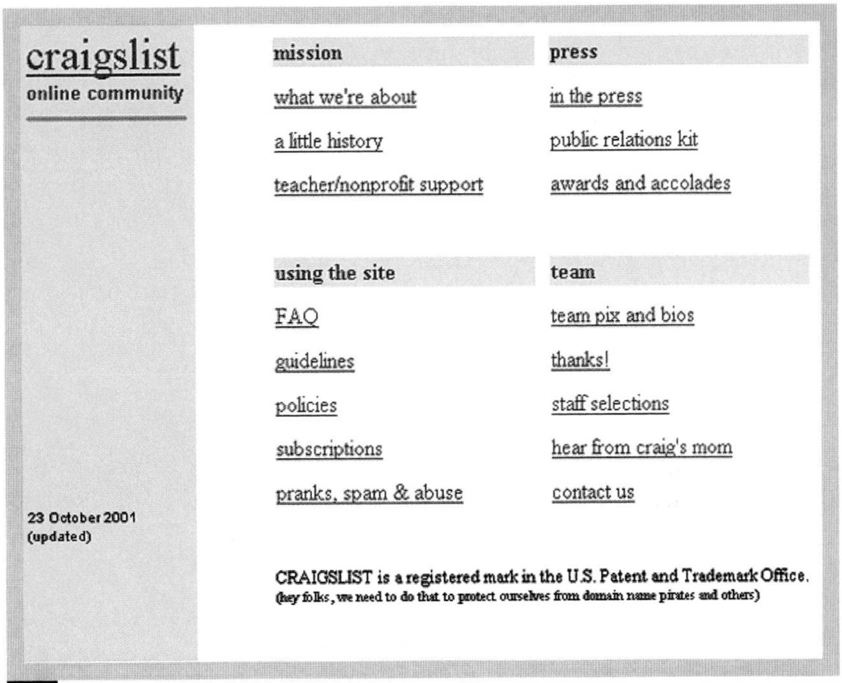

craigslist
online community

mission	press
what we're about	in the press
a little history	public relations kit
teacher/nonprofit support	awards and accolades

using the site	team
FAQ	team pix and bios
guidelines	thanks!
policies	staff selections
subscriptions	hear from craig's mom
pranks, spam & abuse	contact us

23 October 2001
(updated)

CRAIGSLIST is a registered mark in the U.S. Patent and Trademark Office.
(hey folks, we need to do that to protect ourselves from domain name pirates and others)

E5.2

(www.craigslist.org, February 14, 2002)

might not. For example, if you're a law firm, it makes sense to identify the general types of law that you practice. If you're a consulting firm, it makes sense to list your strengths and specialties.

2. Contact Information • Contact information is something that every business must have, such as a physical mailing address, phone numbers, fax numbers, and e-mail addresses. Having a physical address is more important than it may seem on the surface. It is sometimes difficult to tell if the company behind a Web site is a real company or a fly-by-night company. Listing a street address and directions to your company can help allay some of your customers' fears.

Phone and fax numbers are important for the same reason. Maybe a customer is having a problem late at night. Maybe a customer's order is wrong. Maybe someone needs immediate help or just prefers phone and fax over e-mail. For these reasons it's crucial to provide numbers that your customers can use.

On the other hand, some people prefer e-mail. Your customers may want to report a PAGE NOT FOUND (K14) error, or need some tech support, or want to compliment you on how cool and usable your Web site is.

(K14)

Again, whatever the reason, make sure you have e-mail addresses to which your customers can send questions and comments.

3. Disclaimers and Legal Information • Many Web sites have a link to their PRIVACY POLICY (E4) and to their **Terms of Use** page from their **About Us** page. Some Web sites also list rules about the right way to link to the site and provide images that people can use. In addition, some Web sites have disclaimers about the content on the Web site, as well as fair use policies. For example, the LEGO Web site (see Figure E5.3) has a page describing how fans of the toy can create their own Web sites in a way that does not infringe on any copyrighted materials or trademarks.

E4

4. Customers and Partners • Listing some of your customers and partners helps establish your credibility. A list of links to past and present customers and partners is like a list of references that other people can check. It can also illustrate that you have been reliable in the past and are

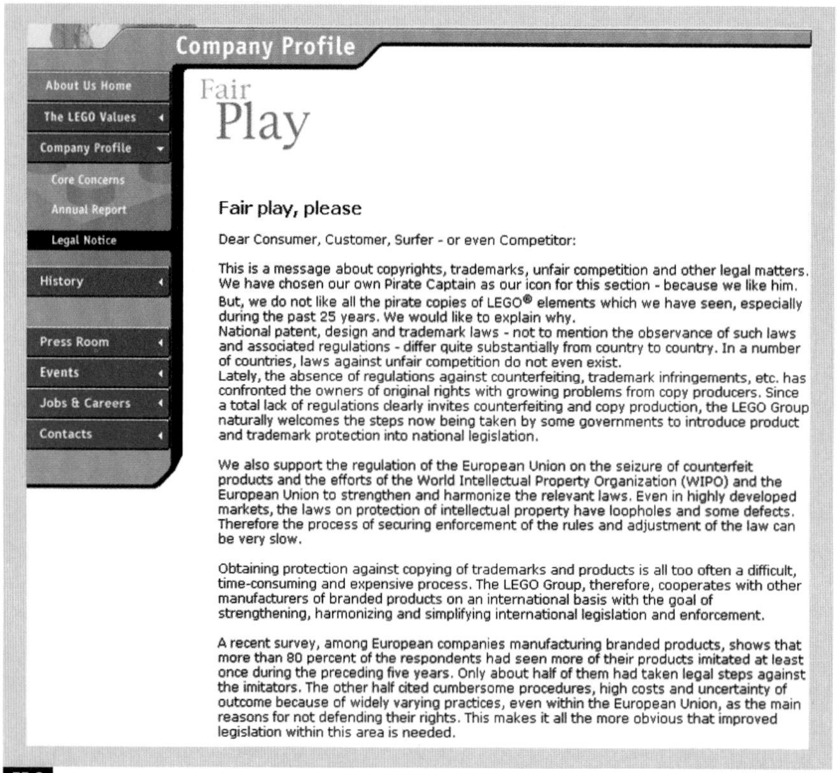
Company Profile

About Us Home
The LEGO Values
Company Profile
Core Concerns
Annual Report
Legal Notice
History
Press Room
Events
Jobs & Careers
Contacts

Fair Play

Fair play, please

Dear Consumer, Customer, Surfer - or even Competitor:

This is a message about copyrights, trademarks, unfair competition and other legal matters. We have chosen our own Pirate Captain as our icon for this section - because we like him. But, we do not like all the pirate copies of LEGO® elements which we have seen, especially during the past 25 years. We would like to explain why.
National patent, design and trademark laws - not to mention the observance of such laws and associated regulations - differ quite substantially from country to country. In a number of countries, laws against unfair competition do not even exist.
Lately, the absence of regulations against counterfeiting, trademark infringements, etc. has confronted the owners of original rights with growing problems from copy producers. Since a total lack of regulations clearly invites counterfeiting and copy production, the LEGO Group naturally welcomes the steps now being taken by some governments to introduce product and trademark protection into national legislation.

We also support the regulation of the European Union on the seizure of counterfeit products and the efforts of the World Intellectual Property Organization (WIPO) and the European Union to strengthen and harmonize the relevant laws. Even in highly developed markets, the laws on protection of intellectual property have loopholes and some defects. Therefore the process of securing enforcement of the rules and adjustment of the law can be very slow.

Obtaining protection against copying of trademarks and products is all too often a difficult, time-consuming and expensive process. The LEGO Group, therefore, cooperates with other manufacturers of branded products on an international basis with the goal of strengthening, harmonizing and simplifying international legislation and enforcement.

A recent survey, among European companies manufacturing branded products, shows that more than 80 percent of the respondents had seen more of their products imitated at least once during the preceding five years. Only about half of them had taken legal steps against the imitators. The other half cited cumbersome procedures, high costs and uncertainty of outcome because of widely varying practices, even within the European Union, as the main reasons for not defending their rights. This makes it all the more obvious that improved legislation within this area is needed.

E5.3

(www.lego.com, February 1, 2002)

Figure E5.3

The LEGO **About Us** Web pages include a page about fair play, describing why LEGO has to protect its trademarks, and what fans may and may not do when creating their own Web sites about the toy.

likely to be reliable in the future. Be sure to ask for permission from any customers and partners before listing them.

5. Employment Opportunities • This page simply describes the kinds of job openings and internships that your company or organization has available. Large companies often provide very advanced database searches, describing positions, responsibilities, and geographic locations. Smaller companies do not need to be as sophisticated, and they often just list all of the open positions.

6. Public Relations • The public relations page contains information published by, as well as for, media outlets. Included are such things as

- Press releases about new products, new partners, changes in management, and so on
- Links to or excerpts of media coverage about the Web site or company
- Awards won
- Contact information for interviews (see Figure E5.4)

Figure E5.4

The LexisNexis **About Us** page contains many of the features described in this section, including an organizational profile, contact information, and disclaimers and legal information.

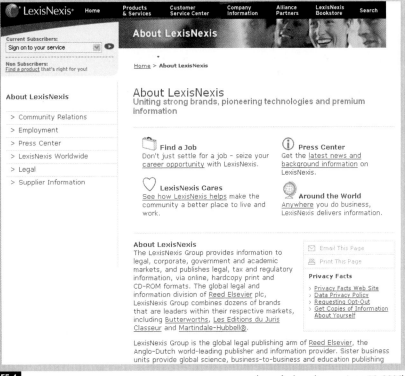

E5.4

(www.lexisnexis.com, June 16, 2006)

7. Investor Relations • The investor relations page contains relevant financial literature about the company. Common items included here are annual reports, Securities and Exchange Commission (SEC) filings, analyst coverage, and positive media coverage.

8. Community Relations • The community relations page describes how the company gives back to the local community, including past charitable events, as well as what the company can provide for future events, such as software, hardware, services, time, people, or money. It is also useful to explain how people can contact your company to request help.

9. Site Credits • The site credits page gives credit to the Web teams that helped develop the Web site. Such a page is often useful for Web design firms because it gives them a little bit of free advertising.

10. Frequently Asked Questions • Some Web sites collect questions that customers often ask and create a FREQUENTLY ASKED QUESTIONS (H7), or **FAQ,** page that answers them.

H7

✳ SOLUTION

Collect background information in About Us pages. These pages should help people learn more about who you are, what you do, and why they can trust you. Include things like an organizational profile, contact information, disclaimers and legal information, customers and partners, employment opportunities, public relations, investor relations, community relations, site credits, and frequently asked questions.

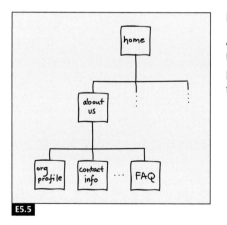

E5.5

Figure E5.5

Although the specific content for the **About Us** pages will vary from site to site, these pages should always be easily accessible from the homepage portal.

❋ OTHER PATTERNS TO CONSIDER

About Us pages should help reinforce the Web site's UP-FRONT VALUE PROPOSITION (C2). They should also contain links to the Web site's PRIVACY POLICY (E4) and FREQUENTLY ASKED QUESTIONS (H7) pages.

　　About Us pages can also be made part of your PAGE TEMPLATE (D1). Contact information should be included in the **About Us** pages, as well as on the PAGE NOT FOUND (K14) error page.

E6 SECURE CONNECTIONS

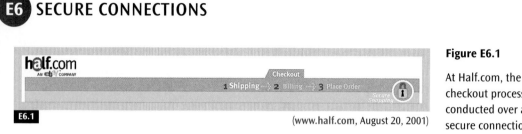

E6.1

(www.half.com, August 20, 2001)

✳ BACKGROUND

One of the requirements of FAIR INFORMATION PRACTICES (E3) is to collect and handle sensitive personal information in a secure manner. One way of doing this is to use secure connections. This pattern deals with interface issues for letting people know that they're entering a secure area. This pattern should be used in conjunction with PREVENTING PHISHING SCAMS (E9) to protect your customers and your Web site from fraud.

E3

E9

✳ PROBLEM

People are often uncomfortable transmitting sensitive personal information over the Web.

Many people are uneasy about sending sensitive information online. They worry that hackers can steal credit card numbers and passwords. One of the ways of tackling this problem is to use secure connections.

You can establish a secure connection with Secure Sockets Layer (SSL), which uses a sophisticated encryption scheme to scramble data sent over the Web, making it very difficult for snoopers to look at the data. You can tell you're using SSL if the Web address begins with *https* instead of just *http*. Most Web browsers also provide feedback that you're using a secure connection, as Figures E6.2 and E6.3 show. (A full discussion of the technical details involved in setting up SSL is beyond the scope of this book. See the Resources section for more information.)

The problem is that this feedback is extremely minimal and easily overlooked. One way of reassuring your customers is to provide better feedback. For example, Figures E6.4 and E6.5 show how an ACTION BUTTON (K4) can be used to make it clear that a secure connection is being used.

K4

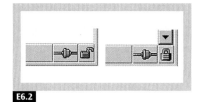

E6.2

E6.3

Figure E6.2

The screen shot on the left shows a nonsecure connection in Netscape 6.1. The one on the right shows a secure connection.

Figure E6.3

The screen shot on the top shows a nonsecure connection in Microsoft Internet Explorer 6.0. The one on the bottom shows a secure connection.

Figure E6.4

Amazon.com uses a labeled button to let customers know that the login information will be secure.

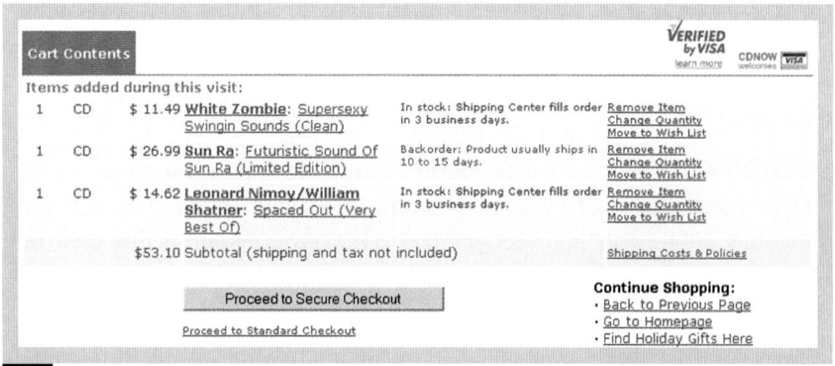

(www.amazon.com, September 22, 2001)

Figure E6.5

CDNOW uses secure connections for its shopping cart. An action button labeled "Proceed to Secure Checkout" reinforces this point.

(www.cdnow.com, February 11, 2002)

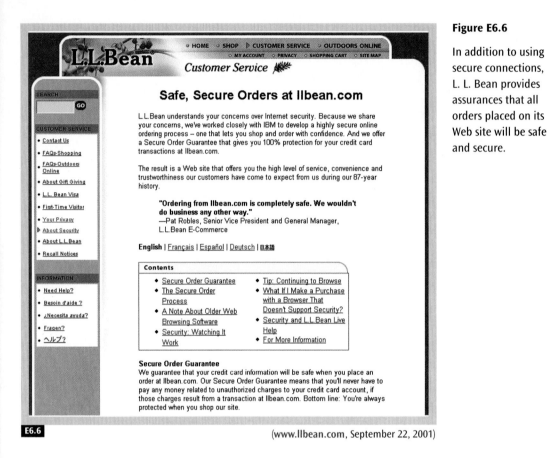

Figure E6.6

In addition to using secure connections, L. L. Bean provides assurances that all orders placed on its Web site will be safe and secure.

(www.llbean.com, September 22, 2001)

Some Web sites provide additional assurances about their security. For example, Figure E6.6 shows L. L. Bean's guarantee that all orders placed on its Web site will be safe and secure.

✳ SOLUTION

Use a labeled icon or a labeled action button to let customers know that they're transmitting information securely. If needed, provide a Web page describing the security practices you use to reassure customers that their personal information will be kept safe.

Figure E6.7

Web pages should provide feedback to let customers know when information is being transmitted securely. Take special care to maintain the secure connection as long as necessary.

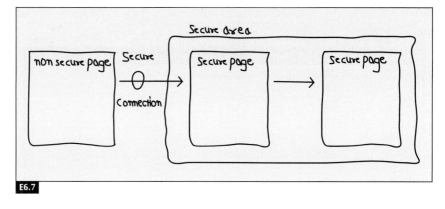

E6.7

✳ OTHER PATTERNS TO CONSIDER

Secure connections help safeguard sensitive personal information that your customers send you, partially addressing the security requirements in FAIR INFORMATION PRACTICES (E3).

Use secure connections in all Web pages where sensitive information is entered by the customer or displayed for the customer. This stipulation includes places such as SIGN-IN/NEW ACCOUNT (H2), QUICK-FLOW CHECKOUT (F1), important PROCESS FUNNELS (H1), ACCOUNT MANAGEMENT (H4), and any Web page dealing with financial information. You can use specially labeled ACTION BUTTONS (K4) to let customers know that the transaction is secure.

E7 E-MAIL NOTIFICATIONS

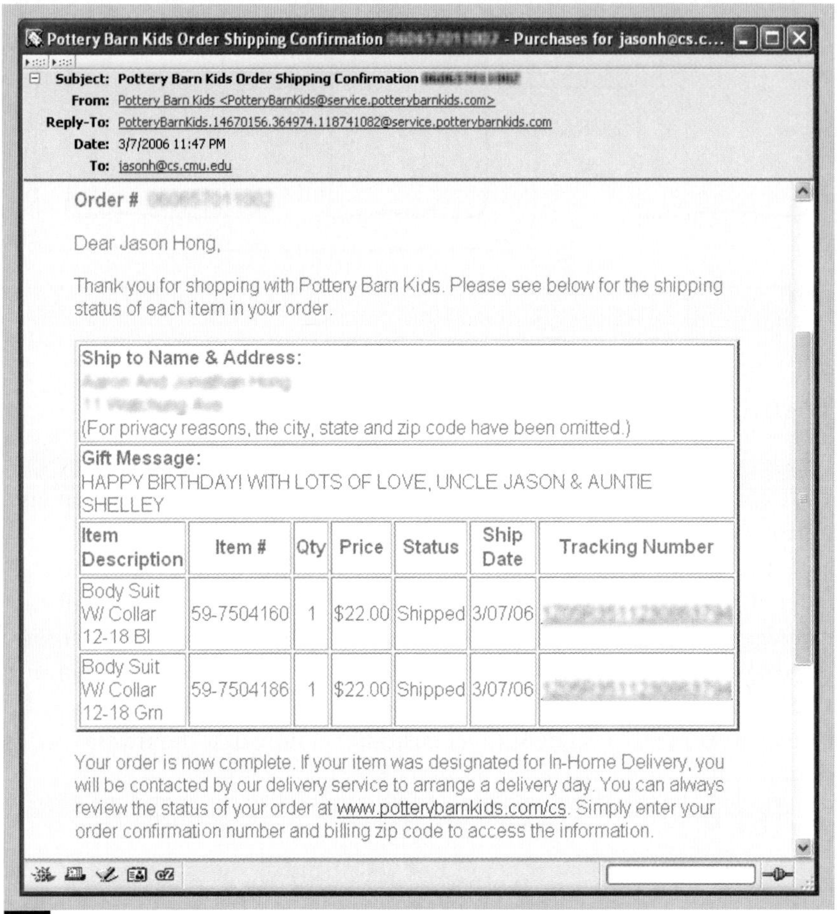
Pottery Barn Kids Order Shipping Confirmation [illegible] - Purchases for jasonh@cs.c...

Subject: Pottery Barn Kids Order Shipping Confirmation [illegible]
From: Pottery Barn Kids <PotteryBarnKids@service.potterybarnkids.com>
Reply-To: PotteryBarnKids.14670156.364974.118741082@service.potterybarnkids.com
Date: 3/7/2006 11:47 PM
To: jasonh@cs.cmu.edu

Order # [illegible]

Dear Jason Hong,

Thank you for shopping with Pottery Barn Kids. Please see below for the shipping status of each item in your order.

Ship to Name & Address:
[illegible]
[illegible]
(For privacy reasons, the city, state and zip code have been omitted.)

Gift Message:
HAPPY BIRTHDAY! WITH LOTS OF LOVE, UNCLE JASON & AUNTIE SHELLEY

Item Description	Item #	Qty	Price	Status	Ship Date	Tracking Number
Body Suit W/ Collar 12-18 Bl	59-7504160	1	$22.00	Shipped	3/07/06	[illegible]
Body Suit W/ Collar 12-18 Grn	59-7504186	1	$22.00	Shipped	3/07/06	[illegible]

Your order is now complete. If your item was designated for In-Home Delivery, you will be contacted by our delivery service to arrange a delivery day. You can always review the status of your order at www.potterybarnkids.com/cs. Simply enter your order confirmation number and billing zip code to access the information.

E7.1

(e-mail from www.potterybarnkids.com, March 28, 2006)

Figure E7.1

E-mail notifications are useful for informing your customers of important transactions, such as purchases from a personal e-commerce site.

BACKGROUND

In contrast to E-MAIL SUBSCRIPTIONS (E2), which are messages that are periodically sent to customers, such as newsletters, e-mail notifications are used to contact customers immediately and notify them of something important, such as an ORDER CONFIRMATION AND THANK-YOU (F8) for a purchase on a PERSONAL E-COMMERCE (A1) site, the creation of a new account with SIGN-IN/NEW ACCOUNT (H2), a change in address, or a change in your PRIVACY POLICY (E4). These notifications need to be written so that they don't look like junk mail, and so that they help PREVENT PHISHING SCAMS (E9). This pattern looks at how to structure your e-mail notifications to make them more effective.

E2 F8 A1 H2 E4 E9

✳ PROBLEM

Web sites need a way of notifying visitors of important events and transactions, but unwanted, dubious, and hard-to-read e-mail notifications are often ignored.

Sometimes a Web site needs to inform visitors of important events and transactions. Because most people are inundated with e-mail, however, it's important to ask yourself certain questions before sending any e-mail notifications. For example, when is it appropriate to send such e-mails? What will engender trust and build a lasting relationship with customers? How can you help ensure that customers will read your e-mails? How can you help customers with routine tasks? Thinking about these questions and reading the discussion that follows can help you design the best solution for your site.

Web sites need to send e-mails for many reasons, some better than others. Here are some examples of e-mails that typical customers want and *expect* to receive:

- An ORDER CONFIRMATION AND THANK-YOU (F8) after completing a QUICK-FLOW CHECKOUT (F1)
- An ORDER TRACKING AND HISTORY (G7) e-mail informing them that their purchased items have been shipped
- For the SIGN-IN/NEW ACCOUNT (H2) page, notifications related to a lost password or the creation of a new account
- Confirmation of changes to the customer's account—for example, confirmation of a change to one's e-mail address, sent to the old address and the new address [see ACCOUNT MANAGEMENT (H4) for more examples]
- Notification of being outbid in an online auction
- Notice of changes in the Web site's PRIVACY POLICY (E4)
- Follow-up posts to a visitor's post on a MESSAGE BOARD (D5) or BLOG (A12)
- Warnings—for example, regarding poor behavior on a Web site's MESSAGE BOARD (D5)
- Notification of billing problems, shipping problems, or other transaction-related problems
- Custom alerts such as event reminders, news updates, or event triggers. Examples might include notification that a library book is due soon or that the price of a stock has dropped below a certain mark.

Use a Simple, Clear Sender Name • People scan senders' e-mail addresses before reading their e-mail, so if your sender's name is unknown, looks like it's made up, or appears odd, your recipient is less likely to read your e-mail notification. You can use a friendly name (such as *Pottery Barn Kids*), or leave the e-mail address exposed (for example, *PotteryBarnKids@ service.potterybarnkids.com*). Many e-mail readers show both, but some show only the friendly name if it's available, saving some space and making the e-mail screen a little less cluttered.

The advantage of using the e-mail address without the friendly name is that you show a little more about where the e-mail came from. Truth be told, though, it's almost as easy to fake an e-mail address as it is to fake a friendly name, so you're not buying much more credibility with a raw address. And since e-mail addresses tend to be longer than their friendly counterparts, you might be better off using a simple and clear friendly name instead.

Using a name that refers to your organization, type of transaction, or department can also help put the e-mail in context. When a personal name (such as *Mary Scott*) is included in a sender's name, if the name is not familiar your recipient may be leery and think the message is spam. A sender name like *XYZ Corp Orders,* however, quickly identifies the company that's sending the message.

Use a Simple Subject Line That Specifies a Past Action or Request • Another way to engender trust and help ensure that people will read your e-mail notifications is to use a simple, straightforward subject line that makes it clear why the recipient is receiving your e-mail. One approach is to have a subject line that reminds people of past actions or requests—for example, mentioning a recent purchase or starting the subject line with the name of your newsletter. Such a subject line will also make it easier to find the message again in the future.

Your subject line should identify the sender of the notification and the reason it was sent. Here are some examples of good e-mail subject lines:

- "Revision to your Amazon.com account"
- "Invoice for Star Wars DVD from xyz.com"

The following examples are not as useful:

- "Thank you for your purchase" (where was the purchase from?)
- "Company ABC customer service" (tells you who the company is, but what's the message about?)
- "Order received" (this e-mail will be difficult to search for and find again)

Make the Purpose of the E-Mail Clear in the Body of the Message • Make it immediately clear to your recipient that the message you're sending is not junk e-mail. You can do this by referring to a recent transaction the customer completed or information that the customer recently requested. In Figure E7.1, for example, the first sentence says, "Thank you for shopping with Pottery Barn Kids." Such a clear statement reminds the recipient of something done or requested, so it's familiar and more trustworthy, and the customer is reassured that it's not spam or phishing e-mail.

Tell Customers How to Follow Up with Questions • Sometimes customers have questions about an e-mail notification that they receive. A natural instinct is to reply to the sender of the e-mail; however, some e-mail addresses are used only to send e-mails, with no one actually reading any e-mails sent to that address. If this is the case, make it immediately clear at the top of the message that recipients should not reply to the e-mail. The message shown in Figure E7.2 begins with such a warning. Use this type of e-mail only for messages that rarely raise questions—for example,

Figure E7.2

If you're using an e-mail address only to send notifications, make sure your recipients are made aware that they should not reply to your e-mail notifications, as this e-mail from Comcast does.

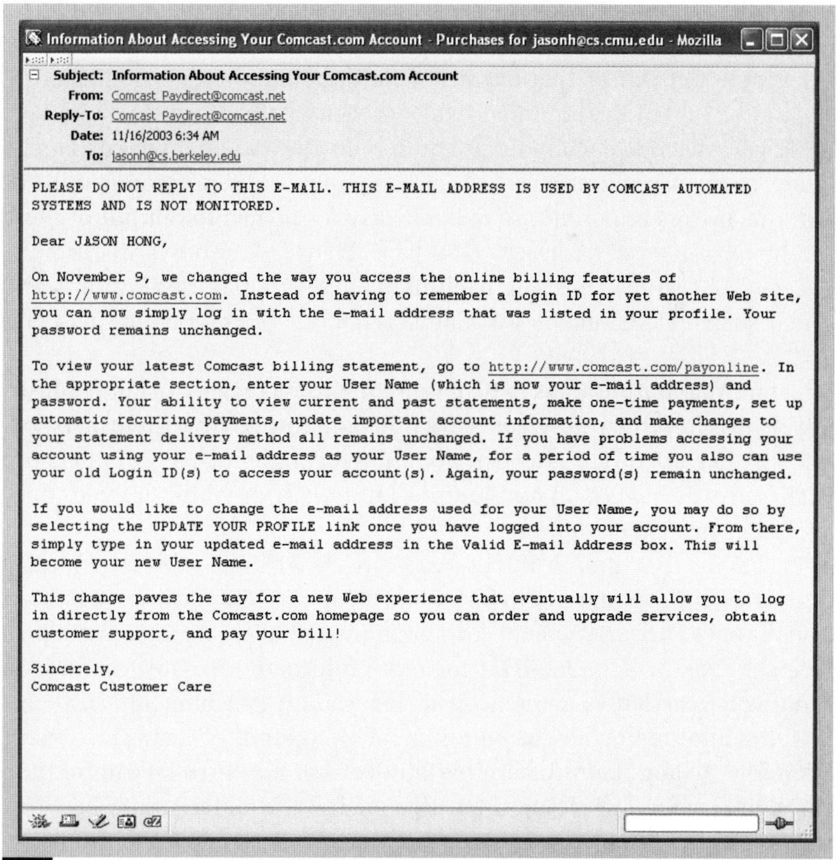

Information About Accessing Your Comcast.com Account - Purchases for jasonh@cs.cmu.edu - Mozilla

Subject: **Information About Accessing Your Comcast.com Account**
From: Comcast_Paydirect@comcast.net
Reply-To: Comcast_Paydirect@comcast.net
Date: 11/16/2003 6:34 AM
To: jasonh@cs.berkeley.edu

PLEASE DO NOT REPLY TO THIS E-MAIL. THIS E-MAIL ADDRESS IS USED BY COMCAST AUTOMATED SYSTEMS AND IS NOT MONITORED.

Dear JASON HONG,

On November 9, we changed the way you access the online billing features of http://www.comcast.com. Instead of having to remember a Login ID for yet another Web site, you can now simply log in with the e-mail address that was listed in your profile. Your password remains unchanged.

To view your latest Comcast billing statement, go to http://www.comcast.com/payonline. In the appropriate section, enter your User Name (which is now your e-mail address) and password. Your ability to view current and past statements, make one-time payments, set up automatic recurring payments, update important account information, and make changes to your statement delivery method all remains unchanged. If you have problems accessing your account using your e-mail address as your User Name, for a period of time you also can use your old Login ID(s) to access your account(s). Again, your password(s) remain unchanged.

If you would like to change the e-mail address used for your User Name, you may do so by selecting the UPDATE YOUR PROFILE link once you have logged into your account. From there, simply type in your updated e-mail address in the Valid E-mail Address box. This will become your new User Name.

This change paves the way for a new Web experience that eventually will allow you to log in directly from the Comcast.com homepage so you can order and upgrade services, obtain customer support, and pay your bill!

Sincerely,
Comcast Customer Care

E7.2

(e-mail from www.comcast.com, November 16, 2003)

changes to a PRIVACY POLICY (E4). Also consider adding a phone number to the e-mail or a Web site that people can use if they do have questions.

E4

In other cases, you might want to structure your e-mails to make it easier for customers to send responses. For example, you could have the **Reply-To** field set to an address that is monitored by customer service representatives. Sometimes subject lines contain case ticket numbers. For example, the computer help desk at Carnegie Mellon University sends responses with subject lines that start with things like *[HD00936522]*, making it easier for the help desk to keep track of who was assigned to a case and the current status of that case.

Declare Your E-Mail Privacy Policies • To assuage any concerns that you will be sending spam e-mails to your customers, you can include a paragraph in your PRIVACY POLICY (E4) that makes clear the conditions under which you will send e-mail notifications. Not everyone will read your privacy policy, but those who are concerned about it will be able to turn to a well-known place.

E4

Let People Opt Out of Less Important Notifications • Some notifications, such as billing information and ORDER CONFIRMATION AND THANK-YOU (F8) messages, are critically important and should always be sent to customers. Other kinds of notifications, such as site updates and promotional information, are less important, so make it easy for people to opt out of these on their ACCOUNT MANAGEMENT (H4) page. Figure E7.3 shows an example.

F8

H4

Table E7.1 shows one way of thinking about e-mail notifications and e-mail subscriptions, and how to handle people's choices for opting in or out.

Structure Your Notifications to Help Prevent Phishing Scams • Online phishing scams, in which miscreants trick people into giving them personal information, are on the rise. One common technique these scammers use is to copy existing e-mail notifications but modify any links to go to their Web page instead of yours.

There are two simple things you can do to help PREVENT PHISHING SCAMS (E9). The first is not to foster bad behaviors like clicking on links in e-mails or to encourage people to sign in to your Web site via e-mail links [see SIGN-IN/NEW ACCOUNT (H2) for more information]. The second is to send your customers periodic warnings about phishing attacks. This includes informing your customers about what kinds of e-mails to expect from you, telling them that you will never ask for personal information through e-mail, and giving them tips on how to differentiate between scams and real e-mails from you.

E9

H2

Figure E7.3

Because some notifications are more important than others, it's a good idea to let customers choose the kinds of notifications that they will receive. In this example, Virgin Mobile lets people receive "promotional information from Virgin Mobile and our Partners," "promotional information from Virgin Mobile only," or "Virgin Mobile service announcements only."

E7.3

(www.virginmobileusa.com, September 19, 2006)

E-Mail Type	When to Use	Examples
High-priority e-mail notifications	High-priority notifications are needed for the operation of an account. Visitors should not be able to opt out of receiving these	Creating a new account with SIGN-IN/NEW ACCOUNT (H2), ORDER TRACKING AND HISTORY (G7)
Low-priority e-mail notifications	Low-priority notifications provide useful but noncritical functionality. Visitors should be able to opt in to receive these. Advertisements should also be used judiciously	Custom alerts, targeted advertisements
E-mail subscriptions	Visitors should be able to opt in for e-mail subscriptions	Newsletters

Table E7.1

E-Mail Notifications versus Subscriptions

H2

G7

Add Images as Attachments Rather Than Using Links to Your Web Site • More and more e-mail clients are blocking links to images for privacy reasons. At one time, e-mail clients downloaded any images specified in the e-mail, but this practice made it possible for senders to track who was reading what e-mail and when. There are three things you can do to compensate for the blocking of linked images. The first is to add any necessary images as attachments. The second is to write your e-mails so that images are not crucial to the message you're trying to convey. The third is to ensure that your images have small file sizes so that they don't clog up your recipients' e-mail inboxes. The FAST-LOADING IMAGES (L2) pattern provides some tips for shrinking image files.

L2

☀ SOLUTION

Make it clear why recipients have received your e-mail notification by having a simple, straightforward subject line, as well as a clear opening sentence. Also make it clear who the sender is so that your customers don't think they're receiving spam, and identify a contact for recipients' questions.

Figure E7.4

A good e-mail notification will have a meaningful sender name, an informative subject line that lets people know why they're receiving the message, useful content, and a way to get answers if there are any additional questions.

To: Customer
FROM: your Organization
SUBJ: straightforward subject
Clear opening sentence.

Contact us:

E7.4

✳ OTHER PATTERNS TO CONSIDER

E-mail notifications are useful for such things as ORDER CONFIRMATION AND THANK-YOU (F8) messages, the creation of new accounts with SIGN-IN/NEW ACCOUNT (H2), and changes in your Web site's PRIVACY POLICY (E4). Specify in your privacy policy the conditions under which you will send out notifications. Also let people change notification receipt selections in their PRIVACY PREFERENCES (E8). Finally, write your e-mail notifications so that they help PREVENT PHISHING SCAMS (E9).

Figure E8.1

The Friendster social networking site lets you configure various preferences for managing your privacy online.

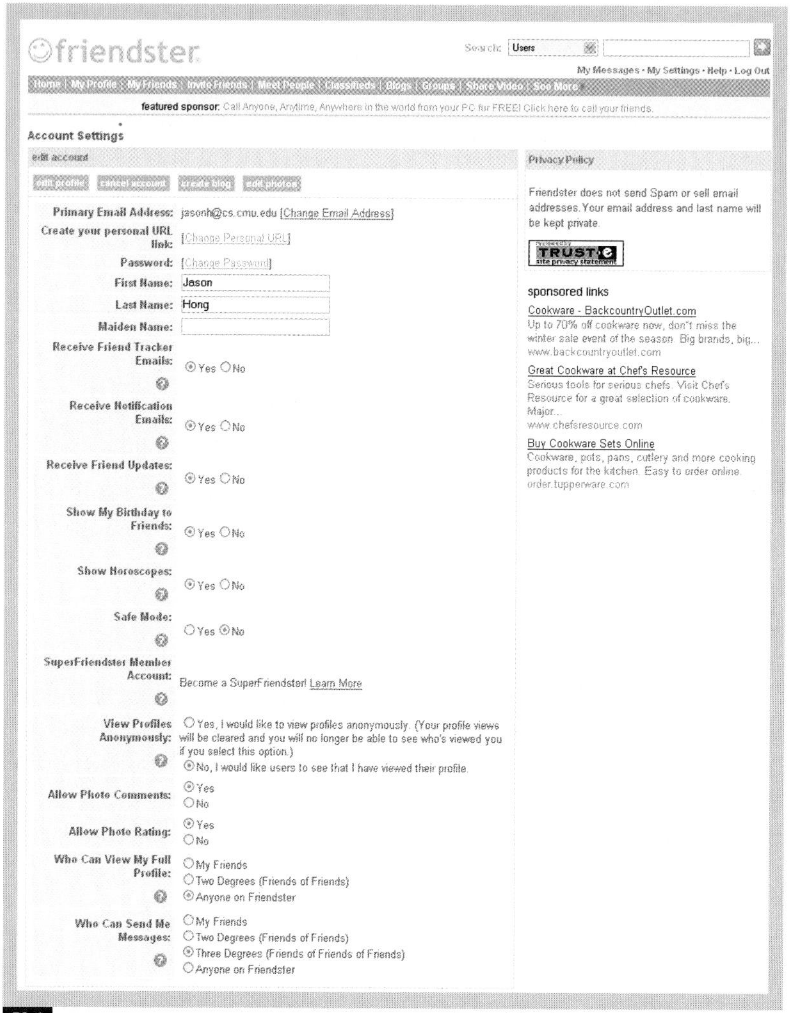

E8.1

(www.friendster.com, February 6, 2006)

✳ BACKGROUND

Customers can share personal information with companies on PERSONAL E-COMMERCE (A1) sites, NEWS MOSAICS (A2), and VALUABLE COMPANY SITES (A7). Customers can also share personal information with other community members on COMMUNITY CONFERENCE (A3) sites. One way of fulfilling the FAIR INFORMATION PRACTICES (E3) and one's PRIVACY POLICY (E4) is to provide a way for customers to see and modify their privacy preferences.

A1 A2

A7

A3

E3 E4

✳ PROBLEM

Customers need an easy way to see and change their privacy preferences.

In many cases, sharing personal information can help streamline online interactions. For example, saved credit card and shipping address information can be used to streamline a customer's QUICK-FLOW CHECKOUTS (F1). Product preferences and ratings can be used to offer PERSONALIZED RECOMMENDATIONS (G3). Information about a customer's hobbies and e-mail address can be used to provide E-MAIL SUBSCRIPTIONS (E2) with highly relevant content.

However, many customers have legitimate concerns about how their personal information is used. According to a poll conducted in 2000 by the Pew Internet & American Life Project, 86 percent of Internet users are concerned about businesses or people they don't know getting personal information about them or their families. Seven of every ten Internet users have concerns about hackers getting their credit card number, and six of ten are concerned about someone learning personal information about them because of their interactions online.

Studies conducted by Alan Westin since the 1970s also indicate that customers in the United States can be roughly divided into three groups:

1. **Privacy fundamentalists** (roughly 25 percent of the population in the United States) are highly concerned about threats to their privacy from businesses, and favor strong government regulation to control business information practices.
2. **Privacy pragmatists** (roughly 60 percent) balance the risks and benefits of sharing personal information, and tend to favor a combination of government regulation and technical solutions.
3. The **privacy unconcerned** (roughly 15 percent) have little or no concerns about their consumer privacy.

Well over a majority of your customers will have concerns about their privacy, and it is thus in your Web site's best interests to clearly show customers what personal information is being collected and, in cases where it is legal and makes sense, to specify how that information will be used.

Many People Like to Keep Contact Information Private • Often people will share their contact information only if your site communicates good reasons for them to do so. With respect to PERSONAL E-COMMERCE (A1),

VALUABLE COMPANY SITES (A7), and other kinds of Web sites where personal information is shared with a company, some examples of privacy preferences that customers might want to indicate include the following:

- Specifying when to receive an E-MAIL NOTIFICATION (E7) from the Web site
- Adding or removing oneself from an E-MAIL SUBSCRIPTION (E2)
- Specifying when it's OK to share one's e-mail address with affiliates
- Specifying if it's OK to receive advertising using a customer's phone number and mailing address

For these kinds of sites, privacy preferences should emphasize the advantages to sharing information, have good defaults where customers can opt in rather than having to opt out, and provide SECURE CONNECTIONS (E6) so that it's clear that personal information is being transmitted safely.

For example, Figure E8.2a shows Yahoo!'s account creation page. Note how this page makes clear what information is being requested, and for what purposes (on the side). Also note, at the bottom, that people can opt in to mailing lists. Figure E8.2b shows a similar page in ACCOUNT MANAGEMENT (H4) that lets customers modify their preferences after creating an account.

One thing worth noting is that, on Yahoo! and many other Web sites, some opt-in options—for example, E-MAIL SUBSCRIPTIONS (E2) to newsletters—are intentionally turned on and then buried in the preferences page. Such cases indicate that marketing is taking precedence over usability, and the result is that many people unintentionally opt in without knowing it. This is a decision that has to be made site by site, but we advocate having people intentionally choose rather than unintentionally choose their options.

People Want to Be Able to Project a Particular Persona on Community-Based Web Sites • For COMMUNITY CONFERENCE (A3) sites, the issue is less what the Web site knows about an individual, and more what other community members can see about an individual. Here, community members are interested in projecting a desired persona when they share personal information. For example, a teenager might want to appear fun-loving and carefree, while a thirty-something might want to avoid looking unprofessional with fellow colleagues.

There is also a wide range of comfort zones for community members, ranging from lurkers who are comfortable sharing only minimal personal information to exhibitionists who are willing to publish every gory detail

Figure E8.2

(a) When customers create a new e-mail account on Yahoo!, they can see what information is being requested and why. At the bottom, customers can also specify whether they want any e-mail subscriptions. (b) Customers can later edit these preferences on a similar page.

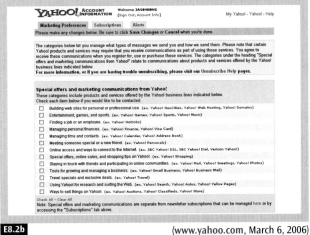

E8.2a   (www.yahoo.com, March 6, 2006)

E8.2b   (www.yahoo.com, March 6, 2006)

of their personal lives online! The challenge here is to provide a design that can accommodate this diverse set of personality types while minimizing foreseeable risks.

Some examples of privacy preferences that customers might want to state with respect to other community members include the following:

- **Selecting who can see one's personal profile.** For example, some social networking sites let only friends of friends see people's descriptions of their own hobbies, favorite movies, and so on, while other social networking sites make that information public to any registered user.
- **Selecting who can see one's wish lists on a** PERSONAL E-COMMERCE **(A1) site, to facilitate** GIFT GIVING **(G6).** A person might be comfortable with making a wish list public to all, or might want to restrict access to that list to a select group of friends, or keep the list entirely private.
- **Selecting who can see one's personal photos on a photo-sharing site.** As with wish lists, a person might want to make some photos public to everyone, public to a group of friends, or entirely private.

Provide a Privacy Mirror to Let Customers See How Others Will See Them • Correctly specifying privacy preferences can be difficult, and a lack of clarity may make people reluctant to share any personal information, making your Web site less useful. A privacy mirror is one way of addressing these concerns. In the real world, a mirror lets you see how others see you, allowing you to groom yourself in private before venturing into the public sphere. Similarly, a privacy mirror lets your customers see how others will see them, before you make any of their personal information public (see Figure E8.3).

For example, a photo-sharing site might show customers a checklist of all photos that they're about to make public. A social networking site might let customers view what a close friend would see, as well as what a distant acquaintance would see.

Privacy Preferences Can Also Be Specified at the End of a Transaction or through Explicit Sharing • On completion of the QUICK-FLOW CHECKOUT (F1), Amazon.com gives you the option to put your purchased items in your public profile, letting others know what types of items interest you. This is a good design because, by default, no personal information is shared (except as you have specified); it is simple to share information [right after a purchase, rather than having to go through various pages in

Figure E8.3

LinkedIn is a social networking site for professionals. When setting up their profiles, customers can use the Web site's privacy mirror to see how others will view them. This figure shows how others will view one of the authors of this book.

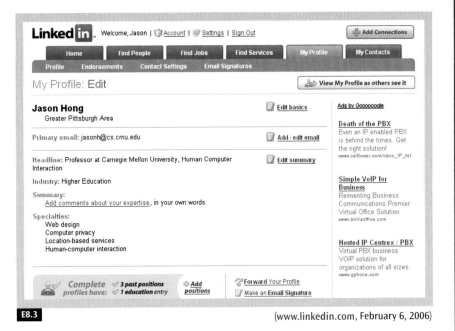

E8.3

(www.linkedin.com, February 6, 2006)

(H4) ACCOUNT MANAGEMENT (H4) to accomplish the same goal]; and people have a clearer idea of precisely what information will be shared.

(D5) As another example, on the craigslist MESSAGE BOARDS (D5), community members can choose whether their messages will show a real e-mail address or an "anonymized" address, before the message is posted (see Figure E8.4). Craigslist also lets customers specify whether it's OK for others to contact them about related products or services.

Photo-sharing sites use a variation of this same idea. Sites like Shutterfly (shutterfly.com) and Kodak EasyShare Gallery (kodakgallery.com) let you explicitly share photo albums simply by selecting which photos you want to share and specifying the e-mail addresses of the people with whom you want to share them. Again, you can do all this without setting any (H4) preferences in ACCOUNT MANAGEMENT (H4).

Let People See and Modify Their Privacy Preferences through Account Management • Customers might discover, after the fact, that they're sharing something they might consider embarrassing, or they may have simply changed their preferences over time. In these cases, it makes sense to make (H4) it easy to modify those preferences. ACCOUNT MANAGEMENT (H4) should be (K2) easy to reach, usually near the NAVIGATION BAR (K2).

Figure E8.4

Before completing a post on its message board, the craigslist community lets members use an anonymous e-mail address and to opt in to getting messages about related services, if desired.

E8.4

(www.craigslist.org, March 6, 2006)

Consider Using a Secure Connection for Highly Personal Content • When highly personal information, such as credit card or medical information, is being sent to a Web site, it is important to use a SECURE CONNECTION (E6) **E6** to reduce the risk of eavesdroppers.

✳ SOLUTION

Provide a way for people to manage their privacy preferences on an account management page, when posting messages to a message board, and when sharing personal information, documents, and images with others.

Figure E8.5

Provide secure access to privacy preferences so that customers can control how their information is shared.

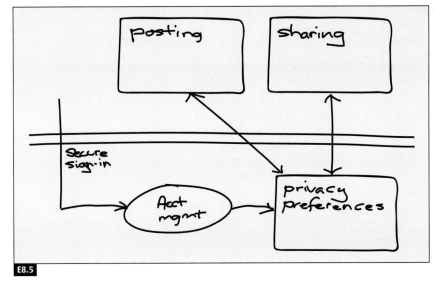

E8.5

✳ OTHER PATTERNS TO CONSIDER

G6
F1 G3

Storing customer information lets you facilitate GIFT GIVING (G6), streamline QUICK-FLOW CHECKOUTS (F1), and offer PERSONALIZED RECOMMENDATIONS (G3). Letting customers easily manage their privacy preferences is one way of fulfilling the requirements of the FAIR INFORMATION PRACTICES (E3) and one's PRIVACY POLICY (E4).

E3
E4

H4
E7 E2

One logical place for managing privacy preferences is the ACCOUNT MANAGEMENT (H4) page. Here, customers can choose when to receive E-MAIL NOTIFICATIONS (E7) and what E-MAIL SUBSCRIPTIONS (E2) they want. Links for account management are often placed near the top-level NAVIGATION BAR (K2), making them highly visible and easy to find.

K2

F1

Another logical place for managing privacy preferences is at the end of a transaction—for example, on completion of the QUICK-FLOW CHECKOUT (F1). However, keep in mind that privacy is more than just setting options; it also includes conveying a consistent appearance to others. Therefore, make it easy to manage privacy preferences in things like personal profiles, wish lists for GIFT GIVING (G6), and MESSAGE BOARDS (D5).

G6 D5

E6

Use a SECURE CONNECTION (E6) if you ever send or receive private information from a customer, such as a credit card number.

E9 PREVENTING PHISHING SCAMS

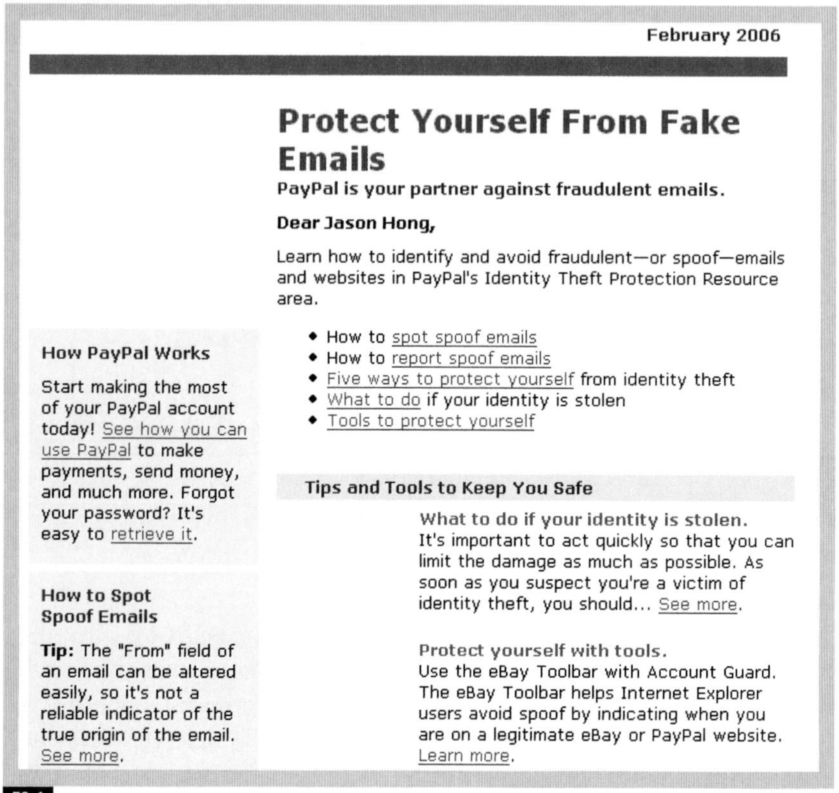

February 2006

Protect Yourself From Fake Emails

PayPal is your partner against fraudulent emails.

Dear Jason Hong,

Learn how to identify and avoid fraudulent—or spoof—emails and websites in PayPal's Identity Theft Protection Resource area.

- How to spot spoof emails
- How to report spoof emails
- Five ways to protect yourself from identity theft
- What to do if your identity is stolen
- Tools to protect yourself

How PayPal Works

Start making the most of your PayPal account today! See how you can use PayPal to make payments, send money, and much more. Forgot your password? It's easy to retrieve it.

How to Spot Spoof Emails

Tip: The "From" field of an email can be altered easily, so it's not a reliable indicator of the true origin of the email. See more.

Tips and Tools to Keep You Safe

What to do if your identity is stolen.
It's important to act quickly so that you can limit the damage as much as possible. As soon as you suspect you're a victim of identity theft, you should... See more.

Protect yourself with tools.
Use the eBay Toolbar with Account Guard. The eBay Toolbar helps Internet Explorer users avoid spoof by indicating when you are on a legitimate eBay or PayPal website. Learn more.

E9.1

(www.paypal.com, February 28, 2006)

Figure E9.1

PayPal (owned by eBay) periodically sends out e-mails that teach its customers about online scams and how to identify them.

✳ BACKGROUND

Many PERSONAL E-COMMERCE (A1), ENABLING INTRANET (A11), and banking sites have faced a rash of online phishing scams in recent years that have resulted in significant financial loss to their customers. These scams often masquerade as legitimate E-MAIL SUBSCRIPTIONS (E2) and E-MAIL NOTIFICATIONS (E7) from a Web site and can cause great harm to your SITE BRANDING (E1).

A1 A11

E2

E7

E1

✳ PROBLEM

Your customers may inadvertently give personal and financial information to online scammers who use your business as part of their scams.

In **phishing,** online scammers impersonate real companies to trick people into giving up personal and financial information. Phishing is a rapidly growing problem. The Anti-Phishing Working Group (apwg.org) reported more than seven thousand new phishing sites in December 2005 alone—a fourfold increase from the seventeen hundred reported the preceding year. The Gartner consulting firm has estimated that phishing affected more than 1.2 million U.S. citizens and cost businesses nearly a $1 billion in 2004 alone. Phishing also leads to additional business losses because of consumer fears of doing business online.

Phishing is an Internet-wide problem that will take a great deal of coordination, technical advances, and political will to combat. Some of these solutions will require the Internet infrastructure to change; others will require customers to use special hardware to verify their identity. In the meantime, here are some site design options that might help minimize problems for your customers and for your business.

Explain What to Expect from Your Web Site • People sometimes fall for phishing scams because they don't know what kinds of messages to expect from you. Many messages that are part of phishing scams pretend to be things like online surveys, account update notifications, or security notices, all of which seem reasonable, since most companies send messages like these.

The first thing you might do is inform your customers that once they create a new account with your Web site, you will never ask for personal information via e-mail. Furthermore, you might promise to limit asking for personal information on your Web site to very few circumstances (for example, asking for a credit card number to confirm a new shipping address, or asking for an e-mail address to request a forgotten password). You can inform customers of this policy as they finish creating a new **H2** account via the SIGN-IN/NEW ACCOUNT (H2) process.

Be aware that if the warning appears too early in the process, customers might become overly concerned and abandon creating an account. However, not warning customers of potential dangers might put them at greater risk to phishing scams. Because people sometimes forget, it's also a good **E7** idea to repeat your warnings with periodic E-MAIL NOTIFICATIONS (E7), and **E5 E4** on your ABOUT US (E5) and PRIVACY POLICY (E4) pages. Of course, you'll want to balance your cautionary statements with everything else you hope to communicate about your site. The level of importance you place on the subject of phishing depends greatly on the sensitivity of the information and services you provide, as well as your vulnerability to potential scams.

The second thing you might do is warn your customers about potential phishing scams and give them a set of simple tips to avoid being tricked. For example, tell your customers to type in your Web address rather than clicking on a link in an e-mail, to look for a SECURE CONNECTION (E6), to check the URL in their Web browser, and to call your company if they're suspicious.

E6

You might include some pages on your Web site educating people about these online scams, and periodically tell your customers about them via E-MAIL SUBSCRIPTIONS (E2). For example, Figure E9.1 shows an e-mail from PayPal that informs people about online scams. Figure E9.2 shows the page to which this e-mail links, which provides more detailed information. You might also have a special page that appears after a customer signs in, providing information about some of these scams and offering additional details if desired. Customers who indicate a deeper interest can be directed to your educational pages. Customers who aren't interested can be taken to the Web page they normally see after signing in.

E2

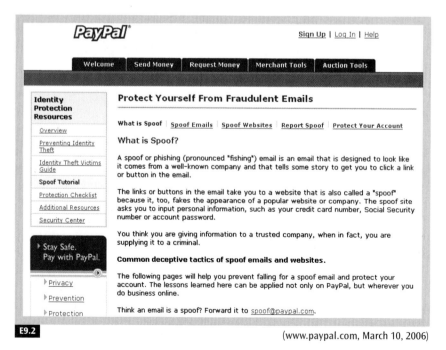

Figure E9.2

PayPal also provides a Web page with more details about how to identify scams and how to protect yourself.

(www.paypal.com, March 10, 2006)

Third, in your E-MAIL SUBSCRIPTIONS (E2) and E-MAIL NOTIFICATIONS (E7), avoid having OBVIOUS LINKS (K10) that lead to a SIGN-IN/NEW ACCOUNT (H2) page. Also avoid having a sign-in form within the e-mail itself. Scammers often include these kinds of links and forms in their fake e-mail notifications but make them go to their Web sites instead of yours. Again, think about how you might teach your customers to be careful of potential scams.

Common Examples of Phishing Scams

Here are some examples of phishing, ranging from the simple to the sophisticated:

- **419 scams.** These scams are also known as *Nigerian money transfer scams,* after a section in the Nigerian Criminal Code. In 419 scams, receivers get an e-mail requesting a loan or money transfer to complete a large transaction, whereupon they are promised to be paid a large multiple of their original investment. In another variant of this scam, the sender claims to represent a Nigerian official or a long lost relative of the receiver, and requests the receiver's bank account number so that money can be wired directly to the receiver. Unless you run a banking Web site, these kinds of scams will probably not directly affect your company.
- **Account suspension scams.** In these scams, people receive messages warning them that their account has been suspended and that they need to verify the account. Variations include confirmation of billing information or warnings that a third party may have accessed the receiver's account.
- **Disaster relief scams.** These scams involve Web sites and e-mails requesting aid immediately after an earthquake, hurricane, or other large-scale disaster.
- **Spear-phishing.** Spear-phishing is perhaps the most sophisticated form of phishing. In this type of scam, a great deal of information about individuals is used to trick them. For example, someone might receive a fake e-mail immediately after winning an auction on eBay, a fake message from a system administrator at the individual's company, or a fake message from a friend whose e-mail address was gleaned from a social networking site like orkut or Facebook.

(Continued)

Common Examples of Phishing Scams (*Continued*)

Phishers also use a variety of increasingly sophisticated techniques to trick people into believing that their fake e-mails are from legitimate sources. These techniques include the following:

- Using forged e-mail addresses—pretending to be from service@chase.com or service@paypal.com, for example.
- Using fake Web addresses such as paypaI.com (an easily overlooked misspelling), similar names such as surveychase.com (pretending to be a survey site for Chase banks), or internationalized domain names (which might be incorrectly displayed in a Web browser and appear to be a legitimate site); or simply hiding the Web domain (for example, http://123.123.123.123/.CU/index.php).
- Hiding the URL by using redirects from other Web sites, for example http:// www.google.com/url?sa=U&start=4&q=http://123.123.123. 123/.CU/ index.php. On casual inspection, this URL would seem to take you to Google rather than to the scam site.
- Opening a fake browser window without an address bar, making it difficult to verify if a site is legitimate.
- Using JavaScript to hide the actual destination URL so that mousing over a link shows the Web address of a real site but clicking on it leads to a fake site.
- Including the person's name in the e-mail, making it seem legitimately personalized.
- Including fake credit card information. A recent scam targeting Mountain America Credit Union included the start of people's credit card numbers in the phishing e-mail—for example, 4053-85**-****-**** (see Figure E9.3). Any of Mountain America's customers who checked their credit card number could verify that this was correct, perhaps not realizing that all of Mountain America's credit card numbers started with the same digits!
- Copying the brand of a legitimate Web site, by using the same images and layout, and even the same HTML Web pages.
- Copying legitimate e-mails and then modifying them.
- Taking advantage of people's fear of being online. Such scams might send messages warning of unauthorized access and urging people to verify their account, nudging them toward doing what seems to be the right thing when they're actually being directed to a scam site.
- Playing off greed—for example, offering money for completing a survey.

Figure E9.3

In this example of a sophisticated phishing scam, note that the fake e-mail looks professional, having a clean design, all the right logos, and a few digits of the person's credit card number (tricking people because the first few digits of credit cards from the same company tend to start with the same digits).

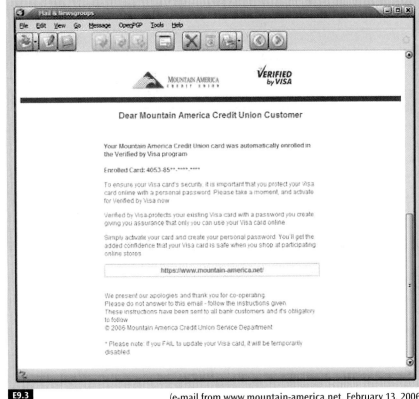

E9.3

(e-mail from www.mountain-america.net, February 13, 2006)

Don't Outsource E-Mail Subscriptions and Notifications • Some people may become suspicious or confused if they see E-MAIL SUBSCRIPTIONS (E2) or E-MAIL NOTIFICATIONS (E7) that seem to contain content from you but are coming from an unknown e-mail address. For example, you have an e-mail subscription with XYZCorp.com, but start getting e-mails from ABCWeb.com with content from XYZCorp.com. This can happen if you outsource your e-mail subscriptions and notifications. We strongly advise not outsourcing subscriptions and notifications, because it will teach your customers bad habits—namely, to expect that e-mails from you do not come from your Web address—and make them more susceptible to phishing scams.

In Designing Your Site, Assume That Some Customers Will Be Phished • No matter how well you attempt to train your customers to avoid phishing scams, some might still be phished. Sometimes malicious hackers use spyware secretly installed on a customer's computer to record every keystroke (called *key logging*). A customer might also let down his guard one day because he's too busy and failed to notice a Web site or e-mail scam.

There are some basic things you can do to minimize the risks of fraudulent transactions. One is to provide an E-MAIL NOTIFICATION (E7) for important transactions, such as a change of e-mail or mailing address. Another is to provide an ORDER CONFIRMATION AND THANK-YOU (F8) when a purchase or other important transaction is completed so that customers can be properly notified. A third is never to show a person's full credit card number on a Web page.

Unfortunately, these "transaction complete" e-mail messages can look like the e-mails that phishers use to trick people in the first place. The difference between your e-mails and phishing attacks is that your e-mails can come directly on the heels of customers' completing an action. If your e-mail servers are slow, however, and these e-mails take more than a few seconds or minutes to send after a transaction completes, they will look more and more like phishing attacks. To minimize customer confusion and vulnerability, it can pay to speed up transaction E-MAIL NOTIFICATIONS (E7).

You can build anti-phishing safeguards into your system. For example, some PERSONAL E-COMMERCE (A1) sites do not allow new shipping addresses to be added on QUICK ADDRESS SELECTION (F4) pages without a complete credit card verification. Although this approach is not scam-proof, since phishers can trick customers into giving them their credit card numbers as well, implementing this feature is fairly straightforward and may help many of your customers avoid financial losses.

Limit Exposure • By limiting the number or size of transactions, you can minimize your vulnerability to phishing scams by limiting your business exposure. If you set up some reasonable limits to prevent a compromised account from being exploited completely and quickly, you give you and your customers time to notice problems and respond before major damage occurs. For the banking site example, you might limit account transfers to $5,000 per day. If you or your customers see money disappearing from the account, you'll have time to act before too much money is lost.

Require Multiple Forms of Identification • The more pieces of verifiable information that scammers need from your customers to break your system, the less likely it is that they'll be able to do so. Depending on your site and services, you might require a user ID and password to log in, but sometimes you might also require a verified e-mail address, validated credit card information (including zip/postal code and security code from the back of the physical card), an ATM PIN, information from a banking statement or other information mailed to a physical address, Social Security number, phone number, birth date, mother's maiden name, secret question/answer, and so on.

Although all of these additional pieces of information can be used to provide more security on your site, they won't keep phishing e-mails and fake Web sites from asking your customers for them as well. However, for more sensitive transactions, such as paying for items or transferring money, if your site requires a second level of identification at the moment of transaction instead of at initial login, a phishing attack that asks for all the information at login will seem very suspicious.

For example, if a banking site requires a login using a Social Security number and secret password to view balance information, but requires an ATM PIN to transfer money to another account, a phishing site that asks for all the information at the beginning will appear noticeably different from the real site. In addition, phishing sites are unlikely to mimic the depth and breadth of a real banking site, because the customer-specific information will be obviously incorrect.

Requiring secondary forms of identification at critical transaction points once a customer is logged in to your site can help prevent more serious business and customer losses.

Consider Setting Up an Explicit Personal Message Area for Each Customer • Some Web sites have set up personal message areas to communicate with customers instead of using e-mail. For example, eBay calls this function *My Messages,* and Chase bank calls this its *Secure Message Center.* Again, communicating in this way is a matter of training customers, letting them know that your company will send only certain kinds of E-MAIL NOTIFICATIONS (E7), and that when your customers receive e-mail messages from your company, they can verify them by seeing the message in these personal message areas on the Web site as well.

It's worth pointing out that this is an extreme measure rather than a quick and easy solution. It is far easier for people to check their e-mail than to have to sign in to multiple Web sites every day, each with their own personal message area, to get important messages.

Actively Search for Web Sites That Are Illicitly Using Your Brand Name • You can help protect your customers and your SITE BRANDING (E1) by actively searching for phishing sites that are impersonating your Web site. One way of doing this is to construct a program that scans your Web logs for

Tips for Your Customers

The Federal Trade Commission has set up a Web page full of tips to avoid phishing, available at ftc.gov/bcp/conline/pubs/alerts/phishingalrt.htm. Try to reinforce these concepts with customers on your SIGN-IN/NEW ACCOUNT (H2) page, through periodic E-MAIL NOTIFICATIONS (E7), and on your FREQUENTLY ASKED QUESTIONS (H7) page.

Here are some of the FTC's tips:

1. If you get an e-mail or pop-up message asking for personal or financial information, don't reply, and don't click on the link in the message.
2. Use antivirus software and a firewall, and keep them up-to-date.
3. Don't e-mail personal or financial information.
4. Review credit card and bank account statements as soon as you receive them.
5. Be cautious about opening any attachment or downloading any files from e-mails.

referring Internet addresses that link directly to your images. Such cases indicate that customers are downloading the images from your Web site without actually visiting it; in other words, they're connecting from a fake Web site. This is a potential warning sign that people are inadvertently going to a phishing site.

Another thing to look for in your Web logs is evidence of people going to your ABOUT US (E5) and PRIVACY POLICY (E4) pages from a site that is neither yours nor a search engine. Many phishers simply link to the real site's Web pages for these kinds of things to make their site look more legitimate and because they're lazy.

In both of these cases, the key thing to look for in your Web logs is the *referer* field.[5] This field will identify the Web site from which people have come to yours. For downloaded images, the referer field will identify the phishing site that's using your images; and for the ABOUT US (E5) and PRIVACY POLICY (E4) pages, referer will identify the phishing site from which your visitors came.

---

5 The term *referrer* was misspelled as *referer* at the beginning of the World Wide Web and has remained so ever since.

Consider Technical Solutions • Many companies are developing technical solutions to minimize the risk of phishing. Although none of these are widely deployed in the United States, we may see more of them in the coming years. One approach that is slowly gaining momentum is e-mail authentication, making it easier for e-mail clients to verify that an e-mail is really from a given site. Another is Web browser toolbars, which are plug-ins that can check whether or not a Web site is a known scam.

Companies have also developed alternatives to simple passwords. One such alternative is **two-factor authentication,** in which a person must sign in using a physical object (such as a smart card or a special key-chain fob, like a small USB device) in addition to entering a password. Many banks in the European Union use two-factor authentication to protect their customers. Another alternative is **biometrics,** in which the computer uses a physical attribute such as a person's fingerprint to verify identity.

At this writing, none of these techniques have seen wide deployment in the United States, but this is an area with a strong need and many interested parties, so it's worth paying attention to updates.

✳ SOLUTION

Train your customers about the risks of online phishing scams and how to identify such scams. Protective tactics include telling your customers what types of information you will request and when, making it more difficult for phished accounts to cause harm to individuals, requiring multiple forms of identification, and actively searching for Web sites that use your brand name.

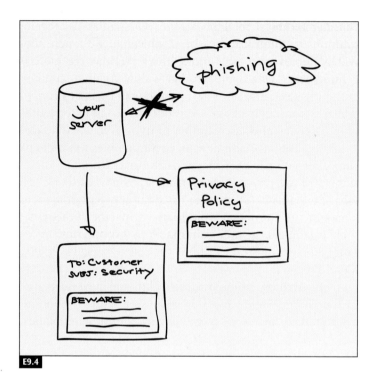

E9.4

Figure E9.4

Educate your customers about how to protect themselves through e-mails and Web pages on your site. In addition, design your Web site assuming that some customers will be phished; that is, make it more difficult for phished accounts to cause harm to individuals.

✳ OTHER PATTERNS TO CONSIDER

It is important for PERSONAL E-COMMERCE (A1), ENABLING INTRANET (A11), and banking sites to help protect their customers from online phishing scams that can cause significant financial loss to customers, as well as hurt your SITE BRANDING (E1).

Inform your customers about the kinds of information you will and will not request. Do this after the customer has created an account or has signed in via the SIGN-IN/NEW ACCOUNT (H2) process. You might also provide periodic E-MAIL SUBSCRIPTIONS (E2) warning your customers about scams, and include information about protecting your customers from online scams on your ABOUT US (E5) and PRIVACY POLICY (E4) pages. Use these e-mail notifications and Web pages to educate your customers about how to detect online scams and what to do if they have been phished. Finally, in E-MAIL SUBSCRIPTIONS (E2) and E-MAIL NOTIFICATIONS (E7), avoid having OBVIOUS LINKS (K10) that lead to a SIGN-IN/NEW ACCOUNT (H2) page.

E7   Consider also providing E-MAIL NOTIFICATIONS (E7) for important transactions, such as verification of a change of e-mail or mailing address or
F8   ORDER CONFIRMATION AND THANK-YOU (F8), letting people know when these have occurred.

   Also assume that some customers will be phished, and minimize any damage by building some anti-phishing safeguards into your system. For
A1   example, some PERSONAL E-COMMERCE (A1) sites do not allow new shipping
F4   addresses to be added on QUICK ADDRESS SELECTION (F4) pages without complete credit card verification.

Basic E-Commerce ◆ **F**

◆◆◆◆◆◆◆◆◆◆◆◆

The ability to find and buy products online is one of the most compelling reasons to use the Web, but for customers to be successful using your Web site, the design must have clean, simple interfaces and support for common tasks. This pattern group discusses how to create the best possible customer experience on your e-commerce Web site. You will notice numerous examples from Amazon.com in this pattern group. We have looked far and wide for good examples but have often come back to Amazon.com because it makes e-commerce work well for the customer—better than any other site we've seen.

F1 QUICK-FLOW CHECKOUT

F2 CLEAN PRODUCT DETAILS

F3 SHOPPING CART

F4 QUICK ADDRESS SELECTION

F5 QUICK SHIPPING METHOD SELECTION

F6 PAYMENT METHOD

F7 ORDER SUMMARY

F8 ORDER CONFIRMATION AND THANK-YOU

F9 EASY RETURNS

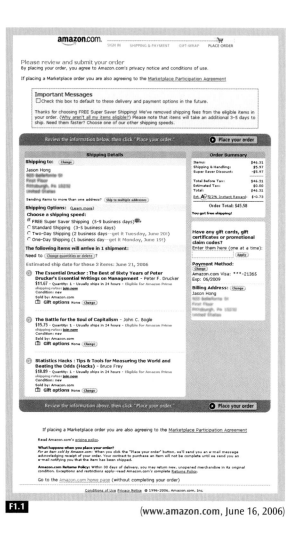

Figure F1.1

Amazon.com's checkout lets the customer specify shipping options, see the important details, and finish quickly.

F1.1

(www.amazon.com, June 16, 2006)

✳ BACKGROUND

PERSONAL E-COMMERCE (A1) calls for an easy shopping experience for customers, with personal benefits. Once shoppers have collected all the items they wish to purchase in a SHOPPING CART (F3), this pattern shows how to have them check out using a quick and simple PROCESS FUNNEL (H1).

✳ PROBLEM

An e-commerce shopping experience will not be enjoyable—or worse, a purchase might not be completed—if the checkout process is cumbersome, confusing, or error prone.

By the time your customers reach the checkout process on your site, they may be impatient to finish the order and move on. Online shoppers do not want surprises, such as hidden charges, unavailable items, tedious text entries, confusing links, or broken pages. Unexpected problems like these frustrate and even scare customers away. Only a straightforward process that is streamlined to include minimal navigation and data entry can make the process feel easy.

Eliminate Distractions • It is easy to complicate the checkout. Shoppers can become distracted during a purchase by following extra links on a page, or by clicking on buttons that don't do what they expect.

Customers who are ready to make a purchase don't like long or complicated instructions. When seeking the next ACTION BUTTON (K4), people tend to look at what's immediately visible on the page. They consult instructions only when the buttons fail to do what they expect. Not only instructions, but also distracting links, should be kept to a minimum during checkout, so this is a good time to stop CROSS-SELLING AND UP-SELLING (G2). In addition, customers want to go through a minimum of pages because each page takes time to download and understand. Make each page a CLEAR FORM (H10) that makes it obvious what information is needed, and why, and that PREVENTS ERRORS (K12) where possible.

Finally, eliminate distractions by using a PROCESS FUNNEL (H1) for the entire checkout sequence, and provide a PROGRESS BAR (H13) to let people know where they are in the checkout and how many steps are left (see Figure F1.2).

Address Potential Deal Breakers • When customers are about to place an order, they may have questions about shipping or return policies, and they will want answers even before they begin to check out. They might wonder any of the following:

- When will my order be shipped?
- Are the products in stock?
- What are my shipping options?
- How much will shipping cost?

Figure F1.2

By the last page of its checkout process, Half.com stops cross-selling and up-selling to customers to ensure that they will complete their orders.

half.com
AN **eb**Y COMPANY

Checkout

1 Shipping ···⟩ 2 Billing ···⟩ 3 Place Order

Secure Shopping

••• **Place my order!**

Order Summary

Martin Archery Mamba (Bow) Seller: beOutdoorsCom (4.4/5.0) Condition: Like New • Notes: 100% Brand New Item. Ideal for short draw archers, the Mamba's compact shape also makes it perfect for bow fishing. The attractive lines and compact look of the Mamba riser is created using select African hardwoods.	Item: $324.99 Ground: $12.95 Subtotal: $337.94
Barrie Archery Ultra, 6-Pack (Arrow Tip) Seller: beOutdoorsCom (4.4/5.0) Condition: Like New • Notes: 100% Brand New Item. Features reinforced, double vented blades that add strength and flight stabilization while the heat treated Power Point cuts on impact and goes through bone for maximum penetration.	Item: $29.99 Ground: $6.95 Subtotal: $36.94
Easton XX75 Camo Hunter (Arrow Shaft) Seller: beOutdoorsCom (4.4/5.0) Condition: Like New • Notes: 100% Brand New Item. Anodized hunter arrows offer a camo finish. Comes complete with quality feathers.	Item: $69.99 Ground: $8.95 Subtotal: $78.94
	Total Merchandise: $424.97 Total Shipping: $28.85 **TOTAL: $453.82**

Ship to

Douglas van Duyne
24915 Soquel-San Jose Rd
Los Gatos, CA 95033

Edit / Change Shipping Address

Bill to

MasterCard ending with 3311
Expires 06/2003
Zipcode: 95033

Edit / Change Billing

☑ Use this shipping and billing information as my Speedy Checkout settings.

••• **Place my order!**

F1.2

(www.half.com, August 20, 2001)

- If some of the products are not in stock, will the available items be shipped?
- What is the return policy?
- Will I be charged tax?
- Is international shipping available?
- Is gift wrapping available?
- Can I ship to multiple addresses?

Your ability to answer these questions can help improve sales. Provide this information using CONTEXT-SENSITIVE HELP (H8) and a FREQUENTLY ASKED QUESTIONS (H7) page before customers add items to their SHOPPING CARTS (F3) or during checkout, depending on their needs (see Figure F1.3).

Build Trust throughout the Process • Customers are sensitive to the amount of information you request and the order in which you request it. Personal information is just that, and at any given moment people don't want to reveal more than they need to. If a Web site asks for too much

Figure F1.3

Amazon.com provides answers to deal breakers on key pages so that customers can have their questions answered quickly.

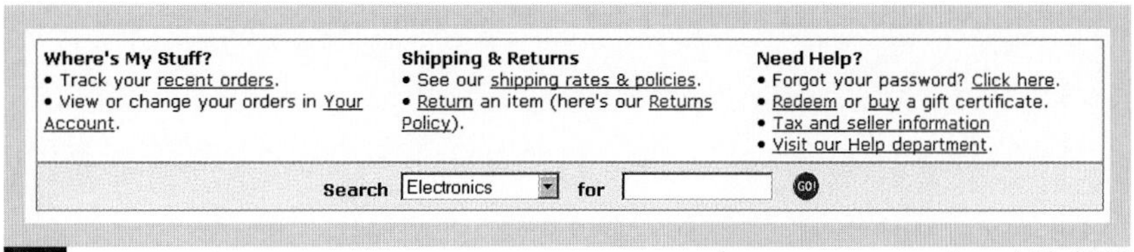

Where's My Stuff?	Shipping & Returns	Need Help?
• Track your recent orders.	• See our shipping rates & policies.	• Forgot your password? Click here.
• View or change your orders in Your Account.	• Return an item (here's our Returns Policy).	• Redeem or buy a gift certificate.
		• Tax and seller information
		• Visit our Help department.

Search [Electronics ▾] for [   ] (GO!)

F1.3

(www.amazon.com, August 19, 2001)

information up front—personal or otherwise—customers become suspicious or negative. Remember that, in a physical store, customers are not asked for any personal information until they check out.

This problem is even worse if you don't provide a clear PRIVACY POLICY (E4). Some site visitors may not want their personal information stored at all, and they will continue with the order only if they know that the information will be used for just the single transaction, as with a GUEST ACCOUNT (H3). At united.com, for example, customers who do not want their personal information stored can create an itinerary and check out as guests. The site explicitly informs them that guest information is not stored online. Other customers may want their personal information stored for convenience because they don't want to reenter it all every time they place an order.

Customers are often not comfortable entering personal information if the Web site is not secure or does not provide a SECURE CONNECTION (E6). And no one wants to try to remember yet another unique user name and password to yet another Web site.

Recap the Order • Shoppers want to make sure all the details of their orders are correct. An ORDER SUMMARY (F7) lets them review the products that they have selected, the total cost, and the shipping information. If any information is incorrect, customers should be able to edit the order summary by changing their orders or any of the delivery or billing information. Customers want to see that the information they entered will be used correctly so that they don't find out later, for example, that the shipping and billing addresses were reversed. Provide an ORDER CONFIRMATION AND THANK-YOU (F8) page that confirms the order, gives the order number, and specifies how to contact the company—all on one page so that customers can print the information for their records (see Figure F1.4).

Retailers need to make sure that funds are available in customer accounts before they process orders because sometimes criminals use stolen credit cards or a customer tries to use a card that has insufficient funds.

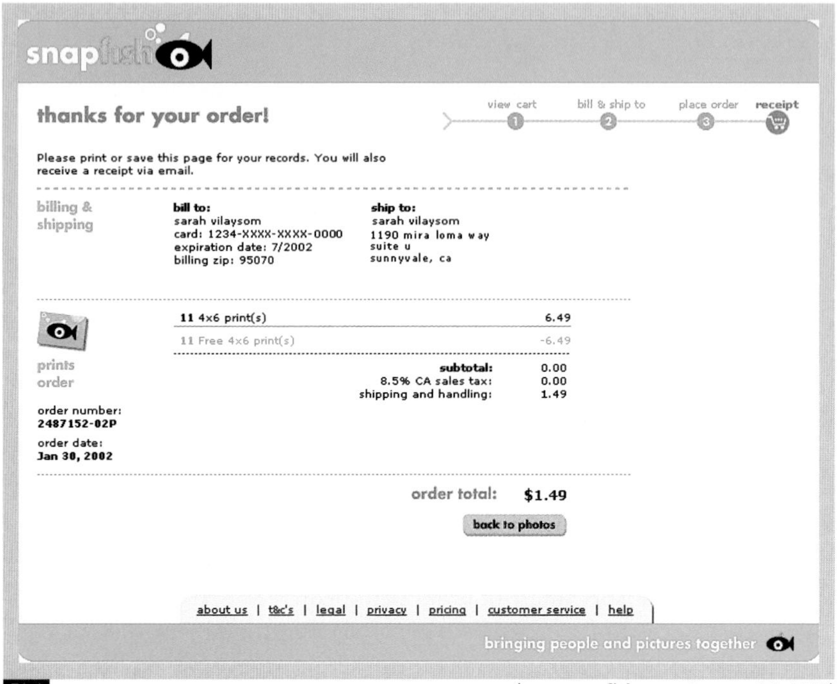

Figure F1.4

A good order confirmation page includes the order number, the order date, shipping and billing details, and an itemized list of all products ordered. Customers can print this page and use it for reference later.

(www.snapfish.com, January 30, 2002)

Verifying the availability of funds at checkout increases the likelihood that a transaction will be completed with sufficient funds. Several commercial services offer systems that plug in to your server to carry out verification and credit card processing.

✳ SOLUTION

Follow a simple four-step approach to make it easy for customers to complete their orders:

1. In a secure area of the site, allow customers to check out without storing their information, or let them create or use a customer identifier so that they don't need to reenter information. Set expectations by providing an overview of the process and answering common questions.
2. Gather shipping and handling information so that you can tabulate the total cost of the order, including taxes, at the next step.

3. Show the total cost of the order along with the order summary so that customers can verify the information. Ask for payment information, and ease any concerns about the security and privacy of your customers' financial information.

4. Confirm that funds for the order are currently available, and give the customer a final opportunity to confirm the order. When the order is complete, provide a printable receipt and invite the customer to return.

On all pages, keep action links visible at all times, and remove all links that do not direct customers to closing the sale.

Figure F1.5

Checking out should be a simple four-step process that funnels customers toward completion of an order.

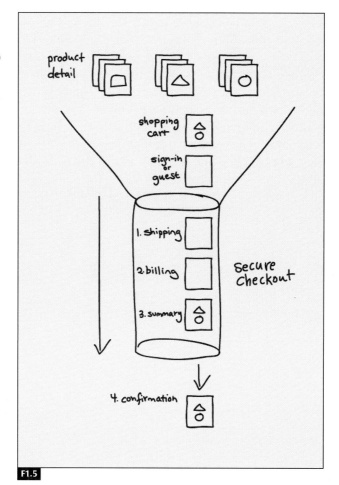

✳ OTHER PATTERNS TO CONSIDER

Establish a SECURE CONNECTION (E6) with the customer before providing a GUEST ACCOUNT (H3) page or asking the customer to register on a SIGN-IN/NEW ACCOUNT (H2) page. Allay concerns about the process that your customers are entering, or answer questions that they may have about particular policies. Give an overview of the process and provide your PRIVACY POLICY (E4), CONTEXT-SENSITIVE HELP (H8), and answers to FREQUENTLY ASKED QUESTIONS (H7). Provide links to your return policy for EASY RETURNS (F9).

Use CLEAR FORMS (H10) that make it obvious what information is needed and why. Use HIGH-VISIBILITY ACTION BUTTONS (K5) because you'll probably have more information than will fit on a single screen. Provide a PROGRESS BAR (H13) on each page so that shoppers know where they are in the process.

Allow customers to use QUICK ADDRESS SELECTION (F4) or MULTIPLE DESTINATIONS (G5), and provide a means of GIFT GIVING (G6) if appropriate. Offer customers QUICK SHIPPING METHOD SELECTION (F5) on the same page.

On the next page, provide an ORDER SUMMARY (F7), as well as links so that people can make changes before you ask for their preferred PAYMENT METHODS (F6). Finally, give customers one last chance to verify the order with an ORDER CONFIRMATION AND THANK-YOU (F8) page. To reduce customer support calls, direct people to ORDER TRACKING AND HISTORY (G7), if you provide this facility.

Figure F2.1

Room & Board's product details page highlights the most important information high on the page to make sure it appears above the fold. The site also makes it easy to find the same product in different sizes and colors, as well as find related pieces of furniture that match the current product.

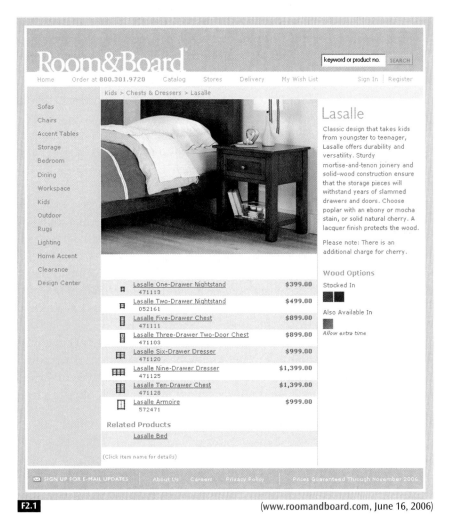

F2.1

(www.roomandboard.com, June 16, 2006)

✳ BACKGROUND

A1
F1
Every PERSONAL E-COMMERCE (A1) site must allow customers to view details about the products it sells because customers will demand that information before they feel comfortable to proceed with a QUICK-FLOW CHECKOUT (F1). This pattern provides the framework for all product pages.

✳ PROBLEM

When shopping, customers want to see product details to help inform their buying decisions. They must also trust a seller before deciding to make a purchase. Many sites do not provide enough in-depth information about their products, or they project an untrustworthy image.

Having plentiful, well-organized, helpful information about your site's products or services helps customers make better and faster purchasing decisions. Shoppers need to scan for basic, valuable blocks of information, including product photos, thorough descriptions, features, prices, and even benefits. When this information is sparse or hard to find, one of the big advantages of online shopping is lost.

Web sites have nearly unlimited space to describe, show, and even critique products. If your customers are unfamiliar with a product, detailed information that includes images and demonstrations can give them what they need to make decisions.

When information is poorly organized, valuable content is not enough. If the presentation is poor, visitors may not find the information that will close the deal, or they may judge a site untrustworthy because of a lack of attention to basics.

On which site in Figure F2.2 are customers more likely to make a purchase? Figure F2.2a shows a product shot with other items in the picture, obscure terms like "Western Wear" and "14.75 oz. Denim," unaligned text and navigation tools, and poor spelling. Figure F2.2b offers a clean

Figure F2.2

(a) Small improvements, such as a better product shot and corrected spelling, would improve this fictional product detail page. (b) This product detail page shows the fabric colors up close, helps with sizing, and has a clean product shot.

F2.2a

F2.2b

product shot, suitable product details, an easy-to-read GRID LAYOUT (I1), sizing assistance, and color examples.

Create a Clean, Standard Template • A product detail page that is quick to scan and read helps customers find the information they need on a conceptual level, and gives them a satisfying experience on an emotional level. A standardized product template helps customers find the details they need as they move from one product page to the next.

On an emotional level, some customers become intrigued with the way a product looks or sounds (if it makes a sound), and the image it portrays.[1] For some people, the first impression of the product can be the most important. Portraying the image that your customers respond to the most— one consistent with your SITE BRANDING (E1)—helps to positively reinforce your company's identity and your brand.

General information is useful to every customer, so providing it at the top of the page is helpful. Some things, like price, are important for almost every customer. Learning what else is useful can take trial and error. You might evaluate one design versus another through an active test online [see Appendix E (Online Research)] to see which page works best on a live site, or more deliberately, through usability research on a page design [see Appendix A (Running Usability Evaluations)]. Investing in evaluating these subtle nuances offers a strategic value to your company because a more effective product page can easily translate into higher sales.

A clean design in a GRID LAYOUT (I1) lets customers scan a page to find information by reading along a line instead of forcing their eyes to jump around the page. Create a PAGE TEMPLATE (D1) that takes into account these elements and the factors described in the sections that follow.

Keep Key Elements above the Fold • The exact information shown ABOVE THE FOLD (I2) depends on what customers need to see first. If you hide crucial facts too far down the page, customers may never

---

1 Direct references to other emotional factors, such as touch, taste, and smell, may be important to your product line, but they are difficult to portray online. Usually companies forgo direct references to these emotional factors for more indirect ones, by portraying a compelling image. For example, perfume ads generally must sell a scent with an image. Wine merchants have developed a special language to help describe their products, using metaphors of fruits and other flavors. Although this is a far cry from the emotional response of actually tasting a wine, it can often be as close as the customer gets without going to the winery for a taste.

see them. The key e-commerce elements to keep above the fold include the following:

- **Standard navigation and shopping tools.** Customers want to use the standard NAVIGATION BARS (K2), shopping tools, and search tools right away if the current product is not the one they want. Forcing customers to backtrack to find a different product only frustrates them.

- **A small, clickable product thumbnail.** Unless all your customers have fast Internet access, use FAST-LOADING IMAGES (L2). To keep the initial product detail page fast and simple, keep your product shot small and in JPEG or GIF format. Provide a higher-resolution, more finely detailed image of each product so that customers can examine it for important particulars that will help them make a purchase decision. Whereas the product shot on the first page must work on the lowest-bandwidth connections with browsers that don't have special visualization plug-ins, for the detailed shot you can use a high-resolution image that can pan,[2] if the product encompasses a room or an outdoor space. For some products, the back might be as important as the front, in which case you can make the link go to a product image that customers can rotate.

- **A needs-oriented description that goes along with the product title.** This description can be just enough to show customers the major differences between this product and others. Make sure the description answers customers' needs, such as how a jacket "keeps out the cold." This brief description may also be used elsewhere on the site.

- **The product price and currency** (unless options change the price greatly). Because nine times out of ten the price is a part of the decision-making process, your customers expect to find this information quickly and easily. Price gives customers a quick understanding of the relative costs of similar products. In some cases, when the product's price varies by 50 percent or more, showing a low price might mislead customers, and showing a high price might turn them away. In these cases, show either a range of prices or a base price and a typically configured price.

- **Product option quick picks or a configuration button.** If a product has several options—whether configuration, style, or something else— quick picks using PREDICTIVE INPUT (H11) or DRILL-DOWN OPTIONS (H12) and configuration buttons are easy ways to let customers select their options

---

2 Visualization plug-ins, like QuickTime, that provide panning and rotating are not always included with Web browsers. Most customers will not download and install these plug-ins just to use your Web site.

H1

while in the context of the current product so that they can browse and choose. Implement this feature with a pick list when short textual descriptions are sufficiently descriptive, or with a PROCESS FUNNEL (H1) that returns customers to the parent product detail page after they select related options, such as size and color (see Figure F2.3).

Figure F2.3

Nordstrom shows the options for this product. The red arrow directs customers to choose size first and then color. The color pick list is generated according to the size chosen.

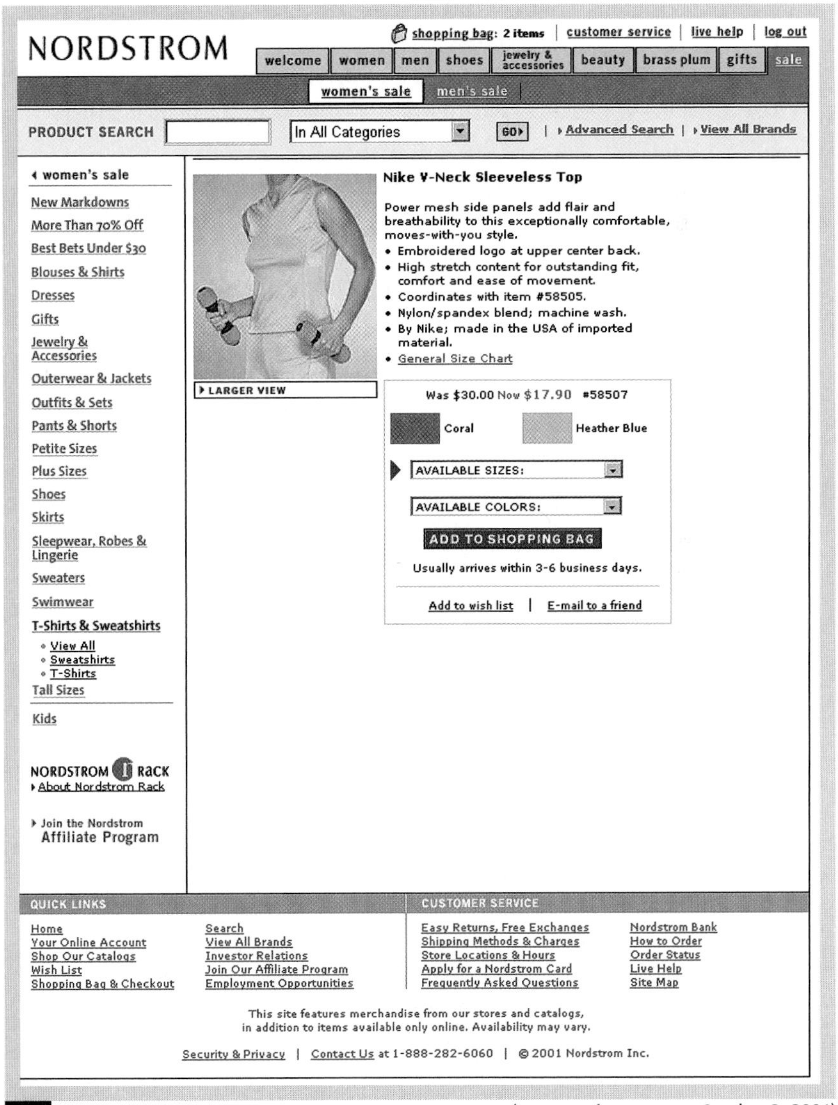

(www.nordstrom.com, October 3, 2001)

In some cases, showing product availability on an option-by-option basis may be difficult. But a customer who wants the blue version of a product, for example, will be frustrated and might cancel a purchase if he finds out late in the process that the blue version is not available after all. The best solution is to show only the options that are currently in stock. See SHOPPING CART (F3) for ideas about how to do this.

F3

- **Overall ratings of your product, if appropriate.** To help your customers understand how the current product stacks up against similar ones, provide a summary of how the company rates the product, how outside experts (magazine reviews or awards) rate it, and how customers rate it. Ratings should use standard scales of either five stars or an industry-specific standard.

- **An idea of when the product will arrive so that the customer can plan for its arrival.** This estimate might come from your inventory system, your production system, or your typical deployment schedule. Failing to include this information, or providing inaccurate information, will greatly increase your support costs.

- **A product item number (if the site is a sales channel).** If customers use the site to find items that they'll be ordering by phone or in person, a product part number greatly simplifies the task of locating the exact product desired.

- **The** Add to Cart **action button.** Customers might be sold by the title, description, photo, ratings, and price alone. Make it easy to order the product by keeping a visible **Add to Cart** ACTION BUTTON (K4) high on the page. If applicable to your site, a **Wish List** link, used for storing products for future purchase or for purchase by friends and family as a gift, works well when it's near the **Add to Cart** button. You should also warn customers if the item is not in stock. For example, Amazon.com changes its **Add to Cart** button to say, "Pre-order this item today," if the item has not yet been released, and hides its **Add to Cart** button if the item is no longer in stock.

K4

- **Links to more detailed information.** Let customers know that more information exists and is only a click away, by making links to these resources visible above the fold. If customers want more in-depth reviews, for example, they should be able to click right to **Reviews.** If customers are concerned about the product's physical dimensions, they should be able to link to **Product Specs.** Both bits of additional information could be on the same page, below the fold, but the links will make customers aware that more information exists and will provide quick routes to it.

Also supply more detailed information through direct product comparison tools. Comparators, recommenders, and selection guides can help simplify the selection process. For complex products with similar features, such tools might even be required for customers to make selections online, without a human attendant to help.

Figure F2.4 shows how two different Web sites manage to keep all this information above the fold.

Put Less Important Information below the Fold • Place secondary elements that are not crucial to customers below the fold. These elements include the following:

- **Full product description.** This description will answer questions about the product's usefulness, its target buyer, and its positive characteristics. Customers are looking to fulfill a need—whether functionality, features, or style. The full product description fills in the blank for a customer who's thinking, "I need something that can do _____."
- **In-depth expert and customer reviews.** License the content or highlight product reviews. Provide a way for customers to add ratings and content directly to your product detail page, creating a RECOMMENDATION COMMUNITY (G4). Highlight the best products with special markings, such as "The best in the category" or "Five stars." Ratings like "G100" are not very useful.
- **Related products and accessories.** List accessories that might be useful, and show related products that complement the current product. Link directly to these products. Or, if they don't require much explanation (such as batteries), creating a separate **Add to Cart** button will make customer purchases even simpler, provided that the customer does not lose the context of the current page.
- **Similar products with numerous features.** Sometimes it's difficult to pick the right product among many. If you have many similar products, provide a means to compare and contrast them. Include expert ratings, customer ratings, popularity scores, and feature-by-feature comparisons.

Figure F2.4

(a) Above the fold (the red dashed line), the Netflix product details page includes a brief movie description, a small product shot, the price, links to more detailed information farther down the page, and obvious action buttons to rent the movie. Below the fold, Netflix provides a detailed synopsis of the movie and lists similar movies and customer reviews.
(b) Cooking.com gives product descriptions and detailed characteristics below the fold.

F2.4a

Figure F2.4

(*Continued*)

❋ SOLUTION

Provide in-depth information in a grid layout. Keep important items that every customer will need above the fold, such as general navigation, product thumbnails, needs-based descriptions, prices, an options pick list or a link to a configuration page, product ratings and delivery time frame, the Add to Cart **action button, and links to more detailed information, even if the information is simply farther down on the page. Put secondary items, such as a full product description, reviews, related products, and a product comparator, if possible, below the fold.**

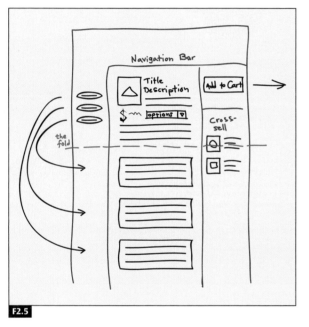

F2.5

Figure F2.5

A good product description page puts the key product details—such as the description, a thumbnail, and the price—above the fold and additional information below the fold.

❋ OTHER PATTERNS TO CONSIDER

Keep the product details page consistent with other SITE BRANDING (E1), and build it with a PAGE TEMPLATE (D1) in a GRID LAYOUT (I1). Make sure the key elements are ABOVE THE FOLD (I2), and put them in CONTENT MODULES (D2) for database updates. Show links to your return policy to ensure EASY RETURNS (F9) and to assure customers that they can change their minds if they're not satisfied. Provide **Add to Cart** ACTION BUTTONS (K4) to keep the shopping experience moving through the PROCESS FUNNEL (H1). For all product detail information, make a PRINTABLE PAGE (D8).

E1
D1 **I1**
I2
D2
F9
K4
H1
D8

Figure F3.1

Amazon.com's shopping cart keeps navigation to the rest of the site clearly indicated at the top of the page, but it makes checking out even clearer. For a business that makes money online through sales, it is critical that customers easily find their way to checkout.

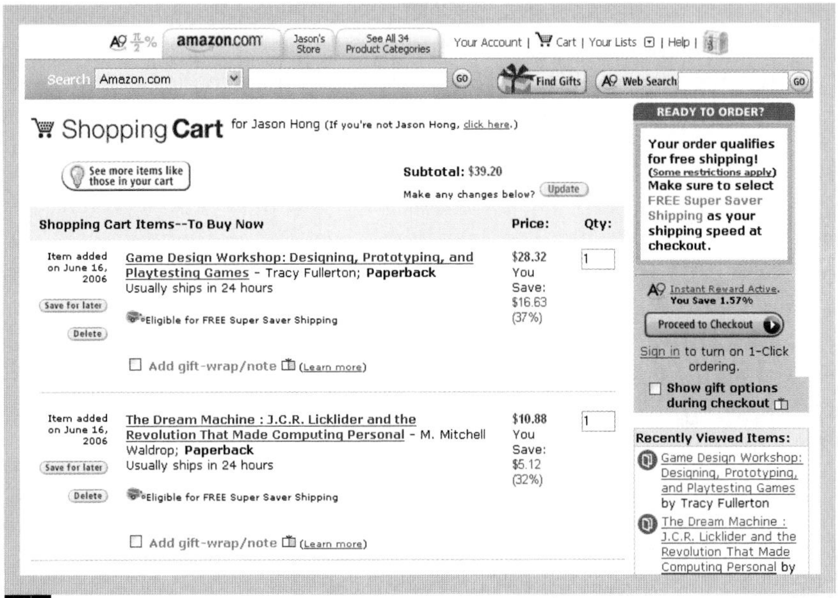

F3.1   (www.amazon.com, June 16, 2006)

✳ BACKGROUND

F2
A1
F1

After customers select products from a CLEAN PRODUCT DETAIL (F2) page, a successful PERSONAL E-COMMERCE (A1) site will use a well-designed shopping cart to lead the customer to the start of a QUICK-FLOW CHECKOUT (F1), removing any barriers to making the purchase.

✳ PROBLEM

Customers want to collect and purchase several items in one transaction. Online shopping carts can provide much more than their offline namesakes, such as making it easy to change the quantity of an item in the cart. However, making shopping carts simple and useful requires restraint.

The shopping cart is a common way to let customers keep track of what they want before they finalize a purchase. Clear ACTION BUTTONS (K4) throughout the site must indicate how to get to the shopping cart and how to put items in it. Let customers use your shopping cart without having to enter personal information. This will encourage them to browse. Once customers arrive at the critical shopping cart page, the existence of too many options can distract them into wandering off without completing their orders. Give shoppers the opportunity to continue shopping at this stage, but encourage them to check out too. **K4**

A clear path to the QUICK-FLOW CHECKOUT (F1) is important for shoppers who are ready to buy. Strike a balance between providing navigation to continue shopping and navigation to check out. **F1**

Provide Easy Access to the Shopping Cart • Customers may decide to check out from any page on the Web site. They start the checkout by reviewing items in their cart to verify products, quantities, and subtotals.

On every page, include a **Go to Shopping Cart** button so that people know how to proceed whenever they're finally ready to say, "I'm done shopping for now." Not everyone understands the shopping cart icon (see the small icon at the top of Figure F3.2), so a text label helps.

Make it easy to add items to the shopping cart from product pages. You might think this is obvious, but you would be surprised at how many Web sites make this a difficult task. Amazon.com does this right, as Figure F3.2 shows. On the right-hand side of the page is a yellow HIGH-VISIBILITY ACTION BUTTON (K5) that draws the eye. **K5**

Let Customers Continue to Shop • One common source of confusion for online shoppers is what to do after adding a product to a shopping cart. Help customers by making their options clear (beyond hitting the **Back** button, of course). For example, you can provide an OBVIOUS LINK (K10) that takes customers back to the last-viewed product CATEGORY PAGE (B8). In the Amazon.com example in Figure F3.1, there is also a SEARCH ACTION MODULE (J1) that lets people search for items they want and CROSS-SELLING AND UP-SELLING (G2) to show related products. Be careful **K10** **B8** **J1** **G2**

Figure F3.2

Each product page should provide a clear way to add the product to the shopping cart. Note how Amazon.com uses an action button to make it look as though customers can push down on the **Add to Shopping Cart** button.

F3.2   (www.amazon.com, June 16, 2006)

that additional links like these do not distract your customers from checking out.

K4
F1
Help Customers Check Out • Use an ACTION BUTTON (K4) labeled "Proceed to Checkout" to lead customers to a QUICK-FLOW CHECKOUT (F1) that allows them to finish their order without distraction. Eliminate distractions on
K2 the shopping cart page itself by maintaining the main NAVIGATION BAR (K2), while eliminating most subnavigation options.

Give Details in the Cart • Each item description in the shopping cart needs to remind the shopper what it is. Provide the following information:

- The name of the item to be purchased and a link to a detailed description
- A short description of the item, such as "book," "CD," or "software"
- The size, color, and other details as appropriate
- The availability and delivery time frame of the item (*especially* important during the holiday season)
- The price of each item

- The quantity to be purchased and a way to modify the quantity
- A way to remove the item from the shopping cart by clicking on a **Remove** button or by unchecking a check box (you might ask people to set the quantity to zero, but not everyone notices these instructions)

A shopping cart must also inform the customer of other charges and offer links to additional information about the purchase:

- Shipping and handling costs (if known), or how they will be calculated
- Any applicable taxes (again, if known)
- Any other charges that contribute to the total cost
- Subtotals for the items in the cart
- Link to the return policy
- Link to shipping information, including costs, acceptable destinations, order processing times, and shipping times

Set Expectations about Availability • Customers become frustrated when they add products to their shopping carts and find out later that the items are not available. For a Web site to reflect product availability in the shopping cart, however, inventory management software must be integrated with the Web server software. Set up business rules to automatically remove products from the Web servers when stock on hand drops below a certain level. Include a buffer in case multiple customers pick the same option at the same time. Keep track of products and product option availability.

Set customers' expectations as well as you can, either with high precision, such as "Ships in 24 hours," or with less precision, such as "Usually ships in 3–6 days." The precision factor depends on the amount of volume your business does and the inventory kept on hand.

Provide availability information as early as possible, on the CLEAN PRODUCT DETAIL (F2) page, as well as in the shopping cart.   **F2**

Store Carts for Later • One serious problem on some e-commerce sites is that the shopping cart disappears if a customer does not do anything on the site for a while. There are dozens of plausible explanations beyond "the customer abandoned the shopping cart." Customers might be comparison-shopping on other Web sites, taking a lunch break, or talking to someone next to them. Save customer shopping carts for *at least 24 hours.* However, a saved cart must be merged with a new cart when a shopper logs in and collects a new cart full of other products. In such cases, be sure to communicate that a customer already has items in the cart as soon as

Figure F3.3

Barnes & Noble's Web site lets customers save items in a wish list, helping them remember the products that they'd like to purchase. It also makes it easy to move items from the wish list to the shopping cart.

F3.3   (www.bn.com, June 16, 2006)

you can. In addition, inform customers about items in the saved carts that are no longer in stock.

Another option to give customers is the ability to store items for later purchase. This option can be provided in one of two ways: as a private list for each customer or as a public list for customers to share with friends and family, also known as a *wish list*. Barnes & Noble's Web site maintains such wish lists (see Figure F3.3). Clearly, wish lists are not useful if they're retained for a relatively short amount of time—for example, a couple of months. The best approach is to retain an item in a wish list until it has been purchased or explicitly removed.

Cross-Sell and Up-Sell • Help your customers and your business by promoting products related to other products that the customer already wants to purchase (see Figure F3.4). For example, printers also need paper and toner. Promoting related products in this way is **cross-selling. Up-selling** highlights products that have more features and benefits than the one that

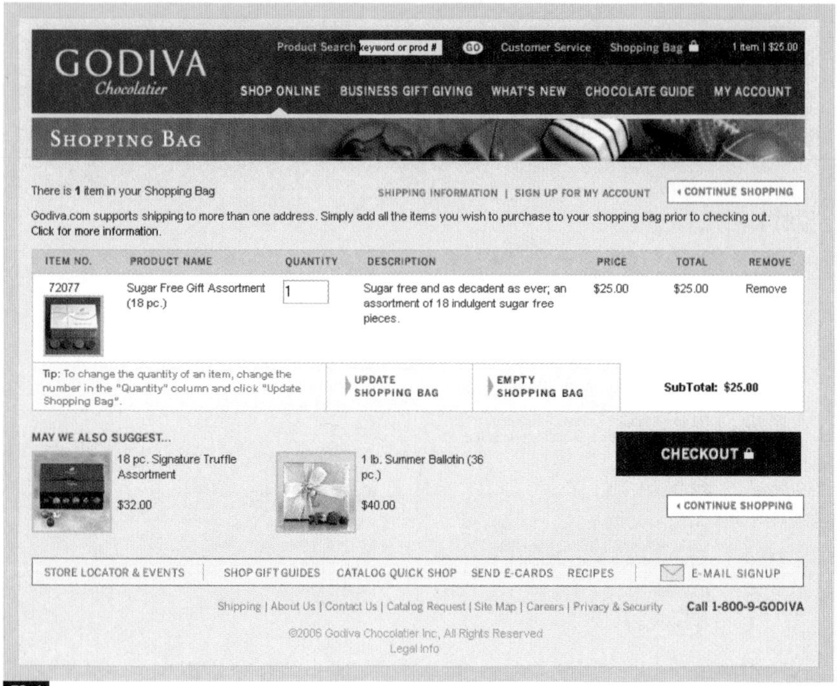

Figure F3.4

Godiva cross-sells additional products on the shopping cart page. This strategy is similar to what supermarkets do when they put magazines and candy next to the checkout stand.

(www.godiva.com, July 21, 2006)

the customer wants to purchase. Products highlighted through up-selling cost more too. For example, if a customer selects a particular mobile phone, a site could recommend a phone with more features in the next price level. Highlight these cross-selling and up-selling opportunities at different points in the purchase process, including in the shopping cart. See the CROSS-SELLING AND UP-SELLING (G2) pattern for more information.

Be careful when cross-selling and up-selling, though, because it's possible to lose your customer by complicating the purchase. Keep the center of attention on the products that your customer wants, and make the cross-selling and up-selling recommendations secondary. See CROSS-SELLING AND UP-SELLING (G2) for more specifics.

Show Cart Contents on Every Page • Every page can provide shopping cart item information so that customers remember what they selected without going back to the cart. Figure F3.5 shows how CDNOW displays the number of items in a customer's shopping cart. The Staples site takes a different approach, providing a mini-shopping cart that includes the start of a description for each product (see Figure F3.6).

Figure F3.5

CDNOW's shopping cart tells customers how many items are in it.

F3.5   (www.cdnow.com, October 26, 2000)

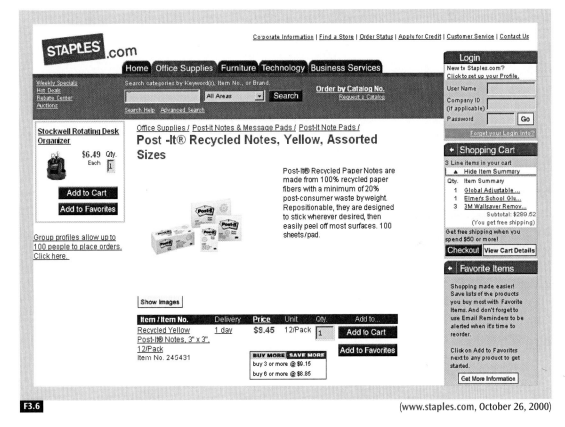

F3.6   (www.staples.com, October 26, 2000)

Figure F3.6

On the right-hand side of each page of its Web site, Staples shows a mini-shopping cart that has a link to the full shopping cart.

These approaches give constant feedback about cart contents, but they also take up precious screen real estate and can cause problems when customers use the **Back** button. In addition, they might curb enthusiasm if the shopper is constantly monitoring how many items are in the cart. Showing a list on every page may help when tens of products are needed and shoppers can't remember what they have in their carts, but for sites with only a few items in a typical order, this approach needs to be tested with customers.

Observe Local Customs • Sometimes the shopping cart metaphor is not the best. In England, the term *shopping basket* is more appropriate, so Amazon.co.uk, for instance, uses that term instead. Other metaphors make more sense on particular types of sites. We have seen the term *shopping bag* on clothing and cosmetics sites, for example. According to research conducted by Heidi Adkisson in 2002 across 75 e-commerce sites, 72 percent of sites use *cart,* 19 percent use *bag,* 7 percent use *basket,* and 2 percent use another term.

☀ SOLUTION

Give customers easy access to the shopping cart from every page of your site. On product detail pages, make the Add to Cart **buttons hard to miss. On the shopping cart page itself, provide highly visible action buttons leading to checkout and action buttons to continue shopping, along with the top-level navigation elements and search features. For each product in the cart, include the product name, a short description, a link to the product page, availability time frame, price, quantity, a button to delete each item, shipping, tax, and subtotal information or links. Display a link to your return policy. Optionally, you might also cross-sell and up-sell other products on the cart page, and put a summary of the cart contents on every site page.**

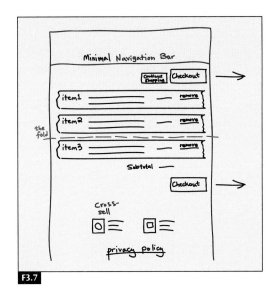

Figure F3.7

A good shopping cart shows customers details about what they're about to buy, including how much the order is going to cost, and then makes it easy to check out without being distracted.

✳ OTHER PATTERNS TO CONSIDER

One common feature on CLEAN PRODUCT DETAIL (F2) pages is to let people add items to the shopping cart. From the shopping cart page, provide a HIGH-VISIBILITY ACTION BUTTON (K5) to let people start the QUICK-FLOW CHECKOUT (F1). The shopping cart is a good place for CROSS-SELLING AND UP-SELLING (G2), recommending products that may be useful, given the current items in the shopping cart. Issues of INTERNATIONALIZED AND LOCALIZED CONTENT (D10) are becoming important as more people worldwide use the Web. Therefore, make sure the title of your shopping cart makes sense for the culture or country using your site. Provide links to your return policy to enable EASY RETURNS (F9) and to assure your customers that they can change their minds if they're not satisfied.

F4 QUICK ADDRESS SELECTION

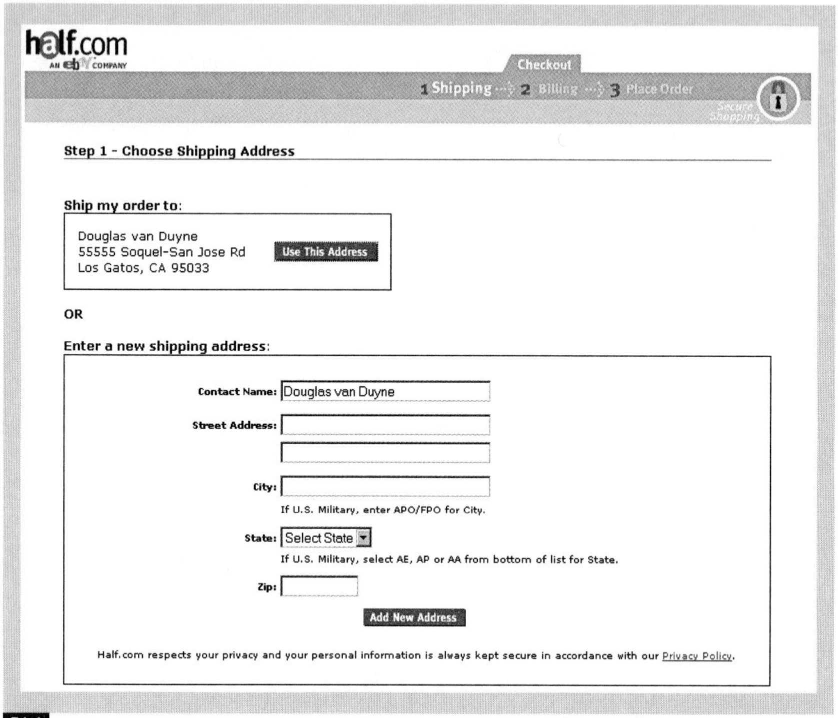

F4.1

(www.half.com, August 20, 2001)

Figure F4.1

Half.com employs an address book and provides a simple, clean, single-column form for entering a new address.

BACKGROUND

For QUICK-FLOW CHECKOUT (F1) on a PERSONAL E-COMMERCE (A1) site, each step must be simple and clearly defined. In the SHOPPING CART (F3) pattern, items are collected and summarized. This pattern provides the mechanism for choosing and entering addresses for shipping and billing.

F1 A1 F3

PROBLEM

Entering addresses need not be cumbersome, especially if customers are ordering from a site for a second time.

Customers must always enter their shipping and billing information if they're using a site for the first time. However, long, complicated, or poorly labeled forms intimidate people. Confusing forms also lead to errors. Furthermore, if customers return, they will likely need the previously entered address, but they might also need to enter an address of a friend (if it's a consumer e-commerce site) or another business location (if it's a business e-commerce site). In fact, customers may need to enter multiple addresses over time. Providing a list of previously entered addresses, as well as a clean, simple form with a space to enter new addresses, gives customers speed and flexibility.

G5   This pattern provides a design solution for simple shipping and billing address pages. The MULTIPLE DESTINATIONS (G5) pattern covers sending one order to multiple locations.

Store Addresses • Customers who are returning to a site will likely use a previous address for shipping and billing. Putting the list of stored addresses at the top of the page ensures that customers will immediately see one or more of their earlier addresses. To select a certain address, all
K4   they have to do is click on the button next to it. An ACTION BUTTON (K4) labeled "Use This Address" next to each address can take the customer to the next step of the order process (see Figure F4.2).

Place a link at the top of the page for entering a new address, which the customer will do in an area beside or below the stored addresses. Even when many addresses are already stored, the link will be visible to the shopper.

Create Clear Forms for New Addresses • For customers who are ordering from
H10   a site for the first time, provide a CLEAR FORM (H10) for adding new addresses at the top of the page. If the customer has stored addresses, the link at the top of the page will scroll the customer to the right place on the page. To make the form for entering a new address easy to use, do the following:

I1
- Build a simple GRID LAYOUT (I1) with all of the field labels right-aligned along a single grid line, and all of the text entry fields in a single column left-aligned along the same grid line. This arrangement helps people scan the labels and fields (see the form for a new shipping address in Figure F4.1).
- Keep the number of fields to a minimum to simplify data entry.
- Keep labels and instructions short because customers tend to skim forms and resort to reading only when necessary.

- Use PREDICTIVE INPUT (H11) or DRILL-DOWN OPTIONS (H12) to simplify data entry in common fields, such as state and country names.

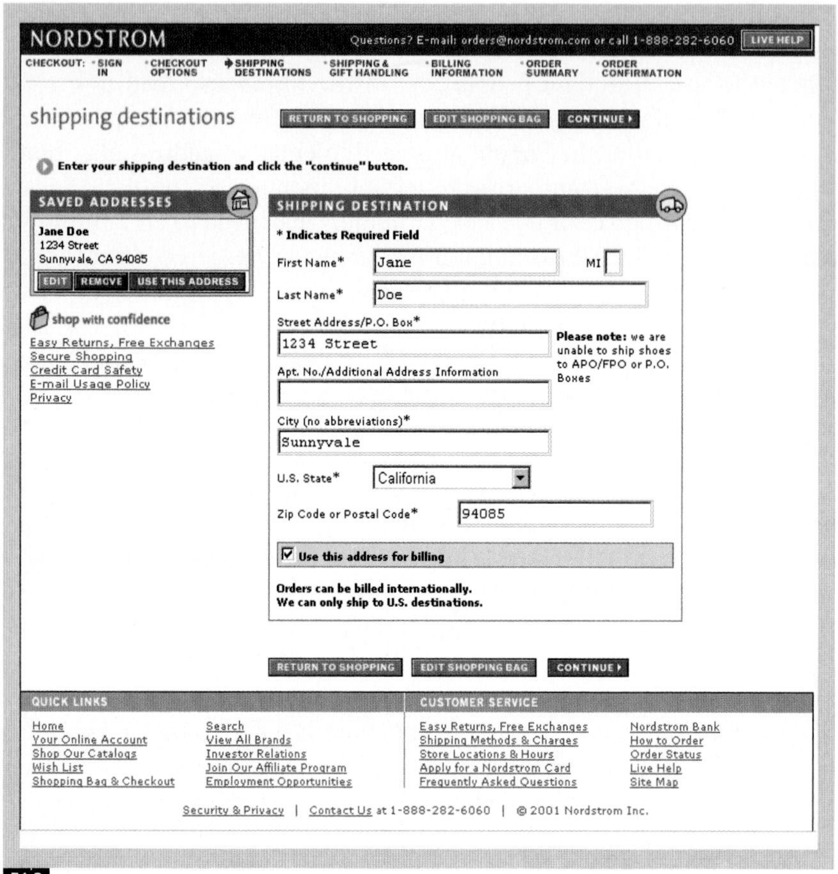

Figure F4.2

To help people check out quickly, Nordstrom stores customer addresses for quick reuse (left) and provides space for a new destination (right).

F4.2

(www.nordstrom.com, October 3, 2001)

Figure F4.3 shows an example of a form that does not follow these conventions. Several reasons why this form would be hard for customers to use are immediately obvious.

Use only the following few fields:

- Full Name
- Address Line 1 (or Company Name)
- Address Line 2 (optional)
- City
- State/Province/Region
- Zip/Postal Code
- Country
- Phone

Figure F4.3

This address form is hard to read and use. There are too many instructions, labels appear inconsistently and are not aligned with the corresponding text entry field, and the text entry fields are not aligned with one another.

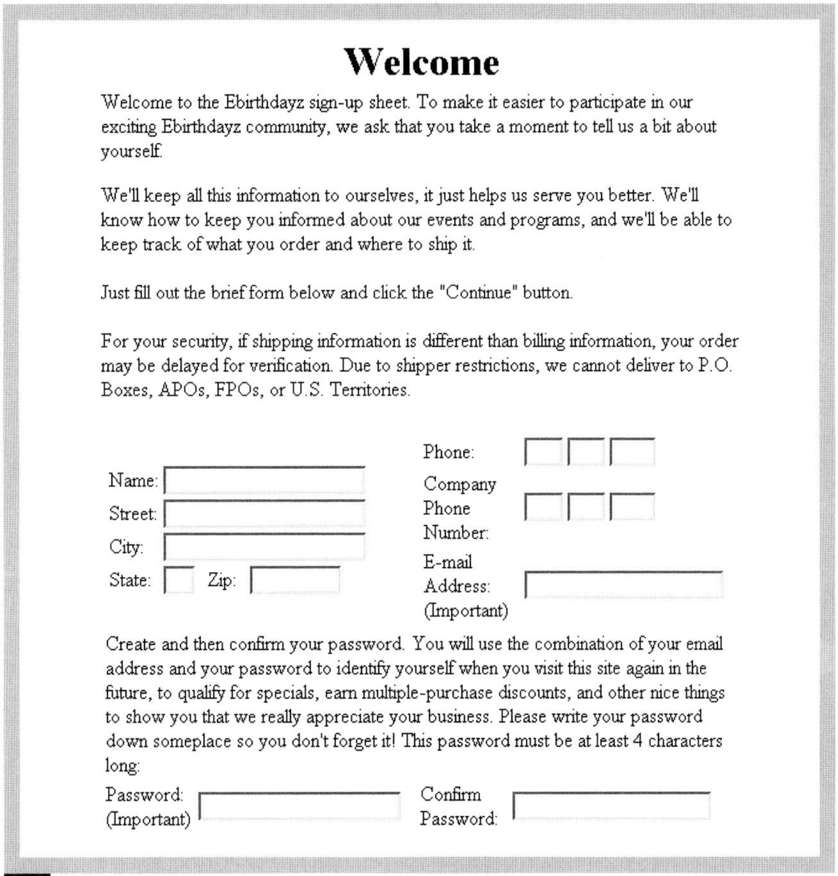

Welcome

Welcome to the Ebirthdayz sign-up sheet. To make it easier to participate in our exciting Ebirthdayz community, we ask that you take a moment to tell us a bit about yourself.

We'll keep all this information to ourselves, it just helps us serve you better. We'll know how to keep you informed about our events and programs, and we'll be able to keep track of what you order and where to ship it.

Just fill out the brief form below and click the "Continue" button.

For your security, if shipping information is different than billing information, your order may be delayed for verification. Due to shipper restrictions, we cannot deliver to P.O. Boxes, APOs, FPOs, or U.S. Territories.

Phone:

Name:

Company Phone Number:

Street:

City:

E-mail Address: (Important)

State: Zip:

Create and then confirm your password. You will use the combination of your email address and your password to identify yourself when you visit this site again in the future, to qualify for specials, earn multiple-purchase discounts, and other nice things to show you that we really appreciate your business. Please write your password down someplace so you don't forget it! This password must be at least 4 characters long:

Password: (Important)

Confirm Password:

F4.3

Typically, having separate fields for first name and last name complicates matters for the customer. On the other hand, having both fields in your database might make other data-processing tasks easier, such as a customer service representative's search for a customer's account. This is a trade-off that you should work through with your software development team.

Use two more fields to handle the address and company name because a company name can be automatically separated (parsed out) later if you need it. A country pick list ensures that country names are not misspelled or spelled in more than one way. You might want to require a phone number for overnight shipments, so provide a single input field for it. Field labels that work in any country help international customers understand how to use the fields (such as Zip/Postal Code).

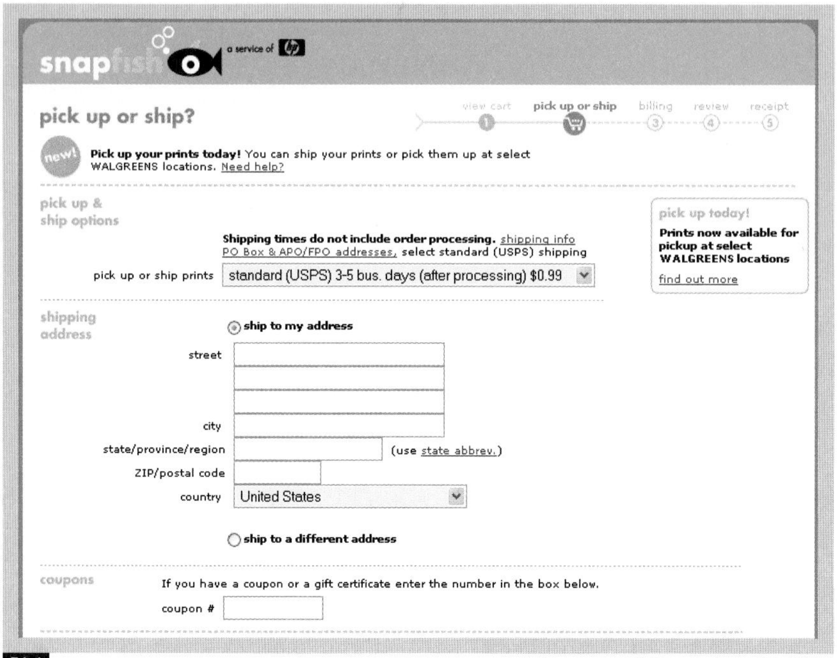

Figure F4.4

Snapfish cleanly incorporates its quick address selection form into its quick-flow checkout.

F4.4   (www.snapfish.com, June 16, 2006)

Next to the form, put a **Use this new address** ACTION BUTTON (K4). Clicking on this button will validate the fields, store the address, and set it as the current address. Figure F4.4 shows how Snapfish lets customers add new addresses as part of the QUICK-FLOW CHECKOUT (F1).

(K4)

(F1)

Validate Fields • Help customers enter correct information by using software to validate their input. Check required fields to ensure that they contain data. Because addresses and city names can be formatted in so many ways, it is difficult to verify the actual content of these fields. For the State field, if all commerce must be conducted within the United States, the field could be restricted to a pick list of states. For international ordering, a pick list for country can guarantee the integrity of the information that customers submit. One trade-off is that pick lists this large can be difficult to navigate. You may want to verify that the phone number contains only numbers and legal punctuation, but if you allow international phone numbers, the formats may be very different. Make PREVENTING ERRORS (K12) your goal, but when they do occur, use field validation and MEANINGFUL ERROR MESSAGES (K13) to help your customer recover.

(K12)

(K13)

✳ SOLUTION

At the top of the page, provide a link to the area where a new address can be entered. Place all previously stored addresses next, with a Use This Address **action button next to each one. Create a form for new addresses that is quick and easy to read: with labels right-aligned and input fields left-aligned along the same vertical grid line, and using a minimum of fields, minimal instructions, and a** Use This Address **action button.**

Figure F4.5

Customers should be able to use addresses that they've entered before, and add new addresses easily.

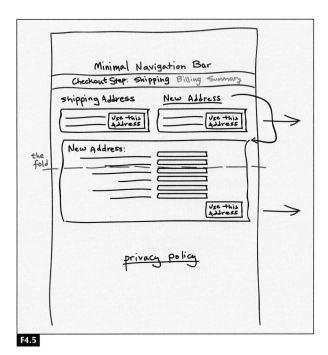

F4.5

✳ OTHER PATTERNS TO CONSIDER

Answer potential questions about your site security by linking directly to your PRIVACY POLICY (E4). Help customers specify an address by having a CLEAR FORM (H10) that helps PREVENT ERRORS (K12) and provides MEANINGFUL ERROR MESSAGES (K13) when errors do occur. Use ACTION BUTTONS (K4) to lead customers to the next step in the checkout process. Organize the text fields in a GRID LAYOUT (I1). If the customer wants to ship to MULTIPLE DESTINATIONS (G5), provide a way to enter multiple addresses. Provide links to your return policy to enable EASY RETURNS (F9) and to assure customers that they can change their minds if they're not satisfied.

F5 QUICK SHIPPING METHOD SELECTION

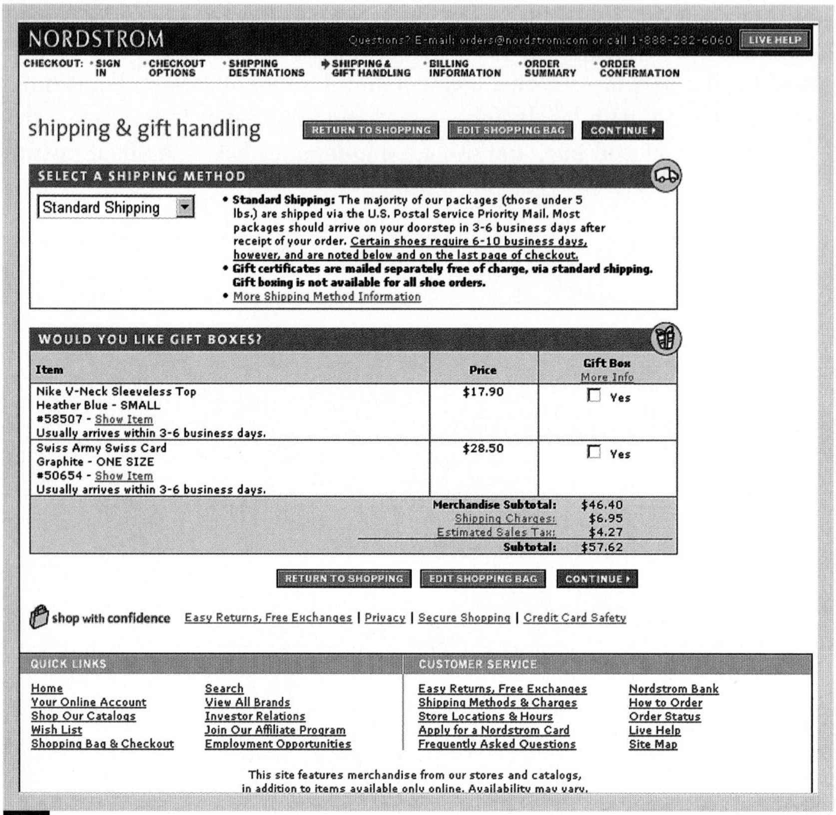

Figure F5.1

Nordstrom provides a pick list right next to the shipping details so that customers can quickly select the best shipping method and see how it affects the price.

(www.nordstrom.com, October 3, 2001)

✳ BACKGROUND

For QUICK-FLOW CHECKOUT (F1) on a PERSONAL E-COMMERCE (A1) site, each step must be simple and clearly defined. In the SHOPPING CART (F3) pattern, items are collected and summarized. This pattern provides the mechanism for choosing a shipping method.

❋ PROBLEM

Customers resent hidden shipping and handling charges, and they want to pick the best shipping option for their situation.

If shoppers encounter previously undisclosed, expensive shipping charges when they reach the checkout phase of an order, they can be quite shocked. With regard to shipping, immediately communicate two things: (1) how long it will take before the items arrive and (2) how much it will add to the cost to speed things up. Other issues, such as customs and insurance for precious cargo, may depend on the particular products being purchased.

Show Delivery Options • Most sites that ship items small enough to be handled by one of the major carriers, such as the U.S. Postal Service, UPS, or FedEx, offer several options for delivery. When you must ship with a carrier that handles large items, you may not be able to offer any shipping choices. But customers still need to know shipping times and costs. Set their expectations for each delivery option with a pick list or radio buttons so that they can choose what's best for them (see Figure F5.2).

Figure F5.2

Customers use Amazon.com's radio buttons to select the shipping method. Although an older version of the Web site required customers to click on an **Update** button, the latest version updates shipping costs automatically when an alternative shipping method is selected.

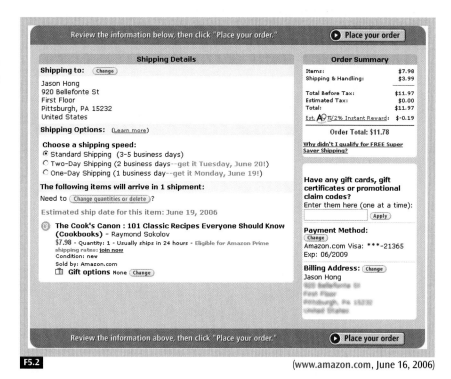

(www.amazon.com, June 16, 2006)

Explain Shipping Times • Even when precise estimates are not possible, providing a range of days that it will take for the customer to receive the goods is better than giving no information at all. Customers appreciate knowing what to expect. Indicate when to expect each item—for example, by saying something like, "Usually ships in 3–5 days."

If an item will take longer to arrive than the time indicated in the order, update the customer with an e-mail explaining the delay and giving the new time estimate. Because the original estimated time frame may have been important (for it to arrive before a birthday or project start day, for example), give the customer an opportunity to update or cancel the order immediately.

International orders may take longer to arrive than estimates indicate, and this information is also important to include on the shipping page. If most customers are local, though, it may be too much detail. Putting this information behind a link that refers to international shipping keeps it from overwhelming the majority of shoppers.

Indicate Costs • The costs of shipping can vary depending on the size and weight of the goods shipped, the time frame the customer requires, insurance for expensive items, and possibly international charges. The specific costs then must be calculated for the items in the cart and the shipping destination. If domestic shipping is standard on the site, you can calculate the shipping on the SHOPPING CART (F3) page using the selected products' size, weight, and insurance requirements. Figure F5.3 shows how babyGap displays shipping type and costs at the same time on its Web site.

F3

Figure F5.3

BabyGap includes the shipping method as a pick list item in its shopping cart, so customers can select it along with the price.

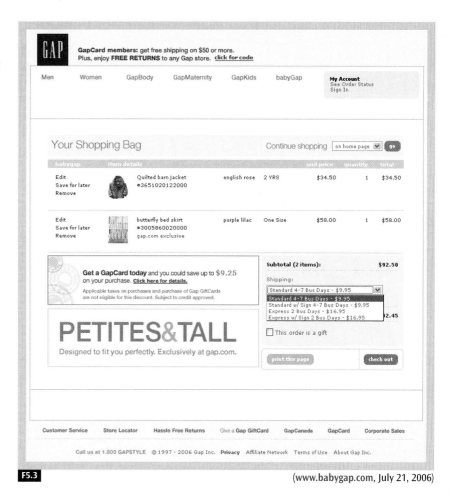

F5.3

(www.babygap.com, July 21, 2006)

✳ SOLUTION

Provide a pick list or radio buttons for selecting shipping options. Give a high-level description of the delivery time frames and the associated costs. Calculate the shipping costs on the basis of size and weight of the products being shipped. Provide links to more in-depth information about shipping issues, including international requirements and insurance.

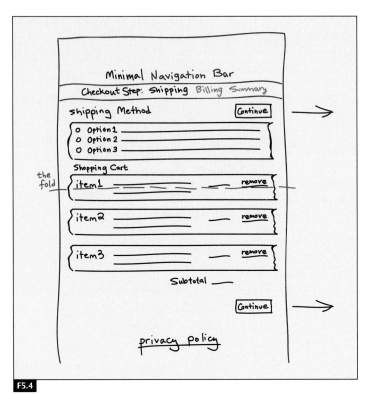

Figure F5.4

The shipping page informs customers of their options and costs for shipping, while moving them through the checkout process with little distraction.

F5.4

✳ OTHER PATTERNS TO CONSIDER

Help customers select a shipping method by having a CLEAR FORM (H10)  that helps PREVENT ERRORS (K12) and provides MEANINGFUL ERROR MESSAGES (K13) when errors do occur. Use ACTION BUTTONS (K4) to lead customers to the next step in the checkout process. Display the shipping information in a GRID LAYOUT (I1), in CONTENT MODULES (D2). Provide links to your return policy to enable EASY RETURNS (F9) and to assure customers that they can change their minds if they're not satisfied.

Figure F6.1

Half.com provides the ability to use previous billing information or quickly enter new billing information. With only a minimum of fields for the credit card details, the billing address can be quickly copied from the shipping address.

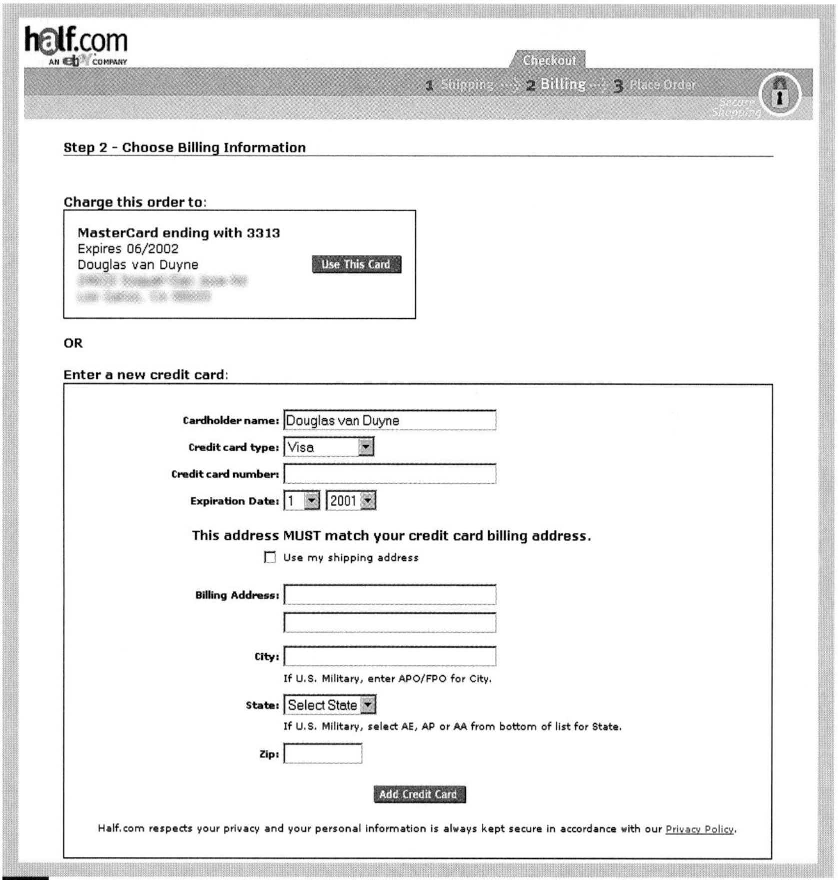

F6.1

(www.half.com, August 19, 2001)

✳ BACKGROUND

For QUICK-FLOW CHECKOUT (F1) on a PERSONAL E-COMMERCE (A1) site, each step must be simple and clearly defined. In the SHOPPING CART (F3) pattern, items are collected and summarized. The QUICK ADDRESS SELECTION (F4) and QUICK SHIPPING METHOD SELECTION (F5) patterns allow the customer to specify where and how to ship the order. This pattern describes the mechanism for specifying how to pay for the order.

✳ PROBLEM

When it comes to paying for an order, people demand security and simplicity.

As with every other part of the online shopping experience, the payment section of the checkout process must be quick and easy. But other concerns are specific to the payment page. Whether making a business or a consumer transaction, customers are concerned about online security because they have heard stories about credit card theft and worse. Although it may be easier for someone to steal a credit card in a real store, people perceive online purchases to be less secure, and the dangers are not well understood.

Take steps to help people overcome their security concerns. Show the lock icon to indicate that the contents of the page have been encrypted. Keep in mind, though, that the lock icon cannot be the full solution, because only savvy customers know to look for it. Make every effort to dispel security concerns and provide a simple mechanism for choosing payment options and entering billing details.

Dispel Concerns about Security • Customers will want to know that your site is secure, and that their information will not be accessible to out-siders. Address concerns by linking to a security or PRIVACY POLICY (E4) **E4** page that explains how the information that customers enter is used, how it is stored on site servers, and who has access to it.

When transmitting credit card information to or from the browser, be sure to encrypt all the checkout pages with a SECURE CONNECTION (E6) **E6** (the Web browser lock icon will indicate that it's secure). Minimize the risk of credit card theft by referring to a customer's credit card by only the last four digits of the card and the expiration date.

Provide Easy Payment Choices • On consumer sites, customers may be ordering with credit cards or gift certificates. They may be using one of many credit cards, and they may have old information in the system, such as expired credit cards or old billing addresses. Business customers might also be ordering with credit cards, but they will probably need to be billed, perhaps against a purchase order. A pick list or radio buttons let customers choose easily among these different payment options.

Provide an Uncomplicated Form for Billing Information • If customers are ordering from a site for the first time, use a CLEAR FORM (H10) and put the billing form at the top of the page, where it's easy to see. If shoppers have stored credit cards, include areas on the page where customers can choose a stored card or input a new one (see Figure F6.1). To make the form for entering new billing information easy to use, do the following:

- Build a simple GRID LAYOUT (I1) with all of the field labels right-aligned along a single grid line, and all of the text entry fields in a single column left-aligned along the same grid line. This arrangement helps people scan the labels and fields (see the form for entering new credit card information in Figure F6.1).
- Keep the number of fields to a minimum to simplify data entry.
- Keep labels and instructions short so that customers can skim forms and resort to reading only when necessary.
- Use PREDICTIVE INPUT (H11) or DRILL-DOWN OPTIONS (H12) where possible to simplify data entry.

Use only the following few fields:

- Full Name
- Address Line 1 (or Company Name)
- Address Line 2 (optional)
- City
- State/Province/Region
- Zip/Postal Code
- Country
- Phone

For business orders, add the following fields:

- Billing Contact E-Mail
- Choice to Be Billed or Pay by Credit Card
- If to Be Billed Option Is Selected by Customer, Add Purchase Order

For support of credit cards, add the following:

- Name on Credit Card
- Credit Card Number [allow multiple formats, as described in PREVENTING ERRORS (K12)]
- Expiration Date

Typically, having separate fields for first name and last name complicates matters for the customer. On the other hand, having both fields in your database might make other data-processing tasks easier, such as a customer service representative's search for a customer's account. This is a trade-off that you should work through with your software development team.

A country pick list ensures that country names are not misspelled or spelled in many different ways. Providing labels that work in any country helps international customers use the fields.

Next to the form, put an ACTION BUTTON (K4) labeled either "Save Billing Info" or "Continue." Clicking on this button will validate the fields, store the address, and set it to be the current address.

Figure F6.2 shows a simple and straightforward form for billing.

K4

Store Credit Card Information • Customers who are returning to a site will likely use a previously entered credit card. Put the list of stored credit cards at the top of the page to ensure that they'll be seen. Provide a **Use This Card**

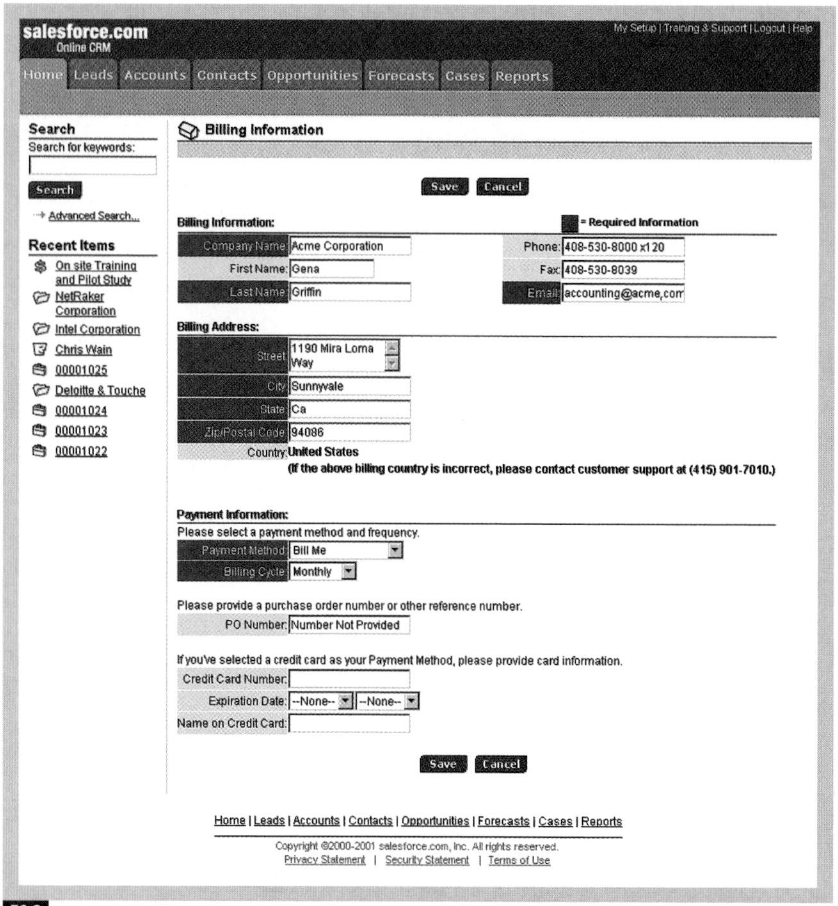

Figure F6.2

The **Billing Information** page on Salesforce.com's Web site shows how few fields are required to process business billing. This process funnel then asks whether to bill by purchase order or charge a credit card.

F6.2   (www.salesforce.com, October 20, 2001)

(K4) ACTION BUTTON (K4) next to each credit card to take the customer quickly to the next step of the order process (see Figure F6.1).

At the top of the page, include a link to a place where the customer can enter new credit card information, which will appear below the stored cards. Even if the customer has already stored many credit cards, the link will be visible. Another approach to this problem is to separate the card selection mechanism from the billing address specification. This way there will always be room to see the new card fields (see Figure F6.3). This approach has the drawback of requiring an additional page to load, and it separates the context of the chosen credit card and the associated billing address, which may lead to errors.

Redeem Gift Certificates • Though they are payment related, gift certificates are not stored as a recurring payment option. Promotion codes and gift certificates are used only once, and then they're gone (any extra money may be stored as credit). Customers want to see a place to enter their certificate information early in the checkout process. If they become concerned that they will not be given the opportunity to use their certificate or promotion code, they might think the promotion and site are misleading or a scam. Customers are reassured if you put the certificate redemption or promotion redemption at the point where a payment option must be selected (see Figure F6.3a).

Figure F6.3

Amazon.com has customers select credit cards and the associated billing address on two pages. (a) On the first page customers pick a stored card or enter a promotion code. (b) On the second page customers select one of the existing billing addresses in their Amazon.com address book or enter a new one.

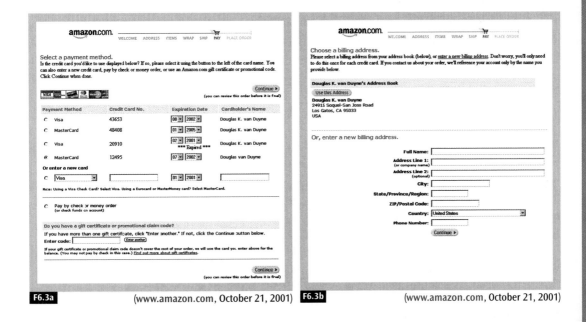

F6.3a (www.amazon.com, October 21, 2001) F6.3b (www.amazon.com, October 21, 2001)

✳ SOLUTION

Dispel any concerns that customers might have about security by addressing them up front with a link to your security or privacy policy. A pick list or radio buttons help customers select the billing options. Create a form for entering new credit card information that is quick and easy to read: with labels right-aligned and input fields left-aligned along the same vertical grid line, and using a minimum of fields, minimal instructions, and a Use This Card **action button. If storing multiple billing addresses, above the new address form include a list of all previously stored addresses with a** Use This Address **action button next to each one.**

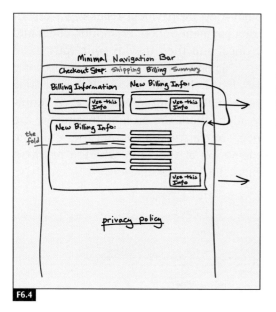

F6.4

Figure F6.4

Customers must be able to easily specify how to pay for their orders, whether by selecting from previously used billing information or by entering new information.

✳ OTHER PATTERNS TO CONSIDER

Answer questions that customers might have about your site security by linking directly to your PRIVACY POLICY (E4). Link to your return policy to enable EASY RETURNS (F9) and to assure customers that they can change their minds if they're not satisfied.

Help customers fill out the form by having a CLEAR FORM (H10) that helps PREVENT ERRORS (K12) and provides MEANINGFUL ERROR MESSAGES (K13) when errors do occur. Use ACTION BUTTONS (K4) to lead customers to the next step in the checkout process. Display the rows of items in a GRID LAYOUT (I1).

ORDER SUMMARY F7

Figure F7.1

Amazon.com offers a single, organized page that summarizes a complete order and provides links to edit the individual elements.

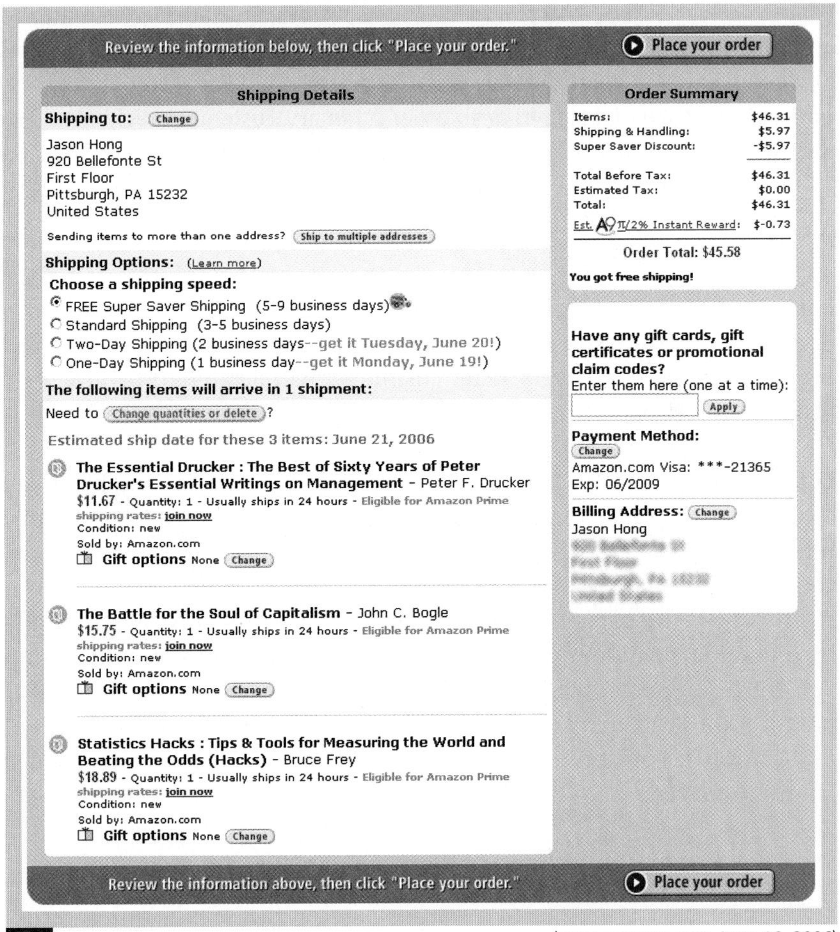

F7.1 (www.amazon.com, June 16, 2006)

BACKGROUND

For QUICK-FLOW CHECKOUT (F1) on a PERSONAL E-COMMERCE (A1) site, customers must be able to double-check orders before finalizing them. In the SHOPPING CART (F3) pattern, items are collected and summarized. Then a QUICK ADDRESS SELECTION (F4) and a QUICK SHIPPING METHOD SELECTION (F5) are made, and a PAYMENT METHOD (F6) is selected. This pattern describes how to present the information entered in these other patterns for final review by the customer.

✳ PROBLEM

When finalizing orders, customers want to see everything related to what they're ordering: the specific products, all the charges, and the billing methods, as well as where, how, and approximately when packages will be delivered. If any one of these elements is missing from an order summary, customers might abandon their purchases.

If the proper information is missing from an order summary, people might wonder whether they entered all the correct information, or they might suspect that the company did not heed the information they entered on previous pages. In any case, it does not foster trust to ignore one of the critical elements of e-commerce: people want to review their orders. If you include every item, customers will be able to review their progress and check out with confidence.

Confirm That the Order Is Ready to Complete • Customers might arrive at the order summary page and think that their order has been submitted already. If they close the browser, though, they will never receive their order and your company will not receive a completed transaction. At the top of the page, highlight the fact that the order is not complete by including a PROGRESS BAR (H13) showing that there's one more step before the order is finalized (see Figure F7.2). To indicate this, provide a HIGH-VISIBILITY ACTION BUTTON (K5) labeled "Place your order" or "Complete your order." See Figures F7.1 and F7.2 for sample order summary pages.

Show Key Elements • The elements to show on the order summary page include everything entered on the site for the specific order, except for customer passwords and full credit card numbers. For shipping information, show the key fields described in QUICK ADDRESS SELECTION (F4), along with an ACTION BUTTON (K4) to change the information.

For shopping cart items, show the key details discussed in the SHOPPING CART (F3) pattern. Again, include ACTION BUTTONS (K4) to change anything in the cart.

For billing information, show the name and address fields that were provided for the billing address, as well as the PAYMENT METHOD (F6) details. Include an ACTION BUTTON (K4) to permit the customer to change any of the billing information.

Figure F7.2

This order summary from Nordstrom alerts the customer that the order is not yet complete and provides high-visibility action buttons above and below the fold so that the customer will see what to click to complete the order, even if scrolling is necessary. The summary also includes a progress bar that shows where the customer is in the checkout process. This page would work better if customers could easily change the shipping or billing information.

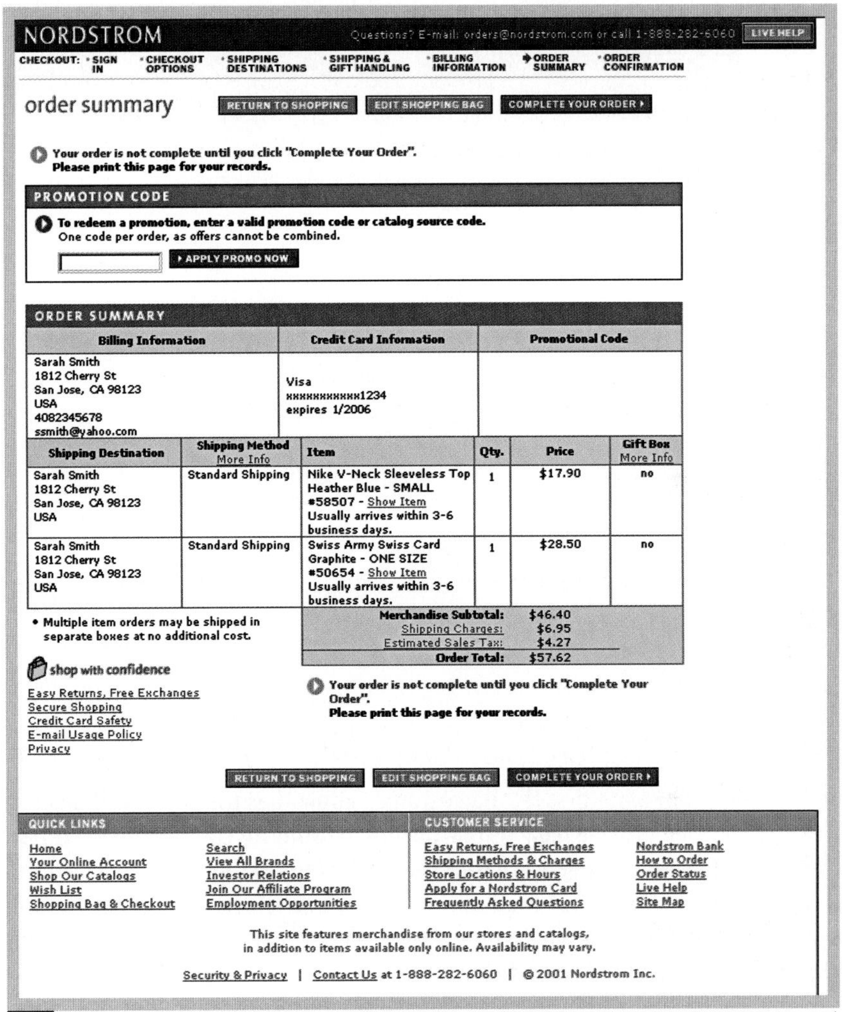

F7.2

(www.nordstrom.com, October 3, 2001)

Finally, be sure to include all other charges and the total:

- Shipping and handling costs
- Any other charges that contribute to the total cost
- Subtotals
- Tax
- Total

Figure F7.3 shows an example of a simple, straightforward order summary page.

Figure F7.3

Once customers have entered their billing and shipping information at snapfish.com, an online photo service, a summary of the order verifies all the items, costs, and taxes.

(www.snapfish.com, January 30, 2002)

✳ SOLUTION

In the order summary, first let the customer know that the order still has not been placed, and provide high-visibility action buttons for completing the order. Then show the items being purchased and all the information that the customer entered: address, payment method, and shipping selections. Provide action buttons to edit these items in case they're incorrect. Finally, calculate and present the total costs, including shipping and taxes.

Figure F7.4

Summarize all infor-
mation that the
customer has entered:
the billing and ship-
ping information,
the items being pur-
chased, and all the
costs. Make it easy
for the customer to
change any of this
information and to
see whether the order
still needs to be
updated.

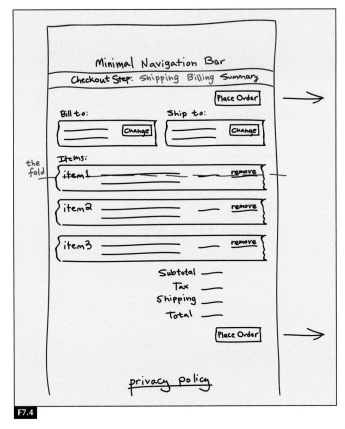

F7.4

✳ OTHER PATTERNS TO CONSIDER

Add a PROGRESS BAR (H13) at the top of the order summary page to
reinforce that this is the final step for customers before the order is
completed. Create HIGH-VISIBILITY ACTION BUTTONS (K5) to encourage shoppers to complete their orders. Provide ACTION BUTTONS (K4) on each of the
element sections for editing, including shipping address, shipping method,
billing method and address, and the items ordered. Display the rows of
items in a GRID LAYOUT (I1), in CONTENT MODULES (D2). Link to your PRIVACY
POLICY (E4) to help answer any final questions that customers might have
about your information use policies. Link to your return policy to enable
EASY RETURNS (F9) and to assure customers that they can change their
minds if they're not satisfied.

F8 ORDER CONFIRMATION AND THANK-YOU

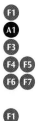

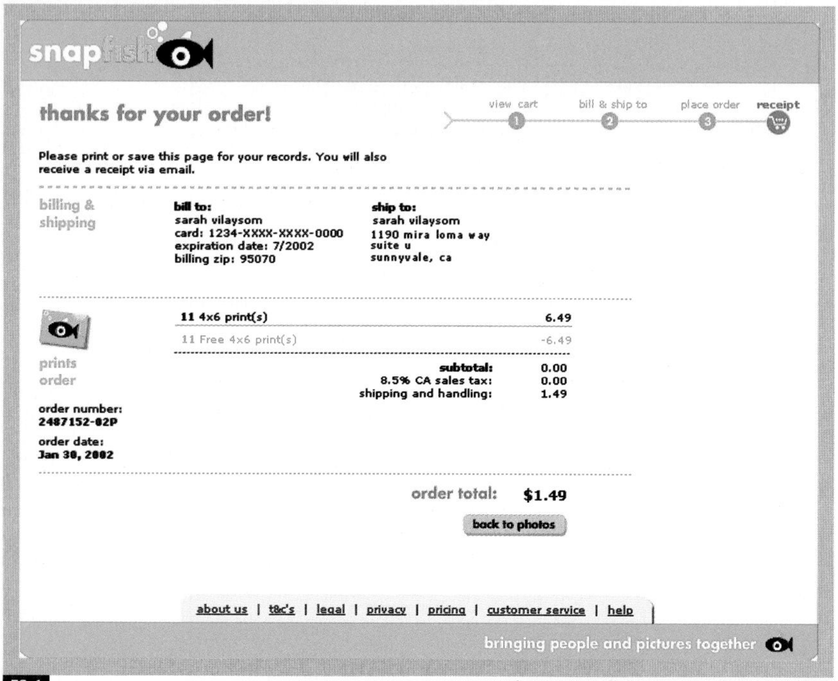

F8.1

(www.snapfish.com, January 30, 2002)

Figure F8.1

The order confirmation and thank-you page makes it clear to the customer that the order has gone through. It also shows the date of the order, the order number, and all items in the order. This is a printable order confirmation and thank-you page from snapfish.com.

BACKGROUND

After completing the QUICK-FLOW CHECKOUT (F1) on a PERSONAL E-COMMERCE (A1) site, customers like to have a receipt for their order. In the SHOPPING CART (F3) pattern, items are collected and summarized. Then QUICK ADDRESS SELECTION (F4), QUICK SHIPPING METHOD SELECTION (F5), and PAYMENT METHOD (F6) selection follow. In the ORDER SUMMARY (F7), customers review their order and decide to finalize it. This pattern, representing the last step in the QUICK-FLOW CHECKOUT (F1), and depicted as the final step in a PROGRESS BAR (H13), confirms the order and items entered in these other patterns.

F1 A1 F3 F4 F5 F6 F7 F1 H13

✳ PROBLEM

If, after completing their orders, customers do not get confirmation or a receipt indicating that the order has gone through, they will be unsure of their order status and have to work to find confirmation evidence.

Online orders are not tangible; that is, customers cannot walk out with goods in their hands. Yet they must trust the online company that their money is not being stolen. What reassures people is a confirmation that shows everything in their order, and an order number to reference in case there's a problem. Without all this detailed information, customers might wonder what they ordered, and they might second-guess the company. If you include every element of an order in a confirmation, the customer can review the details and print out the confirmation for later reference. Suddenly an order becomes somewhat tangible.

Thank Your Customers • After an order is completed, thank the customer for shopping with you. It's just a simple courtesy.

Highlight the Order Number and Date • To help customers organize their various orders, made on various days, display the order number and the date of the order on the confirmation (see Figure F8.2). If they want to go back to the order later, they can look it up by number or date.

Figure F8.2

Nordstrom's order confirmation high-lights the order number and date, but it is missing several key elements. The confirmation should display all of the product items, as well as the shipping and billing information.

(www.nordstrom.com, October 3, 2001)

Show All Key Elements • The elements to show on the confirmation page include everything on the ORDER SUMMARY (F7).

Send an E-Mail Confirmation • Send customers an E-MAIL NOTIFICATION (E7) confirming that their purchase was completed. This message should have all of the key elements found in the ORDER SUMMARY (F7), and it will make it easier for customers to remember what they purchased and track the status of their order.

Make the Page Printable • Customers may want to reference an order later. They can go online to do it, but they may not know where to find this information, or a computer with a network connection might not be within easy reach. In addition, some people like the artifact of a paper receipt for their files. By making the order confirmation and thank-you a PRINTABLE PAGE (D8), you can satisfy both of these needs.

Encourage Customers to Continue Shopping • After placing an order, customers might remember an item that they didn't order and might want to return to shopping. Some shoppers might want to place a separate order for someone else. Make sure your customers can return to your site quickly and easily after placing an order. Use CROSS-SELLING AND UP-SELLING (G2) to highlight other products that might interest them, given the items they just purchased (see Figure F8.3). Use a HIGH-VISIBILITY ACTION BUTTON (K5) labeled "Continue Shopping" to take them back.

Figure F8.3

Amazon.com does a good job of cross-selling products after customers have completed purchases, providing two lists of recommended items ("Recommended for You" and "Customers who bought items in your order also bought").

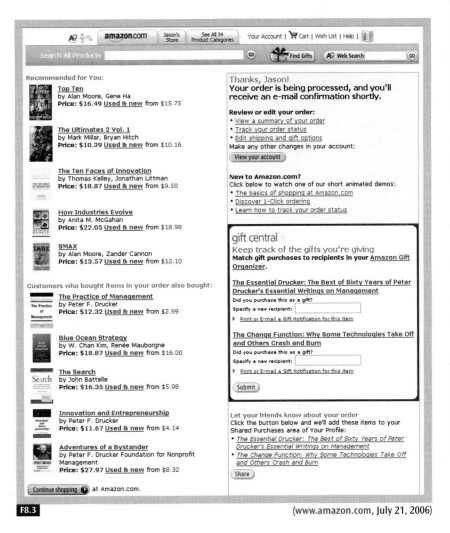

F8.3

(www.amazon.com, July 21, 2006)

✳ SOLUTION

Confirm each order and thank the customer for shopping with you on a printable page that displays the order number, the order date, and all the order information, including items purchased, quantities, product prices, shipping prices, tax, total, and shipping and billing information. Provide an action button that allows customers to continue shopping, and cross-sell them on other products that they might be interested in purchasing.

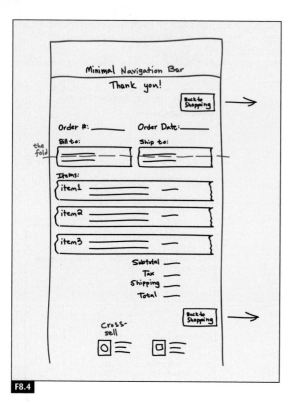

F8.4

Figure F8.4

An order confirmation page lets the customer know that an order has been processed successfully. It provides summary information to record what was purchased and the specifics of the billing and shipping for future reference.

✳ OTHER PATTERNS TO CONSIDER

Provide a PRINTABLE PAGE (D8) that displays all the elements from the previous ORDER SUMMARY (F7) page. Consider sending an E-MAIL NOTIFICATION (E7) that summarizes the order and provides a receipt to let the customer know that the order was received properly. Include a HIGH-VISIBILITY ACTION BUTTON (K5) on the thank-you page that lets customers continue shopping, in case they forgot something. By CROSS-SELLING AND UP-SELLING (G2), suggest other products that might interest them. Link to your return policy to enable EASY RETURNS (F9) and to assure customers that they can change their minds if they're not satisfied.

D8
F7
E7
K5
G2
F9

Figure F9.1

A site can help close sales by letting customers know that returns are not only possible, but also easy. Buying items sight unseen requires trust. Customers are reassured if they know that they can make a mistake and not be charged for it. Buy.com clearly states its return policy and provides a clear link to make a return.

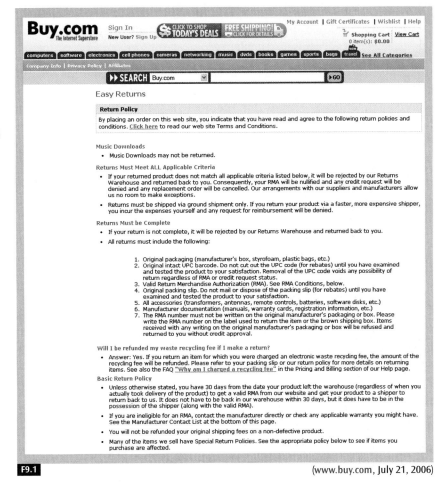

F9.1

(www.buy.com, July 21, 2006)

❋ BACKGROUND

To build trust on a PERSONAL E-COMMERCE (A1) site, each policy and process must center on satisfying the customer. In QUICK-FLOW CHECKOUT (F1), items are purchased. This pattern provides the mechanism for returning goods for replacement or refund.

✳ PROBLEM

When items that are accidentally ordered, damaged during delivery, or just not wanted can be returned quickly and easily, customers are more likely to order. But making returns easy is not simple.

Customers may become tentative during a checkout process if they're not sure the product fits them or their needs. Customers who have not yet placed an order need to know that the site where they're shopping makes the return process easy.

Place Return Policy Links Prominently on All Product and Checkout Pages • For customers to know that the company policy allows returns, they must be able to find the return policy (see Figure F9.2). They want to know things like the following:

- Does the company have a return policy?
- If there's a return policy, can an item be returned for any reason?
- What condition must the products be in?
- Will I be charged return shipping costs?

A return policy answers all these questions, while also providing more specific details about where to send something or how to use an online return process. Put a link to the return policy on all QUICK-FLOW CHECKOUT (F1) pages, on every CLEAN PRODUCT DETAIL (F2) page, on all CATEGORY PAGES (B8), and on the HOMEPAGE PORTAL (C1).

Provide a Return Process Funnel • After receiving a shipment, opening it, and finding that one or more of the items ordered are incorrect, broken, or unwanted, a customer might put the items back in the box and return them immediately. Some customers, however, might not put the items right back in the box, because they don't realize that they have a problem. These customers might throw away the return label or the box itself. By providing a way to generate a label on the site, a company can help customers through the process of returning an item and getting their money back, while at the

Figure F9.2

Putting a link to the return policy on every page helps ensure that people know they can return items. This is the first step in educating customers about your return policy and giving them quick access to the return process. Amazon.com puts these links on every product page.

Where's My Stuff?	**Shipping & Returns**	**Need Help?**
• Track your <u>recent orders</u>.	• See our <u>shipping rates & policies</u>.	• Forgot your password? <u>Click here</u>.
• View or change your orders in <u>Your Account</u>.	• <u>Return</u> an item (here's our <u>Returns Policy</u>).	• <u>Redeem</u> or <u>buy</u> a gift certificate.
		• <u>Tax and seller information</u>
		• <u>Visit our Help department</u>.

Search [Electronics ▾] for [   ] (GO)

F9.2   (www.amazon.com, August 19, 2001)

same time making it easier to sort through the returned merchandise. A
PROCESS FUNNEL (H1) can simplify returns to a few clicks and a page print.

Have customers find the previous order containing the item that needs
to be returned. There might be many orders, so provide a list and the
order contents. Make the order easy to find, even if customers don't know
the order number or exact date, or the order was a gift from someone else.

Display the items in the order, and using DRILL-DOWN OPTIONS (H12),
provide a list of reasons why a customer might legitimately make a return
for each item (see Figure F9.3).

Once customers have selected the items to return and the reasons for
the return, offer to print a label for the package, or tell customers to use
the return shipping label that was included with the original order
(see Figure F9.4). By tagging your order database with the return, the
returns department will know what to expect in the box.

If customers elect to print labels, generate a tracking code that will
tie into the order database when the package returns (see Figure F9.5).

Figure F9.3

Amazon.com
provides a form for
selecting the reason
to return every item
in an order.

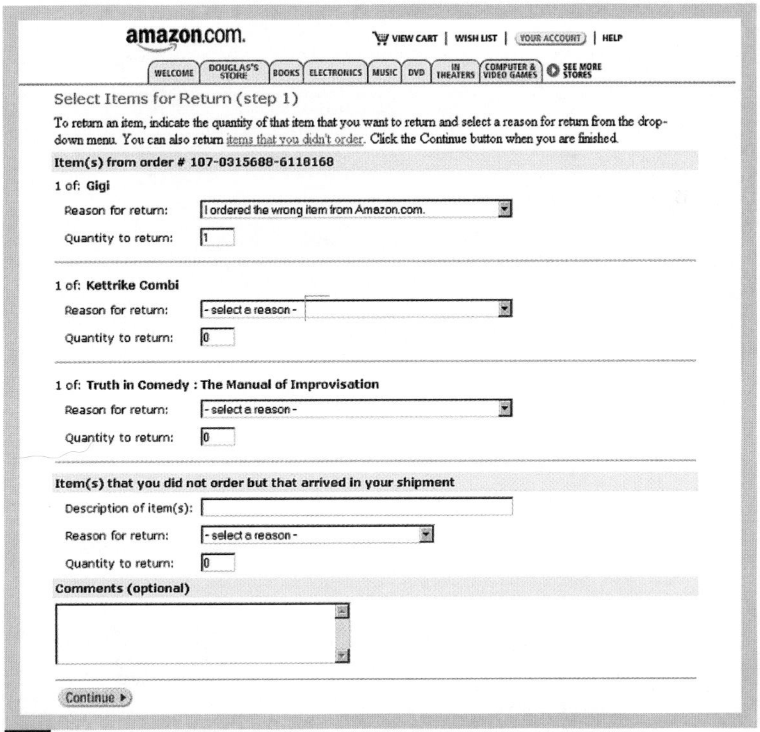

(www.amazon.com, August 19, 2001)

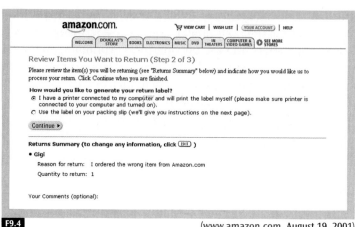

Figure F9.4

Amazon.com asks customers who are returning merchandise if they would like to print a return label.

(www.amazon.com, August 19, 2001)

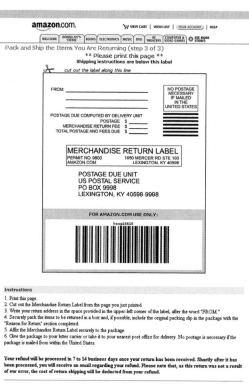
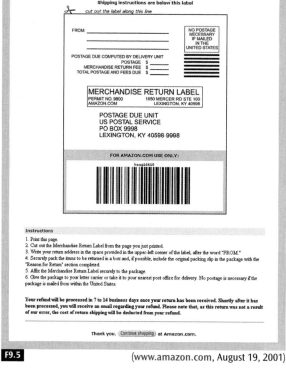

Figure F9.5

If the customer elects to print a return label, Amazon.com automatically generates this label and gives instructions for how to use it.

(www.amazon.com, August 19, 2001)

This will make it easier for your company to credit customer accounts. The faster you can do this, the happier customers will be with your site, and the more likely they will be to place another order later.

✳ SOLUTION

Show the return policy on all product and checkout pages, including a link to a return process. In case customers throw away a return label, give them the ability to print another one, and use the label to track returns as they arrive.

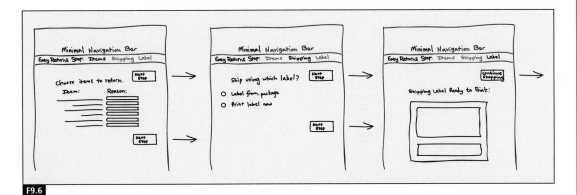

Figure F9.6

Make the return process easy by using a process funnel that takes customers step-by-step through identifying the order, specifying the items to return and the reasons why, and finally printing a shipping label, if necessary.

✳ OTHER PATTERNS TO CONSIDER

On QUICK-FLOW CHECKOUT (F1) pages, CLEAN PRODUCT DETAIL (F2) pages, CATEGORY PAGES (B8), and the HOMEPAGE PORTAL (C1), include a link to the return policy and the return PROCESS FUNNEL (H1). In the process funnel, ask customers to select the order, and the items and reasons for the return. At the end of the process, display a PRINTABLE PAGE (D8) with a mailing label to be used for return purposes.

Advanced E-Commerce ◆ G

Pattern Group F (Basic E-Commerce) established the basic framework for e-commerce. This pattern group discusses advanced and optional features that you may wish to include on your site, such as promoting products, sending gifts, and tracking orders.

G1 FEATURED PRODUCTS

G2 CROSS-SELLING AND UP-SELLING

G3 PERSONALIZED RECOMMENDATIONS

G4 RECOMMENDATION COMMUNITY

G5 MULTIPLE DESTINATIONS

G6 GIFT GIVING

G7 ORDER TRACKING AND HISTORY

(www.1800flowers.com, June 16, 2006)

Figure G1.1

1-800-flowers.com highlights several kinds of featured products, including "Florist Designed," as well as specials like "DOUBLE POINTS!" and "SAVE 10%." The attractive photographs also give the flowers a seductive quality.

❋ BACKGROUND

In PERSONAL E-COMMERCE (A1) we provided a solution for building sites and promoting sales within those sites. Recommendations can make customers more confident in their choices and help close more sales. This pattern, along with CROSS-SELLING AND UP-SELLING (G2), PERSONALIZED RECOMMENDATIONS (G3), and RECOMMENDATION COMMUNITY (G4), describes how to provide useful recommendations. Specifically, this pattern describes the featured-product page, which provides recommendations on or near the homepage.

❋ PROBLEM

Customers find value when sites identify specific products as recommended or featured. Otherwise, product lists can appear bland and tedious.

Having tens, hundreds, thousands, even millions of products on a Web site gives customers a wide selection of choices. But if they can get to those products only through long lists or search engines, they'll find it difficult to browse your site, and you will make fewer sales. If your site presumes that visitors already know what they want and gives them no easy way to explore the site, people who like to browse will be at a loss. The site will not be a place to gather information before making a buying decision.

One way to make it easy to explore your products is to provide a list of featured products. Such a list gives customers an opportunity to window-shop and lets them know that there's always something new to see. On the downside, the site must be set up so that it can be quickly updated either manually or automatically.

Editorialize in Your Product Recommendations • For some customers, simply having the product name, a picture, and the price is not enough. These customers are accustomed to getting personal recommendations from salespeople and friends when they shop in a store. On the Web, however, there is no direct connection, and people are usually alone at their computers. You can minimize their feelings of isolation by editorializing in your recommendations, giving the site a personality and a human touch (see Figure G1.2).

G1.2

(www.brooksbrothers.com, August 10, 2006)

Figure G1.2

Brooks Brothers' homepage recommends several products with editorial comments that seduce customers much more effectively than a simple list would.

Adopting a consistent editorial voice gives the site personality, and it gives customers the sense that they're interacting with a real person instead of a large, faceless company. Decide on your voice and make the copy match. Do you want your site to be friendly? Wisecracking? Authoritative? Friendly? Whatever you choose, be consistent to avoid confusion.

Provide Different Kinds of Recommendations • Shoppers have diverse needs and different values. On a site that sells jewelry, for example, a shopper who likes to see the latest styles may decide to go elsewhere if she can't see what's new. Fashionable shoppers want to see what's gaining popularity; cost-conscious customers may want to see what's on sale. Those who need help with a purchase will want to see a buyer's guide. Featuring products to accommodate all these different slants can dramatically improve your customers' ability to find the desired items. Categories to use for featuring products might include things like "Best-Sellers," "Editors' Picks," "Rare Finds," and "New Releases." Figure G1.3 shows two examples.

Table G1.1 shows another way of thinking about featured products. Any of the questions shown in the table can be used as the basis for categorizing featured products. Start with the most relevant and appropriate products for your customers' needs. Keep in mind that each of these tools takes time to build and that some will be more important than others, depending on how your shopper looks for products. For example, shopping by brand might be very important on a clothing site.

Figure G1.3

Here are two different kinds of recommendations. (a) Barnes & Noble lists top-selling books. (b) RedEnvelope provides the editors' recommendations of favorite gifts.

G1.3a

(www.bn.com, June 16, 2006)

Figure G1.3

(*Continued*)

G1.3b   (www.redenvelope.com, June 16, 2006)

Table G1.2 is more extensive than what you can provide on your site. Pare it down according to your customers' needs, and customize it for your site by naming the appropriate products and categories.

To implement these featured-product schemes, refer also to MULTIPLE WAYS TO NAVIGATE (B1), BROWSABLE CONTENT (B2), ORGANIZED SEARCH RESULTS (J3), PERSONALIZED CONTENT (D4), and RECOMMENDATION COMMUNITY (G4).

Provide Opportunities to Explore • Not everyone will come to your site with a specific question, goal, or product in mind. Yet visitors will not browse through thousands of products. Like a virtual window dresser, you have to give customers chances to explore your products by highlighting imagery and detail that will compel them to click for more information. By featuring several different ways for people to experience your products, you will draw people in according to their varying interests (see Figure G1.4).

Table G1.1

Using Commonly
Asked Questions to
Categorize Featured
Products

		Choose one		Choose one	
I'm interested in	+	all of	+	a product type.	→ Where is it?
		the best of		a product.	
		the least expensive of		a brand.	
		the best for this price of		anything.	
		what's new of		anything on sale. something new. something for a friend.	

Table G1.2

Patterns to Apply

So that your customers can find . . .		Provide these tools
all of/the best of:	a product type	Product type CATEGORY PAGES (B8), SEARCH ACTION MODULE (J1)
	a brand	Brand CATEGORY PAGES (B8)
	anything	SEARCH ACTION MODULE (J1)
	anything on sale	"On Sale" CATEGORY PAGES (B8)
	something new	"What's New" CATEGORY PAGES (B8)
	something for a friend	"Gift Finder" PROCESS FUNNEL (H1) and GIFT GIVING (G6)
the least expensive of:	a product type	Price sort in product type CATEGORY PAGES (B8)
	a brand	Price sort in brand CATEGORY PAGES (B8)
	anything	Price sort after SEARCH ACTION MODULE (J1)
	anything on sale	Price sort in "On Sale" CATEGORY PAGES (B8)
	something new	Price sort in "What's New" CATEGORY PAGES (B8)
	something for a friend	Price criteria in "Gift Finder" PROCESS FUNNEL (H1) and GIFT GIVING (G6)

Pattern markers (left margin): B8, J1, B8, J1, B8, B8, H1 G6, B8, B8, J1, B8, B8, H1 G6

(www.anntaylor.com, July 21, 2006)

Figure G1.4

Ann Taylor's Web site starts editorializing right on the home-page. Note the enticing pictures and tempting phrases, such as "NEW SUMMER DRESSES" and "FINAL SUMMER SALE!"

❊ SOLUTION

To give people a better sense of what's on your site, build category pages that highlight special featured products and editorialize in the product recommendations. Provide different kinds of recommendations, choosing categories such as "Top Sellers," "Editors' Picks," and so on. Let visitors explore by highlighting as many areas of interest as possible.

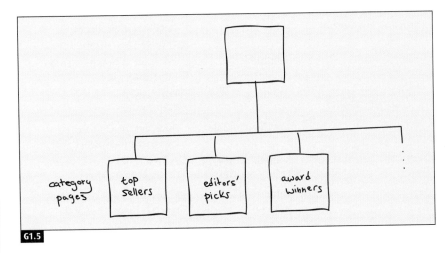

Figure G1.5

Feature products in a variety of ways to recommend and promote sales.

✳ OTHER PATTERNS TO CONSIDER

Provide MULTIPLE WAYS TO NAVIGATE (B1) to the best products on your site, including a SEARCH ACTION MODULE (J1) and BROWSABLE CONTENT (B2). Use PERSONALIZED CONTENT (D4) in a PAGE TEMPLATE (D1), as well as the reviews of a RECOMMENDATION COMMUNITY (G4). Different sets of featured products can be thought of as different CATEGORY PAGES (B8).

G2 CROSS-SELLING AND UP-SELLING

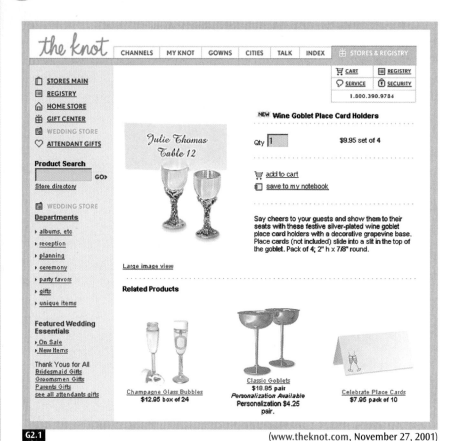

Figure G2.1

Cross-selling and **up-selling** mean promoting products and services that are highly related to the current product. On this page of The Knot's Web site, the assumption is that people who are interested in wine goblets might also be interested in place cards, champagne glasses, and nicer goblets. These cross-selling and up-selling links reduce people's shopping time by helping them find many things they might want at the same time.

❊ BACKGROUND

In PERSONAL E-COMMERCE (A1) we provided a solution for building sites and promoting sales within those sites. Recommendations can make customers more confident in their choices and help close more sales. This pattern, along with FEATURED PRODUCTS (G1), PERSONALIZED RECOMMENDATIONS (G3), and RECOMMENDATION COMMUNITY (G4), describes how to provide useful recommendations. Specifically, this pattern describes cross-selling and up-selling—that is, recommending additional products according to the interests that the customer has already expressed.

❄ PROBLEM

When choosing a product in stores, people appreciate hearing about related products that are complementary to or better than the products that they've chosen. Doing the same thing online requires prudence and planning.

People often come to a site looking for something, whether they have a specific idea of what they need or only a vague notion. While looking around, however, they may be pleased to find something useful that they didn't know about. Cross-selling and up-selling are two techniques for providing information about related products and services right when the customer is making a purchase. These strategies increase your profit on each sale by enticing customers to buy items related to what they're planning to purchase anyway.

Cross-selling is promoting accessories related to the current choice. For example, someone who buys a mobile phone may be interested in buying extra travel chargers and spare batteries. **Up-selling** is promoting a better (and more expensive!) version of the current choice. For example, a person interested in one product line of mobile phones may be interested in more upscale versions or in an extended warranty covering any damages. From the perspective of a fast-food restaurant, cross-selling is, "Do you want fries with that?" and up-selling is, "Do you want to supersize that?"

Although *cross-selling* and *up-selling* have specific meanings in sales, the distinction between the two can sometimes become blurry. In fact, we think it's easier and better to think of both approaches as promoting products and services that are highly related to the current products that interest the customer. The goals in both cases, though, are the same. For customers, the goal is to get help finding useful items and completing purchases more quickly. For the company, the goal is to increase sales and revenue. This pattern describes how to use cross-selling and up-selling on your Web site, and how to implement these techniques without being too aggressive.

Cross-Sell and Up-Sell Related Products • What will customers find useful if they're already looking at a specific product? Such items might include accessories, complementary products, better versions of the current product, or similar products with slight differences (see Figures G2.2 and G2.3).

Figure G2.2

RedEnvelope makes it easy for gift givers to add batteries to their orders so that recipients of electronic gifts won't be disappointed by not being able to try them out right away.

(www.redenvelope.com, November 27, 2001)

Figure G2.3

CD Universe relates products to each other to help its customers make the most useful connections. Here, people thinking of purchasing an audio CD are shown, at the bottom, additional CDs that might be of interest.

(www.cduniverse.com, July 21, 2006)

You can offer all these related products, depending on customer needs. Not all customers will find all of the related products useful, but if enough of them do, your efforts will have been worth the trouble.

Related products are connected in the product database, as well as in customers' minds. The product database must implement the connection to automatically sell related products on the main product pages. In your product database, list all the products that are related to a given product. You can have your Web site update these relationships automatically on the basis of previous customer purchases so that the recommendations change over time.

To create automatic product relationships, do the following:

1. Group together all products that customers purchased with the current product.
2. Rank the products by how many times they were purchased together.

These two steps will tell you which products sell best together, so you will also know exactly which top three to five related products to show on your current product page.

On the other hand, you can manage these relationships by hand, updating them once a month or quarter. Hand-merchandising is much more time-consuming but also gives you the opportunity to give customers some unique insights about the products you sell, such as why two products go well with each other.

Separate and Minimize the Screen Real Estate Devoted to Related Products • Customers must be able to differentiate between related products and current products. A visual distinction that places the related products on the side, or in a special area, helps when people scan the page. Set off the related products in separate CONTENT MODULES (D2), each with its own title showing how the products are related. The titles give customers a quick way to scan the boxes and items. Provide a brief description or picture to help customers identify the value of the items.

At the same time, be sure to minimize the amount of screen space used to advertise related products. In physical stores, customers appreciate salespeople who graciously provide help in finding a product. But salespeople can cross a line when their suggestions become too pushy and annoy customers. You can cross the same line online. The graphics and text promoting related products can make the page look too busy and distract customers from reading about the main product. Make sure that more space is devoted to the main product than to related products. Keep the main product in the center of the screen, and push related products to the bottom or to the side.

Editorialize about Related Products • Customers want to know something about a product before they leave their current Web page to explore it. Giving them a descriptive preview helps them judge whether it's worth checking out that product's CLEAN PRODUCT DETAIL (F2) page. Unless the product name is very descriptive, you might add one or two sentences of editorial description.

(F2)

Allow Quick Purchase of Related Products • When you take customers to a separate page to purchase a related product, they might get lost on their way back or be sidetracked and forget about the original product. Make it easy for customers to buy related products without losing the original product. Give customers enough information about a related product to decide on its value without having to jump to another page (see Figure G2.4).

You can also provide quick-purchase ACTION BUTTONS (K4) or check boxes to make it easy to add related products to the SHOPPING CART (F3) without leaving the current page. For example, suppose the customer is buying a toy that requires batteries. A quick-purchase ACTION BUTTON (K4) can let the customer add batteries to the shopping cart and then update the page or show a FLOATING WINDOW (H6) to indicate that the batteries have been added.

(K4)
(F3)

(K4)

(H6)

Sell Related Products during Checkout • If there are important related products that the customer has not purchased, you can suggest them again from the SHOPPING CART (F3), the ORDER SUMMARY (F7), and the

(F3)(F7)

Figure G2.4

Netflix invites customers to rent movies that other members enjoyed. When a customer clicks on the **Add** button to select one of these, a floating window opens to show additional related movies.

G2.4

(www.netflix.com, August 11, 2006)

F8 ORDER CONFIRMATION AND THANK-YOU (F8) pages (see Figures G2.5 and G2.6). This tactic is similar to what grocers do with impulse buys at the checkout stand, but on a Web site you can provide much more relevant products because you already know what's in your customer's shopping cart and what might be of additional value. Again, you must make it simple and quick to add these related items, because your first priority is to close the primary sale.

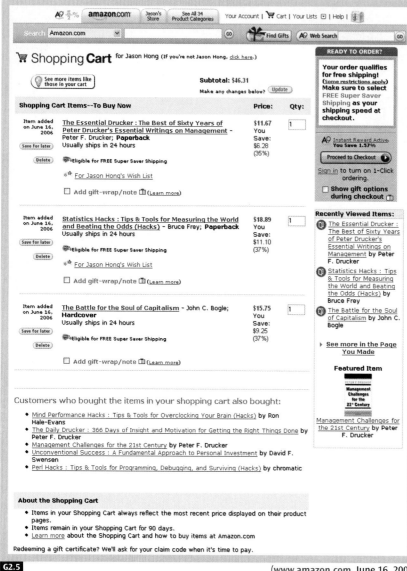

Figure G2.5

On the basis of what customers have placed in the shopping cart, Amazon.com provides links (bottom) to related products.

Figure G2.6

After completing a checkout, Amazon.com provides links to products that the customer might have missed.

✳ SOLUTION

In a subtle and careful way, cross-sell and up-sell related products by indicating the benefit they provide to your customers. Customers will be seduced and will not need to go far to make a purchase if you make it quick and easy to add a related product to a shopping cart without leaving the context of the current page. Make a visual distinction between these promotions and the other content on the page. Sell the related products again later in the checkout process, in case customers missed them the first time.

G2.7

Figure G2.7

Use cross-selling and up-selling to promote products related to the interests already indicated by your customers.

✳ OTHER PATTERNS TO CONSIDER

Editorialize about related products so that customers get a preview of the CLEAN PRODUCT DETAIL (F2) page. For accessories and other related items, add a quick-purchase ACTION BUTTON (K4) to the SHOPPING CART (F3).

Highlight related products in separate CONTENT MODULES (D2), each with its own title showing how the products are related. The titles give customers a quick way to scan the boxes and items in the list. Customers may want to purchase related products after making a purchase. Adding products to a SHOPPING CART (F3) always takes customers forward in the QUICK-FLOW CHECKOUT (F1), and if they want a product that was promoted on an earlier page, they can hit the **Back** button. If the customer has not purchased important related products, suggest them again from the SHOPPING CART (F3), the ORDER SUMMARY (F7), and the ORDER CONFIRMATION AND THANK-YOU (F8) pages.

G3.1

(www.tivo.com, June 16, 2006)

Figure G3.1

TiVo lets you search or browse a database of television shows and offers an **If you like this . . .** tab that suggests other television shows you might like.

❋ BACKGROUND

The core of PERSONAL E-COMMERCE (A1) is to provide an experience that satisfies each customer's unique needs. Making the shopping experience personal requires tailoring it to each customer. This pattern forms the core of personalized recommendations, a form of PERSONALIZED CONTENT (D4) that provides recommendations based on past purchases and on information that customers reveal about themselves. This pattern can be used in conjunction with FEATURED PRODUCTS (G1), CROSS-SELLING AND UP-SELLING (G2), and RECOMMENDATION COMMUNITY (G4) to provide useful recommendations and streamline purchases for customers.

A1

D4

G1 **G2**
G4

✳ PROBLEM

Personalized recommendations can provide customers with a better sense of what's useful and what isn't. But if they require too much effort on the customer's part, or if they're based on what customers perceive as scant evidence, they will fail.

When shopping online, customers can benefit from personalized recommendations. These suggestions can make shopping easier and more enjoyable, helping customers to choose between products and to find new products that they didn't even know might interest them. Unfortunately, personalized recommendations require significant design and engineering, and priming the pump with enough information to make useful comments requires detailed customer information.

When visitors go to your site for the first time, there is very little the site can tell about them. Over time, the site can learn what customers are interested in on the basis of where they go, what they click on, and what they search for. However, basic path and search information is not enough to make strong conclusions about visitor interests, because they might have clicked on a link to a product page but found it was not the one they were looking for, or typed in a search word but did not use the expected words. Recommendations that come from such information, which can be false or misleading, do not always deliver the kinds of personalized recommendations that customers will find useful.

More deliberate expressions of interest, such as actual purchase behavior, make reliable indicators. But requiring customers to purchase something before you can recommend other products does not provide any value to first-time shoppers, the people whom a site wishes to attract to become long-term, repeat customers. Instead, try alternatives such as providing easy-to-perform ratings of products, carrying out recommendation interviews, and using the purchase behavior of other customers. This solution provides you with the framework to create each of these alternatives.

Avoid Using Purely Inferred Data • Referer information from Web server logs identifying the page from which a customer just came, and additional information about other sites that customers have visited can be used to infer customer needs. But such inferences are not always accurate, because navigation errors may have led customers to the

Figure G3.2

Amazon.com bases its category recommendations on customer purchases.

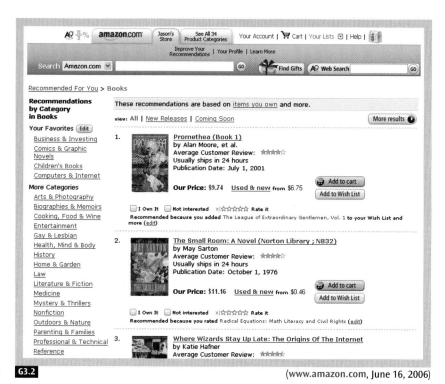

`G3.2`

(www.amazon.com, June 16, 2006)

wrong locations. Product recommendations that are based on false leads can ring hollow.

Recommending products on the basis of pure inference from circumstantial data is different from making recommendations about products that this customer or other customers bought (see Figure G3.2). In both of these other cases, customers vouch for their interest in a particular product by buying it. By itself, visiting a product category or a specific product page does not provide enough information to say it was the right product for someone.

Make It Easy for Customers to Choose Preferred Products • Customers don't want to fill out forms to get product recommendations unless there's a clear and tangible benefit. Give customers a way to rate preferred products without having to purchase them. However, keep in mind that this technique works only if people are familiar with the products you sell, or if they can provide assessments based on information on your site.

F2 Provide customers with a way to rate items on CLEAN PRODUCT DETAIL (F2) pages, letting them indicate how much they liked something. Keep the rating interaction on the current page and reflect the selection made by the customer. Ideally, the rating system will use AJAX (Asynchronous JavaScript And XML) or another technology so that the page will not even have to reload, making the ratings instantaneous and more likely to be used (see Figure G3.3).

Once customers have rated a few products, the Web site can start recommending related products that may interest them.

Invite Customers to State Their Needs • Another way to provide recommendations for customers is through interviews. For example, on a health and nutrition site, an offer of personalized nutrition recommendations might lead to a short series of questions asking about the customer's family medical history, as well as eating and exercise habits. After answering the questions, the customer would receive expert health and nutrition tips, as well as personalized product recommendations.

Figure G3.3

Netflix lets customers rate movies they haven't rented but know about. Here, red stars identify the average rating by other customers, and yellow stars the current customer's ratings. When visitors choose their ratings for a movie, the yellow stars "stick" to that movie for future sessions. After a customer has rated a movie, the Web site can recommend related movies that may be of interest.

G3.3

(www.netflix.com, August 11, 2006)

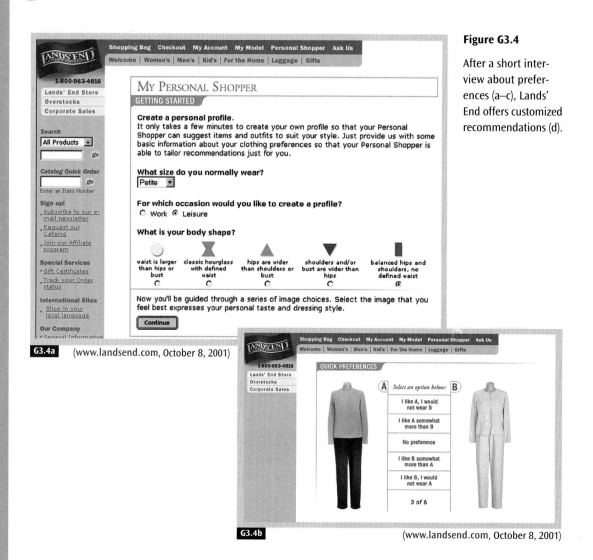

Figure G3.4

After a short interview about preferences (a–c), Lands' End offers customized recommendations (d).

G3.4a (www.landsend.com, October 8, 2001)

G3.4b

(www.landsend.com, October 8, 2001)

The same method could be employed on almost any site where the products are complicated and customers' needs vary widely. Employ a PROCESS FUNNEL (H1) using PREDICTIVE INPUT (H11) or DRILL-DOWN OPTIONS (H12) that takes a customer through a short sequence of choices. Keep the process funnel short and indicate how long the process will take, because customers may balk if too much work is involved with little perceived benefit. Figure G3.4 shows how Lands' End asks customers a few simple questions before providing personalized recommendations.

Figure G3.4

(*Continued*)

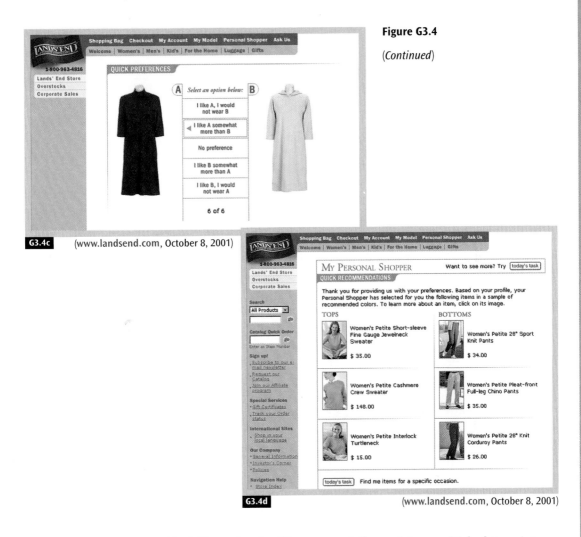

G3.4c — (www.landsend.com, October 8, 2001)

G3.4d — (www.landsend.com, October 8, 2001)

Provide Different Levels of Recommendations • Often multiple data points on each customer's interests can yield useful personalization recommendations. Here are the basic techniques for personalizing recommendations and the information required to generate them:

- Tracking the most popular purchases of customers who like the same things requires the following:
  - A database of product ratings by customers (this is different from just using product purchases, because that approach assumes that customers really liked everything they purchased)
  - The current customer's product ratings

- Tracking the best products, according to information provided by the customer, requires the following:
  - Specific information about customer needs, such as interest in new sports products or in kids' toys
  - Expert recommendations for targeting people with specific interests

Provide Feedback about Why a Recommendation Was Made • One of the biggest problems with personalized recommendation systems is that customers don't know how reliable the recommendations are. One way of addressing this concern is to provide feedback about why a certain recommendation was made. The feedback can be as simple as explaining that the reason for a particular recommendation is that other customers also liked three other similar products. The key here is to avoid describing how the algorithm works at a highly technical level because that will simply confuse customers.

Provide Multiple and Repeated Recommendations • Another way of providing feedback on the reliability of a recommendation is to give several (five to seven) recommendations, and to include items that customers have seen before and liked. This last part is especially important because it gives customers a way of knowing whether or not the system is working. From customers' perspectives, if the Web site is recommending things that they already like, then it's probably working correctly, and the other choices are probably things that they will also like. On the other hand, if the Web site is recommending things that they don't like, they'll think that the site is "broken" and will ignore any personalized recommendations.

Address Privacy Concerns • In an era when more and more marketing is targeted to specific consumers and more and more personal information is recorded in databases, privacy is a primary concern for customers. However, personalized recommendations can help customers find items of interest and value. If your company does not abuse customer information, and discloses clearly and simply how it will use that information, customers are more likely to trust you. Make sure that your PRIVACY POLICY (E4) identifies the kinds of information collected and explains how the information is used. Use PRIVACY PREFERENCES (E8), when necessary, to request permission to use personal data for targeted marketing efforts.

E4

E8

✳ SOLUTION

Figure G3.5

Page templates can be used in conjunction with individual preferences and the product database to present recommendations to new visitors (1). Visitors have their individual preferences stored whenever they explicitly personalize those preferences or purchase something (2). Individual preferences can be combined with the product database to provide personalized recommendations (3). Web site managers can manage the product database through an administrative page that makes it easy to add, remove, and edit content.

Avoid using purely inferred data to make product recommendations, because it will not necessarily reflect real customer choices. Start by offering product and category recommendations based on previous purchases by other customers. Then add recommendations based on past purchases, ratings, and interviews completed by the customer. Integrate this data into your site on product pages, category pages, and personalized recommendation pages. Provide feedback about why a recommendation was made. Provide multiple recommendations, including those that customers have seen before, to help people gauge the quality of the recommendations. Address privacy concerns and how the personalization data will be used.

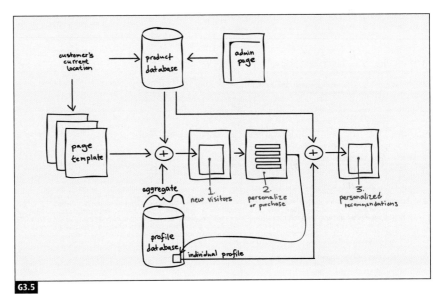

G3.5

✳ OTHER PATTERNS TO CONSIDER

To give customers a way to explicitly state their needs, invite them to participate in a "needs assessment" interview that leads them through a PROCESS FUNNEL (H1). Provide PERSONALIZED CONTENT (D4) based on customer profiles to build product CATEGORY PAGES (B8) and CLEAN PRODUCT DETAIL (F2) pages.

H1 **D4**
B8
F2

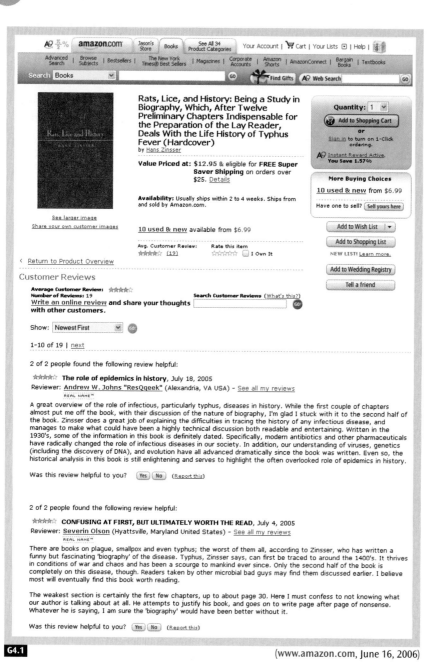

Figure G4.1

Amazon.com's recommendation community provides content for customers. This review content comes from other customers, and it gives the site research value, thereby making it a destination as well as a shopping site.

G4.1   (www.amazon.com, June 16, 2006)

✳ BACKGROUND

In PERSONAL E-COMMERCE (A1) we discussed how COMMUNITY CONFERENCE (A3) tools could augment the shopping experience. This pattern provides the core for giving customers a voice on an e-commerce site and describes how customers' opinions can be used to provide recommendations for other customers. This pattern can be used in conjunction with FEATURED PRODUCTS (G1), CROSS-SELLING AND UP-SELLING (G2), and PERSONALIZED RECOMMENDATIONS (G3) to provide useful recommendations and stream-line purchases for customers. Some recommendation communities share much in common with MESSAGE BOARDS (D5).

✳ PROBLEM

Recommendations from other customers are valuable, but making sure that the community system is not abused is a time-consuming process littered with obstacles.

Within the Web lies a powerful potential for building lasting and sustainable online communities. You can take advantage of this potential on e-commerce sites by creating recommendation communities, letting your community members help each other. The goal of a recommendation community is to empower customers to make informed decisions and thus encourage e-commerce transactions. It's a win–win situation: customers are more satisfied with their purchases, and sites make more sales and thus improve their bottom line.

Customers like recommendations so much that even strangers, especially those who seem knowledgeable, influence them. A past customer's rave review of a product or service is a very strong selling point. Conversely, customers avoid products if they've heard bad things. If we multiply all of the written conversations exchanged by hundreds, even thousands, of customers, we begin to get a small inkling of the power of online communities.

Some of the major obstacles to overcome with recommendation communities are how to deal with obscenities, copyrighted material, reviews by individuals who have a commercial interest in the reviewed product, abusive writers, and negative reviews. You need to make sure that customer-written comments on your site do not include profanity and do not promote competitors' sites. You also need to be able to remove reviews that get past your profanity filters, reviews that are libelous, and reviews that make use of copyrighted material.

For sites that sell a variety of equivalent products, negative reviews are not a crucial problem, as long as customers eventually make a purchase. For sites that sell their own products, though, negative reviews can have a serious, adverse effect on sales. The problem, though, is that customers will keep looking for reviews, even beyond your site if you don't provide them.

According to statistics from the Pew Internet & American Life Project, 73 percent of people research a product or service before buying it.[1] If customers can't do the research on your site, they'll do it on a competitor's site, especially one that has a recommendation community containing an abundance of reviews. In the worst case, customers will make the purchase on a competitor's site! This is a difficult issue, but it is something that the management of a company has to face head-on.

This pattern creates the framework for all recommendation communities.

Help Community Members Write Good Reviews • It can be quite difficult to write reviews, especially for a customer who has never done it before. Help your customers by providing some structure (see Figure G4.2). Having a customer write a review is a two-step PROCESS FUNNEL (H1):　　　　　　　　　　　　　 **H1**

1. Let the customer write a title for the review, and provide a separate area for the text of the review. Include a section to give the product a numerical rating. Provide writing guidelines that specify what to say and how to say it. For example, book reviews should focus on the content of the book and describe why the reader liked or disliked it. However, reviews should avoid giving away book and movie endings, should refrain from profanity, and should not attack the authors personally (although attacking their skills as authors is legitimate). Provide tips for writing good reviews, as well as examples of what to do and what to avoid. For example, you could tell your customers to avoid writing short, one-sentence reviews.
2. Let the customer review what he or she has written, and before it's posted, show how it will appear. Give customers the opportunity to go back and edit if they choose.

Provide Use Policies • Allowing customers to post text or links on a site opens the door to abuses. What if someone posts copyrighted material in a review? If a review allows images, what if someone points to something obscene? What if someone posts an obviously fake review, or an insider such

---

1   Internet Activities, May–June 2000 poll, www.pewinternet.org/reports/chart.asp?img= 4_summary3.gif.

Figure G4.2

The Yahoo! Video site provides review guidelines on the same page as the input form (a), and it shows reviewers their work so that they can proofread what they've written before posting it (b).

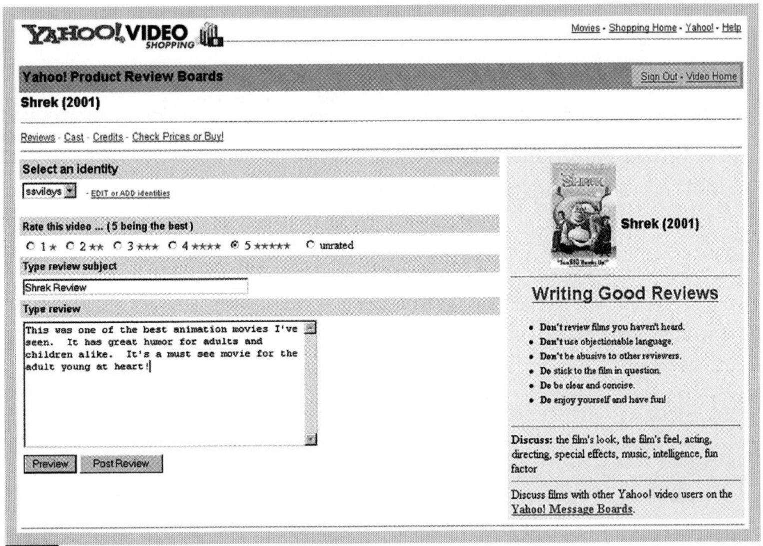

G4.2a   (video.yahoo.com, October 25, 2001)

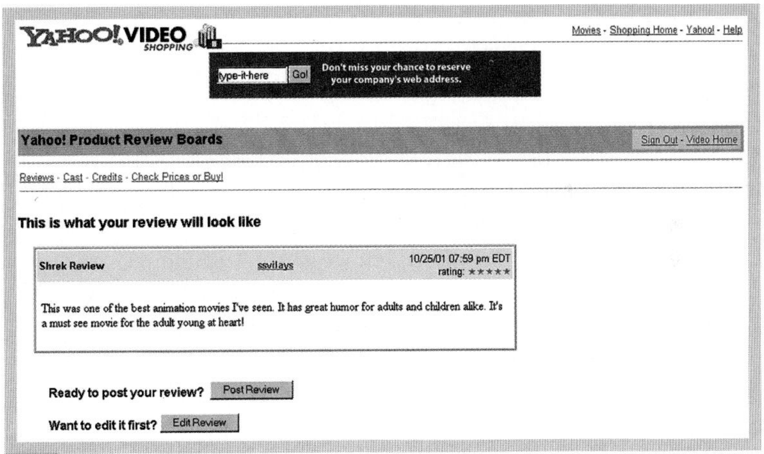

G4.2b   (video.yahoo.com, October 25, 2001)

as a restaurant owner gives his or her own establishment a positive review? In addition, who owns the reviews? What about minors under a certain age? For example, as discussed in PRIVACY POLICY (E4), the U.S. government restricts the kinds of information that can be collected about minors.

The site management team must address all these issues in its FAIR INFORMATION PRACTICES (E3). Many of these issues have potentially serious legal ramifications, so consult legal counsel to develop the best policy. Figure G4.3 shows an example of such a policy.

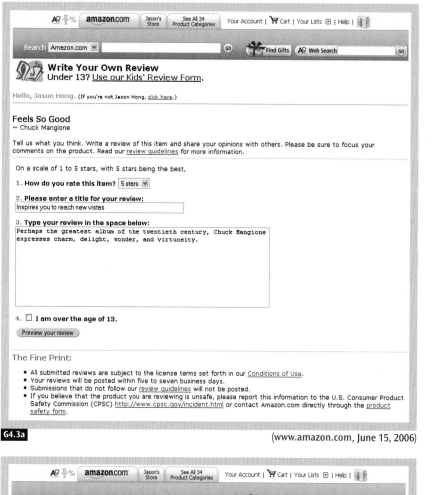

Amazon.com provides links to policies and writing guidelines on the same page as the review form. You can write your review (a), check it (b), and then submit it by clicking **Save.**

A site also needs an editor to check reviews, to ensure that any obscene or possibly libelous material is removed from the review prior to posting. However, it is practically impossible to read and edit every review in a timely manner. One way of managing this responsibility is to randomly spot-check new customer reviews. Another way is to provide a feedback form that lets customers inform the editor of problematic reviews.

Equip Your Site with Meta-ratings • People need a way of knowing which reviews are good and which aren't. One way of providing this information is with **meta-ratings,** or reviews of recommendations. Figure G4.4 shows Amazon.com's meta-rating system. It asks, "Was this review helpful to you?" Reviews with many yes votes are seen as more useful than those with many no votes.

The online auction site eBay uses a similar system for providing feedback about buyers and sellers (see Figure G4.5). The scoring is simpler: −1 for a negative comment, 0 for a neutral comment, and +1 for a positive comment. This approach is novel because it rates not the quality of a product, but the trustworthiness and reliability of people who buy and sell. However, the general theme is still the same: provide information to empower future customers to make informed decisions.

Implement your meta-rating system with ACTION BUTTONS (K4) that give customers the power to rate each recommendation.

Figure G4.4

Amazon.com lets customers comment on reviews in meta-reviews.

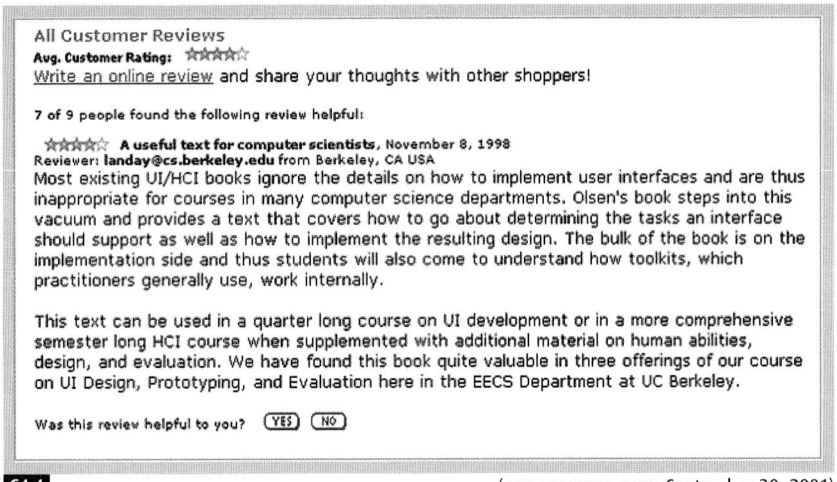

All Customer Reviews
Avg. Customer Rating: ★★★★☆
Write an online review and share your thoughts with other shoppers!

7 of 9 people found the following review helpful:

★★★★☆ **A useful text for computer scientists**, November 8, 1998
Reviewer: **landay@cs.berkeley.edu** from Berkeley, CA USA
Most existing UI/HCI books ignore the details on how to implement user interfaces and are thus inappropriate for courses in many computer science departments. Olsen's book steps into this vacuum and provides a text that covers how to go about determining the tasks an interface should support as well as how to implement the resulting design. The bulk of the book is on the implementation side and thus students will also come to understand how toolkits, which practitioners generally use, work internally.

This text can be used in a quarter long course on UI development or in a more comprehensive semester long HCI course when supplemented with additional material on human abilities, design, and evaluation. We have found this book quite valuable in three offerings of our course on UI Design, Prototyping, and Evaluation here in the EECS Department at UC Berkeley.

Was this review helpful to you? (YES) (NO)

G4.4   (www.amazon.com, September 30, 2001)

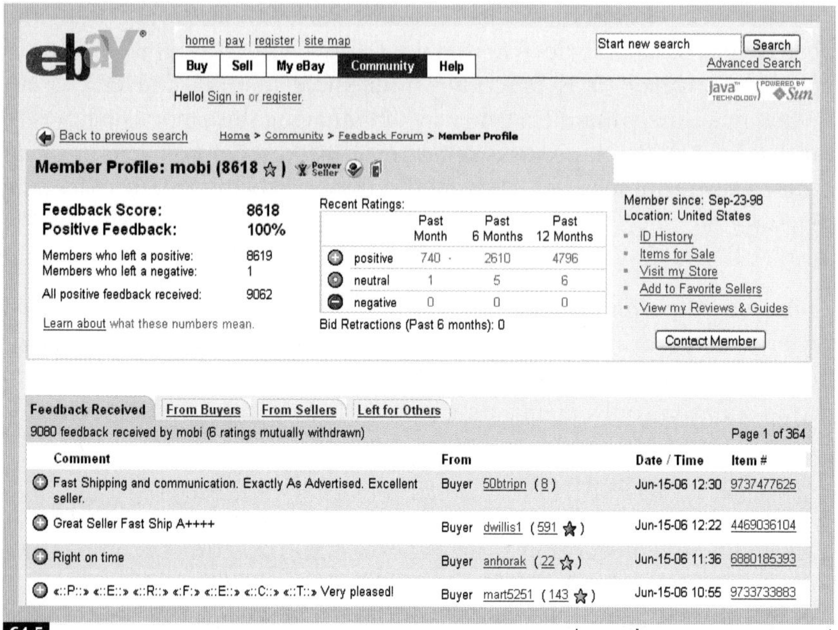

Figure G4.5

eBay shows numerical ratings and comments on sellers and buyers.

G4.5

(www.ebay.com, June 16, 2006)

Prime the Pump • Customers tend to follow the example of a few early adopters, and recommendation communities are no different. Before your site can gain popularity, it must be perceived as having useful recommendations. Use a UNIFIED BROWSING HIERARCHY (K1) to integrate content, commerce, and customer reviews. Put customer reviews on the CLEAN PRODUCT DETAIL (F2) page, and add links to make it easy for visitors to add reviews. Also consider providing motivation to write a review, perhaps entering customers who write their first review into a contest in which they could win a $50 (U.S.) gift certificate.

Remember, the most important resource in a recommendation community consists of the members themselves. Involve them in the development of their community by testing new ideas with those who are active in the community.

❋ SOLUTION

Provide a two-step process to write a review: (1) Have customers enter a review title and text of the review, along with any numerical rating. The text must follow the guidelines of the site. (2) Let customers see the recommendation as it will appear on the site, and allow them to edit it. Filter the title and text for profanity and HTML that might link to another site. Keep an editor on staff to review customer-written recommendations and remove them if they're offensive or libelous. Once the review has been posted, provide a mechanism for other customers to rate the review, giving it a meta-rating. Finally, to get customers to use the community features, offer them an incentive to write the first review.

Figure G4.6

Provide a two-step process funnel to help customers write reviews. Let them (1) write the review and (2) check that their review is formatted correctly before submission. After the publisher makes sure that the review conforms to all stated rules, other customers can see the published review.

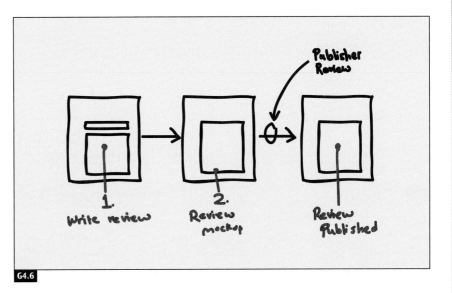

❋ OTHER PATTERNS TO CONSIDER

(K1) (H1) Provide a UNIFIED BROWSING HIERARCHY (K1) to integrate content, commerce, and community on your Web site. Build a two-step PROCESS FUNNEL (H1) for people to (1) write reviews and enter numerical ratings, then (2) review and edit what they wrote. Publish the review guidelines, as well as your (E3) (F2) (K4) FAIR INFORMATION PRACTICES (E3). Integrate the reviews into the CLEAN PRODUCT DETAIL (F2) pages. Once reviews have been posted, let other customers rate them by clicking rating ACTION BUTTONS (K4). Some recommendation communities share much in common with MESSAGE (D5) BOARDS (D5); many of the tips in that pattern apply here as well.

G5 MULTIPLE DESTINATIONS

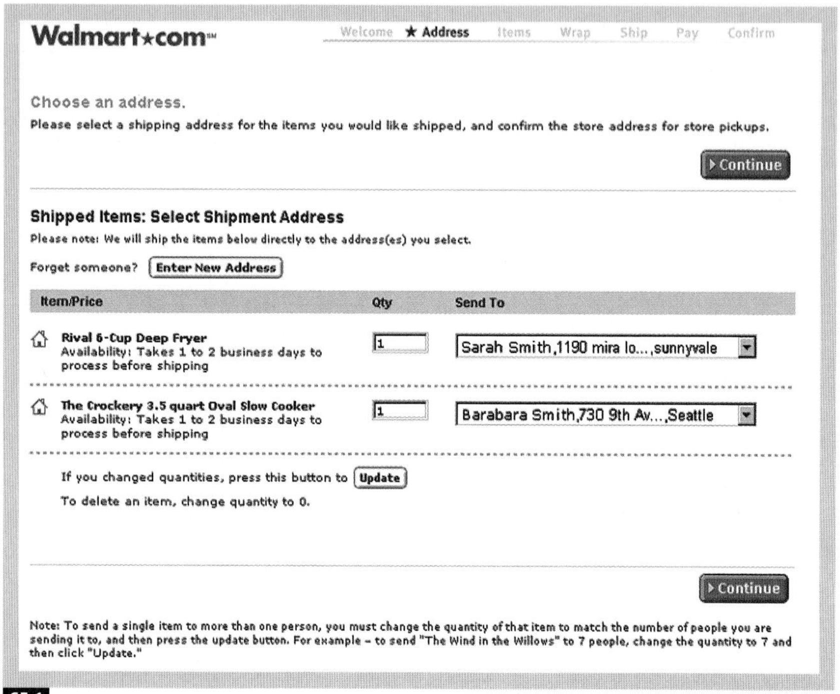

Figure G5.1

Walmart.com provides a quick and easy way to ship items to multiple addresses.

(www.walmart.com, October 28, 2001)

✳ BACKGROUND

Sometimes customers fill their SHOPPING CARTS (F3) and indicate in QUICK ADDRESS SELECTION (F4) that they want to send items to multiple addresses. This pattern provides the framework for shipping to multiple destinations.

✳ PROBLEM

Customers sometimes want to ship items that they've chosen to purchase to multiple addresses. Making this process simple requires changes throughout the checkout process.

Shoppers need to assign items to particular addresses when shipping them as gifts or to multiple destinations. To do this, they have to fill out multiple destination addresses. In QUICK ADDRESS SELECTION (F4), we formulated the pattern for shipping to a single address, but we did not offer a means to assign a particular destination to each product. Once shoppers have assigned destinations to products, they'll want to review which items are going to each address to verify the completeness and correctness of each order. Once they've finished placing the order, they'll want a printable confirmation. This pattern provides the solution.

Let Customers Choose Multiple Destinations • When customers are shopping and selecting items, they leave the specifics of shipping for later, during checkout. On the QUICK ADDRESS SELECTION (F4) page of QUICK-FLOW CHECKOUT (F1), provide a **Ship to Multiple Addresses** ACTION BUTTON (K4), as Walmart.com does (see Figure G5.2).

Figure G5.2

Walmart.com asks shoppers, during quick address selection, if they would like to ship to multiple addresses.

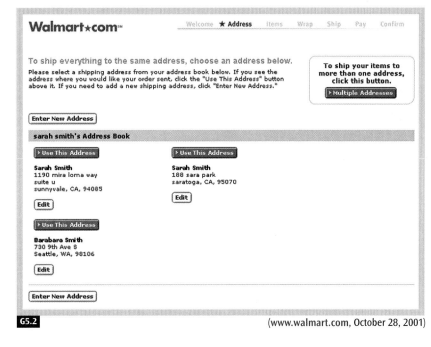

G5.2

(www.walmart.com, October 28, 2001)

Let Customers Choose Addresses from Their Existing Address Book • If customers have purchased products in the past, they will already have an address book with the Web site. On a page listing all the products to be purchased, provide a pick list next to each product, listing all of the possible destinations available from the address book (see Figure G5.3).

On the other hand, in case the customer is new to the site (and thus has an empty address book), or returning customers need to add a new shipping address, provide a page that is essentially the same as the shipping address entry form from QUICK ADDRESS SELECTION (F4).   (F4)

Confirm the Order • Before checking out, customers need to review their orders for correctness and completeness. An ORDER SUMMARY (F7) page   (F7) that categorizes items by destination gives customers a way to quickly review the order before completing it. And if they need to correct anything, an **Edit** ACTION BUTTON (K4) on each address section of the order   (K4) takes them back to the address assignment screen. Figure G5.4 shows an example of an order summary that displays multiple addresses.

Finally, an ORDER CONFIRMATION AND THANK-YOU (F8) page that includes   (F8) the items ordered and their destinations in a printable format gives customers a tangible order record that they can print.

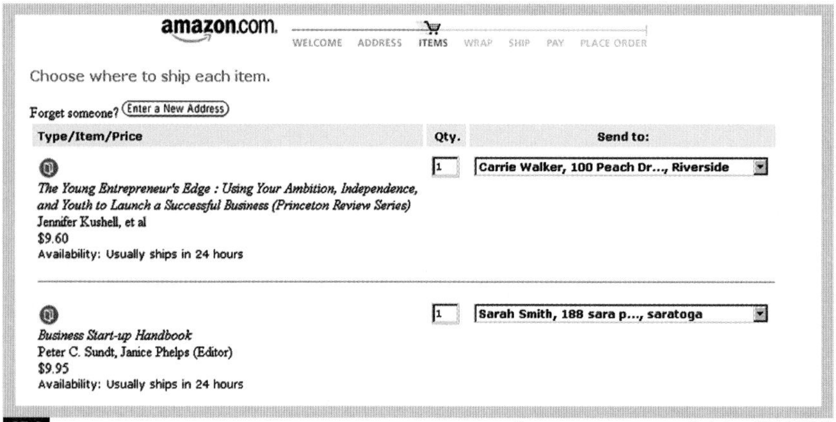

G5.3   (www.amazon.com, October 28, 2001)

Figure G5.3

An address assignment page on Amazon.com shows each product and provides a pick list of prior addresses with each one. Customers can also enter a new address.

Figure G5.4

When purchased items are being sent to more than one address, the order summary page needs to be modified to show the multiple shipping addresses. This is how Amazon.com does it.

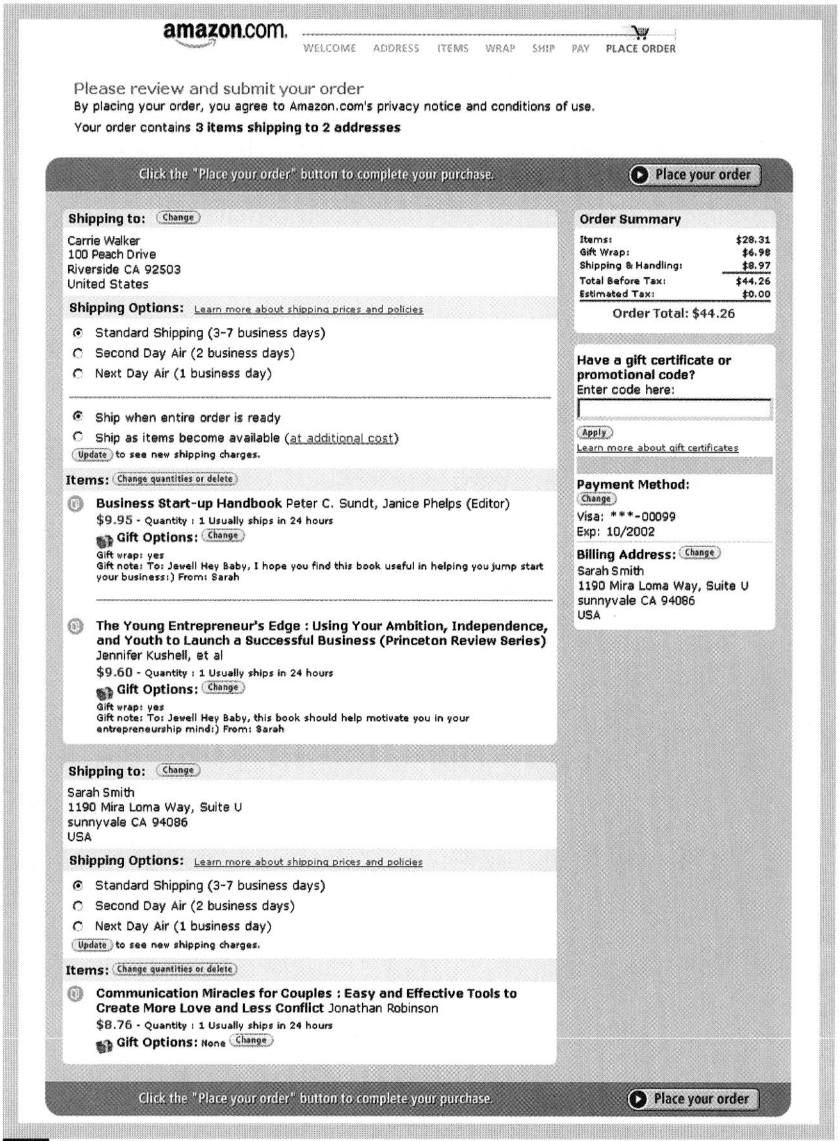

G5.4

(www.amazon.com, October 28, 2001)

✳ SOLUTION

Provide a Ship to Multiple Addresses **action button at the top of the quick address selection page. If the customer clicks it, show a new page with an** Add New Address **action button, a list of all the products in the order, and a pick list next to each product. The pick list provides all the destination options. If there are no existing addresses, as in the case of first-time customers, immediately go to the page for inputting new addresses. On the new-address page, have a new-address form that is quick and easy to read. On the order summary page, separate orders by their destinations, and provide a link to change the items in a destination's order. On the confirmation and thank-you page, separate items by destination.**

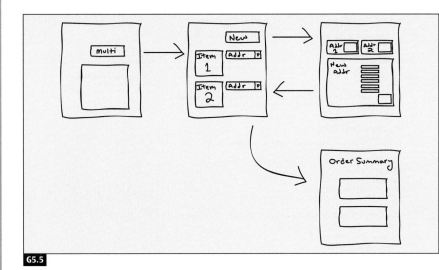

Figure G5.5

Give customers the option to send products to multiple addresses. Let customers choose which items will be shipped where, and provide a way for them to add new addresses. Before the order is finalized, provide a concise order summary that shows where all of the items will be shipped.

G5.5

✳ OTHER PATTERNS TO CONSIDER

Answer questions that customers might have about your site security by providing a direct link to your PRIVACY POLICY (E4). Help customers fill out the form by PREVENTING ERRORS (K12) and providing MEANINGFUL ERROR MESSAGES (K13) when errors do occur. Use ACTION BUTTONS (K4) to lead customers to the next stage in the checkout, and to edit a destination's order on the ORDER SUMMARY (F7) page. Display the rows of items in a GRID LAYOUT (I1), in CONTENT MODULES (D2).

E4
K12
K13 K4

F7
I1 D2

Figure G6.1

Martha Stewart's Web site makes it easy to find gifts for loved ones for a variety of special occasions. And for every order, the options of gift wrapping and a gift message are offered. These features, combined with the site's clean design and navigation, make it a good service-based gift-giving site.

G6.1

(www.marthastewart.com, February 12, 2002)

✳ BACKGROUND

PERSONAL E-COMMERCE (A1) establishes how people can order online and complete their orders through the QUICK-FLOW CHECKOUT (F1) process. Enabling customers to purchase and send gifts online requires a few changes to the standard checkout process. This pattern describes some requirements for gift giving online.

✳ PROBLEM

When ordering gifts online, customers want to write notes to the recipients and to be assured that the price will not be disclosed. If a site does not offer these conveniences, customers will be less likely to order gifts.

If your site offers consumer items, shoppers will want to send them as gifts to family, friends, associates, and customers. Gifts sent online are especially convenient because all the wrapping and mailing is handled by the online store, and because customers can shop for multiple people and send to MUL-TIPLE DESTINATIONS (G5) with one order. But there are variables. Customers will not want their recipients to see an item's price, might want to send gift-wrapped presents, and probably will want to include a personal note. Making the process simple and clear, especially for different items going to different people, is key if you want your site to be a resource for gift giving.

Not all items will necessarily be going to the same person, even if they're being sent to the same location. Especially on holidays, when whole families are celebrating, customers might send gifts to different people at one address. Making the notes customized for each gift ensures that the right person gets the right gift, and that the customer is able to convey any special messages.

Some products may be too big for gift wrapping, but a note could still be attached. Larger products might require more paper and effort to wrap and therefore understandably might cost more to gift wrap. By providing separate prices for gift wrapping each item, you can charge the right amount for both large and small products.

You will need to make changes to the QUICK-FLOW CHECKOUT (F1) PROCESS FUNNEL (H1) to create a gift-giving site (see Figure G6.2). Once customers have selected their gifts by putting them in their SHOPPING CART (F3), the QUICK-FLOW CHECKOUT (F1) process needs to indicate that items can be gift wrapped and gift notes can be attached. It is best to disclose the prices for these services at this point so that customers are not surprised later. Including the price right next to the option means that your customers won't have to bother looking elsewhere.

State That the Packing Slip Will Not List Prices or Items • The packing slip that ships with products usually includes prices of the respective items. When giving gifts, however, customers don't want the recipients to see or know the prices. People receiving gifts that are gift wrapped should not know what's inside before opening the wrap, but recipients do need instructions on how to return items if necessary. If the packing slip for a gift order includes the sender information, the recipient information, the order number, and the return instructions, recipients can make exchanges if they like.

Provide the Ability to Select and Edit Gift Recipients and Notes • After customers have placed items in their SHOPPING CART (F3), but before they have completed QUICK-FLOW CHECKOUT (F1), they will need to identify the recipients of the gifts by attaching notes. Provide a form so that gift givers

Figure G6.2

In this example of specifying gift options during the quick-flow checkout, Walmart.com makes it easy to add gift wrapping and personalized notes to each gift.

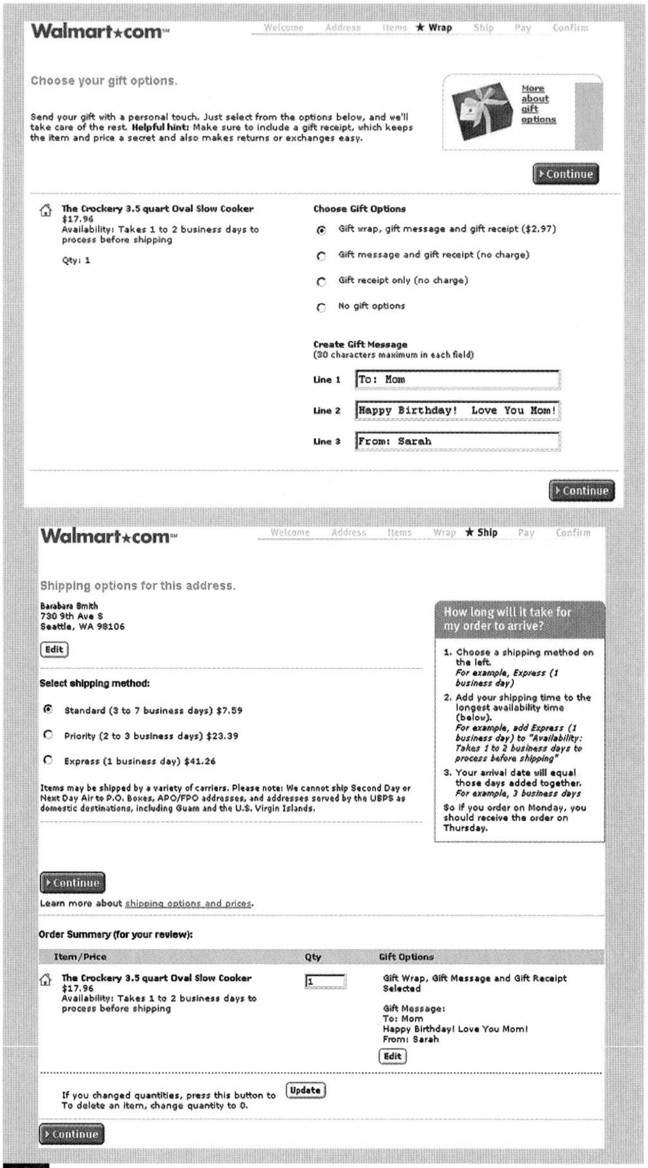

G6.2 (www.walmart.com, October 28, 2001)

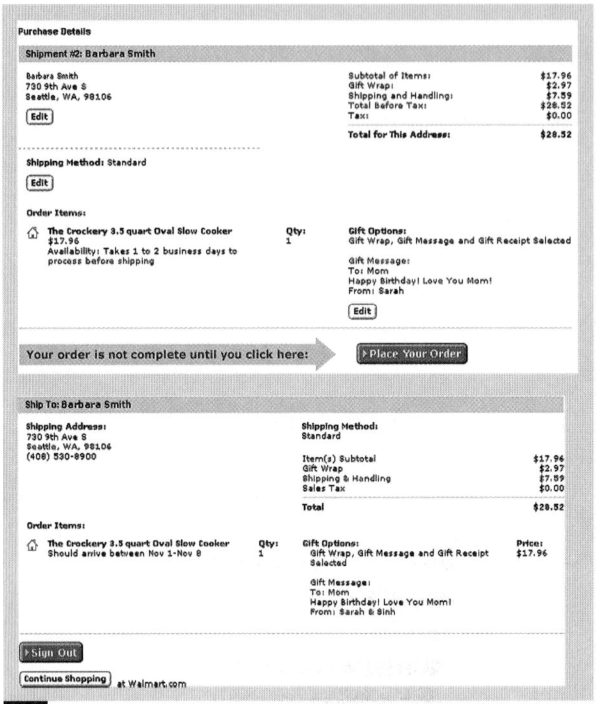

Figure G6.2

(Continued)

G6.2   (www.walmart.com, October 28, 2001)

can enter a personal note per package, to help ensure that the individual items go to the right person, and to give gift givers the chance to say something intimate. Use a **Save Gift Options** ACTION BUTTON (K4) to save the edits and take customers back to the ORDER SUMMARY (F7) page.

Summarize and Confirm the Order • Once customers have made their selections, have decided which items are gifts, have written personal notes, and have selected items to wrap, they'll want to see a summary before confirming the entire order. On the ORDER SUMMARY (F7) page, show each item and indicate any additional costs for wrapping so that there are no surprises later.

Provide an **Edit Gift Options** ACTION BUTTON (K4) on the ORDER SUMMARY (F7) page to take customers back to the gift selection and editing page if there are any problems with the order. If the order is satisfactory, the **Place Order** ACTION BUTTON (K4) takes customers to the ORDER CONFIRMATION AND THANK-YOU (F8) page, where the details are reported again for confirmation and possible printing.

G3

Provide Other Gift-Giving Features • Sometimes customers want help choosing gifts. To provide help, create a PERSONALIZED RECOMMENDATIONS (G3) system for selecting gifts. Such a system takes customers through the process of identifying appropriate gift ideas, and makes recommendations based on editorialized product selections that are currently in stock. Figure G6.3 shows how Amazon.com helps customers find gifts for friends and family.

Figure G6.3

Providing gift ideas can help customers find the right gift.

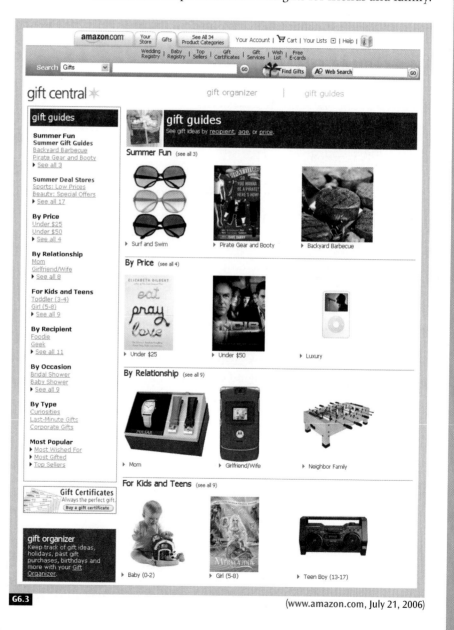

(www.amazon.com, July 21, 2006)

✳ SOLUTION

Make it clear early in the shopping process that the site has gift-giving options so that customers can shop for that reason. On the checkout page, provide a button that takes customers to a form where they can enter gift notes and select gift-wrapping options. And on this form, provide a button that takes customers back to the order summary page, where they can review their whole order, including gift options. When they're done, provide an order confirmation page that shows details of the entire order, including gifts, in case customers want the information for their records.

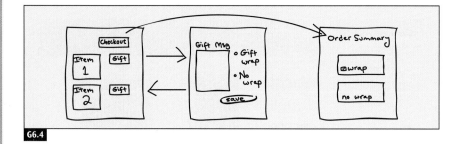

Figure G6.4

Let customers choose which purchases are meant as gifts. Offer the options of wrapping each gift and enclosing a personal message.

✳ OTHER PATTERNS TO CONSIDER

Indicate in the SHOPPING CART (F3) that gift options are available so that customers can plan to send items directly to the gift recipients. Modify the QUICK-FLOW CHECKOUT (F1) PROCESS FUNNEL (H1) by inserting an ACTION BUTTON (K4) that allows customers to change gift options on the ORDER SUMMARY (F7) page. Provide a form with note text input fields and gift-wrapping options for each item, and an ACTION BUTTON (K4) to save gift options. After confirming their gift options on the ORDER SUMMARY (F7) page, customers can click the **Place Order** ACTION BUTTON (K4) and receive the ORDER CONFIRMATION AND THANK-YOU (F8) page. For other gift-giving features, consider offering a gift wizard PROCESS FUNNEL (H1) that provides PERSONALIZED RECOMMENDATIONS (G3).

F3

F1 H1

K4

F7

K4

F7

K4

F8

H1

G3

Figure G7.1

Nordstrom's Web site shows clear order detail, including shipping destination, product detail, quantity, price, gift options, and shipping methods and charges for each item ordered, as well as tax and totals.

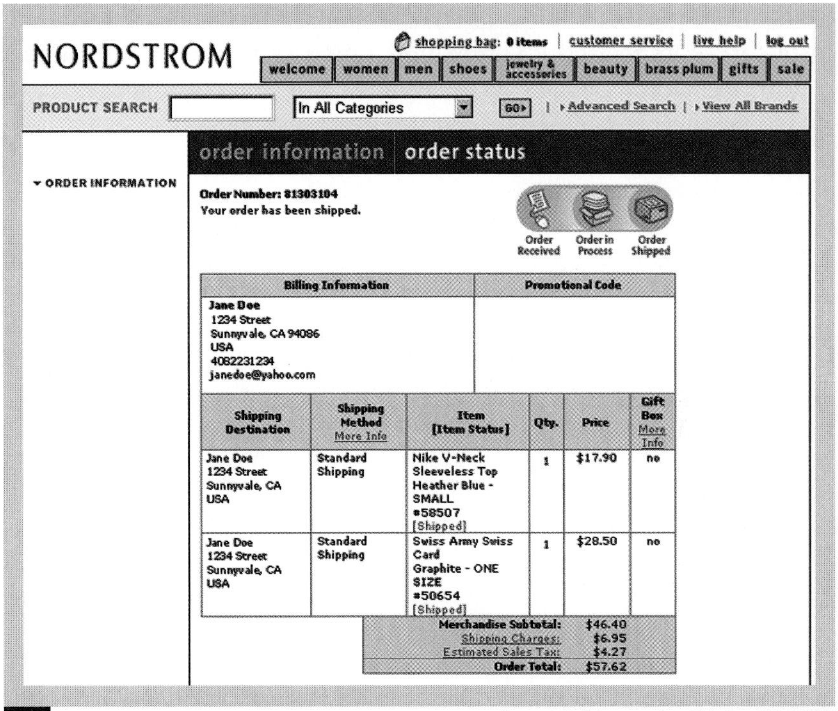

G7.1

(www.nordstrom.com, October 28, 2001)

✳ BACKGROUND

(A1)
(F1)
PERSONAL E-COMMERCE (A1) establishes how people can order online and complete their orders through the QUICK-FLOW CHECKOUT (F1) process. After completing an order, customers receive an ORDER CONFIRMATION AND
(F8)
THANK-YOU (F8) message. Some customers might also like to check the status of their shipment. This pattern provides the core for tracking e-commerce orders.

✳ PROBLEM

When customers place online orders, the details about order status and shipping become important. If this information is not easily available online, the cost of processing customer inquiries increases dramatically.

Shoppers sometimes need to receive packages by a certain date. As a result, they often have questions about the status of their orders and would like to get that information quickly and easily. Usually they can call customer service to get this information. However, because phone centers require significant budgets to manage and operate, companies have looked for cheaper alternatives. On the Web, customers can obtain more information than is typically available over the phone. A site can link directly to the shipper, for example, so that customers can get detailed information about the progress of a package toward its destination.

Building an order-tracking system on the Web requires integrating the site with the order fulfillment department, the part of the company that makes sure products are shipped on time. The customer experience must be smooth, and it must provide the information that customers need for making decisions if items are delayed. This pattern provides the solution.

Provide Access to Orders • Customers sometimes need to modify orders that are still pending. Perhaps the shipping address needs to be changed, the contents of the order need to be updated, or the billing information is not correct. In all of these cases, the ability to update an order online, in the same manner that the order was placed, improves the customer's experience, as long as the process is simple.

To grant access to this information, obtain secure account information by requiring returning customers to sign in on the SIGN-IN/NEW ACCOUNT (H2) page. Customers who created an account can sign in with a user name and password. Customers who used a GUEST ACCOUNT (H3) must reference the order number together with other secure information, such as a billing zip code. Make sure you use a SECURE CONNECTION (E6), to help protect the security and privacy of your customers.

H2

H3

E6

Once they're in the system, customers may not remember the orders that they've placed, and they may wish to review their order history to find a particular order. Give customers a list of their orders organized by the processing stage of each order. For example, let customers review orders by the following categories:

- Pending shipment
- Recently shipped
- Shipped and received

People need a way to skim through the results of these order histories. A logical way to sort order histories is with a CHRONOLOGICAL ORGANIZATION (B6) so that customers can see purchases in sequence. List all the orders by date, and if the list of items is not too long, indicate the contents as well. Figure G7.2 shows how Shutterfly organizes its order tracking and history page.

B6

Figure G7.2

Shutterfly's site provides a convenient order history with status and order detail.

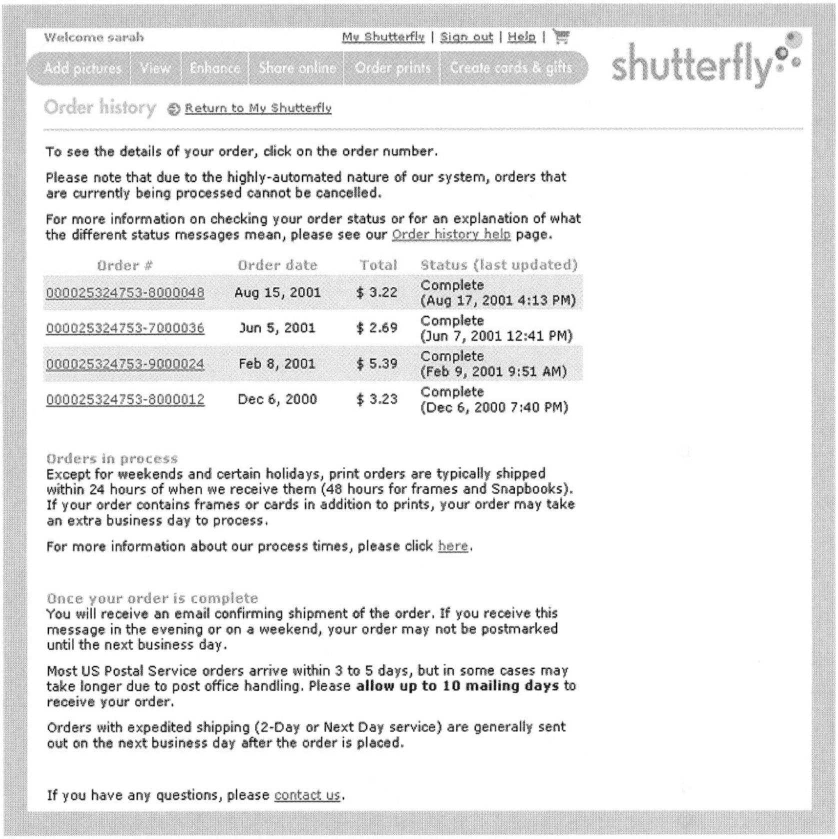

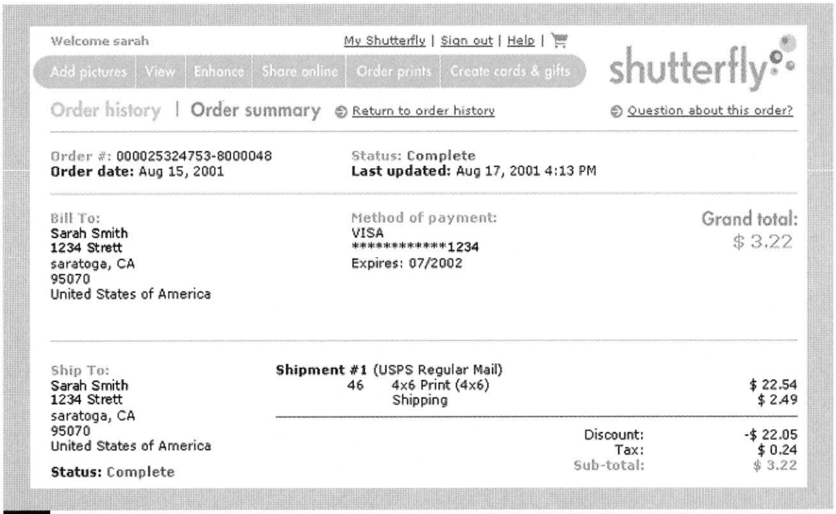

G7.2 (www.shutterfly.com, November 20, 2001)

For Pending Orders, Indicate Product Availability • When products have not been shipped yet, it helps to tell the customer how far along the fulfillment process is for each product. For time-sensitive orders, it is especially important to set customers' expectations by informing them if a product has not been shipped or is not in stock.

While checking out, customers assume that a product is in stock. If it's not in stock and the product is needed by a certain time, customers need to have that information so that they can order something else. In fact, if the product or order changes status in any significant way, notify customers so that they can take action accordingly. Even though it might be bad news, customers appreciate knowing as soon as possible. It is worse to set expectations and not deliver than to adjust expectations along the way.

Table G7.1 specifies the different actions to take when the status of an order changes.

Allow Order Modification, If Possible • Customers might need to change an order in some way if there is a negative change in the status of an order, such as a shipping delay. If customers cannot change orders on the site, they will need to call customer service. If customer service is not available, they will need to send e-mail, which does not provide an immediate resolution to a potentially time-sensitive issue. Providing the means to solve the problem on the site reduces customer service

Table G7.1

Actions to Take on Order Status Changes

Order Status	Automated Action
Product in stock	None
Product out of stock	Inform customer through e-mail
Product discontinued	Inform customer through e-mail
Product delayed	Inform customer through e-mail
Product in stock; order being processed	None
Order shipped	Inform customer through e-mail
Order delivered	None

Table G7.2

Potential Changes to Orders

Items to Be Modified	Navigation Tools
Shipping address(es)	QUICK ADDRESS SELECTION (F4), MULTIPLE DESTINATIONS (G5)
Shipping method	QUICK SHIPPING METHOD SELECTION (F5)
Billing address	PAYMENT METHOD (F6)
Payment method	PAYMENT METHOD (F6)
Product items	CLEAN PRODUCT DETAILS (F2), SHOPPING CART (F3)
Product quantities	SHOPPING CART (F3)
Gift options	GIFT GIVING (G6)

costs but requires complete integration of back-end fulfillment systems with the site. Provide ACTION BUTTONS (K4) to edit different parts of the order.

Table G7.2 lists the parts of the order that might need modification, and the respective patterns that address changes to the order. Figure G7.3 shows how Amazon.com handles order tracking and modification.

Sometimes orders cannot be canceled after processing begins. If customers know this, they might have time to change the order before processing begins.

Allow Order Tracking • If an order is delayed, or if the customer needs the package on a precise day, as in the case of a priority-delivery gift or a business-critical item, order tracking provides the information that customers need to locate the package.

Order tracking provides a direct link to the shipper's database and displays information, such as date and time of receipt, at various way stations. To provide this type of information, your site must store a shipper's tracking number and interface with the shipping database.

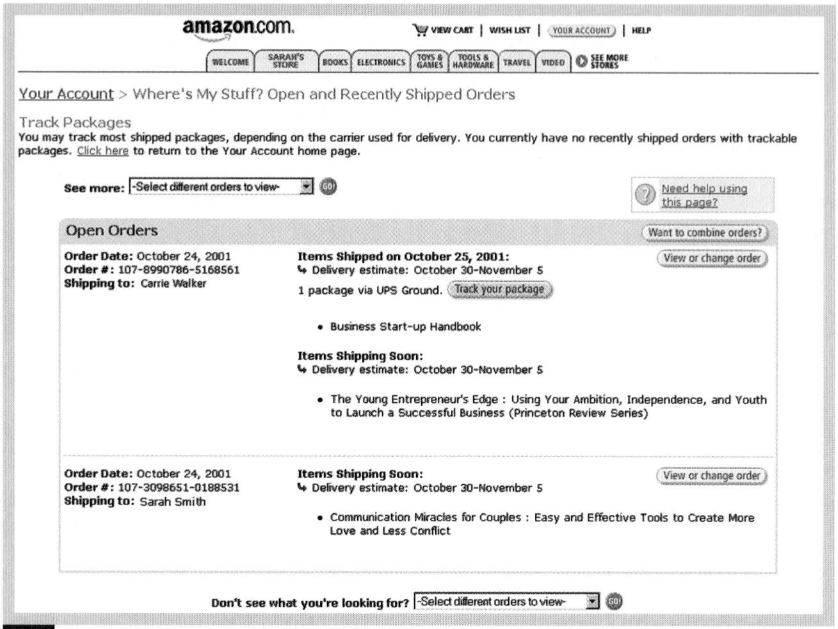

G7.3a

(www.amazon.com, October 27, 2001)

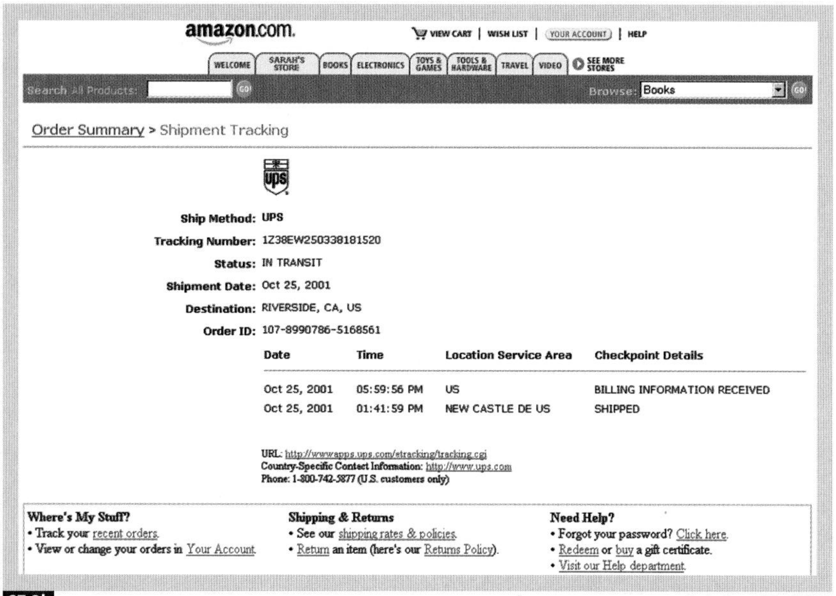

G7.3b

(www.amazon.com, October 27, 2001)

Figure G7.3

(a) Amazon.com offers order histories and modifiable orders. (b) Once an order has shipped, the site provides order tracking.

✳ SOLUTION

Require customers to sign in to review and modify their orders. Give them access to an order history that categorizes orders as pending, shipped, or completed. Display the selected orders chronologically, listing the order number, as well as the contents of the order if the list is not too long. For pending orders, indicate each item's availability, and allow modification of everything from shipping and billing to products and options. For orders you have already shipped, allow order tracking by interfacing with the shipper's database and displaying the shipment way station history.

Figure G7.4

Provide a secure order tracking and history system to let customers check on their past and pending orders.

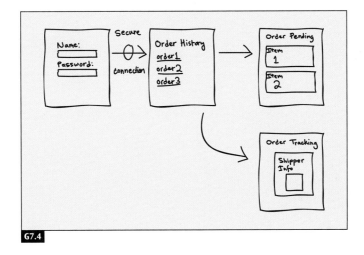

✳ OTHER PATTERNS TO CONSIDER

To gain access to their account information, returning customers must use the SIGN-IN/NEW ACCOUNT (H2) page. Once the account has been accessed, provide customers with their order history sorted by CHRONOLOGICAL ORGANIZATION (B6). If the list of items in an order is not too long, indicate the contents of the order. If a customer wishes to change an order, provide ACTION BUTTONS (K4) to edit different parts of the order. For modifying shipping address and method, use QUICK ADDRESS SELECTION (F4) and MULTIPLE DESTINATIONS (G5). For customers modifying billing information, access the PAYMENT METHOD (F6) page. Allow customers to change items using CLEAN PRODUCT DETAIL (F2) pages and the SHOPPING CART (F3). To update gift options, use GIFT GIVING (G6).

Helping Customers Complete Tasks

◆◆◆◆◆◆◆◆◆◆◆◆◆

Sometimes customers will need help carrying out and completing a task on your Web site. This pattern group describes ways to structure your site to minimize problems and improve your task completion rate.

H1 PROCESS FUNNEL

H2 SIGN-IN/NEW ACCOUNT

H3 GUEST ACCOUNT

H4 ACCOUNT MANAGEMENT

H5 PERSISTENT CUSTOMER SESSIONS

H6 FLOATING WINDOWS

H7 FREQUENTLY ASKED QUESTIONS

H8 CONTEXT-SENSITIVE HELP

H9 DIRECT MANIPULATION

H10 CLEAR FORMS

H11 PREDICTIVE INPUT

H12 DRILL-DOWN OPTIONS

H13 PROGRESS BAR

H1 PROCESS FUNNEL

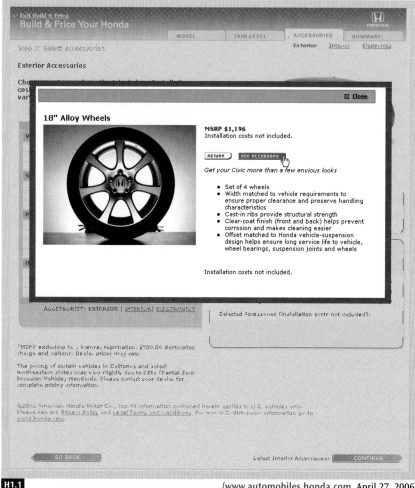

H1.1

(www.automobiles.honda.com, April 27, 2006)

Figure H1.1

Honda uses a process funnel consisting of several logical steps that guide customers to quickly configure a car with the desired options. Information in floating windows shows additional details but keeps customers in the funnel so that they can continue to completion.

✳ BACKGROUND

All Web sites that lead visitors through stepped tasks—PERSONAL E-COMMERCE (A1), SELF-SERVICE GOVERNMENT (A4), WEB APPS THAT WORK (A10), and ENABLING INTRANETS (A11)—need ways to help people succeed at completing the tasks.

✳ PROBLEM

Customers often need to complete highly specific tasks on Web sites, but pages with tangential links and many questions can prevent them from carrying out these tasks successfully.

People enjoy completing the tasks they start. Yet all kinds of distractions—including links that lead off the critical path, extra steps, and extra content—can inadvertently lead them away from accomplishing their goals. These diversions can have legitimate purposes, however, such as providing continuity, giving visitors opportunities to explore, providing instructions, or providing extra details. Striking a balance between these various forces and the actual task can be challenging.

Minimize the Number of Steps Required to Complete a Task • Customers find tasks daunting if there are too many steps. A process funnel might have anywhere from two to six discrete steps. Anything less than two steps is not a process, and a process of more than six steps can be unmanageable. If there are more than six steps, try to split the process into two or more separate process funnels, or try combining multiple steps on one page. You don't want to intimidate customers with too many steps. However, these are not always viable solutions, because one choice may precede another, and not every page can hold all the information that customers might need at certain points.

 Provide a Progress Bar to Let Customers Know Where They Are in the Process Funnel • Showing a PROGRESS BAR (H13) at each step lets your customers know how much farther they need to go to complete the task (see Figure H1.2). Note that it's often not worth your effort to make the individual steps on the progress bar clickable because doing so adds more

Figure H1.2

Many Web sites use a progress bar like this one at Half.com to let customers know where they are in the process funnel and how much farther they have to go.

H1.2   (www.half.com, October 24, 2001)

complexity but little benefit for customers. See the PROGRESS BAR (H13) pattern for situations where it makes sense to allow this.

Remove Unnecessary Links and Content While Reinforcing the Brand • Removing links and content that are unrelated to the task at hand will reduce the number of distractions, making it more likely that your customers will successfully complete their tasks. Remove extraneous NAVIGATION BARS (K2), TAB ROWS (K3), LOCATION BREAD CRUMBS (K6), and EMBEDDED LINKS (K7), leaving only the links and ACTION BUTTONS (K4) that help visitors reach their goals, as well as an obvious exit that cancels the process funnel. Take out any content that is superfluous to the task.

Reinforce the Web SITE BRANDING (E1) to minimize any disorientation that customers might feel from sudden changes in navigation options. Use the same fonts, images, colors, layout, and logo throughout the Web site so that, no matter where they are, people know they're still on the same site.

Use Floating Windows to Provide Extra Information, without Leading Visitors Out of the Process Funnel • Sometimes customers need additional information that you have not provided on a page, such as extra help or product details. Provide a link to a FLOATING WINDOW (H6) containing CLEAN PRODUCT DETAILS (F2) (see Figure H1.1), CONTEXT-SENSITIVE HELP (H8), or information from the FREQUENTLY ASKED QUESTIONS (H7) page, to make the extra information less intrusive. Your challenge is to implement this extra content without detracting from the main purpose.

Make Sure the Back **Button Always Works •** Customers often use the **Back** button on browsers to modify answers that they've typed in on previous pages. If the Web site is not implemented correctly, however, the information that they've already entered may be lost when they hit the **Back** button, forcing them to type everything again. In the worst case, people get a cryptic error message saying that the posted information was lost. You can address this annoying problem by temporarily storing the information entered on each page, redisplaying this information if customers hit the **Back** button, and then overriding the temporarily stored information on the page if it is changed.

Always Make It Clear How to Proceed to the Next Step • Some Web pages are longer than can be displayed on a customer's Web browser, and people sometimes get lost if the critical ACTION BUTTON (K4), the one that takes them to the next step, is hidden below the fold. Place HIGH-VISIBILITY ACTION BUTTONS (K5) both high *and* low on the page, ensuring that at least one of the critical action buttons will always be visible without scrolling.

Allow Customers to Skip Unnecessary Steps • Customers sometimes need to be able to skip unnecessary steps in a process. For example, customers do not always choose the gift-wrap option on Amazon.com during the check-out process. Some steps might automatically be skipped if the required information is automatically supplied, as when name and address information comes from a customer database, such as in SIGN-IN/NEW ACCOUNT (H2), rather than being supplied manually by a customer logging on with a GUEST ACCOUNT (H3). A step also can be skipped, for example, when customers supply a billing address and then check the **Shipping Address Same as Billing Address** box so that they don't have to type the whole address again.

    If a choice that the customer makes early in the process eliminates the need for one or more subsequent steps, then simply skip the subsequent steps in the PROGRESS BAR (H13) and treat them as if they were completed. Don't remove steps from the progress bar in the course of the process (or add them, for that matter) because this might confuse the customer.

Prevent Errors and Provide Error Messages Whenever Errors Do Occur • People will always make mistakes, even with the best of designs. You can help PREVENT ERRORS (K12) if you use CLEAR FORMS (H10) with structured fields, sample input, and PREDICTIVE INPUT (H11). At the same time, provide MEANINGFUL ERROR MESSAGES (K13) whenever errors do occur.

✳ SOLUTION

Minimize the number of steps required to complete a task, keeping them between two and six. Remove unnecessary and potentially confusing links and content from each page, while reinforcing the brand to maintain a sense of place. Use floating windows to provide extra information without leading people out of the process funnel. Make sure the Back button always works so that customers can correct errors. Use high-visibility action buttons to make it clear how to proceed to the next step. Let customers skip steps that may be unnecessary. Prevent errors where possible, and provide error messages whenever errors do occur.

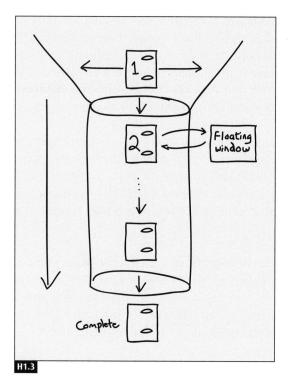

H1.3

Figure H1.3

A process funnel lets people complete their goals by breaking down complicated tasks into a small number of steps, using floating windows for detailed information, and including only critical links, so that people are not distracted.

✳ OTHER PATTERNS TO CONSIDER

Many kinds of Web sites use process funnels, including sites for PERSONAL E-COMMERCE (A1), SELF-SERVICE GOVERNMENT (A4), WEB APPS THAT WORK (A10), and ENABLING INTRANETS (A11). Customers use process funnels when they finalize purchases through QUICK-FLOW CHECKOUT (F1), when they create new accounts through SIGN-IN/NEW ACCOUNT (H2), and when they post new messages to a RECOMMENDATION COMMUNITY (G4), to name some examples.

Remove NAVIGATION BARS (K2), TAB ROWS (K3), irrelevant ACTION BUTTONS (K4), LOCATION BREAD CRUMBS (K6), and EMBEDDED LINKS (K7) to ensure that customers stay on their paths. However, keep strong SITE BRANDING (E1) so that customers still know where they are.

Design process funnels to PREVENT ERRORS (K12) by using CLEAR FORMS (H10) for each step of the process funnel and provide MEANINGFUL ERROR MESSAGES (K13) when errors do occur. Consider also adding a PROGRESS BAR (H13) that tells people where they are in the process and how much farther they have to go.

Track your customers through PERSISTENT CUSTOMER SESSIONS (H5) to avoid problems with the **Back** button, and to save customer-entered information.

Move extra content, such as CONTEXT-SENSITIVE HELP (H8) and FREQUENTLY ASKED QUESTIONS (H7), to FLOATING WINDOWS (H6) to keep the main task page on the screen. Make the next action visible by keeping it ABOVE THE FOLD (I2) and by using HIGH-VISIBILITY ACTION BUTTONS (K5).

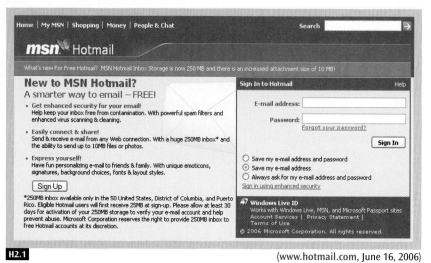

Figure H2.1

MSN Hotmail has an easy sign-in if customers already have an account or if visitors need to create a new account on the spot.

H2.1

(www.hotmail.com, June 16, 2006)

✳ BACKGROUND

To provide PERSONALIZED CONTENT (D4), PERSONALIZED RECOMMENDATIONS (G3), and other individualized services, Web sites need a way for both returning customers and new customers to identify themselves. This pattern covers the sign-in and new account processes, describing how to structure the design of these pages, as well as common mistakes to avoid.

D4 **G3**

✳ PROBLEM

A single process has to handle both returning customers, who sign in and identify themselves to get personalized content, and new customers, who need to create an account before going further on the site.

This pattern solves the problem by using a variation of the PROCESS FUNNEL (H1) to achieve its goals: an easy way for customers to sign in if they already have accounts, and an easy way for visitors to create new accounts. The sections that follow identify some things to consider when creating a sign-in mechanism.

H1

Collect the Minimum Amount of Information for Creating New Accounts • You risk alienating potential customers if creating a new account takes too long, if you ask for too much personal information, or if the process doesn't run smoothly. If creating a new account is simple and painless, more customers will do it (see Figure H2.2). Using CLEAR FORMS (H10) is one way to help ensure this goal. For sites that have a prior *offline* relationship with a customer, consider using your existing customer databases and unique ID numbers that customers can easily find (for example, on the mailing label of a magazine) to simplify the new account process (see Figure H2.3).

Figure H2.2

If you want visitors to create a new account, make the process simple and painless by minimizing the potential for mistakes and by keeping it as short as possible.

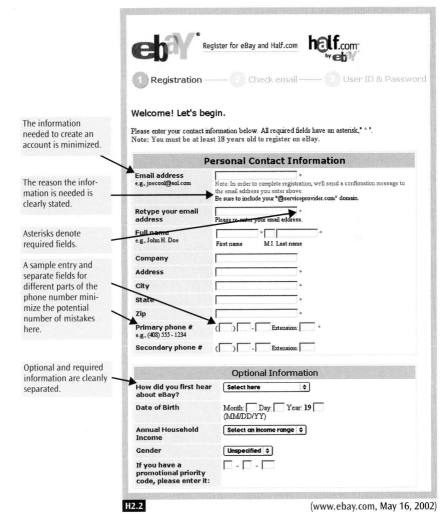

The information needed to create an account is minimized.

The reason the information is needed is clearly stated.

Asterisks denote required fields.

A sample entry and separate fields for different parts of the phone number minimize the potential number of mistakes here.

Optional and required information are cleanly separated.

(www.ebay.com, May 16, 2002)

> **>SIGN IN**
>
> If you have already established an online account with Wine&Spirits Magazine, enter your Login ID and Password below and click the Login button.
>
> If you currently subscribe to Wine&Spirits Magazine but have not yet established a complimentary online account, enter the subscriber code from your mailing label and click the Create Account button to begin the process.
>
> **Login ID:** [   ]
>
> **Subscriber Code:** [   ]
>
> **Password:** [   ]
>
> [Login]   [Create Account]
>
> Forget your Login ID or Password?
>
> ```
> *####################3-DIGIT   900
> 12345SMOLL*90123467     FEB-04
>                                 9/5/2390
> DAVID SMALLEY
> 30 WEST 19TH ST
> LAS VEGAS NV    89104
> ```
>
> Code still not working?

Figure H2.3

Wine & Spirits Magazine makes it easy for subscribers to create an online account by simply entering a subscriber code from their mailing label.

H2.3   (www.wineandspiritsmagazine.com, May 4, 2006)

Make Clear Which Fields Are Required and Which Are Optional • Splitting the information into required and optional fields can help keep account creation short. Many Web sites flag required fields with bold type or asterisks so that customers clearly understand what's optional.

Prevent Errors • Smooth the account creation process by PREVENTING ERRORS (K12), and by providing examples of the data you expect. For example, if you need a phone number, should it be shown in the format (510) 555-5555 or 510 555 5555? Or do you need an international phone number, such as +1 510 555 5555? Develop software that accepts any possible format so that any number typed in can be translated into the format that your databases use.

Provide Your Web Site's Privacy Information • Include a link to your PRIVACY POLICY (E4) on the account creation page, to explain your FAIR INFORMATION PRACTICES (E3). Explain why you need certain pieces of information, and how that information will be used. For an e-commerce site, for example, make it clear that you need customers' e-mail addresses and phone numbers in case there are delays in shipping or problems with the order, and that these pieces of information will not be used for spamming with promotional e-mail or phone calls unless the customers choose those options.

Clearly Specify the Kinds of Information You Will and Will Not Ask For after Creating an Account • *Phishing* is the general term for online scams in which scammers try to trick customers into giving them their passwords and other personal information. One way you can help PREVENT PHISHING SCAMS (E9) is to make it clear what kinds of personal information you will and will not ask for after an account has been created. For example, you can do this immediately after an account is created, and after that periodically, by showing customers a customized page after they success-fully sign in to your Web site. This page might warn your customers about online scams and help them avoid such scams.

Avoid Providing Direct Links to Your Sign-in Pages in E-Mail Messages • Most phishers attack unsuspecting victims by sending an e-mail with an OBVIOUS LINK (K10) to a fake sign-in page. We strongly recommend that you avoid having any kind of sign-in form or hyperlinks to sign-in pages in the body of your E-MAIL SUBSCRIPTIONS (E2) and E-MAIL NOTIFICATIONS (E7), because doing so implicitly trains your customers to click on those links and makes them more vulnerable to phishing attacks.

Have a Process for Handling Forgotten Passwords • People often forget their passwords, especially if they have many accounts on different Web sites. Web sites need mechanisms for helping people remember their pass-words. One approach is to send the password to a customer's e-mail address. You will already have the e-mail address from the customer's sign-up.

However, there are several potential dangers. E-mail systems are not always secure, and although doing so is difficult, hackers could break in and get a visitor's password.

Avoid sending passwords through e-mail if your Web site provides access to sensitive information, such as a student's grades or a customer's bank account. For special cases like these, one partial solution is to have customers create a security question when they open a new account. This security question requests a piece of personal information, such as a favorite pet's name, the person's city of birth, or a mother's maiden name (see Figure H2.4). A customer who forgets the password but can answer the security question either gets a hint as to what the password is, or can reset it. When the customer provides the answer to the security question during account setup, have your software check that the answer to the

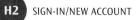

Figure H2.4

(a) eBay asks the customer to choose a security question and answer at the time of account creation. (b) If a customer forgets a password, the security question is used to reset the customer's password.

H2.4a

home | my eBay | site map | sign out
Browse | Sell | Services | Search | Help | Community
overview | registration | buying & selling | my eBay | about me | feedback forum | safe harbor

▸ Check out LIVE auctions on eBay.   Search tips
☐ Search titles and descriptions

Change your Password Hint

Your Hint question should be easy for you to answer but difficult for others to guess.
Note: You cannot use your eBay user ID or password as part of your Hint question or answer.

- Visit the Password Hint help page for tips on creating an effective hint.

Select or create your Password Hint question and enter the answer below.

Choose your Hint question: (required)	Pick a suggested question... ⬍
	OR
	Create your own question:
	Example: "What city would you like to visit?"
Enter the answer to your question: (required)	
	Example: "Rome"

Submit

Pick a suggested question...
✓ What is the name of the street where you grew up?
What is the name of your favorite restaurant?
What is the name of your favorite cartoon character?
What is the name of your favorite fictional character?
What is the title of your favorite book?
Where did you go on your first date?
What is your favorite pet's name?
What is your best friend's last name?
What is your dream occupation?

H2.4b

home | my eBay | site map | sign in
Browse | Sell | Services | Search | Help | Community

Please Sign In...

eBay members, sign in to save time for bidding, selling, and other activities.

eBay User ID   [   ]
You can also use your registered email.

eBay Password   [   ]
Forgot your password?

Sign In or Register Now

☐ Keep me signed in on this computer unless I sign out. Learn more .

⑦ Having problems signing in? Get help now .

Click here to sign in using SSL. For more information about sign in, visit sign in help .

eBay   Register for eBay and Half.com   half.com by eBay

▸ Check out LIVE auctions on eBay.   Search tips
☐ Search titles and descriptions

Your Password Hint

Provide the correct answer to the Password Hint below.

| Your Password Hint question: | What is your favorite pet's name? |
| The answer to your question: | [   ] |

Click Continue and create

Continue...

home | my eBay | site map | sign in
Browse | Sell | Services | Search | Help | Community

▸ Check out LIVE auctions on eBay.   Search tips
☐ Search titles and descriptions

Create your new password

Enter your new password below. Please enter it twice to ensure you typed it correctly.

| Your New password: | [   ] |
| Retype your New password: | [   ] |

Submit

(www.ebay.com, May 16, 2002)

security question is not the same as the password. If it is the same, provide a MEANINGFUL ERROR MESSAGE (K13) explaining the point of the security question and how it works.

Another way to handle forgotten passwords is to create a one-time URL and e-mail that to your customers. When they click on the link, the URL will take them to a unique page on the site where they can change their password. That way the password is never transmitted, and the ability to change the password is given only once with that URL. This technique can be combined with security questions for even more protection.

Another partial solution is to have customers go to a physical location where they show pieces of identification so that someone on your staff can reset the password. This approach makes sense for Web sites that serve a local area, such as a school or a university. It provides more security, but it is still not foolproof, because people can fake identification and the process can be time-consuming for the customer.

Don't Force First-Time Customers to Sign In Too Early • There are two reasons not to hide all your content behind a sign-in screen. First, you could reduce traffic. Pages that require a sign-in will cause most search engines to fail. This means that none of those pages will ever appear when people search sites like Google or Yahoo! Second, visitors dislike having to create a new account just to see the content of a site, particularly when it's a shopping site. Tempt people with enough content to persuade them to stay a little longer.

You can address both of these issues by dividing your Web site into a public portion that is accessible to everyone and a private part that requires people to sign in. The public part is a sampler, which might provide headlines, a few paragraphs of fresh content, or complete access to a few pages.

✳ SOLUTION

Collect the minimum amount of information you need to create new accounts. Make it clear which fields are required and which are optional. Prevent errors where possible. Provide your Web site's privacy information. Have a process for handling forgotten passwords. Don't force first-time customers to sign in too early.

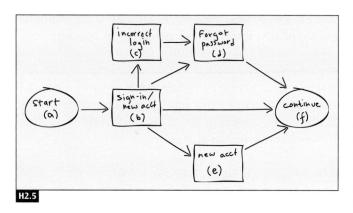

H2.5

Figure H2.5

In general, signing in to a Web site should proceed as follows: Visitors come to an entry point (a) that requires them to sign in (b). Customers who already have an account and remember the password can sign in and continue (f). Visitors who want to create an account do so (e) and then continue (f). Returning customers who enter the wrong account information or password are blocked from continuing (c). A returning customer can ask to receive help remembering the password or to have the password reset (d). After the password has been recalled or reset, the customer can continue (f).

✳ OTHER PATTERNS TO CONSIDER

The sign-in/new account pattern is actually a version of PROCESS FUNNEL (H1), which covers techniques to help customers complete highly specific tasks.

Design your sign-in/new account process to PREVENT ERRORS (K12) and to provide MEANINGFUL ERROR MESSAGES (K13) whenever errors do occur. Also, structure the process to help PREVENT PHISHING SCAMS (E9). One way to do this is to remind your customers of potential dangers and to teach them how to identify such scams. Another approach is to avoid sign-in forms and OBVIOUS LINKS (K10) to your sign-in pages in the body of E-MAIL SUBSCRIPTIONS (E2) and E-MAIL NOTIFICATIONS (E7).

Make your PRIVACY POLICY (E4), which explains your FAIR INFORMATION PRACTICES (E3), prominent when visitors sign in, or when they're creating a new account. Use a SECURE CONNECTION (E6) if sensitive personal information is involved.

Content that requires people to sign in cannot be indexed by search engines. See WRITING FOR SEARCH ENGINES (D6) for more information.

GUEST ACCOUNT H3

Figure H3.1

Pottery Barn Kids lets its customers make purchases as either guests or registered members. When purchasing as a guest, customers are assured that their personal information will be used only for processing the order and will not be kept in the company's database.

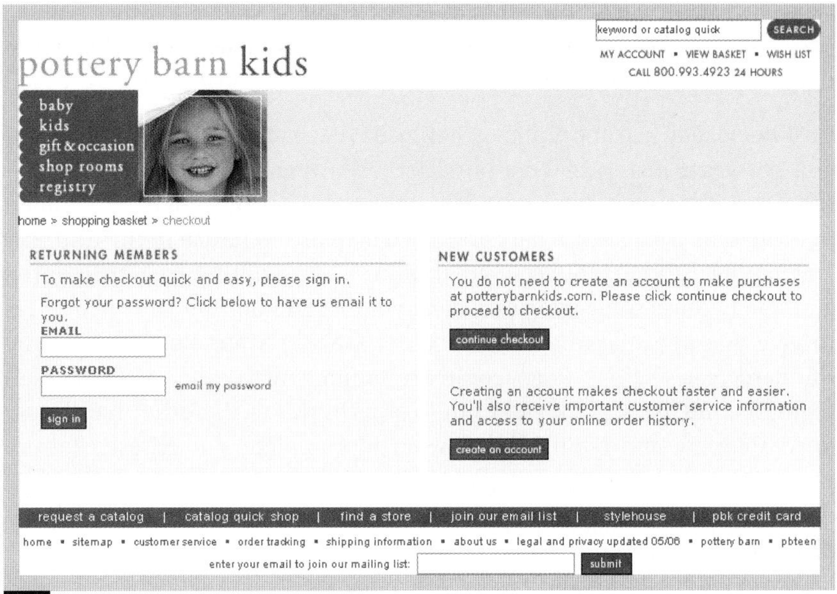

H3.1 (www.potterybarnkids.com, June 16, 2006)

BACKGROUND

F1 H2 Some customers prefer just to use a Web site instead of having to create an account first. For example, they might want to use the QUICK-FLOW CHECKOUT (F1) without having to go through SIGN-IN/NEW ACCOUNT (H2). This pattern describes guest accounts in detail.

✳ PROBLEM

Many customers will be put off and possibly leave a Web site if they have to create an account to use it. However, you need information from customers to support them in their tasks.

Customers may become annoyed if they have to create yet another account and password just to make a purchase on a PERSONAL E-COMMERCE (A1) site. Such a requirement is especially frustrating for customers who intend to make only a single purchase and have no plans to return in the future. **(A1)**

Forcing customers to create an account is just another barrier to entry, and it may cause some people to leave your site. Requiring your customers to give you personal information before making a purchase violates the standard "sales script" that people are familiar with when they shop in regular stores [see QUICK-FLOW CHECKOUT (F1)]. On the other hand, you **(F1)** need shipping and billing information to complete a purchase. Pottery Barn Kids makes a nice compromise by assuring its customers that they don't have to create an account just to make a purchase (see Figure H3.1). The U.S. Mint's Web site makes similar assurances to its customers, as Figure H3.2 illustrates.

This is one instance where guest accounts make sense. In this case the guest account lets customers make purchases first. Once they have completed the QUICK-FLOW CHECKOUT (F1), they are given the option of creat- **(F1)** ing a new account, thus saving all of the information about shipping and billing that they just typed (see Figure H3.3). It can be helpful to inform your customers up front that they will not need to create an account before checking out (see Figure H3.4).

WEB APPS THAT WORK (A10) are another place where guest accounts **(A10)** make sense. For example, you might let first-time customers try out the service, and only when they want to save their information ask them to create a new account.

Figure H3.2

(a) The U.S. Mint's
checkout page lets
customers choose
between **Member
Checkout** and
Continue Checkout.
(b) The second option
leads to the **Billing
Address** page, which
assures customers
that the information
submitted will be
used only for the
purpose of fulfilling
the order.

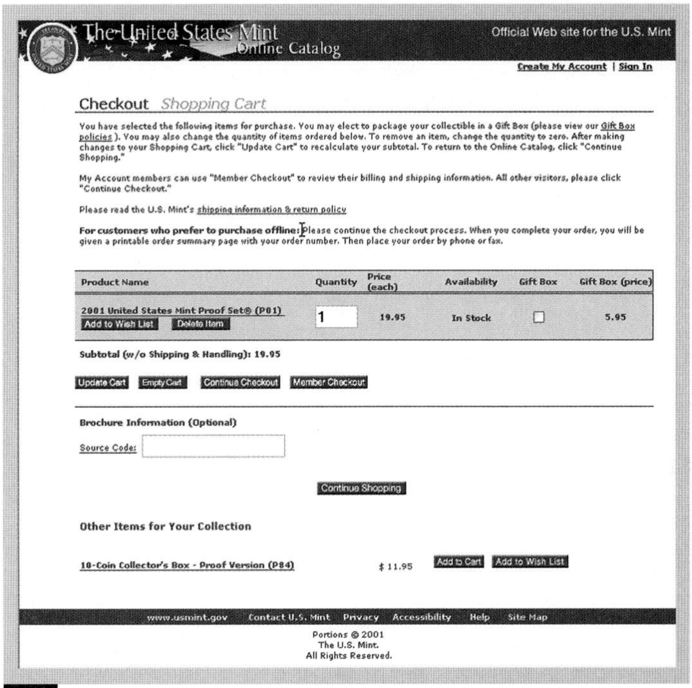

H3.2a

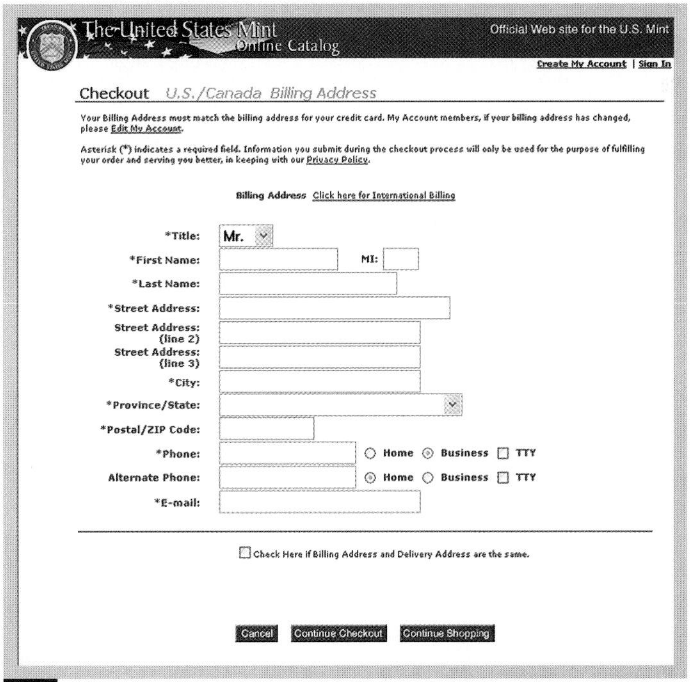

H3.2b

(www.usmint.gov, February 27, 2002)

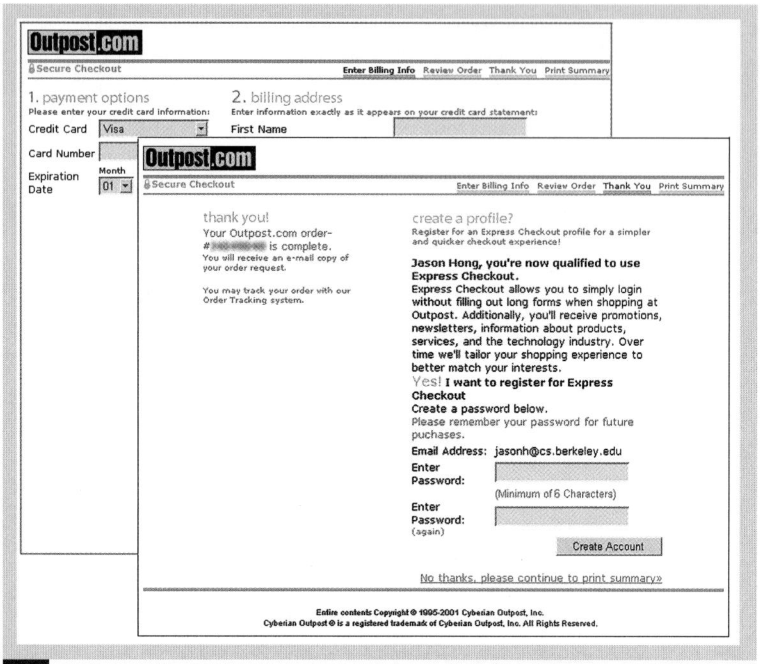

Figure H3.3

Outpost.com lets people without accounts make purchases first and then create an account, if they choose. It also provides an expedited checkout process for customers who already have an account.

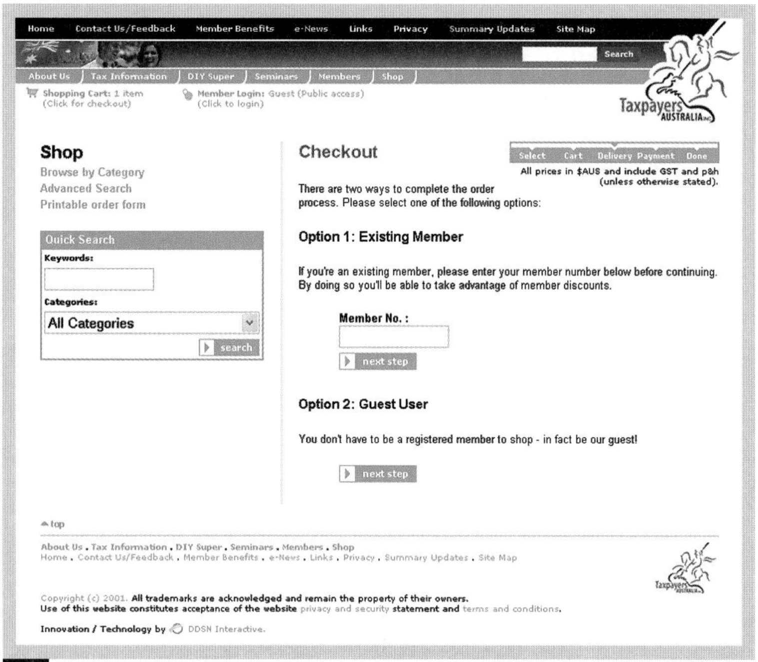

H3.3
(www.outpost.com, October 26, 2001)

Figure H3.4

Taxpayers Australia's Web site makes it very clear to customers that they do not need to be members of the site before purchasing tax information there.

H3.4
(www.taxpayer.com.au, February 27, 2002)

✳ SOLUTION

Give new visitors the option of creating an account at the end of a process, rather than forcing them to create one at the beginning.

Figure H3.5

Make account creation optional, and put it at the end of the process.

✳ OTHER PATTERNS TO CONSIDER

Guest accounts are an alternative to requiring customers to go through the SIGN-IN/NEW ACCOUNT (H2) process at the beginning of QUICK-FLOW CHECKOUT (F1).

To implement guest accounts, use temporary session IDs, as discussed in PERSISTENT CUSTOMER SESSIONS (H5).

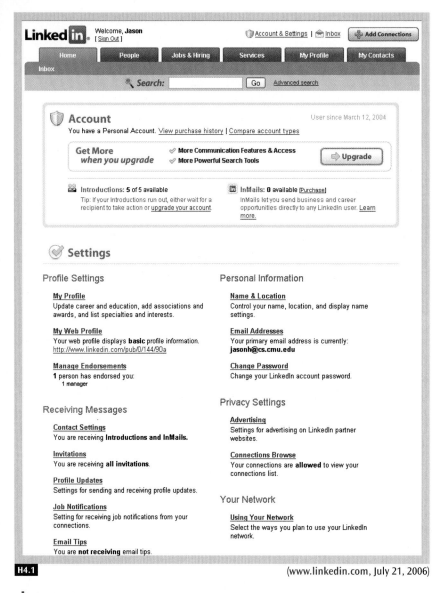

Figure H4.1

This account management page lets customers see and update all the information that LinkedIn manages for them. Customers can update what others see about them, as well as their contact and privacy settings.

H4.1 (www.linkedin.com, July 21, 2006)

✳ BACKGROUND

All Web applications that provide personalization, such as PERSONAL E-COMMERCE (A1), NEWS MOSAICS (A2), and COMMUNITY CONFERENCE (A3), need a way to let customers manage personal data and PRIVACY PREFERENCES (E8).

✳ PROBLEM

Customers need to see and manage the information that a Web site keeps about them.

Web sites need to keep track of a great deal of information about their customers to create highly PERSONALIZED CONTENT (D4) for them. For example, a PERSONAL E-COMMERCE (A1) site might store shipping address, billing address, and credit card information to streamline the check-out process. A NEWS MOSAIC (A2) site might store the kinds of news articles that a specific customer likes, presenting a high-value news site tailored for that individual. A COMMUNITY CONFERENCE (A3) site might store a customer's favorite message boards and favorite participants, making it easy to find new and relevant discussions. A STIMULATING ARTS AND ENTERTAINMENT (A9) site might store a customer's movie and music preferences and provide recommendations.

When you're developing a personalized Web site, remember that one of the FAIR INFORMATION PRACTICES (E3) is *access*. Individuals should be able to see the information that a Web site has about them, correct inaccurate data, and delete undesired data, as well set their PRIVACY PREFERENCES (E8). This is not just a matter of fairness; it's also a matter of practicality. If customers give you their mailing addresses when creating new accounts, it makes sense to let them change addresses if they move.

We call any kind of system designed to help people manage their personal information an **account management system.** Account management systems are essential to any Web site that offers personalized content. In the sections that follow, we offer some ideas about how to design these systems.

Provide a Single Page to Hold All Account Information in One Place • Your Web site can store a great deal of information about individuals. Consolidating all the information in one place makes it easy for people to see and manage their information. Figure H4.2 shows how the U.S. Mint's Web site lets customers manage their address books, wish lists, ORDER TRACKING AND HISTORY (G7), and other information.

As another example, Figure H4.3 shows how CDNOW, a music site, groups all of the information related to an account on a profile page. This page lets customers check whether their contact information, preferences, and financial information are correct and up-to-date.

(www.usmint.gov, February 1, 2002)

Figure H4.2

The U.S. Mint's Web site lets customers manage all their account information in one convenient place.

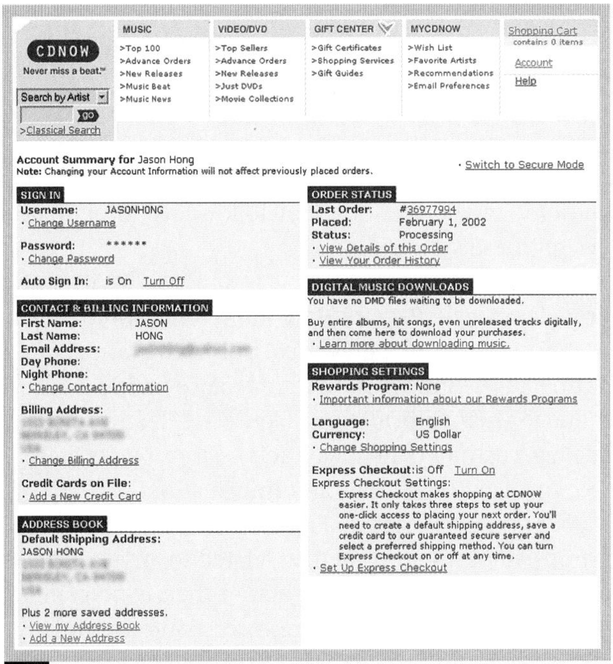

Figure H4.3

CDNOW consolidates all of a customer's account information on a single page.

H4.3   (www.cdnow.com, February 11, 2002)

B4 **Provide a Task-Based Organization Scheme to Let Customers Modify Their Information** • Use a TASK-BASED ORGANIZATION (B4) scheme that lets visitors access their account information while they're in the middle of a task, without having to go back to the account information page to add or update information. For example, Figure H4.4 shows how CDNOW provides links to let customers change their credit card information while they're checking out.

Make the Account Management Page Easy to Access • The key design issue here is where to put the link so that it's easy to find. One approach is to have an account link in the primary navigation, usually near the NAVIGATION **K2** BAR (K2). The ability to modify privacy preferences should always be **H4** available from these highly accessible ACCOUNT MANAGEMENT (H4) pages. Figure H4.5 shows how several Web sites handle links to their account management: **My Account** (for Pottery Barn Kids and Kodak EasyShare Gallery), **Update Profile** (for The Knot), and **My Virgin Mobile** (for Virgin Mobile USA). It's also worth noting that a study carried out at Wichita State University suggests that people expect the account management link to be near the top right of a Web page, as all of the examples in Figure H4.5 have done.

Figure H4.4

CDNOW shows customers their account information in context, when they need it for a specific task. For example, customers can change their credit card information at checkout instead of having to go back to the account information page.

3. Payment Information

Payment Method: Bill To:

Visa Card ending with 123.

Change Payment Method   JASON HONG

Redeem Your CDNOW Gift Certificate

4. Submit Your Order

Please make sure that all of the information above is correct.
You must click on the "Place Order" button to submit your order.

[Place Order]

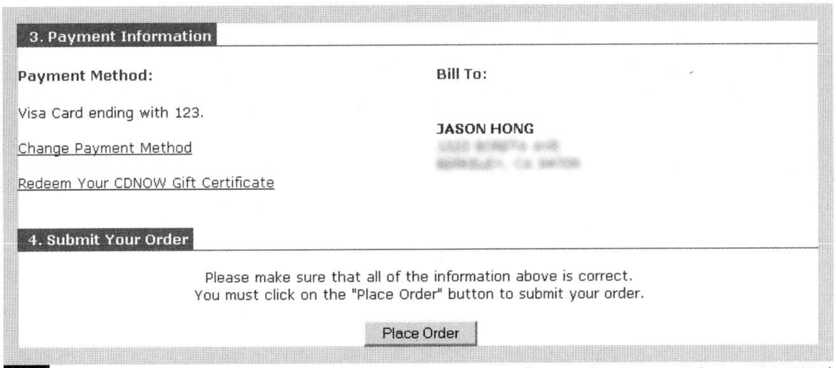

H4.4   (www.cdnow.com, February 11, 2002)

Figure H4.5

These screen shots show how different Web sites provide an obvious link to account management, using terms like *My Account* and *Update Profile* on the site's main navigation bar.

H4.5   (www.potterybarnkids.com, www.kodakgallery.com, www.theknot.com, www.virginmobileusa.com, March 26, 2006)

✳ SOLUTION

Provide a single page that holds all the customer's account information in one place. Use a task-based organization scheme to let people see and modify their information in the context of specific tasks.

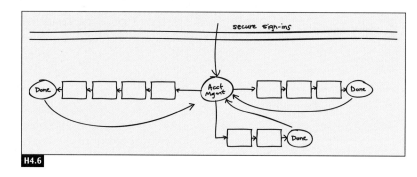

Figure H4.6

An account management system should use a secure connection to protect each customer's personal information and should guide customers through the steps needed to see and change their information.

✳ OTHER PATTERNS TO CONSIDER

As part of the FAIR INFORMATION PRACTICES (E3), every Web site that provides PERSONALIZED CONTENT (D4) should also provide an account management system to let customers manage their personal information and

E8 their PRIVACY PREFERENCES (E8). Such information might include cus-
D5 **E2** tomers' favorite MESSAGE BOARDS (D5), E-MAIL SUBSCRIPTIONS (E2), address
F4 books for QUICK ADDRESS SELECTION (F4), shipping preferences for QUICK
F5 **F6** SHIPPING METHOD SELECTION (F5), PAYMENT METHOD (F6) information, and
G7 ORDER TRACKING AND HISTORY (G7).

Use a centralized organization scheme, with all the information in one
B4 place, as well as TASK-BASED ORGANIZATION (B4), where the information is
spread out according to task.

The more sensitive the data is, the more protection customers need. If
the account management system contains sensitive personal or financial
E6 information, use a SECURE CONNECTION (E6) with extremely strong encryption
to protect the data.

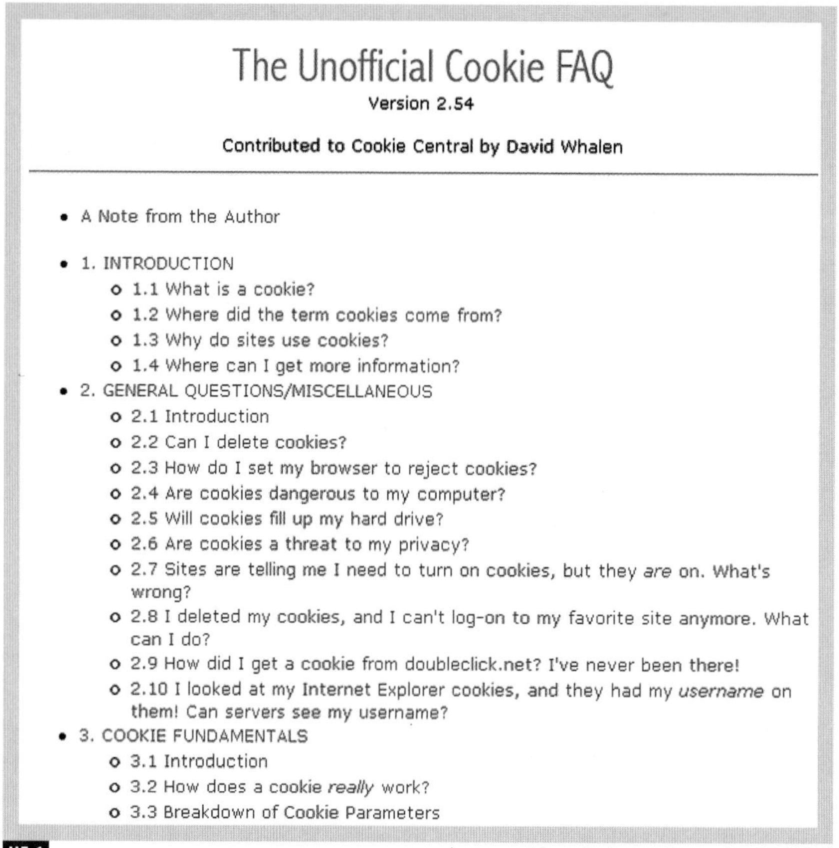

The Unofficial Cookie FAQ
Version 2.54

Contributed to Cookie Central by David Whalen

- A Note from the Author

- 1. INTRODUCTION
    - 1.1 What is a cookie?
    - 1.2 Where did the term cookies come from?
    - 1.3 Why do sites use cookies?
    - 1.4 Where can I get more information?
- 2. GENERAL QUESTIONS/MISCELLANEOUS
    - 2.1 Introduction
    - 2.2 Can I delete cookies?
    - 2.3 How do I set my browser to reject cookies?
    - 2.4 Are cookies dangerous to my computer?
    - 2.5 Will cookies fill up my hard drive?
    - 2.6 Are cookies a threat to my privacy?
    - 2.7 Sites are telling me I need to turn on cookies, but they *are* on. What's wrong?
    - 2.8 I deleted my cookies, and I can't log-on to my favorite site anymore. What can I do?
    - 2.9 How did I get a cookie from doubleclick.net? I've never been there!
    - 2.10 I looked at my Internet Explorer cookies, and they had my *username* on them! Can servers see my username?
- 3. COOKIE FUNDAMENTALS
    - 3.1 Introduction
    - 3.2 How does a cookie *really* work?
    - 3.3 Breakdown of Cookie Parameters

H5.1

(www.cookiecentral.com, November 28, 2001)

Figure H5.1

Cookies are the most common way of implementing persistent customer sessions, which are necessary to provide personalized services. However, cookies pose several implementation and privacy problems.

❊ BACKGROUND

All Web applications that provide any degree of PERSONALIZED CONTENT (D4), such as PERSONAL E-COMMERCE (A1), COMMUNITY CONFERENCE (A3), and WEB APPS THAT WORK (A10), need a way to identify and track customers.

✳ PROBLEM

To provide personalized services, Web sites need to identify and track their customers while the customers are on the site.

HyperText Transfer Protocol (**HTTP**) is the means by which pages are downloaded from a Web server to a Web browser. When HTTP was first invented, it was designed to be stateless, meaning that Web servers had no memory of who was requesting pages or which pages a customer had seen. All customers saw exactly the same Web pages.

This limitation made it difficult for designers to provide personalized services, such as SHOPPING CARTS (F3), PROCESS FUNNELS (H1), and PERSONALIZED CONTENT (D4). It also made it impractical to provide fee-based services, such as monthly subscriptions for viewing an online news site. Customers would have to enter their identity and password for *every* page they downloaded. What was needed was a way of providing **customer sessions** so that Web servers could keep track of who their customers were and what those customers were doing on the site.

Cookies were invented to solve this problem. **Cookies** are small pieces of data used by Web servers to uniquely identify customers. However, it is more useful to think of this problem in terms of *temporary* and *persistent* customer sessions.

Temporary Customer Sessions • Sometimes Web servers remember a customer for a short period of time, usually until the customer closes the Web browser. **Temporary customer sessions** are useful when a Web site needs to maintain only short-lived information about customers, such as what items are in the customers' SHOPPING CART (F3) or which part of the QUICK-FLOW CHECKOUT (F1) they're in.

There are two ways of implementing temporary customer sessions. **Session IDs** temporarily store the identity of a customer in Web addresses. The session ID is usually a long, nonsensical string that is embedded in the URL, such as *http://www. website.com?sessionid=$qoijlgsk185794q$*. This string is passed along in every page that the customer sees, but it is discarded when the customer leaves the site. **Session cookies** also temporarily store the identity of a person. When a customer closes his or her Web browser, however, the session cookie is deleted, making it impossible to track people over long periods of time. The chief difference between session IDs and session cookies is that session cookies are sent to Web servers through HTTP, instead of through the Web address. For all practical purposes, though, the two are equivalent when used to implement temporary customer sessions.

Persistent Customer Sessions • Compared to temporary sessions, **persistent customer sessions** let Web servers remember customers for longer periods of time. Persistent customer sessions are useful when you want to maintain permanent information about a customer, such as when your site generates PERSONALIZED RECOMMENDATIONS (G3) or shows customers their ORDER TRACKING AND HISTORY (G7) information. A good rule of thumb is that, if your customers ever need to go through the SIGN-IN/NEW ACCOUNT (H2) pattern, you probably need to use persistent customer sessions.

G3

G7

H2

Persistent customer sessions are implemented with **persistent cookies,** which are similar to session cookies but are stored on customers' hard drives, allowing your Web site to track customers over longer periods of time.

Differences between Temporary and Persistent Customer Sessions • Table H5.1 not only shows the differences between the two kinds of customer sessions, but also describes when one should be used over the other, as well as which patterns require use of a particular type of customer session.

Most of the patterns you can implement through temporary customer sessions can also be implemented with persistent customer sessions. For example, by having each customer select a specific language on the homepage, you can implement INTERNATIONALIZED AND LOCALIZED CONTENT (D10) with temporary customer sessions. All of the subsequent pages will be displayed in that language, as long as the customer's Web browser remains open. Once the Web browser is closed, however, that information is lost. If you used persistent customer sessions, the Web site could store customers' language preferences so that they wouldn't have to select the language every time they visited.

D10

The only pattern unique to temporary customer sessions is GUEST ACCOUNT (H3), which describes how to implement temporary accounts. This pattern applies when customers are certain they want to purchase something now but they don't plan to return, or simply do not want their personal information retained. A guest account would let customers add items to their SHOPPING CARTS (F3) and proceed through the QUICK-FLOW CHECKOUT (F1) without having to go through the SIGN-IN/NEW ACCOUNT (H2) process of creating a new account and a password.

H3

F3

F1

H2

Choosing between Temporary and Persistent Customer Sessions • Two factors to consider when you're choosing between temporary and persistent customer sessions are complexity and privacy. Temporary customer

Table H5.1

Temporary and
Persistent Customer
Sessions Compared

	Temporary Customer Sessions	Persistent Customer Sessions
Mode of implementation	Session IDs, session cookies	Persistent cookies
Context for use	You want to keep track of and use temporary information, or privacy concerns are important.	You want to keep track of and use permanently stored information, such as the customer's identity, to provide personalized content.
Patterns involved	• INTERNATIONALIZED AND LOCALIZED CONTENT (D10) • PROCESS FUNNEL (H1) • GUEST ACCOUNT (H3) [which implies SHOPPING CART (F3) and QUICK-FLOW CHECKOUT (F1) as well]	• PERSONALIZED CONTENT (D4) • MESSAGE BOARDS (D5) • INTERNATIONALIZED AND LOCALIZED CONTENT (D10) • QUICK-FLOW CHECKOUT (F1) • SHOPPING CART (F3) • PERSONALIZED RECOMMENDATIONS (G3) • RECOMMENDATION COMMUNITY (G4) • ORDER TRACKING AND HISTORY (G7) • PROCESS FUNNEL (H1) • SIGN-IN/NEW ACCOUNT (H2) • ACCOUNT MANAGEMENT (H4)

D4
D10 D5
H1
H3 D10
F1
F3 F3
F1
G3

G4

G7
H1
H2
H4

sessions are easier to implement because you don't need to store most of the information permanently. With persistent customer sessions, however, the customer's preferences and customized information need to be stored in a database, and this data must be retrieved every time the customer returns.

Temporary customer sessions are also better for consumer privacy because lots of data is thrown away after customers close their Web browsers, making it difficult to track a customer's browsing habits over an extended period of time. On the other hand, persistent customer sessions make it easier not only to track customers, but also to provide streamlined, personalized services.

A4

Because of privacy concerns, SELF-SERVICE GOVERNMENT (A4) Web sites are restricted in how they support customer sessions. In June of 2000, the Office of Management and Budget published a memorandum establishing U.S.

federal policy on the use of cookies.[1] In general, the OMB stated, a self-service government Web site should not use cookies unless it

- Provides clear and conspicuous notice of their use
- Has a compelling need to gather the data on the Web site
- Has appropriate and publicly disclosed privacy safeguards for handling information derived from cookies
- Has the personal approval of the head of your organization

Although the memorandum does not explicitly say so, the government is more concerned about the use of persistent cookies than of session cookies on government Web sites. Here, use session cookies rather than persistent cookies because session cookies do not pose the same privacy concerns.

Two Warnings about Customer Sessions • Avoid putting any sensitive data in session IDs. Occasionally customers will see a URL like this:

```
http://www.xyzzyz.com/index.html?user=jhong
```

or worse:

```
http://www.xyzzyz.com/index.html?user=jhong&password=xyzzyz
```

making it easy for snoopers to see the password.

Similarly, cookies are not securely transmitted, meaning that clever hackers can see the cookie data being passed back and forth. If you designed your Web site improperly, a hacker would be able to record a customer's cookie data as it was sent, and then could impersonate that individual.

The first step in solving this problem is to understand the difference between **identification** and **authentication.** A user name is an example of identification, stating who someone is. Passwords are examples of authentication, proving that customers really are who they say they are. Cookies help streamline identification, but don't use them for authentication unless there's nothing sensitive to protect.

If sensitive information is involved, divide the Web site into secure pages (those that require authentication) and nonsecure pages (those that customers can always view). Many e-commerce sites are designed so that customers can browse the site and add items to the SHOPPING CART (F3), but to start the QUICK-FLOW CHECKOUT (F1) they must have a SECURE CONNECTION (E6) and go through the SIGN-IN/NEW ACCOUNT (H2) process.

---

1 OMB Memorandum 00-13, June 2000.

✳ SOLUTION

Use customer sessions to provide personalized services. Use temporary sessions for short-lived temporary data or when privacy concerns dictate, such as on self-service government Web sites. Use persistent sessions for long-lived data, or when the customer's identity needs to be known. Avoid placing any sensitive data in session IDs. Use cookies for identification, but not for authentication.

Figure H5.2

Persistent customer sessions are maintained by cookies, small pieces of information passed between the Web browser and the Web server. This information can be used to create personalized content and services.

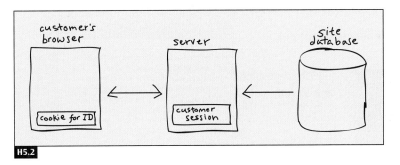

✳ OTHER PATTERNS TO CONSIDER

Any Web site that requires visitors to go through the SIGN-IN/NEW ACCOUNT (H2) pattern, or that provides any form of PERSONALIZED CONTENT (D4), requires persistent customer sessions.

Every Web site needs a clear and well-thought-out PRIVACY POLICY (E4) that explains the FAIR INFORMATION PRACTICES (E3) and how your site uses persistent customer sessions. You can let your customers control the application of these policies using PRIVACY PREFERENCES (E8).

Consider using SECURE CONNECTIONS (E6) when you use persistent customer sessions, especially if potentially sensitive data is involved. Financial information, the authority to make purchases, and personal data are examples of sensitive data.

FLOATING WINDOWS

H6.1

(www.netflix.com, August 9, 2006)

Figure H6.1

Use a floating window to keep the main browser window visible while displaying additional information. Floating windows are useful for showing extra information while maintaining a specific context. They can also be used for surveys and advertisements. In this example, a window provides details about a movie that otherwise would overwhelm the page, or require going to another page.

✳ BACKGROUND

Some PROCESS FUNNELS (H1), CONTEXT-SENSITIVE HELP (H8), CATEGORY PAGES (B8), and EMBEDDED LINKS (K7) need to display information in addition to the current page without taking visitors to another Web page. This pattern describes how you can use floating windows for this purpose.

✳ PROBLEM

You need to be able to show the customer extra information, while maintaining context and keeping the customer's Web browser on the same page.

Sometimes customers need additional information that is not on the current Web page, but at the same time they need to stay where they are. For example, you want customers to remain on the main path of a PROCESS FUNNEL (H1), but you also want them to read extra information that might be useful.

As another example, you may want to use EMBEDDED LINKS (K7) to let your customers see potentially useful and interesting content without spending time loading another page. This is often the case on CATEGORY PAGES (B8), where showing all of the details about each product would consume far too much space.

An older solution was to use pop-up windows to display additional information, ads, or surveys. However, rampant overdone advertising caused such a consumer backlash that many companies now provide pop-up blockers to eliminate unwanted pop-ups.

A better solution than a pop-up window is to use a floating window, letting customers see other information while staying on the same page. Whereas a **pop-up window** is a new browser window, a **floating window** does not create a new browser window, but instead creates what appears to be a window floating over the current browser window. This effect is achieved using the DHTML (Dynamic HTML) <div> tag. In this section we describe the trade-offs of using a floating window.

There are two kinds of floating windows: automatic and link based.

Use Link-Based Floating Windows to Show Related Information While Maintaining Context • A **link-based floating window** appears when a customer clicks on a link designed to open a new window. Use link-based floating windows with EMBEDDED LINKS (K7), EXTERNAL LINKS (K8), CATEGORY PAGES (B8), and PROCESS FUNNELS (H1) to display information related to the current page.

Floating windows are especially useful for PROCESS FUNNELS (H1), like QUICK-FLOW CHECKOUT (F1) and SIGN-IN/NEW ACCOUNT (H2). Floating windows let customers see extra information, such as CONTEXT-SENSITIVE HELP (H8) or an answer to a FREQUENTLY ASKED QUESTION (H7), while keeping them in the funnel. Figure H6.2 shows how Gap uses floating windows to show extra details about clothing, such as sizes and colors, while not leading customers off the CATEGORY PAGES (B8) where all the products are pictured.

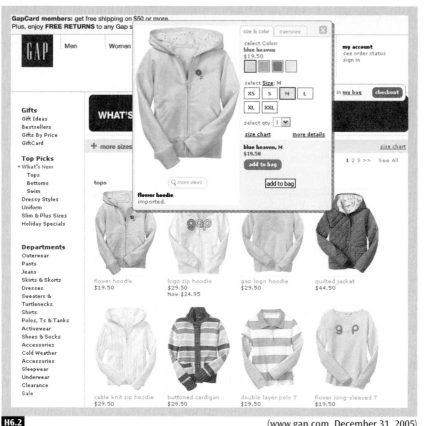

Figure H6.2

Gap uses floating windows to show product detail information on category pages, while maintaining context.

`H6.2`

(www.gap.com, December 31, 2005)

Automatic floating windows appear as a result of a customer's arrival at a Web page, or upon rolling over an OBVIOUS LINK (K10) on a page.

K10

Use Floating Windows to Provide Additional Information Instantly • Sometimes sites show summary information on one page, and detail information on a detail page as in CLEAN PRODUCT DETAIL (F2) pages. Because it takes time to load each additional page, another option is to load the requested information and quickly display it in a floating window instead. These details can be triggered automatically by rolling over items, or with a link.

F2

Use Automatic Floating Windows to Show Unrelated Information upon Page Entry • Another use of automatic floating windows is to survey customers— a powerful tool for understanding the needs of customers and how well the Web site is meeting those needs. Using a bit of JavaScript, you can randomly select customers so that only a small percentage will be shown the floating survey. Figure H6.3 shows an example of a floating survey.

Many people find advertisements in automatic floating windows annoying, but some Web sites have found success with them. One innovation is the *timed* advertisement, which places a floating window containing an advertisement over the site's content temporarily when the page is initially loaded, and minimizes after a brief message. If you want to show floating advertisements, there are many factors to consider, including usability, customer satisfaction, and business revenues. We can't say for sure whether automatic floating windows showing advertisements are good or bad for a Web site. This is something that your team will need to judge on a case-by-case basis.

Figure H6.3

This online magazine article has a floating survey window. The site opens a floating window rather than trying to pop up a window, letting visitors continue to read the main article.

(www.businessweek.com, December 12, 2005)

Use Concurrent Floating Windows Sparingly • Minimize the number of automatic and link-based floating windows that your Web site creates simultaneously because they can quickly overwhelm and frustrate visitors.

Use automatic floating windows when visitors first come to your site. Consider using cookies and PERSISTENT CUSTOMER SESSIONS (H5) so that people see your floating windows only once.

✳ SOLUTION

Use link-based floating windows to show related information while maintaining context. Use automatic floating windows to show surveys and possibly ads when customers enter your Web site. Minimize the use of concurrent floating windows.

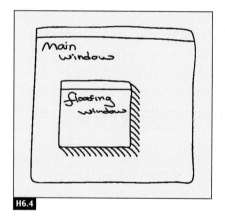

Figure H6.4

Use floating windows to display extra information while still maintaining context.

H6.4

✳ OTHER PATTERNS TO CONSIDER

Use link-based floating windows whenever you need to display information related to the current page—such as a FREQUENTLY ASKED QUESTION (H7), CONTEXT-SENSITIVE HELP (H8), or CLEAN PRODUCT DETAILS (F2)—but you don't want visitors to leave the current page. This situation is common with PROCESS FUNNELS (H1), CATEGORY PAGES (B8), EMBEDDED LINKS (K7), and EXTERNAL LINKS (K8). Consider using DIRECT MANIPULATION (H9) to let customers drag the floating window to a convenient place within the larger window, making it easier for them to see what's underneath.

Figure H7.1

Snapfish has extensive help that includes a FAQ page offering several categories of answers to common questions. The categories and a top-ten list make it easier for customers to find their question in a large set. Snapfish also offers a separate page for customers who need more help.

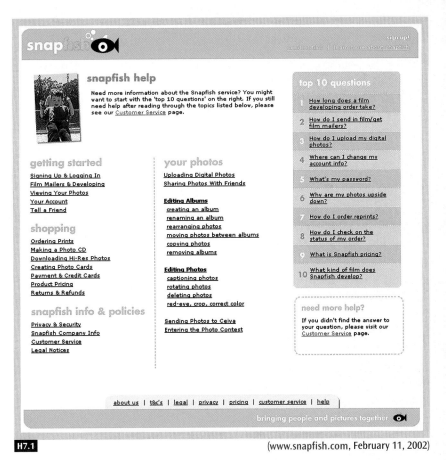

H7.1

(www.snapfish.com, February 11, 2002)

✳ BACKGROUND

Different customers often have the same questions when browsing a Web site, no matter what type of site it is. A good way to answer these repeated questions is through a **frequently asked questions** (**FAQ**) page. This pattern describes how to gather the questions, what the basic structure of a FAQ page is, and where to place the FAQ page so that it's easy to find. Use this pattern in conjunction with CONTEXT-SENSITIVE HELP (H8) to help your customers accomplish their tasks.

✳ PROBLEM

Customers often ask the same questions on a Web site, and it can be expensive and time-consuming to answer these questions over and over.

Visitors to PERSONAL E-COMMERCE (A1) sites, GRASSROOTS INFORMATION SITES (A6), EDUCATIONAL FORUMS (A8), and other types of sites usually ask the same kinds of questions. Although Web sites must answer these questions, it can be expensive to answer the same questions repeatedly.

Let your visitors help themselves by providing a frequently asked questions (FAQ) page—a list of common questions and their answers. A FAQ page makes it easier for people to search for answers themselves, while reducing help desk costs for you and response time for your customers.

First Identify Some Frequently Asked Questions • Start with a list of questions from your design team. Get everyone on the design team—from business and marketing, to design and usability, to programmers—involved in brainstorming. Draft a list of questions, but don't spend too much time organizing and grouping the questions yet. It's important here to come up with questions from your customers' perspective, rather than from a perspective internal to how your company is organized.

Examine Your Competitors' FAQ Pages • Ask yourself which questions on your competitors' Web sites apply to your Web site, and see if their answers have better solutions than yours. Keep these in mind for the next iteration of your Web site.

Collect competitors' questions that are relevant for your Web site, but don't copy the answers. Provide answers that are relevant and appropriate for your Web site instead.

Supplement Your Questions with Those Collected from People in Close Contact with Customers • Collect questions and answers from people who have a great deal of contact with your customers—for example, the people who conduct usability tests. What questions did customers ask when they were using your Web site? Were they unfamiliar with certain concepts? For instance, if you have an auction site, did the testers understand how bidding works? If you offer wish lists, did people understand how they work? What were their concerns? Were they worried about having their credit card information stolen? Were they worried about returning products?

The help desk staff will also be able to suggest questions. Find out which questions customers repeatedly ask by phone or by e-mail. Does the help desk already have a database to help answer questions? Can you get a copy of the help desk's e-mails and replies so that you can see what questions people asked and what answers were sent back?

Also talk to the marketing and sales staff. Inquire about the questions customers ask about the products. What features interest them? What concerns do they have?

3 See Chapter 3 (Knowing Your Customers: Principles and Techniques) for more information about understanding the needs of your customers.

Group Related Questions Together • After collecting questions and answers, decide how to organize the questions. If there are more than 20, use an organization scheme. For example, Figure H7.1 shows how Snapfish uses **B7** a combination of POPULARITY-BASED ORGANIZATION (B7) (see the top-ten **B3** list on the right) and HIERARCHICAL ORGANIZATION (B3) to group frequently asked questions.

On the other hand, if there are only a few questions, the easiest thing to do is to put all of them on one Web page, at the top, and then link the questions to the answers below (see Figure H7.2).

If There Are Many Questions, Add a Search Feature • Browsing through a **J1** long list of questions can be dull. Adding a SEARCH ACTION MODULE (J1) makes it easier to find answers to common questions quickly.

Use Redundant Navigation to Make It Easy to Find the FAQ Page • Provide mul- **K2** tiple links to your FAQ page, including one from the NAVIGATION BAR (K2) to the FAQ page, labeled "FAQ" or "Help." You can also place links to the **E5 K14** FAQ page on the ABOUT US (E5) and PAGE NOT FOUND (K14) pages. **B4** Use a TASK-BASED ORGANIZATION (B4) scheme to link to specific questions on the FAQ page. For example, if the FAQ page contains information about shipping policies, make this information easily accessible **F1** on the QUICK-FLOW CHECKOUT (F1) pages, where customers are more likely to need it.

Use the FAQ Page Only as a Temporary Fix for Usability Problems • Don't rely on the FAQ page to help your customers overcome usability problems. Design the Web site to help customers successfully accomplish their tasks. Consider the FAQ page a redundant source of information. Your customers' goal is not to browse through the FAQ page, but to

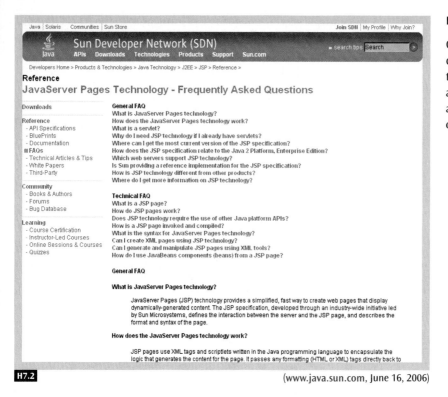

(www.java.sun.com, June 16, 2006)

Figure H7.2

On many FAQ pages, questions are grouped together at the top and linked to the answers below or on separate pages.

accomplish a particular task, and the FAQ page is just one way of helping them do it. If you use links for each question on your FAQ (see Figures H7.1 and H7.2), then a server log analysis of the most popular questions asked can help you improve your site.

Encourage Your Community Site to Create a FAQ Page • The FAQ page can be a significant community-building effort for COMMUNITY CONFERENCE (A3) sites. Usually a few people take the initiative to create the first version of the FAQ page, and they post it to the community site. They collect comments, new questions, and new answers from other members of the community and then iteratively improve the FAQ page (giving due credit to the contributors, of course). Figure H7.3 shows an example of a community conference FAQ page.

Figure H7.3

Many community conference sites feature a FAQ page. This example shows a portion of the rec.birds Usenet newsgroup FAQ page, developed with the help of many members of the community.

```
Archive-name: birds-faq/wild-birds/part1
Last-modified: May 30, 2001
Posting-frequency: Every 37 days

rec.birds Frequently Asked Questions (FAQ) (Part 1/2)

This is part 1 (of 2) of the Frequently Asked Questions list for the Usenet
newsgroup rec.birds.  The FAQ is posted every five weeks.  Its current editor
is Lanny Chambers; send suggestions for new questions and other comments to
him. Remember the FAQ is intended as a living document about rec.birds,
constant updating is welcome!

This section of the FAQ contains information about rec.birds and about
wild birds.  The other section of the FAQ contains pointers to more
information about wild birds.

Do not send articles to the FAQ editor for posting.  rec.birds is an
unmoderated newsgroup, so you may post articles yourself.  If you are a
newcomer to Usenet, please read the official articles about etiquette
in the newsgroup news.announce.newusers before you post.

Contents:

1.0.   All-purpose rec.birds etiquette
1.1.   I have a question about pet birds.
1.2.   Are domestic cats Satan?  --A Non-judgmental Attempt at Consensus.
1.3a.  Can I "count" this bird?
1.3b.  What are "listers"?
1.4.   I found an injured bird; what can I do?
1.5.   I found an abandoned nestling; what can I do?
1.6.   A wild bird is annoying me; what can I do?
1.7.   What is the Migratory Bird Treaty?
1.8.   I saw a rare bird!  What do I do?
1.9.   Why does everybody seem to hate Starlings and House Sparrows so much?
1.10.  Why does everybody seem to hate Cowbirds so much?
1.11.  I saw a bird which I can't identify.  Can someone help me?
1.12.  How do I keep squirrels out of my feeders?
1.13.  How can I make homemade hummingbird nectar?
1.14a. What kind of binoculars should I buy?
1.14b. What kind of scope should I buy?
1.15a. I found a dead bird with a band.  What do I do?
1.15b. I saw a banded or marked bird.  What do I do?
1.16.  If we throw rice at our wedding, will birds eat it and explode?
1.17.  Does providing food at feeders during summer keep birds from migrating?
1.18.  If I stop feeding birds, will they die?
1.19.  Does anyone archive rec.birds?
1.20.  ETHICS FOR BIRDERS
1.21.  Acknowledgements
```

H7.3

(news://rec.birds, August 24, 2001)

✳ SOLUTION

Start by identifying some frequently asked questions with the entire design team. Review the questions and answers in your competitors' FAQ pages to identify any questions your team might have missed. Supplement your questions with those collected from people in close contact with target customers. Use an organizational scheme to group related questions. Add a search feature if there are many questions. Use redundant navigation to make it easy to find the FAQ page on your site. Use the FAQ page only as a temporary fix if there are usability problems.

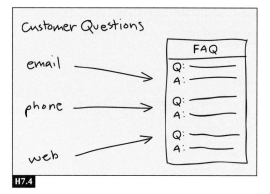

Figure H7.4

A FAQ page contains commonly asked questions and answers, helping customers help themselves. Use questions gathered from people who ask them on the phone, via e-mail, and over the Web.

✳ OTHER PATTERNS TO CONSIDER

FAQ pages are useful for all kinds of Web sites, including PERSONAL E-COMMERCE (A1) sites, GRASSROOTS INFORMATION SITES (A6), EDUCATIONAL FORUMS (A8), and COMMUNITY CONFERENCE (A3) sites.

    Short FAQ lists are usually organized on a single page; longer ones might use HIERARCHICAL ORGANIZATION (B3) and possibly POPULARITY-BASED ORGANIZATION (B7). For large FAQ lists, include a SEARCH ACTION MODULE (J1) to let people quickly search through the FAQ page.

    Link the FAQ page from the main NAVIGATION BAR (K2) as **Help** or **FAQ,** as well as from the ABOUT US (E5) and PAGE NOT FOUND (K14) pages. Use TASK-BASED ORGANIZATION (B4), with pages linking to a specific question and answer on the FAQ page, depending on the task.

Figure H8.1

Dell provides links to context-sensitive help to give customers detailed descriptions of features. This context-sensitive help is contained in a pop-up window, letting customers maintain the context of the task while seeing the information they need.

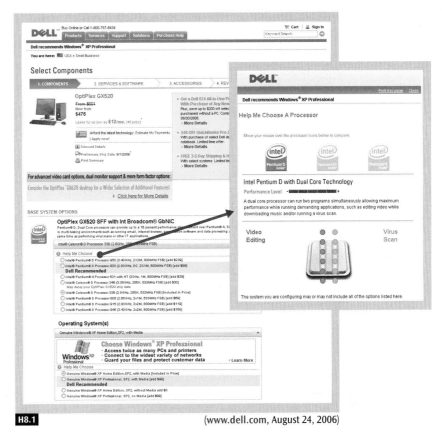

H8.1 (www.dell.com, August 24, 2006)

✳ BACKGROUND

There are always some visitors to a Web site who encounter problems, finding that they need more information to complete a task. Sometimes problems crop up even when a customer is trying to complete a task in a **H1** PROCESS FUNNEL (H1). Help your customers by offering context-sensitive help that provides additional information related to the current task. This pattern describes context-sensitive help in general, presenting guidelines for how to use it most effectively. Use this pattern in conjunction with **H7** FREQUENTLY ASKED QUESTIONS (H7) to help your customers accomplish their tasks.

✳ PROBLEM

Customers sometimes need highly specific help to complete a task.

Sometimes, in the middle of a task, customers have questions that cannot be answered on the current page. Your Web site might already have a help page, but it doesn't make sense to force your customers to go to that page and lose the context of their work.

Address this problem by providing context-sensitive help. This means providing appropriate answers, in both text and links, near where customers are likely to have questions. The content might include any of the following:

- An example of what's expected, helping to PREVENT ERRORS (K12)   **K12**
- A MEANINGFUL ERROR MESSAGE (K13) describing the problem and how to solve it   **K13**
- Detailed descriptions [such as a FLOATING WINDOW (H6) or the pop-up window in Figure H8.1 describing features in great detail]   **H6**
- Steps describing how to do the task
- Part of the FREQUENTLY ASKED QUESTIONS (H7) page   **H7**

In this section we describe some ways of using context-sensitive help on your Web site.

Place Context-Sensitive Help Near Where It's Needed • Place links and text to help your customers spatially. As Figure H8.2 shows, MSN Hotmail puts a **Why Sign Up?** link right next to links that let customers sign up for an e-mail account on its SIGN-IN/NEW ACCOUNT (H2) page. MSN Hotmail also has **Forgot Your Password?** and **Problems Signing In?** links right next to where customers can sign in and check their e-mail.   **H2**

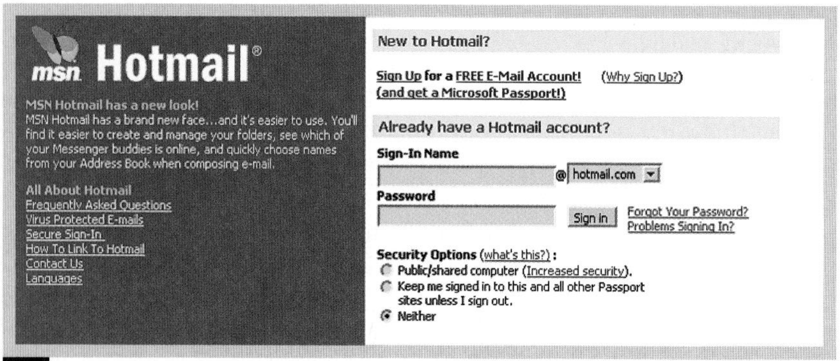

H8.2

(www.hotmail.com, October 26, 2001)

Figure H8.2

MSN Hotmail offers a great deal of context-sensitive help on its sign-in/new account page. Help appears in the form of friendly questions, such as "Why Sign Up?" "Forgot Your Password?" and "Problems Signing In?"

Consider Using Pop-up Windows to Let Customers Maintain Context •
Although we don't generally advocate the use of pop-up windows and
we suggest using FLOATING WINDOWS (H6) instead, when it comes to displaying help when people need to see help pages and continue with their
activities on your site, pop-up windows are the most practical option. A
pop-up window for browsing help allows customers to continue using
multiple pages in your site. That's not possible with floating windows.
The résumé builder service provided by Monster, shown in Figure H8.3,
has links to sample titles and objectives. Clicking on one of these links
opens a pop-up window that contains examples, letting people see the
information and still type their information in the text fields. Amazon.com,
Dell, Yahoo!, and even the most advanced AJAX-based sites use pop-up
windows to show context-sensitive help.

Figure H8.3

Monster, a Web site
that matches job
seekers with employ-
ers, helps prospective
job hunters build
online résumés. This
screen shot shows the
step of the résumé
builder in which job
hunters are expected
to enter a title and an
objective. To help,
Monster provides
links to examples,
which appear in
pop-up windows.

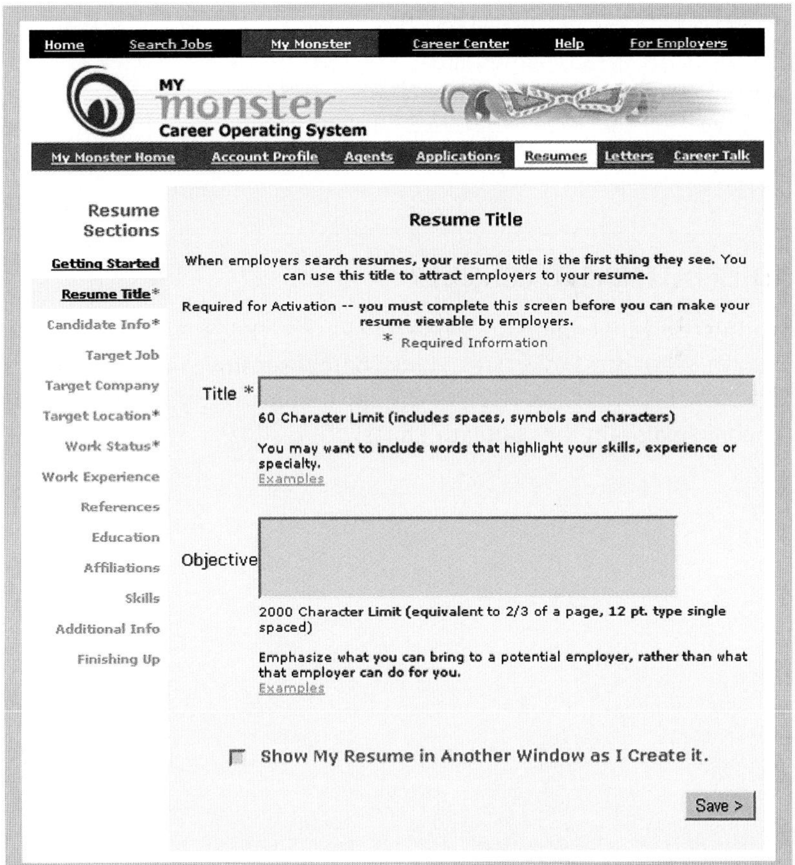

(www.monster.com, October 26, 2001)

✳ SOLUTION

Help customers by placing context-sensitive text and links near where they're needed on a page. Consider using floating windows to display the help, letting people continue with their tasks. If customers need to see the help while navigating multiple pages, use pop-up windows instead.

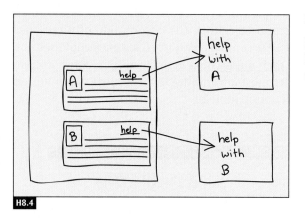

H8.4

Figure H8.4

Place context-sensitive help near the content that needs it.

✳ OTHER PATTERNS TO CONSIDER

Use context-sensitive help to PREVENT ERRORS (K12) and to provide MEANINGFUL ERROR MESSAGES (K13). Link context-sensitive help to a specific FREQUENTLY ASKED QUESTION (H7), or display it in a FLOATING WINDOW (H6) to let people maintain the context of a task.

Figure H9.1

Customers can click on a subject header in the Yahoo! Mail interface to open an e-mail or drag it to another location.

H9.1

(mail.yahoo.com, March 14, 2006)

✳ BACKGROUND

Direct manipulation refers to the ability to manipulate items on a Web page, often by dragging, providing an immediate sense of feedback and control. This technique is often used to simplify complex customization, data organization and manipulation, and control features. Although ubiquitous in most desktop applications, direct manipulation is less commonly found on Web pages, and it is typically implemented in genres that can most benefit from it, especially WEB APPS THAT WORK (A10). Direct manipulation can also exist within or between CONTENT MODULES (D2), and it can also serve as a way to move FLOATING WINDOWS (H6). A direct-manipulation Web interface can be more complex to program, but it can also simplify your system by reducing the number of pages in the site, as well as improving the customer experience.

A10
D2
H6

✳ PROBLEM

Site customization, managing sets, changing views and layouts, and other multistep actions and tasks can be difficult for customers to accomplish by only clicking on links and buttons.

For many common Web page tasks, such as QUICK-FLOW CHECKOUT (F1), product configurators, and other wizards, customers are taken through a PROCESS FUNNEL (H1), a tightly controlled series of forms in which they type information and select check boxes to choose options. This type of step-by-step process is suitable for some applications, but for others, it becomes awkward. In many applications, customers are doing more than just typing in data; they might have to organize information by managing sets, groups, and folders, or by editing designs, layouts, and views.

Although it's possible to create Web pages that let customers perform these tasks using step-by-step processes and forms, the resulting interaction tends to be confusing and cumbersome. The forms may also become extremely long, requiring many page reloads. But the biggest problem with this approach is that forms-based organization and layout tools are abstractions of the actual items and pages. Customers must therefore think of their information abstractly, which makes interacting with things like photos and maps much less intuitive.

Designers can make these tasks simpler by using an interface like the one shown in Figure H9.2, but even this interface requires many clicks and page reloads to perform simple actions. Fortunately, today's browsers have technology that enables site designers to create some of the interface elements that have previously existed only in desktop software applications.

Certain Web Tasks Are Best Suited to Direct Manipulation • From their experience with traditional desktop software applications, customers are accustomed to performing certain types of tasks by directly manipulating on-screen elements. These tasks typically involve the manipulation of elements such as large, customer-created sets, groups, and folders of information (see Figure H9.3). These elements can be textual or graphical in nature, and direct manipulation enables customers to move and organize them visually, instead of through abstract forms and check boxes. Other tasks that are good candidates for direct manipulation are design, layout, and view editing tools, which, because they are visual to begin with, are best suited to visual, direct control.

Figure H9.2

The **Layout and Organization** page from an obsolete Yahoo! site demonstrates a JavaScript-based method for configuring the customer's homepage layout preferences. Although this is a reasonably effective solution, it still requires a lot of trial and error on the part of the customer because the configuration interface does not display the final result. Direct manipulation improves on this method by enabling customers to work with the actual layout elements in real time.

H9.2

(www.yahoo.com, March 14, 2006)

Moving Objects around the Screen Requires Something to Grab • Direct manipulation often involves moving screen elements from one place to another. To select an element for manipulation, the customer clicks on part of the object to "grab" it. As a designer, you must decide how best to implement this procedure in your Web application. Some of the possible interaction techniques are:

- **Grabbing entire objects.** The most intuitive method of direct manipulation is to click anywhere in a screen element to grab it. This approach is practical if the element doesn't have to support other actions when clicked. For example, Flickr lets customers manage their

H9.3

(my.yahoo.com, March 14, 2006)

Figure H9.3

Organizing a personal homepage is a task naturally suited to direct manipulation, because it enables customers to move the screen elements in real time and see the results immediately.

own collections of photographs by clicking anywhere in thumbnails of their photos and dragging them to a particular folder (see Figure H9.4). However, it is also common to support multiple actions on a single element, as in the Yahoo! Mail interface (see Figure H9.1), where individual messages can be clicked to open, as well as moved by clicking, holding, and dragging.

- **Dragging windows using the title bar.** The standard paradigm for desktop windowing systems is to place applications in separate rectangular windows, each with a title bar running across the top. To move a window, you click anywhere in the title bar, drag the window to a new location, and drop it in place. You can emulate this behavior in a Web

Figure H9.4

Flickr lets customers drag and drop photos to make organizing them easy.

H9.4

(www.flickr.com, March 14, 2006)

application, as long as it's appropriate to use CONTENT MODULES (D2) for your movable elements. This practice also enables you to separate window movement from other functions, as in Figure H9.5, which illustrates how a customer can grab the title bar of a section on the Google News site and drag it to a new location without triggering any of the headline links in that section.

- **Grabbing objects using move/grow handles.** A third option is to create a dedicated handle for the customer to grab when manipulating an object. The move/grow handle is the most obvious mechanism for direct manipulation, but it does have a drawback. Handles generate screen clutter, using up screen real estate that could be displaying

H9.5

(www.google.com, March 14, 2006)

Figure H9.5

On personalized Google homepages like this one, customers can select the news departments for which they want to see headlines. Each department is located in a separate windowlike section with a title bar, which customers can grab to move the section to a new location on the page. Below the title bar are the headlines, which are linked to individual news story pages.

valuable content. Because their function is so intuitive to the customer, handles are best employed in situations that are unfamiliar to the customer. For example, it is probably not a good idea to add a handle to a window that has a title bar, because most customers are familiar with the process of grabbing the title bar to move a window, and the handle would waste screen real estate. When the function of the underlying element is less obvious, however, as in the mapping site shown in Figure H9.6, a handle on the zoom control not only provides a convenient means of direct manipulation, but also identifies the function of the screen element.

Figure H9.6

On this mapping site, the upper left corner of the map displays a zoom control to zoom in and out. Adding a handle to the zoom control encourages experimentation on the part of the customer, who will quickly discover and learn the zooming function.

H9.6

(maps.google.com, August 4, 2006)

Create Visual Clues on Movable Objects • One of the most important parts of implementing direct manipulation in a Web page is making sure that customers know which objects they can manipulate and what they have to do to manipulate them. It's important to make these visual clues, or **affordances,** obvious to the customer. Emulating a standard interface element such as a window with a title bar provides a big clue to the customer that the element is movable, but it helps to provide other affordances as well. Most browsers, for example, change the appearance of the mouse cursor when the customer rolls over a hyperlink. You can use the same technique to indicate when a customer is rolling over a movable object. Figures H9.3 and H9.5 both show a page in the midst of a drag, with the mouse cursor transformed into a four-way arrow, indicating that the object can move in any direction.

Change the Look of the Object When Rolled Over • On some Web sites, the object itself changes as the customer rolls the mouse cursor over it. For example, on Flickr's site, rolling over a thumbnail of an image causes that image to enlarge, suggesting that the image has dynamic qualities. However, this does not necessarily mean that the customer will recognize that the object is movable. Customers must actually click and drag to discover the object's mobility.

Provide Feedback • In most desktop applications, when a user clicks and drags something, a translucent shadow or *ghost* of the object moves with the cursor to the new location (see Figures H9.3 and H9.4). When the user drops the object, the ghost becomes solid and the object disappears from its old location. Take advantage of your customers' prior experience with direct manipulation by duplicating this behavior in your Web pages. Customers might not be sure that anything is happening unless something is directly dragged to the new location.

Provide Instruction Where Necessary • If you're not sure that your visual cues are obvious enough, provide some simple instructions so that customers know what to do. The instruction can appear to the side, but it should stand out to a first-time customer. For example, on the Google Maps homepage (see Figure H9.6), a small note on the side tells you that you can "Drag the map with your mouse, or double-click to zoom."

✳ SOLUTION

Create direct-manipulation interfaces when visitors must manage sets, groups, or folders containing a large number of items, or if they're editing designs, layouts, and views. When creating movable objects, think carefully about which part of the object a customer must "grab" to move it. Provide visual cues to an object's functions by using familiar interface elements, such as title bars, file folders, or handles, and by changing mouse cursors. Provide instructions for first-time customers so that they know how to perform these direct-manipulation functions.

Figure H9.7

Direct-manipulation techniques can simplify customers' interaction with visual elements by giving them immediate feedback and control.

H9.7

✳ OTHER PATTERNS TO CONSIDER

Many common Web page actions and PROCESS FUNNELS (H1), including product configurators and page customization of CONTENT MODULES (D2), can benefit from the direct control and feedback provided by direct manipulation. Direct manipulation helps PREVENT ERRORS (K12). You may consider using direct manipulation in MOBILE INPUT CONTROLS (M2), but be aware that not all phones and phone interfaces support DHTML, Flash, or programming languages like J2ME that may be required to implement direct manipulation.

H10 CLEAR FORMS

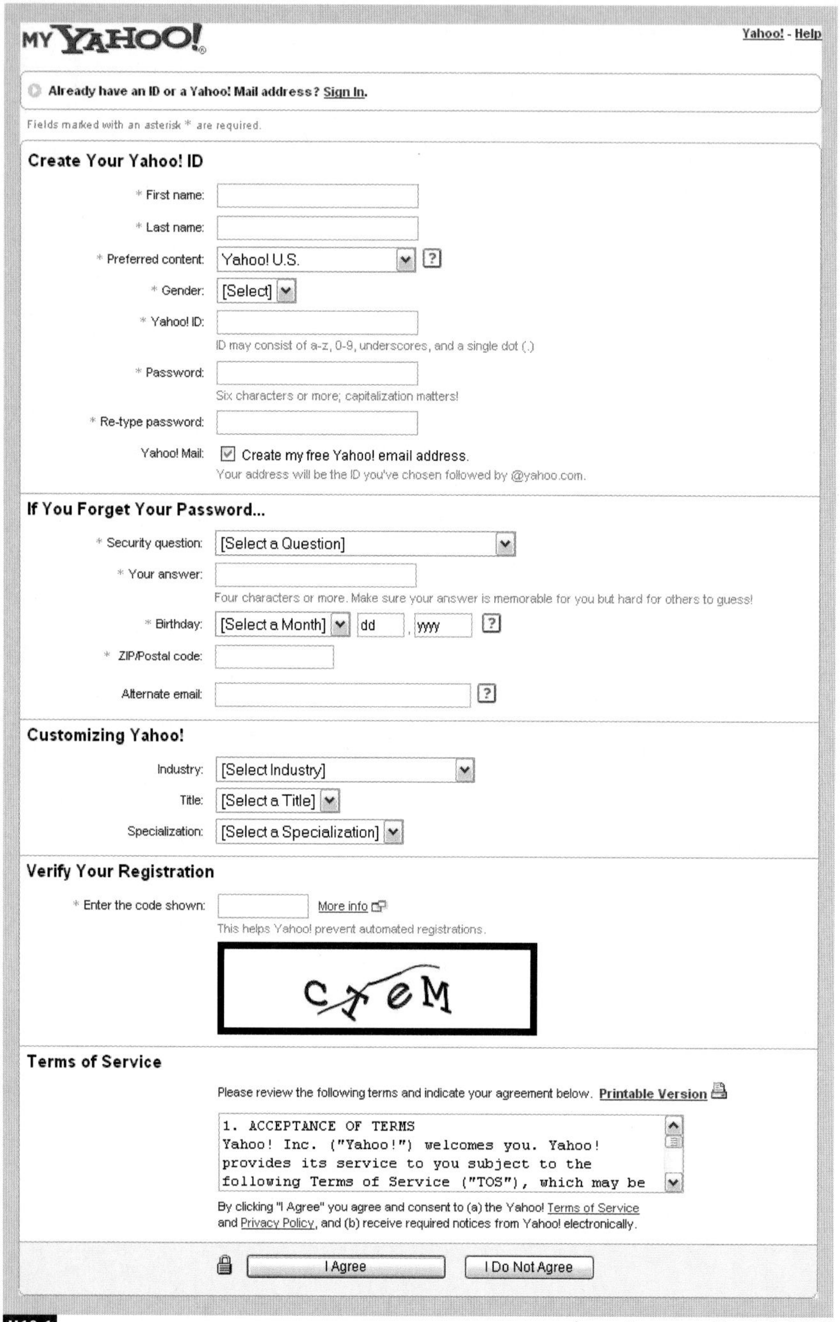

Figure H10.1

By setting the goal of a form at the beginning, creating an easy-to-read layout, and making separate subsections, each with their own purpose, you make it more likely that visitors will spend the time filling out all the fields requested.

H10.1

(my.yahoo.com, March 9, 2006)

✳ BACKGROUND

Whether you're collecting information to provide a QUICK-FLOW CHECKOUT (F1) on a PERSONAL E-COMMERCE (A1) site, identifying customer preferences for a NEWS MOSAIC (A2), or configuring a WEB APP THAT WORKS (A10), forms are essential parts of almost every site. They provide site operators with information about customers, and ideally they also help give customers the information they need, directly or indirectly.

✳ PROBLEM

Forms can be tedious and frustrating to complete, especially when they're long or difficult to understand.

Most Web users don't like to fill out forms and try to avoid them, if possible, for a variety of reasons. If it's not clear why the information is needed, or if a form seems to benefit the site owner more than the customer, visitors are likely to resist completing the form, often by abandoning the site entirely. Another common reason for a customer to avoid a form is that the form is poorly designed. Forms that are too long, have confusing or ambiguous labels, or contain complicated instructions lead to frustrated customers. Some types of design flaws can even make the page designer appear inconsiderate to the visitor, such as requiring that the input data be in a special format, requiring excessive tabbing, or implementing poor error handling that causes visitors to rekey the entire form after making a simple mistake. Designing clear and intuitive forms that avoid these faults can increase customer compliance and avoid the loss of frustrated visitors.

Provide a Payoff for the Form • More than ever before, and with good reason, Internet users are reluctant to give out personal information. When faced with a Web form, many visitors today hesitate to fill it out unless they have something to gain by it. Make sure that your forms provide an UP-FRONT VALUE PROPOSITION (C2) specifying exactly what payoff customers will receive in return for supplying their information (see Figure H10.2), and make sure the payoff is sufficient compensation for the information you're requesting. This helps visitors understand the benefit of filling out all the fields and transforms their task from collecting information for the site into entering information to help themselves.

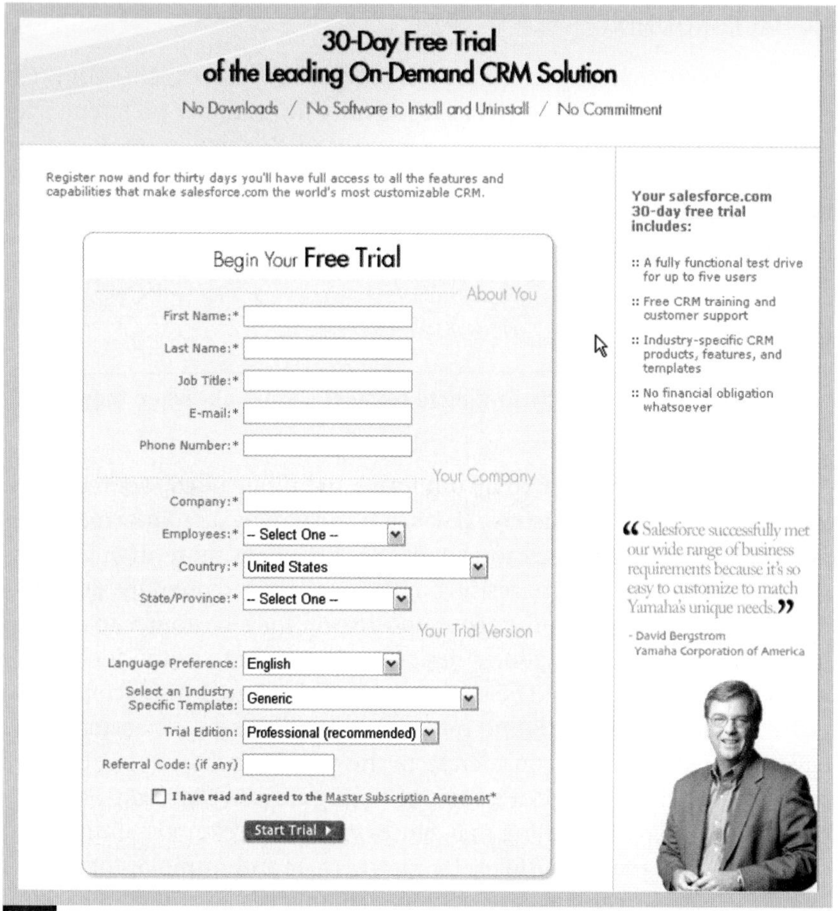

**30-Day Free Trial
of the Leading On-Demand CRM Solution**

No Downloads / No Software to Install and Uninstall / No Commitment

Register now and for thirty days you'll have full access to all the features and
capabilities that make salesforce.com the world's most customizable CRM.

Begin Your **Free Trial**

About You

First Name: *
Last Name: *
Job Title: *
E-mail: *
Phone Number: *

Your Company

Company: *
Employees: * -- Select One --
Country: * United States
State/Province: * -- Select One --

Your Trial Version

Language Preference: English
Select an Industry Specific Template: Generic
Trial Edition: Professional (recommended)
Referral Code: (if any)

☐ I have read and agreed to the Master Subscription Agreement *

Start Trial ▶

Your salesforce.com
30-day free trial
includes:

:: A fully functional test drive
for up to five users

:: Free CRM training and
customer support

:: Industry-specific CRM
products, features, and
templates

:: No financial obligation
whatsoever

❝ Salesforce successfully met
our wide range of business
requirements because it's so
easy to customize to match
Yamaha's unique needs. ❞

- David Bergstrom
Yamaha Corporation of America

H10.2

(www.salesforce.com, March 9, 2006)

Figure H10.2

This form states
explicitly at the top
of the page what
benefits the visitor
will receive in return
for registering. Such
a value proposition is
particularly important
for a form like this,
which serves the dual
purpose of configur-
ing the service's trial
and gathering sales
lead information.

One way of making the payoff clear is to split the form into sections, each
stating a reason for supplying the requested information. In Figure H10.1,
for example, "Customizing Yahoo!" is one of the section labels, and one
of the questions is labeled "Industry." Seeing these headings, customers
realize that they will receive information about their industry by answering
the question—a real payoff and a good reason to answer.

Select Appropriate Field Labels • When asking for specific pieces of information in a form, use FAMILIAR LANGUAGE (K11) so that customers immediately understand what you're asking for. A field labeled "Address" will,

K11

of course, be self-explanatory. However, a label like "Prefix," prompting for a person's title (Mr., Ms., or Dr., for example), or the abbreviation "M.I." for "Middle Initial" might not be understood as easily, especially by visitors whose first language is not English. Ask yourself what the most common names are for the fields, and consider testing your labels with potential visitors. A poorly chosen label can lead to frustration for thousands of customers, reducing your site traffic.

Select Appropriate Label Locations • In the design of a form, labels must be visually associated with only one input field so that people aren't confused about where to put the information or what the field is for. You can put labels above, beside, or below the input fields, using any one of the following techniques:

- **Side labeling.** When labels are placed to the left of the fields they identify, right alignment brings them as close as possible to the fields (see Figure H10.1). However, side labeling takes up a lot of horizontal space, which can cause problems in a multicolumn page. Side labeling also makes it difficult to place multiple fields on a single line, because each field needs its own label; but you can easily arrange subfields that don't require separate labels on one line.
- **Top or bottom labeling.** When labels are placed above or below the input fields, left-aligning both the labels and the fields makes the form easy to read, as long as you leave a blank space between each field and label combination. This arrangement, illustrated in Figure H10.3, enables you to group related fields, like City, State, and Zip Code, all on one line, and it provides more room in each label for instructions because lengthening the label does not displace the input field. Unfortunately, this type of labeling consumes lots of vertical space because each input field requires three lines: label, field, and blank line. Pages are longer as a result, and ACTION BUTTONS (K4) are often no longer ABOVE THE FOLD (I2).
- **Combined side and bottom labeling.** You can complement side labeling with beneath-the-field examples and further instructions. In this case, visual encoding is needed to differentiate the two, as in Figure H10.1, which uses standard black text for the side labels and light gray text for the instructions below the fields.

Use Automatic Input Formatting • Certain types of information require special formatting to be useful to the site owner. For example, dates and telephone numbers can be formatted in several ways, all of which are technically correct,

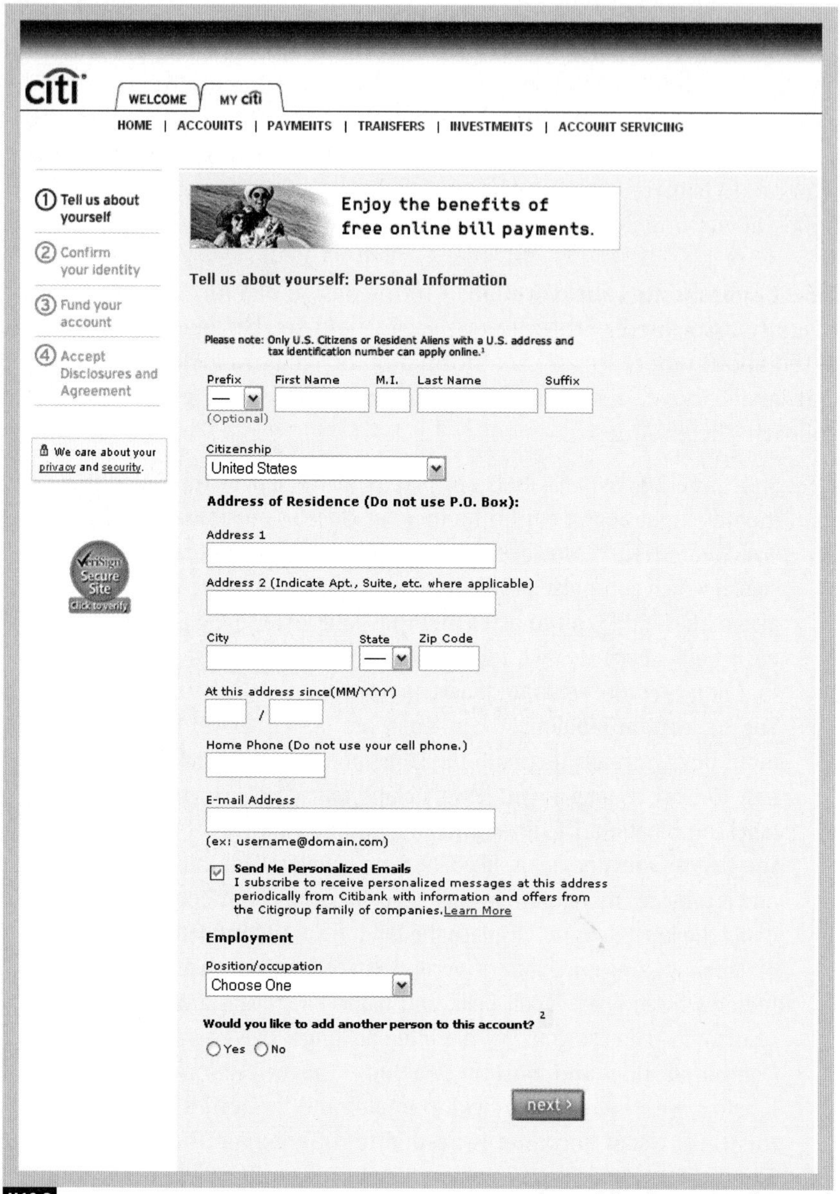

Figure H10.3

Customers tolerate long forms better when they're split into multiple parts on separate pages. The progress bar, shown here in the left margin, shows customers where they are in the form completion process, and how far they have to go.

H10.3

(www.citibank.com, March 9, 2006)

but all of the data collected by a site must be in the same format to be useful. It's possible to use PREDICTIVE INPUT (H11) for some of these fields, such as dates, but others, such as telephone numbers, are not predictable. It's always a good idea to PREVENT ERRORS (K12) and provide instructions for the proper format, such as an input diagram indicating how many digits should be provided for month, day, and year, as in MM/DD/YYYY.

However, simply including instructions does not guarantee compliance, so you may want to consider partially automating the data entry process. When a field consists of separate elements, you can divide it into several subfields, such as a telephone number's area code, exchange, and number, and have the cursor skip from one subfield to another as the customer types in digits, eliminating the need for manual tabs. Another method is to leave the data in a single field and use JavaScript to convert the input to the appropriate format automatically. For example, if "Jan. 31, 2009" were entered in a Date field, the form could convert it to 01/31/2009.

In some cases, an even easier input device for dates is a calendar displayed in a FLOATING WINDOW (H6), which greatly simplifies date entry when date ranges are within a few months. Providing a calendar can be useful on Web sites asking for dates in the near future or recent past. For sites that need dates covering many years, however, paging through years' worth of months can be arduous. By comparison, manual entry is simpler.

Keep Forms Short • The shorter a form is, the better people like it, so avoid asking for information that would be just "nice to have" and stick to the essentials. In addition, it's always a good idea to indicate which fields are required to complete the form, and which are optional. You can use an asterisk (*) and a different color to indicate the required fields, since two redundant indicators are more likely to be noticed. Just be sure to provide a key specifying what your symbols mean (see Figure H10.1). Using both a distinct color and a symbol will improve your SITE ACCESSIBILITY (B9) for customers who are blind and those with color deficiency. Alternatively, you could just add the word *optional* next to unnecessary fields and/or *required* next to necessary ones.

Make Forms Appear Shorter • There are ways to make a form appear shorter without removing any questions or fields. One way is to make your instructions as short and simple as possible. If you can get away without any instructions, that's ideal, but test the page with potential visitors to be sure that the instructions are not needed. Another method is to split a long form into multiple short pages.

Split Long Forms into Multiple Pages • Customers are more frustrated when they see a long, scrolling form on a single page than when they are presented with the brief first page of a multipart form. If an application requires an extensive amount of information from the customer, consider splitting the form into several pages so that most or all of the questions can appear ABOVE THE FOLD (I2) and customers are not faced with a single long, scrolling form. Splitting up a form also helps ensure that data is not lost, because entries must be submitted at the end of each page. Nothing is more frustrating than filling out a long form, only to have the entry lost when a page has errors or a server session times out, forcing visitors to start over. With multipart forms, always include a PROGRESS BAR (H13), as shown in Figure H10.3.

Put Form Elements in a Box • Putting all the elements of a form in one box helps people connect it all in their minds, especially if the ACTION BUTTON (K4) is not ABOVE THE FOLD (I2). Use an outline or background shading to delineate the box, and include the ACTION BUTTON (K4) in the same box so that visitors know immediately that the button allows them to submit their information and move on (see Figures H10.2 and H10.3).

Prefill Fields That Require a Special Format • For form elements requiring dates, e-mail addresses, and the like, prefilling the field can quickly communicate what's expected without taking up a lot of space in the label or in instructions above or below. Prefilling helps in PREVENTING ERRORS (K12). For example, in an E-Mail Address field, provide a generic address, such as "name@company.com," that is automatically cleared when a customer clicks in the field so that the example doesn't have to be deleted manually.

Reduce the Amount of Typing Required • You can also help streamline the process of filling out forms by minimizing the amount of typing required. One simple way to reduce the amount of typing required is not to ask for information that you already have. For example, rather than having customers type in their shipping address, you might let them choose from a QUICK ADDRESS SELECTION (F4) page. Similarly, rather than having customers type in their billing address, you might let them specify that it's the same as the shipping address.

For fields that have a fixed set of answers, you can convert type-in boxes to pick lists, and for fields with long lists of options, you can use

PREDICTIVE INPUT (H11) to speed data entry. If the fields are interdependent, consider using DRILL-DOWN OPTIONS (H12) to reduce the number of options in each field after the customer starts filling out the form.

Pick lists are a common method for reducing the amount of typing needed to complete a form. For example, e-commerce sites typically enable customers to specify their credit card expiration dates using pick lists containing the months and years. Not only does this practice save some typing for the customer, but it also eliminates potential ambiguity caused by differing abbreviations, as well as any need for the site to confirm that a customer's entry is valid.

Use Intelligent Error Handling • When a customer submits a form with an error, such as missing or improperly formatted information, always reload the page with a MEANINGFUL ERROR MESSAGE (K13) and the typed-in data intact so that the customer doesn't have to retype it. Include an error summary at the top of the page, highlighted in a different color and with an icon or bold type that is repeated at the location of each problem. For each field containing a problem, repeat the error icon, and include instructions on how to correct the error. Also be sure to consider SITE ACCESSIBILITY (B9) in using color to signify errors, since some of your customers may have problems distinguishing between certain colors.

✳ SOLUTION

Provide a payoff for the form by specifying what customers will receive if they supply their information. Choose label names carefully, using familiar language and abbreviations, and then test the labels. Place labels beside, above, or below input boxes, but make sure the labels are visually associated with their fields. Help people input data that needs to be specially formatted by automatically skipping from field to field or formatting the data for them. Keep forms short, or split longer forms into multiple pages with a progress bar, or into clear sections on one page. Provide simple instructions, as well as examples that clear when the customer types. Reduce the amount of typing required of customers by using predictive input. Provide intelligent error handling by reloading the page with all information intact, by calling out problems at the top of the page, and by providing instructions next to each problem.

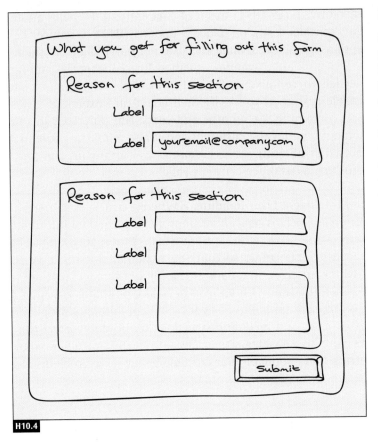

Figure H10.4

Clear forms make the purpose for collecting each data item obvious, simplify data entry, and automatically validate the data, if possible, while also communicating how the customer benefits by filling out the form.

✳ OTHER PATTERNS TO CONSIDER

Use a GRID LAYOUT (I1) to keep all the form elements in alignment. If you can't keep everything ABOVE THE FOLD (I2), include an ACTION BUTTON (K4) in the same box as the form elements. Use PREDICTIVE INPUT (H11) and DRILL-DOWN OPTIONS (H12) to help customers fill out fields more quickly, if the list of options is long but not unlimited. Ensure that your form design is PREVENTING ERRORS (K12) by carefully designing and testing the forms. When errors do occur, present MEANINGFUL ERROR MESSAGES (K13).

Figure H11.1

Dynamically loaded content enables customers to select departure and arrival cities on this travel site. In addition to saving keystrokes, the option lists also prevent ambiguity due to inconsistent abbreviation of city names.

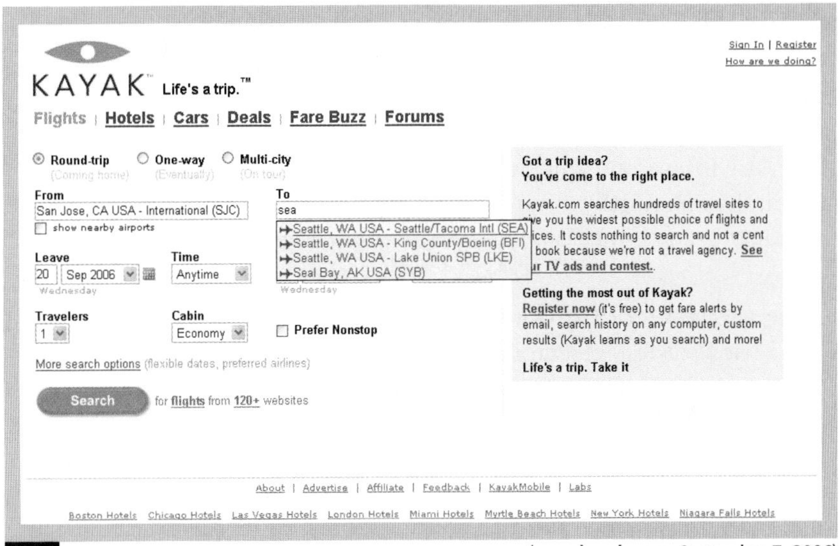

H11.1

(www.kayak.com, September 7, 2006)

✳ BACKGROUND

Used by all patterns in Pattern Group A (Site Genres), this pattern provides a method for simplifying the completion of forms. Predictive input can make a CLEAR FORM (H10) even easier to use.

✳ PROBLEM

Filling out forms can be tedious when lots of typing is required.

Forms are a standard method for gathering information from Web site visitors, but the act of filling in forms, especially long ones, is a chore that most people would prefer to avoid. To encourage people to complete them, use forms only when necessary and make them as easy as possible to complete. Predictive input, a powerful way to improve the speed and accuracy of data input, can be implemented in various ways.

Typing within a Pick List Can Provide Basic Predictive Input • The typical way to use a pick list is to scroll through a set of options and make a selection. This approach can be inconvenient, though, when the list is long, as in the case of a pick list containing the 50 United States. However, most browsers enable customers to jump forward in a pick list by selecting the list and typing the first letter of the desired option. For example, pressing the **M** key will cause a state list to jump to *Maine,* the first state starting with the letter *M.* Unfortunately, this capability is not particularly intuitive, and many customers are unaware of it.

Use Predictive Text Input to Help Speed Entry • Another way to reduce the typing needed to complete a form is to use automatic suggestions. With predictive text input, a list of options, supplied by the site designer, appears when the customer selects a particular field in the form. Customers can choose one of the supplied options, or begin typing something else. As they type, the list of available options is winnowed down to the selections beginning with the supplied letters. The arrow keys can be used to select an option farther down the list, and the **Enter** key to choose the selected option. Alternatively, the mouse can be used to select an option in the list.

Load Predictive Text Input with the Page • Preloading form options with the page, or soon thereafter, works for large lists of options, as in the case of the airport lists shown on the Kayak.com Web site in Figure H11.1. Preloaded options can be supplied by the site designer and loaded with the homepage, or they can be compiled by the browser from responses by this customer to the same question on previous visits and stored in a cookie (see Figure H11.2).

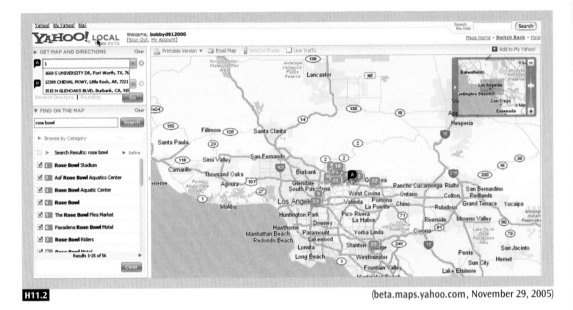

(beta.maps.yahoo.com, November 29, 2005)

Figure H11.2

The simplest form of predictive text input is a list of values that the customer has supplied in the same form field on previous visits to the site, as shown in this mapping site. In this instance, the text is supplied by the customer and stored in a cookie on the customer's computer, so no data has to be supplied by the server.

Sometimes, however, a site-supplied option list would be too long to preload quickly. In these cases, by using AJAX (Asynchronous JavaScript And XML) in a background process, you can load text dynamically from the server, on the basis of what the customer is typing. Taking this approach, you can supply a list of possible values based on the answers supplied by many customers. For example, when a customer starts typing letters in the standard google.com search page, a list of preloaded options appears, taken from the searches that the customer has already performed on that computer. However, in a new service called Google Suggest, typing in the search field displays an aggregated list of search terms supplied by thousands of Google customers (see Figure H11.3). Unlike the preloaded list of terms, which is stored in a cookie on the client computer, this aggregate list is supplied by the server.

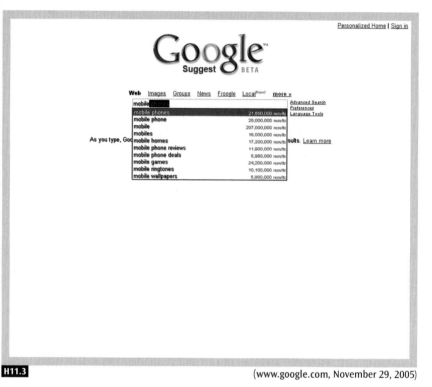

Figure H11.3

The Google Suggest service supplies customers with possible search terms previously employed by thousands of other site visitors. The list of terms is narrowed down by the successive keystrokes supplied by the customer.

H11.3

(www.google.com, November 29, 2005)

Build a List of Viable Text Strings • To create the predictive text input for a Web form, begin by building a list of text strings containing viable options for the particular field in question. The list might contain names, terms, or items, and it should be sorted using a method appropriate to the application. The sorting of the list is a crucial element because the sort is what enables the list to be shortened as the customer types each letter in the form field. For example, a list of U.S. state names for an e-commerce form will nearly always be sorted alphabetically so that customers can press a key to advance through the list, and the list of months for a date field should always be in chronological order. In some cases, the sort might combine two or more criteria, as in the Google Suggest list (see Figure 11.3), which is sorted both alphabetically and by popularity of the search term (while also showing popularity of the search result).

Create a Visible List of Appropriate Size • Predictive text input appears in a window generated by DHTML (Dynamic HTML) <div> tags when a customer types a first letter in the form field. The appearance is much like that of a standard drop-down list. As the customer types additional letters in the field, the list is winnowed down to only those options beginning with the chosen letters. The site designer must decide on the appropriate size for the window, based on the size of the list to be displayed, the nature of the information in the list, and the location of the field on the screen. If the overall list is very large, it might not be possible to display a broad range of options at one time. By keeping the predictive text input field in the page's GRID LAYOUT (I1), you'll make it easy to read.

Keep the visible list small enough to remain ABOVE THE FOLD (I2) so that the customer doesn't have to scroll down to see all of it. Another reason to keep the window relatively small is to reduce the number of items that the customer needs to scan. However, a visible list that is too small reduces the usability of the predictive text input, especially when the list is long. For example, in a form requiring customers to supply a date, the month field is most usable when the pick list is large enough to display all 12 months at one time so that customers do not have to scroll down to select December. A list of the 50 U.S. states, on the other hand, is far too long to appear in a pick list without scrolling. In this case, a visible window showing seven to ten states at once would usually be appropriate.

Provide Multiple Selection Methods • Customers can select an option from the predictive text input list using either the mouse or the keyboard. Be sure to exercise control over the function of the **Enter** key when designing a page that displays predictive text input. In some cases, it is preferable for the **Enter** key to insert the selected option into the field; in other cases, you might want the act of pressing **Enter** to submit the entire form to the server as well.

✳ SOLUTION

Change type-in fields to predictive pick lists when option lists are short. Use predictive text input for medium and large option lists. Configure forms either to preload predictive input with the page or to load it dynamically. Build a list of text strings that can function as viable options for a particular form field, and sort them using an appropriate method for the information: alphabetical, chronological, or by popularity. Create a predictive text input window that appears when the customer begins typing in the field. Size the window appropriately for the amount and type of information to be displayed and its place on the screen. Let customers choose options with both the keyboard and mouse.

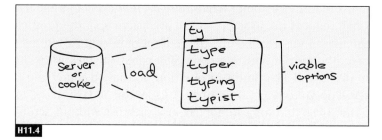

Figure H11.4

Predictive input makes it more likely that your customers will complete forms quickly and accurately.

✳ OTHER PATTERNS TO CONSIDER

Use FAST-LOADING CONTENT (L6) to preload predictive text input options as the page loads, or as visitors type. Put the predictive text input field in the page's GRID LAYOUT (I1). Keep the predictive text input field ABOVE THE FOLD (I2).

L6

I1

I2

Figure H12.1

Yahoo! Autos makes good use of drill-down options to specify car make and model.

H12.1

(autos.yahoo.com, February 25, 2006)

✳ BACKGROUND

It's important to give visitors to your Web site easier ways to enter information into CLEAR FORMS (H10) when option lists are large but limited. An alternative to the PREDICTIVE INPUT (H11) pattern is one that provides drill-down options.

✳ PROBLEM

Specifying a particular option in a long list can be daunting.

There are several techniques for letting customers select from a long list of options. One technique is PREDICTIVE INPUT (H11), which is preferable when the list is extremely long or changes frequently, or when customers must be able to enter an option that is not on the list. Another technique is called *drill-down options,* in the form of hierarchical pick lists and hierarchical menus.

H11

Use Hierarchical Pick Lists for Specifying Interdependent Options • Hierarchical pick lists consist of multiple pick lists on a Web page in which options in the secondary pick list depend on selections made in the primary pick list. This type of drill-down option, made with standard HTML forms, is particularly useful for specifying products in a product family. In Figure H12.2, for example, customers select the manufacturer of their telephone from the primary pick list. This selection activates the secondary pick list, which contains only the models produced by the selected manufacturer. The site can then load a page containing information specific to that exact phone. Alternatively, the hierarchy could continue deeper and include a third pick list, and even more levels, before displaying the results.

Deactivate the Secondary Pick List Until a Primary Selection Is Made • Hierarchical pick lists can be baffling to customers if they're not implemented well. Customers must intuitively understand that they have to make a selection from the primary pick list first. If both pick lists are active when the page loads, simply having one above the other (or one to the left of the other) might not be sufficient to lead visitors to the primary list first. The best practice, therefore, is to deactivate the secondary pick list (and any tertiary or additional lists) so that it appears grayed out until the customer makes a selection in the primary pick list. Another possibility is to have each pick list appear on a separate page (see Figure H12.3), but if your site is slow, your customers will become frustrated with each page load.

Create Pick Lists Containing Generic Options That Appear by Default • A pick list must always have a generic first entry, which is what customers see first. It can be baffling to a customer if specific secondary options, which depend on primary-option choices, appear to be available even before the

Figure H12.2

In hierarchical pick lists, the secondary menu is unavailable until the customer makes a selection from the primary menu. You can implement such a hierarchy by storing secondary options in a JavaScript list until the primary selection has been made.

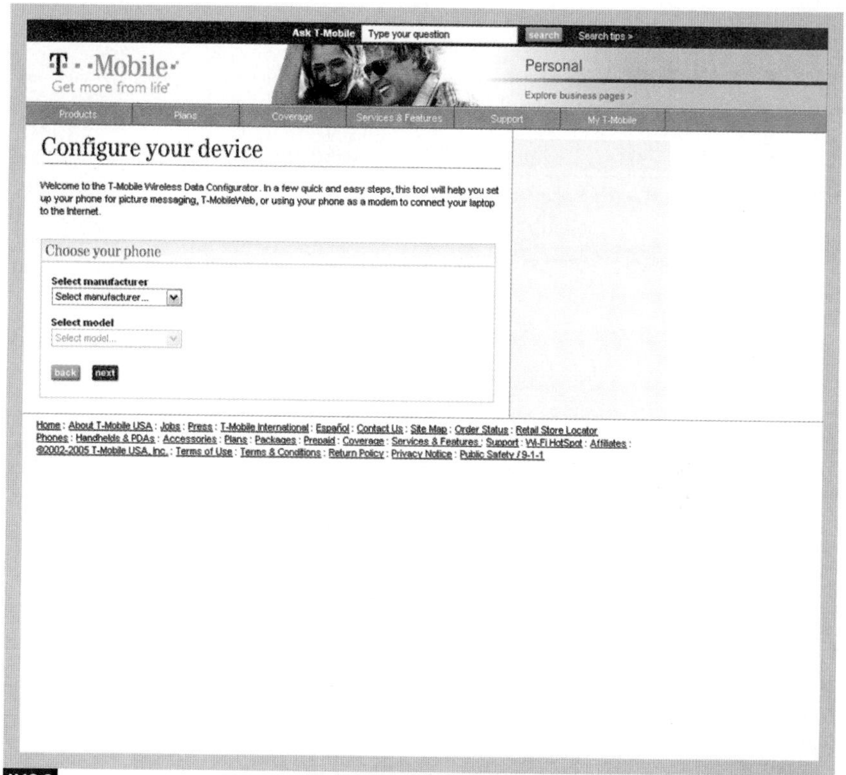

H12.2

(http://tmobileus.wdsglobal.com/phonefirst, February 25, 2006)

customer has made the primary choice. If you display secondary options that are based on the default primary option, visitors might not explore the primary option list first. For this reason, don't display actual options in your secondary or tertiary pick lists by default. Deactivated pick lists should also display a generic entry by default, such as one that says, "Choose a Model," so that people know what step they'll be taking next.

Create Hierarchical Menus • A hierarchical menu is a drill-down option that consists of a combination of primary and secondary (and possibly even tertiary) lists that appear when a customer clicks or rolls the mouse

Figure H12.3

You can create hierarchical pick lists on separate pages so that customers are compelled to make selections in the right order. On this site, after customers select the manufacturer of their computer, a new page loads in which they select the appropriate model. Using separate pages adds loading time, but when you might need to show additional information after the primary selection, this method makes page design and implementation easier.

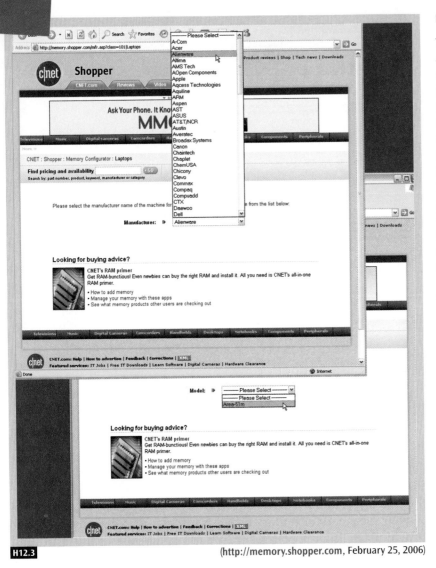

H12.3

(http://memory.shopper.com, February 25, 2006)

over a particular Web page element (see Figure H12.4). On a company site, for example, visitors might roll over a **Products** banner to display a menu containing categories representing the types of products the company sells. When the visitor clicks or points to one of the options on the category menu, a secondary menu appears containing a list of the products in that category. The visitor then selects an entry from the secondary menu

Figure H12.4

On the Cisco Systems homepage, visitors use hierarchical menus to select a category of products or services, and then a specific product or service.

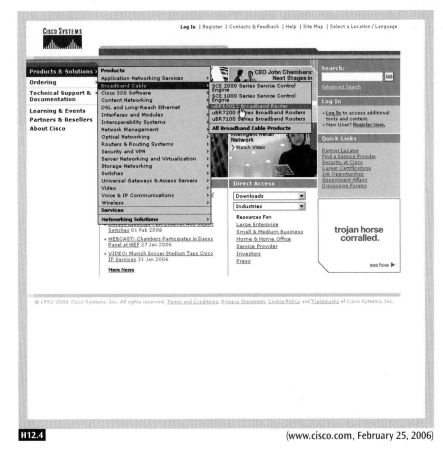

H12.4 (www.cisco.com, February 25, 2006)

and a new product-specific page loads. Although it does not address the problem of creating menus directly, the HIERARCHICAL ORGANIZATION (B3) pattern offers some tips on creating an effective hierarchy.

One problem with hierarchical menus, however, is that in poor implementations, customers need to move the mouse cursor along a narrow path provided by the text of the primary option as they make their way to the secondary option. Precise control of the mouse is required, and this can make it difficult to reach the desired submenu. The problem is only exacerbated if the menus use small fonts. In addition, older browsers and certain devices have difficulty rendering hierarchical menus properly. Even the most current browsers require different coding tricks to implement them consistently.

Fine-Tune the Hierarchical Menu Performance • To make hierarchical menus easier to use, you can configure the secondary menus to appear after a visitor has hovered over a primary menu selection for a second or two, or after the primary menu has been clicked. Once the secondary menu appears, make it "sticky" by locking it in place for a few seconds, even if the visitor moves the mouse off the primary menu selection. Because a visitor can mouse over other primary options without bringing up different secondary menus, the path to selecting the proper secondary option is widened considerably, making it much easier to reach. In addition, keeping the menus visible even if the cursor leaves the menu area entirely for up to a second or two forgives visitors for being a little off the mark with the mouse.

✳ SOLUTION

When you have too many hierarchically organized items to fit in a single pick list, you can create drill-down options using multiple, hierarchical pick lists or menus. If you use multiple pick lists, deactivate the secondary and tertiary pick lists until the customer selects a parent pick list option. If you use hierarchical menus, configure the secondary and tertiary menus to stay visible for a second or two even if customers move the mouse away from the parent option.

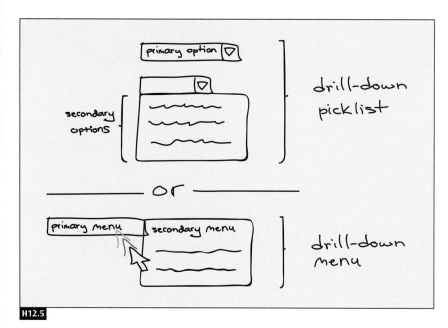

Figure H12.5

Drill-down options allow your customers to quickly pick interdependent options from multiple pick lists or hierarchical menus without having to wade through all of the possible combinations of options.

❋ OTHER PATTERNS TO CONSIDER

Secondary menus can be loaded when the original page loads, or if the lists are too numerous or too long, try FAST-LOADING CONTENT (L6) dynamically as it is needed. If you have many items, consider organizing them into a hierarchy. Although it does not address the problem directly, the HIERARCHICAL ORGANIZATION (B3) pattern offers some ways of making an effective hierarchy.

Drill-down options are an alternative to PREDICTIVE INPUT (H11) for making CLEAR FORMS (H10) easier to fill out. Choose the best option based on how many items will be in the pick list and how dynamic the items are.

H13 PROGRESS BAR

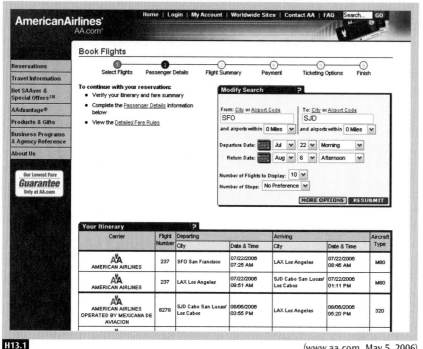

(www.aa.com, May 5, 2006)

Figure H13.1

On its Web site, American Airlines shows the steps that customers need to take to plan a flight and purchase a ticket, setting expectations up front and showing progress along the way.

✳ BACKGROUND

PROCESS FUNNELS (H1) are used by many other patterns, including PERSONAL E-COMMERCE (A1), WEB APPS THAT WORK (A10), and QUICK-FLOW CHECKOUT (F1), to lead visitors through a set sequence of tasks, such as the purchase of a product. Process funnels often need to show customers their progress through the task sequence to help reassure them of where they are in the process.

✳ PROBLEM

Web site visitors become frustrated when a process takes longer than they expect.

H1 Some of the multistep PROCESS FUNNELS (H1) commonly implemented in Web sites can take a long time to complete. However, customers might abandon the process if they have no idea how many steps are left in the process funnel. The frustration that customers experience when they abandon a process creates a bad impression of the Web site, and this dissatisfaction might spread by word of mouth.

Provide Process Feedback • It behooves site owners to explain to their customers what a process entails and approximately how long it will take. A progress bar gives customers feedback on where they are in a multistep sequence (see Figure H13.1), so they know how much more is left. A progress bar can consist of several elements, depending on the nature of the progress and the amount of information you want to provide to site visitors.

Outline the Major Steps • One of the primary functions of a progress bar is to indicate what kinds of information or activities are involved at each step of a process. Most progress bars name the steps in the process to give customers an indication of what's occurring at any given time. For example, Figure H13.2 shows the customer that she is on the "SHIPPING & PAYMENT" step. (A Web site designer might choose not to name the steps in a progress bar for space considerations—when there are many steps or when the steps are too complex to name.) Progress bars also usually specify the overall goal of the process. For example, the final step in Figure H13.2 is "PLACE ORDER," reminding people that they're in a QUICK-FLOW

F1 CHECKOUT (F1).

Visually Indicate Where the Customer Is in the Process • Progress bars commonly provide visual indications of what steps in the process have been completed, what step is currently being performed, and what steps in the process remain to be completed (see Figure H13.1). Completed steps might appear in a dimmer shade of the current step color to indicate that they've been viewed, for example, while the steps remaining might appear in light gray to indicate that they're yet to come. If you use

K5 HIGH-VISIBILITY ACTION BUTTONS (K5), customers move forward only by pressing these buttons.

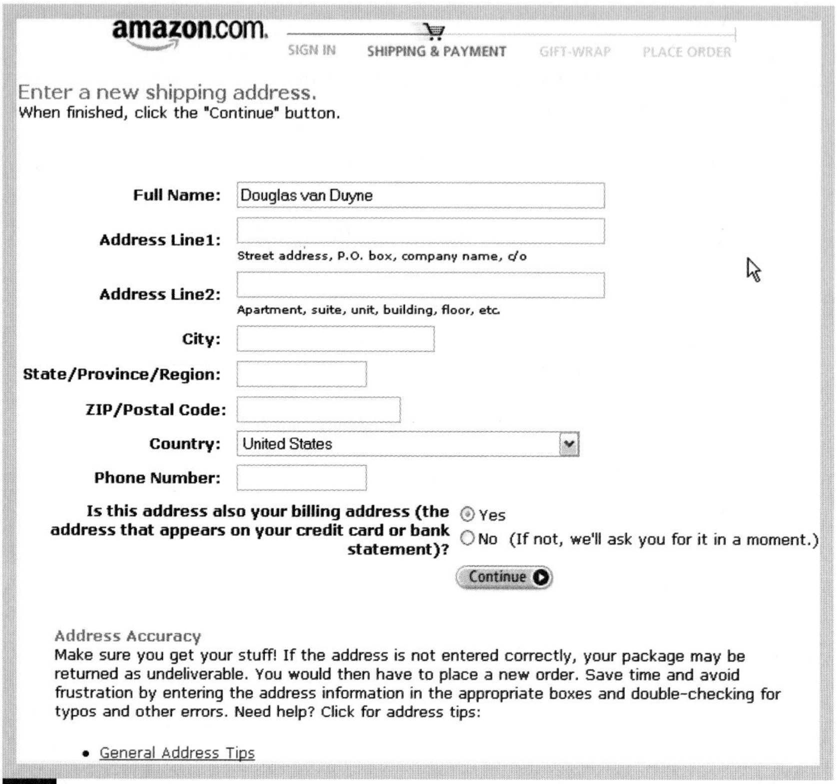

H13.2

(www.amazon.com, May 5, 2006)

Figure H13.2

The progress bar at the top of the Amazon.com checkout page specifies "PLACE ORDER" as the ultimate goal of the process, to which all of the previous steps are leading.

Design the Progress Bar to Communicate Information Clearly • You can place a progress bar anywhere on a Web page, but most progress bars are found running horizontally near the top of the screen. When selecting the steps that will appear in the progress bar, keep in mind that the object of creating the bar in the first place is to comfort your customers and give them strong feedback about where they are in the overall process. Avoid design decisions that will compound their frustration, such as putting too many steps in the bar, which might lead customers to believe that the process will take too long. The progress bar steps do not all have to be exactly proportional, because the steps don't necessarily all take the same amount of time. If a single step is much longer than the others, however, the whole process may appear long.

Provide Direct Step Navigation • Although some processes consist of steps that must be performed in order, others benefit from the customer's ability to navigate directly to any step in the process. To provide this ability, you can convert the steps in a progress bar into buttons or tabs, or create a "wizard" by including **Back** and **Next** buttons at each step of the process (see Figure H13.3).

You might also consider creating a clickable progress bar using a tablike interface in which people can select the step they wish to jump to and **K3** proceed there immediately. Using a TAB ROW (K3) in this way might make sense in a product configurator, if the customer has already selected the product model and no options depend on other options (as in Figure H13.3).

Figure H13.3

Honda's Web site enables customers to configure a custom automobile by selecting a model, trim level, and accessories. Because the configuration steps do not depend on each other once the model has been selected, the elements of the progress bar appear as tabs, which customers can select to jump to any step in the configuration process. Customers can also click the **GO BACK** and **NEXT STEP** buttons to step back and forth through the process.

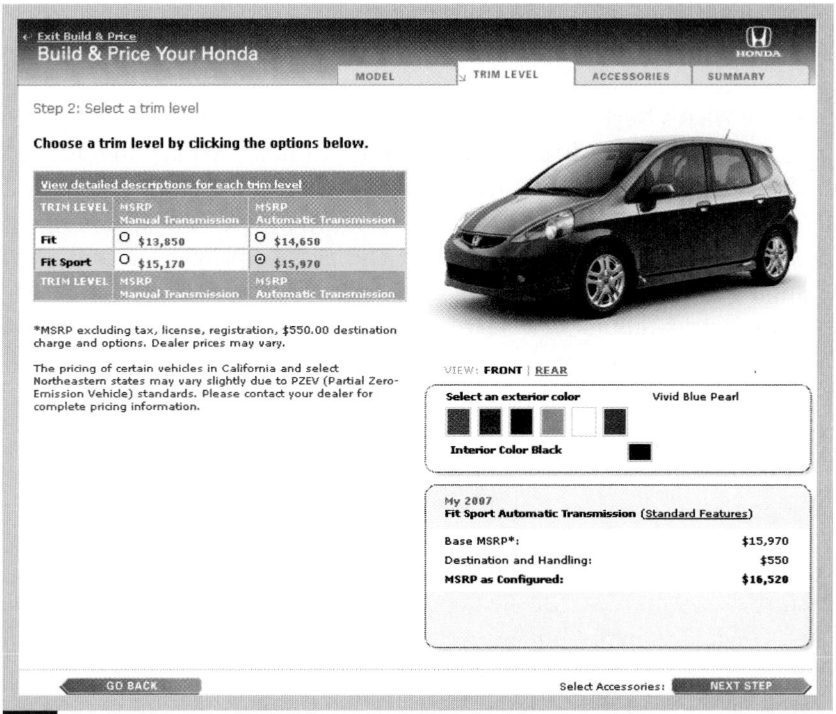

(www.automobiles.honda.com, May 5, 2006)

If some of the options do depend on others, you can have the system update the dependent options once a verification screen indicates to the customer the consequences of the choice.

If you decide to make a clickable progress bar, use text or graphics to make it clear that the individual steps are clickable. You might need other buttons to help people move through the process linearly. Conversely, if you decide to create a progress bar that is nonclickable, avoid making the elements look as though they're clickable and make sure to label them so that they look like steps—for example, "1 2 3 4."

Include Edit **Buttons** • Another method of providing a means to alter the steps of a process is to create buttons that allow customers to edit information that they've already supplied. For example, a QUICK-FLOW CHECKOUT (F1) procedure would typically include a step requiring customers to supply a mailing address. On subsequent screens, an appropriately located edit button would make it possible for customers to modify address information that they had previously entered incorrectly (see Figure H13.4), without losing the data that they entered during the intervening steps of the process. **(F1)**

Indicate What's Next • One method of minimizing customer annoyance with the length of a process is to indicate in detail what's involved in the next step (see Figure H13.5). Although each step in a progress bar is labeled, sometimes these labels are not sufficiently detailed. Adding an explanatory sentence for each step in the process provides more information for the customers and makes them less likely to abandon the process in frustration.

Skip Unnecessary Steps • Customers need to be able to skip unnecessary steps in a PROCESS FUNNEL (H1). If a choice that the customer makes early in a process eliminates the subsequent steps, then simply skip the later steps in the progress bar and show them as if they were completed. Don't remove steps from the progress bar in the course of the process (or add them, for that matter) because this might confuse the customer. **(H1)**

Figure H13.4

The Apple Store contains a progress bar that indicates the customer's place in the checkout process. In this example, the customer has reached the verify/edit stage, meaning that billing and shipping addresses have already been entered. However, the two **Change this address** buttons enable the customer to return to earlier stages in the checkout process to correct any mistakes made during the input of address information.

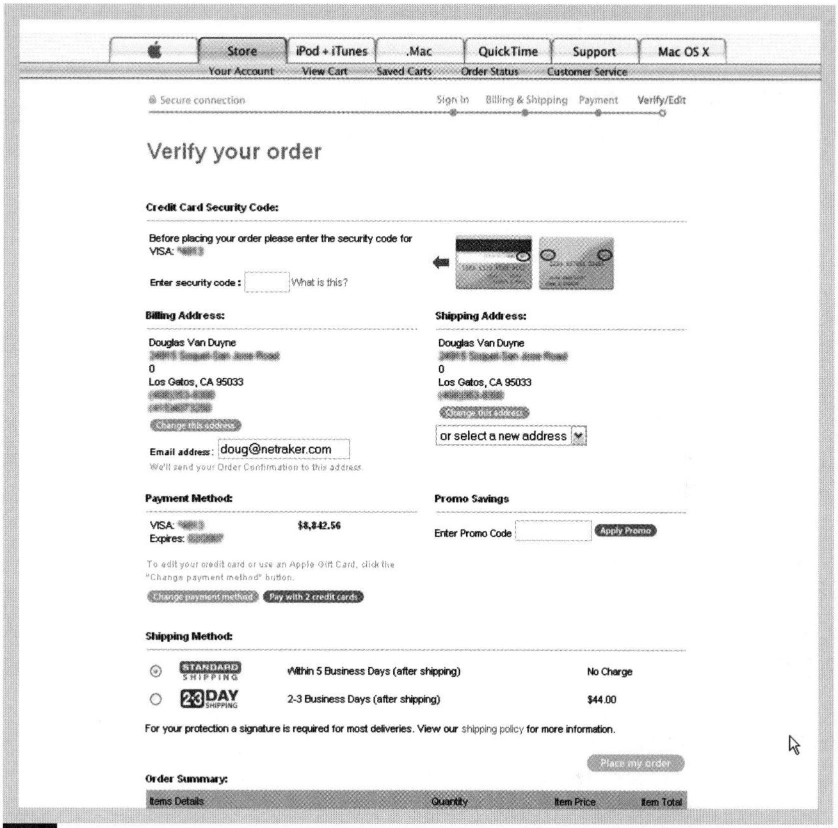

H13.4

(www.store.apple.com, May 5, 2006)

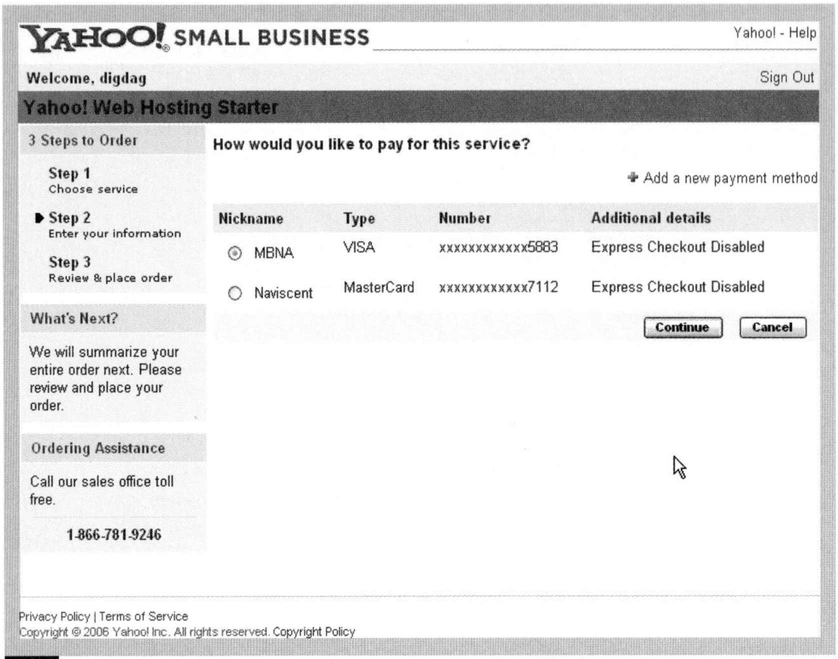

Figure H13.5

The Yahoo! Small Business site uses a progress bar that runs down the left side of the screen rather than across the top, and it includes a **What's Next?** box that explains what will happen during the next step of the process.

(smallbusiness.yahoo.com, May 5, 2006)

✳ SOLUTION

Outline the major steps in a process and visually indicate which steps have been completed, what the current step is, and what steps are yet to come. Label your progress bar steps with a summary of what will be expected, if space allows. You might also indicate what will be coming in the next step. When building a progress bar that can skip from any step to any other step, make the steps appear clickable.

Figure H13.6

Progress bars set customers' expectations as to where they are in a process and how many more steps are left.

H13.6

✷ OTHER PATTERNS TO CONSIDER

Use HIGH-VISIBILITY ACTION BUTTONS (K5) that let your customers move forward and back. When information that completes some steps in a PROCESS FUNNEL (H1) is supplied automatically, such as by the use of SIGN-IN/NEW ACCOUNT (H2) rather than a GUEST ACCOUNT (H3), treat the steps as completed and leave them in the progress bar. Use OBVIOUS LINKS (K10) or a TAB ROW (K3) to make it clear when elements of a progress bar are clickable.

Designing Effective Page Layouts

It can be difficult to design structured, ordered layouts for Web pages. This pattern group describes how to create layouts that your customers will find clear, predictable, and easy to understand.

I1 GRID LAYOUT

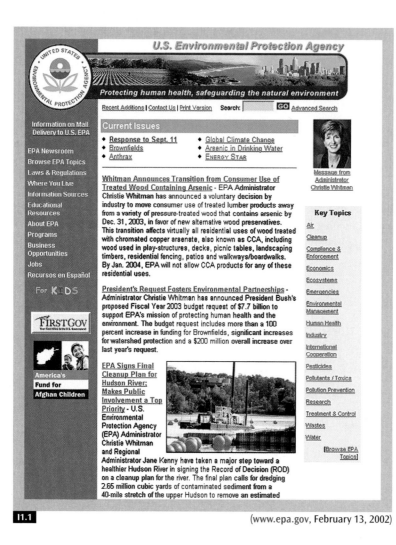

I1.1

(www.epa.gov, February 13, 2002)

Figure I1.1

The Environmental Protection Agency's Web site has a strong grid layout. The navigation bar runs along the left side, and features like **Recent Additions** and **Search** run along the top. The main content is in the center, and relevant side content is on the right.

✳ BACKGROUND

A major step in creating a PAGE TEMPLATE (D1) is designing a clean grid layout, one that will give your Web pages structure and coherence. This pattern describes grid layouts and how to create one. You can use this pattern in conjunction with ABOVE THE FOLD (I2), CLEAR FIRST READS (I3), EXPANDING SCREEN WIDTH (I4), and FIXED SCREEN WIDTH (I5) when you're designing a page template.

D1

I2 **I3**

I4 **I5**

✳ PROBLEM

It is difficult to organize the many competing elements of a Web page in a cohesive manner without creating clutter and overwhelming the reader.

Grid layout is a technique from graphic design used for organizing page layouts for newspapers, magazines, and other documents. It can also be used to organize the content of your Web pages. In a grid layout, a page is divided into rows and columns, and every element is made to fit within this grid. Constant design elements, such as titles and logos, always appear in the same place, giving a consistent theme to every page.

There are three advantages to using grid layout:

1. It gives your entire Web site a coherent visual structure, making it easier for your customers to predict where they'll be able to find elements such as page titles, NAVIGATION BARS (K2), and CONTENT MODULES (D2).

2. It reduces clutter and gives your site visitors strong visual cues to follow, making things easier to find and text quicker to read.

3. Once it has been designed, your design team can reuse it, giving them more time to focus on content development instead of reinventing the wheel. They can place new content into the right place in the grid every time.

The sections that follow present some guidelines for creating grid layouts.

Identify the Elements That Are Common throughout Your Web Site • Decide which elements are essential and which are common to the majority of your pages, such as the logo, NAVIGATION BARS (K2), SEARCH ACTION MODULES (J1), PRIVACY POLICY (E4), and CONTENT MODULES (D2) containing news items, stock quotes, travel information, and sports scores. Use these elements to anchor the structure of your Web pages.

Sketch Out Grid Layouts That Incorporate the Common Elements • Rough out several grids that combine the basic elements of your Web site in a design that you can use consistently. Group related items together; keep unrelated items separate. Keep in mind that people have already developed expectations about where certain design elements will appear. For example, research conducted at Wichita State University suggests that people expect links to the SHOPPING CART (F3), ACCOUNT MANAGEMENT (H4), and CONTEXT-SENSITIVE HELP (H8) to be at the top right; a SIGN-IN/NEW ACCOUNT (H2)

link to be near the top left; and a clickable logo that leads back to the HOMEPAGE PORTAL (C1) to be in the top left corner.

C1

Create Sample Web Pages and Get Feedback • Use your sketches to create rough Web pages, and test them for usability with your customers. See if the placement of your elements makes sense to them. "Greek" the text by changing it to nonsense words, and see if your customers can still guess the basic elements of the Web site on the basis of position and layout.[1] Use this feedback to fix potential errors early in the process, when they are still easy to correct. [For more information on getting feedback in usability tests, see Appendix A (Running Usability Evaluations).]

Make related elements look similar, either by grouping them near each other or by making them the same in size, color, and font. Leave proper spacing between unrelated elements. For example, visually separate your navigation from other images and the main text. Thin lines can also be used to emphasize elements.

Study How Other Web Pages Implement Their Grids • If you understand how other Web sites use and implement their grid layouts, you will find it easier to implement your own. Many older Web pages use HTML tables for grids, making them quite easy to reverse-engineer. Go to a Web site and save one of the Web pages to your computer. Then open the Web page in a text editor. Find every instance of *border="0"* and change it to *border="1"*. Now you're ready to open the local copy of the Web page in your Web browser. You should be able to see the overall grid and how each individual element fits in. Doing this for newer Web sites that make use of XHTML and/or STYLE SHEETS (D11) is just as easy. First save the entire Web page, including images and style sheets. Then open the Web page in a text editor, go to the bottom of the Web page, and add the HTML lines shown in Figure I1.2. Once you save your changes and load the file into your Web browser, you should see a thin border around any <div> and <table> elements in the Web page, making it easy to see how the grid layout is set up.

D11

---

1 Most Web designers use a variation of a poem for greeking. It starts with "Lorem ipsum dolor sit amet." Oddly enough, this poem, written in Latin, historically has always been quoted incorrectly.

Figure I1.2

When this code is added to your pages, it lets you view all the <div> and <table> structures.

```
<style type="text/css">
    div {
        border: solid black 1px;
        }
    table {
        border: solid black 1px;
        }
</style>
```

I1.2

✳ SOLUTION

Create a grid layout that you can use to organize all of the elements on a Web page. Sketch out multiple grid layouts to see if they can accommodate the most important navigation and content elements. Run usability tests on the grid layouts by greeking the navigation and content, and determine if customers can guess the elements solely on the basis of position and layout.

Figure I1.3

Align the navigation and content on your Web pages in a grid layout.

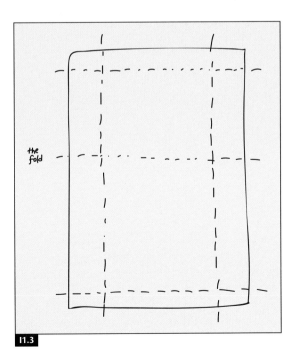

I1.3

✳ OTHER PATTERNS TO CONSIDER

Grid layout is one part of the PAGE TEMPLATE (D1) pattern. The three most important elements of a grid layout are NAVIGATION BARS (K2), SEARCH ACTION MODULES (J1), and CONTENT MODULES (D2).

Grid layouts need to take into consideration which elements will be ABOVE THE FOLD (I2)—that is, which elements customers will be able to see without having to scroll down. Design your layout to emphasize a CLEAR FIRST READ (I3)—that is, the first element that visitors typically see on a page.

Many of the items you place in the grid will be CONTENT MODULES (D2) containing dynamically retrieved content. One issue to consider is that these modules will vary in length, making it more difficult to have precise control over the layout of a Web page.

In older Web sites, grid layouts are often implemented using HTML tables. Splitting large tables into SEPARATE TABLES (L3) can speed up the load time of these Web pages. For newer Web sites, we advocate using XHTML and STYLE SHEETS (D11) rather than using tables for layout.

Figure I2.1

Each of the solid red lines here represents a different fold, or the imaginary line marking the bottom of the area that customers with different screen sizes would see when viewing a Web page without having to scroll down. The most important things should go at the top, where they are visible to all visitors and easy to access.

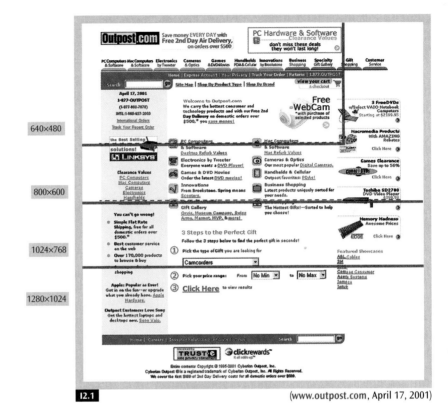

640×480

800×600

1024×768

1280×1024

I2.1

(www.outpost.com, April 17, 2001)

❇ BACKGROUND

Site visitors don't always scroll down, so they can miss important information if it's not positioned well. This pattern describes why your most important information should be at the top of a Web page, and how to design your Web site accordingly. Use this pattern with GRID LAYOUT (I1), CLEAR FIRST READS (I3), EXPANDING SCREEN WIDTH (I4), and FIXED SCREEN WIDTH (I5) when you're designing a PAGE TEMPLATE (D1).

✳ PROBLEM

Customers often miss navigation elements and content if they have to scroll down to see them.

The term *above the fold* comes from the newspaper business because newspapers are folded in half when they're sold on the street. Newspaper editors know to put the most important stories above the fold of the front page to draw attention and drive sales. On the Web, *above the fold* refers to what your customers can see on your Web page without having to scroll down. Visitors don't always realize that they can scroll down, or that there's more information below. Therefore, it makes sense to put all the vital links and content at the top.

The difference between designing for the fold in print and on the Web is that on the Web, you don't always know the size of the customer's screen. Consequently, you can't be sure of what a customer who visits your site will see.

Figure I2.1 shows what visitors with screens of different sizes would see on Outpost.com's Web site. The designers did a good job of positioning the most important elements toward the top left of the page, making these the first things that everyone will see. A common mistake of Web sites is to have too much unimportant information at the top of a page, while pushing more important content below the fold. This problem is common on sites with large logos or advertising banners.

Because what goes above the fold constitutes the most important real estate on the page, marketing people will want to place their ads and featured products there, programmers will want to display the functionality they just implemented, and designers will want to show off their graphic design skills. You will have to combine business needs, usability needs, customer experience needs, and aesthetics to find a design that everyone can agree on.

The sections that follow describe our solution for designing above the fold.

Choose a Minimum Screen Resolution to Support • The first step is to survey your customers to determine their screen resolutions and decide how many customers you want to support. How many view Web pages at a resolution of 800×600 pixels? How many at 1024×768? How many have something better? Ultimately, you will have to decide on the minimum size that your Web site will support. This minimum will not cut out visitors with smaller screens entirely, but it will make reading and navigating your Web pages a little more difficult for those customers.

You can use AnyBrowser.com to open up Web pages at a desired resolution, making it easy to see what your Web site would look like to your customers.

Determine the Elements That Must Be above the Fold • Research conducted at Wichita State University suggests that people have already developed expectations as to where certain design elements will be located. For example, people expected the SHOPPING CART (F3), ACCOUNT MANAGEMENT (H4), and CONTEXT-SENSITIVE HELP (H8) links to be at the top right, a SIGN-IN/NEW ACCOUNT (H2) link to be near the top left, and a clickable logo leading back to the HOMEPAGE PORTAL (C1) to be in the top left corner. Other elements to consider positioning above the fold include the page title, a CLEAR FIRST READ (I3), NAVIGATION BARS (K2), advertisements, and CONTENT MODULES (D2). Try out various layouts and have your clients and customers rank them to see which one works best for the most people.

✳ SOLUTION

Make sure that the most important material is at the top of each page of your Web site, easily visible and easily accessible. Test the page to see how it looks on various screen sizes and to make sure that the important navigation elements and content are always visible.

Figure 12.2

Put the most important navigation elements and content above the fold, where people can see them immediately.

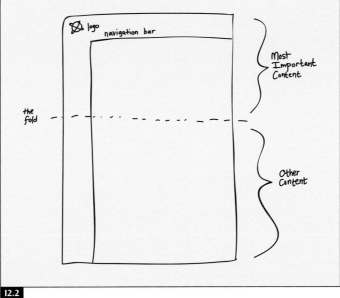

✳ OTHER PATTERNS TO CONSIDER

Page elements that should be above the fold include NAVIGATION BARS (K2), SEARCH ACTION MODULES (J1), and CLEAR FIRST READS (I3). Other page elements to consider include LOCATION BREAD CRUMBS (K6), HEADLINES AND BLURBS (D3), FEATURED PRODUCTS (G1), and PERSONALIZED RECOMMENDATIONS (G3).

Above the fold is especially important for PROCESS FUNNELS (H1) such as QUICK-FLOW CHECKOUT (F1) and SIGN-IN/NEW ACCOUNT (H2). These kinds of processes often use HIGH-VISIBILITY ACTION BUTTONS (K5) to help guide people through a task.

The CLEAR FIRST READS (I3) pattern stresses the use of font, size, color, and position of a single element to give your Web page something that most people will see first. However, first reads need to be balanced with concerns about what material is positioned above the fold, because first reads may take up precious screen real estate and reduce the number of items that can be added. CLEAR FIRST READS (I3) also emphasizes designing for a specific screen resolution, and points out that you have to design at a slightly lower resolution than the screen resolutions that your customers have.

Figure I3.1

What's the first thing you see when you look at this page? Through a combination of position, font, color, size, and graphic design, the image of the shoes and the headline "Slip into the shoe that's taking America by storm" are the items that pop out best. The first read helps to set expectations and conveys a wealth of subtle information to your customers. This first read tells the visitor that these shoes are featured and popular with other customers.

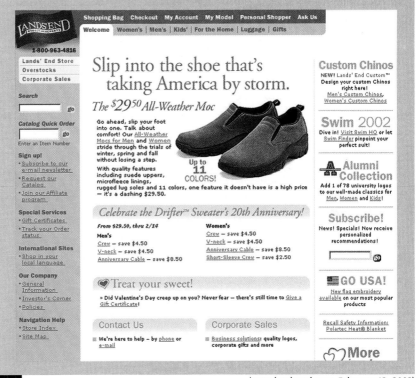

I3.1

(www.landsend.com, February 13, 2002)

✳ BACKGROUND

Although your Web page may contain many elements, your customers must be able to easily find the most important item on the page. This pattern covers first reads, a technique from graphic design that helps focus Web pages and gives readers a clear first impression. You can apply this pattern to the creation of a PAGE TEMPLATE (D1), and you can use it with GRID LAYOUT (I1), ABOVE THE FOLD (I2), EXPANDING SCREEN WIDTH (I4), and FIXED SCREEN WIDTH (I5) when you're designing a page template.

✳ PROBLEM

How can a Web page be designed with a single unifying focus when so many visual elements are competing for attention?

As a Web designer, you have many goals for each page on your Web site. However, these goals often conflict and could cause you to lose focus. With all of the information on each page vying for a customer's attention, you need something that unifies the entire page.

The **first read** is one technique that brings order to your Web pages. Think of it as an overall first impression, a gestalt feeling that sets the theme for the entire Web page. The first read is the dominant visual element that fuses all of the disparate elements of the Web page.

In this section we describe some approaches for creating effective first reads on every page.

Determine the Most Important Element on Each Page • For each group of pages, find a focus. Some common choices include the following:

- Company logo
- Page title
- News headline
- Advertisement
- Product name
- Product image

Use Multiple Features to Differentiate the First Read • By coordinating features such as color, size, font, weight (for example, boldface), and position, you can make an effective first read that stands out. With color, for example, you want to make the first read contrast well with the page background. Complementary colors or colors that have good contrast, such as black text on white, work well here.

In terms of size, it's a good idea to make the first read larger than the surrounding elements. In Figure I3.1, note that the first-read text and the image of the shoes are larger than any other text or image on the entire page. Similarly, the first-read image of the cupcakes in Figure I3.2 dominates the page, and the first-read text "SUMMER SALE" is larger than any other text on the page, with the exception of the brand "Williams-Sonoma" in the upper left corner.

Clean, easy-to-read sans serif fonts, such as **Arial** or **Verdana**, work well. On the first read, these fonts will not look cluttered. (Sans serif fonts make

Figure 13.2

The large picture of cupcakes near the center of Williams-Sonoma's homepage immediately draws people's eyes.

13.2

(www.williams-sonoma.com, July 21, 2006)

clean text headers for the same reason.) Stay away from hard-to-read, overly ornate faces, such as MS Comic Sans.

The first read should be positioned near the top left of the page for two reasons. First, many sites use a page layout that naturally converges at the top left corner. They use "inverse L" NAVIGATION BARS (K2)—that is, navigation bars positioned along the top and left side. Visitors tend to look at the top left first because these navigation bars come together there. Second, most of your customers will be reading from left to right and top to bottom, so it's natural to have the first read at the top left. This is not a firm rule, though. Other constraints may make it necessary to place the first read elsewhere.

Like the concept of ABOVE THE FOLD (I2), this placement strategy also came from newspapers. Readers go to the top of the page, where the designer placed the first read. Then the design lures them through the page to the bottom right, where they turn the page because that's all that's left to do.

Design for Lower-Resolution Displays • One quirk about the Web is that you don't necessarily know what kind of display size your customers will have. Few people still have displays with only 640×480 resolution. Some may still have 800×600 resolution, but most now have at least 1024×700 resolution, and a few will have better resolution. Survey your customers and gather the statistics for your target customers so that you can create the most effective design for them.

Design your Web pages to work at a slightly lower resolution than the resolution of your customers' monitors. Remember that Web browsers, with the browser buttons and scroll bar, take up space themselves. In addition, not all of your customers will have their Web browsers maximized to fit the entire screen. You can use AnyBrowser.com to quickly test what your Web pages will look like at a given resolution.

Test Your First Reads • Create a high-fidelity mock-up of a sample Web page. The mock-up can be anything from an image to an HTML page. Show the mock-up to some representative customers for a few seconds. Ask them what they remember about the page and what they think the page is about. Revise your first read if a majority of these test customers did not understand the point of the page, and keep doing quick tests until you come up with a design that satisfies both you and your customers.

Also try out the first read on a range of screen resolutions that are different from the resolution for which you designed it.

✳ SOLUTION

Use a first read to give each page a unifying focus on the most important message, and to emphasize the most important element of that page. Use color, size, font, weight, and position to differentiate and highlight the first read. Design for lower-resolution displays, and test your first reads with your customers to see if they're effective.

Figure 13.3

Use color, size, font, weight, and position to create a first read that communicates the most important point on each of your Web pages.

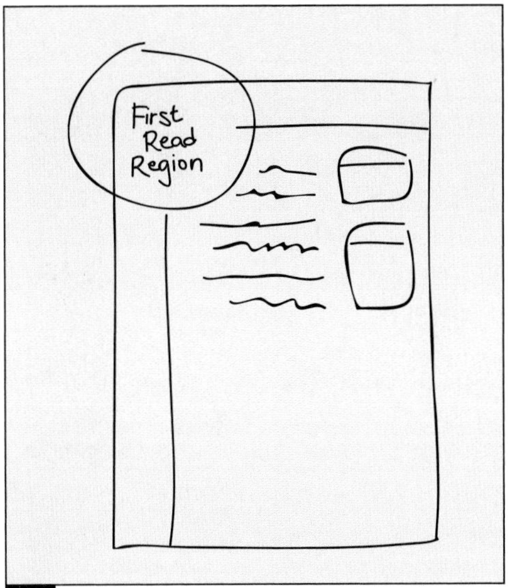

13.3

✳ OTHER PATTERNS TO CONSIDER

Apply clear first reads when you create PAGE TEMPLATES (D1). You can also use clear first reads with the GRID LAYOUT (I1), ABOVE THE FOLD (I2), EXPANDING SCREEN WIDTH (I4), and FIXED SCREEN WIDTH (I5) patterns.

First reads are often located in the top left corner of a Web page, affecting the layout and placement of NAVIGATION BARS (K2).

If you use an image as the first read, make it a FAST-LOADING IMAGE (L2). If you're working on an older Web site that still uses HTML tables for layout, place your first reads in SEPARATE TABLES (L3) for faster loading.

EXPANDING SCREEN WIDTH

Figure I4.1

iWon uses an expanding screen width—one that looks good on varying screen sizes. Note that the left and right columns remain constantly sized, while the center column expands.

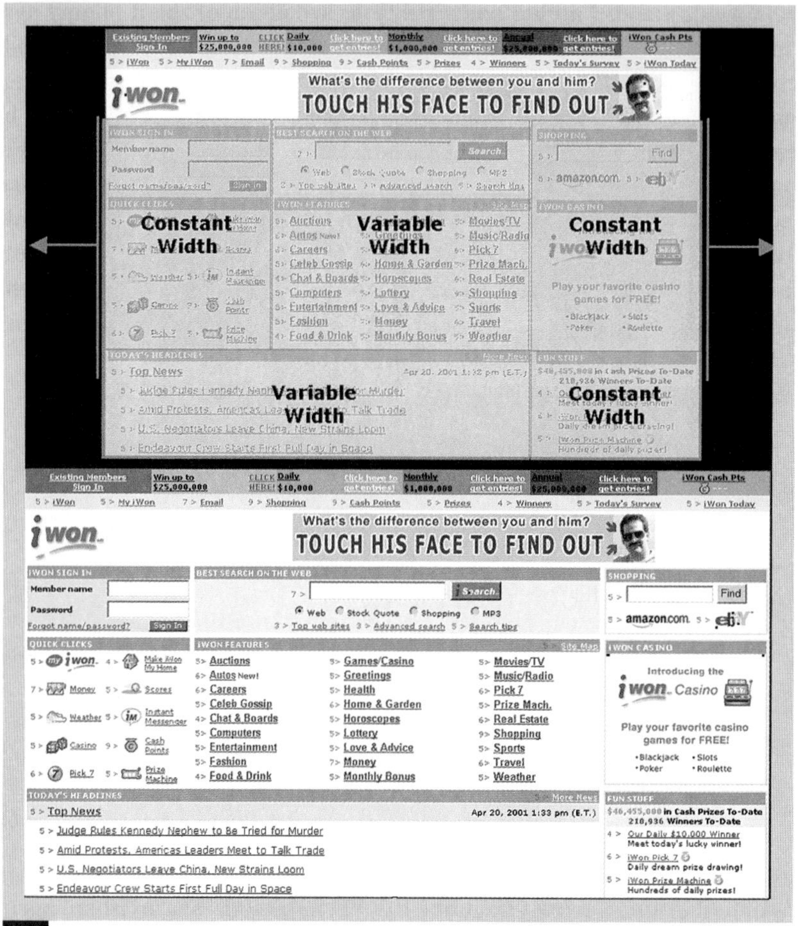

I4.1

(www.iwon.com, April 20, 2001)

✳ BACKGROUND

Designers often create a site for one screen size. In general, this strategy works, but sometimes Web pages, especially those with lots of navigation elements and content, are left with a great deal of wasted empty space. This pattern describes how to design your Web pages to take advantage of a larger than expected screen size. You can apply it when creating a PAGE TEMPLATE (D1), and you can use it together with GRID LAYOUT (I1) and ABOVE THE FOLD (I2).

D1 · I1 · I2

❋ PROBLEM

Many Web pages are packed with navigation elements and content but don't take advantage of extra space when visitors resize the browser to make it larger.

Web sites often don't take advantage of the extra space that results when customers make their browsers bigger, keeping the layout and content of the page the same. But the empty space resulting from such expansion of the screen offers the opportunity for displaying more content.

Use expanding screen width to make Web pages adapt to different widths. Expanding screen width uses features in HTML and STYLE SHEETS (D11) to adjust to the size of the Web browser as it shrinks and grows. In the sections that follow, we describe some techniques for implementing an expanding screen width.

Use Relative Table Widths to Create Expanding-Width Web Pages • Create expanding screen widths by using relative-width HTML tables. In HTML you can specify table widths as either absolute or relative values. Absolute widths are expressed in terms of pixel sizes and are calculated only once by the Web browser. For example, the expression *<table width="60">* would create a table exactly 60 pixels wide.

Relative widths are expressed in terms of percentages and are recalculated dynamically, so they expand properly every time the customer resizes a Web browser window. For example, the expression *<table width="80%">* would create a table that is exactly 80 percent of the current width of the Web browser window.

Mix Absolute and Relative Widths to Fix the Width of Some Parts of a Web Page • You can make specific columns within a table fixed width or relative width. Many Web site designs take advantage of this feature by making the navigation and side content on the left and right sides fixed, while letting the center content expand. Figure I4.2 shows an example of how to do this in HTML.

Figure I4.3 shows what the sample illustrated in Figure I4.2 looks like in a Web browser set at three different browser sizes.

You can obtain the same expanding-width screen using W3C (World Wide Web Consortium) standards–compliant XHTML and STYLE SHEETS (D11). Because of implementation bugs, however, there will be a few minor quirks in how it will be displayed in various Web browsers. Roughly speaking, your HTML will look like Figure I4.4.

```
<html>
<body>

<!-- this makes the entire table expanding width -->
<table width="100%" border="1">
    <tr>

        <!-- the left column is fixed at 170 pixels -->
        <td width="170">
            Fixed width left
        </td>

        <!-- the browser puts any leftover space here -->
        <!-- making this column expand to fill up space -->
        <td>
            Expanding-width content goes over here. This
            sentence is extra long just to underscore this
            point.
        </td>

        <!-- the right column is fixed at 170 pixels -->
        <td width="170">
            Fixed width right
        </td>
    </tr>
</table>

</body>
</html>
```

14.2

Figure 14.2

The center column of this table expands to take better advantage of the full width of the page, while the left and right columns are fixed width.

Design Web Pages with a Minimum Width in Mind • Expanding screen widths work well, up to a point. You will find it relatively easy to create Web pages that still look good when the width is expanded, but not when the width is shrunk beyond a certain size. Currently, there are no good solutions to this problem. The best way to deal with it is to survey the computer platforms and Web browsers used by your target customers and make sure you support all the groups you care about. This point is described in more detail in ABOVE THE FOLD (I2).

I2

Figure 14.3

A common approach to fitting content on a page that will be viewed in browsers with different resolutions is to keep the outer columns fixed width and let the content in the center column expand to fit the size of the individual customer's browser window. The three variations shown here are of the same page at three different resolutions.

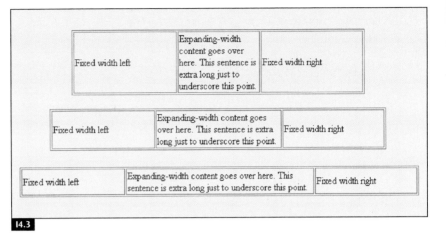

14.3

Figure 14.4

This code shows how to use style sheets to implement an expanding-width center column with fixed-width left and right columns.

```
<?xml version="1.0"?>
<!DOCTYPE html PUBLIC "-//W3C//DTD XHTML 1.0 Strict//EN"
    "http://www.w3.org/TR/xhtml1/DTD/xhtml1-strict.dtd">
<html xmlns="http://www.w3.org/1999/xhtml" xml:lang="en" lang="en">
<head>
    <title>Example title</title>
    <style type="text/css">
        /* the left column is fixed at 170 pixels */
        .boxLeft {
            float: left;
            border: solid gray 1px;
            width: 170px;
        }

        /* the browser puts any leftover space here */
        /* making this column expand to fill up space */
        .boxMid {
            width: auto;
            margin-left: 170px;
            margin-right: 170px;
            border: solid gray 1px;
        }
```

14.4

```
        /* the right column is fixed at 170 pixels */
        .boxRight {
            float: right;
            border: solid gray 1px;
            width: 170px;
        }
    </style>
</head>
<body>

    <!-- here is the left box -->
    <div class="boxLeft">
        Fixed width left
    </div>

    <!-- here is the right box -->
    <div class="boxRight">
        Fixed width right
    </div>

    <!-- here is the middle box -->
    <div class="boxMid">
        Expanding-width content goes over here. This
        sentence is extra long just to underscore this
        point.
    </div>

</body>
</html>
```

14.4

Figure 14.4

(*Continued*)

✳ SOLUTION

Design your Web pages to use an expanding screen width that you create using relative-width HTML tables or XHTML-based style sheets. Keep the basic navigation elements at fixed width, and let the center area containing the main content expand.

Figure I4.5

Use expanding screen widths when you want your Web pages to fill the entire Web browser.

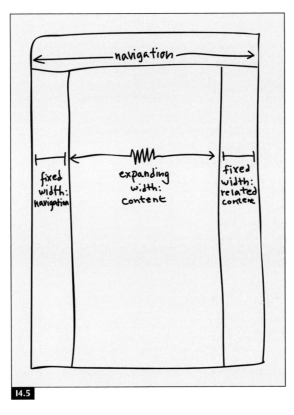

14.5

✳ OTHER PATTERNS TO CONSIDER

Contrasting with expanding screen width is FIXED SCREEN WIDTH (I5). It is useful to make pages fixed width if they contain few navigation elements and the main portion of the page emphasizes a single passage of text. Also make a Web page fixed width if you need strong control over its layout and appearance.

Use expanding screen widths in conjunction with GRID LAYOUT (I1) and ABOVE THE FOLD (I2) when creating PAGE TEMPLATES (D1) that can be reused throughout the Web site. If you're modifying older Web sites, you may want to continue using HTML tables for layout. If you want to create Web sites compliant with newer standards, use XHTML and STYLE SHEETS (D11) to control your layout.

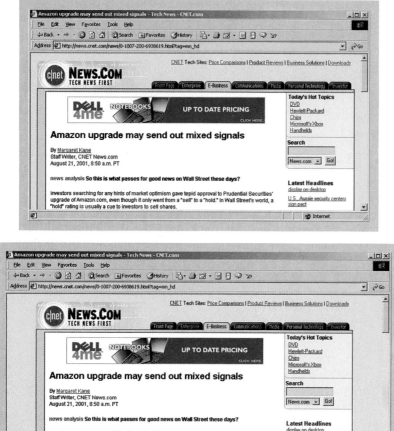

Figure I5.1

CNET News.com keeps its Web pages at a fixed width so that the content stays in the center of the page.

(www.news.com.com, August 21, 2001)

✳ BACKGROUND

Articles, essays, and other forms of online writing need to be designed for comfortable reading on computer screens. Text width is a factor that influences readability. Text that is too wide can be awkward to read. This pattern describes how to keep the text width at a fixed size for easy reading. You can apply this pattern when creating a PAGE TEMPLATE (D1), and you can use it together with GRID LAYOUT (I1) and ABOVE THE FOLD (I2).

✳ PROBLEM

Customers' browser sizes affect the amount of text they can see on the screen. When people make their browsers too large, each line of text becomes too long to read comfortably.

When text is too wide, it is difficult to skim and to find the next line of text. Use fixed screen widths to correct this problem. In contrast to EXPANDING SCREEN WIDTHS (I4), fixed screen widths keep a Web page at exactly the same width, regardless of the size of your customer's Web browser (see Figure I5.2). This is a useful technique for news and magazine articles, essays, and other long passages of text.

Usually you can implement fixed screen widths by making the table containing the main content a fixed width. Place the main content of your page either in the center of the page or on the left.

I5.2

(www.ifilm.com, February 2, 2002)

Figure I5.2

IFILM keeps its Web pages at a fixed width, choosing to keep the content on the left side of the page when the Web browser window is expanded.

If you're modifying an older Web site that uses HTML tables for its fixed-width layout, see Figure I5.3 for an example of how to place the content in the center.

Some Web sites keep the content on the left. This is the default if the designer does not set the <align="center"> attribute in the main table. There is no real difference between having the content on the left or in the center. It's simply a matter of style.

If you're creating a new Web site, we advise using standards-compliant XHTML and STYLE SHEETS (D11) to control layout. Figure I5.4 shows an example of how to accomplish the same layout as in Figure I5.3.

Figure I5.3

This code shows how to use tables to build an fixed-width center column and a fixed-width left column.

```
<html>
<body>

<!-- this makes the entire table fixed width -->
<table border="1">
    <tr>

        <!-- the left column is fixed at 170 pixels -->
        <td width="170">
            Fixed width left
        </td>

        <!-- the center column is fixed at 430 pixels -->
        <td width="430">
            Fixed-width content goes over here. This
            sentence is extra long just to underscore this
            point.
        </td>

    </tr>
</table>

</body>
</html>
```

I5.3

Figure 15.4

This code shows how to use style sheets to achieve the same format—fixed-width center column and fixed-width left column—that tables accomplish in Figure 15.3.

```
<?xml version="1.0"?>
<!DOCTYPE html PUBLIC "-//W3C//DTD XHTML 1.0 Strict//EN"
    "http://www.w3.org/TR/xhtml1/DTD/xhtml1-strict.dtd">
<html xmlns="http://www.w3.org/1999/xhtml" xml:lang="en"
lang="en">
<head>
    <title>Example title</title>
    <style type="text/css">

        /* the left column is fixed at 170 pixels */
        .boxLeft {
            float: left;
            border: solid gray 1px;
            width: 170px;
        }

        /* the browser puts any leftover space here */
        /* making this column fixed at 430 pixels */
        .boxMid {
            width: auto;
            margin-left: 170px;
            border: solid gray 1px;
        }

        /* lets us center everything and specify total width */
        .boxAll {
            width: 600px;
        }
    </style>
</head>
<body>
    <div class="boxAll">
        <!-- here is the left box -->
        <div class="boxLeft">
            Fixed width left
        </div>

        <!-- here is the middle box -->
        <div class="boxMid">
            Fixed-width content goes over here.
            This column is not resized.
        </div>
    </div>

</body>
</html>
```

15.4

❉ SOLUTION

Use a fixed screen width to make long tracts of text more readable by constraining the width of the text column. Create fixed screen widths by using absolute widths in your HTML tables or XHTML-based style sheets.

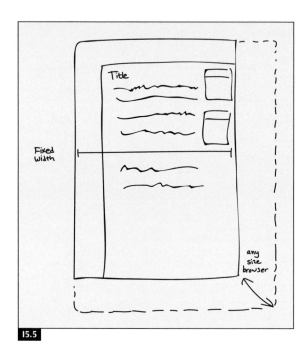

Figure I5.5

Use fixed screen widths when you want the width of your Web pages to remain constant regardless of the size of the Web browser.

❉ OTHER PATTERNS TO CONSIDER

Contrasting with fixed screen width is EXPANDING SCREEN WIDTH (I4). Expanding width is useful for pages that contain many navigation elements or a wide variety of content instead of a single passage of text. However, making a Web page expanding width reduces the amount of control you have over its overall layout and appearance.

Use fixed screen widths in conjunction with GRID LAYOUT (I1) and ABOVE THE FOLD (I2) when creating a PAGE TEMPLATE (D1) that can be reused throughout the Web site. If you're modifying older Web sites, you may want to continue using HTML tables for layout. If you want to create Web sites compliant with newer standards, use XHTML and STYLE SHEETS (D11) to control your layout.

Figure I6.1

Beliefnet, a multifaith community Web site, uses sidebars to highlight special content. This example shows **news** and **Today's Top Picks** sidebars.

I6.1

(www.beliefnet.com, January 16, 2002)

✳ BACKGROUND

In CROSS-SELLING AND UP-SELLING (G2), we discuss how it can be useful to showcase accessories and more expensive versions of the current product, to entice customers to spend more money. In UNIFIED BROWSING HIERARCHY (K1), we discuss reasons why community, content, and commerce should be combined instead of being separated into distinct categories. In HEADLINES AND BLURBS (D3), we look at ways of promoting content found on other parts of your Web site. This pattern discusses how to use a sidebar to feature these kinds of related BROWSABLE CONTENT (B2) on a Web page.

✳ PROBLEM

Finding related content on a page can be frustrating.

On content pages, such as news articles or CLEAN PRODUCT DETAILS (F2) **F2**
pages, people often want to see related items—things like similar products,
PERSONALIZED RECOMMENDATIONS (G3), other news articles on similar topics, **G3**
or MESSAGE BOARDS (D5) for further discussion. The key idea here is to **D5**
encourage customers to explore more content. The main problem is
presenting these related links to visitors in a clear and obvious manner,
without distracting them from the main content and without taking up
too much valuable page space.

One way of doing this is to place related content at the bottom of the
Web page. A potential problem, however, is that some visitors might not
see the content, especially if they have to scroll down to get to the bottom
of the page. Another way is to use consistent sidebars of related content.
These sidebars feature the related content but are placed near the top of
a Web page on the side (see Figure 16.2). This kind of layout makes the
related links easy to see and visually distinct from the main content.

The sections that follow give some tips on using sidebars of related
content.

Make the Location of Sidebars Consistent • Because NAVIGATION BARS (K2) **K2**
generally run along the top and the left of a page, and because the main
content is generally placed in the center, sidebars of related content usually
lie on the right side of a page. The easiest way to make sidebars appear in
a consistent location is to create a GRID LAYOUT (I1) for your page, parti- **I1**
tioning some space for sidebars, creating a PAGE TEMPLATE (D1) that **D1**
reflects the layout, and then using this page template for new pages.

Determine a Maximum Length for Sidebars • As discussed in CONTENT
MODULES (D2), one potential problem with sidebars is that they might be **D2**
longer than the main content, making the page layout look awkward.
One solution is to impose a maximum number of lines for each sidebar,
which can be enforced manually by editors or automatically if the content
in the sidebar is retrieved from a database.

Figure 16.2

CNN places related news stories, photo essays, and video clips in sidebars. Note the visual separation of the sidebar titled "2002 Winter Olympics, CNN/SI Winter Olympics Coverage" from the rest of the page.

16.2

(www.cnn.com, February 15, 2002)

✳ SOLUTION

Make the location of sidebars consistent by using a grid layout and page templates. Also determine a maximum length for sidebars so that the page layout will be balanced.

16.3

Figure 16.3

Consistent sidebars of related content appear in the same place on every page so that customers know where to find them.

✳ OTHER PATTERNS TO CONSIDER

Consistent sidebars of related content are often used for HEADLINES AND BLURBS (D3), CROSS-SELLING AND UP-SELLING (G2), UNIFIED BROWSING HIERARCHY (K1), and EXTERNAL LINKS (K8). EMBEDDED LINKS (K7) are sometimes used instead of sidebars.

Sidebars are often implemented as CONTENT MODULES (D2) to make it easier to automatically serve up related content. Sidebars are sometimes used to feature PERSONALIZED CONTENT (D4). A PAGE TEMPLATE (D1) can be used to make it easy to include sidebars on new pages. PRINTABLE PAGES (D8) are often stripped of sidebars to make them easier to print.

Making Site Search Fast and Relevant

Search is an essential feature of most Web sites. Make sure you have search features that are useful and usable. Pay special attention to which words customers type in, how you present the results, how customers interact with the results, and what happens if they can't find what they're looking for. This pattern group deals with designing the interaction so that your customers' searches are more effective.

J1 SEARCH ACTION MODULE

Figure J1.1

IMDb's Web site provides an effective search feature—one that is both simple and powerful.

J1.1

✻ BACKGROUND

As a standard element of MULTIPLE WAYS TO NAVIGATE (B1) and a counterpart to BROWSABLE CONTENT (B2), this pattern explains the search half of the search and browse combination.

B1
B2

✳ PROBLEM

Customers sometimes want to jump quickly from one location to another, but search pages are often too complex for such functionality.

When entering your site, customers sometimes know exactly what they're looking for. A quick and simple search function on the homepage is critical to win these visitors' confidence. Other visitors may browse through a site and then perform a search. If they don't spot a search tool immediately, or they have to go through a complex search page, they are less likely to spend the time. Building a simple search action module into every page is the best way to serve the needs of all customers.

Create a Simple Search Tool • A simple tool for searching, when possible, is much easier to understand than a complicated search page. Although advanced search tools might allow customers to look for words near another word, to search for specific words and not others, and to enter other complex search expressions, most customers would rather have a simpler tool that works well and returns ORGANIZED SEARCH RESULTS (J3). Use simple phrasing to identify the search field and provide an ACTION BUTTON (K4) for starting the search.

Some large Web sites use a search selector to help narrow the focus of a search. Figure J1.2 shows the search selector at Barnes & Noble's Web site. When designing a search selector, keep in mind two important issues. The first is to make sure that the search selector has the right default, in case it goes unnoticed. For example, the default for Barnes & Noble's site is to search on "Books." Anyone who types in something without changing the default will expect to find books on the site of a

Figure J1.2

Barnes & Noble's Web site provides a search selector that lets people search on specific categories, such as "Books" and "Music."

J1.2

(www.bn.com, January 30, 2002)

store known primarily for selling books. The second issue is size. Smaller sites that have fewer than a couple hundred pages in various categories will not be able to yield enough results to warrant a subsection search selector.

We advocate starting simply, using a straightforward search mechanism that lets people type in whatever terms they want. However, when your site becomes large and produces dozens of results to common searches, it's time to add a search selector to let people narrow their searches.

Put the Search Tool in a Consistent Place • People expect to find the search tool in the same place on every page. They might use the search function from any page on your Web site, so place the search action module ABOVE THE FOLD (I2) in the top left, middle, or right, and keep it there on every page.

✳ SOLUTION

Build a search action module into every page, using simple phrasing that indicates the search space for typing in words or phrases and providing an action button for starting the search. If you have a large site and want to give customers the ability to search a subsection, add a list of subsections and the word *for* to indicate the string to look for.

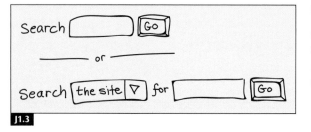

Figure J1.3

Customers will readily use the search action module if it is simple and appears on every page.

✳ OTHER PATTERNS TO CONSIDER

I2 Keep your search tool in a consistent place on every page, ABOVE THE FOLD (I2) at the top left, middle, or right.

D6 If you're WRITING FOR SEARCH ENGINES (D6) when you develop your site's search facility, customers will use your site's content more readily because the search action module will exist on every page.

Make the button that starts the search, which is often labeled "Search"
K4 or "Go," an ACTION BUTTON (K4).

When necessary, customers can fill out more detailed STRAIGHTFORWARD
J2 SEARCH FORMS (J2). Results will always be returned on an ORGANIZED
J3 SEARCH RESULTS (J3) page.

J2 STRAIGHTFORWARD SEARCH FORMS

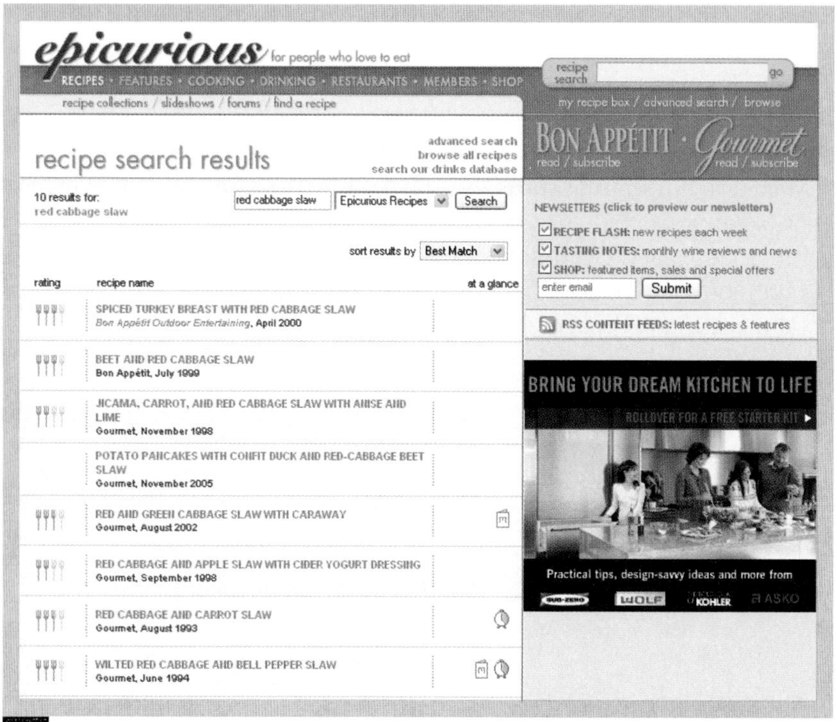

J2.1

(www.epicurious.com, June 16, 2006)

Figure J2.1

Epicurious's search form does not require much precision from the customer. Searching for "red cabbage slaw" results in recipes that have the exact term *red cabbage slaw* near the top, with variants like *red cabbage and carrot slaw* included as well.

BACKGROUND

SEARCH ACTION MODULES (J1) make it easy for your customers to find the search feature on your site. However, the way search terms are specified can confuse customers. This pattern describes how to avoid common errors with search entry forms. J1

✳ PROBLEM

Search forms are often ineffective because they require too much precision.

Search is an essential feature for most Web sites. However, most search facilities have limited value because they're designed to make searches easy for the computer to process, instead of being useful and usable for customers.

Boolean Expressions Are Hard to Understand • Boolean searches use the terms *and* and *or*. For example, the search "computer and monitor" would find all Web pages containing both *computer* and *monitor*, whereas "computer or monitor" would find all Web pages containing at least one of *computer* or *monitor*.

It's easy to add Boolean searches to a search engine. However, many studies have shown that customers find Boolean searches difficult to understand. The basic problem stems from how we use *and* and *or* in everyday conversation. For example, whereas a person would say, "I want to search for information about cats *and* dogs," the corresponding search term for computers is actually "cats *or* dogs." Help your customers by providing a search engine that does not use Boolean operators at all, or by providing a search form that has explicit phrasing, such as Google's "with *all* of the words" and "with *any* of the words."

Exact Matches Mean No Matches • Some search engines require exact matches. For example, a customer searching for "presentation" might not get any results if she types in the plural "presentations" or misspells it as "presentatino." Getting the response "no matches were found" may make customers think that there are no results at all. Web search engines can help compensate by using a dictionary to check for plurals and for misspellings.

The problem of exact matches also crops up with product names. For example, is it a *laptop* or a *notebook* computer? Is it *apparel* or *clothes?* Your customers will use different terms to mean the same thing, and the development team should design the search engine to take synonyms into consideration. Analyzing your log files, as described in ORGANIZED SEARCH RESULTS (J3), is one way to do this.

Provide Defaults for Category Searches • Some search forms require visitors to specify a category for each search. For example, a music Web site might let people search on categories such as "Artist Name" or "Album Title." But it's easy for customers to end up with no matches because they overlook the category field. To ensure that your customers will get some results, set the default action to be a search on all categories.

✳ SOLUTION

Use a search engine that does not require extreme precision. Avoid Boolean searches and exact matches. Compensate for the use of different terms to mean the same thing. Set the search engine to look across all categories by default.

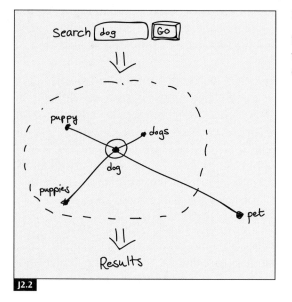

Figure J2.2

Search results should include words and concepts that are closely related.

✳ OTHER PATTERNS TO CONSIDER

Straightforward search forms need to be part of a visible SEARCH ACTION MODULE (J1) that visitors can easily find on a Web page. To assist your customers with searching, it's important to implement CLEAR FORMS (H10). In addition, ORGANIZED SEARCH RESULTS (J3) will make it easier for your customers to understand what the search engine has found for them.

Figure J3.1

In its extensive online restaurant guide, Zagat lets its customers sort by name, cuisine, area, food (F), décor (D), service (S), and cost (C). It also shows a restaurant's address and phone number, as well as a short excerpt from the review.

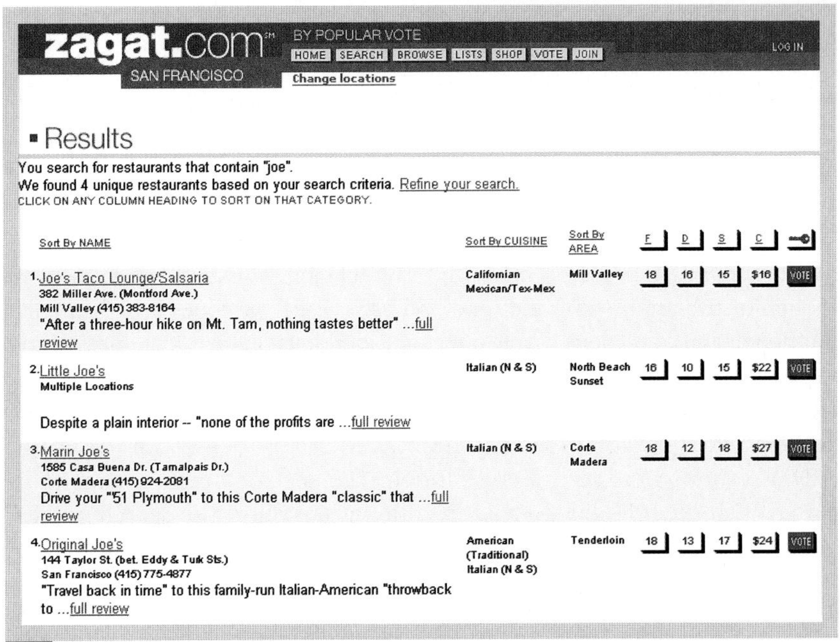

(www.zagat.com, August 21, 2001)

✳ BACKGROUND

A visible SEARCH ACTION MODULE (J1), a STRAIGHTFORWARD SEARCH FORM (J2), and CLEAR FORMS (H10) address some of the common problems that site visitors have using search engines. However, it might still be difficult for your customers to comprehend search results, especially when there are a large number of them. Structuring and organizing search results can make them much easier to understand. This pattern covers ways of arranging and categorizing search results to make them more valuable to your customers. It applies to both local searches on your site and Web-wide search engines.

✳ PROBLEM

It can be difficult for site visitors to understand search results if there are too few or too many results.

A search engine is only as good as the results it presents. It doesn't matter if it's fast and can simultaneously support thousands of queries per second if people can't understand the results.

Provide Relevant Summaries with the Search Results • The Zagat restaurant guides are indispensable for many city dwellers, providing an overview of all the major restaurants in a metropolitan area. Zagat provides a high-quality online version of its popular restaurant guidebooks. Figure J3.1 shows how zagat.com provides useful, domain-specific information in its search results, including a short excerpt from the full review, as well as ratings of the food, décor, service, and cost of the restaurant.

There are no hard rules here, though. The specific needs of each individual Web site will dictate what should be shown in the search results. On e-commerce sites, for example, it makes sense to show the price and availability of products. And search results on community message boards could show the author and date of posting.

Clearly Organize the Search Results • No one likes sifting through hundreds of hits to find the right one. One way of addressing this problem is to group the hits according to a coherent, logical scheme, such as alphabetically or chronologically. For example, Figure J3.2 shows how Amazon.com groups related search results. This is one way to make sure your search results present customers with BROWSABLE CONTENT (B2).

B2

Provide Good Hyperlinked Titles for Each Hit • Search engines typically display a Web page's HTML title as the name of the search result. Because these titles are what visitors see, it is crucial to give your Web pages DISTINCTIVE HTML TITLES (D9).

D9

Use Log Files to Tailor Results for the Most Common Search Terms • Search engines by themselves don't always provide the best results. The key to better results for your customers lies in your analysis of the log files, which keep track of the terms your customers use to search.

Find the most common terms, and make sure that search results using those terms point to the right place. This approach solves two problems. First, it compensates for the fact that customers use different words to

Figure J3.2

Amazon.com groups search results by category. On a search for "addison wesley computer," the various hits are grouped by "Books" and "zShops."

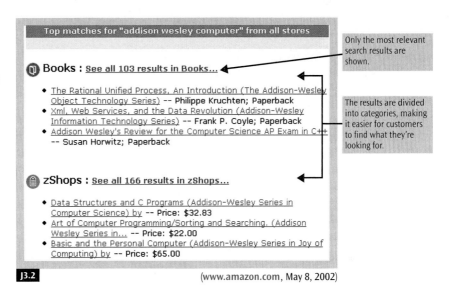

Top matches for "addison wesley computer" from all stores

Books : See all 103 results in Books...

- The Rational Unified Process, An Introduction (The Addison-Wesley Object Technology Series) -- Philippe Kruchten; Paperback
- Xml, Web Services, and the Data Revolution (Addison-Wesley Information Technology Series) -- Frank P. Coyle; Paperback
- Addison Wesley's Review for the Computer Science AP Exam in C++ -- Susan Horwitz; Paperback

zShops : See all 166 results in zShops...

- Data Structures and C Programs (Addison-Wesley Series in Computer Science) by -- Price: $32.83
- Art of Computer Programming/Sorting and Searching. (Addison Wesley Series in... -- Price: $22.00
- Basic and the Personal Computer (Addison-Wesley Series in Joy of Computing) by -- Price: $65.00

Only the most relevant search results are shown.

The results are divided into categories, making it easier for customers to find what they're looking for.

J3.2   (www.amazon.com, May 8, 2002)

mean the same thing. Figure J3.3 shows how IBM does this on its Web site. The search terms "notebook" and "laptop" point to the same page, greatly increasing the chance that a customer will find the right page.

Second, this approach lets you create the best possible hit for search terms. Look at Figure J3.3 again, and you'll notice a special area for tailored search results. Whenever a customer searches on "notebook," or "laptop," the search page shows a special promotion for selling these computers. However, the regular searches on the site show only ordinary search results. IBM keeps these ordinary search results in case their customers' "best" hits are not what they're looking for.

Compensate for Common Misspellings • Figure J3.4 shows how Amazon.com handles misspelled search terms. At the top of the Web page, it notes that there are no search results for the exact search terms entered, but then it corrects the spelling and searches on the new terms. Many customers will not notice that they misspelled the terms, nor will they see the message at the top of the Web page stating that they misspelled the terms, but Amazon.com does the right thing and shows them the results anyway! This is a customer-savvy, elegant design.

Compensating for spelling mistakes means you have to tailor the spell checker's dictionary to your specific domain. An ordinary spell checker's dictionary will not be useful for Web sites dealing with legal matters, for example, because it will not contain legal terms.

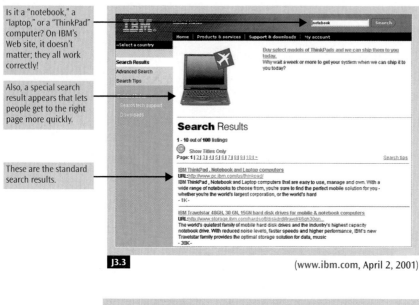

Is it a "notebook," a "laptop," or a "ThinkPad" computer? On IBM's Web site, it doesn't matter; they all work correctly!

Also, a special search result appears that lets people get to the right page more quickly.

These are the standard search results.

J3.3

(www.ibm.com, April 2, 2001)

Figure J3.3

IBM presents specially tailored search results for common searches, such as "notebook" and "laptop," in addition to the standard search results.

States that it couldn't find any results.

Does the next search, what a person would do anyway, instead of presenting "No results."

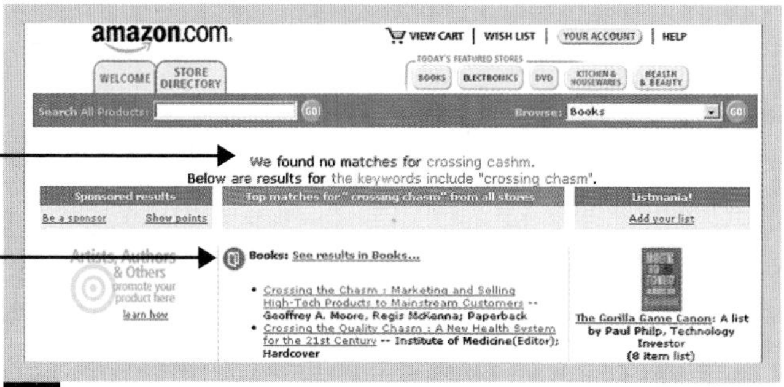

J3.4

(www.amazon.com, April 14, 2001)

Figure J3.4

Amazon.com automatically corrects certain misspellings. In this case, it corrects the search "crossing cashm" to read "crossing chasm."

Another way to compensate is to scan your Web server log files for the most commonly misspelled search terms. You will have to tweak your search engine so that these misspellings point to the right terms. This is clearly a tedious proposition, especially if there are a huge number of search terms. Concentrate on finding the most popular terms, perhaps by limiting your corrections to the top one hundred or five hundred.

Provide Support for Common Search Tasks • Common search tasks include things like going to the next page of results, starting a new search, and refining a current search. Figure J3.5 shows a good example of how the Google search engine handles these tasks. The top of the page provides a search entry form, letting visitors quickly create a new search if they did not

Figure J3.5

Google has a clean, minimalist design for displaying search results and supporting common tasks.

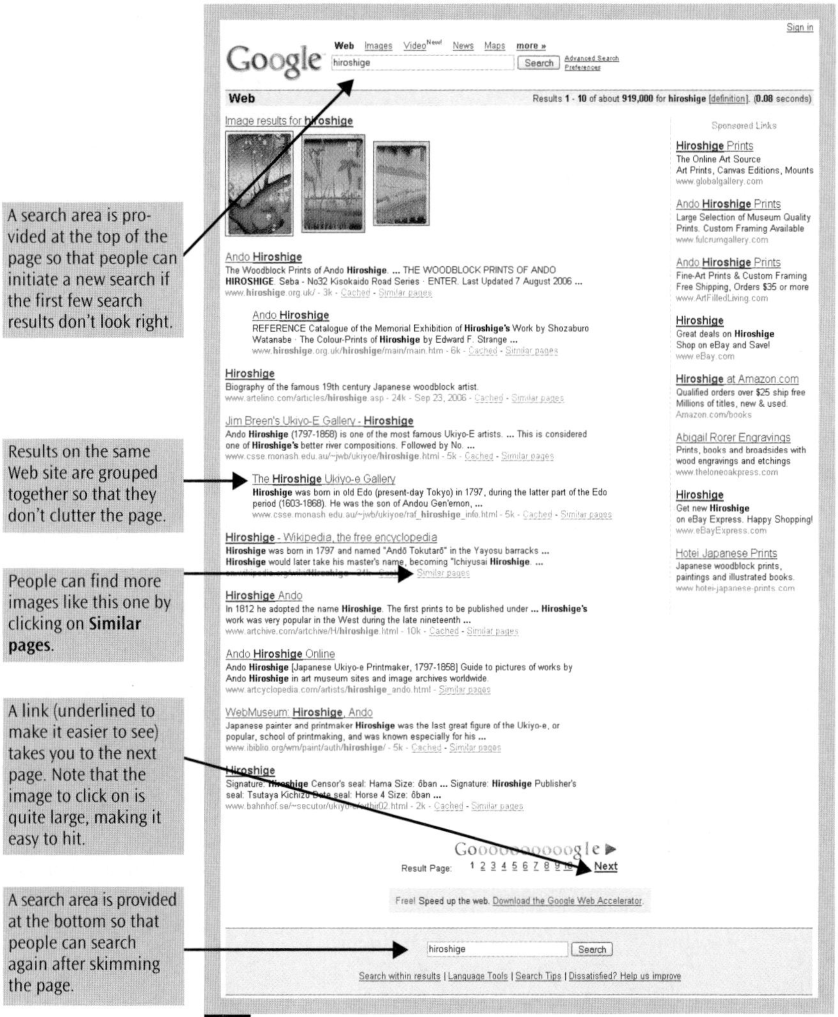

A search area is provided at the top of the page so that people can initiate a new search if the first few search results don't look right.

Results on the same Web site are grouped together so that they don't clutter the page.

People can find more images like this one by clicking on **Similar pages**.

A link (underlined to make it easier to see) takes you to the next page. Note that the image to click on is quite large, making it easy to hit.

A search area is provided at the bottom so that people can search again after skimming the page.

J3.5

(www.google.com, April 15, 2001)

get the results they wanted. In addition, the new-search form includes the search terms that the customer originally typed in, making it easy for them to remember what they entered and to edit it if necessary.

The bottom of the page has a second search entry form because the customer may look through all of the search results for a page, reach the bottom, and then decide to start a new search or refine the existing one. This design is more considerate than forcing the customer to scroll back to the top of the page.

The bottom of the page also contains links to the next set of search results. One subtle but very useful thing that Google's designers have done here is to make the "gle" part above the **Next** button part of the link to the next page of search results. Therefore, the target that customers must click on to go to the next page of search results is fairly large. Incidentally, designs with large targets are also good for improving SITE ACCESSIBILITY (B9) because they help customers with poor motor control, as well as those on a Mobile Web platform.

B9

At first glance, the controls at the bottom might seem to argue against designing for ABOVE THE FOLD (I2). But visitors tend to read the page from top to bottom. If they have not found what they want by the time they reach the bottom, they can go to the next page of results.

I2

❋ SOLUTION

Provide relevant summaries in your customers' search results. Clearly organize the results. Provide hyperlinked titles for each hit on the search results page. Use log files to tailor the search engine for the most common search terms and to compensate for common misspellings. Support your customers' common search tasks.

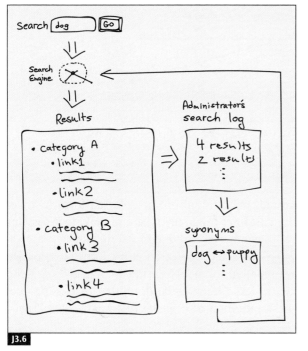

Figure J3.6

Organize search results, and continue to update the search database with common synonyms.

J3.6

✳ OTHER PATTERNS TO CONSIDER

3 You can use the card-sorting techniques described in Chapter 3 (Knowing Your Customers: Principles and Techniques) to find common search terms, but do this before launching the site and before performing a log file analysis. This strategy can help you prevent errors, instead of waiting for them to happen and then fixing the problems after the fact.

B9 Use the SITE ACCESSIBILITY (B9) pattern to ensure that the results you return can be used by all of your potential customers, including those with disabilities.

D6 When WRITING FOR SEARCH ENGINES (D6), give your Web pages DISTINCTIVE
D9 HTML TITLES (D9), and construct the pages using simple HTML that a search engine's Web crawlers can understand.

M3 On mobile platforms, consider using LOCATION-BASED SERVICES (M3) to emphasize nearby places in the search results.

Making Navigation Easy ◆ **K**

◆◆◆◆◆◆◆◆◆◆◆◆◆

Navigation is an integral part of every Web site, but customers cannot always find links and don't always know where links will take them. This pattern group describes several well-known techniques for organizing and displaying navigation elements to make them easy to find and easy to understand.

K1 UNIFIED BROWSING HIERARCHY

K2 NAVIGATION BAR

K3 TAB ROWS

K4 ACTION BUTTONS

K5 HIGH-VISIBILITY ACTION BUTTONS

K6 LOCATION BREAD CRUMBS

K7 EMBEDDED LINKS

K8 EXTERNAL LINKS

K9 DESCRIPTIVE, LONGER LINK NAMES

K10 OBVIOUS LINKS

K11 FAMILIAR LANGUAGE

K12 PREVENTING ERRORS

K13 MEANINGFUL ERROR MESSAGES

K14 PAGE NOT FOUND

K15 PERMALINKS

K16 JUMP MENUS

K17 SITE MAP

UNIFIED BROWSING HIERARCHY

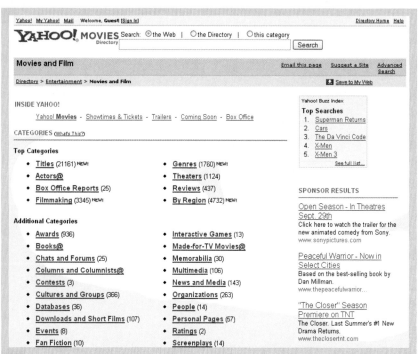

Figure K1.1

Yahoo! brings together content, community, and commerce in its site directory, creating a unified browsing hierarchy.

K1.1

(www.yahoo.com, June 16, 2006)

✳ BACKGROUND

We have considered designing for MULTIPLE WAYS TO NAVIGATE (B1) and BROWSABLE CONTENT (B2), but what about cases in which a site offers content, commerce, and community all around the same topic or topics? This pattern provides a navigable design for sites that have these features.

B1

B2

✳ PROBLEM

When Web sites have distinct community, content, and commerce sections, it's hard for people to find related topics in each of these sections, and the community areas can grow stale.

Putting content, commerce, and community about the same topics on different pages creates a challenge for Web site visitors. If they're interested in all three, they have to go to three separate sections, which means more work. To avoid this situation, link separate elements from the three sections or even combine them into one unified whole.

Your customers want quick access to all your site's benefits. Forcing them to navigate back to the homepage, only to navigate down another branch, is cumbersome, especially when the branches could be connected.

Why Always Force Visitors to Go Home? • Many designs require customers to return from the content section to the homepage before going to commerce or community sections. Some visitors will miss the related areas entirely because either they don't know they're there or they don't have the energy to look for them. Such a design might look like this:

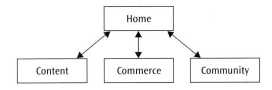

However, site information is related by a unified purpose. Even if these sections are written by different people, making the site a unified whole reinforces the value of all the sections.

Granted, unifying the sections requires making someone responsible for the unification process—someone who has the time and capability to add mechanisms to link from one section to the next—but your customers benefit by having full use of your site.

Create Links for Easier Navigation • Link related content, commerce, and community categories so that customers have easier access. You could keep the sections separate and accessible from the homepage but connect related content through special links in each area. Such a design might look something like this:

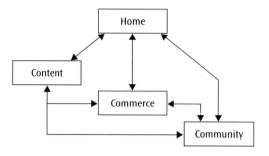

Another approach is to connect sections directly within one page, providing two or three of the different types of elements on a single page—something like this:

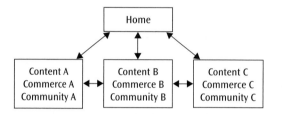

Either of these solutions will work. As long as the content, commerce, and community sections are related by cross-linking in one unified browsing hierarchy, you benefit from CROSS-SELLING AND UP-SELLING (G2) content and products, providing more value to your customers.

✳ SOLUTION

If your site offers content, community, and commerce on the same topics, integrate the three elements into one unified browsing hierarchy, either by directly linking the three elements or by integrating the elements into one page.

Figure K1.2

Provide links among your content, commerce, and community Web pages, integrating them into a unified whole.

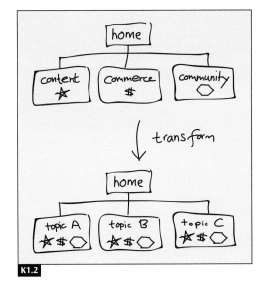

K1.2

✳ OTHER PATTERNS TO CONSIDER

If content, community, and commerce are not integrated on one page, give customers immediate access to the separate elements of the site through your NAVIGATION BAR (K2) or through CONSISTENT SIDEBARS OF RELATED CONTENT (I6). Provide strong feedback on the customer's location with LOCATION BREAD CRUMBS (K6).

K2
I6
K6

K2.1

Figure K2.1

Epicurious has a top-running navigation bar—one that runs across the top of the page—on its Web site.

(www.epicurious.com, June 16, 2006)

✳ BACKGROUND

From MULTIPLE WAYS TO NAVIGATE (B1), we know we need a consistent interface for browsing and searching a site. The BROWSABLE CONTENT (B2) and SEARCH ACTION MODULE (J1) patterns provide the fundamentals for building a browsable structure and straightforward search. Navigation bars are a common way to provide access to the main parts of your Web site. This pattern describes how to create navigation bars that your customers will find useful.

B1
B2
J1

✳ PROBLEM

Customers need to be able to reach the most important parts of your Web site in a structured, organized way that is easy to understand and use.

Large-scale Web sites need a clear and systematic scheme to make it easy for visitors to navigate them. Web sites on this scale are usually organized into subsites that focus on a specific topic, or into categories that focus on a specific product or type of information.

One common pattern that has emerged for helping people move across subsites and categories is the navigation bar. There are three types of navigation bars. The first type, the **top-running navigation bar,** stretches across the top of a Web page (see Figure K2.1). Top-running navigation bars often act as top-level navigation—that is, navigation linking directly to different subsites or categories.[1]

The second type is the **side-running navigation bar.** Side-running bars often are positioned along the left side of a Web page. It is fairly rare to see a navigation bar on the right, even on sites designed for languages that read from right to left. Side-running navigation bars have more space to work with than top-running navigation bars. They usually show more categories, too, often providing second-level navigation that provides links within a subsite.

The third type of navigation bar is the **top-and-left navigation bar,** which resembles an upside-down letter *L* and is sometimes referred to as an *inverted L.* This bar runs across the top and along the left side of a Web page. Often the top-running portion provides broad navigation across subsites, and the side-running portion provides deep navigation within the current subsite (see Figure K2.2).

Navigation bars link to the most important portions of a Web site either through text links or through icons and text. Icons by themselves are usually not effective because they're not always universally understood across cultures or even within a culture. It helps to have a text description to augment an icon (see Figure K2.3).

---

1 Here the word *top* is being used in two different ways. *Top-running* refers to the fact that the navigation bar is positioned across the top of a Web page. *Top-level* means that the navigation bar provides access to all of the major portions of a site.

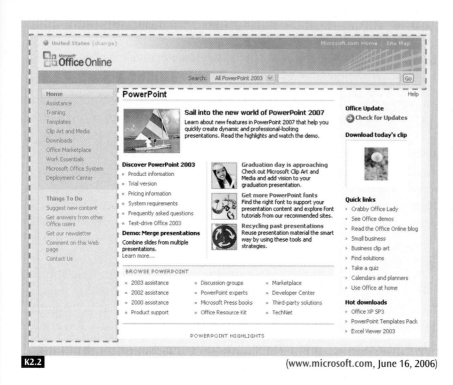

K2.2

(www.microsoft.com, June 16, 2006)

Figure K2.2

Microsoft's Web site has a navigation bar that runs across both the top and the left. The top part of the bar contains a search action module and links to help and to the site map. The left part contains links to specific topics in the site.

K2.3

(www.yahoo.com, June 16, 2006)

Figure K2.3

The text under the icons here makes it clear what the images represent.

✳ SOLUTION

Coordinate top-level and second-level navigation in a navigation bar along the top and/or left side of each Web page. Use text, or both icons and text, as links inside the navigation bar.

Figure K2.4

Create a navigation bar that runs along the top and/or left side.

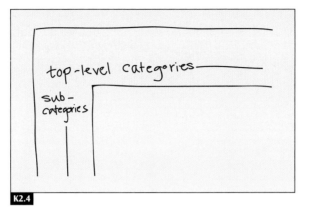

K2.4

✳ OTHER PATTERNS TO CONSIDER

If your navigation bar uses images, make sure they're FAST-LOADING IMAGES (L2). Navigation bars that use OBVIOUS LINKS (K10) are the clearest. Alternatively, by using HTML POWER (L4) to create a background color distinct from the body copy background color, and by keeping the navigation bar to the left or the top, you can bend the rules of OBVIOUS LINKS (K10) and remove the underlines or change the link color to something other than blue.

TAB ROWS (K3) are often used for top-level navigation. One advantage of tab rows is that they clearly show customers which category they're currently viewing.

CLEAR FIRST READS (I3) are sometimes placed at the top left corner of a Web page, affecting the placement of navigation bars.

K3 TAB ROWS

Figure K3.1

Well-designed tab rows provide visual cues that help customers recognize and use them more effectively.

K3.1

(www.theknot.com, June 16, 2006)

✱ BACKGROUND

MULTIPLE WAYS TO NAVIGATE (B1), BROWSABLE CONTENT (B2), and NAVIGATION BARS (K2) show the value of providing clear and consistent navigation indicators. One type of NAVIGATION BAR (K2) is a tab row, which offers clear visual cues about what your customer can click on, as well as straightforward feedback about the currently selected item.

✳ PROBLEM

Sites need to let customers navigate through categories of content and give them feedback on where they are. To make tab rows work well, however, requires including specific details in the visual elements.

Tab rows are cues that people find familiar. They are reminiscent of tabs on file folders at the office and in school. When implemented well, they clearly indicate what's active and open, while showing customers which other sections they can access. This design provides a simple but powerful navigation aid to quickly orient visitors and give added visual appeal to a site. Making tab rows work on the Web, though, involves creating some specific graphical devices.

Clearly Identify the Active Tab • Customers need to be able to see which tab is active. Make the active tab stand out from nonactive tabs by giving it a different color and accentuating the contrast in brightness for visitors who cannot distinguish by color differences alone. Making a tab active, even when customers first come to a site, will be another visual clue that the row of rectangles is a collection of tabs. Use color, contrast, and pre-selection to make active tabs stand out (see Figure K3.2).

Figure K3.2

On LinkedIn's Web site, the active tab is differentiated by color and contrast, and the **Home** tab is preselected when a customer first arrives at the site.

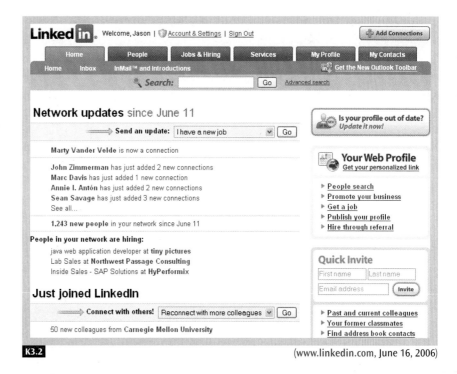

(www.linkedin.com, June 16, 2006)

Create an Indicator Line • To reinforce the illusion that the row of tabs is just that, and to bring content to the foreground, give visitors an indicator showing that the content of the page is controlled by tabs. Showing a line below the active tab in the same color—one that extends from left to right over all the content—indicates that the tab is not only a switch, but also a control over the content that customers see (see Figure K3.3).

Tab Rows Have Limitations • Tab rows can do only so much. The number of categories that a tab row can effectively manage on one line is about ten, and when you use multiple rows of tabs the screen begins to look cluttered—too much of it consumed by tabs (see Figure K3.4). An alternative design is to combine a tab row with a JUMP MENU (K16), as shown in Figure K3.5.   **K16**

Figure K3.3

K3.3   (www.amazon.com, August 25, 2001)

Although Amazon.com no longer uses multiple individual tabs for its product categories, this figure is still a good example of how to make an effective tab row. The indicator line covers the width of the page, giving the impression that all content on the page belongs to that tab.

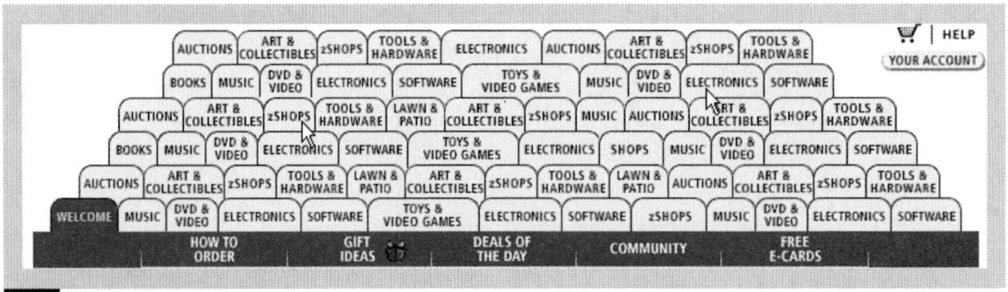

K3.4   (www.dack.com/web/amazon.html, April 2000)

Figure K3.4

This is an extreme (and fictional) example, but it makes a point: Too many tabs clutter the screen.

Figure K3.5

(a) The most recent version of Amazon.com's tab rows has dramatically cut down on the number of tabs, instead (b) placing them in a floating window that appears when you mouse over or click on a tab.

K3.5a

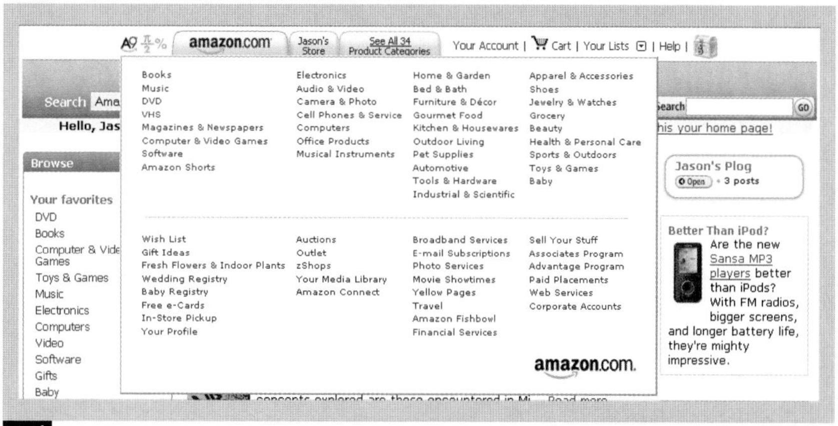

K3.5b

(www.amazon.com, June 16, 2006)

✳ SOLUTION

Create tab rows using an active tab and indicator line, but with no more than ten items, or whatever can fit on one line of tabs. Differentiate an active tab by color and contrast, as well as through preselection. Include an indicator line that extends across the page to create the impression that the whole page below the line belongs to the active tab.

Figure K3.6

Use tab rows to let customers navigate through different categories of information.

topic A   topic B   topic C

K3.6

✳ OTHER PATTERNS TO CONSIDER

Create your tab rows graphically with a LOW NUMBER OF FILES (L1) and
FAST-LOADING IMAGES (L2), or use HTML POWER (L4) to build them with
HTML. If there are too many tabs, consider combining your tab row with
a JUMP MENU (K16). If you're modifying an older Web site that still uses
HTML tables for layout, you can use SEPARATE TABLES (L3) to download
the tab row portion of the page first, giving the impression that the page
is loading faster than it really is. For newer Web sites, we advocate using
XHTML and STYLE SHEETS (D11) to create tab rows.

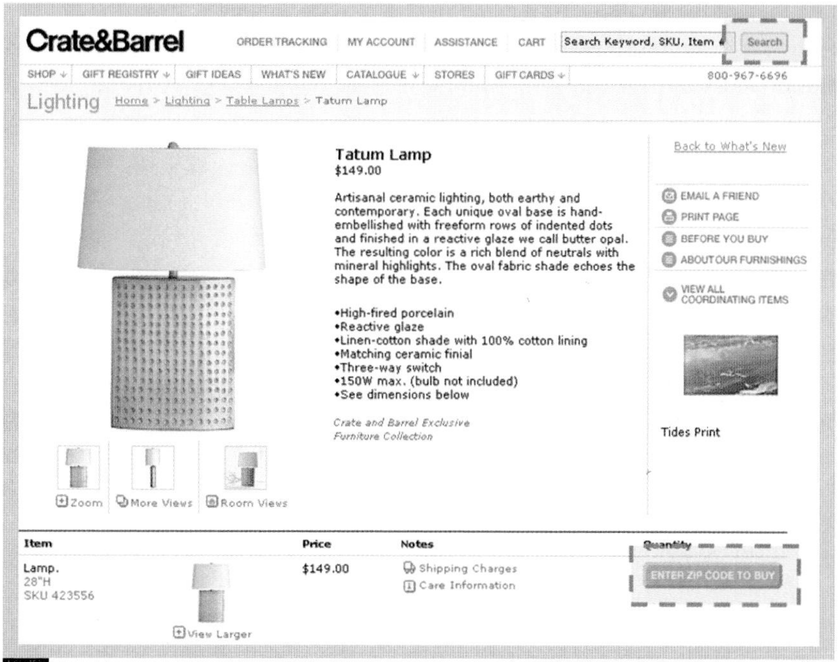

Figure K4.1

Action buttons (enclosed here by dashed lines) highlight the most important actions that you want customers to take.

K4.1   (www.crateandbarrel.com, June 16, 2006)

✳ BACKGROUND

As described in MULTIPLE WAYS TO NAVIGATE (B1), a navigation framework needs to support both impulse- and intention-based activity. Most links on a Web page simply take you to another page. Some links, however, represent actions that cause other actions to happen. In a PROCESS FUNNEL (H1) we know that moving from step to step requires a clear call to action. This pattern looks at how to differentiate ordinary links from action links through the use of buttons.

✳ PROBLEM

Text hyperlinks are good for moving from one page to another, but they're not quite right for representing actions that do something important, such as authorizing a purchase or submitting a message to a message board.

Text hyperlinks are well understood as words that customers can click on to bring up another page. There are no side effects or consequences. However, text hyperlinks are not quite right for representing *transactions,* in which important information is being sent back to a Web server for processing.

For cases like these, buttons make more sense than text links because in the physical world buttons cause action. Pushing a button on a remote control causes the television to change channels. Pushing an elevator button causes the elevator to come to your floor. Pushing the power button on a computer turns the computer on.

There are two kinds of buttons on the Web: graphical action buttons and HTML action buttons.

Graphical Action Buttons • Graphical action buttons are made from images, but they are modified to look like they can be pressed. With many great-looking Web pages, often it's not clear what's clickable and what isn't. Customers end up moving the mouse all over the page trying to figure out what to click on next. By adding slight lighting touches around the border of an image, you can make the image look like it's raised, providing a visual cue that it's clickable (see Figure K4.2).

Where possible, provide supporting text or labels for graphical action buttons to help explain their purpose. The text can be part of the graphical image (as in Figure K4.3). The text can also be part of the HTML, but in this case it's a little harder to align the image and the text correctly. Including a textual label with a graphical icon is an example of relying

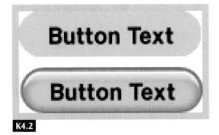

Figure K4.2

These two images illustrate the difference between flat images (top) and graphical action buttons (bottom). Graphical action buttons are tailored to look like real buttons, making them appear as if they could be physically pressed.

Figure K4.3

Buttons should be accompanied by text describing what they do.

K4.3 (www.amazon.com, www.geocaching.com, December 4, 2001)

on recognition over recall, one of the design principles introduced in Chapter 4 (Involving Customers with Iterative Design). The label helps the user learn the meaning of the icon so that, in the future, it can simply be recognized quickly.

If graphical action buttons are too small, they'll be hard to see and hard to click on. On the other hand, if they're too large, they'll take up too much screen space. As we mentioned in Chapter 3 (Knowing Your Customers: Principles and Techniques), human motor skills are predicted by what's known as Fitts's Law, which says that it takes customers a lot longer to hit objects that are far away or small. You will have to decide the size of your buttons on a case-by-case basis, but we recommend a minimum of 20 × 20 pixels.

One trick you can use with GIF images is to have a transparent "halo" around them, making their effective size much larger than they appear. Both Yahoo! and Amazon.com use this technique for some of their buttons.

HTML Action Buttons • HTML action buttons are encoded directly in HTML, and in most Web browsers they're represented as gray buttons (see Figure K4.4).

HTML action buttons are faster to download than graphical action buttons, but they offer less control over layout and appearance beyond the text inside of the button. One consequence of this lower amount of control is that HTML action buttons with a lot of text become very wide, making them visually unattractive. Another consequence is that the Web browser may make wide buttons wrap to the next line if there's not enough space. The best solution is to keep the text of an HTML action button short so that the button will be small and will be more likely to be positioned where you want it.

Figure K4.4

The **Search** button on the right is an example of an HTML action button. HTML action buttons are created directly in HTML.

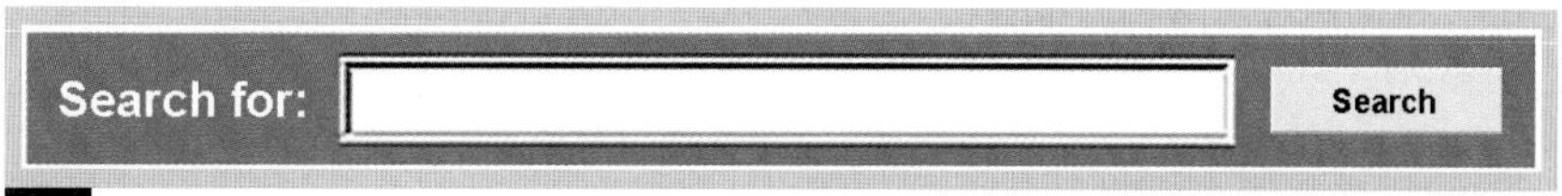

Search for: [   ] **Search**

K4.4

✳ SOLUTION

Use buttons to represent actions. If you use images, make them look like they can be clicked on by giving them a three-dimensional appearance. Also provide clear, concise labels to explain what the buttons will do.

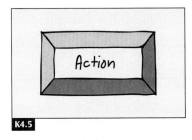

Figure K4.5

Use buttons for actions, and make it clear that these buttons can be clicked on.

✳ OTHER PATTERNS TO CONSIDER

For important action buttons that are critical to completing a task, use HIGH-VISIBILITY ACTION BUTTONS (K5), which are placed in redundant locations ABOVE THE FOLD (I2), as well as below it.

You can use buttons in NAVIGATION BARS (K2). However, these buttons do not represent actions, just navigation. The same techniques for making images look three-dimensional can be applied to images in navigation bars. Avoid using HTML action buttons in these bars, though, because of the lack of control you have over layout and appearance.

Graphical action buttons work against the goal of a LOW NUMBER OF FILES (L1) unless the images are combined. Having many of these buttons can make your Web pages slower to load. To compensate, make graphical action buttons into FAST-LOADING IMAGES (L2). Shrink images by reducing the number of colors, combining many nearby images in a single image, and using a different file format. You'll want to use the GIF image format for most graphical action buttons so that they can have transparent backgrounds.

SITE ACCESSIBILITY (B9) is an important factor to consider for action buttons. Making graphical action buttons universally accessible entails adding <alt> attributes to all of them, describing what they will do when selected.

Figure K5.1

Nordstrom's key checkout button is visible both above and below the fold, so customers can always see how to proceed to checkout.

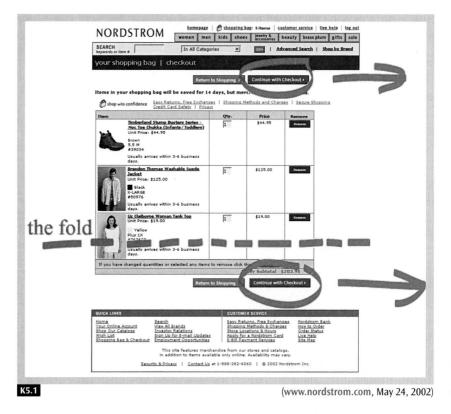

K5.1

(www.nordstrom.com, May 24, 2002)

❋ BACKGROUND

This pattern assists in the completion of PROCESS FUNNELS (H1) and QUICK-FLOW CHECKOUT (F1). To help customers finish tasks, put ACTION BUTTONS (K4) and other critical information ABOVE THE FOLD (I2) and create OBVIOUS LINKS (K10). If your pages are longer than a screen, this pattern describes how to handle ACTION BUTTONS (K4) in a way that makes sense for your customers.

✳ PROBLEM

People can easily be derailed from completing a task if the next step is not obvious.

When working on a task, customers become frustrated if they reach a roadblock and can't figure out the next step. If all the buttons are the same size, shape, and color, or are ambiguously named, people have a tough time deciding which button is most important. If the link they think should be next is not visible on the page, some people will not have the patience to scroll down to look for it. On certain pages, customers need to scroll to make selections or verify information. On other pages, they can see that the information at the top is correct, and they will assume that the rest of the page is correct.

Mind the Fold • Designing pages for different Web browsers and configurations poses a challenge. Web pages "fold" in different places, depending on the browser type, the browser's window size, and optional configurations, such as the default font size. Some people set their browsers to the maximum window size; others shrink their windows so that they can see multiple windows at once. Customers who shrink their browser windows see less of what's on your Web page. The maximum browser window size depends on a computer screen's resolution. A large window on one machine could be a medium window on another, and a small window on a third. Putting the critical buttons at the very top of a page, however, can confuse customers if the buttons are the first thing to draw the eye. If customers don't see the site brand first and recognize the site they're on, they might feel lost.

   To be obvious, the critical buttons that take people to the next step in a process must obey the following rules: Because browser size cannot be controlled, critical buttons must be as close to the top of a page as possible, without being at the absolute top. To make it easier for customers to move forward after reading the content, provide duplicate critical buttons (which do not increase page download time) below the fold, at the bottom of critical content. Differentiate action buttons from other buttons so that customers notice them right away.

✳ SOLUTION

On every page that is part of a process

1. Provide your action button(s) right below the top navigation bar, tab row, or progress bar.

2. If critical content cannot be placed above the fold, repeat action buttons at the bottom of the content.

3. Make action buttons larger than all other buttons on the screen, and give them a color that contrasts well with the background color. Choose button labels that are descriptive and different from the names of other buttons on the page. Make the buttons that move a task forward the largest ones on the page.

Figure K5.2

Task-critical action buttons should be distinct and appear near the top of the page, as well as below the fold, so that customers always know how to complete their tasks.

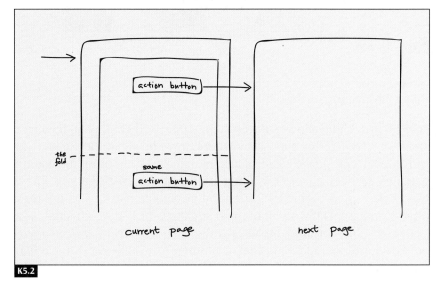

✳ OTHER PATTERNS TO CONSIDER

Use ACTION BUTTONS (K4) to make buttons highly visible. Place these buttons both ABOVE THE FOLD (I2) and below it. Put the button at the top near the NAVIGATION BAR (K2) or TAB ROW (K3).

Use FAMILIAR LANGUAGE (K11) and DESCRIPTIVE, LONGER LINK NAMES (K9) for button names, and make sure each is different from other links on the same page. Use the same image at the top and bottom of a page so that you have a LOW NUMBER OF FILES (L1).

K6 LOCATION BREAD CRUMBS

K6.1

(www.eddiebauer.com, June 16, 2006)

Figure K6.1

The area at the top of this Web page enclosed by the dashed line shows location bread crumbs, which identify where customers are on the Web site. Bread crumbs also provide a quick way of back-tracking to previously viewed pages.

✳ BACKGROUND

Part of providing BROWSABLE CONTENT (B2) is including a feedback mechanism that lets people know where they are. NAVIGATION BARS (K2) and TAB ROWS (K3) provide feedback on their own, but other navigation schemes do not. It can be quite a challenge for customers to know where they are on some Web sites and how to get back to where they came from, especially on large sites. SITE MAPS (K17) are effective as a last resort, but location bread crumbs, also known as *trail markers*, provide location indicators that customers can also use for navigation. This pattern describes ways of using location bread crumbs effectively.

B2
K2
K3

K17

✳ PROBLEM

Customers can get lost easily on Web sites, losing track of where they are in relation to other pages on the site.

In the traditional fairy tale, a wicked stepmother leads a young Hansel and Gretel into a dark forest. Hansel leaves a trail of bread crumbs to mark their path so that they can return home to their father.[2] So what does this fairy tale have to do with the Web? Every Web site's navigation design must answer the following three questions for the customer:

1. Where am I now?
2. Where did I come from?
3. Where can I go from here?

The term **bread crumbs** refers to the bar at the top of a Web page showing the trail of pages that a customer took from the homepage to the current page (see Figure K6.1). Showing this trail helps visitors answer the first two questions. NAVIGATION BARS (K2), EMBEDDED LINKS (K7), EXTERNAL LINKS (K8), and other links on a page help answer the third question.

Provide Bread Crumbs for Visitors to Backtrack • Each page in the bread crumb bar is hyperlinked, letting customers quickly backtrack through the site. Bread crumbs also let people see where they are in relation to the homepage, providing information about the Web site structure in the process. Visitors who jump directly into a Web page through a bookmark, an e-mailed link, or a search engine may find bread crumbs extremely helpful to orient themselves.

Use Separators to Show Relationships among Categories • Location bread crumbs can be implemented in many different ways. To show how each category leads from one to the other, designers use symbols such as >, /, and |. Although each of these symbols has a different meaning in another context, we recommend > as the best separator because it suggests that one category "points" to the next level of detail. Also, this symbol is widely understood in the most popular directories, such as Yahoo! Here's an example of how this symbol might be used:

Home > Arts > Performing Arts > Acting

---

2 Unfortunately for the children, birds eat the bread crumbs, leaving the children lost in the woods.

❋ SOLUTION

Provide bread crumb links that show how to get from the homepage to the current page and back. Use a string of back links and separate them by a "pointing" (>) character.

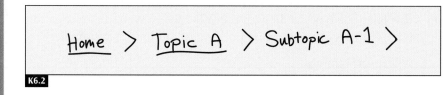

K6.2

Figure K6.2

Use bread crumbs to show people where they are on the Web site.

❋ OTHER PATTERNS TO CONSIDER

Use OBVIOUS LINKS (K10) for bread crumbs to make them easy to see and understand. Bread crumbs are usually placed at the top of a page's GRID LAYOUT (I1). They can interfere with NAVIGATION BARS (K2) that run across the top. In these cases, it is usually better to place the bread crumbs underneath the navigation bar.

Figure K7.1

On this page from WhatIs.com, a site that explains in simple language what technical terms mean, note how many of the links appear in the middle of the text. These kinds of embedded links encourage visitor exploration and help provide more context for identifying where a link goes.

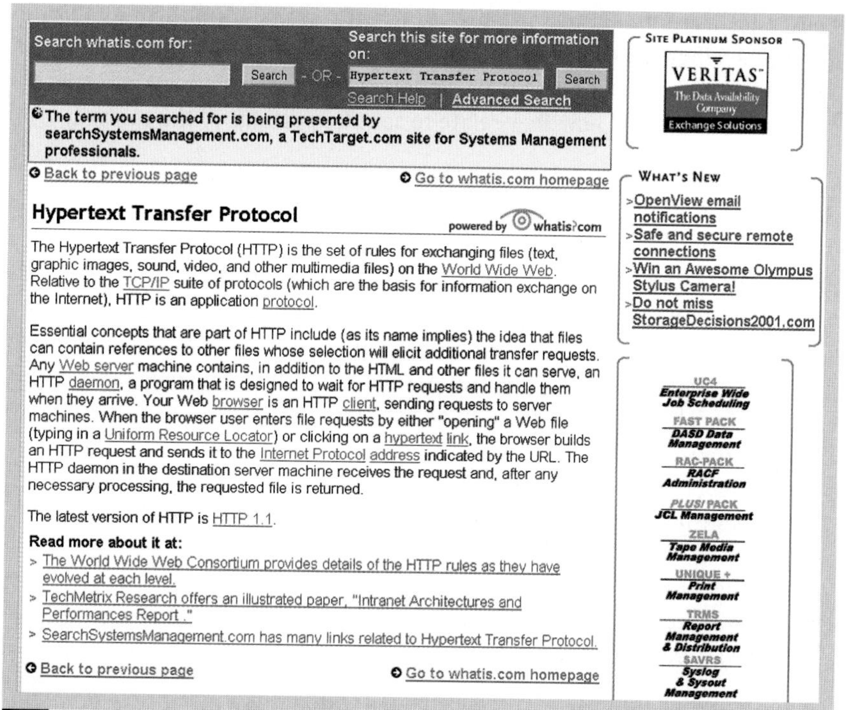

K7.1

(www.whatis.com, August 17, 2001)

✳ BACKGROUND

B1
B2

As we claimed in MULTIPLE WAYS TO NAVIGATE (B1) and BROWSABLE CONTENT (B2), customers need more than one way to find things on a site. When you're reading, it can be tedious to go elsewhere on the page for additional information. One way around this problem is to embed

K10

OBVIOUS LINKS (K10) in the body of the text. In this pattern we discuss the pros and cons of using embedded links and ways of maximizing their effectiveness.

❊ PROBLEM

Sometimes visitors want to delve deeper into a certain subject that appears in the text, or they need an explanation but don't want to go searching for it. Links off to the side or at the end of the text may lack the context necessary for readers to understand how they relate to specific portions of the content.

One of the most common approaches to using hypertext links is to place them in the body of the text, letting customers jump to other pages if they're interested. This approach allows people to explore more about a topic if they choose. Embedded links also stand out from the rest of the text, making them easy for people to find while skimming.

However, one disadvantage of embedded links is that they make it difficult to maintain a coherent experience for the reader. People might leave the original page and never return. Furthermore, if too many links are embedded, the text becomes hard to read and hard to skim because everything looks important. So where's the balance? This pattern describes how to get the most out of embedded links.

Use Helpful Link Names • Take more words from the surrounding text and use them to create DESCRIPTIVE, LONGER LINK NAMES (K9). For example, consider the following (somewhat) fictitious paragraph:

> Although the number of Web pages is increasing dramatically with every passing month, it is quite clear to any Web surfer that the overall Web experience has not improved at the same fast-paced rate. In fact, a recent Web usability survey revealed that most customers do not return to sites that they consider hard to use.

Now suppose we wanted to make a link to the survey page. Here are three good ways to do it:

1. In fact, a recent <u>Web usability survey</u> revealed that most customers do not return to sites that they consider hard to use.
2. In fact, <u>a recent Web usability survey</u> revealed that most customers do not return to sites that they consider hard to use.
3. In fact, a recent Web usability survey revealed that <u>most customers do not return to sites that they consider hard to use.</u>

Which is the best choice? It depends. Link 1 sounds like it might go to the actual survey, which is good if you want to send people there. Link 2 sounds like it could go to the survey or an article about the survey. Link 3 sounds like it will go to a specific part of the results or to an article about the survey, which is good for impatient Web surfers who like to read summaries only.

How Many Links Are Too Many? • A page with too many links feels cluttered and makes it difficult for visitors to tell what's important. Avoid linking to arbitrary things that do not really matter. We once saw a Web page that looked like this sentence, with every word in its text linked to an online dictionary. This is an extreme case, but it illustrates the minimalist philosophy quite well: less is more.

Consider Having Some Embedded Links Open Floating Windows • You can maintain coherence on a page by having the links open up FLOATING WINDOWS (H6). The benefit to this approach is that customers can view the linked material in the new window, without losing track of the original page. This technique is useful, for example, when a visitor needs to see extra information, such as a definition, or when a visitor is going through a PROCESS FUNNEL (H1).

In considering floating windows for your links, remember that having a lot of new windows can quickly become confusing. Furthermore, no patterns have emerged for representing links that open up new windows. For now, use this technique sparingly and only where it really makes sense.

✲ SOLUTION

Embed links within a text passage to allow more free-form exploration. Use descriptive, longer link names to let customers know where the links will take them. Keep the number of embedded links per page of text low, so as not to overwhelm readers. Use floating windows for some embedded links, to provide additional information while maintaining the context and to keep visitors from jumping to other pages.

Figure K7.2

Use embedded links to let people explore.

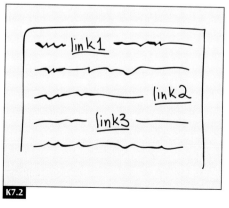

K7.2

✳ OTHER PATTERNS TO CONSIDER

Use OBVIOUS LINKS (K10) with embedded links to make it easier for cus- K10
tomers to skim through the text. Embedded links need DESCRIPTIVE,
LONGER LINK NAMES (K9) to help visitors understand where the links will K9
take them.

FLOATING WINDOWS (H6) help keep people from losing the context of the H6
existing page. Embedded links often go to other Web sites. Use EXTERNAL
LINKS (K8) to label and group these kinds of links to maintain coherence. K8

Figure K8.1

External links point to other Web sites and let people see how your Web site is connected with other people, places, and things. Some external links in this screen shot include the related stock quotes on the left, the content module on the bottom left labeled "ELSEWHERE ON THE WEB", and the link to Rite Aid under "On the Net" near the bottom.

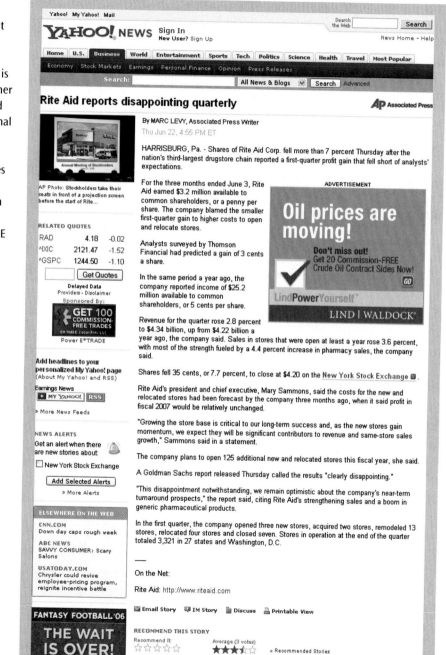

K8.1

(news.yahoo.com, June 23, 2006)

✳ BACKGROUND

It can be difficult for customers to know if a link points to something in your Web site or goes to an outside site. Including links to external Web sites can improve your credibility, as in GRASSROOTS INFORMATION SITES (A6), but it also makes it easy for customers to leave your Web site unintentionally. This pattern explains some techniques for organizing external links so that there are no surprises for your customers.

A6

✳ PROBLEM

Most sites have links to other Web sites. These external links need to be treated in a special manner so that customers understand that they lead to other Web sites that are not managed by the current Web site.

Providing external links is important for a site because it helps build trust and credibility. Visitors appreciate a site owner who is willing to reference another site to keep customers better informed and satisfied. But site owners are rightly concerned that customers will leave their sites to follow an external link. And visitors are sometimes surprised when they click on a link and unexpectedly leave a site. You can address these concerns by building in some safeguards, as described in the sections that follow.

Consider Including Links That Lead to External Web Sites • Help your customers by providing additional useful information that you don't have on your site. Links might go to partner Web sites, client Web sites, press releases, articles, reviews, products, and services that complement your own.

Minimize Link Rot • A site operator could change the content of a page or decommission a page address, and you would never know about it until you tested your external links. This problem is often called **link rot.** If your site has many external links, testing the links can be time-consuming. In addition, the external site to which you link may not want you to link to it.

There are three things you can do. The first is to use tools to help check the hyperlinks on your Web site, to ensure that they're still going to the right place. The second is to link to PERMALINKS (K15), which are links

K15

that are intended to always work. The third is to get permission from the external site. Getting permission is useful for several reasons:

- External site operators can give you their conditions for linking to their sites, perhaps agreeing to link to you as well.
- You can inform the external site operators that your site relies on their current link structure, thereby hopefully reducing link rot.
- Talking to another site operator helps you understand how to link to other sites so that the same page addresses will contain the content you wish to reference, again reducing link rot.

Receiving permission does not guarantee that the external links will continue to work in the future, but you will be much better informed as a result.

Set Expectations, Mark External References • News sites that reference other news sites often collect all their external references in one clearly marked area. For example, the CNN Web site places external links at the bottom of each news article. Other news aggregators, like Yahoo!, put a marker—such as *[external]*—before each link to another site. These strategies inform customers that if they click the link, they will no longer be on the current site, so that they will not be surprised to be transported away. You can use similar strategies by putting external content in specific areas or clearly marking an external reference on the link itself.

Consider Combining Embedded Links with External Links • One technique that the *New York Times* uses for its news articles is to merge embedded links with external links. If customers click on an embedded link, they jump to the bottom of the page, where there is a section identified as external links.

The advantage of this approach is that it makes it easy for readers to see all of the external links after reading a news article. It also lets customers go to external Web sites, making clear which links point to those sites.

Open New Windows for External Links • Open a new window for an external link when you want customers to maintain the context of the original site, especially when they're in the middle of a process. Pop-up windows can be problematic, as explained in FLOATING WINDOWS (H6), but if used judiciously, they can work well. Keep in mind that too many open windows can be annoying, and because not every link comes in the middle of a process, not all external links need to open new windows.

❄ SOLUTION

External links can help build trust and credibility among your customers, while reducing the amount of work required to create new content. Take special care to ask permission from external site operators, and learn their policies on page addresses and dynamic content creation so that you can avoid most link rot. Let your customers know that they're about to be sent to an external site by explicitly marking each link, or by putting external links in a well-marked area on your page. Use pop-up windows for external links only when the context of your site must be maintained so that customers don't lose their place in a process.

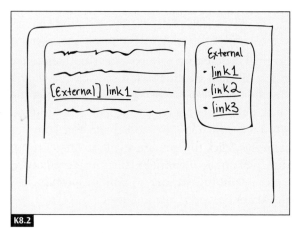

K8.2

Figure K8.2

Group external links at the end of a page (left) or in a module separated from the actual content (right).

❄ OTHER PATTERNS TO CONSIDER

Use DESCRIPTIVE, LONGER LINK NAMES (K9) so that customers will know that they're going to another site, or put all external links in their own CONTENT MODULES (D2).

K9

D2

Figure K9.1

CNET News.com's links clearly describe where customers will go if they click on them.

F9.1

(www.news.com.com, June 16, 2006)

✳ BACKGROUND

B1
K2 **B2**
K8 **I6**

From MULTIPLE WAYS TO NAVIGATE (B1) we know that customers will be navigating your site using NAVIGATION BARS (K2), BROWSABLE CONTENT (B2), EXTERNAL LINKS (K8), and CONSISTENT SIDEBARS OF RELATED CONTENT (I6). Poorly worded text links can be confusing. This pattern describes how descriptive and longer link names can guide visitors to the right place easily.

✳ PROBLEM

Text hyperlinks must be made predictable and understandable in terms of the Web pages to which they link. Otherwise, when browsing, customers will repeatedly follow links, arrive at something that doesn't interest them, and continually "pogo" back and forth in frustration.

The text of a link is a preview of the linked page. Your customers should be able to guess the content of the linked page before they click on a link. In fact, researchers at PARC[3] have developed a notion of how people follow links, called **information scent.** The basic idea is that given a link, its text, its location, and the previous pages that they've seen, people should be able to tell if a link will take them closer to the desired information.

Generic Terms Make Poor Link Names • Many Web sites have generic links like <u>click here</u> or <u>download</u> or even <u>http://www.click-this-link.com</u>. "Click here" for what? "Download" what? What is "http://www.click-this-link.com," and why should anyone go there? Compare these link names to the ones in the CNET News.com example (see Figure K9.1). Take one of its links at random, and guess what kinds of things you would see if you clicked on it. In most cases, you will guess correctly. That's the mark of a good link name.

Longer Link Names Improve Site Accessibility • Descriptive, longer link names can also foster SITE ACCESSIBILITY (B9) in three ways. First, longer link names are easier to click on than short ones, making your Web site easier to use for people with poor motor skills, such as senior citizens and children. Second, descriptive link names are more useful to people who are blind because they often skip over content and listen to just the links on a Web page. Longer link names, such as <u>three recent articles on e-commerce</u>, will therefore be more useful to customers with impaired vision than short ones, such as <u>articles</u>. Third, a new page has to be downloaded every time customers click on a link. For the many people who still have slow Internet connections, a good link name will help customers feel confident that they're downloading the right page.

(B9)

Longer Link Names Make a Page Easier to Skim • Longer link names make long passages of text easier to skim. Customers often browse through text, looking for EMBEDDED LINKS (K7). More descriptive link names can help them understand what the text is about and find the right link.

(K7)

---

3 Formerly Xerox PARC.

Summarize the Linked Page with a Few Choice Words • Remember the five *W*s: who, what, when, where, and why. Answering these questions will help you create a descriptive link name. If you're using an INVERTED-PYRAMID WRITING STYLE (D7), a good link name will come straight from the title of the page.

Use Familiar Language • Avoid jargon. If your site customers are consumer car buyers, for example, avoid technical details that they won't understand. Instead of a link name such as <u>Torque and traction to avoid hydroplaning</u>, use something like <u>Driving safely on wet roads</u>.

A corollary of this rule is to use link names that everyone else is using. For example, nearly everyone calls the area where you can see what you plan to purchase a *Shopping Cart* or a *Shopping Bag.* Other common names include *Home* for the homepage, *Search* or *Find* for the search page, and *My* for a personalized Web page. Stick to names your customers already know.

The reverse of this corollary is also true: Avoid using these terms when they don't mean what people expect. For example, some e-commerce sites have Home departments and use the term *Home* to point there. *Home* on a Web site means the homepage, so a Home department needs a link name like *Home Department* or *Household.*

Differentiate or Eliminate Links That Have Similar Names • If customers see links that sound similar, they may become confused. For example, which link would you click on for help: <u>Service</u>, <u>Tech Support</u>, or <u>Help</u>? As another example, what's the difference between <u>Shopping Cart</u>, <u>Checkout</u>, and <u>Order List</u>? FAMILIAR LANGUAGE (K11) describes some techniques for addressing this type of problem.

The problem of inconsistent terminology tends to crop up on large Web sites, which often name the same thing differently in different places. Is it *email* or *e-mail?* Is it *notebook computer* or *laptop computer?* Overcome the problem of inconsistent terminology by establishing a style guide that all your site designers follow. As we discussed in Chapter 4 (Involving Customers with Iterative Design), strive for consistency by choosing a consistent vocabulary and stick with it throughout the Web site. In addition, be consistent with standard terminology that your customers will see elsewhere.

Separate Links That Word-Wrap • Because of the way HTML works, sometimes your link names will word-wrap, making a single link look like multiple links (see Figure K9.2). Use the layout of the Web page to give hints about the number of links you have. CNET News.com avoids the problem of word wrapping well (see Figure K9.1). Headlines are in larger fonts and thus are visually separated from the text below. Figure K9.3 demonstrates how you can use bulleted lists or dividing bars to separate links.

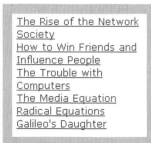

The Rise of the Network Society
How to Win Friends and Influence People
The Trouble with Computers
The Media Equation
Radical Equations
Galileo's Daughter

K9.2

Figure K9.2

How many links does this list contain? If you guessed six, you're correct, but why use a design that makes your customers guess?

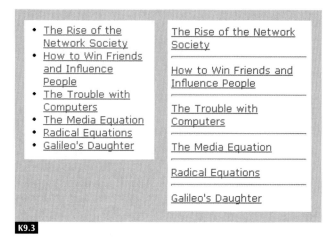

- The Rise of the Network Society
- How to Win Friends and Influence People
- The Trouble with Computers
- The Media Equation
- Radical Equations
- Galileo's Daughter

The Rise of the Network Society
_____
How to Win Friends and Influence People
_____
The Trouble with Computers
_____
The Media Equation
_____
Radical Equations
_____
Galileo's Daughter

K9.3

Figure K9.3

Bullets or dividing bars can be used to separate links that word-wrap.

✳ SOLUTION

Use descriptive, longer link names that act as a preview of the linked page. Create the link name by summarizing the linked page in a few words. Use familiar language, and differentiate links that have similar names. Finally, make sure that any links with long names that word-wrap are clearly differentiated from other links.

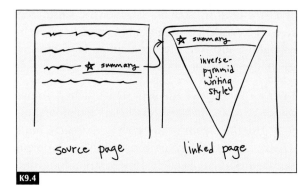

K9.4

Figure K9.4

Use descriptive, longer link names to link to other content pages.

❋ OTHER PATTERNS TO CONSIDER

(K11) Write descriptive, longer link names in FAMILIAR LANGUAGE (K11). Use
(K10) them with OBVIOUS LINKS (K10) to make it clear they're links that cus-
(K7) tomers can click on. EMBEDDED LINKS (K7) also benefit from descriptive,
longer link names. It's easy to create link names for pages with content
(D7) written in an INVERTED-PYRAMID WRITING STYLE (D7) because the title is
usually a good summary of the content.

(B9) Improve SITE ACCESSIBILITY (B9) with better link names so that customers with limited access can jump over and navigate through links
without having to move slowly through an entire page.

K10 OBVIOUS LINKS

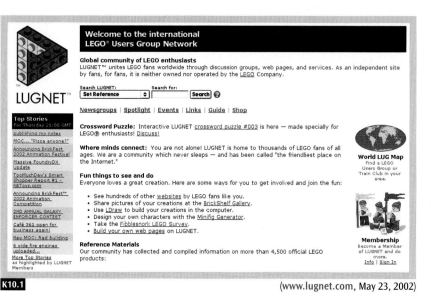

K10.1

(www.lugnet.com, May 23, 2002)

Figure K10.1

Note how quickly you can determine on LUGNET's site which links have already been visited and which have not. Pages that use colors other than blue for links can be confusing because visitors have to learn new rules.

✳ BACKGROUND

Text links can come in the form of NAVIGATION BARS (K2), LOCATION BREAD CRUMBS (K6), EMBEDDED LINKS (K7), and EXTERNAL LINKS (K8). However, it is not always clear which text on a Web page is a link. Most of your customers will know that a blue underlined link is an unvisited link. It's possible to change this color or remove the underline, but doing so comes with the risk of confusing some of your customers. This pattern describes the advantages of sticking with blue underlined links and discusses some of the trade-offs.

✳ PROBLEM

It's not always clear which bits of text are clickable links.

As you undoubtedly know, most Web sites normally use <u>blue underlined text</u> for unvisited links. You might think that blue links are ugly, are hard to read, and clutter the page, but there is an advantage to using blue underlined text.

Blue links have been part of the Web experience from the very beginning, and customers expect unvisited links to be blue and underlined. Most Web sites still follow this convention. In fact, according to Alexa's "traffic rankings," of the 25 most-visited Web sites worldwide, 19 used blue links for a significant portion of their Web site.[4] Furthermore, a study of 75 e-commerce Web sites conducted by Heidi Adkisson in 2002 found that 50% of the sites used blue links.

Changing your link colors might help differentiate you from the crowd, but Web sites have to provide as many reasons as possible to keep customers coming back. Research shows that ease of use is a critical factor, and because your visitors will spend far more time on other Web sites than on yours, it makes sense to do what everyone else is doing. Blue links may not be the best design, but you have to remember that your Web site is just one of several million out there.

We're not saying that every Web site should have only blue links. You have to balance the trade-offs. Here are some tips for making the most of your link colors.

Avoid Using Blue Text for Anything Other than Web Links • Blue is harder to see than other colors because of the basic physiological structure of the human eye. More importantly, though, blue text looks like a Web link, and customers will be misled by what appears to be something they can click on. For these reasons, avoid blue text.

Avoid Underlining Anything Other than Web Links • Underlined text often looks like a link and can confuse your customers. Underline nonhyperlinked text sparingly, if at all.

---

4 Alexa (www.alexa.com/site/ds/top_500).

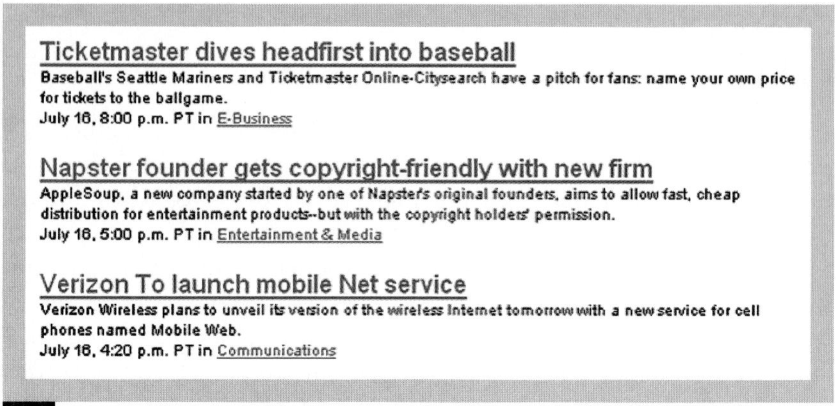

Ticketmaster dives headfirst into baseball
Baseball's Seattle Mariners and Ticketmaster Online-Citysearch have a pitch for fans: name your own price for tickets to the ballgame.
July 16, 8:00 p.m. PT in E-Business

Napster founder gets copyright-friendly with new firm
AppleSoup, a new company started by one of Napster's original founders, aims to allow fast, cheap distribution for entertainment products--but with the copyright holders' permission.
July 16, 5:00 p.m. PT in Entertainment & Media

Verizon To launch mobile Net service
Verizon Wireless plans to unveil its version of the wireless Internet tomorrow with a new service for cell phones named Mobile Web.
July 16, 4:20 p.m. PT in Communications

K10.2

(www.news.com.com, July 2001)

Figure K10.2

CNET News.com uses Arial and a larger font size to differentiate headlines from other text.

Make Links More Attractive by Using Different Font Sizes and Styles • If you're building a menu, experiment with blue links in a sans serif font like **Verdana, Geneva, Arial,** or **Helvetica.** If you're formatting a headline, try making the headline link a little larger and using a sans serif font for it, to make it look cleaner.[5] Figure K10.2 shows how CNET News.com uses larger, sans serif fonts for headlines.

Use the <title> Attribute with Text Links • If you have text-based HTML links that use the <a href=". . ."> tag, familiarize yourself with the <title> attribute. The new <title> attribute introduced in HTML 4.0 allows you to annotate links with a description, in a way similar to how the <alt> attribute works for the <img> tag. Most modern Web browsers display the <title> attribute as a tool tip. It is also possible for audio-based Web browsers to read the <title> attribute to know where a link goes, providing better SITE ACCESSIBILITY (B9).

B9

Here's an example of the <title> attribute:

```
<a href="http://www.site.com" title="Your comment">Link text</a>
```

---

5 A general rule of thumb is to use sans serif fonts for titles and headers and serif fonts for text.

And here's how this <title> attribute looks in Microsoft's Internet Explorer 5.0:

Avoid Using Colors Associated with Color Deficiency • Color deficiency (commonly known as *color blindness*) is a common problem among males [see Chapter 3 (Knowing Your Customers: Principles and Techniques)]. For this reason, if you choose to change your link colors, avoid red and green (the most commonly indistinguishable colors) as a color pair for unvisited and visited links.

Use Different Link Colors for Artistic, Entertainment, or Experimental Purposes • If you're designing an interface for deliberate exploration or artistic purposes, you can break the rules that we've established in the preceding sections because visitors come to your site for fun. Figure K10.3 shows the Web site for the quirky band They Might Be Giants. The strange design of the Web site successfully reflects the personality of the band.

Figure K10.3

The primary goal of this Web site is fun, not ease of use. In cases like this, conventions like using blue text for links may not necessarily make sense.

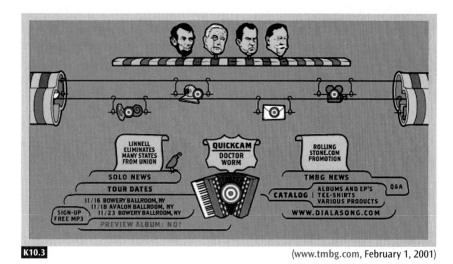

(www.tmbg.com, February 1, 2001)

❋ SOLUTION

Use blue underlined text for hyperlinks. Avoid using blue or underlining for anything other than Web links. Make links more attractive by using different font sizes and styles. Use the <title> attribute with text links. To improve site accessibility, avoid using colors associated with color deficiency (especially red and green). Try different colors or links if you're designing a Web site as a puzzle, as an art piece, or for fun.

blue underlined link

K10.4

Figure K10.4

Stick with blue underlined text for hyperlinks.

❋ OTHER PATTERNS TO CONSIDER

NAVIGATION BARS (K2) are one place where blue underlined links don't always make sense. People know they can click on certain things on a Web page, and navigation bars have become so common that it's not always necessary to make such text blue and underlined.

Use obvious links with EMBEDDED LINKS (K7), EXTERNAL LINKS (K8), and LOCATION BREAD CRUMBS (K6) to make them all easier to see. Use obvious links with FAMILIAR LANGUAGE (K11) and DESCRIPTIVE, LONGER LINK NAMES (K9) to make them easier to understand.

As an alternative to obvious links, use ACTION BUTTONS (K4), but only sparingly and only when you need customers to take a specific action. Graphical buttons take up more space and can take longer to download.

Using obvious links can make access to your Web site easier for people who are blind and for people who use mobile phones to connect to the Internet. For these reasons, obvious links improve your SITE ACCESSIBILITY (B9).

K2

K7 K8
K6
K11 K9

K4

B9

Figure K11.1

Edmunds.com has a friendly site that provides detailed information about automobiles using simple, understandable language.

K11.1

(www.edmunds.com, June 16, 2006)

✳ BACKGROUND

BROWSABLE CONTENT (B2) discussed techniques for structuring the entire Web site in a way that customers understand. This pattern is an extension of that one, continuing the process of naming links on individual pages, and extending it to all text on the site, including CLEAR FIRST READS (I3) and INVERTED-PYRAMID WRITING STYLE (D7). This pattern describes why it's important to use language familiar to your customers throughout your site, and how you can identify which terms to use to simplify the task of navigation.

✳ PROBLEM

Unfamiliar terms and link names make understanding and navigating a Web site difficult.

Sometimes Web sites are hard to use because there's a chasm between how you see the world and how your customers see the world. One cause of this rift is the mismatch in the language used. Words familiar to you may not be familiar to your customers. Customers often get confused when faced with unfamiliar terms, and this confusion can lead them to become lost in your Web site.

The key to bridging this chasm is understanding the target customers from their point of view. What terms and concepts are familiar? What words do they use to describe things? What expressions and idioms do they use to talk about the world? Understanding how customers think is crucial for writing content and creating link names that they will find understandable and predictable.

Observe and Interview Your Customers • Understand the customer's perspective by ethnographically observing how your customers go about doing things. To do this you will have to follow some of your customers around for a few days to see the types of people with whom they communicate, the kinds of forms and tools they use, and the kinds of things they do. Another approach is to interview customers in their workplaces. Have them take you through the steps of their work. These two techniques— ethnographic observation and interviewing—are described in greater detail in Chapter 3 (Knowing Your Customers: Principles and Techniques). **3** Note the types of terminology and language that your customers use. Also try to write at a ninth- or tenth-grade reading level unless your audience is highly sophisticated or much less sophisticated.

Use Card Sorting to Help Structure the Information on Your Web Site • Card sorting is intended to provide a better idea of how customers organize information. Give participants a stack of cards, each of which has a label representing a Web page or a set of Web pages, and have participants organize the cards in a way that is meaningful to them, grouping the cards and explaining the reasons for their grouping choices. See what names they use for the groups. These might be good names to use on your site. This technique is also used for creating BROWSABLE CONTENT (B2) and is **B2** described in more detail in Chapter 3 (Knowing Your Customers: Principles **3** and Techniques).

Test Link Names through Category Identification and Description • Use two related techniques—category identification and category description—to test the usefulness and usability of your link names, independent of visual design and layout.

In **category identification,** present recruited participants with a list of link names that would appear on a page. The links might be grouped together as they would be on the Web page, but there is no other content or layout. Also give participants a set of tasks. For each task, ask them to select the link that they think will take them to the right page, and to rate the confidence of their choice on a scale of 1 to 3. This technique provides useful feedback about how well potential customers can map from a given task to the navigation provided on your Web page to complete the task. It also checks if potential customers can differentiate link names. Link names that are too similar will cause people to choose the wrong link. Category identification will help you spot this problem early in the design process.

Category description is the flip side of category identification. In category description, ask participants to examine the same list of links and describe what they expect to find by clicking on each. This technique helps identify unfamiliar or potentially ambiguous link names. It also checks if other people's expectations of page content match yours.

✳ SOLUTION

Use language that your target customers understand. Observe and interview representative customers so that you can empathize with the way they see and understand the world. Use techniques such as card sorting, category identification, and category description to get a better feel for how they organize, structure, and describe things. Use all of this information to create content and links that your customers will find understandable and predictable.

Figure K11.2

Ask your customers to review the language you intend to use on your site.

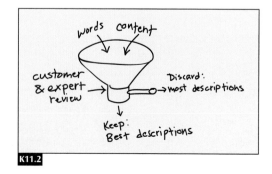

K11.2

✳ OTHER PATTERNS TO CONSIDER

Whereas BROWSABLE CONTENT (B2) addresses issues dealing with the entire site structure, this pattern deals more with the names of links on specific pages.

Apply this pattern when you're developing names for links in NAVIGATION BARS (K2) and OBVIOUS LINKS (K10). This pattern is key for developing DESCRIPTIVE, LONGER LINK NAMES (K9).

Figure K12.1

MSN Hotmail makes it clear what kinds of information and formatting are required for creating a new account.

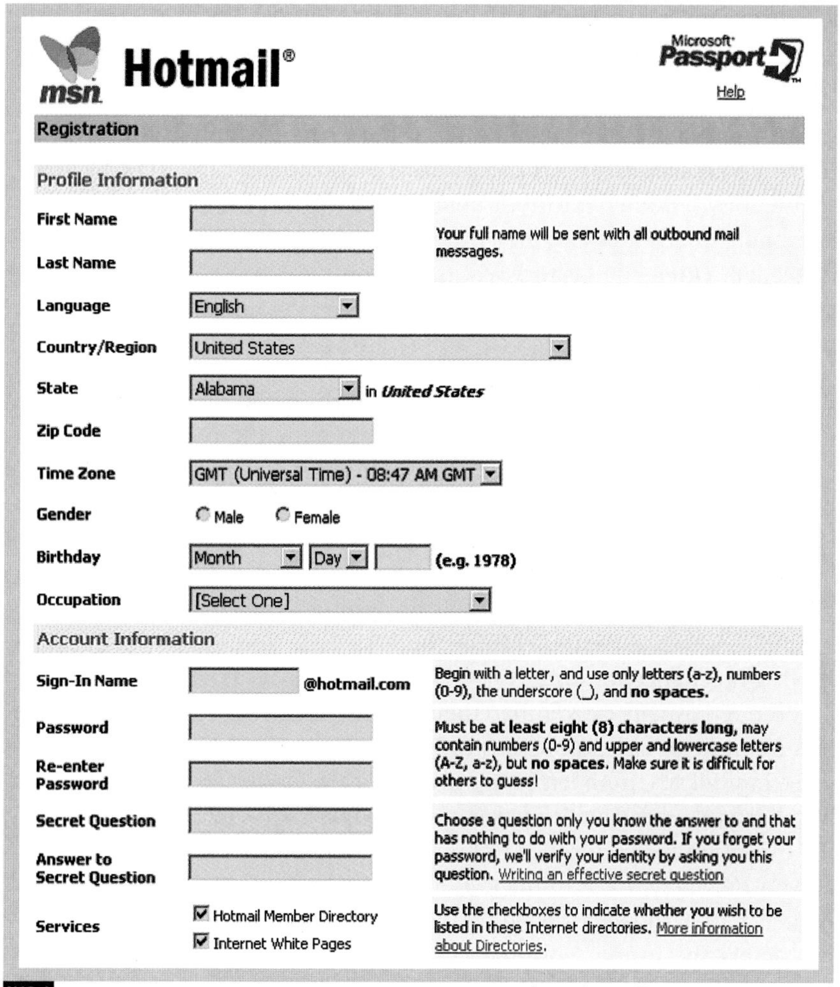
msn Hotmail®

Microsoft® Passport™

Help

Registration

Profile Information

First Name		Your full name will be sent with all outbound mail messages.
Last Name		
Language	English	
Country/Region	United States	
State	Alabama in ***United States***	
Zip Code		
Time Zone	GMT (Universal Time) - 08:47 AM GMT	
Gender	Male Female	
Birthday	Month Day **(e.g. 1978)**	
Occupation	[Select One]	

Account Information

Sign-In Name	**@hotmail.com**	Begin with a letter, and use only letters (a-z), numbers (0-9), the underscore (_), and **no spaces.**
Password		Must be **at least eight (8) characters long,** may contain numbers (0-9) and upper and lowercase letters (A-Z, a-z), but **no spaces.** Make sure it is difficult for others to guess!
Re-enter Password		
Secret Question		Choose a question only you know the answer to and that has nothing to do with your password. If you forget your password, we'll verify your identity by asking you this question. Writing an effective secret question
Answer to Secret Question		
Services	Hotmail Member Directory Internet White Pages	Use the checkboxes to indicate whether you wish to be listed in these Internet directories. More information about Directories.

K12.1

(www.hotmail.com, August 27, 2001)

BACKGROUND

Web sites need to be engineered for errors, minimizing the number that
K13 can occur and providing MEANINGFUL ERROR MESSAGES (K13) when they inevitably happen. This pattern focuses on minimizing the errors from a common source: online forms.

✳ PROBLEM

Customers will make errors and generate erroneous data when faced with online forms that have little structure, include no formatting directions, and are not designed to account for errors from the start.

Errors cause frustration, result in poor performance, and lead to a lack of trust in your site. Errors are common when customers are asked to fill out online forms. Some text input fields require a specific kind of data, such as a name or a phone number, but give very few hints as to what exactly is needed. Often site visitors will try to complete these forms with what they think is the right data, only to get obscure error messages saying that they did something wrong.

Provide Hints about the Expected Format • Minimize errors by providing fields that clarify the required format by showing the required structure, by giving examples, or by including explanatory text. Figure K12.2 shows two text input fields asking for a customer's phone number. The first one is error prone. Is "555.5555" acceptable? Is "(510) 555 5555" acceptable? What about "510-555-5555"? It simply is not clear, and it's likely that whatever the person types in will be wrong. Now look at the second example. It has separate fields for the area code and the phone number, leaving no chance for error.

Although usually clearer than their unstructured counterparts, structured text input fields can also be misleading. In Figure K12.3, for example, the three input fields, from left to right, are supposed to be for area code, phone number, and extension. However, some people might mistakenly think that the extension field is for the last four digits of the phone number.

Another way of minimizing errors is to provide sample values. Figure K12.4 shows a text field with a sample phone number to show customers the format you expect. Providing explanatory text is a third way of helping to prevent errors (see Figure K12.5).

Make Sure the Software Accepts Multiple Formats • A fourth approach to preventing errors in text input fields—slightly more complex from a

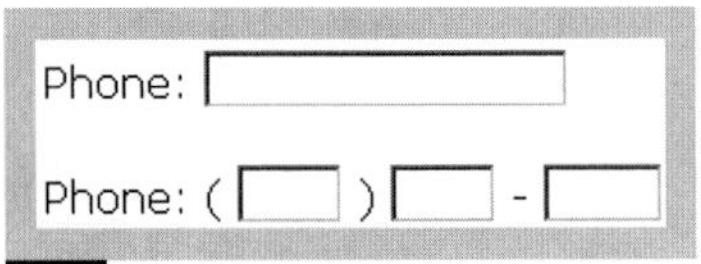

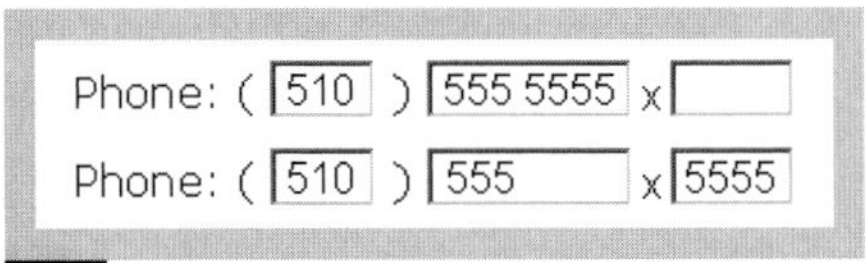

Figure K12.2

Here are two text input fields for a customer's phone number. The first one gives no hint as to how the visitor should format the phone number. The second one makes the required formatting clear.

Figure K12.3

These two examples show how even structured text input fields can sometimes be misleading.

Figure K12.4

Providing a default value of how the data should look helps prevent errors.

Figure K12.5

The example showing how the data should look can also be provided in the form of explanatory text.

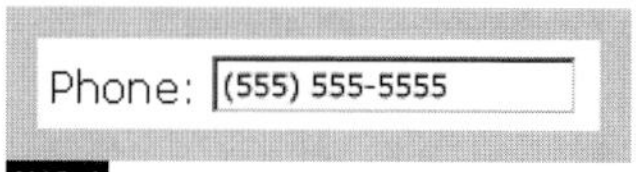
Phone: (555) 555-5555

K12.4

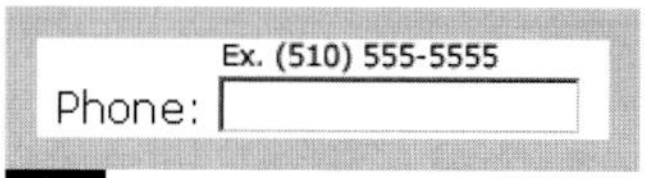
Ex. (510) 555-5555
Phone:

K12.5

programming standpoint—is to allow multiple kinds of formatting and have the computer figure out what the value should be. For example, a credit card field could let people type in credit card numbers with or without spaces. A phone number field could allow all the different kinds of formatting for phone numbers. When the processing is straightforward and unambiguous, as with credit card numbers, allow flexible formatting.

Make Clear Which Fields Are Required and Which Are Optional • A fifth approach to error prevention informs customers which fields are required so that they can focus on the important information. These fields must be clearly marked with a symbol that is explained in a footnote (see Figure K12.6) or a text label such as *required*.

Figure K12.6

Prevent errors by indicating which fields are required. The site pictured here uses the asterisk for this purpose. It is important to explain the required symbol in a place where it will be read.

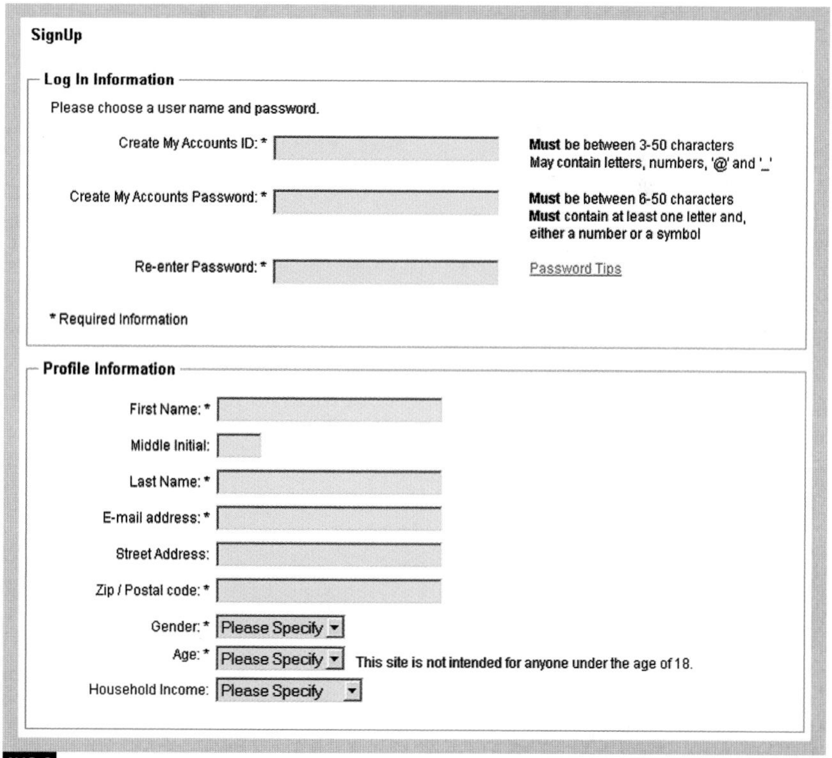
SignUp
Log In Information
Please choose a user name and password.
Create My Accounts ID: *
Must be between 3-50 characters
May contain letters, numbers, '@' and '_'
Create My Accounts Password: *
Must be between 6-50 characters
Must contain at least one letter and, either a number or a symbol
Re-enter Password: *
Password Tips
* Required Information
Profile Information
First Name: *
Middle Initial:
Last Name: *
E-mail address: *
Street Address:
Zip / Postal code: *
Gender: * Please Specify
Age: * Please Specify
This site is not intended for anyone under the age of 18.
Household Income: Please Specify

K12.6

(www.myciti.com, August 21, 2000)

✳ SOLUTION

Provide hints about what kind of text input you expect from your customers. You can do this by providing fields showing formatting, by providing sample values in the fields, or by providing explanatory text. Whenever it is simple to do so, allow flexible formatting and have the computer determine the correct format. Also make clear which fields are required and which are optional so that customers will not have to guess.

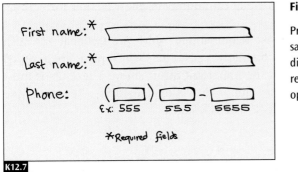

K12.7

Figure K12.7

Prevent errors by providing sample formatting and differentiating between required fields and optional fields.

✳ OTHER PATTERNS TO CONSIDER

No matter how well a site is designed to prevent errors, some errors will still occur. In these situations, provide MEANINGFUL ERROR MESSAGES (K13) to help people recover. Preventing errors is especially important for PROCESS FUNNELS (H1), such as SIGN-IN/NEW ACCOUNT (H2) and QUICK-FLOW CHECKOUT (F1). Since forms are often a source for errors, see CLEAR FORMS (H10) for more on how to prevent errors on forms.

K13

H1 H2

F1

H10

Figure K13.1

Dell's Web site handles errors during account creation with two error messages, which are positioned near the problem area. Each message states the problem and what the customer must do to fix it.

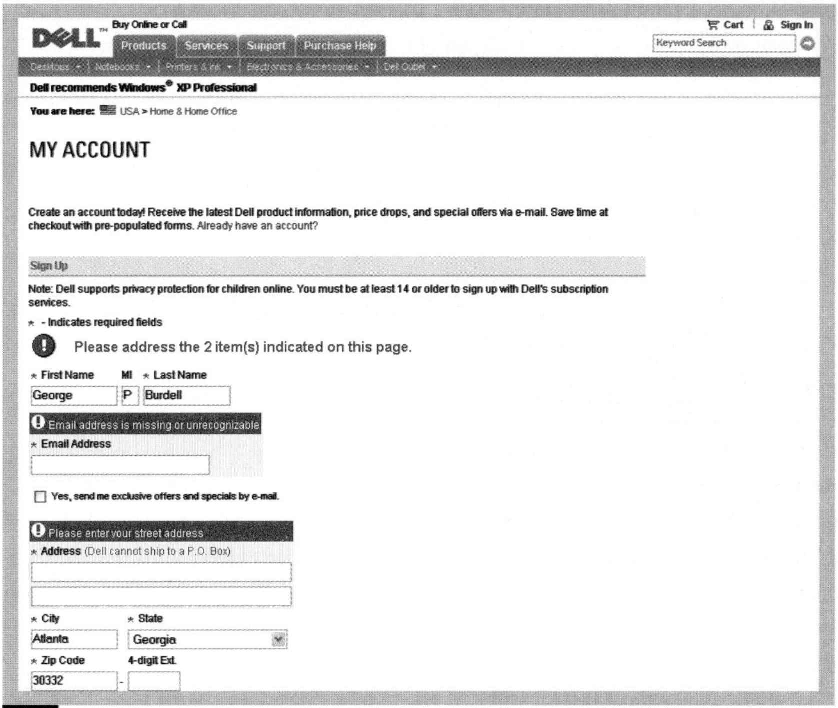

K13.1   (www.dell.com, August 24, 2006)

✳ BACKGROUND

(K12) Web sites need to be engineered for PREVENTING ERRORS (K12), as well as making it easy to recover from errors. This pattern focuses on providing meaningful error messages that facilitate recovery.

✳ PROBLEM

When customers make mistakes, they need to be gently informed of the problem and how to recover gracefully, or the error condition may persist.

No matter how well a Web site is designed, people will make occasional errors—some accidental and some because of misunderstanding. In both cases, your Web site needs to provide meaningful error messages designed to help your customers recover from errors. Meaningful error messages have four characteristics in common:

1. Clear statement of the problem
2. Avoidance of humor
3. Explanation of how to recover
4. Positioning near the problem

Provide Clear Error Messages without Assigning Blame • A meaningful error message clearly states the problem in FAMILIAR LANGUAGE (K11) and without blame. Examples of poor error messages include "Error code 15," "Invalid syntax," and "You entered bad data." The first two examples provide no useful information about the problem. The third example places blame by using a "you" statement, as in "You did this wrong." These kinds of statements can usually be rewritten to avoid placing any blame.

K11

Avoid Humor in Error Messages • Also avoid injecting humor into error messages. Errors can be frustrating, and although humor may help some people, it may aggravate others. Furthermore, what's funny in one language, culture, or mood may not be funny in another.

Explain How to Recover from the Error • Meaningful error messages provide steps that people can take to recover from the problem. Some examples include offering an explanation of what went wrong and how to recover, listing an e-mail address for questions, and providing a phone number that people can call for more information.

In the case of providing explanation, it's better to tell people how to use the system instead of describing how the system works. For example, rephrase the message "Items can be removed from the shopping cart by clicking on the **Remove** button" as follows: "To remove an item from the shopping cart, click on the **Remove** button."

Place the Error Message Near the Problem It Identifies • Good error messages are presented spatially near the problem area in a visually apparent manner.

A common design mistake is to put error messages on a completely separate page, with no context. This approach forces people to remember the problem, hit the **Back** button, wait for the previous page to load, find the problem area, and then try to fix it. Figure K13.1 shows a better design: re-creating the page where the error occurred and placing error messages near the problem areas. This approach makes it easy to find and fix problems.

Another common design mistake is to make error messages look like the rest of the Web page. Such error messages are hard to find because they don't stand out, and they often leave customers puzzled about why they're still on the same page. Use fonts, icons, and colors that are distinct from the rest of the Web page to highlight the error message and direct your visitors' attention to the right place.

Keep Previously Entered Text Intact • One of the most irritating experiences on the Web is to fill out all of the fields on a page and submit it, only to get an error message and find out that the page has been reset, forcing you to type the same information again. PERSISTENT CUSTOMER SESSIONS (H5) can help you avoid this problem, by keeping track of information already entered and redisplaying that information when a customer gets an error message.

✳ SOLUTION

Provide meaningful error messages in familiar language without assigning blame and without trivializing the problem with humor. State the severity of the problem and provide steps that customers can take to recover. Display the error message near the problem area, and highlight it to make it stand out visually.

Figure K13.2

Provide simple, blame-free error messages that let people know what's wrong and what to do to fix the problem.

✳ OTHER PATTERNS TO CONSIDER

In your Web site design, focus first on PREVENTING ERRORS (K12), resorting to error messages only as a fallback. Always use FAMILIAR LANGUAGE (K11) in error messages. Also use PERSISTENT CUSTOMER SESSIONS (H5) so that customers do not have to reenter the same information after an error message is displayed.

Meaningful error messages are especially important for PROCESS FUNNELS (H1), such as SIGN-IN/NEW ACCOUNT (H2) and QUICK-FLOW CHECKOUT (F1), where they help maintain focus so that the customer does indeed complete the process.

Figure K14.1

If it can't find a requested page, Microsoft's Web site displays a special page describing the problem. This page helps customers who may be lost by providing a meaning-ful error message, a site map with an overview, a search form, and basic navigation to the main portions of the Web site.

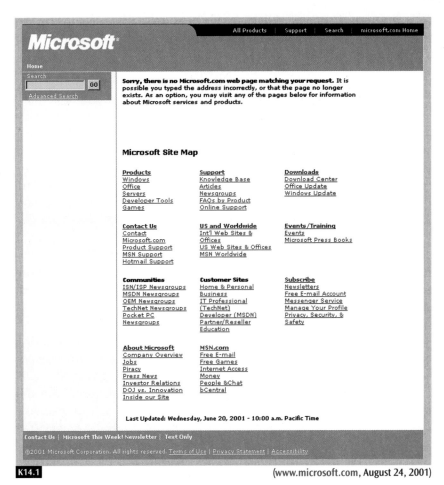

`K14.1`
(www.microsoft.com, August 24, 2001)

✳ BACKGROUND

Because pages are moved around as a Web site evolves, invariably some customers will get a "Page not found" error. This pattern looks at cus-tomizing the error message to make it easier for visitors to recover from this error.

❋ PROBLEM

Sometimes customers click on links, type in URLs, or have bookmarks for pages that no longer exist, resulting in the dreaded "Page not found" error message or, even worse, "Error 404."

Customers might try to access a page that does not exist. Perhaps the page they came from had a bad link, perhaps the page was moved, or perhaps they typed the address incorrectly. In any case, you need to inform visitors that the page they're looking for cannot be found, and give them some ways of recovering.

Fortunately, most Web servers let you customize the **Page not found** page. You can make this page display an error message saying that the page cannot be found. You can also add a SEARCH ACTION MODULE (J1) and a NAVIGATION BAR (K2), making it easy for customers to continue browsing and searching (see Figure K14.1). Providing a SITE MAP (K17) along with the most common links can help your customers see the overall structure of the Web site and direct them to the right place. Finally, including a link to whoever maintains the Web site makes it easy for visitors to send e-mail describing any problems with the site.

Check your Web log files to find out where people are encountering "Page not found" errors. If these customers are all coming from a specific Web site, send a message to whoever maintains that Web site, stating what the old link was and requesting that they update it with the new link. Also create a Web page at the old location that will take visitors to the new location. You can do this using the "refresh" <meta> tag as follows:

```
<meta http-equiv=Refresh
content="0;url=http://www.yoursite.com/newlocation.html">
```

❋ SOLUTION

Create a custom Page not found **Web page that makes it easy for customers to browse or search for the content they were expecting to find.**

Figure K14.2

A **Page not found** page should let customers know that the page they want is missing and help them find their way back into the Web site.

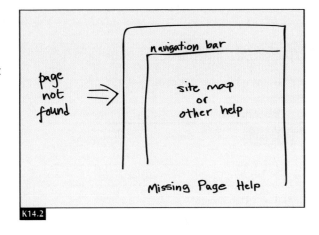

K14.2

✻ OTHER PATTERNS TO CONSIDER

On your **Page not found** page, provide a MEANINGFUL ERROR MESSAGE (K13) explaining that the requested page could not be found. Also give customers some ways to continue navigating the Web site from the **Page not found** page, such as a NAVIGATION BAR (K2), a SEARCH ACTION MODULE (J1), and relevant portions of your SITE MAP (K17).

K15 PERMALINKS

K15.1

(www.nytimes.com, January 8, 2006)

Figure K15.1

A newspaper Web site adds dozens of new pages every day, and visitors frequently want to bookmark a Web page they find interesting and even share it with others. A properly formatted permalink, in this case based on the date of the news story and the category of its content, lets visitors return to the page later. Here the permalink, as shown in the address bar, is *http://www.nytimes.com/2006/01/08/politics/08cnd-policy.html.*

❋ BACKGROUND

Permalinks are a way to ensure that site visitors can save URLs and return to them as needed or share them with other people. Permalinks are useful for any site genre (Pattern Group A) that has BROWSABLE CONTENT (B2).

✳ PROBLEM

It's frustrating for visitors to try to return to a site that they found interesting, only to discover that the page they bookmarked is no longer there.

When visitors to your site discover useful information, it's natural for them to want to return later to reread that information. Many people also share URLs with others through e-mail. Web browsers make finding a site again easy by letting visitors save a Web page's URL as a bookmark or favorite.

Whether a day, a week, or a year later, visitors to your Web site might want to return to the information they found there, and they expect to be able to use the link that got them to the site in the first place to return to the same page. Depending on how you've designed your site, however, the bookmark may or may not work. The URL might lead to a Web page that is constantly updated with content and thus may no longer have what someone is looking for, or worse, it might lead to a PAGE NOT FOUND (K14) error. This can be a frustrating experience for visitors, who must then either browse or search the site to find the information they want. In the worst case, they might abandon the site entirely, breaking the positive connection that you previously established with them.

You can avoid this problem by using appropriately designed permalinks that will always let people find the content they want.

Reserve Generic Permalinks for Category Pages • The designer of a news site might create a CATEGORY PAGE (B8) called *TopStories.html* that contains the headlines for the most important news of the day. The designer reasons that visitors can bookmark the URL so that when they return to the site, they'll see the latest news. But what about visitors who want to return to one of Tuesday's stories a few days later? They need to bookmark the individual article itself, which therefore needs its own non-generic permalink.

The problem of retrieving new content with an old link arises with any page that is constantly updated with new content, as is often the case with NEWS MOSAICS (A2) and BLOGS (A12). Although generically named permalinks are useful because they're easy for visitors to remember, to minimize the impact of this problem for these types of sites we advocate limiting the use of such generic URLs to HOMEPAGE PORTALS (C1) and CATEGORY PAGES (B8).

Tables K15.1 through K15.3 show examples of how three different Web sites use generic and content-specific permalinks.

Link	Target
http://nytimes.com	Homepage, updated daily
http://nytimes.com/pages/national/index.html	Category page, updated daily
http://nytimes.com/2006/02/05/national/05friedan.html	Specific story
http://nytimes.com/2006/02/05/magazine/05lying.html	Specific story

Table K15.1

Permalinks on the *New York Times* Web Site

The New York Times online uses permalinks in a variety of ways (see Table K15.1). The first two links in Table K15.1 are to the HOMEPAGE PORTAL (C1) and to a CATEGORY PAGE (B8), respectively—pages where visitors would probably expect the content to be updated. The third and fourth links refer to specific stories, and those stories can always be accessed from these URLs.

Metacritic collects reviews for movies, music albums, TV shows, and the like. The first link listed in Table K15.2 is to Metacritic's HOMEPAGE PORTAL (C1). The next two are to CATEGORY PAGES (B8). These kinds of pages are updated periodically. The fourth and fifth links are to specific pieces of media, which are always accessible from these links.

Tiffany.com is the Web site of the famous Tiffany & Co. jewelers (see Table K15.3). Each of its category pages has a short and simple permalink. Individual product pages also use permalinks that can be bookmarked and e-mailed, but these URLs are longer and are not meant to be read or typed in.

Link	Target
http://www.metacritic.com	Homepage, updated daily
http://www.metacritic.com/music	Category page, updated periodically
http://www.metacritic.com/film/weekendboxoffice.shtml	Category page, updated weekly
http://www.metacritic.com/film/titles/goodnightandgoodluck	Specific movie
http://www.metacritic.com/music/artists/clearlake/amber	Specific music album

Table K15.2

Permalinks on Metacritic's Web Site

Table K15.3

Permalinks on
Tiffany's Web Site

Link	Target
http://www.tiffany.com	Homepage, updated periodically
http://www.tiffany.com/shopping/default.aspx?category=Diamonds	Category page, updated periodically
http://www.tiffany.com/shopping/default.aspx?category=Gifts	Category page, updated periodically

Temporary URLs Are Important for Certain Types of Web Sites • Temporary URLs are essential for Web sites that want to prevent visitors' Web browsers from caching sensitive information. For example, designers of banking sites and other secure Web applications want customer data to be forgotten when a session ends so that other people using the same computer cannot access someone else's confidential information.

One solution is to configure the application to create temporary URLs for the secure pages displayed during the session. Even if the customer creates a bookmark to one of these secure pages, any attempt to access the page later will fail because that URL no longer exists. The designer typically configures the site so that when visitors attempt to access the temporary URLs, they are automatically returned to the site's homepage or to a secure login page. Note that the site's HOMEPAGE PORTAL (C1) and secure SIGN-IN/NEW ACCOUNT (H2) page are assigned permalinks so that customers can come back to them again and again.

Use Permalinks to Establish Positive Connections with Customers • For non-secure content like that found on NEWS MOSAICS (A2), information sites, public-access Web applications, e-commerce catalog pages, BLOGS (A12), and social networking sites, each page contains information that the site owners hope visitors will save and share. Even pages deep in the site should have permalinks that remain perpetually active so that customers can always return to information where they originally found it.

Identify the Immutable Aspects of the Page • To devise appropriate permalinks for your site, think about the elements of the page that are unchangeable, and that define its essence. Use these elements to create a pattern for your URL naming conventions. For example, sites providing the latest news about a particular topic usually consist of pages that are associated with a particular date (see Figure K15.2). *News,* in this case, need not refer to "hard" news, such as crime and politics; a site could be

Figure K15.2

News sites, blogs, and other sites that are updated on a regular basis frequently use URLs that are based on the date that each page is published. In the case of this blog, the site designer has created separate directories representing the year, month, and day that each page was created. Because the pages created on succeeding days will be located in a different directory, the page shown here can always be accessed using the same URL.

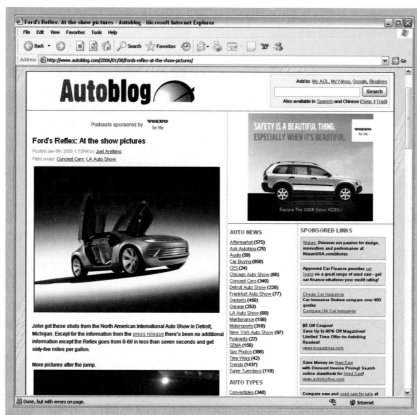

K15.2 (www.autoblog.com/2006/01/08/fords-reflex-at-the-show-pictures, January 8, 2006)

devoted to the latest news about a particular hobby or special interest, or even an individual person or family, such as in a BLOG (A12). Using the date the story was posted as part of the URL is a common way of making news pages perpetually available to site visitors.

Include Text Suggesting the Content of the Page • Here's an example of a good permalink from the popular blog Boing Boing:

www.boingboing.net/2006/02/06/2006_mayan_calendars.html

Even without knowing anything about this blog, you could correctly guess that the content was published in 2006 and is about Mayan calendars, which is our main point: including meaningful text in your URLs makes it easier for people to guess what the focus of a Web page is.

Figure K15.3

On a mapping site, the content is created on demand according to the customer's request so URLs based on dates would be useless. Instead, this site creates URLs that contain the location shown on the map, so that when the customer attempts to access the same page later using a bookmark, the site displays the same content.

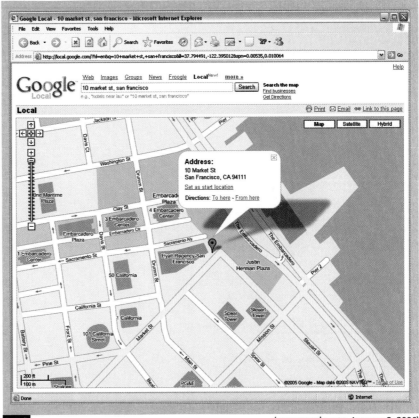

K15.3

(www.google.com, January 8, 2006)

However, although a URL based on the publication date might be suitable for some types of sites, it is clearly not appropriate for others. For example, on a mapping site like the one shown in Figure K15.3, a more useful URL might be based on the precise location displayed on the map, including a street address, a business name, or even latitude and longitude.

On a search engine site (see Figure K15.4), the site designer can establish a URL naming pattern for search result pages based on the search string the visitor used when initiating the search. With this convention, accessing a bookmark containing the URL will cause the same search to be performed again. Many PERSONAL E-COMMERCE (A1) sites with a large number of products or with seasonal content use this approach as well. See Table K15.3 for an example of how Tiffany & Co. uses these kinds of URLs for its CATEGORY PAGES (B8).

K15.4

(www.google.com, January 8, 2006)

Figure K15.4

Search engine sites typically use permalinks that contain the search string supplied by the customer. Accessing a bookmark of the page therefore causes the site to perform the same search again whenever the customer accesses the bookmark. Note, however, that although the URL might be permanent, it will not necessarily yield the exact same results later, because the information found by the search engine is likely to have changed.

Create a Naming Convention for Your URLs and Stick to It • For the sake of both administrators and visitors, devise a convention for naming permalinks and then apply it throughout the site without exception. A consistent set of rules for URL formation helps visitors navigate around the site and enables different administrators to modify and maintain the site without creating conflicting URL patterns.

Create Short URLs That Are Practical and Readable • Making your permalinks as brief and as readable as possible is preferable for several reasons. Short, readable URLs are easier to remember, often enabling visitors to return to a site even when they haven't created a bookmark. Furthermore, many Web browsers offer predictive URL completion for previously visited Web pages, and readable URLs are easier to recognize. Figure K15.5 shows an example of a short, readable URL.

Figure K15.5

The Yahoo! Groups site uses permalinks that contain the name of a group and a section within that group. This naming formula keeps the URL relatively short and easily understandable.

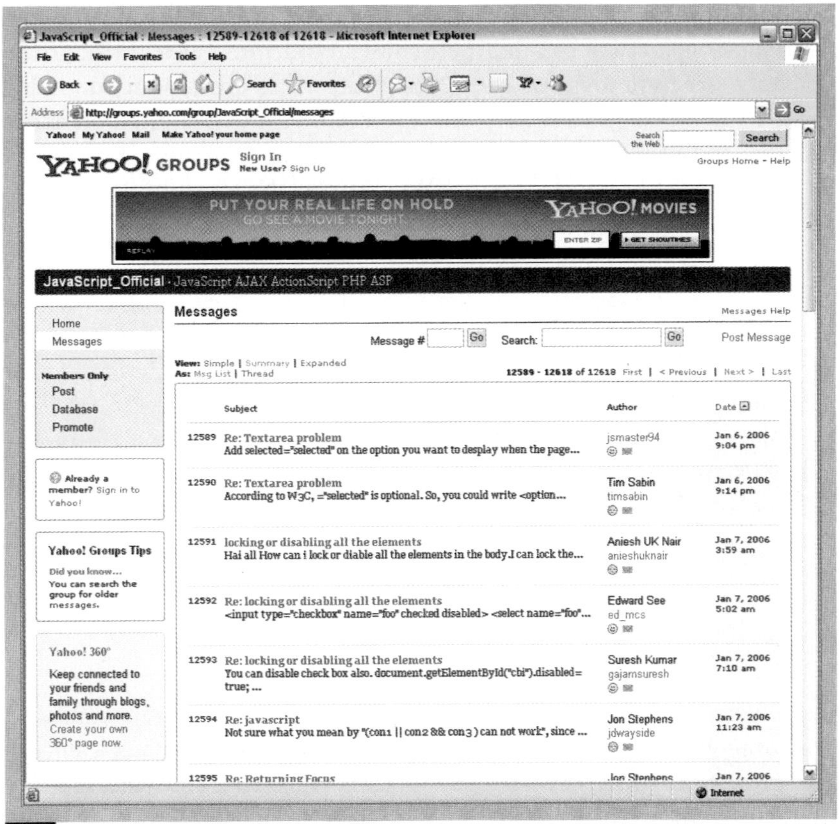

K15.5

(groups.yahoo.com, January 8, 2006)

Short URLs are also less likely to cause problems when they're shared. Long URLs are frequently broken across two or more lines when e-mailed. Many e-mail readers do not handle this situation correctly, however, and often the result is a PAGE NOT FOUND (K14) error.

When creating URLs for your Web site, also be careful of blank spaces and punctuation because these kinds of special characters are replaced by strings like *%20*, making the URL difficult to read. For example, the fictitious URL

http://www.example.com/[category news]

is automatically converted by many Web browsers into

http://www.example.com/%5Bcategory%20news%5D

Implement a Storage Solution So That Your Pages Can Persist Forever • When devising a means for creating permalinks, you must also consider the directory structure for your site. Even if the URLs are unique, dumping them all into a single directory will eventually cause a site maintenance problem and possibly slow down server performance. As noted in several of the previous examples, permalinks can contain categorical elements, such as dates, that translate easily into directory names.

Design Dynamic Elements into Static Pages • Creating permalinks for your homepages does not necessarily mean that all of the content on these pages has to remain static forever. You incorporate dynamic content, such as banner ads and navigation links, into a permanent page by using appropriately designed PAGE TEMPLATES (D1) and CONTENT MODULES (D2). In the future, a visitor returning to a bookmarked page will see all of the original content, but the ads and navigation links are likely to change.

✳ SOLUTION

Create permalinks for site content that you want to be perpetually available. Temporary URLs are suitable for confidential content that you don't want visitors' browsers to cache. Use immutable aspects of the page (like date, topic, or street address) and view-specifying parameters to devise a naming pattern for permalinks. If a URL is meant to be saved or shared, design a naming convention that permits short (and preferably human-readable) URLs. Incorporate a directory structure into your URLs that will enable your servers to store large amounts of content perpetually.

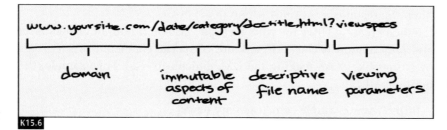

K15.6

Figure K15.6

Permalinks are short URLs that incorporate the immutable aspects of the page to make the page perpetually available.

✳ OTHER PATTERNS TO CONSIDER

Consider using generic URLs for HOMEPAGE PORTALS (C1) and for CATEGORY PAGES (B8). Giving your site's HOMEPAGE PORTAL (C1) and secure SIGN-IN/NEW ACCOUNT (H2) page permalinks will help visitors come back to them again and again. If you include a visitor's search terms in the URL for a search result, the search can be saved as a permalink on PERSONAL E-COMMERCE (A1) sites, NEWS MOSAICS (A2), BLOGS (A12), or any other site genre. Beware that many e-mail readers do not handle URLs longer than one line, leading to a PAGE NOT FOUND (K14) error, so try to keep your URLs short. You can incorporate dynamic content, such as banner ads and navigation links, into a permalink page by using appropriately designed PAGE TEMPLATES (D1) and CONTENT MODULES (D2).

K16 JUMP MENUS

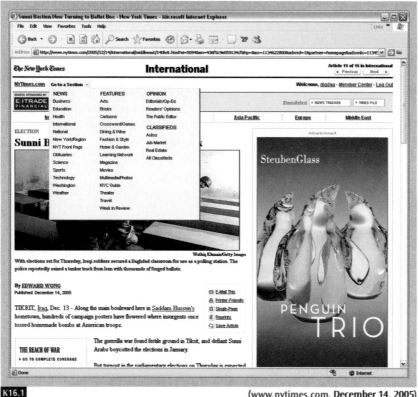

Figure K16.1

This jump menu on the *New York Times* Web site provides access to subareas of the site, much as a table of contents provides access to the sections of a newspaper.

K16.1
(www.nytimes.com, December 14, 2005)

✳ BACKGROUND

Jump menus are an alternative or a supplement to NAVIGATION BARS (K2) and can be used in most site genres (Pattern Group A). A jump menu is one way of providing MULTIPLE WAYS TO NAVIGATE (B1), as well as BROWSABLE CONTENT (B2).

K2

◆ A

B1

B2

✳ PROBLEM

Providing copious navigation links to key site areas can make large sites easier to use, but too many links on a page can be overwhelming.

Organizing the homepage of a large site with a great deal of content can be quite a challenge. A NAVIGATION BAR (K2) is an excellent way to provide customers with direct links to all areas of a site, but on a large site, the sheer number of links can be problematic and start to dominate the page. For large sites, each of the three types of NAVIGATION BARS (K2) has its limitations:

1. A *top-running* navigation bar typically does not provide enough space for all the necessary links, even if used only for section or subsite links.

2. A *side-running* navigation bar provides more room for links but can still grow too large very quickly. A side-running bar requires a line for every section name and every individual item. On a large site, the list of sections and links can grow too long, preventing a portion of it from appearing ABOVE THE FOLD (I2). The list can also grow to the point of taking up too much screen real estate and becoming the dominant feature of the page rather than a helpful peripheral tool.

3. A *top-and-left* (or *inverted L*) navigation bar spreads out the menu by separating the section links from the individual items for each section, and it makes it easier to keep the entire menu system above the fold, but it still requires a substantial amount of screen real estate. In addition, this type of navigation bar requires a page reload to update the left-hand menu whenever the customer selects a new item in the top-running menu (unless the page has been designed to dynamically update itself using JavaScript). These page reloads take time, possibly adding to customer frustration, although PERSONAL E-COMMERCE (A1) sites can take advantage of these reloads to provide other promotional options.

Create a Jump Menu to Retain Full Navigation While Preserving Screen Space •
Jump menus let you provide direct links to a large number of pages across a large site without using more screen real estate. A **jump menu** is a navigation menu that expands when it's needed and collapses when it's not. When a customer clicks on the trigger for the jump menu, identified by an instruction or a heading, a box containing OBVIOUS LINKS (K10) appears. The customer can select one of the links and proceed directly to that page, or click outside of the jump menu, causing it to collapse into its original form.

For example, Figure K16.1 shows a jump menu for a newspaper Web site that provides customers with access to all of the paper's various sections.

The jump menu is accessible from a top-running navigation bar, providing many more links than could possibly fit on that navigation bar in its standard form or even on a side-running navigation bar.

Make the Function of a Jump Menu Immediately Obvious • Jump menus can perform a variety of navigation functions, and they can appear anywhere on a homepage. Therefore, visitors to the site must be able to recognize the function of each jump menu immediately and intuitively. You can indicate the function of a jump menu by placing a heading above or beside the trigger for the box (specifying the types of links that the jump menu provides), by including an instruction informing visitors how to use the box, or by adding a small arrow nearby to suggest that visitors can click on the menu to open it. In Figure K16.2, for example, the "Browse by Make" label indicates the function of the jump menu just beneath it. In the

K16.2

(www.collectablediecast.com, December 15, 2005)

Figure K16.2

A jump menu requires some type of label or instruction to inform customers of its function. The jump menu also has a trigger (usually a down arrow) that enables customers to expand and collapse it.

same way, a general jump menu might have a label saying, "Go to Section," and a banking site might have a jump menu for "Account Services."

Note that you can also use the first entry in the jump menu list itself to provide instruction. In its collapsed state, the jump menu in Figure K16.2 displays only "Select" which is neither a link nor an entry in the alphabetical list of automakers. When a customer clicks the "Select" entry (or the down arrow next to it), the jump menu containing the full list of automakers appears. Adding two hyphens before and after the instruction word distinguishes it from the actual links in the jump menu list, and ensures that the instruction appears first in the alphabetical list of terms.

Create a Pick List Using Standard Organizational Options • The simplest type of jump menu is an expandable/collapsible pick list containing navigation links, as shown on the right in Figure K16.3 under "Custom Rate Search."

Figure K16.3

The **Custom Rate Search** option on the right in this screen shot contains a simple jump menu that lets E-LOAN visitors navigate by selecting the type of loan they need. You can use the same technique to permit navigation by category, by task, or by any other organizational paradigm.

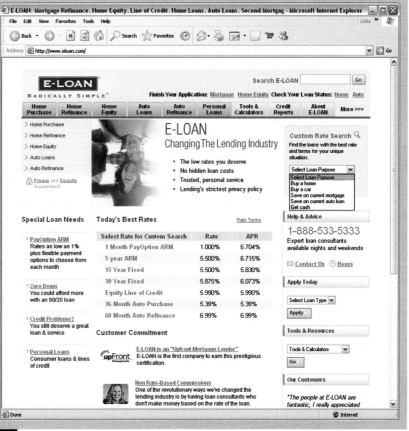

K16.3

(www.eloan.com, December 15, 2005)

As with other types of navigation menus, you can arrange the items in the pick list using any form of organization suitable to the site. For a navigation jump menu, HIERARCHICAL ORGANIZATION (B3) is often suitable, with separate groups of links separated by category titles. TASK-BASED ORGANIZATION (B4) is common in a jump menu that provides a list of specific functions, such as one for an online banking site or the loan site shown in Figure K16.3. Links can also appear in order of popularity [see POPULARITY-BASED ORGANIZATION (B7)], or in any other suitable order. ALPHABETICAL ORGANIZATION (B5) is common in jump menus containing a long list of terms, such as in the list of automakers shown in Figure K16.2.

A Simple Form-Based Pick List Requires a Button • Using a simple pick list is the easiest way to program a jump menu. But because a simple pick list is actually an element of an HTML form, you must include a mechanism that enables the customer to submit the form, which in this case causes the browser to send the list item selected by the customer to the server hosting the site. The submit mechanism is typically a small square button containing the word *Go* placed just to the right of the text entry box for the form (see Figure K16.4). In addition to its form-processing function, the **Go** button serves as an indicator of the pick list's function.

Use JavaScript to Submit the Form Automatically • You can use JavaScript to program the jump menu to submit a form automatically when a customer selects one of the links in the pick list, eliminating the need for the customer to click the **Go** button. However, most automated jump menus include the button even when it's not strictly necessary, either as a backup trigger mechanism or simply as a visual clue (affordance) to the pick list's function. Beware that jump menus that automatically submit in this way can cause the customer to navigate to the wrong page if an item is accidentally selected.

Use DHTML to Build More Complex Jump Menus • Simple HTML form–based jump menus are limited to a single column of links, but by using DHTML (Dynamic HTML), you can create larger jump menus containing more links, using horizontal as well as vertical layout. Using the <div> element to build a DHTML jump menu enables you to create a more

Figure K16.4

The jump menu on this online banking page enables customers to display different types of account information by selecting an item from the list and clicking the **Go** button. However, this page could just as well use JavaScript to submit the form automatically, eliminating the need for the customer to click the button.

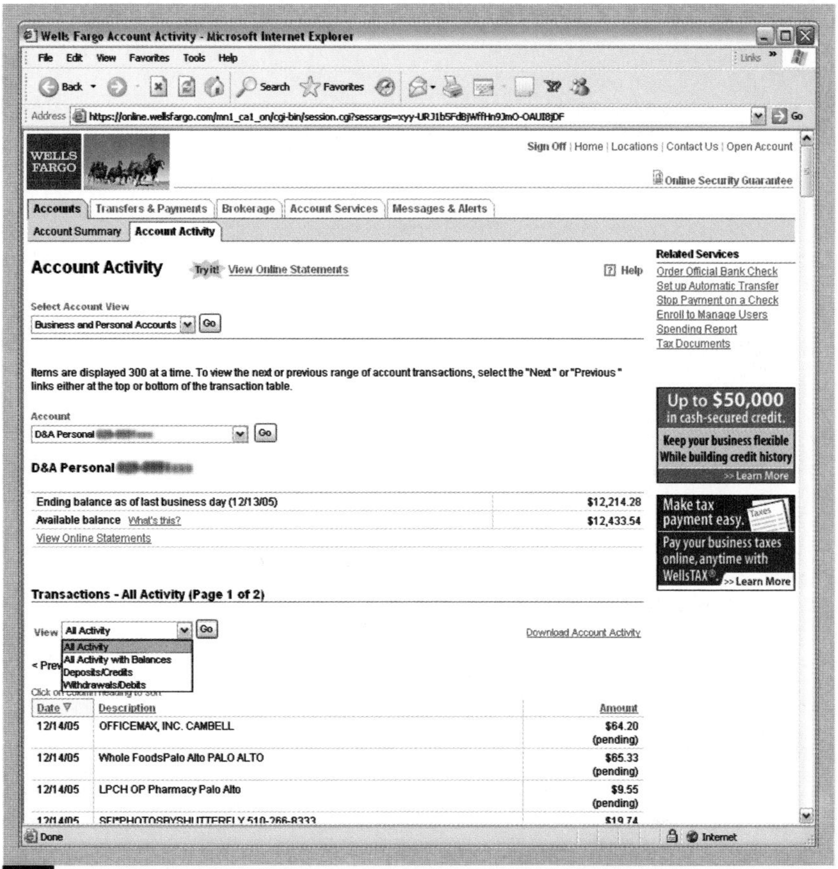

K16.4

(www.wellsfargo.com, December 15, 2005)

complex navigation menu, like the one shown in Figure K16.5. As with other two-dimensional menu designs, you can organize the content in whatever manner is appropriate for your site. Complex jump menus commonly use a GRID LAYOUT (I1), which makes the links easy to use and helps keep the content ABOVE THE FOLD (I2).

Without visual clues that the options are clickable, the DHTML menu will not serve its purpose. As with a simple jump menu, use OBVIOUS LINKS (K10) to make sure that customers recognize the menu items as links. Also make sure that the design you select for the jump menu is consistent with any other types of navigation menus used on the site.

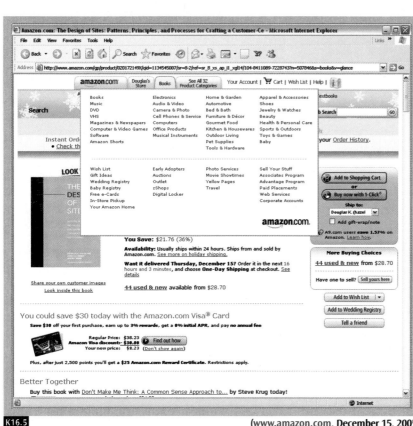

Figure K16.5

A DHTML-based jump menu can take any size or shape and can contain multiple columns and rows of links, as well as additional content, such as the logo shown here.

K16.5   (www.amazon.com, December 15, 2005)

✳ SOLUTION

Create a jump menu to provide a large navigation menu without using an excessive amount of screen real estate. Use standard organization options, such as subject categories or task-based organization, when creating your list of menu options. Include a title for the jump menu to inform customers of its purpose. Choose between a simple forms-based pick list and a more complex DHTML-based jump menu. For a pick list, reinforce the function of the jump menu by including a Go button, and by using the first item in the list to provide instructions to the customer. For a DHTML-based jump menu, create menu options horizontally and vertically using a grid-based layout, and make sure that the menu options are immediately identifiable as links.

Figure K16.6

Jump menus let your visitors quickly get to a particular part of your site without cluttering your pages with too much navigation content.

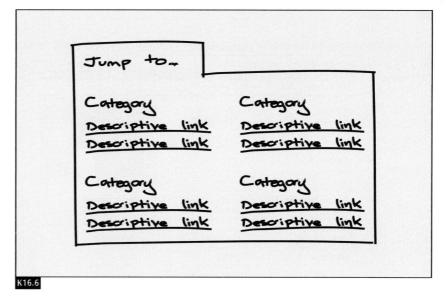

K16.6

✳ OTHER PATTERNS TO CONSIDER

All Web site visitors must pass through the HOMEPAGE PORTAL (C1), and for small to medium-sized sites, a NAVIGATION BAR (K2) is sufficient to provide access to other areas of the site. For large sites, a SITE MAP (K17) can display many more links than a navigation bar, but a site map is intended more as a fallback for customers encountering navigation problems. HIERARCHICAL ORGANIZATION (B3) is often suitable for navigation jump menus, with separate groups of links separated by category titles. TASK-BASED ORGANIZATION (B4) is common in a jump menu that provides a list of specific functions, such as one for an online banking site. ALPHABETICAL ORGANIZATION (B5) is common in jump menus containing a long list of terms. Like the other navigation options on your site, jump menus need to use OBVIOUS LINKS (K10) and fit as much content as possible ABOVE THE FOLD (I2).

K17 SITE MAP

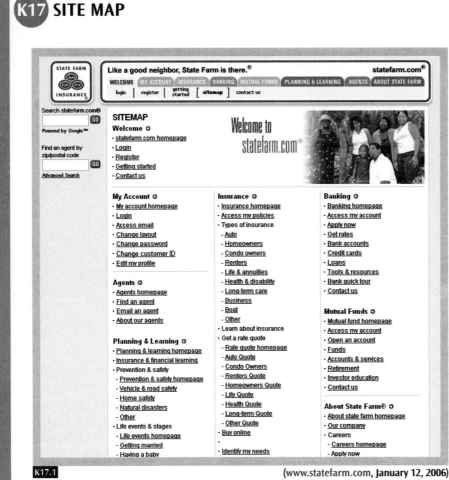

Figure K17.1

State Farm uses a site map with a grid-based hierarchical organization that provides links to category pages and enables visitors to locate specific functions within each category quickly.

`K17.1`

(www.statefarm.com, January 12, 2006)

✳ BACKGROUND

Used by most site genres (Pattern Group A), a site map offers an overview of the entire Web site and is used as a backup form of navigation. It is one way of providing MULTIPLE WAYS TO NAVIGATE (B1), as well as BROWSABLE CONTENT (B2).

A

B1

B2

✳ PROBLEM

Finding specific information in a site can sometimes be difficult, especially if it's not obvious where to start looking.

A typical homepage must accommodate visitors that have many different needs. An ideal homepage provides easy access to all areas of the site without overwhelming visitors with too much content. In working toward this ideal, however, designers inevitably have to make compromises, meaning that not every visitor will be equally well served. For example, a VALUABLE COMPANY SITE (A7) designed primarily for use by customers might not be able to devote much homepage space to the needs of other types of visitors, such as job seekers, investors, or the press. These other visitors often have highly specific needs and don't want to spend time browsing or searching through the site to find the latest job postings, financial documents, or press releases.

One way of addressing this problem is to provide MULTIPLE WAYS TO NAVIGATE (B1). However, it's not always possible to provide access to all of the site's features using every navigation method. For example, some visitors prefer to browse using links, but the homepage might not have enough room to link to every section of the site. Other visitors might prefer to search for specific documents, but for various reasons a search engine might not produce the exact results the visitor wants. A site map is a navigation option that functions as an ultimate fallback or backup, providing visitors with access to all of the functions of a site. Site maps provide an overview of the entire Web site, outlining all of the major portions in a meaningful manner. This pattern offers guidelines for creating effective site maps.

Design Site Maps as a Backup to Other Site Navigation • Because visitors often use the site map as a last resort for site navigation, it must provide access to all of the features of the site. Visitors who are unable to locate the feature they need in the site map are most likely to assume that the site lacks that feature. For this reason, you must keep the site map complete, periodically updating it whenever new features are added to your site. A useful method for creating this list of features is to conduct a task analysis, as described in Chapter 3 (Knowing Your Customer: Principles and Techniques).

Don't Let Site Maps Substitute for Well-Designed Navigation • Site maps are the navigation mechanism of last resort for frustrated visitors, so make every effort to avoid having your visitors need to use one. Overreliance on the site map might be a good indication that you need to revamp your overall navigation or include links to more sections, using JUMP MENUS (K16) on every page. By examining the site logs, you might be able to identify trends that indicate which site visitors are not being served adequately by your other means of navigation. For example, if your logs show that a disproportionate number of visitors are using the site map to access the ABOUT US (E5) pages containing the company telephone numbers, assume that those pages are not easily accessible by other means, and take steps to improve their visibility.

A Well-Organized Site Map Can Provide a Highly Detailed Site Overview • A site map provides access to a Web site's content with more detail than a HOMEPAGE PORTAL (C1) or even CATEGORY PAGES (B8) can. A site map might also include links to sections intended for specific types of visitors that might not fit on the homepage. For example, a site map might have an entire section for investors, containing links to press releases, financial disclosures, and the company's current stock price.

A Site Map Needs to Serve Everyone • Unlike a HOMEPAGE PORTAL (C1), a site map has to accommodate all types of visitors to a site. Whereas a homepage should be designed to serve the needs of the most common visitors, a site map must be more equitable in its arrangement. As a result, a site map typically does not contain many of the cosmetic elements usually found on other pages, such as large graphics and complex backgrounds. In most cases, a site map is a simple page of OBVIOUS LINKS (K10) arranged in a GRID LAYOUT (I1) that combines HIERARCHICAL ORGANIZATION (B3) with TASK-BASED ORGANIZATION (B4) (see Figure K17.2). Using all-text links and HTML POWER (L4) for the site map enables the page to load quickly, even though it might contain a huge amount of information. In addition, when you're WRITING FOR SEARCH ENGINES (D6), the site map will provide an alternative destination to successfully fulfill a customer's search.

We discuss some of these design issues in more depth in the sections that follow.

Don't Let Your Site Map Directly Reflect Your Web Directory Structure • It's tempting just to create a simple page of text links that reflects the underlying directory structure of your Web site. However, this straightforward approach rarely yields the best results, because it reflects how your Web designers think of the Web site rather than how visitors think of it.

A site designer must do a good job building BROWSABLE CONTENT (B2) and organizing the content in a way that's meaningful for visitors.

Figure K17.2

Google's site map consists of a grid containing headlines for the site's major categories and bulleted text links for the individual features in each category.

K17.2

(www.google.com, January 12, 2006)

An endless list of undifferentiated text links can result in a site map that is difficult to use and only compounds the frustration of the visitor.

As noted already, we advocate using a combination of HIERARCHICAL ORGANIZATION (B3) and TASK-BASED ORGANIZATION (B4) for most site maps. For example, Figure K17.2 shows Google's site map, which is divided into several categories useful for different kinds of visitors. Keep in mind that, if it makes sense to do so, you can put an item in more than one category in a site map. This way, people approaching your site map with different goals will be more likely to find what they're looking for.

Finally, except in rare circumstances, such as a personnel list, ALPHABETICAL ORGANIZATION (B5) is not suitable for a site map.

Link Categories to Category Pages Where Possible • Another way of improving the usability and usefulness of your site map is to include content categories. Content categories make it easy for visitors to scan the page quickly, and linking the categories to CATEGORY PAGES (B8) using OBVIOUS LINKS (K10) enables people to access more general content in a single step.

Use a Grid to Compress Information As Much As Possible • A site map can be a single, long column of text links, but such an arrangement wastes screen space and frustrates visitors by forcing them to scroll down repeatedly. To reduce frustration and increase efficiency, keep as much information as possible ABOVE THE FOLD (I2) by using multiple columns in a GRID LAYOUT (I1). A possible alternative is to include multiple links in each line of text (see Figure K17.3).

Make the Site Map Available from Every Page • A site map that no one can find is not helpful. If you include a link to your site map in the header or NAVIGATION BAR (K2) of your page, it will be hard to miss, but it will also take up valuable real estate ABOVE THE FOLD (I2) of every page. This might

	Store	iPod + iTunes	.Mac	QuickTime	Support	Mac OS X
Hot News	Switch	Hardware	Software	Made4Mac	Education	Pro	Business	Developer	Where to Buy

Apple.com Site Map

About Apple

- Contacting Apple — Phone Numbers | Website Feedback | International Sites
- Investor Relations — Stock Info | Earnings Releases | Calendar
- Job Opportunities — College | Internships | Benefits
- Legal Information — Privacy Information
- Public Relations — Contacts | Exec Bios | Press Release Library
- Where to Buy — Apple Store Online | Retail Stores | Find a Reseller
- **Additional Info** — Accessibility | Environment | Ergonomics | Supplier Diversity | Web Badges

News & Events

- eNews — Subscribe | Current eNews | eNews Schedule
- Hot News
- **Additional Info** — Macintosh Products Guide | Seminars & Events | User Groups

Switch

- Switch — Considering a Mac | Choosing a Mac | Buying a Mac | How To | Getting Started

iPod + iTunes

- iTunes — Free Download | iTunes Music Store | Overview
  - Music | Podcasts | Audiobooks | Create Playlists | Sync with iPod | Share & Stream |Burn CDs
  - Working with iTunes | Labels & Artists | Buy Volume Songs | Sales & Music Marketing | iTunes Link Maker
  - Buy Music Now | Send Gift Certificates | Redeem Gift Certificates | New Music Tuesday | Music Requests | Music Store Support
- iPod — Features | Sync Your Music | Accessories | Car Integration | Tech Specs
- iPod nano — Features | Sync with iTunes | Accessories | Car Intergration | Tech Specs
- iPod shuffle — Tech Specs | Music to Go | Accessories | Shuffle Your Music

Hardware Products

- AirPort Express — Tech Specs | AirTunes | Unwire Your Living Room | On the Go
- AirPort Extreme — Tech Specs | Wireless Hotspots | At Home | On Campus
- Displays — Tech Specs | Design | Technology | Digital | Environment
- eMac — Tech Specs | SuperDrive | Graphics | Software

K17.3

(www.apple.com, January 12, 2006)

Figure K17.3

Apple's site map, instead of using a grid, places multiple text links on each line of an unnumbered list. Notice how this design employs categories in two dimensions: vertically, with headlines separating groups of bullets; and horizontally, with a subcategory heading at the beginning of each line.

be necessary if you see that visitors use the site map very often, but again, frequent use of the site map is a red flag indicating that your overall site navigation might have problems. If you put the site map link below the fold at the footer of every page, people will find it quickly by scrolling there, and they'll know to expect it on every page.

We suggest placing a link to your site map in at least one of these two areas, and ideally in both. This approach is similar to the placement of **K5** **I2** HIGH-VISIBILITY ACTION BUTTONS (K5) both ABOVE THE FOLD (I2) and below it.

Consider Making Portions of Your Site Map Part of a Page Not Found **Error Page •** If your visitors encounter a "Page not found" error message, provide a page that makes it easy to see what content you have on your Web site. **K14** **K2** This PAGE NOT FOUND (K14) error page might include a NAVIGATION BAR (K2), **J1** a SEARCH ACTION MODULE (J1), and relevant portions of your site map.

❋ SOLUTION

As a backup to site navigation and search, create a site map page that contains links to all of the features offered on the site, and organize the page to serve the needs of all types of visitors equally. Keep the site map page simple— containing only text and HTML—so that it loads quickly. Use a grid layout to keep as many links visible as possible, and place most of the content above the fold. Organize the page using a suitable hierarchy, with categories to separate links for different functions, visitors, or types of content. Link the categories to category pages for quick access to general content. Include a link to the site map from the header or footer of every page.

Figure K17.4

Site maps can help your customers navigate the site when all other navigation options have failed.

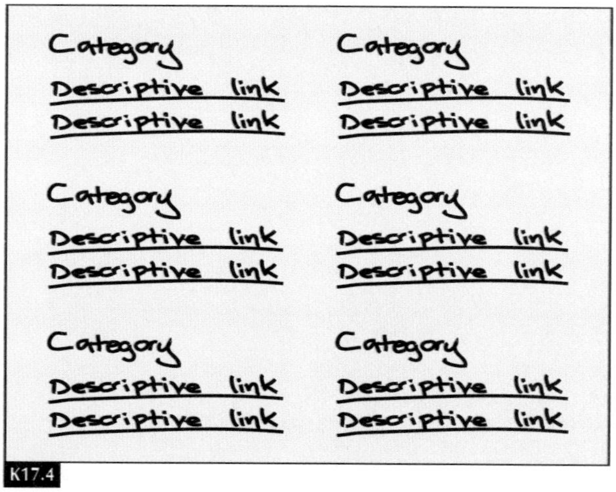

K17.4

✳ OTHER PATTERNS TO CONSIDER

A site map provides access to the content of a Web site with more detail than a HOMEPAGE PORTAL (C1) or even CATEGORY PAGES (B8) can. A JUMP MENU (K16) can enable access to more pages and takes up less space than primary and secondary NAVIGATION BARS (K2) do, but it still won't provide as comprehensive a list of destinations as a site map can.

Like every other page on your site, your site map needs to use OBVIOUS LINKS (K10) and fit as much content as possible ABOVE THE FOLD (I2), arranged in a GRID LAYOUT (I1) and with HIERARCHICAL ORGANIZATION (B3), and possibly with TASK-BASED ORGANIZATION (B4) as well. Using all-text links and HTML POWER (L4) for the site map enables the page to load quickly, even though it might contain a huge amount of information, and provides an alternate destination when you're WRITING FOR SEARCH ENGINES (D6).

A site designer must do a good job building BROWSABLE CONTENT (B2) and organizing the content in a way that's meaningful for visitors. If your visitors encounter a PAGE NOT FOUND (K14) error, provide a page that makes it easy to see what content you have on your Web site. This page might include a NAVIGATION BAR (K2), a SEARCH ACTION MODULE (J1), and relevant portions of your site map.

Speeding Up Your Site ◆ L

Slow Web sites are frustrating to use. A slow homepage can have a major impact on customers' first experience with a site. They might not wait around to find out what you have to offer. Remember, many customers still connect to the Web using slow, analog modems. In March 2006, the Pew Internet & American Life Project estimated that roughly 42 percent of Americans had high-speed Internet access at home, up from 30 percent the previous year. Even if you're designing a business site, many of your customers will be accessing your site from home, after work hours, or from a laptop on the road. Furthermore, many customers are starting to access the Web from their mobile phones. These devices will probably always trail behind office network speeds. We have done some research on the techniques you can apply to speed up your Web site. Keep in mind, however, that it's just as important to improve the *perceived* speed of your site. This pattern group describes ways to make your Web site look and feel fast.

L1 LOW NUMBER OF FILES

L2 FAST-LOADING IMAGES

L3 SEPARATE TABLES

L4 HTML POWER

L5 REUSABLE IMAGES

L6 FAST-LOADING CONTENT

L1 LOW NUMBER OF FILES

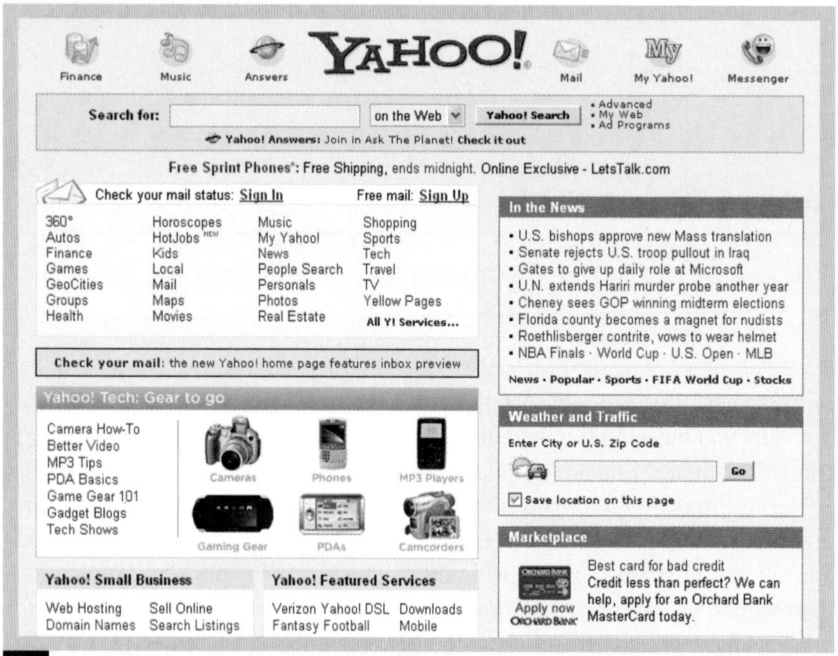

L1.1

(www.yahoo.com, June 16, 2006)

Figure L1.1

Yahoo!'s homepage has a minimalist design with very few images, making it fast to load.

✴ BACKGROUND

You can make your Web site pages load faster by minimizing the number of files contained in those pages. This pattern can be used by itself, or in conjunction with other patterns for creating fast-loading Web pages, such as FAST-LOADING IMAGES (L2), SEPARATE TABLES (L3), HTML POWER (L4), and FAST-LOADING CONTENT (L6).

✳ PROBLEM

Web pages that have many images, audio/video files, applets, and plug-ins are slow to load.

Web surfers are an impatient bunch. The Internet is not called the "World Wide Wait" for nothing. As a Web designer, you face a dilemma. You want your customer to see many items, such as the company logo, navigation bars, a good-looking background, maybe an ad or two, a few images, and lots of text. However, the more image, audio/video, applet, and plug-in files you put on a Web page, the longer it takes for visitors to load it, and the more frustrated they become.

The key is to minimize the number of files that absolutely must be transferred. Fewer files equals shorter download time because there are fewer bytes to transfer, and because the Web browser does not have to communicate as often with the Web server.

Four approaches minimize the number of files that must be loaded:

1. Removing unnecessary image, audio, applet, and plug-in files
2. Using HTML features instead of images, where it makes sense
3. Reusing images
4. Removing slow, large files from pages that need to be fast

Remove Unnecessary Image, Audio/Video, Applet, and Plug-in Files • This approach applies our aesthetic and minimalist design principle [see Chapter 4 (Involving Customers with Iterative Design)]. If removing the file does no harm to the site, take it out. Every extra element draws attention away from the elements that really matter. Removing the extra elements means that Web pages load faster.

Use HTML Features Instead of Images, Where It Makes Sense • This approach takes advantage of the fact that HTML supports buttons, lines, and backgrounds, so you don't have to use images. The features that you implement using HTML POWER (L4) will load much faster.

Reuse Images • This approach makes use of how Web browsers temporarily store (cache) files that the browser has already downloaded. Images that are reused do not have to be loaded again.

Remove Slow, Large Files from Pages That Need to Be Fast • This approach advocates moving large image, audio, applet, and plug-in files to a separate, linked page. That way customers get a fast response, and they can preview the large file and decide whether they want it without having to download the whole thing. A good way to create FAST-LOADING IMAGES (L2) is to present a page of **thumbnails,** or small versions of the original image, each linked to larger versions. You can also link thumbnails to video files. **L2**

The number of files that require transfer must be reduced on a page-by-page basis. Prioritize your site's pages, and then focus your efforts on making the most important pages faster. If your site has not yet been deployed, you will have to make an educated guess as to which pages are the most important. Likely candidates are the homepage and the pages supporting the most common tasks that you expect visitors to want to do. If you already have a live site, analyze your server logs to find the most popular pages.

✳ SOLUTION

Determine your most important pages and focus your efforts on tuning those pages for download performance. Minimize the number of files that absolutely must be loaded for each page. Take advantage of features in HTML and in Web browsers that minimize the number of images customers have to download. In addition, move slow-loading objects from the most important pages to other pages, and provide links to and previews of them instead.

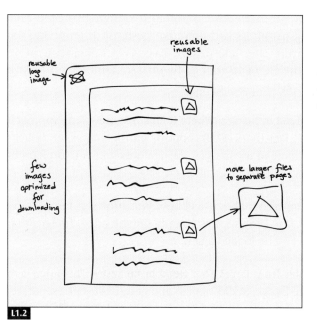

L1.2

Figure L1.2

Use a variety of techniques to minimize the number of files that are downloaded with each Web page.

✳ OTHER PATTERNS TO CONSIDER

(L4) Apply HTML POWER (L4) to use HTML in place of images. Use REUSABLE
(L5) IMAGES (L5) throughout your site so that you can minimize the download cost.

(L2) Use a low number of files in conjunction with FAST-LOADING IMAGES (L2)
(L3) and SEPARATE TABLES (L3) to greatly improve the download time of individual
Web pages.

Two important pages that you can optimize for a low number of files
(C1) (F1) are the HOMEPAGE PORTAL (C1) and the QUICK-FLOW CHECKOUT (F1).

...ADING IMAGES

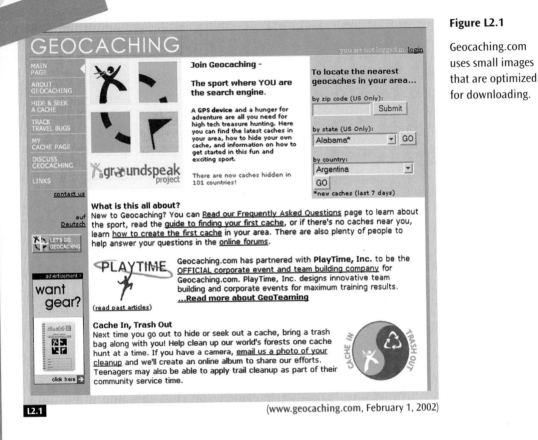

Figure L2.1

Geocaching.com
uses small images
that are optimized
for downloading.

L2.1

(www.geocaching.com, February 1, 2002)

✳ BACKGROUND

Images are often the slowest-loading part of a Web page. Reducing the size of an image can have a significant impact on how visitors perceive your Web site. This pattern describes techniques for reducing the sizes of images, and it can be applied to images you already use or to images that you're about to deploy. This pattern can be used by itself or in conjunction with other patterns for making fast-loading Web pages, such as LOW NUMBER OF FILES (L1), SEPARATE TABLES (L3), HTML POWER (L4), and FAST-LOADING CONTENT (L6).

L1 L3 L4
L6

✳ PROBLEM

Large images are slow to load.

Reducing the sizes of images can significantly speed up customers' experience on your Web site. However, reducing the size of an image can also reduce its quality. There are trade-offs to consider when balancing image quality and image size. Three main approaches to reducing the file size of images are **cropping** (reducing the file size of an image by trimming unneeded portions of it), **shrinking** (scaling down the entire image), and **compressing** (reducing the number of colors used in an image or intentionally degrading the overall quality of an image, thereby reducing the amount of information required to encode the image).

Understand the Strengths and Weaknesses of Different Image File Formats • At this writing, the two most popular file formats for images are **GIF** (Graphics Interchange Format) and **JPEG** (Joint Photographic Experts Group). GIF images can have up to 256 colors and are good for small icons and buttons. GIF images can be compressed without losing any information. GIF images also support transparency, which means that parts of the images can have the same color as the background. This transparency is useful when you want to make ACTION BUTTONS (K4) larger than they actually appear (and thus easier to click), as well as when you're using tables and one-pixel images to ensure that your Web site looks correct, no matter what Web browser your visitors use.

JPEG images are good for photograph-quality images. The JPEG file format can have several million colors, but it does not support transparency, and it throws away some data to get better compression.

A newer file format is **PNG** (Portable Network Graphics). Developed by the World Wide Web Consortium (W3C), PNG is an improvement on GIF and JPEG. PNG was created as an alternative to GIF because Unisys Corporation decided to enforce its patent on GIF, specifically on software tools that output it. PNG images are technically superior to GIF images in several ways; for example, they have more flexible transparency, wider color depth, and better compression, as we'll see shortly. Furthermore, most popular Web browsers and image processing tools now support PNG.

Reduce the Number of Colors • Reducing color depth works only in certain cases. For GIF and PNG files, it can help make files smaller. For JPEG images, though, reducing color depth can sometimes make files *bigger,* and it will have a significant impact on image quality. Experiment with these different formats to find what works for your images. Employ gradients sparingly because they require a much larger color palette and thus larger file sizes.

Crop and Shrink Images • Cropping and shrinking are two common techniques for making images smaller. **Cropping** means cutting out the edges of an image; **shrinking** means resizing the entire image (see Figure L2.2).

Cropping and shrinking are often used to create thumbnails, the small images that we mentioned earlier. Thumbnails load quickly, but they also provide access, by their links, to the larger images or videos. A smart way to make small yet legible thumbnails is to first crop the image to the relevant portion of the material, and then shrink the cropped image.

A common way of presenting a large number of images is the thumbnail page (see Figure L2.3). This design allows customers to browse through a large set of images quickly. You can also provide the file size or a download time estimate for the larger image so that people will know if it will take a long time to load.

Use Higher Compression Ratios on Images • Compression is a common technique for making image files smaller. GIF and PNG files are compressed automatically, via **lossless compression,** meaning that image file sizes are reduced without any loss in image quality. However, GIF images are limited to 256 colors or less, whereas PNG images can have 16 million colors. This means you might need to reduce the number of colors in your GIF images, either by dithering or color averaging, or convert them to PNG files instead.

With JPEG, by contrast, you must choose a compression rate. The problem is that JPEG uses **lossy compression,** meaning that some of

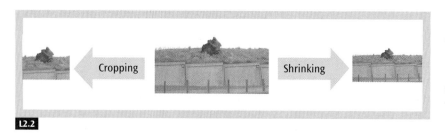

L2.2

Figure L2.2

Cropping makes an image smaller by removing a portion of it; shrinking resizes the entire image.

Figure L2.3

Clicking on a thumbnail image (left) brings up the full-sized version (right).

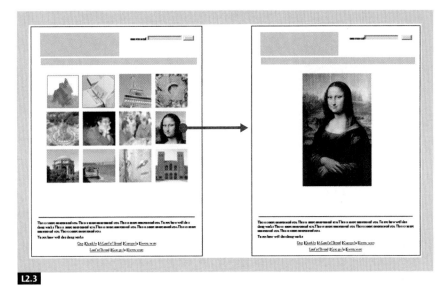

L2.3

the image quality is sacrificed for smaller file sizes. In other words, the higher the compression rate, the smaller the file size but the lower the image quality. When you're dealing with JPEG files, you have to be careful because you can lose a lot of image quality as you keep working with them. One workaround is to save your image in a different file format and convert it to a JPEG when you're ready. Another is to keep older versions of JPEG images so that you can always revert to one of higher quality.

Figure L2.4 compares techniques that reduce image sizes. Note the degradation in the image quality as higher levels of compression are used.

Use Progressive-Scan and Interlaced Images • Progressive-scan and **interlaced images** let visitors see the image as it's loading, making the Web page feel more responsive. Figure L2.5 shows a progressive-scan JPEG image as it's loading. Figure L2.6 shows an interlaced GIF image as it's loading. PNG images can be interlaced as well.

With progressive-scan JPEG images, the files are usually smaller than regular JPEG files. The opposite is true of interlaced GIF images. It can cost a few extra kilobytes to make an interlaced GIF file, but in many cases the faster response time is worth the extra storage space.

Original photo is a progressive JPEG with low compression. The size of the image is 34K.

Original photo, shrunk by 50%. The size is now 11K.

Original photo, cropped by 50%. The size is now 10K.

Original photo, medium compression. The size is now 12K.

Original photo, high compression. The size is now 8K.

Original photo with very high compression. The size is now 5K.

L2.4

Figure L2.4

Various techniques can be used to reduce the size of images. Higher levels of compression yield images of lower quality.

Use the <height> and <width> Attributes for Images • Specifying a height and width makes it easier for Web browsers to lay out the entire page. The browser does not have to wait for all the images to be loaded before displaying content. Your customers will think that the page is loading faster, especially if some of the images are below the fold. Note that the speed-up here is more substantial for older Web browsers than for newer ones.

Use the <alt> Attribute with All Images • Using the <alt> attribute with all images (on <img> tags) lets customers with slow network connections see the names of images even before they have loaded (see Figure L2.7). For more details on how to use the <alt> attribute, see SITE ACCESSIBILITY (B9). **B9**

Consider Combining Small Images That Are Close Together • If you design a page with lots of small images, it can take a long time to load because of

Figure L2.5

When a progressive-scan JPEG image is loading, visitors see the image load from top to bottom.

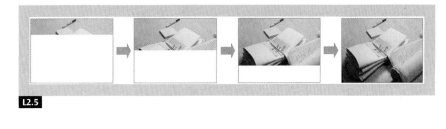

L2.5

Figure L2.6

When an interlaced GIF image is loading, visitors see first a blurry image, then progressive refinement. Note the graininess in the third image and compare it to the cleaner lines in the fourth. Also compare the quality of the final image to that of the example shown in Figure L2.5.

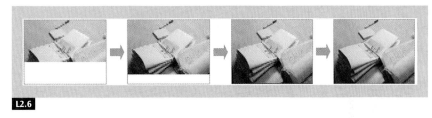

L2.6

the communication overhead of requesting and sending each image. Reduce the overall number of bytes that are downloaded by combining small images into a larger image (see Figure L2.8). If you use the small images as links, the larger image can be made clickable by the use of client-side image maps in the HTML. One trick to be aware of is entering

Figure L2.7

The top screen shot here shows what a customer sees on a Web page that uses image <alt> attributes as it loads. Customers can click on the links without waiting for the images to load. The bottom screen shot shows the same Web page without <alt> attributes.

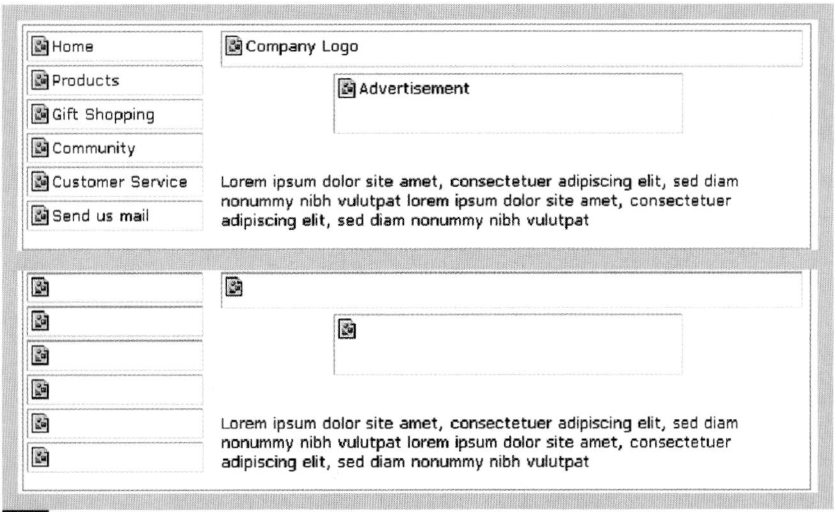

Home	Company Logo
Products	
Gift Shopping	Advertisement
Community	
Customer Service	Lorem ipsum dolor site amet, consectetuer adipiscing elit, sed diam nonummy nibh vulutpat lorem ipsum dolor site amet, consectetuer adipiscing elit, sed diam nonummy nibh vulutpat
Send us mail	

Lorem ipsum dolor site amet, consectetuer adipiscing elit, sed diam nonummy nibh vulutpat lorem ipsum dolor site amet, consectetuer adipiscing elit, sed diam nonummy nibh vulutpat

L2.7

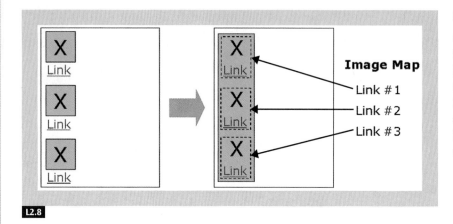

L2.8

Figure L2.8

Combining small
images into one
larger image speeds
up the download.
Place an image map
on top of the larger
image to make it
clickable.

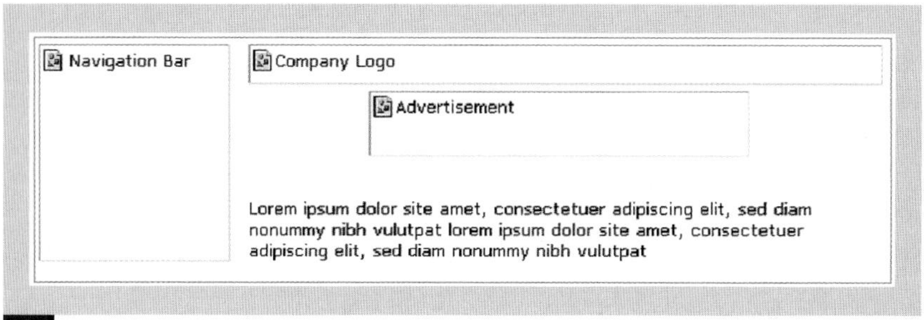

L2.9

Figure L2.9

If you combine small
images, as has been
done with the navi-
gation bar images in
this screen shot, visi-
tors can no longer see
each individual bit of
<alt> text. (Compare
Figure L2.7.)

the text name of the link as part of the image. See ACTION BUTTONS (K4)
for an example.

One disadvantage of combining small images is that you lose the ability
to display <alt> text for each individual image (see Figure L2.9). You can
still label each active region in an HTML image with <alt> text, but currently Web browsers do not display these labels.

Focus on the Main Web Pages First • Consider shrinking, cropping, compressing, or moving large images off of your homepage and other heavy-
traffic Web pages first. These are the pages that customers use the most,
so make them fast first.

❋ SOLUTION

Use a combination of techniques to speed up the loading of images. To the image itself, consider applying the following techniques: changing the image file format, reducing colors, cropping and shrinking, using higher compression, and using progressive-scan or interlaced images. Use other techniques—such as including the <height> and <width> attributes in the HTML, using the <alt> attribute for the <img> tag, and combining small images that are near each other into larger images—to determine how the image is best used on a Web page and to help improve the perceived speed of loading the image.

Figure L2.10

Apply a variety of techniques, both on the image itself and in how the image is used in the Web page, to make images faster to load.

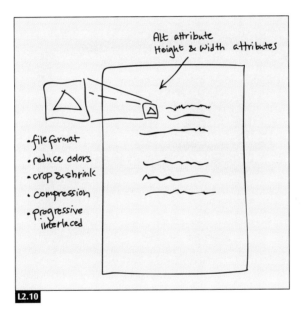

❋ OTHER PATTERNS TO CONSIDER

 REUSABLE IMAGES (L5) appear to load very quickly, in the eyes of the customer.

ACTION BUTTONS (K4) and NAVIGATION BARS (K2) often contain images that you can tune for download speeds.

L3 SEPARATE TABLES

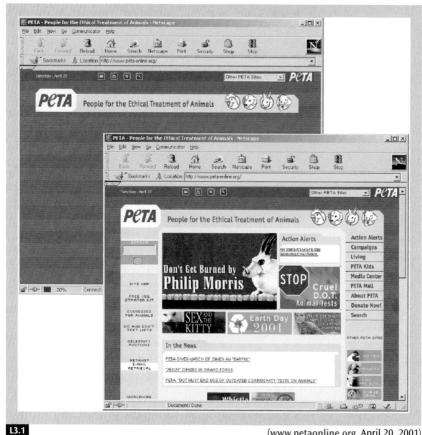

Figure L3.1

This example from the People for the Ethical Treatment of Animals (PETA) site shows separate tables in action. In the background is what a customer sees while the Web page is loading. Note that the logo and some navigation elements are already displayed. In the foreground is what the customer sees after the page has finished loading.

L3.1

(www.petaonline.org, April 20, 2001)

✳ BACKGROUND

This pattern describes ways of simplifying tables and dividing them into smaller tables to make them display faster in Web browsers. The pattern can be applied to speed up older Web sites that still make use of HTML tables for layout. Use this pattern alone or in conjunction with other patterns for making fast-loading Web pages, such as LOW NUMBER OF FILES (L1), FAST-LOADING IMAGES (L2), HTML POWER (L4), REUSABLE IMAGES (L5), and FAST-LOADING CONTENT (L6).

✱ PROBLEM

Web pages with long, complex HTML tables take a long time to be displayed in Web browsers.

Newer Web sites often use XHTML and STYLE SHEETS (D11) to handle page layout. However, older Web pages created before style sheets were popularized typically use HTML tables to control the layout of a page. The problem is that it can take a long time, especially for older browsers, to load these tables. The browser has to calculate the height and width of all the text, images, and plug-ins before displaying anything. The end result is that the Web page feels sluggish.[1]

To make navigation bars and advertisements appear quickly while the rest of the page is still loading, you can split the page into separate tables instead of using one large table. With this approach, the images, text, and tables near the top are displayed first, while the rest of the Web page loads.

The main thing to consider when using separate tables is what should be at the top of the page (see Figure L3.2). Include things like NAVIGATION BARS (K2) and, if possible, CLEAR FIRST READS (I3) and advertisements. Also keep in mind that not everything has to be in an HTML table. See if

Figure L3.2

Because the top of this page is a separate table, customers can get immediate feedback while the bottom table is still loading.

Table 1 loads first

Table 2 loads next

L3.2   (www.babycenter.com, November 16, 2001)

---

1   Newer Web browsers minimize this problem by recalculating how the table should look as text and images are loading, instead of all at once at the end. However, until you're sure that the majority of your customers have the latest Web browsers, we recommend dividing long tables into shorter ones.

you can move elements out of a table while maintaining the basic GRID LAYOUT (I1) you desire. It will be a little harder to align things in a grid. In some cases, the alignment is more important, but this is a trade-off you have to consider case by case.

✳ SOLUTION

For older Web sites that use HTML tables for layout, split large tables into completely separate, smaller tables so that each one can be loaded and displayed independently.

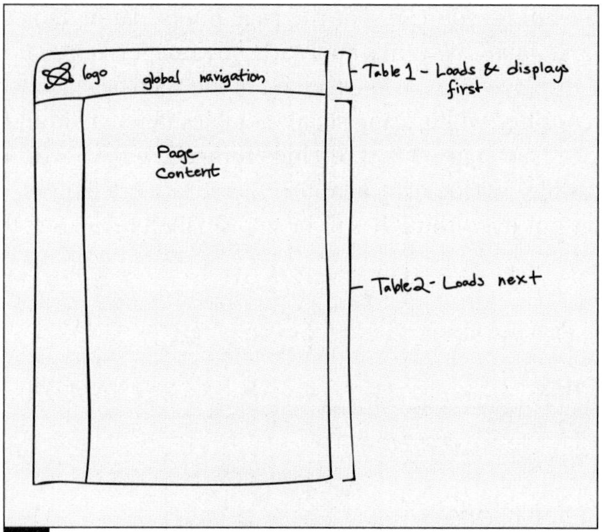

Figure L3.3

Use separate tables so that the top portion of the page can load first. Put important navigation elements and content in the first table so that people will see them first, while the rest of the page is loading.

L3.3

✳ OTHER PATTERNS TO CONSIDER

For newer Web sites, consider using STYLE SHEETS (D11) to specify page layout. For older Web sites, use separate tables when implementing a GRID LAYOUT (I1) in HTML. In some cases, separating the tables or moving things out of them may make it harder to implement a clear grid.

Decide what will go into the table at the top. Some things to consider include a CLEAR FIRST READ (I3) and NAVIGATION BARS (K2).

Figure L4.1

Craigslist provides a clean, functional, and popular Web site without using any images.

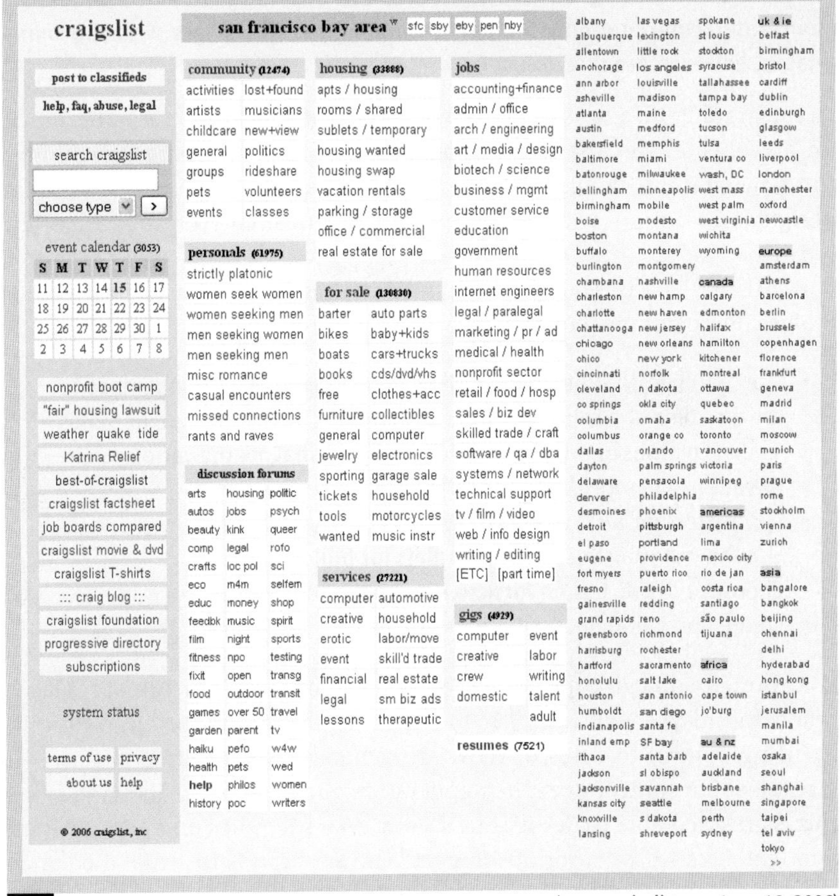

L4.1

(www.craigslist.org, June 16, 2006)

✳ BACKGROUND

This pattern describes features built into HTML that help you reduce the number of images on a page so that Web pages have a LOW NUMBER OF FILES (L1) to be transferred. This pattern can be applied to Web sites that you're about to develop or sites that you've already developed and deployed. It can be used alone or in conjunction with other patterns for making fast-loading Web pages, such as FAST-LOADING IMAGES (L2), SEPARATE TABLES (L3), REUSABLE IMAGES (L5), and FAST-LOADING CONTENT (L6).

✳ PROBLEM

Images are critical to good Web site design because they provide visual clues about interaction and how the page is organized. Web pages with too many images, however, are slow to load.

Great graphic design is an important part of a customer's experience on a Web site. But the more images you put on your site, the longer the pages take to load. Some designers advocate extreme minimalist design as a solution, with few or no images, but such Web sites are often boring.

HTML has many features built into it that you can use in place of images. For example, you might do any of the following:

- Use the <bgcolor> attribute in the <body> tag in place of an image to set the color of a solid background. Use the same technique in tables so that columns or rows have different colors, making the various areas of your page more obvious.
- Choose text for NAVIGATION BARS (K2).   **K2**
- Use the <ul> tag to create the bullets for bulleted lists.
- Choose an HTML button for ACTION BUTTONS (K4).   **K4**
- Create horizontal lines with the <hr> tag.

Although you can consider all these alternatives as functional replacements for images, you will have to think through an important trade-off: by using built-in features of HTML to achieve faster-loading pages, you give up some control over the appearance of a Web page. In some cases this is an acceptable trade-off, but if your Web site relies on a unique look and feel, it can have a serious impact. The solution is to strike a balance between using images and using HTML (see Figure L4.2).

Figure L4.2

The Lincoln Highway site uses HTML features instead of images to handle layout, background colors, and bullets. The result is a simple and clean design that loads quickly.

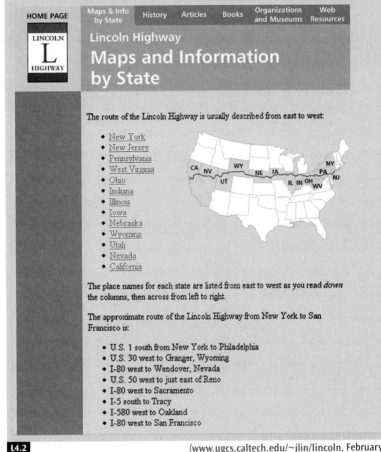

L4.2 (www.ugcs.caltech.edu/~jlin/lincoln, February 11, 2002)

✳ SOLUTION

Wherever it's still functional and aesthetically pleasing to do so, use built-in HTML features instead of images.

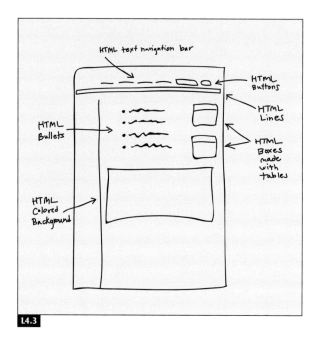

L4.3

Figure L4.3

Often HTML features, including navigation bars, action buttons, dividing lines, bullets, and backgrounds, can be used in place of images for faster loading.

✳ OTHER PATTERNS TO CONSIDER

Use this pattern along with REUSABLE IMAGES (L5) to achieve a LOW NUMBER OF FILES (L1).

If you need ACTION BUTTONS (K4), use HTML as a faster alternative to a custom image. Pure HTML and text can also be used in place of images for NAVIGATION BARS (K2).

L5
L1
K4

K2

Figure L5.1

Napster uses many small, reusable graphics to accent its Web pages, including its logo, small play buttons for quickly playing music, **SHARE IT** links that provide HTML that you can paste into your Web pages, and small arrows highlighting links (for example, **Launch NapsterLinks** and **Go To Narchive**).

L5.1

(www.napster.com, June 16, 2006)

✳ BACKGROUND

This pattern expands on the ideas in LOW NUMBER OF FILES (L1) and focuses on how you can improve the download speed of your Web site using a special feature found in most Web browsers. Apply this pattern if you're about to develop a site, or if you've already developed and deployed a site. Use this pattern alone or in conjunction with other patterns for making fast-loading Web pages, such as FAST-LOADING IMAGES (L2), SEPARATE TABLES (L3), HTML POWER (L4), and FAST-LOADING CONTENT (L6).

✳ PROBLEM

A Web browser must download every image that it has not encountered before.

Every well-designed Web browser has the notion of a **cache,** where Web pages and images that have already been downloaded are stored. The basic idea of the cache is that, if customers go back to a Web page they've seen before, it will display faster because it does not have to be downloaded again.

Images are also cached. In fact, if you design your Web pages to reuse the same images, they will seem to display faster (see Figure L5.2). Make sure the images you want to reuse have the same URL. Here's a list of the most reused images on Web sites:

- Accent graphics, such as "New" or "Hot"
- Logos
- NAVIGATION BARS (K2) and TAB ROWS (K3)
- Stylistic images, such as dividing lines
- Icons, such as those representing mail or SHOPPING CARTS (F3)

K2 **K3**

F3

Some Web sites make the mistake of using one set of images for the NAVIGATION BARS (K2) or TAB ROWS (K3) on their HOMEPAGE PORTAL (C1), and another set of images for the rest of the Web site. The result is a slower customer experience because Web browsers have to download both sets of images. Having a single set of images for navigation will solve this problem.

K2 **K3** **C1**

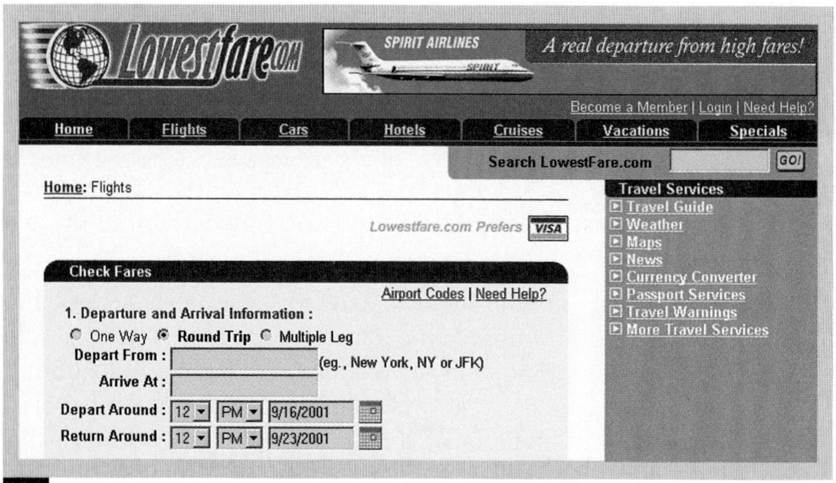

L5.2   (www.lowestfare.com, August 26, 2001)

Figure L5.2

For stylistic purposes, Lowestfare.com makes use of many reusable images, such as the small images used to make curved tabs in the tab row and the small white arrows to mark different travel services offered.

✳ SOLUTION

Design your Web pages to use a core set of reusable images. These images will be cached by Web browsers and will be faster to display the next time they're viewed because they will have been downloaded already.

Figure L5.3

Reusable images include logos, navigation bar images, stylistic images, and accent graphics.

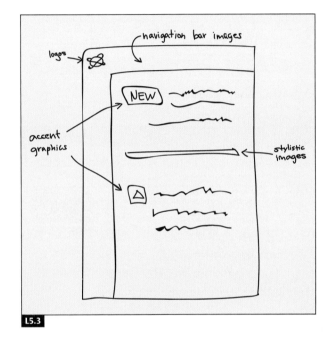

L5.3

✳ OTHER PATTERNS TO CONSIDER

Customers will not have to download reused images again. Use this pattern along with HTML POWER (L4) to achieve a LOW NUMBER OF FILES (L1). One trade-off is that in some cases it's easier to reuse many smaller images than to use one large image that contains the smaller images.

Use this pattern in conjunction with other techniques for creating fast Web pages, such as FAST-LOADING IMAGES (L2) and SEPARATE TABLES (L3). This pattern should also be applied to the HOMEPAGE PORTAL (C1), creating a smoother experience for customers as they visit the rest of your Web site.

NAVIGATION BARS (K2) and TAB ROWS (K3) that use images can also be designed to use only text labels, reducing the number of images that must be downloaded.

Figure L6.1

Optimize server code on your site to make pages load as fast as possible. When they cannot be optimized any further, load data as it comes in and show progress bars so that your customers can start using the initial information and anticipate the delay for the rest.

L6.1

(www.sidestep.com, January 25, 2006)

✳ BACKGROUND

This pattern focuses on the engineering details, as well as customer feedback issues, in tasks that can generate delays in the customer experience. The pattern applies to all sites that perform resource-intensive tasks at either the browser or the server, including PERSONAL E-COMMERCE (A1) sites, NEWS MOSAICS (A2), WEB APPS THAT WORK (A10), and other sites that use PROCESS FUNNELS (H1). To speed up your Web site, you can use this pattern alone or in conjunction with other patterns, such as LOW NUMBER OF FILES (L1), FAST-LOADING IMAGES (L2), SEPARATE TABLES (L3), HTML POWER (L4), and REUSABLE IMAGES (L5).

A1 A2
A10 H1

L1 L2
L3 L4 L5

❋ PROBLEM

Sites sometimes require a long time to process or load information, but making people wait can cause frustration.

Your site might include features and functions that cause delays for visitors. These delays might be as short as a few seconds, as a graphic-intensive page loads, or as long as a few minutes, for more complex processes like credit card authorizations. Delays can occur because the client's browser is busy loading data, such as a large movie file or a great many small files, or because a back-end server is processing information, searching a database, or accumulating results. In some cases, such as the AJAX (Asynchronous JavaScript And XML) application shown in Figure L6.2, the browser might be working in conjunction with the server, causing a delay for the customer. No matter what the cause, though, too much waiting leads to frustrated customers, so make every effort to minimize that frustration.

Is Anything Happening? • Web site visitors faced with loading or processing delays experience the most frustration when they can't see what, if anything, is going on. The server could be calculating or searching, or the browser could be loading data, but if there's no visible feedback that something is occurring, a customer might think that the site is broken, that the connection to the Internet is down, or that the client computer or browser has crashed. In such cases, the customer might leave the site, either temporarily or permanently. This is a particularly aggravating situation when the site requires customers to work, by filling out forms or performing other tasks, resulting in wasted effort when they leave the site in frustration.

Locate the Bottlenecks Affecting Site Performance • The first step in identifying the source of a site performance problem is to determine what elements of the client/server process are causing the slowdown. For example, adding another T1-speed network link to your server's Internet connection will not speed up a customer's performance if the site delays are being caused by the amount of server processing occurring. Work with your engineering team to locate the component, server, connection, or browser that is causing the delay, and then do what you can to eliminate it. The sections that follow offer some specific suggestions.

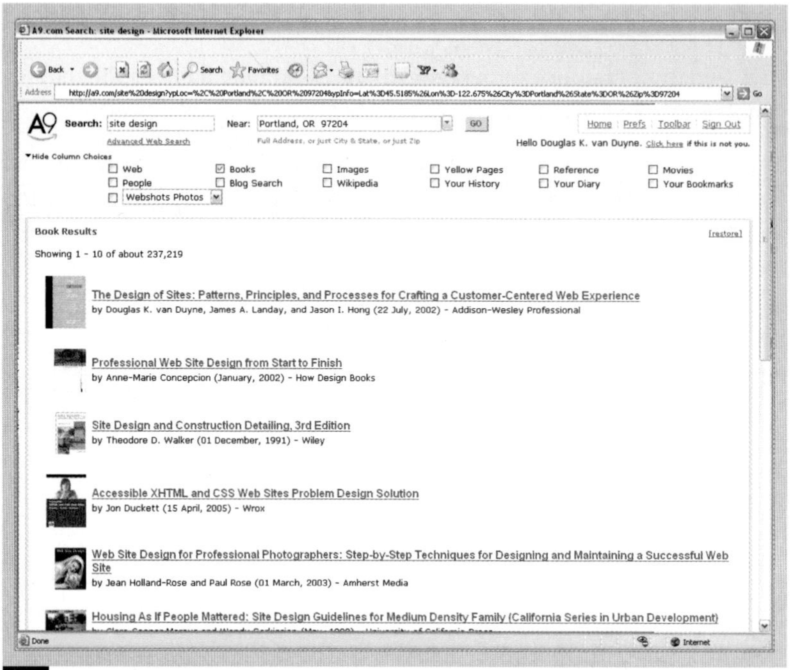

L6.2a

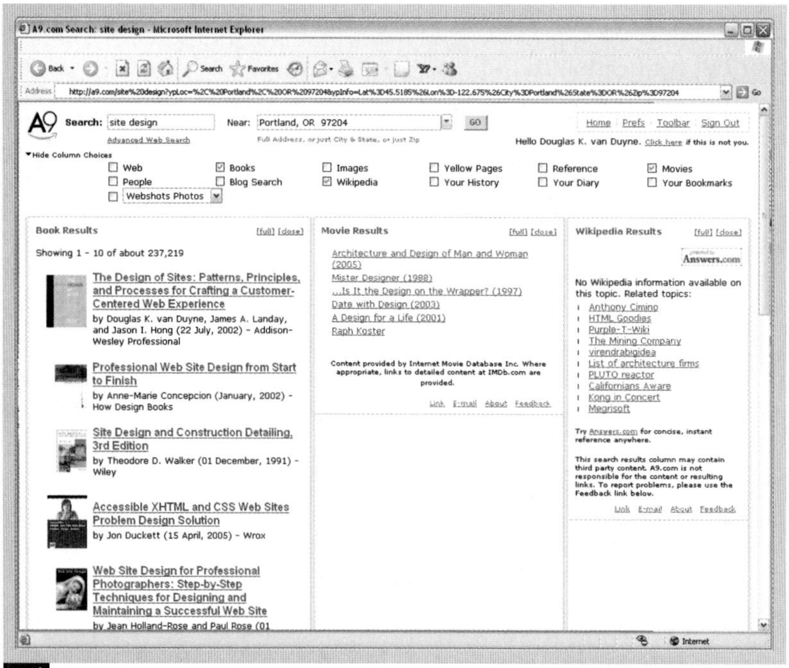

Figure L6.2

The A9.com Web site enables customers to run a search of several different media interactively and simultaneously. (a) When only the **Books** check box is selected, there is a brief delay as the server performs the single search and sends the results to the browser. (b) Selecting additional check boxes causes the server to search for the same string in other media, and display all of the results on the screen at once. Each check box that the customer selects causes the server to perform an additional search, incurring another processing delay.

L6.2b

(www.a9.com, January 25, 2006)

Optimize Server Functions to Load Pages Faster • Managing applications and infrastructure to ensure quick responses is a critical component of any complex Web site. If you determine that your site visitors are experiencing delays due to server processing, you have several avenues to explore to minimize those delays. The first step is to examine your server functions and attempt to optimize them in any way possible. For example, if the server is performing database queries, you might want to examine the query language you're using, to see if it can be optimized. You might also try optimizing the database itself, by recompiling the data or defragmenting the drive on which it's stored. If your server application is already running at peak efficiency, you might want to consider upgrading the server to a computer with more memory or a faster processor. Finally, if traffic levels are high, you might think about increasing the number of servers, using a clustering solution to balance the traffic load between them.

Use Design Strategies to Load Pages Faster • If your site visitors are experiencing delays because pages are loading slowly, you may be able to improve loading times by using page design strategies such as the following:

(L1)
- Using a LOW NUMBER OF FILES (L1), to reduce the number of requests that the browser must make to the server
(L2)
- Creating FAST-LOADING IMAGES (L2), to improve the speed of existing graphics
(L3)
- For older Web pages, using SEPARATE TABLES (L3), to display a portion of each page while downloading more content or processing information
(L4)
- Redesigning graphically intense pages to use HTML POWER (L4) instead
(L5)
- Taking advantage of REUSABLE IMAGES (L5) to optimize use of the browser cache

Show Progress • Sometimes sites depend on services provided by other sites, or on computationally intensive functions, and there's nothing you can do to increase the performance of your site's back end. If this is the case, then other steps will be required to keep visitors from leaving your site in frustration. Showing progress, even if it's slow progress, lets visitors know that the site, the browser, and the computer have not stopped, and that the results will appear eventually.

Use Static Progress Indicators • At its simplest, a progress indicator can consist of a message—such as "Please wait. This may take a minute to process." or "Page loading"—that is displayed to the customer during the delay. For example, Figure L6.3 shows a screen shot of Yahoo! e-mail. When you

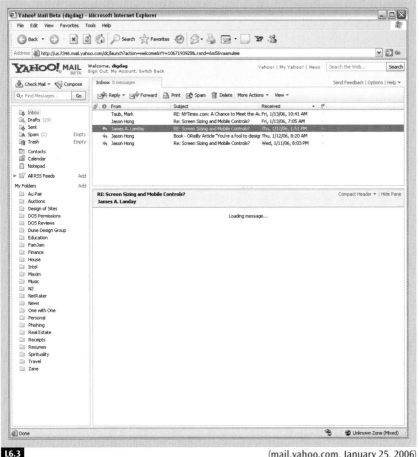

Figure L6.3

The Yahoo! Mail site displays a static "Loading message…" indicator as the browser downloads and displays an e-mail message. This indicator informs the customer that the e-mail message might take some time to load, but if the browser freezes or the site server experiences a stoppage, the customer could be left hanging indefinitely.

L6.3   (mail.yahoo.com, January 25, 2006)

click on a message in the top half of the screen, the text of the message will be shown in the bottom half. As the message is being loaded, the bottom half says "Loading message…", indicating that everything is still OK.

These kinds of messages inform customers that the site designer is aware of the delay and that the desired results are forthcoming. However, although a static progress indicator is better than nothing, it can conceivably backfire. Because a static indicator does not display continuing activity, it is conceivable that the site or the browser might actually freeze while the customer is being told to wait. If that happens, the customer has no way of distinguishing between an actual crash and a delay anticipated by the designer. The result could be more frustration than if there were no progress indicator at all.

Use Animation to Demonstrate Progress • An animated progress indicator is always preferable to a static indicator, because it demonstrates to the customer that the browser is still functioning. The simplest type of animated progress indicator is the "marching ants" type, a line of dots or periods that grows longer with each second of delay, as shown with the five dots in the center of Figure L6.4. The benefit of this type of progress indicator is that it is graphically simple, and no elaborate skills are required to implement it; a designer can create the "ants" with HTML using a simple graphic image or periods in a text display. Additional text near the indicator can inform visitors what's happening, tell them how long they will have to wait, and assure them that the system is still working. The object is to demonstrate the site's value and give the customers a reason to stick around.

You can also use more elaborate animated progress indicators, such as the horizontal barber pole shown in Figure L6.5. This type of indicator is more eye-catching to visitors, and might do more to avert frustration at the wait than a static or "marching ants" indicator would. The barber pole

Figure L6.4

Expedia's Web site displays a "marching ants" indicator when running a search. A large period repeatedly pulses through a line of smaller periods, giving people feedback that the Web site is still active.

L6.4   (www.expedia.com, August 24, 2006)

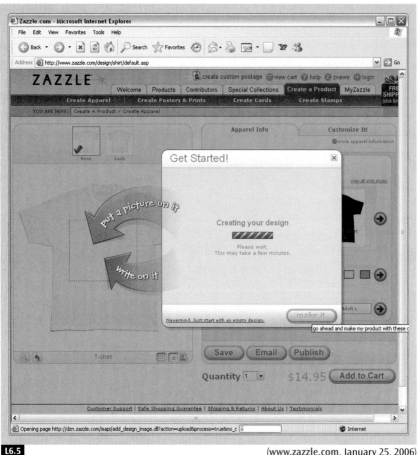

(www.zazzle.com, January 25, 2006)

Figure L6.5

Zazzle's barber pole progress indicator is more difficult for a designer to implement than simpler types of progress indicators are, but it's also more attractive to most customers.

appears to rotate indefinitely, and it is intriguing to the eye (at least at first), but it imparts no other information to the visitor. There is no way for visitors to know how long they've been waiting or how much longer they'll have to wait.

Use a Thermometer for Accurate Progress Reporting • A thermometer-style progress indicator displays an animated progression from the beginning to the end of the wait, as shown at the top left of Figure L6.6. Unlike the barber pole indicator, a thermometer lets customers know approximately how much time has passed since the beginning of the delay, and how

Figure L6.6

Kayak.com uses a thermometer-style progress indicator to let customers know how long their searches will take. The site works by sending the same search criteria to dozens of different travel sites and displaying the results to visitors in a unified interface. As a result, the Kayak.com server is able to use the completion of the search at each distinct site to gauge the overall progress of the customer's request. The server also displays the name of the airline that it's currently searching as part of the thermometer display.

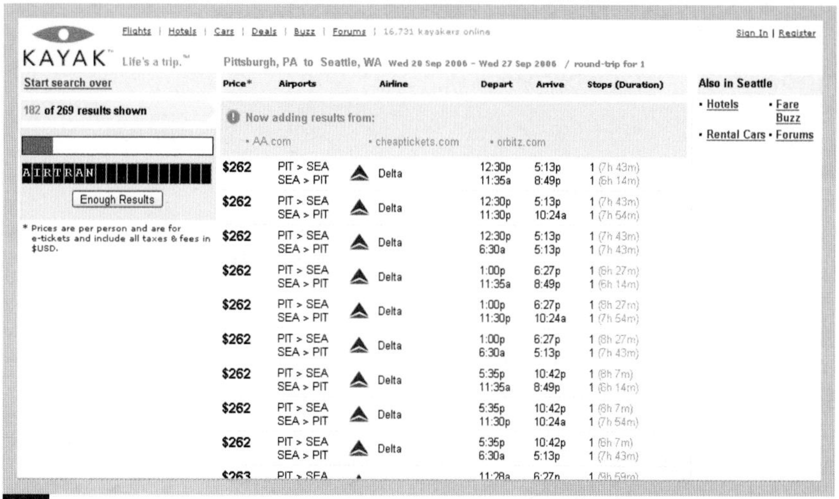

L6.6

(www.kayak.com, September 7, 2006)

much longer they have to wait. Thermometers are the most difficult type of progress indicator to implement because they require the designer to have a reasonably accurate knowledge of how long the process causing the delay will take. When the thermometer is half filled, the task at hand should be approximately half completed. If the thermometer is not accurate, it can cause customers to experience even more frustration than if there were no progress indicator at all.

Display Items As They're Loading • One of the best ways to indicate the ongoing progress of a lengthy Web procedure is to show individual items or parts of a page as they become available (see Figure L6.7). Not all types of content are suitable for this treatment, but for those that are, the gradual completion of the page serves three purposes: (1) the continued activity demonstrates to the customer that the process is still running, (2) the

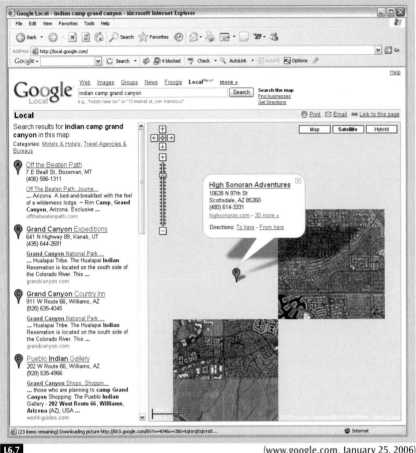

(www.google.com, January 25, 2006)

Figure L6.7

The Google Maps site displays individual segments of the map requested by the customer as they are downloaded from the server. This gradual download enables the customer to decide whether the results are satisfactory early in the process and also demonstrates that the rendering process is ongoing.

amount of information displayed indicates how close the process is to completion, and (3) the partial content serves as a preview of the final results, hopefully convincing the customer that the payoff is worth the wait. Sometimes the partial content returned can already be good enough for the customer to make a decision without returning all of the results. For example, on a travel site, an answer to the question, "Can I find a flight to LA next weekend for under $400?" might be revealed long before the entire page has downloaded.

✳ SOLUTION

Make your site as fast as possible by optimizing server code, bandwidth, and page designs. For pages that still take time to load, use a progress indicator to demonstrate to customers that the system is working. You can simply inform people with a text message such as "Loading," use "marching ants" to draw the customer's eye, create graphical indicators such as barber poles or thermometers, or ideally display parts of the content as they load instead of waiting for the entire page.

Figure L6.8

Optimizing your server code and pages to load quickly and giving customers feedback when there must be a delay will improve the customer experience on your site.

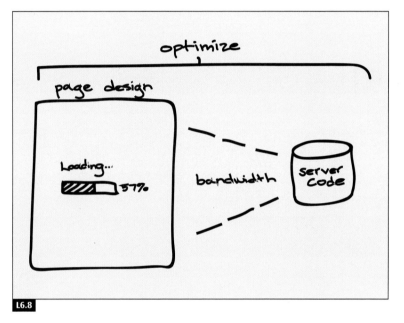

L6.8

✳ OTHER PATTERNS TO CONSIDER

Keep pages loading fast by speeding up your site. Use a LOW NUMBER OF **(L1)** FILES (L1) to reduce the number of requests that the browser must make **(L2)** to the server. Create FAST-LOADING IMAGES (L2) to improve the speed of **(L3)** existing graphics. Use SEPARATE TABLES (L3) to display a portion of each page while downloading more content or processing information. Redesign **(L4)** graphically intense pages to use HTML POWER (L4) instead. Take advantage **(L5)** of REUSABLE IMAGES (L5) to optimize use of the browser cache. Let people know how much more to expect and that the content is still loading by **(H13)** using a PROGRESS BAR (H13).

The Mobile Web

◆◆◆◆◆◆◆◆◆◆◆◆◆◆

An increasing number of people are starting to access the Web from mobile devices. However, designing for mobile devices is not the same as designing for desktops. Mobile devices have smaller screens and impoverished input capabilities. This pattern group describes near-term research, as well as pragmatic issues in preparing your Web site for the Mobile Web.

M1 MOBILE SCREEN SIZING

M2 MOBILE INPUT CONTROLS

M3 LOCATION-BASED SERVICES

M1 MOBILE SCREEN SIZING

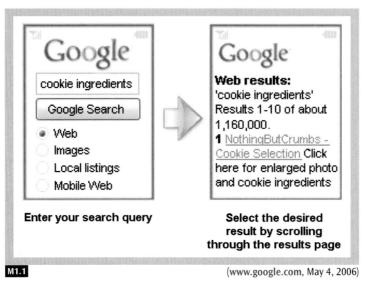

M1.1

Enter your search query

Select the desired result by scrolling through the results page

(www.google.com, May 4, 2006)

Figure M1.1

Google offers a special homepage for visitors using mobile phones. This stripped-down version of the main homepage offers access to all of the most important tools at a size that is large enough to easily read on a mobile device.

✳ BACKGROUND

Screen sizes are an ever-present problem for Web designers. As discussed in EXPANDING SCREEN WIDTH (I4) and FIXED SCREEN WIDTH (I5), the site designer can never be sure what screen resolution site visitors are using, or how large their browser windows are. Making this problem even more complex is the increasing popularity of Web-capable handheld devices that use extremely small screens.

✳ PROBLEM

Small screens are harder to read than large ones, and Web sites can be much more difficult to use on small-screen mobile devices because of their page layout.

On handheld screens, small text requires people to focus even more closely than they do for print or for typical computer screens. The result is greater eye strain and fatigue, reducing the likelihood that the average customer will be willing to read a large amount of text. In addition, the extreme smallness of the handheld screen itself places a limit on how much information it can display. The same amount of information that fits on a standard-size screen, even at low resolution, almost never fits on the screens found in today's mobile devices, since the text has to be relatively larger on the small screen to remain legible.

How Small Is Small? • Web sites complicate the task of reading on a small screen by presenting too much information on a single page, making the volume of information that visitors need to scroll through daunting. This is especially true in the case of the extremely small screens found on many mobile devices. Whereas typical monitors have screen sizes of at least 100 square inches, PDAs, such as Palm and Pocket PC devices, typically have screens that are approximately 10 to 12 square inches in size, and mobile phones have screens as small as 2 to 4 square inches. Figure M1.2 shows an example of how little of a Web page a typical PDA can display, illustrating how much scrolling would be required to see anything interesting.

Complicating the matter further are the wide range of form factors and resolutions. Desktop screens (which are wider than they are tall) tend to use a landscape orientation, but handheld devices typically use portrait orientation, in which the screen is taller than it is wide.

The main point is that mobile devices will always be limited in terms of screen size. No matter how much screen resolution improves, screen sizes will always be roughly the size of a Post-it note, which is capable of holding only so much information before it becomes unreadable.

How Do Browsers Render Web Sites on Handheld Devices? • Handheld devices vary widely in their methods of rendering Web pages designed for larger desktop screens. Some, like the BlackBerry, omit graphics entirely and assume that the text supplies sufficient information to make the page comprehensible. Other devices—for example, Palm and Windows Mobile

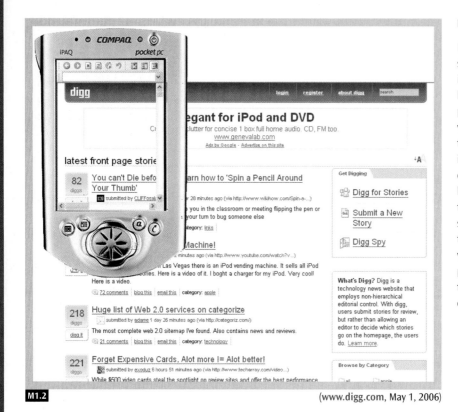

M1.2

(www.digg.com, May 1, 2006)

Figure M1.2

Browsing the Web on small-screen devices is very difficult because only a small part of a Web page is visible at any given time. Simply shrinking the page to fit doesn't work, because the text is then too small to see. Wrapping the text also doesn't work, because then people have to scroll too much to find the content they want.

devices—offer multiple formats that the customer can select, including the following alternatives:

- **Full layout.** The entire page is laid out as it would be on a desktop screen, but only a small portion of the page is displayed (see Figure M1.2). Some browsers now render the entire page, showing only a portion but providing convenient full-view and scrolling capabilities. Some of these advanced browsers even offer full JavaScript support, enabling DIRECT MANIPULATION (H9).

- **Columned.** Table columns that would be side by side on a full-sized screen are stacked one on top of the other (see Figure M1.3). This generic rerendering is not particularly intelligent, because it can't determine the relative importance of a Web page's various elements, and therefore doesn't know which element to put first, second, third, and so on.

H9

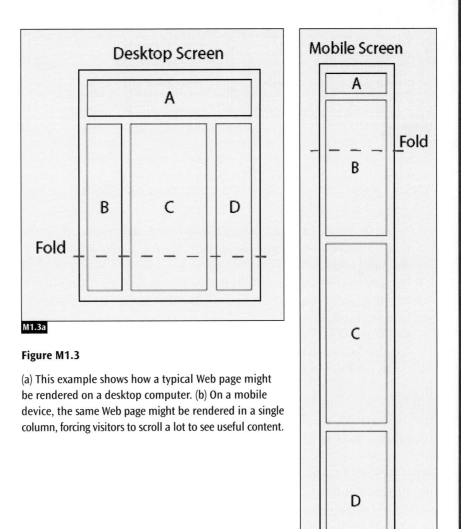

M1.3a

M1.3b

Figure M1.3

(a) This example shows how a typical Web page might be rendered on a desktop computer. (b) On a mobile device, the same Web page might be rendered in a single column, forcing visitors to scroll a lot to see useful content.

Opera is an increasingly popular Web browser for both desktop computers and mobile devices. One particularly nice feature of the desktop version of Opera is that you can render Web pages and view them as though you were using a mobile device. For site designers, this feature makes it easier to rapidly iterate on a design without having to use any mobile devices.

1 Acuson Solutions	1 Acuson Literatur	1 Acuson Brochures	http://www.acuson.co
2 Acuson Home	2 Brochures	2 Aspen System	Select a service:
3 Acuson Offices	3 Echoes Customer	3 WorkPro Producti	1 i About
4 Acuson Literatur	4 White Papers	4 AEGIS System	2 Read
5 650-969-9112	5 Navigation...	5 OBPro Enhanced O	3 Mail
6 800-422-8766	6 Offsite...	6 DBPro Database E	4 FAXFax
Open Svcs	Open Svcs	Open Svcs	Select Cancel

M1.4a, b, c, d   (www.fxpal.com/?p=MLinks, May 5, 2006)

Figure M1.4

M-Links is a research project at Fuji Xerox Palo Alto Laboratory (FXPAL) examining how to support Web browsing on mobile phones. The key idea behind M-Links is that when people browse Web pages on mobile devices, they are often seeking highly specific information. M-Links supports this primary goal by extracting key links, documents, and phone numbers and making them easy to navigate. These screen shots show (a) what you might see on a sample Web site, (b) drilling down through the options, (c) selecting a document, and (d) choosing what to do with the document.

There's also been a fair amount of research into making Web page navigation on mobile devices easier, as the following examples illustrate.

- Figure M1.4 shows M-Links, a Web browser on mobile phones that makes it easier to accomplish mobile tasks, such as finding a specific document or phone number.
- Figure M1.5 shows Summary Thumbnails, a technique that makes a Web page more readable by enlarging the first few words of each paragraph and hyperlink.
- Figure M1.6 shows collapse-to-zoom, a technique that lets Web site visitors collapse the parts of a Web page that don't interest them, opening up more space for parts that do.

All these techniques have been developed in research labs but have not yet made their way into actual products.

Do Web Sites Need to Be Completely Redesigned for the Small Screen? • In most cases, it is difficult or impossible to design a Web site that can accommodate all of the different screen sizes in use today. Because handheld devices account for only a relatively small fraction of Web browsers, designers typically create their sites for full-sized desktop screens and only then consider the handheld market. For sites that would find heavy use in a mobile setting, such as LOCATION-BASED SERVICES (M3), it makes sense to design a special version for small screens. This could be a substantial undertaking, however, in terms of both time and money, so consider questions like the following before you commit to this path:

- **How big could your mobile customer base become?** Depending on the nature of the information and services provided by your site, you must decide if developing a mobile site will benefit a sufficient number of mobile customers to be profitable.
- **Will additional features become possible if you offer a mobile version?** In some cases, a site might be able to offer additional services to mobile customers based on the capabilities of the technology they use.

Figure M1.5

Simply shrinking a page to fit small screens makes things unreadable. With Summary Thumbnails (a technique developed at Microsoft Research), the first few words of each link and each paragraph are enlarged to make them more readable, while the same relative layout for the Web page is maintained.

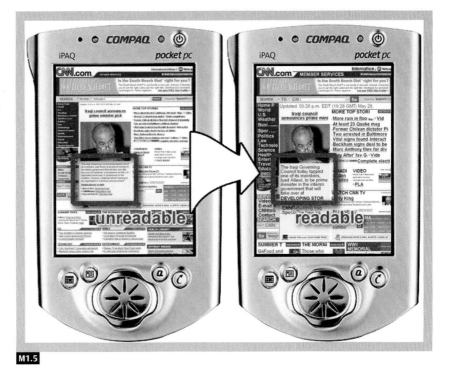

M1.5

For example, Microsoft's local.live.com site offers a toolbar that can use the visitor's current location to offer tailored search results, such as nearby restaurants.

- **How much work will be required to make the site work on a small screen?** In some cases, it might make sense to do some minor restructuring of your design layouts to make the pages easier to use on a mobile device. However, if your pages are complex and hard to read on small screens, or if your navigation mechanisms consume much of the top of each page, forcing customers with small screens to scroll down to the content, it probably makes sense to create a new version just for mobile devices.

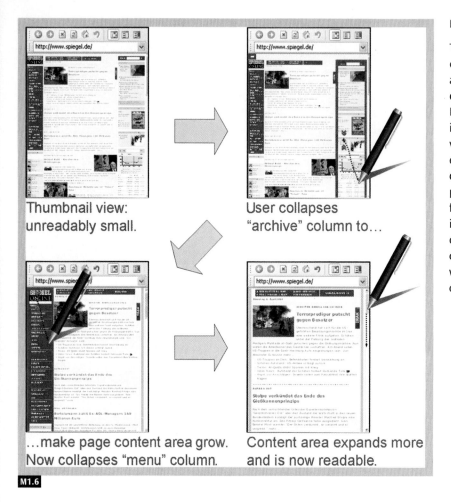

Thumbnail view: unreadably small.

User collapses "archive" column to...

...make page content area grow. Now collapses "menu" column.

Content area expands more and is now readable.

M1.6

Figure M1.6

The main idea of collapse-to-zoom, another technique developed at Microsoft Research, is to let Web site visitors collapse parts of the screen that don't interest them, providing more space for content that does interest them. People can bookmark collapsed pages, as well as zoom back in on collapsed parts.

Site Designers Have Multiple Options • To accommodate mobile customers, site designers have five basic alternatives:

1. **Do nothing and allow the site to be interpreted by mobile browsers as needed.** Currently, most mobile Web browsers do a poor job of rendering pages on mobile devices. Unless mobile Web browsers improve significantly or you expect to have few mobile visitors, this option does not make much sense.

2. **Format the site to fit the device used to view it.** New definitions for STYLE SHEETS (D11) enable a single Web page to accommodate both desktop and mobile layouts. For example, in the desktop style the page might show normally, while in the mobile style, custom navigation providing useful "jump links" to important parts of the main content might be shown first, followed by the main content area, and any advertisements might be stripped out.

3. **Redesign the content.** If it's not possible to create a good enough site using mobile style sheets, it may be necessary to go to the next step and redesign the content as well. Redesigning content is often difficult and expensive, but it might be justified if sufficient profit is to be made by having a high-quality mobile site.

4. **Use WAP.** Wireless Application Protocol, or **WAP,** is similar to HTTP but designed specifically for mobile phones with small screens (see Figure M1.7). WAP includes **WML** (Wireless Markup Language), which is similar to but much simpler than HTML. The advantages of WAP include a large base of mobile phones that can use it, as well as a feature set that is good enough for many simple mobile applications. The disadvantages include having to rewrite content and navigation in WML (or deploying a system that can automatically convert your Web pages to WML), a lack of good authoring tools, and limited capabilities.

Figure M1.7

Yahoo!'s WAP page offers only the key capabilities that are available on the standard desktop Web site.

(www.yahoo.com, May 4, 2006)

5. Create a completely custom application, such as Google Maps for Mobile (www.google.com/gmm). This option can provide customers with a service that is easier to use because it takes advantage of DIRECT MANIPULATION (H9), MOBILE INPUT CONTROLS (M2), mobile screen size optimization, and dynamic screen updates. Such an application can be a big plus to customers and a competitive advantage for your Web site, but it has the disadvantage of requiring a download, which can be complicated for customers to install and launch. An application also costs more to implement than a new style sheet, because it is typically implemented in a programming language such as Java.

(H9) (M2)

The Advantages of Being Mobile Enabled Often Outweigh the Costs • The advantages of enabling a site for mobile use are especially high when the costs are minimized by the development of a simple mobile style sheet rather than a custom site or application. A mobile style sheet can be relatively easy to implement, and it will make the site much more usable than the standard, generic rerendering provided by today's mobile browsers.

Lay Out Content and Navigation to Minimize Scrolling • Scrolling on a mobile device, even more than on a desktop, should not be required without a compelling reason. Though scrolling is not out of the question for mobile visitors, it is often harder than for desktop customers because of the small buttons and imprecise targeting mechanisms typically found on mobile devices.

Therefore, keep the most important content and navigation ABOVE THE FOLD (I2), and reduce the navigation elements to the absolute minimum required (such as a single search box for a directory site or links jumping to entries for a blog). Start with the primary content immediately following the major navigation elements. Content can continue below the fold, but by starting it above the fold, you draw visitors in to read more. Put everything else farther down on the page, including nonessential navigation elements and content of secondary importance, such as CONSISTENT SIDEBARS OF RELATED CONTENT (I6). Figure M1.8 shows how Google has tailored its Gmail service for mobile devices.

(I2)

(I6)

Figure M1.8

Google's Gmail service has a simplified user interface that is more effective for mobile devices.

M1.8 (www.google.com, May 4, 2006)

✳ SOLUTION

When making a Web site available to mobile visitors, adding a mobile style sheet is the quickest way to reorganize each page, putting the most important content and navigation above the fold to make it easy to find and to minimize scrolling. If your site offers primarily a service, make sure the tools that customers need are above the fold. If your site provides content, make sure the primary content is above the fold. If your business justifies the expense, designing a custom application that is even easier for mobile customers to use might be appropriate.

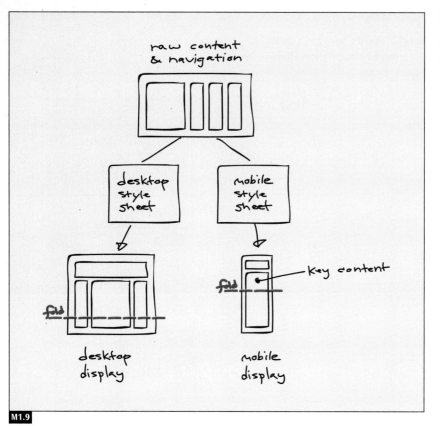

Figure M1.9

A style sheet can format the contents of your site specifically for mobile devices.

M1.9

✳ OTHER PATTERNS TO CONSIDER

Consider the techniques discussed in EXPANDING SCREEN WIDTH (I4) and FIXED SCREEN WIDTH (I5) when designing sites for mobile customers. Complement the mobile output described in this pattern with MOBILE INPUT CONTROLS (M2). If your site can justify a custom application, more advanced interaction techniques, such as DIRECT MANIPULATION (H9), will be easier to deliver to your customers and offer them a richer experience.

Figure M2.1

Google's mobile Web site keeps the navigation simple, offering only a text box and a radio button panel for the relevant features of the desktop site. This makes the site usable on a mobile phone with limited input capabilities.

M2.1   (www.google.com, June 26, 2006)

✳ BACKGROUND

Although most Web pages can be rendered on mobile Web browsers, this does not mean that they're easy to navigate. Mobile devices have limited input capabilities, making it hard to do things like entering text and scrolling. This pattern looks at how to design your Web pages to improve mobile navigation. Together with MOBILE SCREEN SIZING (M1) and LOCATION-BASED SERVICES (M3), this pattern forms the basis for mobile applications. This pattern is also useful for SITE ACCESSIBILITY (B9).

M1
M3
B9

✳ PROBLEM

Web page designs need to take into account the often limited input capabilities of mobile devices.

Mobile phones today are a fashion statement, with manufacturers attempting to differentiate their phones by releasing a constant parade of new designs. These physical phone designs, while appealing to people's desire for style, often employ different hard and soft button configurations, which can make common browser tasks such as selection and cursor movement difficult.

Customers are also being urged to adopt new mobile phone trends as often as they update their wardrobe, forcing phone users to learn new button positions and cursor controls for almost every phone. These constant design changes are a challenge for Web site developers, who must create site designs that work with the broadest range of phones (the lowest common denominator). Further complicating the issue are the Web browsers built into phones, which often reformat pages for their small screens and consequently change the locations of on-screen buttons.

This pattern provides an overview of the various kinds of input mechanisms available on mobile devices today, and then describes how to tailor your Web site so that mobile customers can easily use these mechanisms to navigate it.

Controlling the Cursor • There are three major types of mobile input cursor controls:

1. The **five-way rocker switch,** as shown on the Palm Treo in Figure M2.2
2. The **five-way joystick,** as used by the Windows Mobile unit shown in Figure M2.3
3. The **scroll wheel** (or *track wheel*), as used by the BlackBerry shown in Figure M2.4

Minimize the Number of Links and Buttons on Web Pages for Mobile Devices • Most Web-capable mobile phones let you traverse links and buttons using the cursor controls as described in the preceding section. However, moving through large numbers of links and buttons can be tedious. Some phones also have a touch-sensitive screen, letting customers press buttons using a fingernail or stylus. On mobile devices with small screens, however, using a stylus to precisely control the browser can be difficult because of the tiny on-screen controls.

Figure M2.2

The Palm Treo is a popular smart phone (combination PDA and phone) offering multiple input controls: a five-way rocker switch, a touch-sensitive screen, and a thumb-type keyboard. Its Web browser can take advantage of all of these input styles.

Five-Way Rocker Switch

M2.2

Figure M2.3

Windows Mobile devices have a five-way joystick that functions in much the same way that the rocker switch on the Treo does. Customers can scroll through the links on a Web page and press the joystick down to activate the currently selected link. This phone's screen is also touch sensitive, so Web links, buttons, scroll bars, and other on-screen controls can be tapped directly.

Five-Way Joystick

M2.3

Figure M2.4

The BlackBerry has a wheel on the side that enables customers to scroll through the items on a Web page, as well as the Web page as a whole when the top or bottom of the page has been reached. In addition, when pushed in like a button, the wheel activates the item that the customer has selected while scrolling the wheel. This simple, single-hand control is one of the features that makes the BlackBerry one of the more popular mobile devices.

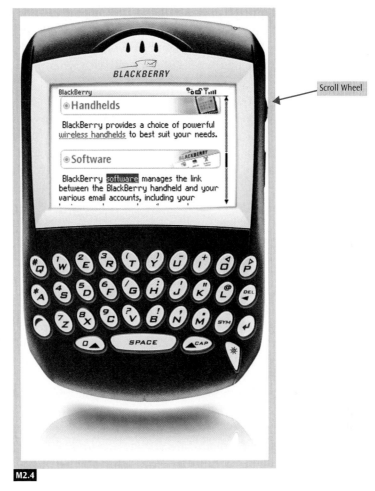

M2.4

To address this problem, consider creating custom STYLE SHEETS (D11) or custom Web pages for mobile devices to minimize the number of links and buttons.

Make the Positions of Links and Buttons Convenient • As described in MOBILE SCREEN SIZING (M1), some mobile Web browsers render pages in the same full-page format that is used for standard-size screens, leaving on-screen buttons and other page elements in the same location as on the desktop version [as long as the Web pages have not been reformatted using a STYLE SHEET (D11) customized for mobile devices]. Although the full-page format preserves the original layout of the Web page, the entire width of the page cannot fit on the phone's small screen. As a result, the device displays only the top left corner of the page when the site loads. The site designer must therefore be concerned not only with what information is placed ABOVE THE FOLD (I2), but also with what content and navigation elements are located on the left side of the page.

I2

Furthermore, when the customer is traversing the links or buttons on a page, if the next link is located to the right of the visible screen, the page automatically scrolls to the right when the cursor is moved to that link. The same is true for automatic scrolling to the left, upward, or downward when a link or button is located to the left of, above, or below the visible screen. This automatic scrolling can confuse someone who is navigating your Web pages. We suggest trying to make the position of your links consistent, to minimize excessive automatic scrolling.

Minimize Text Entry • Mobile devices have a range of text entry methods, including stylus-based methods like Graffiti and Jot, soft keyboards on which people can select letters from a keyboard displayed on the screen, multitap and T9 for mobile phones, and actual QWERTY keyboards. Despite this rich design space, however, text entry is slow on all mobile devices, and it is made more difficult by the fact that people often use their mobile devices while walking or otherwise occupied.

Consequently, we advocate minimizing the amount of text entry required for your Web pages. Help your mobile customers by using PERSISTENT CUSTOMER SESSIONS (H5) when people use the SIGN-IN/NEW ACCOUNT (H2) page, using PREDICTIVE INPUT (H11), and remembering previously entered information to provide things like QUICK ADDRESS SELECTION (F4) and QUICK SHIPPING METHOD SELECTION (F5).

H5

H2 **H11**

F4 **F5**

Avoid Pick Lists and Image Maps • Pick lists, also known as *drop-down boxes*, let visitors select one item from a list of items. Avoid using pick lists on Web pages for mobile devices, because they increase the number of navigation steps required and may not work for all mobile Web browsers. Also avoid image maps, because they require visitors to click on specific parts of the image, which may not always be possible with limited navigation controls.

Minimize the Use of AJAX Technologies • AJAX technologies can be used to improve the customer experience on Web sites, but they are often designed only for desktop computers where visitors have a keyboard and mouse.

Thus, AJAX makes certain kinds of rich interactions, such as DIRECT
H9 MANIPULATION (H9), quite difficult on mobile devices. To address this problem, we suggest minimizing the use of AJAX technologies for mobile Web pages, and providing meaningful alternatives that don't require people to drag or select arbitrary points on the screen.

D11 **Use Style Sheets** • STYLE SHEETS (D11) offer a way to reorganize your Web pages by changing one file on your server instead of writing all new pages or creating a custom application. If you reformat your Web pages with a
D11 STYLE SHEET (D11) customized for mobile devices, button positions are largely under your control. You can strip the primary links and buttons down to those left visible at the top of the page, and even trim the number of images so that the pages will load more quickly over relatively slow mobile phone networks. You can also order the content and navigation according to their priority, making it easy for mobile customers to get to them.

SOLUTION

Mobile devices have limited input capabilities, making Web page navigation a challenge. To make mobile navigation easier, minimize the number of links and buttons on your Web pages and make the position convenient, minimize text entry, avoid pick lists and image maps, and limit rich interactions from AJAX technologies to those that can be easily used on small devices.

Figure M2.5

A style sheet can reconfigure your site's inputs for your customers' mobile devices.

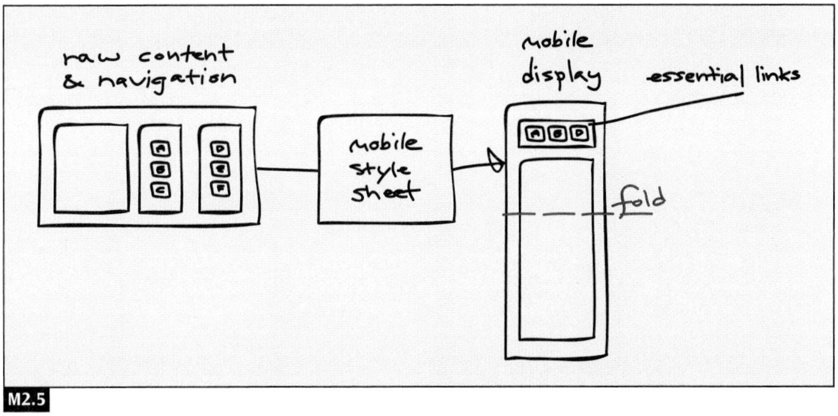

✴ OTHER PATTERNS TO CONSIDER

MOBILE SCREEN SIZING (M1) and LOCATION-BASED SERVICES (M3) can be used in conjunction with mobile navigation to create effective mobile applications. Use STYLE SHEETS (D11) to rearrange navigation elements and content, helping to ensure that the most important navigation and content are ABOVE THE FOLD (I2), and that the positions of links and buttons are convenient.

Minimize text entry with PERSISTENT CUSTOMER SESSIONS (H5) when your customers use the SIGN-IN/NEW ACCOUNT (H2) form, with PREDICTIVE INPUT (H11), and with techniques that reuse previously entered information [such as QUICK ADDRESS SELECTION (F4) and QUICK SHIPPING METHOD SELECTION (F5)].

Figure M3.1

Emerging location-based services on phones provide a simple but compelling value proposition: "find where you want to go, and never get lost again." These screen shots are from an NTT DoCoMo service in Japan that lets customers search for nearby businesses and restaurants and see maps showing how to get there.

M3.1

✳ BACKGROUND

Location-based services are an emerging class of applications that let you create PERSONALIZED CONTENT (D4) based on a visitor's current physical location. Location-based services let you customize the customer experience for STIMULATING ARTS AND ENTERTAINMENT (A9) sites, emphasize nearby places for ORGANIZED SEARCH RESULTS (J3), and enable new ways of doing PERSONAL E-COMMERCE (A1).

✳ PROBLEM

What kinds of compelling location-based services are emerging, and how do you design them well?

Because location-based services are not yet widespread, this pattern is more speculative than others in this book. However, we believe that location-based services are emerging as an important capability for personal wireless devices.

Location information is already available on many mobile phones. Today, when a person reports an emergency from a mobile phone by dialing 911 in the United States or 112 in Europe, the caller's phone number and general location (within about a hundred meters) are displayed to the dispatcher. Add to this the fact that computing and communication technologies are finally converging. Many mobile phones can run a host of powerful applications and include mobile Internet access. Most notebook computers also offer high-speed wireless connectivity as a standard feature, and researchers have also developed ways for these notebooks to calculate their location within about twenty meters. It's only a matter of time before all these factors converge to enable location-based services on a wide scale.

What are the benefits of location-based services? How do we design them so that customers will have positive experiences? The goal of this pattern is to give you a flavor of some of the emerging uses for location-based services and some of the design issues that have to be addressed.

Guides for Exploration and Navigation Are the Most Popular Location-Based Service • The most common use of location-based services is for navigation while driving. For example, the TomTom ONE (see Figure M3.2), the Magellan RoadMate, and Garmin nüvi are three in-car navigation systems that can display maps and read out directions while you're driving.

Similar to these in-car systems are newly emerging handheld location-enhanced devices that can be used as portable tour guides to help people explore areas they've never visited before. Figure M3.3 shows two screen shots from Cyberguide, a mid-1990s research project at Georgia Tech investigating this technology. On the left is a map that shows people where they currently are and what points of interest (the stars on the map) are nearby. People can click on this form of PERSONALIZED CONTENT (D4) to get more details, as shown on the right.

Guides for exploration and navigation have also been developed for mobile phones. Figure M3.1 shows screen shots from a location-based

Figure M3.2

The TomTom ONE is an in-car navigation system.

M3.2

Figure M3.3

Cyberguide is a portable tour guide that can help customers explore areas they've never visited before. The map on the left shows people where they currently are and what points of interest are nearby.

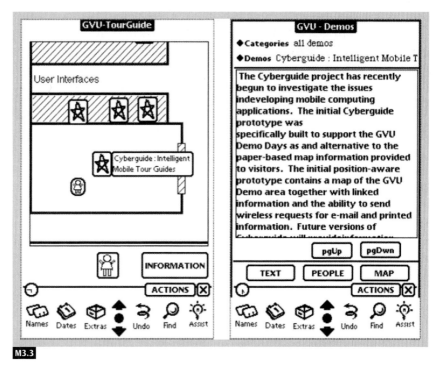

M3.3

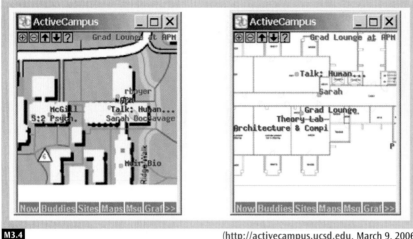

(http://activecampus.ucsd.edu, March 9, 2006)

Figure M3.4

UCSD's ActiveCampus provides the location of your friends, making it easier to meet up.

service on an NTT DoCoMo phone in Japan. Customers can search for nearby businesses and shops, and they can display ORGANIZED SEARCH RESULTS (J3) with a map showing nearby parking lots and parks.

ActiveCampus is a system developed at the University of California at San Diego (UCSD) to support education (see Figure M3.4). One feature of ActiveCampus is a real-time map that shows where your friends are, as well as what talks (lectures) are in progress inside buildings. This display makes it easy to coordinate with friends and to make serendipitous findings. Social coordination is another location-enhanced application type that will take off, as additional examples will illustrate.

The notion of serendipity is more important than it may first sound. Certain people dislike preplanned tours. An alternative is to support serendipity by letting customers freely explore. For example, rather than providing an omniscient overhead map, a conceptual design called the (De)Tour Guide lets people discover districts and landmarks "only upon approach, as if by chance." It also allows people to "get lost on purpose, or to follow the idiosyncratic paths of unusual strangers."[1] For example, a person might choose to be lost for one hour but be at a certain location at the end of that hour. The (De)Tour Guide would let that person wander around, while gently nudging her closer and closer to the final destination.

---

1 From Gaver, B., and Martin, H. (2000) Alternatives: Exploring information appliances through conceptual design proposals. In *CHI 2000 Conference Proceedings (Conference on Human Factors in Computing Systems)*, pp. 209–216. The Hague, Netherlands.

You might also want to consider supporting customer-created content. For example, one idea is to let customers post and share virtual "Post-it" notes that can be attached to places, sort of a MESSAGE BOARD (D5) attached to a physical location. Creating compelling content is difficult and expensive, and in many cases it makes sense to have your customers be part of a community that creates such content.

Tagging Content Automatically by Location Can Make It Easier to Find Later •
Many cameras and camera phones have built-in global positioning systems, making it simple to record location information for each photo taken. Figure M3.5 shows a sample user interface developed at Stanford

Figure M3.5

Location information can be used to automatically tag multimedia data. (a) This research prototype for browsing through tagged photos lets people browse for photos by time, location, season, weather, and so on. (b) When people click on a specific location (in this case "United States"), they can drill down on more locations and view some sample photos.

M3.5a

Time		Time of Day	
2002 (398)	2003 (3306)	Afternoon (12pm-5pm) (1573)	Late night (12am-3am) (28)
		Early morning (3am-6am) (22)	Morning (6am-12pm) (923)
Location		Evening (5pm-8pm) (650)	Night (8pm-12am) (508)
Cambodia (151)	Italy (146)		
France (167)	Sri lanka (512)	**Weather Status**	
Hungary (176)	Thailand (60)	Clear (944)	Mist (61)
Israel (670)	United states (1822)	Fog (2)	Mostly cloudy (373)
		Haze (135)	Overcast (110)
Elevation		Heavy rain (6)	Partly cloudy (590)
-2000–1001 (36)	10000-10999 (85)	Light rain (237)	Patches of fog (1)
-1000–1 (327)	11000-11999 (59)	Light rain showers (3)	more...
0-999 (2425)	12000-12999 (37)	Light snow showers (3)	
1000-1999 (151)	13000-13999 (40)		
2000-2999 (53)	14000-14999 (33)	**Temperature**	
3000-3999 (43)	more...	20-40 (87)	80-100 (239)
4000-4999 (57)		40-60 (972)	Unknown (1646)
		60-80 (760)	
Season			
Autumn(sep 21st-dec 20th) (1007)	Summer (june 21st- sep 20th) (1059)	**Time Zone**	
Spring (march 21st-june 20th) (953)	Winter (dec 21st-march 20th) (685)	-5 (8)	2 (670)
		-7 (180)	5 (512)
Light Status		-8 (1634)	7 (211)
Dawn (47)	Dusk (495)	1 (489)	
Day (2367)	Night (789)		

Location: United States

Time (group results)
2002 (398)   2003 (1424)

1822 items (grouped by location)

Location: all > United States
Around: san francisco, berkeley, sonoma,ca (876)
Around: stanford, mountain view, monterey,ca (284)
Colorado (219 miles w of denver,co) (180)
Long beach,ca (35 miles s of los angeles,ca) (90)
Philadelphia,pa; pennsylvania (8)
Seattle,wa; washington (39)
Sequoia np (153 miles e of fresno,ca) (133)
South lake tahoe; bear valley,ca (96)
Yosemite np; yosemite valley,ca (116)

Around: San Francisco, Berkeley, Sonoma,CA

000000.jpg
Oct 31, 2002 10:...

000001.jpg
Oct 31, 2002 10:...

Around: Stanford, Mountain View, Monterey,CA

M3.5b

M3.6

Figure M3.6

AT&T offers a Find Friends application that lets customers request the location of friends.

University for browsing tagged photos. On the basis of time and location information, other kinds of metadata for the photos, such as season, temperature, and weather status, are automatically generated to provide MULTIPLE WAYS TO NAVIGATE (B1). For example, one can browse first for photos in 2003 and then for photos in Cambodia, or vice versa.

Retrieving content by location can also provide memory aids. Location-based reminders—for example, reminding a customer to purchase milk while at the grocery store—are a popular idea.[2]

Location-Based Services Can Enhance Social Coordination and Communication •
AT&T offers a service called Find Friends (see Figure M3.6). Customers can query the locations of their friends and see roughly where a person is at the street level.

Researchers at Intel Research Seattle developed a system called Reno that lets people share their location with others (see Figure M3.7). Reno supports both explicit requests (for example, Alice requests Bob's location) and automatic disclosures (for example, Alice automatically sends her location information to Bob when she gets home). An experiment showed

---

2 One variant that the authors of this book are waiting for someone to invent is a key-chain system that records where you parked your car, to make it easier to find in large parking lots!

Figure M3.7

An example of a manual request and disclosure using Reno. (a) An explicit request from Phoebe for Ross's location. (b) Ross's selection to indicate where he is (this manual selection is due to a limitation in how fine-grained the location information is). (c) The message that Phoebe gets from Ross saying that he's at Merchant Mick's.

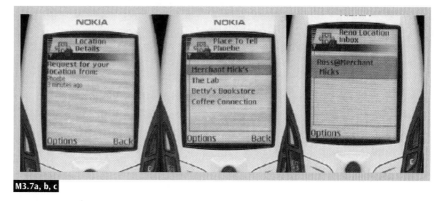

M3.7a, b, c

that the explicit request was generally preferred over automatic disclosures, which occasionally made for some clumsy interactions. Sometimes the problem was an error in location information. Other times the problem was awkward social interaction, such as when one family member went out for a late-night errand and discovered that her phone had sent a notification as she was coming home.

Reno also supported something called *okayness checking*, whereby people could check that their loved ones were OK. For example, working parents could ask their children to set their phones to send a message when the children got home. This use of location information is more for peace of mind than for coordination.

Wherify has developed a wearable watch for monitoring and locating one's children (see Figure M3.8). Parents can bring up a street map or an

Figure M3.8

This children's watch, developed by Wherify, can communicate location information to a web site and thus tell parents where their children have been.

M3.8

aerial photo on a Web site and display a child's current location and movements over time. Other kinds of trackers are being developed for helping elderly adults who have Alzheimer's disease, as well as for monitoring parolees.

Games That Fuse the Virtual and Physical Worlds Often Require Location • Augmented reality games are another example of an emerging application for location-based services. One popular form of STIMULATING ARTS AND ENTERTAINMENT (A9) is geocaching, a game in which people hide small caches of goodies in the physical world and post the GPS (Global Positioning System) location of the cache on a well-known Web site (see Figure M3.9). These caches are often placed in scenic areas, and some caches are abstract, consisting of the scenic spot itself. Geocaching is an example of **user-created content,** in which the Web site's customers drive new innovations and new adventures.

A9

Games are also being developed for smaller settings. Pirates! is a game developed by the PLAY group in Sweden. It uses wirelessly networked devices to create a virtual world of islands, pirates, and treasure overlaid on the physical world. People can wander around with these devices and be notified when the area that they've entered contains an island, search for treasure, and fight other pirates (other players) when they come near each other.

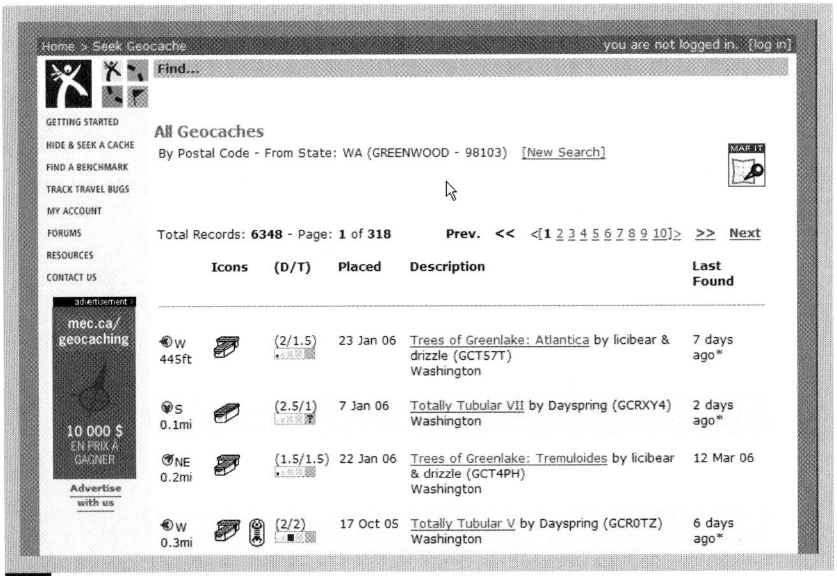

Figure M3.9

In geocaching, people hide small "treasures" for others to find using GPS devices.

M3.9   (www.geocaching.com, March 26, 2006)

Location-Based Services Can Enhance Vehicle Security, Fleet Management, and Transit Services • Location-based services have also been used to streamline business operations. For example, Bobcat has developed specialized GPS hardware that provides real-time data about construction equipment, including when a specific piece of equipment is being used and where it is being used. Customers can also set up a "geo-fence" and be notified if the equipment enters or leaves a certain boundary. This feature is useful for being notified, for example, when a truck carrying critical cargo arrives at its destination.

Location information is also useful for fleet management. For example, many delivery trucks are being outfitted with location sensors so that the locations of all vehicles can be tracked at all times. Such tracking can simplify routing, as well as identifying the nearest vehicle to send for a pickup or delivery. These kinds of fleet management systems are also being installed on vehicles such as buses so that commuters can know how much longer it will be before a bus comes, and on garbage trucks for managing complaints and increasing efficiency.

Location-Enhanced Applications Must Be Designed for Privacy from the Start • It's easy to imagine numerous scenarios in which information about a person's location and/or availability might be abused—for example, between employers and employees, between overzealous parents and independent-minded teens, and between governments concerned with security and citizens concerned about civil rights. For this reason, it is important that location-based services have clear PRIVACY POLICIES (E4), follow FAIR INFORMATION PRACTICES (E3), and let people tailor their PRIVACY PREFERENCES (E8) so that they're comfortable using the service. Try to address these issues when designing location-enhanced applications, because it may be hard to add privacy protections after the fact.

Also note that privacy is not just secrecy. As Chuck Darrah and his fellow sociologists at San Jose State University have noted, people tend to devise strategies "to restrict their own accessibility to others while simultaneously seeking to maximize their ability to reach people."[3] Furthermore, as noted by famed sociologist Erving Goffman, an important aspect of privacy is projecting a consistent persona to others. For example, we project our "professional" personas to our work colleagues, but we're more relaxed with close friends and family. In other words, when designing for privacy for location-based services, success requires balancing many different forces.

3 From *Families and Work: An Ethnography of Dual Career Families (Grant Number 98-6-21)* (Final report to the Alfred P. Sloan Foundation). (2001, July 22) (www.sjsu.edu/depts/anthropology/svcp/pdfs/sloanrpt.pdf), p. 29.

❋ SOLUTION

Location-based services are useful as guides for exploration and navigation, for tagging and retrieving information, for coordinating better with other people, for augmented reality games, and for vehicle tracking. In all of these applications, be sure to design for privacy from the start.

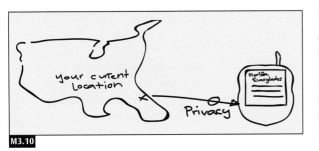

Figure M3.10

Customers benefit from receiving location-specific information on their mobile devices, while maintaining their privacy.

❋ OTHER PATTERNS TO CONSIDER

Location-based services let you provide PERSONALIZED CONTENT (D4), more relevant ORGANIZED SEARCH RESULTS (J3), MESSAGE BOARDS (D5) attached to physical locations, MULTIPLE WAYS TO NAVIGATE (B1) for tagged multimedia, and new kinds of STIMULATING ARTS AND ENTERTAINMENT (A9). However, privacy is an important concern, so provide a clear PRIVACY POLICY (E4), follow FAIR INFORMATION PRACTICES (E3), and let people tailor their PRIVACY PREFERENCES (E8) so that they'll be comfortable using your services.

D4
J3 D5
B1
A9
E4
E3
E8

Location-based services are an emerging area of commercial activity, and we'll be seeing more kinds of compelling applications in the near future.

PART III

Appendixes

Running Usability Evaluations

Running a usability test with real customers is essential to good Web site design. You may know a lot about your customers, but it's hard to predict how people will react to and interact with a Web site. Usability tests are also effective in ending those constant opinion wars in which members of the design team argue about what people like and don't like. The best way to answer questions about your customers is to recruit some participants,[1] run a quick test, and see what they say and do. This appendix describes the steps for running both formal and informal usability tests, from setting up the test to running the test to analyzing and presenting the results.

You probably want to run a usability test in which both you and the participant are in the same place. Keep in mind, though, that an alternative approach is **remote usability testing**—that is, recruiting and testing many participants online without having to be present yourself. We discuss how to do this in Appendix E (Online Research).

A.1 Setting Target Goals

The initial steps in planning a usability test are figuring out what you would like to learn from the test, devising a specific strategy to learn that information, and deciding whether you will be collecting qualitative or quantitative data.

Identifying What You Want to Learn

The first thing to do is to decide what you want to learn from the test. Do you want to find out if people are having problems with a specific part of

---

[1] In psychology and other fields, the term *subjects* has traditionally been used, but we have always felt that the term *subjects* has a slightly sinister tone. Nowadays, most fields are switching to using the term *participants*.

the Web site? Do you want to see how well a proposed design works? Or do you just want to get general feedback about the existing Web site?

Getting the Information You Want

After deciding what you want to learn, think about how you'll get the information. If people are having problems with a portion of the Web site, the straightforward thing to do is to test tasks that rely on that part and see what the problems are. If you want to test a new design, it's useful to compare it to the old design or to a competitor's Web site. This approach is also useful for getting general feedback about an existing Web site.

Process Data versus Bottom-Line Data

Usability tests yield two kinds of data: process data and bottom-line data. **Process data** consists of informal, qualitative observations of what people are thinking and doing—an overall feeling of what works on a Web site and what doesn't. The key things to look for here are **critical incidents,** points during testing at which participants are confused, frustrated, or even swear. Critical incidents also include cases in which people are pleasantly surprised or say something positive about the site.

In contrast, **bottom-line data** consists of formal, quantitative measurements of what happens, such as the time it takes to learn or complete a task, or the number of errors that occur.

In general, focus on obtaining process data first because it gives a good overview of where the problems in a Web site are and because it's easier to get. Process data can also be obtained from low-fidelity paper prototypes, making the collection of process data a handy technique for the early stages of design.

It takes more work to get and use bottom-line data. One reason is that you need to have lots of participants to get statistically reliable results. Another is that bottom-line data does not always tell you what problems need to be fixed; it just tells you, for example, that people are going too slowly or making too many errors. Bottom-line data is better for later phases of design, when you're tuning the performance of an existing Web site. It is also better for comparing two Web site designs, to show that one is superior to another in a particular measurable aspect. Such a comparison can be especially important when you're trying to convince management to make either a major change or a change on an important page, such as the homepage of a high-traffic site.

A.2 Setting Up the Tasks

The next step is to choose several representative tasks. By *representative,* we mean realistic tasks that your target customers are likely to do on your Web site. Choose some tasks that are simple, some that are of medium difficulty, and some that are hard. Ideally, these tasks will have already been worked out in the task analysis you carried out when learning to know your customers and can just be taken from there [see Chapter 3 (Knowing Your Customers: Principles and Techniques)].

3

Levels of Tasks

Simple Tasks Are Short and Performed Often • Simple tasks include things like finding the latest news article about parenting or finding the phone number and e-mail address of the help desk. Success on simple tasks is a binary result: the person either succeeds or fails.

Tasks of Medium Difficulty Are a Little Longer and Harder than Simple Tasks • Examples of medium-difficulty tasks include purchasing the cheapest printer available, printing a list of all previous purchases, and adding a message to the gourmet cooking community board. These tasks span a few Web pages, but they're reasonable things that people would do. Some medium-difficulty tasks will have binary success metrics; that is, they will either succeed or fail. The results of other medium-difficulty tasks will be more open-ended and require further interpretation of the results.

Hard Tasks Span Many Web Pages and Are Fairly Involved • Examples of hard tasks include making the Web site show only the stocks that interest you, buying a digital camera for a friend that he or she will like, and buying a toy for your friend's one-year-old child. Most hard tasks are free-form, so it will take some judgment to determine how successful participants are.

Designing Effective Tasks

To ensure that the tasks you design will yield the information you need, it's important to keep in mind some simple principles.

Tasks Should Be about What People Want to Do • Be careful not to tell participants *how* to do the task. For example, instead of saying, "Go to **My Profile** and find your previous purchases," say something like, "Find all of your previous purchases." Again, the task should be worded in the way people would ordinarily think about the problem—that is, *what*, not *how*. Another example of careful wording is, "Make the Web site show you only the stocks that interest you." Not as realistic would be a task like "Customize your profile to show you the stocks that interest you," because the words *customize* and *profile* are not likely to be part of people's regular vocabulary. Such wording also might give away leading information, especially if there are links labeled "customize" or "profile."

Tasks Should Be Realistic • As you're developing tasks for your test, think about how real people would approach real tasks. For example, creating a new customer account is something that many people do on a Web site, but not because they want to. People create an account only because they have to, to get something else done. In other words, creating an account is more of a secondary task that people do to accomplish a primary task.

"Buy a digital camera for a friend that he or she will like" is a very open-ended direction, but it's likely to be the way people approach the problem. It's important that tasks be realistic, because you want to find out what people are thinking and see if the design provides the right cues to support them.

Tasks Should Form a Complete Story • Taken as a whole, the tasks in your test should be complete, forming a cohesive and believable story. For example, it does not really make sense to specify tasks in the following order: "Find previous purchases," "Add a message to a community board," and then "Find the privacy policy." The tasks need to flow logically. For example, the following order makes more sense: "Find the privacy policy," "Purchase a printer," and then "Purchase additional ink toner cartridges."

Also be careful not to fragment tasks: "Purchase the best printer for under $300" makes more sense than (1) "Create an account," (2) "Find and compare printers for under $300," and (3) "Purchase the printer you found." Testing fragmented tasks may show that customers can complete the subtasks just fine, but when they're combined in a more realistic situation, the results may not be nearly as good.

The number of tasks you specify depends on how extensively you want to test your Web site. Five to ten tasks is about right for most cases— enough to cover a lot of functionality without taking a lot of time for each participant.

_____ **A.3** **Recruiting Participants**

After you've defined some tasks, begin recruiting participants. These participants need to be representative of eventual customers in terms of vocabulary, general knowledge, and desired tasks. If the Web site is aimed toward college students, then advertise at a nearby college. If the Web site is for mothers of young children, then get friends of friends who are also mothers or advertise with local mom's groups.

Avoid Friends and Family As Participants • One thing to avoid is recruiting close friends or family to help, unless you're sure that they'll give honest feedback. They may be reluctant to criticize something that you've worked on so hard. Also don't recruit coworkers from down the hall, because they're likely to know too much about what you're doing. It's OK to use friends, family, and coworkers for a first pass, as a way of getting quick comments on a design and piloting your experimental procedures, but don't rely solely on feedback from these tests. Again, get people who would realistically use the Web site.

Compensate Participants with Gifts and Prizes • One way to recruit people is to compensate them for their time. You might be surprised what some people will do for a free T-shirt.[2] Some other ways of enlisting participants include giving away small toys, coffee mugs, gift certificates, or money; raffling off an iPod; or giving a large cash prize of $200 to $300 to the participant who "does the best." This last type of compensation works well for experiments where creative performance is important. For straight cash payments, we normally offer about $20 per hour for university students and about $50 per hour for other participants.

If you don't have time to recruit participants, several market research firms can recruit participants who meet the profile you need for about $100 per participant, not including the compensation you must pay each participant. Many usability practitioners and designers go this route, although this approach may double your direct costs for running the tests.

Get the Right Number of Participants • You don't need many participants to obtain process data. If you're in the early stages of design, five or six people will be fine, especially for paper prototypes. In later stages of design, you'll need more people—often about 10 to 20 participants—to evaluate the site. However, you'll need to increase these numbers if you

2 Then again, if you've been working in the computer industry, you might not!

have a large and diverse audience to cover, or if your Web site is very large. Getting so many people right at the outset might seem expensive, but consider how much trouble this investment will save you later when you've created a more useful and usable Web site for your customers.

Getting bottom-line data requires a lot more people. Ten to 20 participants can provide initial data, but most tasks will still have a large amount of variability. Section A.5, Analyzing the Data, will provide more details about the relationship between the number of people and variability in the data.

When you're recruiting participants, get a few more people than are really needed. The first few tests you run may be a little rough, and you may have to change some things to make the evaluation flow smoothly. In addition, not everyone remembers to show up.

There are two important things to do when you're recruiting people. First, give them a general overview of the experiment, describing what the Web site is about, what they'll be doing, and approximately how long the whole thing will take. Don't provide too many details, because you don't want to bias the test. Second, tell them about any prizes or compensation that will be given for participating. For each participant, schedule a time and place for the test, and then get the person's name and either a phone number or an e-mail address so that you can provide a reminder before the test.

Select an Appropriate Experimental Design • One important consideration in experimental design is whether each participant participates in more than one experimental condition. If you're testing two versions of a Web site to compare them, for example, there are two experimental conditions. In a **between-groups experiment,** you break your pool of test participants into two groups and each group uses only one of the Web sites. In a **within-groups experiment,** by contrast, you have only one group of test participants, and each participant uses both sites.

These two types of experimental design have trade-offs. For example, a within-groups experiment may not require as many test participants before producing statistically significant results. If you're after bottom-line data, the within-groups approach can save you considerable time and money. On the other hand, a within-groups experiment can raise issues of validity if learning effects are involved. For example, if you test the same tasks on two versions of the same Web site, your participants might be quicker completing a task the second time because they learned how to do it on the first site. You can alleviate some of these problems by randomizing or counterbalancing the order of sites tested and other experimental conditions.

In general, within-groups experiments work better when a low-level interaction technique is being tested, such as finding the best position for a particular button on the page. Use between-groups experiments when you want to compare tasks on two versions of a site or between two competitive sites. Try to make sure that the participants in the two groups match as well as possible in terms of demographics, Internet experience, and familiarity with the problem domain.

A.4   Running the Test

Several considerations about the test itself are important—from where you run it to what you say to the participants. In this section we look at these issues.

Setting Up the Test Location

If you're evaluating a paper prototype, you can conduct the test practically anywhere. All you need is a large table and places for everyone to sit. For online prototypes, the testing location just needs to be a quiet place with a networked computer.

Video cameras and audio recorders are useful to have in both cases, but they're not required. You can accomplish some tests simply by taking notes on paper, though audio and video recordings make it easy to clarify specific issues later. In contrast, some companies have special rooms for testing, complete with expensive recording equipment, eye-tracking devices, and one-way mirrors for observers. These kinds of setups are useful for gathering bottom-line data but are not necessary for process data.

Ethical Considerations

Tests can be a grueling experience for some people. Participants have been known to leave in tears, embarrassed by their mistakes or their inability to complete the tasks successfully. You have a responsibility to alleviate these kinds of problems. One way is to avoid pressuring people to participate. Get participants' informed consent regarding the subject matter of the test, and then make it clear that the test is voluntary and that participants can stop the test at any time for any reason [see Appendix C (Sample Consent Form)]. Also stress that you're testing the Web site and not the participants themselves, and that they're really helping you by finding problems with the site. If they have problems, it's the Web site's fault, not theirs.

If other people besides you will see the collected data, make the data as anonymous as possible. Remove names and other pieces of identifying information, and blur out people's faces in any pictures and video footage. In some cases a videotape of a person struggling with a user interface has been played for an audience that included that very person! Making the data anonymous will help prevent any potentially awkward situations.

Test Roles

The key role in running a usability test is the facilitator. The facilitator greets participants, introduces any other people in the room, explains the procedure for the test, and answers participants' questions.

The other people act simply as observers, watching what participants do. Their role is to take notes and keep quiet. Observers can also be remote if the setup allows them to view things from another location or through a one-way mirror.

If you're running a test on a paper prototype, another role you'll need is the computer. The job of the person playing computer is to run the interface, updating the paper interface as needed.[3]

Running a Pilot Test

Before running the tests with actual participants, carry out a **pilot test** with two or three people. Coworkers and friends are acceptable participants for this initial test. The key is to get used to the procedure of running a test and to work out any bugs in the procedure. A pilot also helps you figure out how long the test will take so that you know whether you need to cut or possibly add more tasks.

After you've finished the pilot tests, try analyzing the collected data. This data should not be used in the final analysis, but do the analysis to make sure that you're collecting the right data. During one Web site evaluation that we conducted without first analyzing data from a pilot test, we asked people to sort a list of features according to importance. Although the exercise was useful, it turned out that the resulting data was extremely difficult to analyze properly. One person mentioned that only the top two things in the list were really important to her; another identified the top four items as important. In retrospect, a better way of gathering this information would have been to ask people to rate the importance of each feature from 1 (not important) to 7 (very important).

---

3 A secondary job is to just smile at all the bad jokes about being slow and needing to upgrade the computer.

If we had tried analyzing data from the pilot test, we would have caught the problem before conducting the real test.

Testing Paper Prototypes

Paper prototypes are useful for obtaining data early in the process, but don't use them for bottom-line data, because they are too far removed from the final implementation. Most people have not seen paper prototypes before. You'll have to explain the concept, but the majority of people catch on pretty quickly.

Ask participants to point at things with a finger, using it as a mouse. If they click on a link, the person playing the computer switches to another piece of paper representing the next page. If they click on a drop-down menu, the computer can place an index card with the choices on top. Note that having a paper prototype that is larger than it would be in reality makes it easier for everyone to see where the participant is pointing (see Figure AppA.1).

Figure AppA.1

It's easier to run usability tests with oversized paper prototypes because everyone can see what's happening.

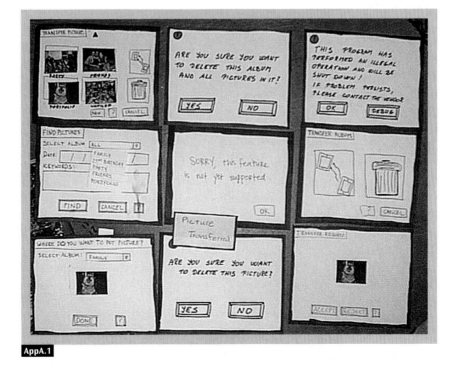

It is difficult to simulate highly interactive elements such as mouse rollovers and animations with paper prototypes. In most cases, this restriction is a good thing because it forces design teams to focus on the core issues first. Be aware of this limitation of paper prototypes, and plan accordingly.

Testing Online Prototypes

Online computer–based prototypes can be used for obtaining either process data or bottom-line data. If you're testing a high-fidelity prototype, make it clear to the participants that they'll be testing an early design and not the final Web site. They might mistakenly believe that the Web site is nearly done when it's really in the early stages of design. Setting their expectations properly will help them give you the type of high-level feedback you need at this stage, rather than, for example, comments on the visuals, such as colors and fonts. Later you can test again to evaluate these details.

Before starting a test, be sure to clear the Web browser's history and cache so that it will be as if the participant had never been to the Web site before, making all the links unvisited.

Starting and Carrying Out the Test

Greet Participants • Tests are generally broken into three major phases: preliminary instructions and paperwork, performing the tasks, and a debriefing. Start by introducing yourself and the rest of the team. Then describe the purpose of the test at a high level, and be sure to emphasize that you're testing the Web site and that you're not testing the participants in any way. Say something like, "We're asking you to help us improve the Web site by helping us find problems with it. We're testing the Web site and not you."

Also make it clear that you will not provide help as participants tackle the tasks, because you want to see how they would go through the Web site normally. However, emphasize that it's all right for them to stop the test at any time for any reason.

This is also a good time to put a "Do Not Disturb" sign on the door saying that a customer research study is in progress. You don't want any interruptions (unless the effect of an interruption is one of the things you want to observe).

Have Participants Fill Out Paperwork • After greeting the participants, have them fill out any paperwork that you have. The paperwork may request such things as basic demographic information, a name and address to which you can send a check if you're paying them, and consent. Any consent forms should explain what the test is, what kinds of data will be collected, and how the data will be used. Make sure you have two copies of the signed consent forms—one for you and one for the participant to keep.

Ask Participants to Think Aloud • If you're gathering process data, ask the participants to think aloud, to say what they're looking for and what they're trying to do. Although some people are really good at this, others find it a little awkward. The facilitator should prompt participants every so often if they stop talking, asking things like, "So, what are you looking for now?" or "What are you trying to do now?"

Don't do this if you're collecting bottom-line data, because thinking aloud may cause participants to make more errors or to go through the Web site more slowly.

Instruct Participants on How to Start • Ask participants if they have any questions before starting. Then hand them any instructions you may have, any special information, such as a fake credit card number to use, and the first task to complete on a piece of paper or an index card. To help them start thinking aloud, ask them to read the task aloud.

You may want to have participants fill out a very short survey after completing each task. You can ask questions such as how easy or hard they thought the task was. You can also ask questions to make sure that they found the right piece of information. For example, if the task is to find and add a specific item to the shopping cart, you can ask them how much the item cost. This is just a redundant check, to make sure that they really did complete the task successfully.

Take Good Notes during Each Task • While observing participants during the test, take notes about what each participant says and does. It also helps to record audio and video if possible. Use a digital watch or a clock to keep track of time too. If a certain task takes far too long, tell the participant that it's OK to move on to the next task.

If you're measuring bottom-line data, make sure everyone knows what to measure. For example, is it an error if someone hits the **Back** button on the browser? Is it an error if someone goes back to the homepage? The criteria need to be decided beforehand. And what happens if someone does not finish a task? There are no hard rules here, but a common technique is to throw out the data for that participant with a clarifying

Some Common Mistakes in Running Usability Tests

- Failing to run a pilot test to work out any bugs in the study design
- Testing a Web site using unrealistic tasks
- Collecting the wrong data or data that is hard to analyze
- Using significantly leading or biased tasks when comparing Web sites
- Recruiting participants who do not represent your expected customers
- Forgetting to clear out the Web browser file cache and history list before starting
- Using only a computer that has a fast network connection, a high-resolution monitor, and a fast processor (unless all or most of your customers really do have these)

note in the final report or to assign to that participant a very large time and a large number of errors, just to keep everything numerical.

Watch Closely • Yes, it will be frustrating to watch people struggle with something in which you have invested so much time, clicking on the wrong link or not seeing the text right in front of them. But bite your lip and keep your mouth closed; you're here to watch and learn how to improve the Web site. Make sure that none of the observers laugh, groan, or make any other inappropriate response. These types of things can unnerve your participants.

If a participant does something really interesting, ask a follow-up question. Ask open-ended questions, such as, "What are you looking for?" Let the participants know that things are going all right. Prompt them to keep speaking and tell you what they're thinking. Also look out for nonverbal cues, such as a furrowed brow or a puzzled look.

Answer any general questions that participants may have, but don't help them with the tasks. Also try not to help some participants more than others. Decide in advance which things you'll help with and which you won't. For example, it is common to decide that you'll help participants when they run into known bugs or functionality that has not been implemented yet, simply to get them back on track.

Follow Up with a Quick Survey • After all the tasks have been completed, follow up with a short survey. Get the participants' overall impressions and comments about the Web site, asking what they liked and disliked about it. Also ask them where they felt they had problems with the site and where they thought it worked well.

Debrief Participants after the Test • Wrap up by debriefing each participant, telling them what you were looking for, as well as discussing any interesting behavior on the participant's part. People often don't remember performing specific actions, so it may be useful to go through the Web site again or to show video segments to help prompt their memory.

Ask participants if they have thoughts on how to fix any problems they encountered. Take the responses with a grain of salt because participants usually don't have an understanding of design or the underlying technology. Nevertheless, these comments are useful to hear. Afterward, finish by asking participants if they have any final questions, and then thank them for their time.

A.5 Analyzing the Data

Analyzing the collected data will differ depending on whether you collected process data or bottom-line data.

Analyzing Process Data

Think about what you saw and what the participants said. Did they understand the things you thought they would? Were they confused by any terms or concepts? If so, maybe you need to rename things using FAMILIAR LANGUAGE (K11) or explain them in greater detail. If the concept in question is a concept fundamental to the Web site, be sure to make that fact clear on the homepage because otherwise people might leave without ever bothering to figure it out.

What errors could participants recover from? For example, did they click on a link but then quickly realize that it was the wrong one? It's important to minimize these kinds of problems, but these are usually just minor annoyances. A bigger problem would be indicated by systematic "ping-ponging"—that is, repeated back and forth attempts from one page down unfruitful paths. Such behavior would suggest a need for more DESCRIPTIVE, LONGER LINK NAMES (K9), which would provide more information scent to help participants find a particular page.

Focus first on the errors from which participants could not recover. Did participants have problems filling out forms? Perhaps a CLEAR FORM (H10) that helps PREVENT ERRORS (K12) and has MEANINGFUL ERROR MESSAGES (K13) will help. What about navigation? Could they make their way through the site adequately? If not, having MULTIPLE WAYS TO NAVIGATE (B1) and BROWSABLE CONTENT (B2) may be what's needed. Did they make any errors where they didn't even notice there was a problem?[4] These could be fundamental problems of the site and should be addressed first when you're fixing the site.

The most important question to ask is why the error occurred. Was the navigation too confusing, making it difficult to go to other pages? Was the information disorganized, making it hard to find things across pages? Was the Web page too cluttered, making it hard to find anything within a page? Was the site too slow, causing participants to lose track of what they wanted to do? Just like a doctor, you get to see only the symptoms, but you need to keep asking yourself if any fundamental issues are causing all of these problems.

Another thing to keep in mind is that people don't give up in usability tests as easily as they would in the real world. Realize that no matter what you do, you're still putting an implicit amount of pressure on participants to try their best to successfully complete the task. People are more attentive and willing to go through a few more pages when they know they're being observed.

Analyzing Bottom-Line Data

Be careful when analyzing bottom-line data. For example, suppose our target goal is to ensure that a person new to a Web site can find and purchase an item in 20 minutes or less. When running our test, we get times of 20, 15, 45, 10, 5, and 25 for our six participants. The mean or average time is 20 minutes; that looks pretty good! And the median for this set of numbers is 17.5—even better!

However, the problem is that there is very little certainty here because there are only six participants and the results are highly variable. The standard deviation, a measure of how spread out the numbers in a set are, is approximately 14 for this data set. If we divide the standard deviation by the square root of the number of samples we have (6), we get 5.8. This is the *standard error of the mean*, and it tells us how much variation we can expect in the typical value. It is plausible that the typical value is as small as the mean minus twice the standard error of the mean, resulting in a lower bound of 8.5, or as large as the mean plus twice the standard error of the mean, or 32. This latter value would clearly be far from our stated goal of 20 minutes!

We can say more precisely what we mean by *plausible*. The best thing to do here is to use statistical techniques. Using basic statistical methods, you can calculate with 95 percent confidence that the actual average time

---

4 A perfect example of this is the infamous butterfly ballot used in several Florida counties in the 2000 U.S. presidential election. Statistical analysis of neighboring counties suggests that at least several thousand citizens unintentionally voted for the wrong candidate, but the voting process lacked a simple verification process that would let people check their votes.

will be 20, plus or minus 11, minutes. In other words, you are 95 percent likely to be correct in saying that the actual time will be in this range, but 5 percent of the time you'll be wrong.[5]

Usability test data is often quite variable, which means that you need lots of participants to get good estimates of typical values. In addition, the breadth of range depends on the square root of the number of participants. In other words, if you have 4 times as many participants, you narrow the range of typical values by an average factor of only 2. Continuing the example, in general, quadrupling the number of participants from 6 to 24 will narrow the spread of the average time from 20 plus or minus 11 minutes, to 20 plus or minus 6 minutes (assuming that the mean and the standard deviation stay about the same). This is where online usability evaluation methods, as described in Appendix E (Online Research), become useful, because they make it easier to scale up the number of participants and thus tighten your confidence intervals.

Basic statistics is beyond the scope of this book, but a great introduction on the topic is *The Cartoon Guide to Statistics* by Larry Gonick and Woolcott Smith. This book covers the main concepts that you will want to be familiar with when doing basic statistical analyses, including mean, variance, standard deviation, correlation, regression, *t*-test, and ANOVA.

A.6 Presenting the Results

After collecting and analyzing the data, present the results to the design team or to the clients. Results can be reported in the form of a written report or an oral presentation. Here's a short outline of the sections your report should include:

- Executive Summary
- Tasks
- Participants
- Problems Found
- Participant Feedback
- Suggested Improvements
- Appendixes

Start with the "Executive Summary," which gives a quick overview of what you did in the test, a summary of the results, and a rundown of the

---

5 If you use Microsoft Excel, you can calculate this range using the CONFIDENCE function. If you use a more advanced tool, like SPSS (Statistical Package for the Social Sciences, www.ssps.com), you probably already know how to do this calculation.

recommendations for improvement. Next, in "Tasks," talk about the tasks that you had participants carry out, describing why these tasks were chosen. Continue with "Participants," a short description of the number of participants, general demographics, and any defining characteristics.

In the next section, "Problems Found," list the problems encountered, prioritized by severity. Show screen shots of problem Web pages, using circles and arrows to point out where critical incidents occurred. Graphs showing the success rates of participants at completing tasks will also help people understand the results. If you're presenting the results orally, this is a good time to show video clips to help convey your message. Video is extremely valuable for convincing skeptical programmers and management that there are problems with the Web site. You can also include video clips in written reports that you plan to put online.

The "Participant Feedback" section contains both positive and negative feedback from participants. This section can include summaries of surveys taken by participants after they finished the test, or direct quotes from them during the test.

The next section, "Suggested Improvements," outlines what needs to be changed to improve the Web site. Triage the improvements into "must do," "should do," and "could do" categories. The "must do" improvements are the showstoppers, the ones that caused serious problems from which people could not recover. They also include really simple improvements that take only a short time to fix, such as misspellings or broken links. The "should do" improvements represent problems that are annoying but tolerable—problems that most people can figure out. The "could do" improvements are changes that will take too much effort to implement for the resulting benefits. Keep these ideas on the back burner for the next iteration.

The last section, "Appendixes," contains any test materials used during the experiment, such as demo scripts and instructions, as well as all of the raw data in a cleaned-up form.

Your evaluation plan can often be used as the basis for your usability test report. See Appendix B (Sample Web Site Evaluation Plan).

Sample Web Site Evaluation Plan[1]

Roles

- **Facilitator.** The facilitator reads instructions, handles transitions from one section of the test to another, fields participants' questions, and if necessary, helps participants recover from software bugs or places where they are clearly stuck far too long.
- **Observers.** Observers record times and on-screen events, and tally tracked metrics.

Introduction

Thank you very much for helping us evaluate two Web sites. We are testing people's perceptions of Web sites that are in the early stages of design. Here's what we have planned for the next [insert time frame here]:

1. *First we will start a Web browser, open a start page, and ask you to read the introductory text.*
2. *Next we will ask you to perform some tasks on the first Web site. Interspersed will be some survey questions asking you about your perceptions of the tasks and of the Web site.*
3. *Steps 1 and 2 will be repeated for the second Web site.*
4. *At the end, we will ask you for any overall comments.*

We're asking you to help us improve the Web site by finding problems with it. We would like to stress that we're testing the Web site, not you. If you have trouble with some of the tasks we ask you to perform, it's the Web site's

---

[1] Throughout Appendix B, italic typeface indicates text that is meant to be spoken to participants.

fault, not yours. Don't feel bad; trouble spots are exactly what we're looking for. And please remember that this test is totally voluntary. Although we don't know any reason why this would happen, if you become uncomfortable or find this evaluation objectionable in any way, feel free to quit at any time.

Hand the participants two consent forms—one for your files, one for them as a copy—as well as any forms for obtaining demographic information or contact information for receipt of any prizes or checks.

This consent form says simply that you understand what this test is about, that you understand we will respect your privacy wishes, and that you will allow us to publish any results from this study.

Wait until the participants complete the forms.

Before we begin, we'd like to ask you to say what comes to your mind as you work. We have found that we get a great deal of information from these informal observations if we ask people to think aloud as they work through the exercises. It may be a bit awkward at first, but it's really very easy once you get used to it. All you have to do is speak your thoughts as you work. If you forget to think aloud, I'll remind you to keep talking.

Do you have any questions before we start?

Tasks

Be sure to do the following for all participants:

1. Provide scrap paper and a pen.
2. Provide a sample address and sample credit card number, if necessary for the tasks.[2] *(The two Web sites we will be asking you to test are e-commerce Web sites. Here's an address and fake credit card number to use. No actual purchases will be made.)*
3. Start the Web browser.
4. Clear out the browser cache and history.
5. Set the Web browser window to a typical size.
6. Provide the first task on a sheet of paper or an index card.

---

2 Be sure to do some tests in which you do give your participants money to complete purchases all the way through. Otherwise, you won't know if the entire checkout process works.

7. Ask participants to read the first task aloud.
8. After they complete each task, ask them what they thought was hard and what was easy about the task. Ask them to rate the difficulty of the task on a scale of 1 to 7.
9. Repeat steps 6 through 8 for each task.

Debriefing

Do you have any final comments about the Web sites, this study, or anything else?

Sample Consent Form

Our names are [*insert your names here*], and we are [*describe your position and the organization you work for here*]. We would like you to participate in our research by evaluating two e-commerce Web sites. Your participation in this study should take about [*insert time frame here*] and poses no risks to you other than those normally encountered in daily life.

All the information that we obtain from your session will be kept confidential. It will be tagged with a code number, and the correspondence between your name and number will be treated with the same care as our own confidential information. We will not use your name or identifying information in any reports of our research (unless you allow it by signing the second line below).

To protect your ideas, please do not discuss with us any personal plans, inventions, or patents that you think you may pursue in the future, or that you may not want us to be able to access.

Your participation in this research is voluntary. You are free to refuse to participate. Whether or not you choose to participate will have no bearing on your standing in relation to [*insert organization name here*].

If you have any questions about the research, you may call [*insert contact person here*] at [*insert contact phone number here*], or send e-mail to [*insert contact e-mail here*]. You may keep the copy of this form for future reference.

By signing this form you accept the following statements:

I agree to participate in the evaluation of two Web sites. I know that the researchers are studying [*insert description here*]. I realize that I will be asked to test the Web sites and discuss perceptions of those two Web sites over [*insert time frame here*].

I understand that any information obtained during this study will be kept confidential.

I give [*insert your names here*] and their associates permission to present the results of this work in written or oral form, without further permission from me.

_____	_____
Signature	Date

I also agree to allow my name or other identifying information, such as a picture or video, to be included in all final reports and publications resulting from my participation in this research.

_____	_____
Signature	Date

Sample Observer Form

Participant ID: _____

Date: _____

Time started: _____   Time ended: _____

Tallies (make a mark for each incident)

Site A	Site B	Incident
		Could not figure out what to do next for more than 30 seconds
		Was visibly lost in the Web site
		Was visibly frustrated with the Web site
		Said something clearly negative about the Web site
		Said something clearly positive about the Web site
		Cursed out loud
		Other: _____
		Other: _____

Tasks Completed (mark whether successfully completed or not)

Site A	Site B	Task
❏	❏	1. Find the Web site's privacy policy.
❏	❏	2. Find the two cheapest MP3 players on the Web site.
❏	❏	3. Find a gift for a friend and add it to the shopping cart.
❏	❏	4. Find a gift for yourself and add it to the shopping cart.
❏	❏	5. Check out and finalize the purchase.
❏	❏	6. Check the status of the purchase.
❏	❏	7. Subscribe yourself to the Web site's newsletter.

Notes

Online Research

There are many good ways to better understand your customers, from traditional usability research, which we covered in Appendixes A through D, to newer forms of research enabled by the Web—what we call *online research*. Although traditional in-lab usability studies are especially useful for formative research that helps qualitatively determine which site design alternatives work best, certain forms of online research can also be employed for formative research, while other forms of online research are best for summative studies that quantify how much better one design is over another.

We define two types of online research:

1. **Remote usability research** provides a live connection between researcher and participant, sharing screens and on the phone, giving the researcher the opportunity to present designs, pose questions, assign tasks, and ask follow-up questions based on earlier answers and actions. Remote usability research is often used at the formative stages of Web site design.

2. **Automated online research** combines some of the best aspects of market research and usability research, gathering data on attitudes, intentions, behavior, and performance by asking preprogrammed questions, assigning tasks, and tracking behavior. Automated online research is frequently used for summative studies.

At Naviscent,[1] usability research (both in-lab and remote) is used to test site prototypes and quickly eliminate bad ideas, iteratively create better and better ideas, and ultimately build the best design. In addition, automated online research is used to perform quantitative usability benchmarks with

---

1 Note that one of this book's authors, Douglas van Duyne, is the principal of Naviscent.

a broader sample of participants, conduct competitive comparisons between sites, and measure the effectiveness of marketing messages. Each type of research has its place, its advantages, and its disadvantages.

One of the benefits of automated online research is that you can use it to gather feedback from a large number of people in a short period of time. It's important to sample many people when you're studying how your overall customer base feels about your site, and how your customers act. As you sample more people, you decrease the margin of error and your confidence in the data increases. You may measure customers' level of satisfaction, or you may want to know what percentage of customers can find products. We have found that this type of research is especially valuable when you're evaluating changes to important sections and pages, such as the SIGN-IN/NEW ACCOUNT (H2) form, the QUICK-FLOW CHECKOUT (F1), and the HOMEPAGE PORTAL (C1). The validity of the data is important because people will make major decisions based on it.

Automated online research can reduce or eliminate problems typically associated with traditional research—problems such as the following:

- **Sample bias.** If the pool of research participants is too small or is not representative of the overall population, it will not accurately reflect the demographics or psychographics of your target customers.
- **Undersampling bias.** If the pool of participants is too small, the sample will not be statistically valid.
- **Question bias.** To ensure that just the asking of a question does not lead people to answer in a certain way, the questions must be asked in exactly the same way every time.

However, automated online research is not suited to all situations. Here are some of the challenges you will face:

- **Complexity of research design.** To predict what people might do and say, you need to think of all your questions up front. Any follow-up questions must be anticipated and automated.
- **Statistical analysis.** With a large sample you need to calculate the margin of error and many other statistical functions, and then use the results appropriately. If you're willing to make the effort to perform these calculations, your results enable more accurate prediction of how your overall customer population would respond to the same research questions and designs. In lab studies, the cost of including enough people to do this (50 participants might be considered a minimum threshold to create a statistically valid sample) is too high.

- **Behavioral analysis.** With multiple paths through each task, evaluating behavioral issues is yet another analytical challenge.
- **Bad data.** When people click through a page of questions without really reading them so that they can get a promised incentive, the result is bad data. You can identify bad data by repeating the same question with slight wording variations to see if you get wildly different responses. You'll need to eliminate participant results that include bad data to keep them from skewing your statistics.

Remote usability research can provide many of the benefits of in-lab studies, without location limitations and travel costs. What you miss with this form of research, unless the participant has a Webcam, are subtle unspoken facial expressions and gestures. But by sharing screens and asking your participant to think aloud over the phone, you can make many of the observations you would make in a lab setting, learning about task completion, about where people get stuck in a particular design, and about what people find important, to name a few.

Given the pace of business, running research quickly can be critical to your Web site's success. Data that, in the past, traditionally took months to generate can now be collected online in only hours or days. This speed can provide a competitive advantage.

The speed with which data is collected and the geographic reach are the main reasons for using online methodologies. With regard to data quality, however, be careful about both speed and geographic spread. If you wish to quickly iterate on many design prototypes, remote usability research is a good option. If you need statistically accurate information, automated online research might be best.

To get the most out of your online research, there are a number of critical steps we recommend you follow. The next few sections provide these suggestions.

E.1 Getting Started: Define Your Research Goals Up Front

The first step in developing a remote usability evaluation plan is to determine what your research goals are.

Understand Customer Retention • Achieving business revenue and savings goals through Web sites and Web-based applications requires a new level of understanding of customer retention. In many cases you can answer the question "What will make a site more successful?" by asking, "What will make customers come back?"

Online research provides many solutions to this problem, as well as to other problems facing site developers—specifically, why customers abandon sites and whether customers can complete tasks.

Learn Why Customers Abandon Sites • The reasons that visitors leave a Web site become particularly important when you're evaluating what to redesign on your site and how the proposed improvements might affect the retention of customers. For any site that attempts to lead customers through a process, whether from the homepage to a product page or from start to completion of a transaction, understanding why customers leave a Web site is critical.

Find Out Whether Customers Can Complete Tasks • The inability of a customer to complete a task on a Web site even though the task *is* possible indicates a failure of design and a failure to test the design. Task testing provides a view into customers' experiences on a site as they attempt to complete specific tasks. You see where they go, what they try to do, and what works and doesn't work on the site. The success or failure of each customer helps the researcher and designer to understand the customer experience better and build a better Web site.

Research by Design Phase E.2

The goal of every Web site, regardless of its stage of development, is to be the best—a site to which customers return regularly. In this section we present suggestions for each development phase to help make this goal a reality.

The Discovery and Exploration Phases

Even in the conceptual phase of designing a Web site, you need to evaluate the needs of the customer to validate or invalidate site goals, messages, and rough designs. Proper testing at this phase helps guarantee that a bigger, more expensive reworking will not be required later. Automated online research is especially valuable for quickly testing goals and messages with large numbers of prospective customers. Remote and in-lab usability research let you test your prototypes and alternative designs quickly, and iteratively. A mix of online research solutions (see Section E.6, Comparison of Research Methods) can provide both the market research capability to validate product concepts, priorities, and goals, and the usability research capability to help you refine early prototypes.

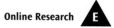

The Refinement, Production, and Implementation Phases

When you're developing a site, invariably issues arise that cause the design to change, such as underlying software technology issues or a change due to a better understanding of the flow of the customer through your site. Whenever you make a change, and as the dynamics of a site evolve, conduct additional testing to analyze the customer response. Bringing participants to your company for in-person testing might be too time-consuming for every change. Online solutions (see Section E.6, Comparison of Research Methods) that let you test a live site work well in this phase and can make it easy to rerun the same tests conducted previously and see how your changes have affected the results.

The Launch and Maintenance Phases

Once a site has been launched and real customers are visiting and experiencing it, it's important to continue testing and analysis. You will probably add new features and designs while the mix of customers changes, so you may need alternative methods of accomplishing the same tasks. All these factors lead to new problems in the live site. Online site satisfaction indices (see Section E.6, Comparison of Research Methods) provide ways to understand and improve a live site. These tools can be your early warning system, and help you stay on top of problems with your site. You can use these alerts to follow up with more in-depth research, using traditional laboratory methods or deeper online research and analyses.

Site Redesign

When you make major design changes to your site, you have the opportunity to fix many existing problems. Find the biggest problems and quantify them. Decide what will have the biggest impact on customer retention. Research your existing site and your new ideas with online usability, audience identification surveys, and competitive comparisons. Your site development team also needs to know whether its new designs will really work for customers. Online solutions (see Section E.6, Comparison of Research Methods) can provide ways to test, analyze, and recommend design improvements.

E.3   Types of Research

There are several kinds of research you might want to conduct on your site. Traditionally, two types have been used to improve companies' understanding of their customers and how they use computer interfaces: market research and usability research.

Market Research

The types of marketing analyses that online research tools can provide include the following:

- **Segmentation analysis,** to see which segments of the population respond best to different products or services
- **Cross-category analysis,** to see which customer groups are alike and which are different
- **Ongoing site assessments and benchmarked competitive comparisons,** to see how well the site is perceived in general and how well it is perceived at a high level with respect to competitors' sites
- **In-depth comparisons with competitors' sites,** to identify which features of your site are better and how to improve your site with respect to your competitors' sites
- **Online usage analysis,** to find out where customers are going on your site and why

Usability Research

Online research tools enhance traditional usability processes by conducting remote usability tests anywhere, anytime. With more advanced systems, you can conduct these tests using screen sharing and recording technology, or click-path recording, also known as *clickstream recording.*

Using automated online research tools allows you to increase the number of participants you include, thereby increasing the validity of data and the breadth of issues covered. You also spend more time *observing* the test participants' actions and less time *capturing and recording* their answers and actions.

The types of usability testing that online research tools can provide include the following:

- **Quantitative automated online research usability task completion analysis,** including clickstream analysis, to see whether customers can complete tasks on your site
- **Qualitative remote usability task completion analysis,** including remote screen viewing and clickstream analysis, to see where and why customers are being tripped up when they try to complete tasks on your site
- **Ongoing site assessments and benchmarked competitive comparisons,** to see how well customers perceive the usability of your site in general and how well they perceive it at a high level with respect to competitors' sites

- **In-depth comparisons with competitors' sites,** to identify tasks that are easier to accomplish or more efficient on your site and ways to improve task completion and efficiency on your site with respect to your competitors' sites
- **Site exit analysis,** to see where customers are leaving your site and why
- **Online usage analysis,** to see how customers are using certain pages on your site and why

Here are some key questions you can answer with online research:

- Who is visiting my site—specifically,
  - What are my visitors' ages?
  - What percentage of my visitors are male/female?
  - How much computer experience do they have?
  - How much online experience do they have?
  - What are their occupations?
  - What specialized experience do they have?
  - What specialized products do they own?

- When visiting my company's Web site, what are visitors' attitudes and impressions about the following?
  - The company
  - The company's products and services
  - The look and feel of the site
  - The messages on the site

- What behavior do visitors exhibit on the Web site?
  - Can they complete tasks and transactions?
  - Can they do what they need to do on the site?
  - What works well on the Web site?
  - What does not work on the site?
  - How can I improve the site?

- Compared with how they interact on competitors' sites, what do visitors think and exhibit as behavior about the following?
  - The company
  - Site messaging
  - Site content
  - Ease of use
  - The level of fun on the site
  - Task completion rates

Online research can also generate recommendations to improve your site. Data collected from real customers through online research can reveal trends, usability issues, and design improvement opportunities.

Running the Test

E.4

The first step is to create a research plan, choose how it is to be delivered, and select the type of research you wish to run. Online tools use templates to give you a set of prewritten questions and tasks based on the type of research and characteristics of your site. You can edit the questions, manage the layout of the questionnaire, add a nondisclosure agreement, and specify a reward for participation in the research. The last step is to add a list of participants to your research (if you have chosen to use e-mail recruiting for delivery of the research), edit the messages to participants, and then review the research one last time before you start it. In this section we'll describe these elements in more detail.

The Participants' View

An important aspect of any product is how it looks to the end customer. Figures AppE.1 through AppE.3 provide some guidelines for how to design the research for your participants.

Online research should always start with disclosures about the research and assurances to the test participants, as well as a chance for them to decline to participate (see Figure AppE.1). In addition, if you plan to video-record the session, the research participant should be informed and explicitly asked to agree. You may include a reference and link to your company's privacy policy to assuage the participant's privacy concerns.

Most online research takes one of two forms. In the first type of research, you might ask participants to complete tasks on the site or to give you their impressions of the site. In this case you'll want to show them the site in one window while asking them questions in another. A third window on the researcher's machine may show the participant's face transmitted via Webcam (see Figure AppE.2). In the second type of research, you might simply ask participants questions about themselves or their experience, without tying in directly to a particular Web site.

Setting Up Your Research

A question editor lets you edit your research questions before launching them. You can use the editor to change the question text, option text, question types, and Web page you show as research participants view and complete the questions.

Figure AppE.1

The introduction screen invites visitors to participate in research and makes it clear that the test is designed to evaluate not them, but the site. Any plan to use a video recording of the test must be divulged in the consent agreement. Nondisclosure agreements may also be included at this time.

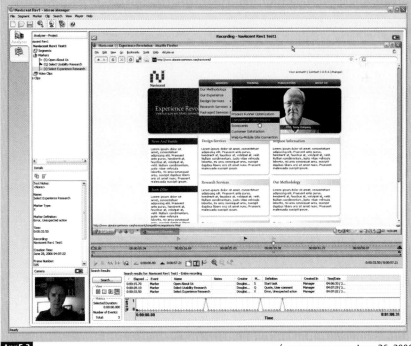

Concept Test (Service)

Thank you for agreeing to help Naviscent evaluate our web site. Your feedback is extremely important. Please respond tot he following series of questions and instructions as well as you can.

The purpose of the following questions is to gain feedback about the Naviscent web site.

We are not testing your abilities in any way, nor are we attempting to judge the "correctness" of your responses. If you have trouble carrying out any instructions or answering any questions, it is a reflection of the web site or on the questions themselves, and not on your abilities. While we value your feedback and would very much like to get your repossess to all of the questions contain in this study, we also respect your time and wishes. You may elect to leave the study at any time.

Any information you share, including your responses to any questions, will be kept strictly confidential. All information is used for research purposes only and does not involve sales of any kind, now or in the future.

START SURVEY!

POWERED BY
zoomerang

Copyright ©1999-2006 MarketTools, Inc. All Rights Reserved.
No portion of this site may be copied without the express written consent of MarketTools, Inc.

AppE.1

(www.zoomerang.com, June 26, 2006)

Figure AppE.2

Video of the participant's face, paired with the Web site screen being viewed at the time, allows the researcher to see nonverbal cues like confusion and frustration.

AppE.2

(www.morae.com, June 26, 2006)

confirmit√.   web site survey

0%   25%   50%   75%   100%

4. Would you tell us why you chose "Yes" in the previous question?
(Previous question: Would you recommend www.confirmit.com to a colleague?)

5. After visiting Confirmit.com, please indicate how strongly you agree or disagree with the following statements about FIRM.
Using a scale of 1 to 5 where 1 means 'Strongly disagree' and 5 means 'Strongly agree' please rate the following:

	Strongly disagree 1	2	3	4	Strongly agree 5
The company provides innovative technology	○	○	○	○	○
The company offers solutions to the global marketplace	○	○	○	○	○
The company is committed to customer satisfaction and loyalty	○	○	○	○	○
The company provides a secure and ethical environment	○	○	○	○	○

6. Please rate the following aspects of the Confirmit.com Web site **design**.
Using a scale of 1 to 5 where 1 means 'Poor' and 5 means 'Excellent' please rate the following:

	Poor 1	2	3	4	Excellent 5
Overall Site Design	○	○	○	○	○
Ease of Navigation	○	○	○	○	○
Download Time	○	○	○	○	○

7. What modifications (if any) would you make to the Confirmit.com Web site **design**?

8. With regards to visiting Confirmit.com, on average, how long did it take you to find the content you were looking for?

○ Less than 1 minute
○ 1 to 2 minutes
○ 3 to 5 minutes
○ Greater than 5 minutes

9. Please rate the following aspects of the Confirmit.com Web site **content**.
Using a scale of 1 to 5 where 1 means 'Poor' and 5 means 'Excellent' please rate the following:

	Poor 1	2	3	4	Excellent 5
Clarity of Message	○	○	○	○	○
Value of Content	○	○	○	○	○

10. What modifications (if any) would you make to the Confirmit.com Web site **content**?

Please provide your email address below to be entered for the iPod mini prize drawing:

OK

Powered by Confirmit

AppE.3   (www.confirmit.com, June 26, 2006)

Figure AppE.3

For sections of research that don't need to show a Web site, a full-screen survey is useful.

Choose the correct question types for the information you need during analysis. Good systems offer a range of question types:

- **Single choice.** Participants choose one option using radio buttons or drop-down pick lists.
- **Multiple choice.** Participants choose one or more options using check boxes or a list box.
- **Rank.** Participants order each option according to priority.
- **Rate: Yes/No.** For each option, participants select "Yes" or "No" using radio buttons.
- **Rate: Agree/Disagree.** For each option, participants select one of five levels of agreement, ranging from "Strongly Agree" to "Strongly Disagree," using radio buttons. This kind of measurement is also known as a *Likert scale*.
- **Rate: Would Not/Would.** For each option, participants select one of four levels of likelihood that they would take action, ranging from "Definitely Would Not" to "Definitely Would," using radio buttons.
- **Rate: 1–5.** For each option, participants select a value between 1 and 5 using radio buttons.
- **Rate: 1–7.** For each option, participants select a value between 1 and 7 using radio buttons.
- **Rate: 0–10.** For each option, participants select a value between 0 and 10 using radio buttons.
- **Semantic differential.** Participants choose a point on a scale between two extremes. For each option of the form "phrase one: phrase two," a scale is displayed.
- **Customized ratings.** The researcher defines any sort of scale, from 1 to 5, 1 to 6, 1 to 7, and so on, to "Never, Rarely, Sometimes, Often, Always."
- **Instruction.** Question text is treated as an instruction. No options are displayed.
- **Free-form.** Participants type responses in a text box. No options are displayed.
- **Task.** Participants are asked to carry out instructions and are given a fixed set of options asking whether the task was completed.

Other options that some online research systems offer are

- Nondisclosure agreements for beta sites and confidential information
- Reward systems that provide, for example, gift certificates
- Customizable e-mail messages
- Customizable welcome messages and thank-you messages
- Cobranding of the survey presentation to reflect the logo and color scheme of your site

If the sequence of questions in a segment of research must change depending on responses, the research can be programmed to handle that situation. Programming gives you the ability to rotate blocks of questions to control for answer bias, to send participants to various questions on the basis of responses, and to show different options to respondents depending on certain criteria. For example, you might want the questionnaire to branch to different questions depending on the participant's previous use of the site being tested. Not all systems have these capabilities, but research programming logic can greatly improve the quality of data captured.

When setting up online research, choose whether you need videos and **clickstreams**—the paths people take through sites—to be captured during the research. Some clickstream tools provide visualization tools that allow you to quickly analyze many participants' clickstreams in one graph. Use clickstreams to pinpoint problem pages on a site. Use videos when participant behavior on a page needs further analysis. Because clickstreams only identify problem pages, videos captured during online research can be valuable for revealing exactly what went wrong.

Recruiting the Right Participants

One of the most important parts of successful online and offline research is recruiting the right participants. Procure your participant base through existing customer lists, partner lists, or site intercept research, or contract with an online research company to find your audience.

To pull existing customers from a customer database, all you need are e-mail addresses. If you need specific types of participants, such as customers who have bought a product multiple times before on your site, or customers who spend less than 15 minutes during each session on your site, store this information in your databases. If you don't have this second level of information, use **intercept research;** that is, pop up a short questionnaire to a random sample of site visitors, to screen and qualify participants.

Research companies like Naviscent can help by selecting a group of participants tailored to your specific needs. If you contract with a research company, make sure they do the following:

- Meet with you to determine which audience the research needs to reach, and how to identify the audience with a screening questionnaire
- Once the screening questionnaire exists, acquire participants from specific pools of potential participants
- Once the customized list of participants has been created, send you the list of e-mail addresses for inclusion in your research participant invitations

E.5 Analyzing the Data

Most online research tools have multiple ways to analyze the resulting data. Typically, online analysis tools provide cross-tabulations (commonly referred to as *cross-tabs*), analysis and filtering of sets, video playback, clickstream analysis, and raw data reporting.

One of the best ways to delve deeper into your data is to have it **cross-tabulated.** Tabulating respondent answers against the key questions in your research, and viewing the results side by side, is the essence of a cross-tab (see Figure AppE.4). Cross-tabs help identify the similarities, trends, and distinctions among groups of research participants.

Many research tools also let you export raw data to software analysis packages like SPSS, SAS, WinCross, Minitab, and Excel. Once you've done this, you can cross-tabulate the data and perform other statistical analyses (such as regression analysis) on it.

If you decide to use online research, you can make the capture, analysis, and reporting of quantifiable results quick and affordable.

Figure AppE.4

A cross-tabulation tool can show correlations between two sets of responses.

Select the **questions** that you would like to cross-tabulate putting a checkmark in the checkboxes next to the questions that you want to add to the columns and rows.

Rows	Columns	
☑	☐	**1.** Did you find the demonstration video helpful?
		2. Please rate the following aspects of the demo video (7 being the best)
☐	☑	Video quality
☐	☐	Audio quality
☐	☐	Narration pace

Click the **Submit** arrow to generate a cross tabulation report.

Did you find the demonstration video helpful?:

	Total	Please rate the following aspects of the demo video (7 being the best): Video quality						
		Not so good	2	3	OK	5	6	Great!
Total	98	1	0	0	11	15	31	40
Yes	96	1	0	0	11	14	30	40
No	2	0	0	0	0	1	1	0

AppE.4

(www.zoomerang.com, June 26, 2006)

Comparison of Research Methods

E.6

This section offers a brief comparison of features of online research and traditional in-lab usability methods, summed up in Table AppE.1. Depending on your project, certain methods might be more appropriate than others.

Features/Benefits	In-Lab Usability Research	Remote Usability Research	Automated Online Research
FLEXIBILITY			
Usability Research			
Task testing	Yes	Yes	Yes
Competitive comparison	Yes	Yes	Yes
Random site visitor task analysis	No	Yes	Yes
Wireless testing	Yes	Yes	Yes
Testing physical interfaces (without emulators)	Yes	No	No
Market Research			
Concept testing	No	No	Yes
Brand value	No	No	Yes
Price elasticity	No	No	Yes
Invitation Methods			
Link invitation	No	Yes	Yes
Multiple intercept invitation methods	No	Yes	Yes
Site exit intercepts	No	Yes	Yes
E-mail invitation	Yes	Yes	Yes
Easy-to-change welcome and invitation text	Yes	Yes	Yes
Research Scripting			
Branching	Yes	Yes	Yes
Quotas	Yes	Yes	Yes
Block rotation	Yes	Yes	Yes
Automatic validation of task completion	No	Yes	Yes

Table AppE.1

Research Methods Compared

Table AppE.1

(Continued)

Features/Benefits	In-Lab Usability Research	Remote Usability Research	Automated Online Research
Question Types			
Multiple question types	Yes	Yes	Yes
Customized ratings (e.g., 1–10, 1–7, 1–6, 1–5, Hot/Warm/Cold)	Yes	Yes	Yes
Reporting			
Real time	No	Yes	Yes
Cross-tabs	Yes	Yes	Yes
Filtering	Manual	Yes	Yes
Online videos	Maybe	Yes	No
Video archives	Yes	Yes	No
DATA ACCESS			
Client ownership of data	Yes	Yes	Yes
Collaborative work environment	Yes	Yes	Yes
REAL CUSTOMER FEEDBACK			
Online view and playback of customer mouse movements, clicks, and typing	Maybe	Yes	No
Evaluation of your Web site by real people	Yes	Yes	Yes
Insights into customers' subjective thoughts	Yes	Yes	Yes
REAL-TIME CUSTOMER OBSERVATION			
Capture of participant actions on video	Yes	Yes	No
Tracking of behavior of real site customers	Yes	Yes	Yes
REMOTE SITE EVALUATION			
No complex software download	No	Maybe	Maybe
Platform independent	No	Maybe	Maybe
Browser independent	No	Maybe	Maybe
Flexibility to participate anywhere, anytime	No	Maybe	Yes
Evaluation of customers in their own environment	No	Maybe	Yes
Clickstream path analysis of pages visited	No	Maybe	Maybe
Automatic clickstream page aggregation	No	Maybe	Maybe

(continued)

Features/Benefits	In-Lab Usability Research	Remote Usability Research	Automated Online Research
DATA ACCURACY AND INTEGRITY			
Large sample used	No	No	Yes
Findings based on geographically dispersed participants	No	Yes	Yes
Depth of information			
Video	Yes	Yes	No
Clickstream	No	Yes	Yes
Self-report	Yes	Yes	Yes
BENCHMARK DATA			
Ongoing customer satisfaction metrics 24/7	No	Maybe	Maybe
Inexpensive competitive comparisons	No	Maybe	Maybe
Tracking against historical data, industries, and best of the best	Maybe	Maybe	Maybe
Drill-down and filtering capability	No	Maybe	Yes

Table AppE.1

(Continued)

In evaluating tools for remote usability or automated online research, look for the following critical features:

- **No complex software download.** Research participants don't like to install software on their computers to take part in online research. Furthermore, requiring a software download may exclude both corporate customers and novices, who may be blocked from installing software. All of these factors result in a biased sample.
- **Platform independence.** Although we see Microsoft Windows at most sites where we work, it's not everywhere. If you don't embrace the Mac platform, you will be excluding 100 percent of the Mac users in the market.
- **Browser independence.** Because Web sites have to be tweaked for different operating systems, to ensure browser independence it's important to have your research participants conduct the research on a variety of browsers.

E.7 Take-away Ideas

A variety of remote usability and automated online research tools exist, for both qualitative and quantitative research. Some are quite pricey, others are inexpensive, and a few are free. With a little creativity, researchers can greatly extend their budgets by also exploring the less expensive options for online qualitative research. Products like TechSmith's Morae or WebEx, together with a conference phone call, can be used to gather qualitative online data at a very affordable price.

This glossary is meant to be a comprehensive resource that you can go to when you have a question about Web design. Even if a topic may not be covered exhaustively in the book, we include it here to give you the important distinctions you need to get your job done.

24/7 • Twenty-four hours a day, seven days a week. Usually this term refers to the reliability of a system, one that cannot fail under any circumstances. Sometimes found as *24/7/365,* meaning 365 days a year as well. Also found as *24/7/360,* meaning 360 degrees around the globe.

A

accelerator • A way to speed up a task for the customer, such as a keyboard shortcut, a macro, or automatic storage of information.

access provider • See *Internet service provider.*

account management system • Any system designed to help people manage the personal information stored by a Web site. For more information, see ACCOUNT MANAGEMENT (H4).

acquisition cost • The cost to acquire a new customer.

Active Server Pages • See *ASP* (definition 1).

Adobe Illustrator • A graphic design software tool that is useful for creating high-fidelity prototypes.

affinity diagramming • A way of organizing data in which all the individual points and concepts that have been gathered are arranged on a wall-sized, hierarchical diagram. For an example, see Figure 3.4 in Chapter 3 (Knowing Your Customers: Principles and Techniques).

affordance • A clue, often visual, to how an object works. For example, most door handles provide an affordance for grasping. Buttons in modern graphical user interfaces, such as action buttons, look three-dimensional, providing affordances for pushing.

For more information, see SITE ACCESSIBILITY (B9), DIRECT MANIPULATION (H9), and ACTION BUTTONS (K4).

AJAX • Asynchronous JavaScript And XML, a set of technologies that enables the creation of Rich Internet Applications that have high levels of interactivity. For more information, see WEB APPS THAT WORK (A10), BROWSABLE CONTENT (B2), DIRECT MANIPULATION (H9), CLEAR FORMS (H10), PREDICTIVE INPUT (H11), DRILL-DOWN OPTIONS (H12), and FAST-LOADING CONTENT (L6), and MOBILE INPUT CONTROLS (M2).

alert • A brief message that notifies a customer of special events that may be of interest, such as the imminent due date of a library book or a particular stock's price drop below a certain mark. Compare *focused advertisement* and *newsletter.* For more information, see E-MAIL SUBSCRIPTIONS (E2).

alpha • Referring to the first cut of a Web site created in the Implementation phase of Web development. An alpha version of a site contains basic functionality and major page types but is not yet polished or ready to be deployed. Compare *beta.*

<alt> text • Text that appears before an image is loaded, when an image is rolled over with the mouse, and if an image fails to load and is not being displayed. For more information, see WRITING FOR SEARCH ENGINES (D6) and FAST-LOADING IMAGES (L2).

anchor text • The hypertext label that is used to link to a particular page.

antialiasing • Smoothing out jagged edges in images or fonts, creating gradual transitions instead of sharp transitions on the borders of images. Antialiased images usually look more professional, but they take a little more time to produce than unantialiased images.

Apache • One of the most popular Web servers. Apache is an example of open-source software.

API • Application programming interface, the means for using an existing piece of software in the source code for a new piece of software.

application programming interface • See *API.*

application service provider • Sometimes abbreviated *ASP,* a Web site or company that provides individuals or enterprises access over the Internet to applications and related services that would otherwise have to be located in their own personal or enterprise computers. Some ASPs focus on providing highly specific services that can be integrated into another Web site, such as search engines or providers of stock information. ASP can be used to outsource certain functions of a Web site, such as local search functionality, thereby making it easier to add the search function to a Web site.

ASP • (pronounced by speaking each letter individually) 1. Active Server Pages, a technology created by Microsoft that mixes HTML and software code. The code is executed when a client Web browser makes a request, enabling the creation of dynamically generated HTML. Compare *JSP,* a competing Java-based technology, and *PHP,* a competing Perl-based technology. 2. See *application service provider.*

asynchronous communication • A communications setup in which customers can leave messages that others can respond to later, such as in e-mail or on a message board. Compare *synchronous communication.* For more information, see COMMUNITY CONFERENCE (A3).

Asynchronous JavaScript And XML • See *AJAX.*

authentication • A process that proves a person really is who he or she claims to be. One example of an authentication process is the use of passwords. Compare *identification.* For more information, see PERSISTENT CUSTOMER SESSIONS (H5).

H5

automated online research • Methods for querying hundreds of people (or more) automatically, to gather their attitudes, intentions, behavior, and performance on a Web site. For more information, see Appendix E (Online Research).

automatic floating window • A floating window that appears simply as a result of a customer's arrival at or departure from a Web site. Automatic floating windows usually contain advertisements or surveys for improving the quality of a Web site. Compare *link-based floating window.* For more information, see FLOATING WINDOWS (H6).

H6

B

b2b • Business-to-business. In e-commerce, a b2b business sells products or services to another business.

b2c • Business-to-customer. In e-commerce, a b2c business sells products or services to end customers or consumers.

b2e • Business-to-employee. In e-commerce, a b2e business provides services and productivity applications online to employees.

b2g • Business-to-government. In e-commerce, a b2g business sells products or services to the government.

back-end cost • A cost incurred as a result of responding to customer needs not addressed by the basic Web site—for example, through support calls, returns, and the like. For more information, see Chapter 1 (Customer-Centered Web Design: More Than a Good Idea).

1

bandwidth • A measure of data transmission speeds over a network connection. Bandwidth is often measured in kilobits per second (kbps) or megabits per second (mbps). Typical modem speeds are 28.8 kbps and 56 kbps. Bandwidth should not be confused with *latency,* which refers to the amount of time it takes to transfer data from one point to another. See also *broadband, cable modem,* and *DSL.*

banner ad • A small horizontal advertisement, usually at the top of a homepage. Visitors click it to link to a Web site. Banner ads are often animated and have standard sizes. Most advertisements on Web pages are banner ads.

beta • Referring to the second version of a Web site, created in the Implementation phase of Web development. It contains nearly all of the desired functionality and is more polished than the *alpha* release.

between-groups experiment • An experiment in which the pool of test participants is divided into two groups and each group is assigned to a different condition. For example, if there are two different Web sites to test, each participant uses only one of the two sites. Compare *within-groups experiment.* For more information, see Appendix A (Running Usability Evaluations).

biometrics • A security alternative to simple passwords in which the computer uses a physical attribute such as a person's fingerprint to verify identity. For more information, see PREVENTING PHISHING SCAMS (E9).

E9

bits per second (bps) • A measure of bandwidth. See *bandwidth* and *latency*.

blog • An abbreviation for *Web log,* a blog is a Web page with dated entries. Blogs are used for a variety of genres, including personal diaries, describing new services provided by a Web site, providing internal communications to employees, and aggregating news, to name just a few. For more information, see BLOGS (A12). **A12**

blurb • A continuation of the headline on a Web page. A blurb provides details of the customer benefit, reinforcing what is important and unique about the content. Blurbs must be short and precise, not more than one or two sentences. Compare *headline.* For more information, see HEADLINES AND BLURBS (D3). **D3**

bookmark • A mechanism built into most Web browsers that saves the location of a Web page so that the customer will not need to type in the address each time. Also called *favorite.* For more information, see DISTINCTIVE HTML TITLES (D9). **D9**

Boolean search • A search that uses the term *and* or *or.* For example, the search "computer and monitor" would find all Web pages containing both *computer* and *monitor,* whereas "computer or monitor" would find all Web pages containing either *computer* or *monitor.* For more information, see STRAIGHTFORWARD SEARCH FORMS (J2). **J2**

bot • Short for *robot,* a bot is a software program that does a repetitive action. Typically carrying a negative connotation, bots are used for things like spamming MESSAGE BOARDS (D5), signing up for thousands of e-mail addresses (which are later used for e-mail spam), and so on. For more information, see BLOGS (A12). **D5** **A12**

bottom-line data • Quantitative usability data, often collected in later stages of design. Examples include time to complete a task, number of errors made, rate of learning, and retention of learned material over time. Compare *process data.* For more information, see Chapter 4 (Involving Customers with Iterative Design) and Appendix A (Running Usability Evaluations). **4**

bps • See *bits per second.*

brand • What customers remember or feel about a Web site or the company behind it. Brand can be shaped by images, graphic look, or the logo of a company. For more information, see SITE BRANDING (E1). **E1**

bread crumb • A small navigation cue giving some indication of where a visitor is currently located on a Web site and where he or she came from. Also called *trail marker.* For more information, see LOCATION BREAD CRUMBS (K6). **K6**

brick-and-mortar • Referring to a company that has a strong real-world presence but a weak or no Web presence. Compare *click-and-mortar* and *e-tailer.*

broadband • Referring to a network connection with high bandwidth, such as DSL or cable modem. Typical speeds range from 256 kbps to 2 mbps.

brochureware • A derisive term for a simple Web site that does no more than promote a company and its products. For more information, see Chapter 1 (Customer-Centered Web Design: More Than a Good Idea). **1**

browser • See *Web browser.*

browsing • One of two major strategies that visitors use to find information on a Web site, in which they examine pages and click on links that seem to take them closer to their target Web page (regardless of whether that page actually exists). Compare *searching*. For more information, see BROWSABLE CONTENT (B2).

bug report • A report of a problem that is provided in a customer e-mail, a Web site evaluation, quality assurance testing, or server log file analysis.

business analysis document • A document, produced during the Discovery phase of Web development, that spells out the business needs of both the client and the customers. For more information, see Chapter 5 (Processes for Developing Customer-Centered Sites).

business plan • A high-level proposal that spells out a company's business model, the basic strategy for how a company will make money. For more information, see Chapter 5 (Processes for Developing Customer-Centered Sites).

C

cable modem • A form of broadband communication that transfers data across a cable television network. Compare *DSL*.

cache • 1. To store information nearby. 2. The space used to store cached information. Web browsers cache Web pages that visitors have already seen so that the pages will load more quickly if viewed again. For more information, see REUSABLE IMAGES (L5).

CAPTCHA • Short for **c**ompletely **a**utomated **p**ublic **T**uring test to tell **c**omputers and **h**umans **a**part, a CAPTCHA is a computer test meant to distinguish between humans and computers. A typical example is to discern letters within a distorted image, something that is relatively easy for people to do but difficult for modern computer systems. CAPTCHAs are used to prevent *bots* from completing SIGN-IN/NEW ACCOUNT (H2) processes or adding spam to MESSAGE BOARDS (D5). Sometimes called *human interactive proof* (*HIP*).

card sorting • A method of categorization by which customers help you organize and label large groups of content. Simply put, customers are asked to organize cards labeled with site content into stacks. For more information, see Chapter 3 (Knowing Your Customers: Principles and Techniques).

Cascading Style Sheets (CSS) • A language for specifying how to present the information in an HTML Web page. With CSS, designers can control things like layout, fonts, and colors without modifying individual Web pages directly. For more information, see STYLE SHEETS (D11).

category description • A technique for testing the usefulness and usability of link names, independent of visual design and layout, in which participants are asked to describe what they think a given category contains. Compare *category identification*. For more information, see HIERARCHICAL ORGANIZATION (B3) and FAMILIAR LANGUAGE (K11).

category identification • A technique for testing the usefulness and usability of link names, independent of visual design and layout, in which participants are given a list of category names and a list of tasks, and are asked to choose the category that they think would help them complete each task. Compare *category description*. For more information, see HIERARCHICAL ORGANIZATION (B3) and FAMILIAR LANGUAGE (K11).

certification authority • A trusted third-party vendor that issues digital certificates for Web servers. For more information, see Chapter 5 (Processes for Developing Customer-Centered Sites).

CGI • See *Common Gateway Interface.*

click-and-mortar • Referring to a company that has both a strong Web presence and a strong real-world presence. Compare *brick-and-mortar* and *e-tailer.*

clickstream • The click path or page path that visitors take when they go through a site. Some server log tools and online usability research applications provide clickstream analysis tools. For more information, see Appendix E (Online Research).

click-through • The number of visitors who click on a banner ad. Usually expressed as a percentage, click-through is calculated as the total number of banner ads clicked on, divided by the total number of banner ads displayed. See also *CPM.*

client • 1. The specific computer or software that requests information, or any other resource, from a server. Web browsers are the most common clients. Compare *server.* See also *client–server architecture* and *Web browser.* 2. A person or company for whom you're doing Web design and development work; the person (company) providing the funding. Compare *customer.*

client–server architecture • A common form of software architecture in which a server contains information or other resources, and clients request the information or resources. The Web is an example of client–server architecture. Compare *peer-to-peer architecture.*

Common Gateway Interface (CGI) • The standard way of processing Web-based forms. CGI is also used to create dynamically generated HTML. Programming languages used for CGI include Perl, Python, and Java. Alternatives to CGI are the ASP, JSP, and PHP technologies.

community • A group of people tied together by shared interests or common values. For more information, see COMMUNITY CONFERENCE (A3), MESSAGE BOARDS (D5), and RECOMMENDATION COMMUNITY (G4).

company-centered design • A design strategy in which the needs and interests of the company dominate the structure and content of the Web site. Compare *customer-centered design, designer-centered design,* and *technology-centered design.* For more information, see Chapter 1 (Customer-Centered Web Design: More Than a Good Idea).

competitive analysis • An analysis that evaluates competitors' Web sites, including the features they offer, as well as which features are important to customers and which are not. For more information, see Chapter 5 (Processes for Developing Customer-Centered Sites).

compressing • An approach to reducing the file size of an image in which either redundant information is encoded more compactly or the number of colors is reduced, thereby reducing the amount of information required to encode the image. Compare *cropping* and *shrinking.* For more information, see FAST-LOADING IMAGES (L2).

conversion rate • A value representing the number of visitors who become buying customers on a Web site. Usually expressed as a percentage, the conversion rate is calculated as the total number of unique customers, divided by the total number of unique visitors. Higher conversion rates are better than low ones.

cookie • A browser feature that allows Web sites to keep information on a visitor's computer. Typically cookies are used for personalization, but they can also be used for tracking a customer's movements through the Web. For this reason, cookies are at the center of a growing privacy debate. For more information, see PERSONALIZED CONTENT (D4), PERSISTENT CUSTOMER SESSIONS (H5), FAIR INFORMATION PRACTICES (E3), and PRIVACY POLICY (E4).

CPM • Cost per thousand impressions. CPM is the cost per 1,000 people delivered by a medium or media schedule. For banner ads, CPM is the cost per 1,000 ads seen by visitors. See also *click-through.*

crawler • A program that gathers and processes content for later use by starting from a list of a few sites and going from link to link, opening pages and indexing the words on those pages. Crawlers make use of meta-information about the content, as well as the content itself, to create a search index. Also called *spider.* For more information, see WRITING FOR SEARCH ENGINES (D6).

critical incident • An incident during a usability test, in which the participant has either a positive or a negative reaction. Negative reactions include frustration, anger, or confusion during a task. Expletives can be strong indicators of negative critical incidents. Positive reactions include cases in which people are pleasantly surprised or say something positive about the site. For more information, see Chapter 4 (Involving Customers with Iterative Design) and Appendix A (Running Usability Evaluations).

CRM • Customer relationship management—methods and software to manage the long-term relationship between a company and a customer.

cropping • An approach to reducing the file size of an image in which unneeded portions of the image are trimmed. Compare *compressing* and *shrinking.* For more information, see FAST-LOADING IMAGES (L2).

cross-selling • Promoting products related to those that a customer already wants to purchase. Compare *up-selling.* For more information, see SHOPPING CART (F3) and CROSS-SELLING AND UP-SELLING (G2).

cross-tabulation • A method of evaluating research results in which answers from respondents are compared with the key questions in the research, and the results are viewed side by side. For more information, see Appendix E (Online Research).

CSS • See *Cascading Style Sheets.*

customer • A person who will use the Web site that you're designing. Also called *target customer.* Compare *client* (definition 2).

customer analysis document • A document, developed during the Discovery phase of Web development, that provides a deep understanding of the needs, tools, and existing practices of a Web site's target customers. For more information, see Chapter 5 (Processes for Developing Customer-Centered Sites).

customer-centered design • A design strategy that (1) focuses on understanding people, their tasks, the technology available, and the larger social and organizational context of where they live, work, and play; (2) keeps the customer involved in the design process; and (3) elicits from visitors to a Web site consistently high marks for content, ease of use, performance, trustworthiness, and overall satisfaction—that is, it provides a positive experience for all customers, whether they're there to find information, to be part of a community, to purchase items, or to be entertained. Compare *company-centered design, designer-centered design,* and *technology-centered design.* For more information, see Chapter 1 (Customer-Centered Web Design: More Than a Good Idea).

customer-centered Web site • A Web site that provides real value and delivers a positive customer experience. Customer-centered Web sites receive consistently high marks for content, ease of use, performance, trustworthiness, and overall satisfaction from visitors. For more information, see Chapter 1 (Customer-Centered Web Design: More Than a Good Idea).

customer experience • The whole experience that a customer has, both online and offline, when using a Web site. Customer experience includes such online factors as ease of use and content, as well as offline factors such as fulfillment and customer service.

customer relationship management • See *CRM.*

customer session • A set of interactions by a customer with a Web site during one sitting. Web servers typically use cookies to track who the customer is and what he or she did on-site during the session. For more information, see PERSONALIZED CONTENT (D4) and PERSISTENT CUSTOMER SESSIONS (H5).

customization • A customer-driven process in which customers enter data and change the layout of a Web site to fit their tastes and interests. Customization is one way of achieving *personalization.* For more information, see HOMEPAGE PORTAL (C1), PERSONALIZED CONTENT (D4), and DIRECT MANIPULATION (H9).

D

default setting • The normal setting for something, before a customer changes it.

deliverable • The end product of a milestone phase (Discovery, Exploration, Refinement, Production, Implementation, Launch, or Maintenance) of Web development. Common deliverables include interactive prototypes and specification documents.

demographics • Detailed characteristics of customers, such as age, education, income, and hobbies. Compare *psychographics.*

design document • A document, created during the Production phase of Web development, that describes how a Web site works in great detail and uses site maps, storyboards, and schematics to describe the flow of interaction. For more information, see Chapter 5 (Processes for Developing Customer-Centered Sites).

designer-centered design • A design strategy in which the needs and desires of the designer, not necessarily of the customers, dominate the structure and content of the Web site. Compare *company-centered design, customer-centered design,* and *technology-centered design.* For more information, see Chapter 1 (Customer-Centered Web Design: More Than a Good Idea).

design guidelines • See *guidelines.*

design style guide • General rules for site design that are intended to be followed on every Web page to minimize inconsistencies.

desktop metaphor • The conceptual model around which modern computer interfaces are organized, consisting of files, folders, trash cans, and so on. See also *GUI*.

DHTML • See *Dynamic HTML.*

digital certificate • Proof that a Web server has the identity it says it has. Digital certificates are issued by a variety of certification authorities. For more information, see Chapter 5 (Processes for Developing Customer-Centered Sites).

Digital Subscriber Line • See *DSL.*

directory • A form of organizing information, in which content appears in categories, usually alphabetically, sequentially, or hierarchically. The best-known example of a directory is Yahoo! Also called *index*. For more information, see 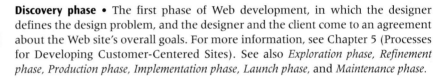 GRASSROOTS INFORMATION SITES (A6) and HIERARCHICAL ORGANIZATION (B3).

Discovery phase • The first phase of Web development, in which the designer defines the design problem, and the designer and the client come to an agreement about the Web site's overall goals. For more information, see Chapter 5 (Processes for Developing Customer-Centered Sites). See also *Exploration phase, Refinement phase, Production phase, Implementation phase, Launch phase,* and *Maintenance phase.*

disintermediation • The removal of middlemen. For example, e-commerce can simplify the ordering and distribution of products by giving customers a direct line to the manufacturer. All the people who distribute the product to local stores, and all of the local stores, are removed.

Document Object Model (DOM) • A standard way of representing HTML and XML documents as objects that can be manipulated in programming languages. Developed by W3C as an open standard.

document type definition • See *DTD.*

DOM • See *Document Object Model.*

domain name • Technically, a way to name computers on the Internet. It is more common to use the domain name to identify a Web site, such as berkeley.edu, than to use its numerical IP address.

DSL • Digital Subscriber Line, a form of broadband network connection for the home that uses existing telephone lines. Compare *cable modem.*

DTD • Document type definition, a specification that accompanies a document and identifies the codes that separate paragraphs, identify topic headings, and so forth, as well as how each is to be processed. For example, a DTD is used by HTML and XML to define tags such as <html> and <b>, and to define any tag-ordering constraints.

Dynamic HTML (DHTML) • Not to be confused with *dynamically generated HTML,* DHTML uses the Document Object Model to dynamically change Web pages after they have been downloaded to a customer's browser.

dynamically generated HTML • A Web page that is generated on the fly when a visitor requests it. The HTML in the Web page does not fully exist until the request is made. A simple use of dynamically generated HTML is to include the last time the HTML file was updated. A more sophisticated use is to provide personalization. Usually dynamically generated HTML is created by the use of CGI, ASP, JSP, or PHP. Dynamically generated HTML should not be confused with *Dynamic HTML,* a Web standard that is being developed by W3C.

E

e-commerce • The business of selling products or services online. The two major forms of e-commerce are business-to-business (b2b) and business-to-consumer (b2c). For more information, see PERSONAL E-COMMERCE (A1) and Pattern Group G (Advanced E-Commerce).

embedded link • A link that is contained in the body of a text (as opposed to being listed at the end of an article). For more information, see INVERTED-PYRAMID WRITING STYLE (D7) and EMBEDDED LINKS (K7).

encryption • Translation of data into a secret form so that unauthorized people cannot easily understand it. SSL is a way of encrypting information transferred over the Web. For more information, see SECURE CONNECTIONS (E6).

e-tailer • Short for *electronic retailer,* an e-tailer is a company that sells products online exclusively. Compare *brick-and-mortar* and *click-and-mortar.*

ethnography • A formal technique used in sociology and anthropology to observe and interact with people in their normal environments. See also *field observation.*

Exploration phase • The second phase of Web development, following Discovery, in which the developer generates multiple designs. For more information, see Chapter 5 (Processes for Developing Customer-Centered Sites). See also *Discovery phase, Refinement phase, Production phase, Implementation phase, Launch phase,* and *Maintenance phase.*

Extensible Markup Language • See *XML.*

Extensible Hypertext Markup Language • See *XHTML.*

extranet • A private portion of a company's Web site intended for suppliers, vendors, partners, and customers. An extranet can also be an extension of a company's intranet. Compare *intranet.*

F

false positive • A problem with a Web site interface that is identified by heuristic evaluation but never found to exist in a usability study of the same interface.

FAQ • Literally, frequently asked questions. A FAQ page provides answers to questions commonly asked by visitors to a Web site. For more information, see FREQUENTLY ASKED QUESTIONS (H7).

favorite • See *bookmark.*

field observation • An experimental technique in which people are watched in their own environment, at home or at work, to see how they use a Web site and other tools, as well as how they interact with other people in their environment.

firewall • A proxy that limits the kind of information transferred over a network. Companies often use firewalls to protect their computers from unauthorized external access.

first read • The dominant visual element of a Web page that draws the customer's eyes. For more information, see HOMEPAGE PORTAL (C1) and CLEAR FIRST READS (I3).

Fitts's Law • An empirically determined law used to calculate the time it takes to move from a given point to a target object. Intuitively, the law states that objects that are far away or small take longer to point to than objects that are close or large. Fitts's Law has implications for the size of clickable links and images. For more information, see Chapter 3 (Knowing Your Customers: Principles and Techniques) and ACTION BUTTONS (K4).

five-way joystick • A small joystick on a mobile phone or other mobile device that provides up, down, left, and right options, as well as a "select" option, when pushed.

five-way rocker switch • A small button or two on a mobile phone or other mobile device that can be pushed on different sides, providing up, down, left, and right options, as well as a "select" option, when pushed.

Flash • The tool and the browser plug-in, developed by Macromedia, for creating and viewing interactive multimedia presentations.

floating window • A small window that appears on the screen without creating a new browser window, and that seems to float over the current Web site. For more information, see FLOATING WINDOWS (H6).

flow • 1. An interaction sequence through or navigation structure of a Web site, often illustrated with a storyboard. 2. Natural and easy movement of a customer on your Web site from goals to fulfillment of those goals.

focused advertisement • An advertisement that draws attention to a new promotion, special offer, or new product. Compare *alert* and *newsletter*. For more information, see E-MAIL SUBSCRIPTIONS (E2).

focus group • A group of representative target customers who are gathered to provide feedback on their motivation for visiting a Web site, describe their response to it, and identify the tasks they want to accomplish there. For more information, see Chapter 3 (Knowing Your Customers: Principles and Techniques).

fold • An imaginary line on a Web page that delineates what is visible in a browser without making the visitor scroll down. The content below the line is "below the fold." Because a potential customer may not necessarily see content below the fold at first, the most important information should be placed above it. For more information, see ABOVE THE FOLD (I2).

force • A key issue or constraint that comes into play when you're trying to solve a particular design problem.

frequently asked questions • See *FAQ.*

fulfillment • All of the surrounding processes required to deliver and support products that customers have purchased, including logistics, inventory management, parcel management, and customer service. Fulfillment is a component of back-end costs.

G

GIF • (pronounced "jiff" or "giff") Graphics Interchange Format, a widely supported and popular way to store images. GIF is usually used for small images and images requiring transparency. See also *JPEG, PNG,* and *SVG.* For more information, see FAST-LOADING IMAGES (L2).

gold-plating • Trying to get a Web site absolutely perfect before launch.

graphical user interface • See *GUI.*

graphic design • Visual communication of information, using elements such as color, images, typography, and layout. Also called *visual design*. Compare *navigation design*.

Graphics Interchange Format • See *GIF*.

greeking • A visual design and usability testing technique in which nonsense text is placed on a Web page. Greeking allows those who view a design or participants testing the interface to focus on the layout and visual design of a page, instead of its content. Typical tasks that participants are asked to do on a greeked page include pointing to what they think is the page title, and pointing to what they believe are the news items. Greeking is often used in low-fidelity prototypes. For more information, see GRID LAYOUT (I1).

grid layout • A technique for organizing Web pages that is borrowed from graphic design (where it is used for organizing page layouts for newspapers, magazines, and other documents), or the end result of that technique. In a grid layout, a page is divided into rows and columns, and every element is made to fit within this grid. Constant design elements, such as titles and logos, always appear in the same place, giving a consistent theme to every page. For more information, see GRID LAYOUT (I1).

GUI • (pronounced "gooey") Graphical user interface. This term often refers to the desktop interface, such as the interface found in Microsoft Windows or the Macintosh operating system. However, GUI can refer to any interface that uses graphics. See also *desktop metaphor*.

guidelines • Suggestions for how to build a Web site, but not as detailed or as rigid as specifications. Guidelines do not have to be as comprehensive, and they can leave more details to your discretion. Compare *specification document*. For more information, see Chapter 5 (Processes for Developing Customer-Centered Sites).

H

Handheld Device Markup Language • See *HDML*.

HCI • Human–computer interaction, a discipline concerned with the design, evaluation, and implementation of interactive computing systems for human use and with the study of major phenomena surrounding them. HCI includes a multitude of other disciplines, such as user interface design, the study of group work, human factors, human physiology, cognitive modeling, and universal accessibility.

HDML • Handheld Device Markup Language. Similar to HTML, HDML is a way to format information for small devices, such as mobile phones. WML is considered the successor to HDML. For more information, see SITE ACCESSIBILITY (B9).

headline • A sentence fragment, roughly ten words or less so that it can appear in large type in a small space, that articulates a Web page's hook in the shortest form possible. Compare *blurb*. For more information, see HEADLINES AND BLURBS (D3).

heuristic evaluation • An informal method for assessing the usability of a Web site, in which three to five expert judges evaluate a site independently, using a list of usability heuristics, or principles. For more information, see Chapter 4 (Involving Customers with Iterative Design).

high-fidelity prototype • A finished and highly detailed prototype, rich with typography, colors, and images. Often presented to clients, high-fidelity prototypes are usually created with computer-based tools. A mock-up is a high-fidelity representation of an individual Web page. Compare *low-fidelity prototype* and *medium-fidelity prototype*. For more information, see Chapter 4 (Involving Customers with Iterative Design).

HIP • See *CAPTCHA.*

hit • A metric that measures the number of requests to a Web server. Hits are generally ineffective as a metric because each image file downloaded also counts as a hit. However, hits can be used as a rough approximation of the popularity of a Web site or pages within a Web site. Compare *impressions.*

horizontal prototype • A prototype that shows a broad swath of what the eventual Web site will support. A horizontal prototype might show the top-level pages, but without much depth behind them. Compare *vertical prototype*. For more information, see Chapter 4 (Involving Customers with Iterative Design).

hortal • Horizontal portal, a portal that covers a broad range of interests and topics. We hope this terrifying-sounding term never becomes mainstream. This term should not be confused with the art nouveau architect Victor Horta, or the *Star Trek* species known as *horta*. Compare *vortal.*

HTML • HyperText Markup Language, the information that represents the content on a Web page, as well as how the content is displayed.

HTTP • HyperText Transfer Protocol, the means by which HTML Web pages are transferred from a Web server to a Web browser. For more information, see PERSISTENT CUSTOMER SESSIONS (H5).

HTTPS • An encrypted and secure form of HTTP, typically used for financial transactions on the Web. HTTPS is implemented as *HTTP* on top of *SSL*. For more information, see SECURE CONNECTIONS (E6).

human–computer interaction • See *HCI.*

human interactive proof (HIP) • See *CAPTCHA.*

hypertext • Units of information connected and associated with other units. An instance of such an association is called a *link* or *hypertext link.* The most pervasive form of hypertext is the Web, though it is by no means the only form.

HyperText Markup Language • See *HTML.*

HyperText Transfer Protocol • See *HTTP.*

I

I18N • Abbreviation for *internationalization.* The *18* comes from the fact that there are 18 letters between the initial *i* and the final *n* in the word *internationalization.* Compare *L10N*. For more information, see INTERNATIONALIZED AND LOCALIZED CONTENT (D10).

identification • Something that states who someone is. One form of identification is a user name. Compare *authentication*. For more information, see PERSISTENT CUSTOMER SESSIONS (H5).

IE • Internet Explorer, Microsoft's standard Web browser. Typically followed by a version number, such as IE4 or IE5.5.

IIS • Internet Information Server, Microsoft's standard Web server. See also *Apache*.

image map • An image on a Web page whose individual parts can be clicked on to take visitors to other Web pages. Image maps can be either on the client side (where the Web *browser* processes the mouse click) or on the server side (where the Web *server* processes the mouse click). Client-side image maps are usually faster to process and provide better accessibility than server-side maps.

Implementation phase • The fifth phase of Web development, following Production, in which a software development team creates the HTML, images, database tables, and software necessary for a polished and fully functional Web site that can be rolled out and used by its target customers. For more information, see Chapter 5 (Processes for Developing Customer-Centered Sites). See also *Discovery phase, Exploration phase, Refinement phase, Production phase, Launch phase,* and *Maintenance phase.*

5

impressions • The number of times people see a specific advertisement. Compare *hit.*

index • 1. See *directory.* 2. The data gathered during a search engine Web crawl.

informal evaluation • A quick method for evaluating the effectiveness of a Web site. Typically, five to ten people representative of target customers help critique a prototype by trying to carry out some tasks from the task analysis.

information architecture • The way information is organized and presented on a Web site. From a usability standpoint, information architecture involves understanding how customers name things, how they categorize and group objects, how they navigate through information, and how they search for information. From an implementation standpoint, information architecture involves creating a structure that scales, or one that can grow as you add more content. Sometimes called *information design.* For more information, see Chapter 4 (Involving Customers with Iterative Design) and Pattern Group B (Creating a Navigation Framework).

4
B

information design • See *information architecture.*

information scent • The perceived proximity to desired information, delivered by cues such as text, link names, images, headings, grouping, page layout, and previous pages seen. For more information, see BROWSABLE CONTENT (B2), HOMEPAGE PORTAL (C1), and DESCRIPTIVE, LONGER LINK NAMES (K9).

interactive prototype • A computer-based prototype that is generated to give clients and customers a general understanding of what the completed product should feel like and what it will be capable of doing. See also *wire frame.* For more information, see Chapter 5 (Processes for Developing Customer-Centered Sites).

5

intercept research • A method of recruiting participants to a research study by popping up a short questionnaire on a Web site to a random sample of visitors or to visitors who perform a targeted action on the site (for example, they reach a particular page or leave the site). Intercept research is often used for qualifying research participants for more in-depth research. For more information, see Appendix E (Online Research).

interlaced image • An image that, when loading, appears blurry at first and then is progressively refined, allowing customers to see the image before it fully loads. Compare *progressive-scan image*. For more information, see FAST-LOADING IMAGES (L2).

internationalization • The process of making software support different languages, dates and times, currencies, weights and measures, and number formats. Sometimes abbreviated *I18N*. Compare *localization*. For more information, see INTERNATIONALIZED AND LOCALIZED CONTENT (D10).

Internet Explorer • See *IE*.

Internet Information Server • See *IIS*.

Internet Protocol (IP) • See *TCP/IP*.

Internet service provider (ISP) • A company that sells Internet connections to customers. Some ISPs provide cable modem, DSL, and modem access. Also called *access provider*.

interstitial • A page inserted in the normal flow of a task, typically for advertising purposes.

intranet • A Web site designed to be used internally within a company. Compare *extranet*. For more information, see ENABLING INTRANETS (A11).

inverted-pyramid writing • A common journalistic style in which the most important idea is stated first and the text continues to the least important idea. For more information, see INVERTED-PYRAMID WRITING STYLE (D7).

IP • Internet protocol. See *TCP/IP*.

ISP • See *Internet service provider*.

iterative design • A cyclical design process consisting of three stages: design, prototype, and evaluate. Iterative design is a simple and proven technique for developing useful and usable Web sites. For more information, see Chapter 4 (Involving Customers with Iterative Design).

J

JAR file • A standard way of packaging a collection of Java files into a single file, for faster download. *JAR* stands for *Java archive*.

Java • A general-purpose programming language designed by Sun Microsystems, specifically for network applications. For more information, go to javasoft.com.

Java archive • See *JAR file*.

JavaScript • A scripting language designed specifically for Web pages that can, among other things, control the look of the page through the *Document Object Model*.

JavaServer Pages • See *JSP*.

Joint Photographic Experts Group • See *JPEG*.

JPEG • (pronounced "jay-peg") Joint Photographic Experts Group, a widely supported file format for saving images with many colors, usually photographs. Sometimes seen as *JPG*. See also *GIF, PNG,* and *SVG*. For more information, see FAST-LOADING IMAGES (L2).

JSP • JavaServer Pages, a technology created by Sun Microsystems that combines HTML and Java code. The code is executed when a site visitor makes a request, enabling the creation of dynamically generated HTML. JSP uses Java servlet technology. Compare *ASP* (definition 1), a competing technology from Microsoft; and *PHP*, a similar Perl-based technology.

jump menu • A navigation menu that expands when it's needed and collapses when it's not. For more information, see JUMP MENUS (K16). **(K16)**

K

kbps • Kilobits per second.

keyword • A significant, illustrative word that describes something about the content or services offered by a Web site.

L

L10N • Abbreviation for *localization*. The *10* comes from the fact that there are ten letters between the initial *l* and the final *n* in the word *localization*. Compare *I18N*. For more information, see INTERNATIONALIZED AND LOCALIZED CONTENT (D10). **(D10)**

language • A common vocabulary that allows people to coordinate action.

latency • The amount of time it takes to transfer data from one point to another. Latency should not be confused with *bandwidth*. Here's how they relate to one another: The number of lanes in a highway can be considered the bandwidth, and the amount of time it takes to get from one city to another is the latency. In some cases, increasing the number of lanes will decrease the latency, but clearly, this will work only up to a certain point.

Launch phase • The sixth phase of Web development, following Implementation, in which the finished Web site is made available to its intended customers. For more information, see Chapter 5 (Processes for Developing Customer-Centered Sites). See also *Discovery phase, Exploration phase, Refinement phase, Production phase, Implementation phase,* and *Maintenance phase.* **(5)**

lead • The first few paragraphs of a story or longer text. The lead reinforces the headline and entices the visitor to read more. For more information, see INVERTED-PYRAMID WRITING STYLE (D7). **(D7)**

link-based floating window • A floating window that appears when customers click on a link. Compare *automatic floating window*. For more information, see FLOATING WINDOWS (H6). **(H6)**

link rot • The problem of a link on your Web site becoming invalid because your site is out of date or the operator of an external site has changed the content of the page or decommissioned the page address without your knowledge. For more information, see EXTERNAL LINKS (K8). **(K8)**

localization • The process of redesigning a Web interface and translating content to support a local culture. Sometimes abbreviated *L10N*. Compare *internationalization*. For more information, see INTERNATIONALIZED AND LOCALIZED CONTENT (D10). **(D10)**

lossless compression • Reduction in the size of an image file without any loss in image quality. Compare *lossy compression*. For more information, see FAST-LOADING IMAGES (L2). **(L2)**

lossy compression • Reduction in the size of an image file that results in some loss of image quality. Compare *lossless compression.* For more information, see FAST-LOADING IMAGES (L2).

low-fidelity prototype • A quick and informal prototype of a Web site design, often created by sketching on paper, using common art supplies. A low-fidelity prototype contains few details, focusing instead on high-level ideas. It is typically done in the early stages of design. Compare *medium-fidelity prototype* and *high-fidelity prototype.* For more information, see Chapter 4 (Involving Customers with Iterative Design).

M

Macromedia Flash • See *Flash.*

maintenance document • A document that details how to maintain a completed Web site. For more information, see Chapter 5 (Processes for Developing Customer-Centered Sites).

Maintenance phase • The final phase of Web development, following Launch, in which the development team supports the existing site by fixing bugs and making minor improvements, gathers and analyzes metrics for success, and prepares for the next redesign. For more information, see Chapter 5 (Processes for Developing Customer-Centered Sites). See also *Discovery phase, Exploration phase, Refinement phase, Production phase, Implementation phase,* and *Launch phase.*

mbps • Megabits per second.

m-commerce • Mobile e-commerce, such as purchasing items through a mobile phone or PDA.

medium-fidelity prototype • A cleaned-up prototype that gives a feel for the final product without showing too many details, such as typeface, color, and images. Medium-fidelity prototypes are typically done in the early stages of design. Unlike low-fidelity prototypes, they are usually presented to clients. Compare *low-fidelity prototype* and *high-fidelity prototype.* For more information, see Chapter 4 (Involving Customers with Iterative Design).

mental model • The way a person believes a system works. People who have used computers extensively, for example, know that most computers consist of a central processing unit (CPU), a monitor, a hard drive, and a keyboard. An engineer will have a more detailed mental model; a novice may have a much simpler (and possibly incorrect) mental model. Usability problems often occur when a customer's mental model does not match the actual workings of a system. The mental model helps set expectations, making the system predictable and understandable.

meta-information • Additional information about content, but not part of the content. Examples of meta-information include the author, the creation time, the last modification time, and the type of information, such as document, image, or audio file. Meta-information is sometimes encoded within <meta> tags.

<meta> tag • A marker in a file that indicates to software applications, including search engine crawlers, what a site or page contains. <Meta> tags are used on all Web pages to provide additional keywords not included in the text, including synonyms, phrases, and language translations. A <meta> tag is often stored with but is separate from the content it represents. Here's a sample <meta> tag representing the keywords on a Web page:

```
<meta name="keywords" content="chocolate,candy,treats,truffles">
```

For more information, see WRITING FOR SEARCH ENGINES (D6).

metrics for success • Measurements to determine whether the design team has reached its goals and requirements. For more information, see Chapter 5 (Processes for Developing Customer-Centered Sites).

mock-up • A high-fidelity representation of a Web page that shows exactly how the page will appear. Usually produced with a graphics application such as Adobe Photoshop, mock-ups are not interactive. Mock-ups contain images, icons, typography, and sophisticated color schemes. Unlike schematics, mock-ups have graphic design that is meant to be taken literally. In some cases, mock-ups are the final deliverable of a design project, perhaps accompanied by written guidelines or specifications.

moderated forum • A forum in which messages are filtered and processed by one or more moderators that must approve all messages to make sure that they follow the established rules and norms. Compare *unmoderated forum*. For more information, see COMMUNITY CONFERENCE (A3).

Mozilla • See *Netscape*.

N

navigation design • The design of methods to help customers find their way around the information structure of a Web site. Navigation design is one part of information architecture. Compare *graphic design*.

Navigator • See *Netscape*.

NDA • See *nondisclosure agreement*.

Netscape • One of the original Web browser companies, now owned by America Online. The term *Netscape* is typically used to refer to the Mozilla or Navigator browser.

network effect • An increase in benefit as more individuals use a particular service. For more information, see NONPROFITS AS NETWORKS OF HELP (A5).

newsletter • A periodic e-mail message sent from a Web site to self-selected customers, informing them of special news, offers, deals, and so on. Compare *alert* and *focused advertisement*. For more information, see E-MAIL SUBSCRIPTIONS (E2).

nondisclosure agreement (NDA) • A legal document specifying that the signer agrees not to discuss any aspect of your product or services with others.

O

open-source software • Software that is distributed with the source code (the files used to construct the software in the first place), with few limitations on what others can do with the source code.

P

p2p • 1. Path to profitability, a business term referring to the strategy needed for companies to become profitable and self-sustaining. 2. See *peer-to-peer architecture*.

page template • See *template.*

participant • A friendly term for someone who helps test an interface design. Meant to replace the not-so-friendly term *subject,* which more and more research disciplines are discarding.

pattern • A design rule that communicates insight into a design problem, capturing the essence of the problem and its solution in a compact form. Design patterns form a language, or common vocabulary, that allows articulation of an infinite variety of Web designs. Patterns are a powerful conceptual framework for building compelling and effective Web sites that are easy to use.

PDA • Personal digital assistant, a small computing appliance for storing personal information. More and more PDAs include wireless connections, making Web access through these small devices possible. For more information, see SITE ACCESSIBILITY (B9) and MOBILE SCREEN SIZING (M1).

PDF • Portable Document Format, a common file format for documents. Compare *PostScript.*

peer-to-peer architecture • Sometimes abbreviated *p2p,* peer-to-peer architecture is a communications model in which all customers are at the same level and have the same access to content and capabilities. A common example of peer-to-peer architecture is Skype, a free telephone application using Voice over Internet Protocol (VoIP). Many people believe peer-to-peer architecture will become more important in the years to come. Compare *client–server architecture.*

periodic backups • Backups of the entire Web site that are stored far away from the building that contains the Web server.

Perl • A programming language often used as part of the Common Gateway Interface.

persistent cookie • A cookie that is stored on the customer's hard drive, allowing a Web site to track that customer over a relatively long period of time. Compare *session cookie.* For more information, see PERSISTENT CUSTOMER SESSIONS (H5).

persistent customer session • A Web session that lets the Web server remember a customer for a relatively long period of time. Compare *temporary customer session.* For more information, see PERSISTENT CUSTOMER SESSIONS (H5).

persona • A detailed profile of a potential customer, including name, home address, background, and hobbies. The goal in creating personas is to make each customer seem as real as possible. Compare *profile.* For more information, see Chapter 3 (Knowing Your Customers: Principles and Techniques).

personal digital assistant • See *PDA.*

personalization • A service-driven process that tailors Web pages to individuals or groups of individuals. Two examples of personalization are having a customer's name on a Web page, and remembering a previously entered mailing address. Personalization makes use of information gathered both explicitly (through customization) and implicitly (such as through server log files and previous purchases). Personalization is typically done on the Web server through dynamically generated HTML. Compare *customization.* For more information, see PERSONALIZED CONTENT (D4).

phishing • A form of fraud in which scammers try to trick people into giving up sensitive information, such as account names, passwords, and credit card numbers. Phishing is typically implemented by scammers sending fake e-mails purportedly from legitimate entities such as banks, directing victims to a Web site that looks like the legitimate Web site but is actually a copy that simply stores victims' information. Compare *spam*. For more information, see PREVENTING PHISHING SCAMS (E9). **E9**

PHP • PHP: Hypertext Preprocessor (yes, the name is part of the acronym), a technology that mixes HTML and Perl code. The code is executed when a site visitor makes a request, enabling the creation of dynamically generated HTML. Compare *ASP* (definition 1), a competing technology from Microsoft; and *JSP*, a similar Java-based technology.

pilot test • A quick trial of a proposed evaluation method, such as a survey or a usability test, performed by coworkers and friends, to help solve problems in wording or procedure. For more information, see Appendix A (Running Usability Evaluations).

PKI • See *public key infrastructure*.

plug-in • An application that can be embedded into a Web browser. Examples of popular plug-ins include Adobe Acrobat Reader (for PDF files) and Shockwave Flash.

PNG • (pronounced "ping") Portable Network Graphics, a format for storing images designed specifically for transport across networks. PNG was once not widely supported by Web browsers. See also *GIF, JPEG,* and *SVG*. For more information, see FAST-LOADING IMAGES (L2). **L2**

pop-under • A pop-up window that is positioned under the customer's browser window so that the customer will not see it until the browser is closed.

pop-up window • A small window that appears in a Web browser, often containing advertising messages or definitions of a term. Pop-ups are created with JavaScript. For more information, see FLOATING WINDOWS (H6). **H6**

Portable Document Format • See *PDF*.

Portable Network Graphics • See *PNG*.

portal • A major Web site designed for a specific audience that uses it to enter the Web, such as America Online (AOL). Portals contain a broad range of content and often make extensive use of customization and personalization. See also *hortal* and *vortal*.

PostScript • A relatively old but common file format for documents that is understood by many printers, typically with the file extension *ps*, as in *printout.ps*. Compare *PDF*.

principle • A high-level concept that guides the entire design process and helps maintain focus.

process • A well-defined series of steps for accomplishing something. For the purposes of this book, a process is how principles are put into practice.

process data • Qualitative data collected in evaluations, giving an overall gestalt of what works and what doesn't. Compare *bottom-line data*. For more information,

[4] see Chapter 4 (Involving Customers with Iterative Design) and Appendix A (Running Usability Evaluations).

Production phase • The fourth phase of Web development, following Refinement, in which a fully interactive prototype and/or a design specification are created. Some design firms use the term *production* to mean the actual creation of the Web **[5]** site—what we have termed *implementation*. For more information, see Chapter 5 (Processes for Developing Customer-Centered Sites). See also *Discovery phase, Exploration phase, Refinement phase, Implementation phase, Launch phase,* and *Maintenance phase.*

professional respondent • A focus group member who makes money on the side by participating in group after group.

profile • 1. On a Web site, details about a customer, including information explicitly provided by that customer (such as an e-mail address) and information implicitly collected (such as which Web pages the person has seen). Profiles are used for personalization. 2. In the Discovery phase of Web development, a detailed narrative describing an individual. Some profiles are short; others can be long and descriptive. Some profiles are made up in the imagination of the design team; others are based on actual people. Here's an example: "Gail is a 16-year-old teenager interested in reading and talking about insects. She wants to learn more about how to collect insects and how to take care of them. She started using a computer only recently and is new to the Web, but she is a quick learner and eager to learn more." Compare *persona.*

progressive-scan image • An image that loads from top to bottom. Compare *interlaced* **[L2]** *image.* For more information, see FAST-LOADING IMAGES (L2).

protocol • A formal and precise definition of what kind of information is transferred and how it is transferred between two or more parties. HTTP is an example of a protocol.

prototype • A first cut at a functional model of a user interface such as a Web site. Prototypes include site maps, storyboards, schematics, mock-ups, and HTML prototypes. We use the term *interactive prototype* to refer to a prototype that clients can use on a computer. See also *low-fidelity prototype, medium-fidelity prototype,* and *high-fidelity prototype.*

proxy • An intermediate computer between the Web server and the end customer's Web browser. Typical uses of proxies are to cache Web pages for multiple customers and to act as a firewall.

ps • See *PostScript.*

pseudonym • The false name that a person who wants to hide his or her true identity assumes within a given community. For more information, see COMMUNITY CONFERENCE (A3).

psychographics • The beliefs and personality traits of customers. Compare *demographics.*

public key infrastructure (PKI) • A technology for encryption on the Internet.

Python • A programming language sometimes used as part of the Common Gateway Interface.

Q

quality assurance • The process of testing all code, graphics, and HTML code thoroughly so that the Web site works as intended and downloads quickly.

question bias • Skewing of a research result because the wording of questions leads people to answer in a certain way. For more information, see Appendix E (Online Research).

R

Really Simple Syndication • See *RSS*.

red–green deficiency • A form of color vision deficiency characterized by the inability to distinguish between red and green. Red–green deficiency affects mostly males. For more information, see Chapter 3 (Knowing Your Customers: Principles and Techniques) and SITE ACCESSIBILITY (B9).

Refinement phase • The third phase of Web site development, following Exploration, in which the design team polishes the navigation, layout, and flow of the selected design. For more information, see Chapter 5 (Processes for Developing Customer-Centered Sites). See also *Discovery phase, Exploration phase, Production phase, Implementation phase, Launch phase,* and *Maintenance phase.*

reliable data • Results that would be found consistently if you ran a survey or a usability test over and over with the same type of audience under the same conditions.

remote usability research/testing • Online recruitment and usability testing of a Web site, often with many participants. For more information, see Appendix A (Running Usability Evaluations) and Appendix E (Online Research).

response time • The time it takes a customer to initiate an action when given a stimulus. Response times on the order of 100 milliseconds are needed for things like dragging icons and typing text. Response times on the order of 1 second (1,000 milliseconds) are required to maintain an uninterrupted flow of thought when completing a routine action, such as clicking on a button.

RIA • See *Rich Internet Application.*

Rich Internet Application (RIA) • A Web application that provides a high level of interactivity and functionality similar to a traditional desktop application. AJAX is one set of technologies that enables such applications.

rollout • The official deployment of a completed Web site. See also *Launch phase.*

rollover • A graphical icon that changes when the mouse moves over it. Currently, rollovers require visitors to have JavaScript activated in their Web browsers. Compare *tool tip.*

RSS (Really Simple Syndication) • A way of syndicating the content of one Web site on other sites. RSS makes it easy for other Web sites to take summaries of your content and show them on their Web sites, helping to make your content available and increasing traffic to your Web site. RSS also makes it easy for people to track updates and see what new content you have on your Web site. For more information, see BLOGS (A12).

S

sample bias • Skewing of a research result because the composition of participants does not accurately reflect the demographics or psychographics of the target customers. For more information, see Appendix E (Online Research).

Scalable Vector Graphics • See *SVG*.

scale • A measure of how well something works if it increases in size, such as how well an information architecture performs when lots more information is added to a Web site compared to what it was originally designed for, or whether a Web server works as well for 10,000 customers as it does for many fewer customers.

scenario • A story rich in context that focuses more on what people will do than on how they will do it. Also called *use case*. For more information, see Chapters 3 (Knowing Your Customers: Principles and Techniques) and 4 (Involving Customers with Iterative Design).

schematic • A representation of the content that will appear on an individual Web page. Schematics are usually devoid of images, though they may indicate with a label where an image should be placed. Unlike mock-ups, schematics typically do not make heavy use of color, typography, and graphics. Compare *site map* and *storyboard*. For more information, see Chapters 4 (Involving Customers with Iterative Design) and 5 (Processes for Developing Customer-Centered Sites).

screen reader • A special hardware device or software program, designed to assist people with impaired vision, that takes all the text on a page and uses computer-based speech synthesis to read it out. For more information, see SITE ACCESSIBILITY (B9).

scroll wheel • A small dial on a mobile device that lets people move the virtual window up or down in the physical window. Also called *track wheel*.

search engine optimization (SEO) • Strategies and techniques for ensuring that a site is listed close to the top of search results for particular terms that are important to drive customer traffic to a site.

searching • One of two major strategies that visitors use to find information on a Web site. Searching makes use of local or Internet-wide search engines. Compare *browsing*. For more information, see Pattern Group J (Making Site Search Fast and Relevant).

Secure Electronic Transaction • See *SET*.

Secure Sockets Layer • See *SSL*.

SEO • See *search engine optimization*.

server • A centralized repository of information or other resources, usually a Web server. Clients send requests to servers, and servers send results back to clients. Compare *client* (definition 1). See also *client–server architecture*.

servlet • A small Java-based application that runs on a server, commonly used in JSP pages. Servlets are similar in concept to the Common Gateway Interface.

session cookie • A cookie that temporarily stores the identity of a person. When a customer closes his or her Web browser, the session cookie is deleted, making it impossible to track people over long periods of time. Compare *persistent cookie* and *session ID*. For more information, see PERSISTENT CUSTOMER SESSIONS (H5).

session ID • A string that temporarily stores the identity of a customer in a Web address. Compare *session cookie.* For more information, see PERSISTENT CUSTOMER SESSIONS (H5). **(H5)**

SET • Secure Electronic Transaction, a relatively new technology supporting secure financial transactions on the Internet.

shopping cart/bag • A common mechanism, often symbolized by an icon that pictures a shopping cart, for helping customers on the Web keep track of what they want before they finalize a purchase. For more information, see SHOPPING CART (F3). **(F3)**

shrinking • An approach to reducing the file size of an image in which the entire image is resized. Compare *compressing* and *cropping.* For more information, see FAST-LOADING IMAGES (L2). **(L2)**

Simple Object Access Protocol • See *SOAP.*

site map • A high-level diagram showing the overall structure of a site. A site map is used primarily to reflect the information structure of the site, as it is being built, and to a limited extent it shows the navigation structure. Compare *storyboard* and *schematic.* For more information, see Chapters 4 (Involving Customers with Iterative Design) and 5 (Processes for Developing Customer-Centered Sites), and SITE MAP (K17). **(4) (5) (K17)**

SOAP • Simple Object Access Protocol, a way of making requests and returning responses to a Web service, typically using XML. SOAP lets organizations create distributed applications over the Web. See also *WSDL.*

solution diagram • Part of a Web design pattern; a drawing that captures the essence of the pattern in graphical form.

spam • Unwanted and often unsolicited e-mail, often related to advertising. The term comes from a Monty Python skit. Compare *phishing.*

specification document • A detailed document, also called a *spec,* that attempts to describe the intent of a design exhaustively and precisely. The specification document contains a set of exact instructions about how to build a site, usually accompanied by an interactive prototype. Directed toward developers who will implement the site, the specification document gives instructions for how to extrapolate from the prototype to the finished site. Compare *guidelines.* For more information, see Chapter 5 (Processes for Developing Customer-Centered Sites). **(5)**

spider • See *crawler.*

splash screen • An opening screen, often heavy with multimedia, shown before the homepage. Splash screens are often implemented with Flash and are frequently of little value.

SSL • Secure Sockets Layer, a form of encryption designed specifically for Web browsers, with the goal of maintaining the security and integrity of information transferred on the Web. SSL is typically used for e-commerce transactions, such as sending credit card information to a Web site. You can tell that you're using SSL if the URL begins with *https://* instead of just *http://.* For more information, see SECURE CONNECTIONS (E6). **(E6)**

statistical validity • A standard for evaluating a study in which it is determined that the study actually measures what it claims to, and that no logical errors have been made in the conclusions drawn from the data. Having enough research participants in a usability study and getting a high enough response rate in a survey are important to achieving validity.

stickiness • The measure of a Web site's ability to retain visitors and drive repeat visits.

storyboard • A sequence of sketches depicting how a customer would accomplish a given task. Typically depicting low-fidelity representations of Web pages, a storyboard is often accompanied by a narrative describing customer tasks. Storyboards are typically not presented to anyone outside the design team, but are used to construct the walk-throughs presented to clients. A walk-through can be thought of as a medium-fidelity or high-fidelity storyboard. Compare *site map* and *schematic*. See also *flow* (definition 1). For more information, see Chapters 3 (Knowing Your Customers: Principles and Techniques), 4 (Involving Customers with Iterative Design), and 5 (Processes for Developing Customer-Centered Sites).

streaming • A method for data transfer, in which small portions of a file are continuously sent to a computer, instead of all at once. The advantage of streaming media is that visitors can view the file as they receive it, instead of having to wait until the entire file is downloaded. Streaming is a common technique used for video and audio files.

style guide • A list of rules for how to spell common words and phrases so that a Web site will have consistent spelling and word usage. A style guide may also specify fonts, colors, and positioning of common design elements (for example, logos). One of Addison-Wesley's styles, for example, is to spell *Web site* as two words, with a capital *W.* The term appears that way throughout this book.

subsite • A major portion of a Web site in which the individual pages are strongly related in content and navigation.

SVG • Scalable Vector Graphics, an XML-based graphics format supporting the creation of dynamic images. Site visitors can pan and zoom in on SVG images, for example. SVG holds promise for products beyond the desktop computer, such as handheld devices, interactive television, large wall-sized displays, and even printing, because of the way the graphics data is stored. See also *GIF, JPEG,* and *PNG.*

synchronous communication • A communications setup in which all parties have to be online simultaneously and interaction takes place in real time. Compare *asynchronous communication.* For more information, see COMMUNITY CONFERENCE (A3).

T

T-1 • A piece of hardware needed for a network connection. The term is commonly used to refer to a type of Internet connection provided by telephone companies. T-1 lines transfer data at 1.5 megabits per second and are typically leased by ISPs and businesses.

tag cloud • A visual depiction of content tags used on a Web site. Often, more frequently used tags are depicted in a larger font or otherwise emphasized, while the displayed order is generally alphabetical.

target customer • See *customer*.

task • A specific goal that a customer wants to accomplish when using a Web site, such as sending an online birthday card to a grandparent, or finding and purchasing the best digital camera for less than $500.

task analysis • The process of identifying common tasks that customers will perform on a Web site.

task and customer analysis • An analysis performed by the design team to articulate who the customers are, what they will do on the Web site, the things they act on, and the things they need to know. For more information, see Chapter 3 **3** (Knowing Your Customers: Principles and Techniques).

TCP/IP • Transmission Control Protocol/Internet Protocol, the core set of protocols that control how data is transferred over the Internet. HTTP, used for transferring Web pages, is built on top of TCP/IP.

technology-centered design • A design strategy that results in a Web site over-loaded with animations, audio, and streaming video banners, built with little up-front research about business and customer needs. Compare *company-centered design*, *customer-centered design*, and *designer-centered design*. For more information, see Chapter 1 (Customer-Centered Web Design: More Than a Good Idea). **1**

template • A sample HTML file that contains the basic structure, layout, and scripts for a set of Web pages of a Web site. Templates typically contain the navigation elements global to the Web site, as well as sections that can be edited for specific local navigation and specific content. Templates are used to ensure consistency throughout a site. For more information, see PAGE TEMPLATES (D1), CONTENT MODULES (D2), and Chapter 5 (Processes for Developing Customer-Centered Sites).

temporary customer session • A Web session that lets the Web server remember a customer for only a short period of time, usually until the customer closes the Web browser. Compare *persistent customer session*. For more information, see PERSISTENT CUSTOMER SESSIONS (H5). **H5**

think-aloud protocol • An experimental setup in which participants say out loud what they're thinking as they use a test Web site, in order to give site designers an idea of how customers will use the site. Also called *verbal protocol*. For more information, see Chapter 4 (Involving Customers with Iterative Design). **4**

thumbnail • A small version of an image that is linked to a larger version. Clicking on a thumbnail brings up the larger image on-screen. For more information, see LOW NUMBER OF FILES (L1) and FAST-LOADING IMAGES (L2). **L1 L2**

tool tip • A piece of text that appears when the mouse cursor hovers over a button or an image. Compare *rollover*.

track wheel • See *scroll wheel*.

trail marker • See *bread crumb*.

Transmission Control Protocol/Internet Protocol • See *TCP/IP*.

tutorial • An online, instruction-based class used for training.

two-factor authentication • A security alternative to simple passwords in which a person must sign in using a physical object (such as a smart card or a special

key-chain fob, like a small USB device) in addition to entering a password. For
more information, see PREVENTING PHISHING SCAMS (E9).

U

UI • See *user interface.*

undersampling bias • Skewing of a research result because there are not enough participants to have a statistically valid sample. For more information, see Appendix E
(Online Research).

Uniform Resource Locator • See *URL.*

unmoderated forum • A free-for-all discussion in which anything goes. People can
say whatever they want, and it is up to the members of the community to enforce
any rules and social norms. Compare *moderated forum.* For more information, see
COMMUNITY CONFERENCE (A3).

up-selling • Promoting products that have more features and benefits (and cost
more) than those that a customer wants to purchase. Compare *cross-selling.* For
more information, see SHOPPING CART (F3) and CROSS-SELLING AND UP-SELLING (G2).

URL • Uniform Resource Locator, the official Web word for *address.* Any address
beginning with *http://* is a URL.

use case • See *scenario.*

user-centered design • An effort pioneered in the 1980s for engineering useful and
usable computer systems. We have broadened and expanded this concept for Web
design into *customer-centered design.* For more information, see Chapter 1 (Customer-
Centered Web Design: More Than a Good Idea).

user-created content • Content that site customers share with other customers.

user experience • See *customer experience.*

user interface (UI) • The part of a system with which a customer interacts. See
also *GUI.*

V

value proposition • A brief statement of what a Web site offers to target customers.
For more information, see UP-FRONT VALUE PROPOSITION (C2).

value ranking • The method that a search engine uses to order the different results
it returns for a particular search. For more information, see GRASSROOTS INFORMATION
SITE (A6).

verbal protocol • See *think-aloud protocol.*

vertical prototype • A prototype that implements only a few key Web pages along
with the path for completing a particular task. Creation of a vertical prototype is
appropriate when a complex feature is poorly understood or needs to be explored
further. Compare *horizontal prototype.* For more information, see Chapter 4 (Involving
Customers with Iterative Design).

Virtual Private Network • See *VPN.*

virtual testing • Evaluation of a Web site in which a few select customers see a
proposed updated site, and they can be observed to see what they do compared to
what they do on the regular Web site.

visual design • See *graphic design*.

vortal • Vertical portal, a portal that specializes in a specific topic, such as law or medicine. Compare *hortal*.

VPN • Virtual Private Network, a way of establishing a private communications network on top of a public network. VPNs are typically used within a company to secure e-mail and other services.

W

W3C • World Wide Web Consortium, the group that coordinates protocols and standards used on the Web, including HTTP, HTML, and XML. For more information, go to w3.org.

walk-through • A sequential presentation of Web pages narrated by the designer, who explains what customers will do on each page. Designers can also use a storyboard for a (low-fidelity) walk-through.

WAP • Wireless Application Protocol, used primarily by small devices, such as mobile phones, to access e-mail and the Web. See also *WML*. For more information, see MOBILE SCREEN SIZING (M1). **(M1)**

Web browser • The software used to navigate Web sites from a computer. The two most popular Web browsers are Internet Explorer and Firefox, also called Mozilla. Other browsers include America Online's Web browser, Opera, and the text-based browser Lynx. A Web browser is an example of a client in a client–server architecture.

Web interface guidelines • A checklist to ensure that a final product has no obvious problems. Often these guidelines address only how a Web site is implemented.

Web log • See *blog*.

Web server • A server, such as Apache or IIS, that delivers Web pages upon request.

Web Services Description Language • See *WSDL*.

white space • The area on a page that is intentionally left blank to create a feeling of spaciousness and a more readable design. Most bad designs would benefit from more white space.

widget • An interactive object such as a button or slider.

wire frame • A simple but functional interactive prototype of a Web site. Typically a wire frame contains text, layout, links, and overall structure, but few if any graphics.

Wireless Application Protocol • See *WAP*.

Wireless Markup Language • See *WML*.

within-groups experiment • An experiment in which there is one group of test participants, each assigned to the same condition. For example, when testing two Web sites, each participant uses both sites. Compare *between-groups experiment*. For more information, see Appendix A (Running Usability Evaluations).

WML • Wireless Markup Language. A markup language similar to HTML, WML is designed specifically for small devices, such as mobile phones. See also *WAP* and *HDML*. For more information, see MOBILE SCREEN SIZING (M1). **(M1)**

World Wide Web Consortium • See *W3C*.

WSDL • Web Services Description Language, a way of precisely specifying what services a Web service offers. WSDL can also be thought of as an API for a Web service. Each service offered can be accessed through a *SOAP* request.

X

XML • Extensible Markup Language, a standard created by W3C for specifying information formats. Although it is similar to HTML, XML can be extended for use in any domain.

XHTML • Extensible Hypertext Markup Language, a markup language that has the same expressive possibilities as HTML, but a stricter syntax.

Part I: Foundations of Web Site Design

Chapter 1: Customer-Centered Web Design: More Than a Good Idea

Books, Research Papers, and News Articles

Beyer, H., and K. Holtzblatt. (1998) *Contextual Design: Defining Customer-Centered Systems*. San Francisco: Kaufmann.

> Beyer and Holtzblatt have written a fantastic book on their process for customer-centered design. As this philosophical and practical guide explains, their process is centered on gaining a deep understanding of customer needs by interviewing people about the way they work, how their organization works, and other constraints. The ideas they present can be used most effectively in the Discovery phase of the Web site development process, when you're trying to understand who your target audience is and what they want.

Bias, R., and D. Mayhew. (1994) *Cost-Justifying Usability*. San Diego, CA: Academic Press.

> This book is a collection of essays that describe various methods and techniques for quantitatively showing how usability affects the bottom line.

Dembeck, C. (2000, January 11) Report: B2B Web sites fail usage test. *E-Commerce Times* (www.ecommercetimes.com/perl/story/2183.html).

> In this news article on a Forrester Report, "Why Web Sites Fail," one of the results described is that when customers have a bad experience on a Web site, they tell an average of ten other people.

Moore, G. (1999) *Crossing the Chasm: Marketing and Selling High-Tech Products to Mainstream Customers* (rev. ed.). New York: HarperBusiness.

> The author describes how high-tech products sell well initially, mainly to a technically literate customer base, but then hit a lull as marketing professionals try to cross the chasm to mainstream buyers. *Crossing the Chasm* was a milestone in high-tech marketing when it was first released in 1991.

---

1 All online resources were accessed in August 2006.

NetRaker Corporation. (2000, September 7) *NetRaker's eShopping Study Reveals the Web Site Drivers of Success with Visitors* [press release] (www.netraker.com/nrinfo/company/20000907.asp).

This study looked at the factors driving repeat visits and purchases at online shopping sites. It found that although a few Web sites offer a great customer experience, there is still plenty of room for improvement. In a comparison study between Yahoo! Shopping, Amazon.com, and AOL Shopping, none of these firms scored over an 8.02 on a scale of 0 to 10 when rated by consumers. The lowest score was below 6.5. By comparison, when leaders in offline industries are evaluated on the key components that drive repeat visits and satisfaction, we see scores typically in the high 8s and low 9s.

Tedeschi, B. (1999, August 30) Good Web site design can lead to healthy sales. *New York Times E-Commerce Report* (www.nytimes.com/library/tech/99/08/cyber/commerce/30commerce.html).

This article reports on IBM's efforts to redesign its Web site and on how sales increased after overall usability was improved. It emphasizes how improvements in Web site design can boost the bottom line. It looks at issues like having a unified information architecture, page templates to help enforce consistency across large Web sites, and short process funnels to help customers quickly finish tasks.

Web Sites

Boxes and Arrows (www.boxesandarrows.com).

Boxes and Arrows is a Web site devoted to "the practice, innovation, and discussion of design; including graphic design, interaction design, information architecture and even business design." The site features articles from practitioners, as well as message boards for fostering thoughtful discussion of issues.

Creative Good (http://creativegood.com) and Good Experience (www.goodexperience.com).

Creative Good is a strategy firm that helps clients focus on the customer experience. Good Experience is a Web log by Mark Hurst, the founder and president of Creative Good. He provides insights about what's right and what's wrong with the Web experience today, as well as an occasional tidbit about technology-related issues. The site is updated fairly often, but you may find it more useful to get the weekly e-mail updates instead.

useit.com: Jakob Nielsen's Website (www.useit.com).

Jakob Nielsen is one of the best-known Web personalities today, for his hard-line stance in favor of usability. Useit.com is his Web site, where he publishes Alertbox, a biweekly newsletter on Web-related usability issues.

Chapter 2: Making the Most of Web Design Patterns

Books, Research Papers, and News Articles

Adkisson, H. (2003, October 13) *Examining the Role of De Facto Standards on the Web* (www.boxesandarrows.com/view/examining_the_role_of_de_facto_standards_on_the_web).

This article describes the results of a study demonstrating that people already expect certain kinds of design patterns on Web pages—for example, clickable logos to go to the homepage and the shopping cart. (See also the Web Design Practices entry under "Web Sites" below.)

Alexander, C., S. Ishikawa, and M. Silverstein. (1977) *A Pattern Language: Towns, Buildings, Construction.* New York: Oxford University Press.

> This book originally introduced the idea of patterns in the field of architecture. Alexander has inspired many, including the authors of the book you have in hand, with his idea that patterns could be an effective way of doing design, and a way that customers could express their needs and desires.

Bernard, M. (2002) Examining user expectations for the location of common e-commerce web objects. *Usability News* 4(1) (http://psychology.wichita.edu/ surl/usabilitynews/41/web_object-ecom.htm).

> This study asked hundreds of people where they would look for a shopping cart, login button, help button, and other e-commerce related buttons. The results indicate where people most often look to find these features.

Fry, J. (2001, August 13) Web shoppers' loyalty isn't so crazy after all. *Wall Street Journal* (http://ebusiness.mit.edu/news/WSJ_Story8-13-01.html).

> This article looks at a phenomenon known as *cognitive lock-in,* in which people find things that are familiar more attractive. One result is that people tend not to shop around as much as economists expect, sticking to retailers they already know, because the time to learn a new interface might not be worth the money that might be saved at a competitor's site.

Gamma, E., R. Helm, R. Johnson, and J. Vlissides. (1995) *Design Patterns.* Reading, MA: Addison-Wesley.

> This book brought the concept of patterns to software design and programming.

Malone, E., Leacock, M., and Wheeler, C. (2005, April 29) *Implementing a Pattern Library in the Real World: A Yahoo! Case Study* (www.boxesandarrows.com/view/ implementing_a_pattern_library_in_the_real_world_a_yahoo_case_study).

> This article describes a case study of how Yahoo! developed and managed its pattern library.

Web Sites

Erickson, T. *The Interaction Design Patterns Page* (www.visi.com/~snowfall/ InteractionPatterns.html).

> This Web site contains resources on pattern languages for interaction design, including pointers to other pattern Web sites and patterns for user interface design.

Tidwell, J. (1999) *Designing Interfaces: Patterns for Effective Interaction Design* (http://designinginterfaces.com).

> This companion Web site to a book on design patterns features about 60 user interface design patterns, running the gamut from content design to navigation to attractiveness.

UW E-Business Consortium Best Practice Reports: B2C Website Design Standard Practices and Benchmarks (www.uwebc.org/opinionpapers/ue).

> This Web site presents the results of an analysis of 19 e-commerce Web sites, comparing how basic design elements such as the HOMEPAGE PORTAL (C1), SEARCH ACTION MODULE (J1), SHOPPING CART (F3), and CLEAN PRODUCT DETAILS (F2) page are done.

Web Design Practices (www.webdesignpractices.com).

This Web site presents an analysis of common Web design practices for navigation and e-commerce, describing how various Web sites use specific design elements, such as SHOPPING CARTS (F3), LOCATION BREAD CRUMBS (K6), and OBVIOUS LINKS (K10). (See also the article by Heidi Adkisson under "Books, Research Papers, and News Articles" above.)

WebPatterns (http://webpatterns.org).

In its own words, "WebPatterns is a place to discuss, document and collaborate on patterns for web design and development." The site features both a blog and a wiki for discussing new developments in user interface design patterns.

Welie, M. van. *Web Design Patterns* (www.welie.com/patterns).

This Web page lists about 70 patterns for Web design, focusing on navigation, searching, page elements, and e-commerce.

Yahoo! Developer Network. *Design Pattern Library* (http://developer.yahoo.com/ypatterns) and *Yahoo! User Interface Library* (http://developer.yahoo.com/yui).

Yahoo! provides a design pattern library, as well as some user interface widgets that will facilitate the construction of high-quality Web sites. Note that the pattern library deals primarily with low-level interaction techniques like menus and transitions, rather than higher-level patterns like the ones in this book.

Chapter 3: Knowing Your Customers: Principles and Techniques

Books, Research Papers, and News Articles

Beyer, H., and K. Holtzblatt. (1998) *Contextual Design: Defining Customer-Centered Systems.* San Francisco: Kaufmann.

See the description under Chapter 1 (Customer-Centered Web Design: More Than a Good Idea).

Cooper, A. (1999) *The Inmates Are Running the Asylum: Why High-Tech Products Drive Us Crazy and How to Restore the Sanity.* Indianapolis, IN: Sams.

This book introduces some of the problems with developing user interfaces. Told in narrative form, it also presents techniques to apply for improving the state of the art. In addition, it describes how to create *personas,* hypothetical and detailed descriptions of typical customers, and explains why personas are a useful way of thinking about design. (However, we would argue that personas should be based on interviews and observations of real people instead of being made up.)

Lewis, C., and J. Rieman. (1994) *Task-Centered User Interface Design: A Practical Introduction* (http://hcibib.org/tcuid).

This shareware book on user interface design has some great material on learning about your customers' tasks. Our Web-based banking example is based on Lewis and Rieman's telephone banking example.

Norman, D. (1988) *The Psychology of Everyday Things.* New York: Basic Books.

This book is an eye-opener, and it should be one of the first books you read to learn about design. Norman points out the importance of design and how it affects our everyday lives. You will never look at doorknobs or oven stoves in the same way again. (Also published as *The Design of Everyday Things.*)

Palen, L. (1999) Social, individual and technological issues for groupware calendar systems. CHI 1999, ACM Conference on Human Factors in Computing Systems. *CHI Letters,* 2(1): 17–24 (http://doi.acm.org/10.1145/302979.302982).

> This study examines calendar systems used by groups, finding that current practices have influenced calendaring habits and technology adoption decisions. (This resource requires access to the ACM Digital Library, at www.acm.org/dl.)

Rubinstein, R., and H. Hersh. (1984) *The Human Factor: Designing Computer Systems for People.* Bedford, MA: Digital Press.

> This early UI design text includes the list of questions we ask when performing a task analysis.

Saffo, P. (1996) The consumer spectrum. In *Bringing Design to Software,* T. Winograd, J. Bennett, L. De Young, and B. Hartfield (Eds.), pp. 87–99. Reading, MA: Addison-Wesley.

> This chapter in Winograd's influential book discusses the fact that consumers' willingness to put up with technology products is measured both by how expensive the technology is and by how much complexity they have to deal with to get the benefits of the product.

Shneiderman, B. (1997) *Designing the User Interface: Strategies for Effective Human–Computer Interaction* (3rd ed.). Reading, MA: Addison-Wesley.

> This textbook is an overview of academic research in the field of human–computer interaction, and it is a great book about the field in general. In addition, the book's Web site, at www.awl.com/DTUI, has many lecture notes and overviews, as well as extensive lists of links.

Software

National Institute of Standards and Technology (NIST). *Web Category Analysis Tool (WebCAT)* (http://zing.ncsl.nist.gov/WebTools/WebCAT/overview.html).

> The Web Category Analysis Tool (WebCAT) is a free tool that helps designers set up, run, and analyze card-sorting experiments.

Chapter 4: Involving Customers with Iterative Design

Books, Research Papers, and News Articles

Beyer, H., and K. Holtzblatt. (1998) *Contextual Design: Defining Customer-Centered Systems.* San Francisco: Kaufmann.

> See the description under Chapter 1 (Customer-Centered Web Design: More Than a Good Idea).

Kelley, T. (2001) *The Art of Innovation: Lessons in Creativity from IDEO, America's Leading Design Firm.* New York: Currency/Doubleday.

> Skim through the first few chapters, but pay attention when Kelley gets to brainstorming. He describes how the design teams at his company, IDEO, combine their observations of how customers really do things with an extremely creative brainstorming process to create innovative, award-winning products.

McConnell, S. (1996) *Rapid Development: Taming Wild Software Schedules.* Redmond, WA: Microsoft Press.

> McConnell has a chapter about user interface prototyping in his manual for managing the software development process. Although he focuses entirely on software-based prototypes, he lists many of the same advantages of prototyping that we describe in this book, including reduced risk, smaller systems, less complex systems, reduction in creeping requirements, and improved schedule visibility.

Mullet, K., and D. Sano. (1994) *Designing Visual Interfaces: Communication Oriented Techniques.* Englewood Cliffs, NJ: SunSoft Press.

> Although this book came out before the Web took off, the information on how to create effective visual interfaces is still valuable. This book is handy in the Refinement and Production phases of the Web site development process, as you build polished and high-fidelity mock-ups of your site.

Nielsen, J. (No date) *How to Conduct a Heuristic Evaluation* (www.useit.com/ papers/heuristic/heuristic_evaluation.html).

> This tutorial explains a fast and relatively inexpensive method of finding potential usability errors by employing a checklist of usability heuristics.

Nielsen, J. (1993) *Usability Engineering.* Boston: Academic Press.

> This book is great for developing products with usability as the key goal. Issues such as prototyping, iterative design, heuristic evaluation, and usability testing are discussed.

Rettig, M. (1994) Prototyping for tiny fingers. *Communications of the ACM,* 37(4): 21–27 (www.acm.org/pubs/citations/journals/cacm/1994-37-4/p21-rettig).

> This is a great article on the motivation behind low-fidelity prototypes, how to make a low-fidelity prototype, and how to run informal usability tests. (This resource requires access to the ACM Digital Library, at www.acm.org/dl.)

Shneiderman, B. (1997) *Designing the User Interface: Strategies for Effective Human–Computer Interaction* (3rd ed.). Reading, MA: Addison-Wesley.

> See the description under Chapter 3 (Knowing Your Customers: Principles and Techniques).

Snyder, C. (2003) *Paper Prototyping: The Fast and Easy Way to Design and Refine User Interfaces,* San Diego, CA: Kaufmann.

> This is a primer on using paper prototypes not only to design, but also to test and iterate on designs.

Tufte, E. (1983) *The Visual Display of Quantitative Information.* Cheshire, CT: Graphics Press.

> Tufte's book is a classic on presenting complex information graphically, stressing simplicity, elegance, and efficiency.

Winograd, T., J. Bennett, L. De Young, and B. Hartfield (Eds.). (1996) *Bringing Design to Software.* Reading, MA: Addison-Wesley.

> This collection of essays takes a broad look at interaction design as a profession. Issues such as the design process, prototyping, art, and people are discussed.

Software

DUB, University of Washington. *DENIM* (http://dub.washington.edu/projects/denim).

> Developed by two of the authors of the book you have in hand, DENIM is a sketch-based design tool for quickly prototyping Web sites.

Chapter 5: Processes for Developing Customer-Centered Sites

Books, Research Papers, and News Articles

Brinck, T., D. Gergle, and S. Wood. (2002) *Usability for the Web: Designing Web Sites That Work.* San Francisco: Kaufmann.

> This book covers a spectrum of topics, including project management, user needs analysis, information architecture, page layout, writing for the Web, visual design, and usability.

McConnell, S. (1996) *Rapid Development: Taming Wild Software Schedules.* Redmond, WA: Microsoft Press.

> This book is really about software development, not Web site development. However, it is an excellent resource on project management, and it is full of best practices, common mistakes, and lessons about planning, scheduling, designing, and creating software. If you're interested in the Discovery and Implementation phases of the Web site development process, this is the book for you.

Newman, M. W., and J. A. Landay. (2000, August) Sitemaps, storyboards, and specifications: A sketch of web site design practice as manifested through artifacts. In *Proceedings of ACM Conference on Designing Interactive Systems*, pp. 263–274. New York (http://guir.berkeley.edu/projects/denim/pubs/iwd-dis-2000.pdf).

> This paper reports on our interviews with Web designers, leading to valuable conclusions about the Web design process, the artifacts, and the deliverables.

Part II: Patterns

Pattern Group A: Site Genres

A1 PERSONAL E-COMMERCE

Cialdini, R. B. (2000) *Influence: The Psychology of Persuasion.* New York: Collins.
> This is the definitive book on what kinds of techniques are effective in persuading people. Cialdini describes how factors like reciprocity, consistency, social proof, liking, authority, and scarcity are effective in getting people to do what you want.

E-Commerce Times (www.ecommercetimes.com).
> *E-Commerce Times* offers up-to-date news about e-commerce–related issues from financial, marketing, and management perspectives.

Frenkel, K. (2000, June 7) Portals struggle to convert browsers to shoppers. *New York Times E-Commerce Report* (www.nytimes.com/library/tech/00/06/biztech/technology/07fren.html).
> This news article looks at many of the issues confronting e-commerce sites, such as poor usability, lack of support for comparison shopping, privacy, security, and shipping costs. It also discusses the approaches that many sites are taking to address these issues.

New York Times E-Commerce Report (http://tech.nytimes.com/top/news/technology/columns/ecommercereport).

> This weekly report, published by *The New York Times,* focuses on issues like Web site design, e-mail, and online marketing. Many older e-commerce reports are archived at www.nytimes.com/library/tech/reference/indexcommerce.html.

Tedeschi, B. (2000, March 29) Now that they've come, what can we sell them? *New York Times E-Commerce Report* (www.nytimes.com/library/tech/00/03/biztech/technology/29tede.html).

> This piece examines the common lament that it's easy to attract visitors but difficult to make profitable Web sites.

A2 NEWS MOSAICS

Pew Internet & American Life Project (www.pewinternet.org).

> This nonprofit initiative conducts and publishes research on "the impact of the Internet on families, communities, work and home, daily life, education, health care, and civic and political life."

Pew Research Center for the People and the Press. (2000, December 3) *Youth Vote Influenced by Online Information; Internet Election News Audience Seeks Convenience, Familiar Names* (www.people-press.org/dataarchive).

> This discussion of the impact of the Internet on the 2000 U.S. presidential election shows that 33 percent of online customers took advantage of Internet news sources to help make their election decisions.

Shapiro, A. (1999) *The Control Revolution: How the Internet Is Putting Individuals in Charge and Changing the World We Know.* New York: PublicAffairs.

> Shapiro takes a critical look at the Internet and its impact on society, analyzing a broad range of topics, including copyright, free speech, communities, and personalization. One of his most interesting conclusions is that a high degree of personalization may actually be detrimental to society because people will tend to gravitate toward others with similar interests and beliefs, resulting in pockets of society that talk only to themselves but not to each other.

A3 COMMUNITY CONFERENCE

Coate, J. (1998) *Cyberspace Innkeeping: Building Online Community* (www.cervisa.com/innkeeping.html).

> This article talks about some of the issues in running online communities, including anonymity, free speech, and leveling the playing field.

Kim, A. J. (2000) *Community Building on the Web: Secret Strategies for Successful Online Communities.* Berkeley, CA: Peachpit Press.

> This excellent and practical book provides detailed explanations and case studies of why communities form and how they grow. It also provides suggestions for how to make your site a nurturing place for communities.

Nielsen-Hayden, T. (2005, January 27) *Virtual Panel Participation on "Spam, Trolls, Stalkers: The Pandora's Box of Community"* (http://nielsenhayden.com/makinglight/archives/006036.html).

> This article discusses one blogger's opinions on moderating online communities and handling the inevitable arrival of malcontents.

Online Community Report (www.onlinecommunityreport.com).

This twice-monthly newsletter offers the latest in online communities, featuring articles on such topics as distance learning, online auctions, massively multiplayer games, and group collaboration.

Pew Internet & American Life Project (www.pewinternet.org).

See the description under NEWS MOSAICS (A2).

Powazek, D. (2001) *Design for Community: The Art of Connecting Real People in Virtual Places.* Indianapolis, IN: New Riders.

This book discusses various aspects of online communities, including design, moderation, e-mail, chat, and other issues intrinsic to online communities. It also features interviews with many people who run large online communities.

Preece, J. (2000) *Online Communities: Designing Usability and Supporting Sociability.* New York: Wiley.

This is one of the best books of academic research on online communities, focusing on issues such as sociability, usability, development, and evaluation.

Rheingold, H. (1998) *The Art of Hosting Good Conversations Online* (www.rheingold. com/texts/artonlinehost.html).

This Web page outlines the role of the Web site in hosting an online community, describing what the goals should be and ways of achieving those goals.

Rheingold, H. (2000) *The Virtual Community: Homesteading on the Electronic Frontier* (rev. ed.). Cambridge, MA: MIT Press.

This book chronicles the start and continued growth of the first thriving online community, The WELL. More of a collection of stories than a practical guide, the book nonetheless contains many insights about the nature of online communities.

A4 SELF-SERVICE GOVERNMENT

Center for Democracy and Technology (www.cdt.org).

The Center for Democracy and Technology is devoted to promoting "democratic values and constitutional liberties in the digital age." Its interests include technology with respect to free speech, privacy, surveillance, cryptography, domain names, and international governance.

Federal Computer Week (www.fcw.com).

Federal Computer Week is a valuable resource for anyone working on information technology for the U.S. government. You will find news articles on a range of technology-related issues, including accessibility, privacy, telecommunications, and training.

FirstGov.gov (www.firstgov.gov).

FirstGov.gov is the official U.S. government portal, a comprehensive directory containing references to all online information created by the U.S. government.

Hart, P., and R. Teeter. (2000) *E-Government: The Next American Revolution* (http://www2.excelgov.org/index.php?keyword=a432c10480be99).

This survey on e-government shows that Americans strongly support electronic government, with the ultimate goals of making government "more accountable to citizens," providing "greater public access to information," and making a "more efficient and cost-effective government." However, Americans have many concerns about privacy and security.

Pew Internet & American Life Project (www.pewinternet.org).
See the description under NEWS MOSAICS (A2).

A5 NONPROFITS AS NETWORKS OF HELP

Idealist (www.idealist.org).
Idealist, a project of Action Without Borders, provides many links to articles about creating, running, and managing nonprofit organizations. It focuses on logistical, legal, financial, and advertising issues as opposed to Web site design.

Nonprofit Online News (http://news.gilbert.org).
Nonprofit Online News provides news about online nonprofits, and links to such topics as use of e-mail, getting grants, and research about nonprofits.

A7 VALUABLE COMPANY SITES

Nielsen, J., and M. Tahir. (2001) *Homepage Usability: 50 Websites Deconstructed.* Indianapolis, IN: New Riders.
This text dissects and analyzes 50 different homepages in detail.

Uchitelle, L. (2000, June 7) It's just the beginning. *New York Times E-Commerce Report* (www.nytimes.com/library/tech/00/06/biztech/technology/07uchi.html).
This article talks about some of the issues that Honeywell, an established company, dealt with in creating its Web site. It focuses on some of the business-to-business aspects involved, including integrating a number of legacy databases, improving access to suppliers and consumers, and managing inventory.

A8 EDUCATIONAL FORUMS

Center for LifeLong Learning and Design (www.cs.colorado.edu/~l3d).
The Center for LifeLong Learning and Design is a group at the University of Colorado at Boulder that researches and theorizes about the "scientific foundations for the construction of intelligent systems that serve as amplifiers of human capabilities."

Computer Support for Collaborative Learning (www.cscl-home.org).
Computer Support for Collaborative Learning (CSCL) is an international conference devoted to all issues related to computers and learning, including research, education, training, and technology.

Distributed Learning Workshop (www.dlworkshop.net).
The Distributed Learning Workshop is a nonprofit group that creates high-quality Web-based instructional materials for college students.

Pew Internet & American Life Project (www.pewinternet.org).
See the description under NEWS MOSAICS (A2).

Pittsburgh Advanced Cognitive Tutor (PACT) Center (http://pact.cs.cmu.edu).
This research group at Carnegie Mellon University is developing state-of-the-art computer-based tutors designed to teach students in a variety of subjects, including science, mathematics, and foreign languages.

Resnick, M., A. Bruckman, and F. Martin. (1996) Pianos not stereos: Creating computational construction kits. *Interactions*, 3(6): 40–50 (http://lcs.www.media.mit.edu/groups/el/Papers/mres/pianos/pianos.html).

   This article argues that computer systems need to be built for more than just ease of use, especially for educational purposes.

A9 STIMULATING ARTS AND ENTERTAINMENT

ACM SIGGRAPH (www.siggraph.org).

   ACM SIGGRAPH is the Association for Computing Machinery's Special Interest Group on Computer Graphics. In addition to publishing magazines and maintaining online art galleries, it holds an annual conference that features the latest in tools, research, and computer-based art.

Laurel, B. 1993. *Computers as Theatre*. Reading, MA: Addison-Wesley.

   Although this book was first published before the Web took off, there is still a great deal of relevant material. Laurel's main point is that designing pleasing user interfaces is similar to producing a play in theater, with multiple actors, a story, and a climax.

McCloud, S. (1993) *Understanding Comics: The Invisible Art*. Northampton, MA: Kitchen Sink Press.

   Although this book is a comic about comics, it is really about communicating through text and images in a static medium (such as Web pages). It's a fun read that takes a critical look at comics as a medium.

Shedroff, N. (2001) *Experience Design*. Indianapolis, IN: New Riders.

   More of a thought provoker than a how-to guide, this book takes the reader through a diverse set of design ideas, focusing on feeling and emotion and on visual quality.

A10 WEB APPS THAT WORK

Drummond, M. (2001) The end of software as we know it. *Fortune/CNET Tech Review*, 52–66 (www.catalytic.com/archive/cnetfortune.htm).

   This article looks at how software may be delivered as a Web service in the future, covering such issues as standards, intellectual property, maintenance, pricing, and business models.

The Unofficial Web Applications List (www.webapplist.com).

   This Web site lists a large number of (often quite creative) Web applications. Entries range from fun time-wasting games (like Sudoku Combat and Othello) to business-related applications such as Web-based spreadsheets.

A11 ENABLING INTRANETS

CIO. (No date) *Knowledge Management - Intranet/Extranet* (www.cio.com/research/intranet).

   This topic is one of a large collection of links, newsletters, interviews, white papers, and reports about building corporate intranets that can be found on CIO's Web site.

Fabris, P. (1999, April 1) You think tomaytoes, I think tomahtoes. *CIO Web Business Magazine* (www.cio.com/archive/webbusiness/040199_nort.html).

This article tells the story of the creation of a large intranet to support more than seven thousand employees at Bay Networks. It describes some of the difficulties involved in understanding how information flowed through the company and the different ways in which people organized things.

Nielsen, J. (1999) *Designing Web Usability: The Practice of Simplicity.* Indianapolis, IN: New Riders.

This book discusses a wide-ranging number of Web usability topics, such as page design, link names, link colors, writing for the Web, search, navigation, intranet design, accessibility, and internationalization. Many screen shots are included to illustrate concepts.

A12 BLOGS

Larson, C. (2005, July 25) Blogging bosses. *U.S. News & World Report* (www. usnews.com/usnews/biztech/articles/050725/25eeblogs.htm).

This article describes how corporate executives are reaching out to employees, customers, and industry analysts with blogs.

Nielsen-Hayden, T. (2005, January 27) *Virtual Panel Participation on "Spam, Trolls, Stalkers: The Pandora's Box of Community"* (http://nielsenhayden.com/ makinglight/archives/006036.html).

See the description under COMMUNITY CONFERENCE (A3).

ProBlogger (www.problogger.net).

ProBlogger is a blog devoted to helping bloggers earn money with their Web sites. It includes tips and case studies on such topics as writing style, advertising, sponsorship, and better search engine results.

Technorati (www.technorati.com).

Technorati is an Internet search engine designed specifically for blogs. It also maintains rankings for the most-cited blogs in the so-called blogosphere.

Pattern Group B: Creating a Navigation Framework

B1 MULTIPLE WAYS TO NAVIGATE

Brinck, T., D. Gergle, and S. Wood. (2002) *Usability for the Web: Designing Web Sites That Work.* San Francisco: Kaufmann.

See the description under Chapter 5 (Processes for Developing Customer-Centered Sites).

Garrett, J. J. (No date) *Information Architecture Resources* (www.jjg.net/ia).

This is a great resource for learning more about information architecture.

InfoDesign: Understanding by Design (www.informationdesign.org).

This Web site is a hub for books, organizations, mailing lists, and other Web sites devoted to information design.

Lakoff, G. (1990) *Women, Fire, and Dangerous Things.* Chicago: University of Chicago Press.

This book analyzes categories of language and thought from a cognitive science perspective. Its title, one of the coolest of any book published in the twentieth century, refers to how an Australian aboriginal language uses the same classifier to describe women, fire, and dangerous things.

Larson, K., and M. Czerwinski. (1998) Web page design: Implications of memory, structure and scent for information retrieval. CHI 1998, ACM Conference on Human Factors in Computing Systems, *CHI Letters*, 1(1): 25–32.

> This study examines the trade-off between breadth and depth for information architectures with respect to preference and performance. *Breadth* means that the architecture is designed so that many pieces of information are displayed per page (leading to a broad and shallow graph), and *depth* means that there are fewer pieces of information (leading to a narrow and deep graph). A total of 512 items from Microsoft Encarta were arranged into three Web sites differing in breadth and depth. Overall, increased depth led to longer browsing times, while a balance between breadth and depth outperformed the broadest and shallowest structure. These findings lend more evidence to the theory that fewer clicks and fewer levels work better for organizing large amounts of information.

Rosenfeld, L., and P. Morville. (2002) *Information Architecture for the World Wide Web* (2nd ed.). Cambridge, MA: O'Reilly.

> This book describes techniques for organizing, labeling, and indexing the information on a Web site for browsing and searching.

Selingo, J. (2000, August 3) A message to Web designers: If it ain't broke, don't fix it. *New York Times E-Commerce Report* (www.nytimes.com/library/tech/00/08/circuits/articles/03desi.html).

> This article looks at the fact that many customers are resistant to change, wanting the power that familiarity and expertise afford. Web sites have had to make changes to accommodate this reality, including homepages that have both directories and search engines, homepages with many organized links instead of just a few, and a consistent structure behind the information.

Sigia-1: SIG Information Architecture (www.asis.org/AboutASIS/SIGEmailLists/ia.html).

> This e-mail list is devoted to practitioner, researcher, and student issues in information architecture.

Tufte, E. (1984) *The Visual Display of Quantitative Information*. Cheshire, CT: Graphics Press.

> See the description under Chapter 4 (Involving Customers with Iterative Design).

Tufte, E. (1997) *Visual Explanations*. Cheshire, CT: Graphics Press.

> Another classic by Tufte, this book presents evidence relevant to cause and effect, for decision making and presentations.

Zaphiris, P., B. Shneiderman, and K. Norman. (1999, June) *Expandable Indexes versus Sequential Menus for Searching Hierarchies on the World Wide Web* (ftp://ftp.cs.umd.edu/pub/hcil/Reports-Abstracts-Bibliography/99-15html/99-15.html).

> This study looks at the effectiveness of expanding menus for Web sites. Expanding menus show top-level hierarchies, revealing the next level of that hierarchy when the mouse is rolled over an item. The results indicate that reducing the depth of hierarchies improves browsing performance, lending more evidence to the theory that fewer clicks and fewer levels work better for organizing large amounts of information.

B2 *BROWSABLE CONTENT*

See the references listed under MULTIPLE WAYS TO NAVIGATE (B1).

B3 *HIERARCHICAL ORGANIZATION*

See the references listed under MULTIPLE WAYS TO NAVIGATE (B1).

B4 *TASK-BASED ORGANIZATION*

See the references listed under MULTIPLE WAYS TO NAVIGATE (B1).

B5 *ALPHABETICAL ORGANIZATION*

See the references listed under MULTIPLE WAYS TO NAVIGATE (B1).

B6 *CHRONOLOGICAL ORGANIZATION*

See the references listed under MULTIPLE WAYS TO NAVIGATE (B1).

B7 *POPULARITY-BASED ORGANIZATION*

See the references listed under MULTIPLE WAYS TO NAVIGATE (B1).

B8 *CATEGORY PAGES*

See the references listed under MULTIPLE WAYS TO NAVIGATE (B1).

B9 *SITE ACCESSIBILITY*

Assistivetech.net: National Public Website on Assistive Technology (www.assistivetech.net).

> This Web site provides information about assistive technology devices and services. It features a database of assistive technology products, links to other public and private resources, and a convenient search function.

IBM Corporation, Human Ability and Accessibility Center. (No date) *Web Accessibility* (www.ibm.com/able/guidelines/web/accessweb.html).

> IBM offers this checklist for making sure your Web site has basic accessibility built in. The site includes links to further reading.

Mankoff, J., H. Fait, and T. Tran. (2005) Is your web page accessible? A comparative study of methods for assessing web page accessibility for the blind. In *Proceedings of the SIGCHI Conference on Human Factors in Computing Systems, Portland, Oregon, April 02–07, 2005*. New York: ACM Press (http://doitest.acm.org/10.1145/1054972.1054979).

> This research paper presents the results of a study comparing the effectiveness of four different techniques for evaluating the usability of Web sites for blind users. The authors found that having multiple developers do an expert review with a screen reader was the most successful technique for finding usability problems, discovering roughly 50 percent of the problems identified by an actual laboratory study. (This resource requires access to the ACM Digital Library, at www.acm.org/dl.)

Section 508 (www.section508.gov).

This U.S. government Web site provides a wide range of information about Section 508 of the Rehabilitation Act, which requires that electronic and information technology used by federal agencies be made accessible to people with disabilities.

UniversalUsability.org (www.universalusability.org).

The ultimate goal of this group is to make information and communication technologies affordable to and usable by everyone. The Web site has some material describing the salient issues, as well as references on long-term social, legal, and technological approaches to addressing the problems.

WebXACT (www.webxact.watchfire.com).

This online service checks for the basic accessibility of Web sites. It does not ensure accessibility but does help pinpoint potential problems.

World Wide Web Consortium (W3C) (www.w3.org).

The W3C's mission is "to lead the World Wide Web to its full potential by developing protocols and guidelines that ensure long-term growth for the Web." Thus it has a special interest in making Web sites accessible to everyone. Check out the W3C's Web Accessibility Initiative at w3.org/wai. You will find tools, checklists, and guidelines at w3.org/tr/wcag (WCAG stands for Web Content Accessibility Guidelines).

Pattern Group C: Creating a Powerful Homepage

C1 HOMEPAGE PORTAL

Nielsen, J., and M. Tahir. (2001) *Homepage Usability: 50 Websites Deconstructed.* Indianapolis, IN: New Riders.

See the description under VALUABLE COMPANY SITES (A7).

Selingo, J. (2000, August 3) A message to Web designers: If it ain't broke, don't fix it. *New York Times E-Commerce Report* (www.nytimes.com/library/tech/00/08/circuits/articles/03desi.html).

See the description under MULTIPLE WAYS TO NAVIGATE (B1).

UW E-Business Consortium Best Practice Reports: B2C Website Design Standard Practices and Benchmarks (www.uwebc.org/opinionpapers/ue).

See the description under Chapter 2 (Making the Most of Web Design Patterns).

C2 UP-FRONT VALUE PROPOSITION

Cialdini, R. B. (2000) *Influence: The Psychology of Persuasion.* New York: Collins.

See the description under PERSONAL E-COMMERCE (A1).

Ogilvy, D. (1987) *Ogilvy on Advertising.* New York: Vintage Books.

This is an excellent read on advertising by one of its preeminent creators.

Pattern Group D: Writing and Managing Content

D1 PAGE TEMPLATES

Code-Sucks.com. *CSS Layouts* (www.code-sucks.com/css%20layouts).

This Web site provides many templates for one-column, two-column, three-column, and four-column page layouts.

CSS Tinderbox (www.dbfnetwork.info/tinderbox/index.html).

This Web site provides high-quality HTML and STYLE SHEETS (D11) that you can use for your Web pages. The examples are provided under the Creative Commons license, which means that you can use and adapt these templates as you see fit.

Open Source Web Design (www.oswd.org).

This Web site allows you to view, download, and share free Web page designs.

Tedeschi, B. (1999, August 30) Good Web site design can lead to healthy sales. *New York Times E-Commerce Report* (www.nytimes.com/library/tech/99/08/cyber/commerce/30commerce.html).

See the description under Chapter 1 (Customer-Centered Web Design: More Than a Good Idea).

D2 CONTENT MODULES

Tedeschi, B. (1999, August 30) Good Web site design can lead to healthy sales. *New York Times E-Commerce Report* (www.nytimes.com/library/tech/99/08/cyber/commerce/30commerce.html).

See the description under Chapter 1 (Customer-Centered Web Design: More Than a Good Idea).

D3 HEADLINES AND BLURBS

Nielsen, J. (1999) *Designing Web Usability: The Practice of Simplicity.* Indianapolis, IN: New Riders.

See the description under ENABLING INTRANETS (A11).

D4 PERSONALIZED CONTENT

Eads, S. (2000, August 4) The Web's still-unfulfilled personalization promise. *BusinessWeek Online* (www.businessweek.com/bwdaily/dnflash/aug2000/nf2000084_506.htm).

This article discusses the advantages of personalization but focuses more on the software and financial costs involved in integrating such a system into a Web site, as well as the difficulties involved in measuring effectiveness.

Hansell, S. (2000, December 11) In search for online success, "easy does it" is good theme. *New York Times E-Commerce Report.*

This article talks about simplicity in design as one of the dominant factors of success. It looks at issues such as the fact that underlined text links are more likely to be clicked on than buttons, the fact that basic security systems built into Web browsers work better than sophisticated systems that people have to download and install, and the fact that recommendation systems work only if they are easy and painless to use.

Kramer, J., S. Noronha, and J. Vergo. (2000, August) A user-centered design approach to personalization. *Communications of the ACM*, 43(8): 45–48 (http://doi.acm.org/10.1145/345124.345139).

> This article argues that customer-centered design is the key to successful design and implementation of systems that make use of personalization. This is one of several articles about personalization in the August 2000 issue of *Communications of the ACM*. (This resource requires access to the ACM Digital Library, at www.acm.org/dl.)

Manber, U., A. Patel, and J. Robison. (2000, August) Experience with personalization of Yahoo! *Communications of the ACM*, 43(8): 35–39 (http://doi.acm.org/10.1145/345124.345136).

> This article discusses the experiences and lessons learned in building and maintaining My Yahoo!, one of the earliest Web sites to use personalization on a large scale. Many interesting points about scalability, privacy and security, and user interface are covered. The article also talks about the fact that people often don't change the defaults. This is one of several articles about personalization in the August 2000 issue of *Communications of the ACM*. (This resource requires access to the ACM Digital Library, at www.acm.org/dl.)

Shapiro, A. (1999) *The Control Revolution: How the Internet Is Putting Individuals in Charge and Changing the World We Know*. New York: PublicAffairs.

> See the description under NEWS MOSAICS (A2).

Stellin, S. (2000, August 28) Internet companies learn how to personalize service. *New York Times E-Commerce Report* (http://nytimes.com/library/tech/00/08/cyber/commerce/28commerce.html).

> This article looks at several ways in which Web sites can apply personalization to improve the customer experience. It also discusses some of the problems involved in personalization, including too much work, bad data, and privacy.

D5 MESSAGE BOARDS

Kim, A. J. (2000) *Community Building on the Web: Secret Strategies for Successful Online Communities*. Berkeley, CA: Peachpit Press.

> See the description under COMMUNITY CONFERENCE (A3).

Nielsen-Hayden, T. (2005, January 27) *Virtual Panel Participation on "Spam, Trolls, Stalkers: The Pandora's Box of Community"* (http://nielsenhayden.com/makinglight/archives/006036.html).

> See the description under COMMUNITY CONFERENCE (A3).

Preece, J. (2000) *Online Communities: Designing Usability and Supporting Sociability*. New York: Wiley.

> See the description under COMMUNITY CONFERENCE (A3).

Rheingold, H. (1998) *The Art of Hosting Good Conversations Online* (www.rheingold.com/texts/artonlinehost.html).

> See the description under COMMUNITY CONFERENCE (A3).

Rheingold, H. (2000) *The Virtual Community: Homesteading on the Electronic Frontier* (rev. ed.). Cambridge, MA: MIT Press.

> See the description under COMMUNITY CONFERENCE (A3).

Cunningham, J. P., J. Cantor, S. H. Pearsall, and K. H. Richardson. (2001) Industry briefs: AT&T. *Interactions: New Visions of Human Computer Interaction,* 8(2): 27–31.

> This short piece discusses some of the experiences in building AT&T's Web site. Of particular interest is the fact that, when people search, they often use the term *AT&T,* as in "AT&T long distance." Unfortunately, this keyword isn't very useful on the AT&T Web site because every page has *AT&T* on it! Included in the article is a discussion of the use of <meta> tags to improve searching on this site.

Search Engine Watch (http://searchenginewatch.com).

> Search Engine Watch provides tips on submitting your Web site to search engines, as well as to newsletters and reviews on search engines.

Tedeschi, B. (2001, December 10) Striving to top the search lists. *New York Times E-Commerce Report.*

> This article discusses how shoppers use search engines and describes the difficulties involved in trying to get to the top of the search results.

Webopedia. (No date) *Search Engine* (www.webopedia.com/TERM/s/search_ engine.html).

> Webopedia is an online reference for technical terms. This Web page contains a short explanation of search engines and how they work, as well as references on writing Web pages for search engines.

D7 *INVERTED-PYRAMID WRITING STYLE*

Brinck, T., D. Gergle, and S. Wood. (2002) *Usability for the Web: Designing Web Sites That Work.* San Francisco: Kaufmann.

> See the description under Chapter 5 (Processes for Developing Customer-Centered Sites).

Morkes, J., and J. Nielsen. (1997) *Concise, Scannable, and Objective: How to Write for the Web* (www.useit.com/papers/webwriting/writing.html); and Morkes, J., and J. Nielsen. (1998, January 6) *Applying Writing Guidelines to Web Pages* (www.useit.com/papers/webwriting/rewriting.html).

> These two articles discuss a series of studies on people's attitudes and behaviors toward writing on the Web. Their main recommendations are that text should be concise and easy to scan. They observe that most people skim text anyway, and that halving the length of the text, using bulleted lists, and highlighting keywords helps the skimming process. In addition, they suggest that text should be objective in tone, avoiding jargon and self-promotion, which is disliked by readers and negatively affects usability.

Nielsen, J. (1999) *Designing Web Usability: The Practice of Simplicity.* Indianapolis, IN: New Riders.

> See the description under ENABLING INTRANETS (A11).

D9 *DISTINCTIVE HTML TITLES*

Ivory, M. (2001) *An Empirical Foundation for Automated Web Interface Evaluation.* Doctoral dissertation, University of California, Berkeley, Computer Science Division.

> This PhD dissertation combines quantitative metrics calculated on hundreds of Web sites with the judges' ratings for the 2000 Webby Awards to validate and invalidate many popular Web design guidelines. Distinctive HTML titles were found to be a common trait of highly rated Web sites.

Nielsen, J. (1999) *Designing Web Usability: The Practice of Simplicity.* Indianapolis, IN: New Riders.

> See the description under ENABLING INTRANETS (A11).

D10 *INTERNATIONALIZED AND LOCALIZED CONTENT*

I18n Guy. (No date) *Internationalization (I18n), Localization (L10n), Standards, and Amusements* (www.i18nguy.com).

> This Web site provides a wide variety of Web-based resources on internationalization.

ICU User Guide. (2000) *Overview of Software Internationalization* (http://icu. sourceforge.net/userguide/i18n.html).

> This discussion focuses on internationalization and localization issues from a software development perspective, including how to structure the code.

Marcus, A., J. Armitage, and V. Frank. (1999, June 3) Globalization of user-interface design for the Web. In *Proceedings of the 5th Human Factors and the Web Conference.* Gaithersburg, MD (www.amanda.com/resources/HFWEB99/ HFWEB99.Marcus.html).

> This paper looks at the issues of designing Web sites for a global audience, including metaphors, mental models, navigation, interaction, and appearance.

Marcus, A., and E. Gould. (2000, June 19) Cultural dimensions and global Web user-interface design: What? So what? Now what? In *Proceedings of the 6th Conference on Human Factors and the Web.* Austin, TX (www.amanda.com/ resources/hfweb2000/hfweb00.marcus.html).

> This paper considers how user interface design might be affected by dimensions of culture, looking at factors like authority, collectivism and individualism, femininity and masculinity, uncertainty, and time.

MultiLingual Computing (www.multilingual.com).

> This Web page contains references to excellent information about Web site internationalization and localization, including featured articles, product reviews, and book reviews.

Nielsen, J. (1999) *Designing Web Usability: The Practice of Simplicity.* Indianapolis, IN: New Riders.

> See the description under ENABLING INTRANETS (A11).

World Wide Web Consortium. (No date) *W3C Internationalization (I18n) Activity* (www.w3.org/international).

> This Web page looks at computer-related internationalization and localization issues, including writing HTML in many writing systems, representing dates and times, and fonts.

D11 *style sheets*

Code-Sucks.com. *CSS Layouts* (www.code-sucks.com/css%20layouts).
See the description under PAGE TEMPLATES (D1).

CSSplay (www.cssplay.co.uk/index.html).
This Web site provides lots of experimental style sheets showing the range of what can be done with CSS alone.

CSS Tinderbox (www.dbfnetwork.info/tinderbox/index.html).
See the description under PAGE TEMPLATES (D1).

Guy D2. *SeeSS Widget 1.0* (www.guyd2.com/widget/seess).
This is a handy Mac OS X dashboard widget for quickly finding documentation about CSS.

HTML Dog (www.htmldog.com).
This Web site discusses beginner as well as intermediate and advanced CSS topics.

Meyer, E. (2002) *Eric Meyer on CSS: Mastering the Language of Web Design.*
Indianapolis, IN: New Riders.
Meyer provides a practical and hands-on guide to CSS, taking you through multiple examples of how to use CSS to get the layout and style you want.

Open Source Web Design (www.oswd.org).
See the description under PAGE TEMPLATES (D1).

W3Schools. (No date) *CSS Tutorial* (www.w3schools.com/css).
This is a comprehensive tutorial on most aspects of style sheets.

Pattern Group E: Building Trust and Credibility

E1 *site branding*

Cialdini, R. B. (2000) *Influence: The Psychology of Persuasion.* New York: Collins.
See the description under PERSONAL E-COMMERCE (A1).

Crawford, F. A., and R. Mathews. (2001) *The Myth of Excellence: Why Great Companies Never Try to Be the Best at Everything.* New York: Crown Business.
Crawford and Matthews surveyed 5,000 consumers to explore their purchasing behavior. The authors found that values such as respect, honesty, trust, and dignity were more important to consumers than value. This finding led to a new model of "consumer relevancy" based on price, service, quality, access, and customer experience. The book suggests that, in order to be successful, companies need to dominate on only one of these five factors.

Fry, J. (2001, August 13) Web shoppers' loyalty isn't so crazy after all. *Wall Street Journal* (http://ebusiness.mit.edu/news/WSJ_Story8-13-01.html).
See the description under Chapter 2 (Making the Most of Web Design Patterns).

Johnston, D. (2000, October 23) A glass of wine helps show what buyers want.
New York Times E-Commerce Report (www.nytimes.com/library/tech/00/10/biztech/technology/25cay.html).
This article discusses the fact that price is not the only consideration in online shopping. Factors such as convenience, quality, reliability, brand recognition, and good product information also weigh in.

E2 E-MAIL SUBSCRIPTIONS

Stamler, B. (2001, April 18) You want repeat customers? Try e-mail. *New York Times E-Commerce Report.*

> This piece looks at the issues that Saturn, Eddie Bauer, and Esperya have had to address when using e-mail for advertising.

Stellin, S. (2000, August 21) Marketers get help from e-mail experts. *New York Times E-Commerce Report* (www.nytimes.com/library/tech/00/08/cyber/commerce/21commerce.html).

> This news article discusses the emergence of an entire industry to help marketers deal with the technical and policy issues involved in e-mail advertising.

Tedeschi, B. (1999, August 9) Personalized e-mail ads: Low cost, high response rate. *New York Times E-Commerce Report* (www.nytimes.com/library/tech/99/08/cyber/commerce/09commerce.html).

> This article reveals that e-mail advertisements are an effective form of advertising for customers who opt in. It also discusses sophisticated marketing techniques, like combining demographics with promotions, or using linked photographs of products to let customers immediately purchase items.

E3 FAIR INFORMATION PRACTICES

European Parliament and the Council of the European Union. (1995) *Directive 95/46/EC of the European Parliament and of the Council of 24 October 1995 on the Protection of Individuals with Regard to the Processing of Personal Data and on the Free Movement of Such Data* (www.cdt.org/privacy/eudirective/EU_Directive_.html).

> This is an online version of the text of a European Parliament directive on fair use of information.

Garfinkel, S. (2001) *Database Nation: The Death of Privacy in the 21st Century.* Beijing, China: O'Reilly.

> This book describes many of the potential dangers to individuals when companies collect large amounts of information about them.

The Privacy Act of 1974 (www.usdoj.gov/foia/privstat.htm).

> This Web page contains the text of the Privacy Act of 1974.

Privacy.Org (www.privacy.org).

> Privacy.Org provides news, information, and resources about privacy in general.

U.S. Department of Commerce, Safe Harbor (www.export.gov/safeharbor).

> The Safe Harbor Web site contains detailed information on the safe harbor agreement, as well as documents about becoming compliant with safe harbor.

U.S. Federal Trade Commission. (No date) *Privacy Initiatives* (www.ftc.gov/privacy).

> This report details privacy initiatives taken by the U.S. government, including news releases, related laws, reports, and design guidelines for protecting privacy.

U.S. Federal Trade Commission. (2000, May) *Privacy Online: Fair Information Practices in the Electronic Marketplace: A Report to Congress* (www.ftc.gov/reports/privacy2000/privacy2000.pdf).

> This report describes the FTC's conclusion that legislation is necessary to ensure the implementation of fair information practices online, and it recommends a framework for such legislation.

E4 *PRIVACY POLICY*

Fox, S. (2000, August 20) *Trust and Privacy Online: Why Americans Want to Rewrite the Rules*. Washington, DC: Pew Internet & American Life Project (www. pewinternet.org/pdfs/PIP_Trust_Privacy_Report.pdf).

This reports details a study looking at Americans' concerns about privacy online.

U.S. Federal Trade Commission, Kidz Privacy (www.ftc.gov/bcp/conline/edcams/ kidzprivacy).

This Web site, created by the U.S. Federal Trade Commission, contains additional details and resources on protecting children's privacy online.

See also the references listed under FAIR INFORMATION PRACTICES (E3).

E5 *ABOUT US*

Cialdini, R. B. (2000) *Influence: The Psychology of Persuasion*. New York: Collins.

See the description under PERSONAL E-COMMERCE (A1).

Fogg, B., J. Marshall, O. Laraki, A. Osipovich, C. Varma, N. Fang, J. Paul, A. Rangnekar, J. Shon, P. Swani, and M. Treinen. (2001, March 31–April 5) What makes web sites credible? A report on a large quantitative study. CHI 2000, ACM Conference on Human Factors in Computing Systems, *CHI Letters*, 3(1): 61–68 (www.webcredibility.org/studies/p61-fogg.pdf).

This paper presents the results of a survey of more than fourteen hundred people from the United States and Europe, reporting how various factors in Web design affected people's perceptions of credibility. Some interesting results include the facts that providing quick responses to customer service questions, listing the organization's physical address, having a contact phone number and e-mail address, and having photos of the organization's members helped increase credibility.

E6 *SECURE CONNECTIONS*

UCLA Center for Communication Policy. (2003, February) *The UCLA Internet Report: Surveying the Digital Future: Year Three* (www.digitalcenter.org/pdf/ InternetReportYearThree.pdf).

This survey of more than two thousand people found many interesting results about people's attitudes and behaviors online. For example, most people waited between 15 and 22 months before purchasing anything online. The single most-cited reason for this hesitation was "concerned about giving a credit card number," followed by "no products or services available" and "concerned about deception." Over two-thirds of the people surveyed were also very concerned about privacy when buying online.

Webopedia. (No date) *SSL* (www.webopedia.com/TERM/S/SSL.html).

Webopedia is an online reference for technical terms. This Web page contains a short explanation of how Secure Sockets Layer works, as well as references for further reading.

E7 *E-MAIL NOTIFICATIONS*

See the references listed under E-MAIL SUBSCRIPTIONS (E2) and PREVENTING PHISHING SCAMS (E9).

E8 PRIVACY PREFERENCES

Kumaraguru, P., and L. F. Cranor. (2005, December) *Privacy Indexes: A Survey of Westin's Studies* (http://reports-archive.adm.cs.cmu.edu/anon/isri2005/CMU-ISRI-05-138.pdf).

> This technical report analyzes a series of privacy surveys run by Alan Westin since the 1970s (see the next resource for more information on Alan Westin). It also describes survey questions that you can use to help assess how your customers feel about privacy.

U.S. House, Subcommittee on Commerce, Trade, and Consumer Protection. (2001, May 8) *Opinion Surveys: What Consumers Have To Say About Information Privacy* (testimony by Dr. Alan Westin to the House Committee on Energy and Commerce) (http://energycommerce.house.gov/107/hearings/05082001Hearing209/Westin309.htm).

> This article provides a privacy expert's opinion on people's attitudes toward privacy. It also provides a nice overview of the key issues for real-world commerce, most of which is applicable to e-commerce as well.

See also the references listed under PRIVACY POLICY (E4).

E9 PREVENTING PHISHING SCAMS

Anti-Phishing Working Group (http://apwg.org).

> The Anti-Phishing Working Group (APWG) is a consortium consisting of companies and law enforcement agencies devoted to fighting phishing. The group holds periodic conferences, and its Web site features some of the latest kinds of attacks.

Kerstein, P. L. (2005, July 19) *How Can We Stop Phishing and Pharming Scams?* (www.csoonline.com/talkback/071905.html).

> This article describes the business and personal costs of phishing scams, as well as some techniques that Web sites are deploying to protect their customers.

U.S. Federal Trade Commission. (2005, June) *How Not to Get Hooked by a "Phishing" Scam* (www.ftc.gov/bcp/conline/pubs/alerts/phishingalrt.htm).

> This consumer alert page, maintained by the U.S. Federal Trade Commission, warns people of online phishing scams.

Pattern Group F: Basic E-Commerce

F1 QUICK-FLOW CHECKOUT

Bidigare, S. (2000, May) *Information Architecture of the Shopping Cart: Best Practices for the Information Architectures of E-Commerce Ordering Systems.* Argus Center for Information Architecture (http://argus-acia.com/white_papers/shopping_cart_ia.pdf).

> This white paper analyzes four different shopping cart and checkout designs and extracts some design principles for making these processes simple to use.

Tedeschi, B. (1999, August 30) Good Web site design can lead to healthy sales. *New York Times E-Commerce Report* (www.nytimes.com/library/tech/99/08/cyber/commerce/30commerce.html).

> See the description under Chapter 1 (Customer-Centered Web Design: More Than a Good Idea).

UW E-Business Consortium Best Practice Reports: B2C Website Design Standard Practices and Benchmarks (www.uwebc.org/opinionpapers/ue).
See the description under Chapter 2 (Making the Most of Web Design Patterns).

F2 CLEAN PRODUCT DETAILS

Johnston, D. (2000, October 23) A glass of wine helps show what buyers want. *New York Times E-Commerce Report* (www.nytimes.com/library/tech/00/10/biztech/technology/25cay.html).
See the description under SITE BRANDING (E1).

Ogilvy, D. (1987) *Ogilvy on Advertising.* New York: Vintage Books.
See the description under UP-FRONT VALUE PROPOSITION (C2).

Tedeschi, B. (1999, August 23) Online sales can be messy, especially those pesky returns. *New York Times E-Commerce Report* (www.nytimes.com/library/tech/99/08/cyber/commerce/23commerce.html).
This article looks at the difficulties with handling product returns, as well as at some of the approaches that companies are using to address these problems, including better management, better product details to give customers realistic expectations, and integration of returns with physical stores.

UW E-Business Consortium Best Practice Reports: B2C Website Design Standard Practices and Benchmarks (www.uwebc.org/opinionpapers/ue).
See the description under Chapter 2 (Making the Most of Web Design Patterns).

F3 SHOPPING CART

Adkisson, H. (2003, October 13) *Examining the Role of De Facto Standards on the Web* (www.boxesandarrows.com/view/examining_the_role_of_de_facto_standards_on_the_web).
See the description under Chapter 2 (Making the Most of Web Design Patterns).

Bidigare, S. (2000, May) *Information Architecture of the Shopping Cart: Best Practices for the Information Architectures of E-Commerce Ordering Systems.* Argus Center for Information Architecture (http://argus-acia.com/white_papers/shopping_cart_ia.pdf)).
See the description under QUICK-FLOW CHECKOUT (F1).

UW E-Business Consortium Best Practice Reports: B2C Website Design Standard Practices and Benchmarks (www.uwebc.org/opinionpapers/ue).
See the description under Chapter 2 (Making the Most of Web Design Patterns).

Web Design Practices (www.webdesignpractices.com).
See the description under Chapter 2 (Making the Most of Web Design Patterns).

F9 EASY RETURNS

Tedeschi, B. (1999, August 23) Online sales can be messy, especially those pesky returns. *New York Times E-Commerce Report* (www.nytimes.com/library/tech/99/08/cyber/commerce/23commerce.html).
See the description under CLEAN PRODUCT DETAILS (F2).

Pattern Group G: Advanced E-Commerce

G1 *FEATURED PRODUCTS*

Cialdini, R. B. (2000) *Influence: The Psychology of Persuasion.* New York: Collins.
See the description under PERSONAL E-COMMERCE (A1).

Ogilvy, D. (1987) *Ogilvy on Advertising.* New York: Vintage Books.
See the description under UP-FRONT VALUE PROPOSITION (C2).

G2 *CROSS-SELLING AND UP-SELLING*

Cialdini, R. B. (2000) *Influence: The Psychology of Persuasion.* New York: Collins.
See the description under PERSONAL E-COMMERCE (A1).

Ogilvy, D. (1987) *Ogilvy on Advertising.* New York: Vintage Books.
See the description under UP-FRONT VALUE PROPOSITION (C2).

G3 *PERSONALIZED RECOMMENDATIONS*

See the references listed under PERSONALIZED CONTENT (D4).

G4 *RECOMMENDATION COMMUNITY*

Kim, A. J. (2000) *Community Building on the Web: Secret Strategies for Successful Online Communities.* Berkeley, CA: Peachpit Press.
See the description under COMMUNITY CONFERENCE (A3).

Preece, J. (2000) *Online Communities: Designing Usability and Supporting Sociability.* New York: Wiley.
See the description under COMMUNITY CONFERENCE (A3).

Sinha, R., and K. Swearingen. (2002) The role of transparency in recommender systems. In *Conference Companion: Proceedings of Human Factors in Computing Systems: CHI 2002,* pp. 830–831. Minneapolis, MN: ACM Press.
Preliminary results from this research indicate that people felt more confident about recommendations from a recommendation system if they understood why a particular recommendation was made.

See also the references listed under PERSONALIZED CONTENT (D4).

Pattern Group H: Helping Customers Complete Tasks

H1 *PROCESS FUNNEL*

Schwartz, M. (2000, June 12) Sharper Staples. *Computerworld* (www.computerworld.com/printthis/2000/0,4814,45787,00.html).
This short article examines the redesign of the Staples Web site. During the process the designers learned that visitors were suspicious of entering their zip code information until being informed about how doing that could help them with shipping information, that the search results had to be culled and organized more efficiently, and that reducing the account creation process from four pages to two reduced the number of customers who balked, among other things. The article also describes how Staples integrated its paper catalogs with its Web site.

Tedeschi, B. (1999, August 30) Good Web site design can lead to healthy sales. *New York Times E-Commerce Report* (www.nytimes.com/library/tech/99/08/cyber/commerce/30commerce.html).

    See the description under Chapter 1 (Customer-Centered Web Design: More Than a Good Idea).

H2 SIGN-IN/NEW ACCOUNT

Schwartz, M. (2000, June 12) Sharper Staples. *Computerworld* (www.computerworld.com/printthis/2000/0,4814,45787,00.html).

    See the description under PROCESS FUNNEL (H1).

H4 ACCOUNT MANAGEMENT

Bernard, M. (2002) Examining user expectations for the location of common e-commerce web objects. *Usability News* 4(1) (http://psychology.wichita.edu/surl/usabilitynews/41/web_object-ecom.htm).

    See the description under Chapter 2 (Making the Most of Web Design Patterns).

Web Design Practices (www.webdesignpractices.com).

    See the description under Chapter 2 (Making the Most of Web Design Patterns).

H5 PERSISTENT CUSTOMER SESSIONS

Persistent Client State: HTTP Cookies. (1999) (http://wp.netscape.com/newsref/std/cookie_spec.html).

    This Web page describes many of the technical details underlying cookies.

Webopedia. (No date) *Cookie.* (www.webopedia.com/TERM/c/cookie.html).

    Webopedia is an online reference for technical terms. This Web page contains a short explanation of cookies, how they work, and references for further reading.

H7 FREQUENTLY ASKED QUESTIONS

Webopedia. (No date) *FAQ* (www.webopedia.com/TERM/F/FAQ.html).

    Webopedia is an online reference for technical terms. This Web page contains a short explanation of FAQs, as well as references for further reading.

H8 CONTEXT-SENSITIVE HELP

Greyling, T. (1998, May) Fear and loathing of the Help menu: A usability test of online help. *Technical Communication Online,* 45(2): 168–179 (http://tc.eserver.org/10347.html).

    This article reports results of a usability test on an online help system. None of the findings are especially surprising: People avoid using online help systems, read any help information hastily, leave quickly if they don't think they're on the right help page, and ignore broad overviews. However, the testers did find that, for their specific application, people liked online help that was context specific and relevant to the current task. They also found that people liked help that was obvious and just one mouse click away.

Web Design Practices (www.webdesignpractices.com).

See the description under Chapter 2 (Making the Most of Web Design Patterns).

H10 CLEAR FORMS

Crescimanno, B. (2005, December 19) *Sensible Forms: A Form Usability Checklist* (www.alistapart.com/articles/sensibleforms).

This article provides a nice analysis of how to design useful and usable forms for the Web. Topics include choosing the right type of field, having enough room for people to see what they're typing, marking mandatory fields, and providing informative error messages.

Pattern Group I: Designing Effective Page Layouts

I1 GRID LAYOUT

Bernard, M. (2002) Examining user expectations for the location of common e-commerce web objects. *Usability News* 4(1) (http://psychology.wichita.edu/surl/usabilitynews/41/web_object-ecom.htm).

See the description under Chapter 2 (Making the Most of Web Design Patterns).

Brinck, T., D. Gergle, and S. Wood. (2002) *Usability for the Web: Designing Web Sites That Work.* San Francisco: Kaufmann.

See the description under Chapter 5 (Processes for Developing Customer-Centered Sites).

Krug, S. (2006) *Don't Make Me Think!: A Common Sense Approach to Web Usability* (2nd ed.). Indianapolis, IN: Que.

The title identifies the main point of this fun book, which says that customers usually know what they want to do, but most Web pages force them to think too much about how to do it. Krug describes a host of tips, techniques, and examples for getting this done.

Marcus, A. (1992) *Graphic Design for Electronic Documents and User Interfaces.* Reading, MA: Addison-Wesley.

This book takes a broad look at visual design. It discusses issues like layout, typography, symbols, icons, color, charts, diagrams, and maps.

Marcus, A., and Aaron Marcus and Associates. (1994) Principles of effective visual communication for graphical user interface design. In *HCI-2000,* R. Baecker, B. Buxton, J. Grudin, and S. Greenberg. (Eds.), pp. 425–441. Palo Alto, CA: Kaufmann.

This chapter looks at techniques for achieving effective visual communication, providing an overview of organization, consistency, screen layout, and color use for graphical user interfaces.

Mullet, K., and D. Sano. (1994) *Designing Visual Interfaces: Communication Oriented Techniques.* Englewood Cliffs, NJ: Prentice Hall.

See the description under Chapter 4 (Involving Customers with Iterative Design).

12 *ABOVE THE FOLD*

Bernard, M. (2002) Examining user expectations for the location of common e-commerce web objects. *Usability News* 4(1) (http://psychology.wichita.edu/surl/usabilitynews/41/web_object-ecom.htm).

> See the description under Chapter 2 (Making the Most of Web Design Patterns).

Krug, S. (2006) *Don't Make Me Think!: A Common Sense Approach to Web Usability* (2nd Ed.). Indianapolis, IN: Que.

> See the description under GRID LAYOUT (I1).

Marcus, A. (1992) *Graphic Design for Electronic Documents and User Interfaces.* Reading, MA: Addison-Wesley.

> See the description under GRID LAYOUT (I1).

Marcus, A., and Aaron Marcus and Associates. (1994) Principles of effective visual communication for graphical user interface design. In *HCI-2000,* R. Baecker, B. Buxton, J. Grudin, and S. Greenberg. (Eds.), pp. 425–441. Palo Alto, CA: Kaufmann.

> See the description under GRID LAYOUT (I1).

Mullet, K., and D. Sano. (1994) *Designing Visual Interfaces: Communication Oriented Techniques.* Englewood Cliffs, NJ: Prentice Hall/SunSoft Press.

> See the description under GRID LAYOUT (I1).

Spool, J., T. Scanlon, W. Schroeder, C. Snyder, and T. DeAngelo. (1998) *Web Site Usability.* San Francisco: Kaufmann.

> This book discusses the results of many informal usability tests conducted by the authors. Although the sites that the study evaluated have since evolved, there are still many interesting tidbits here, including link labeling, embedded links, searching, page layout, and keeping important content above the fold.

13 *CLEAR FIRST READS*

See the references listed under GRID LAYOUT (I1).

14 *EXPANDING SCREEN WIDTH*

CSS Tinderbox (www.dbfnetwork.info/tinderbox/index.html).

> See the description under PAGE TEMPLATES (D1).

Niederst, J. (1999) *Web Design in a Nutshell: A Desktop Quick Reference.* Beijing, China: O'Reilly.

> This book discusses many of the low-level implementation issues that you will face in the Production and Implementation phases of Web site development. It covers the different versions of HTML, browser compatibility, forms, and frames.

Open Source Web Design (www.oswd.org).

> See the description under PAGE TEMPLATES (D1).

UW E-Business Consortium Best Practice Reports: B2C Website Design Standard Practices and Benchmarks (www.uwebc.org/opinionpapers/ue).

> See the description under Chapter 2 (Making the Most of Web Design Patterns).

Weijers, J. (No date) *WebThings* (www.weijers.net/guide).

> This Web site discusses all the basics and some advanced topics of HTML. With a nice clean design, it also provides many useful examples.

I5 *FIXED SCREEN WIDTH*

Code-Sucks.com. *CSS Layouts* (www.code-sucks.com/css%20layouts).
 See the description under PAGE TEMPLATES (D1).

CSS Tinderbox (www.dbfnetwork.info/tinderbox/index.html).
 See the description under PAGE TEMPLATES (D1).

Niederst, J. (1999) *Web Design in a Nutshell: A Desktop Quick Reference.* Beijing,
China: O'Reilly.
 See the description under EXPANDING SCREEN WIDTH (I4).

Open Source Web Design (www.oswd.org).
 See the description under PAGE TEMPLATES (D1).

UW E-Business Consortium Best Practice Reports: B2C Website Design Standard
Practices and Benchmarks (www.uwebc.org/opinionpapers/ue).
 See the description under Chapter 2 (Making the Most of Web Design Patterns).

Weijers, J. (No date) *WebThings* (www.weijers.net/guide).
 See the description under EXPANDING SCREEN WIDTH (I4).

I6 *CONSISTENT SIDEBARS OF RELATED CONTENT*

Fogg, B., J. Marshall, O. Laraki, A. Osipovich, C. Varma, N. Fang, J. Paul,
A. Rangnekar, J. Shon, P. Swani, and M. Treinen. (2001, March 31–April 5) What
makes web sites credible? A report on a large quantitative study. CHI 2001, ACM
Conference on Human Factors in Computing Systems, *CHI Letters,* 3(1): 61–68
(www.webcredibility.org/studies/p61-fogg.pdf).
 See the description under ABOUT US (E5).

Pattern Group J: Making Site Search Fast and Relevant

J1 *SEARCH ACTION MODULE*

Bernard, M. (2001) Developing schemas for the location of common web objects.
Usability News, 3(1) (http://psychology.wichita.edu/surl/usabilitynews/3W/
web_object.htm).
 This study asked 304 participants how they expected to see common Web
 objects on a page, such as the <u>Home</u> link, internal links, external links, the
 search engine, and advertisements. The participants expected the <u>Home</u> link to
 be at the top left and at the center bottom of a Web page, internal links to run
 along the left side, external links to run on the bottom left and on the right-
 hand side, search engines to be at the top right or near the top center, and
 advertisements to be at the top.

English, J., M. Hearst, R. Sinha, K. Swearingen, and K. Yee. (2002) *Flexible Search
and Navigation Using Faceted Metadata* (http://bailando.sims.berkeley.edu/
papers/flamenco02.pdf).
 This paper describes Flamenco, an advanced search and navigation system that
 lets nonexperts explore large information spaces. The key idea is to provide
 a flexible interface that lets people search and navigate through metadata
 (additional data describing the actual content—for example, the author, date,
 and publisher of a news article).

Nielsen, J. (1999) *Designing Web Usability: The Practice of Simplicity.* Indianapolis, IN: New Riders.

See the description under ENABLING INTRANETS (A11).

UW E-Business Consortium Best Practice Reports: B2C Website Design Standard Practices and Benchmarks (www.uwebc.org/opinionpapers/ue).

See the description under Chapter 2 (Making the Most of Web Design Patterns).

Web Design Practices (www.webdesignpractices.com).

See the description under Chapter 2 (Making the Most of Web Design Patterns).

Webopedia. (No date) *Search Engine* (www.webopedia.com/TERM/s/ search_engine.html).

See the description under WRITING FOR SEARCH ENGINES (D6).

J2 STRAIGHTFORWARD SEARCH FORMS

Baeza-Yates, R., and B. Ribeiro-Neto. (1999) *Modern Information Retrieval.* Reading, MA: Addison-Wesley.

This book presents extremely technical details about the inner workings of modern information retrieval engines, of which search engines are one type. It includes a great deal of ongoing research in the field. And it looks at many interface techniques related to information retrieval.

Cunningham, J. P., J. Cantor, S. H. Pearsall, and K. H. Richardson. (2001) Industry briefs: AT&T. *Interactions: New Visions of Human Computer Interaction,* 8(2): 27–31.

See the description under WRITING FOR SEARCH ENGINES (D6).

English, J., M. Hearst, R. Sinha, K. Swearingen, and K. Yee. (2002) *Flexible Search and Navigation Using Faceted Metadata* (http://bailando.sims.berkeley.edu/ papers/flamenco02.pdf).

See the description under SEARCH ACTION MODULE (J1).

J3 ORGANIZED SEARCH RESULTS

Cunningham, J. P., J. Cantor, S. H. Pearsall, and K. H. Richardson. (2001) Industry briefs: AT&T. *Interactions: New Visions of Human Computer Interaction,* 8(2): 27–31.

See the description under WRITING FOR SEARCH ENGINES (D6).

English, J., M. Hearst, R. Sinha, K. Swearingen, and K. Yee. (2002) *Flexible Search and Navigation Using Faceted Metadata* (http://bailando.sims.berkeley.edu/ papers/flamenco02.pdf).

See the description under SEARCH ACTION MODULE (J1).

Schwartz, M. (2000, June 12) Sharper Staples, *Computerworld* (www. computerworld.com/printthis/2000/0,4814,45787,00.html).

See the description under PROCESS FUNNEL (H1).

Tedeschi, B. (2001, December 10) Striving to top the search lists. *New York Times E-Commerce Report* (www.nytimes.com/2001/12/10/technology/ebusiness/ 10ECOM.html).

See the description under WRITING FOR SEARCH ENGINES (D6).

Pattern Group K: Making Navigation Easy

K2 NAVIGATION BAR

Bernard, M. (2001) Developing schemas for the location of common web objects. *Usability News,* 3(1) (http://psychology.wichita.edu/surl/usabilitynews/ 3W/web_object.htm).

See the description under SEARCH ACTION MODULE (J1).

Krug, S. (2006) *Don't Make Me Think!: A Common Sense Approach to Web Usability* (2nd Ed.). Indianapolis, IN: Que.

See the description under GRID LAYOUT (I1).

UW E-Business Consortium Best Practice Reports: B2C Website Design Standard Practices and Benchmarks (www.uwebc.org/opinionpapers/ue).

See the description under Chapter 2 (Making the Most of Web Design Patterns).

K3 TAB ROWS

Krug, S. (2006) *Don't Make Me Think!: A Common Sense Approach to Web Usability* (2nd Ed.). Indianapolis, IN: Que.

See the description under GRID LAYOUT (I1).

K4 ACTION BUTTONS

Card, S. K., T. P. Moran, and A. Newell. (1983) *The Psychology of Human–Computer Interaction.* Hillsdale, NJ: Erlbaum.

This is the classic book on *human–computer interaction* research, the one that coined the term. It delves deeply into low-level psychological and cognitive research on human performance, including physical motion, memory, and decision making. Of interest here are the sections on evaluating a design using Fitts's Law.

Krug, S. (2006) *Don't Make Me Think!: A Common Sense Approach to Web Usability* (2nd Ed.). Indianapolis, IN: Que.

See the description under GRID LAYOUT (I1).

Raskin, J. (2000) *The Humane Interface.* Boston: Addison-Wesley.

This book looks at user interface development from a fairly low-level, psychological and cognitive science standpoint. It has a short section about Fitts's Law and how it applies to user interfaces.

K5 HIGH-VISIBILITY ACTION BUTTONS

Krug, S. (2006) *Don't Make Me Think!: A Common Sense Approach to Web Usability* (2nd Ed.). Indianapolis, IN: Que.

See the description under GRID LAYOUT (I1).

K7 *EMBEDDED LINKS*

Bernard, M., S. Hull, and D. Drake. (2001). Where should you put the links? A comparison of four locations. *Usability News,* 3(2) (http://psychology.wichita.edu/surl/usabilitynews/3S/links.htm).

> This study compared the placement of links and its effect on performance. Links were embedded in the document, placed at the bottom or top left of the page, or provided in a sidebar right next to their associated content. The study showed no significant differences in the four arrangements in terms of search accuracy, time, or efficiency. However, the 20 participants preferred embedded links because they felt that these links made the test document easier to navigate, and because they made it easier to search for specific information.

Spool, J., T. Scanlon, W. Schroeder, C. Snyder, and T. DeAngelo. (1998) *Web Site Usability.* San Francisco: Kaufmann.

> See the description under ABOVE THE FOLD (I2).

K8 *EXTERNAL LINKS*

Bernard, M. (2001) Developing schemas for the location of common web objects. *Usability News,* 3(1) (http://psychology.wichita.edu/surl/usabilitynews/3W/web_object.htm).

> See the description under SEARCH ACTION MODULE (J1).

Bernard, M., S. Hull, and D. Drake. (2001). Where should you put the links? A comparison of four locations. *Usability News,* 3(2) (http://psychology.wichita.edu/surl/usabilitynews/3S/links.htm).

> See the description under EMBEDDED LINKS (K7).

Fogg, B., J. Marshall, O. Laraki, A. Osipovich, C. Varma, N. Fang, J. Paul, A. Rangnekar, J. Shon, P. Swani, and M. Treinen. (2001, March 31–April 5) What makes web sites credible? A report on a large quantitative study. CHI 2001, ACM Conference on Human Factors in Computing Systems, *CHI Letters,* 3(1): 61–68 (www.webcredibility.org/studies/p61-fogg.pdf).

> See the description under ABOUT US (E5).

K9 *DESCRIPTIVE, LONGER LINK NAMES*

Nielsen, J. (1999) *Designing Web Usability: The Practice of Simplicity.* Indianapolis, IN: New Riders.

> See the description under ENABLING INTRANETS (A11).

Spool, J., T. Scanlon, W. Schroeder, C. Snyder, and T. DeAngelo. (1998) *Web Site Usability.* San Francisco: Kaufmann.

> See the description under ABOVE THE FOLD (I2).

K10 *OBVIOUS LINKS*

Hansell, S. (2000, December 11) In search for online success, "easy does it" is good theme. *New York Times E-Commerce Report* (www.nytimes.com/2000/12/11/technology/11SIMP.html).

> See the description under PERSONALIZED CONTENT (D4).

Nielsen, J. (1999) *Designing Web Usability: The Practice of Simplicity*. Indianapolis, IN: New Riders.

See the description under ENABLING INTRANETS (A11).

Web Design Practices (www.webdesignpractices.com).

See the description under Chapter 2 (Making the Most of Web Design Patterns).

K11 FAMILIAR LANGUAGE

See the references listed under MULTIPLE WAYS TO NAVIGATE (B1).

K12 PREVENTING ERRORS

Linderman, M., and Fried, J. (2004) *Defensive Design for the Web: How to Improve Error Messages, Help, Forms, and Other Crisis Points*. Indianapolis, IN: New Riders.

This book features many screen shots of Web error messages, both good and bad. It also has some tips on preventing errors.

K13 MEANINGFUL ERROR MESSAGES

Linderman, M., and Fried, J. (2004) *Defensive Design for the Web: How to Improve Error Messages, Help, Forms, and Other Crisis Points*. Indianapolis, IN: New Riders.

See the description under PREVENTING ERRORS (K12).

K14 PAGE NOT FOUND

404 Research Lab (www.plinko.net/404).

In addition to containing several humorous examples and jokes about the dreaded "Page not found" error, this Web site has some practical tips for helping customers if they do encounter "Page not found" errors.

Pattern Group L: Speeding Up Your Site

L1 LOW NUMBER OF FILES

Niederst, J. (1999) *Web Design in a Nutshell: A Desktop Quick Reference*. Beijing, China: O'Reilly.

See the description under EXPANDING SCREEN WIDTH (I4).

Rhodes, J. (2001, July 25) *The Usability of Usability: An Interview with Jared Spool* (www.webword.com/interviews/spool2.html).

This interview presents an interesting counterpoint to the argument for speedy download times. Jared Spool, a noted usability consultant, claims his research shows that download speed has no correlation with the usability of a site. In fact, his data says that it is the customer's ability to complete tasks that best correlates with the perception of the site's speed.

L2 FAST-LOADING IMAGES

CNET Builder.com. (No date) *Graphics* (http://builder.com.com/1200-31-5084829.html).

This Web page gives tips and tricks for creating and publishing images on the Web.

Marcus, A. (1992) *Graphic Design for Electronic Documents and User Interfaces.* Reading, MA: Addison-Wesley.

See the description under GRID LAYOUT (I1).

Marcus, A., and Aaron Marcus and Associates. (1994) Principles of effective visual communication for graphical user interface design. In *HCI-2000,* R. Baecker, B. Buxton, J. Grudin, and S. Greenberg. (Eds.), pp. 425–441. Palo Alto, CA: Kaufmann.

See the description under GRID LAYOUT (I1).

Niederst, J. (1999) *Web Design in a Nutshell: A Desktop Quick Reference.* Beijing, China: O'Reilly.

See the description under EXPANDING SCREEN WIDTH (I4).

Spalter, A. (1999) *The Computer in the Visual Arts.* Reading, MA: Addison-Wesley. This book looks at many of the technology-related issues involved in creating visual images, including terminology, input devices, displays, projectors, printing, color spaces, three-dimensional worlds, and a little bit about the Web. It is an excellent book for visual designers wanting to learn more about technology, or for technologists wanting to learn more about the visual arts.

L3 SEPARATE TABLES

Niederst, J. (1999) *Web Design in a Nutshell: A Desktop Quick Reference.* Beijing, China: O'Reilly.

See the description under EXPANDING SCREEN WIDTH (I4).

Weijers, J. (No date) *WebThings* (www.weijers.net/guide).

See the description under EXPANDING SCREEN WIDTH (I4).

L4 HTML POWER

Niederst, J. (1999) *Web Design in a Nutshell: A Desktop Quick Reference.* Beijing, China: O'Reilly.

See the description under EXPANDING SCREEN WIDTH (I4).

Weijers, J. (No date) *WebThings* (www.weijers.net/guide).

See the description under EXPANDING SCREEN WIDTH (I4).

L5 REUSABLE IMAGES

Niederst, J. (1999) *Web Design in a Nutshell: A Desktop Quick Reference.* Beijing, China: O'Reilly.

See the description under EXPANDING SCREEN WIDTH (I4).

Pattern Group M: The Mobile Web

M1 MOBILE SCREEN SIZING

McLaughlin, B. (2005, November 22) *Retrofit Your Web Pages for Wireless Compatibility: Create More Flexible Web Pages with XHTML and CSS* (www-128.ibm.com/developerworks/wireless/library/wi-css/?ca=dgr-lnxw01WirelessPages).

This Web resource provides some concrete examples of how to use XHTML and style sheets to create Web pages that can be more easily viewed by mobile devices.

Smith, M. (2005) *You're a Fool to Design Only for the Un-mobile Web* (www.onlamp. com/pub/wlg/8817).

> This Web page provides some simple steps you can take to make your Web pages more friendly for mobile users, including (1) adding "jump" links so that mobile users can jump to each of the major parts of the page, (2) adjusting the physical layout of your Web page so that the most important parts are at the top and will be loaded first, (3) testing your Web page first with desktop computers, and (4) splitting up your Web pages into smaller, more digestible chunks.

W3C. (2002) CSS Mobile Profile 1.0 (www.w3.org/TR/css-mobile).

> CSS Mobile is a recommended standard that provides a way for site designers to design once for desktops and CSS-based Mobile Web devices.

W3C. (2005) WICD Mobile 1.0 (www.w3.org/TR/WICDMobile).

> This is a working draft of a standard that provides a way for site designers to design a site once and then publish to desktops, XHTML (WAP), and other Mobile Web devices using CSS and SVG.

M2 MOBILE INPUT CONTROLS

See the references listed under MOBILE SCREEN SIZING (M1).

M3 LOCATION-BASED SERVICES

Pfeiffer, E. W. (2003, September) WhereWare. *Technology Review* (www.cs.cmu.edu/ %7Ejasonh/courses/ubicomp-f2004/papers/05-whereware.pdf).

> This article gives a nice overview of some ways of determining one's location, as well as some emerging applications and players in this field.

Part III: Appendixes

Gomoll, K. (1990) Some techniques for observing users. In *The Art of Human–Computer Interface Design*, B. Laurel (Ed.), pp. 85–90. Reading, MA: Addison-Wesley.

> Some of the material in Appendix A (Running Usability Evaluations) of the book you have in hand is based on this chapter's list of ten things to do when running a usability study.

Gonick, L., and W. Smith. (1993) *The Cartoon Guide to Statistics.* New York: HarperPerennial.

> This book is a good introduction to basic statistical terms, as well as procedures, explaining what they're good for and how to do them. It is presented as a large comic book, with fun illustrations to hold the reader's interest.

McQuarrie, E. (1996) *The Market Research Toolbox: A Concise Guide for Beginners.* Thousand Oaks, CA: Sage.

> This is a great book for people new to market research, discussing the various objectives, techniques for discovering customer needs, and expected payoffs of those techniques. The book looks into secondary research, customer visits, focus groups, surveys, choice modeling, and experimentation; and it details costs, uses, tips, and trade-offs of each.

Rettig, M. (1994) Prototyping for tiny fingers. *Communications of the ACM*, 37(4): 21–27 (www.acm.org/pubs/citations/journals/cacm/1994-37-4/p21-rettig).

See the description under Chapter 4 (Involving Customers with Iterative Design).

Rubin, J. (1994) *Handbook of Usability Testing: How to Plan, Design, and Conduct Effective Tests*. New York: Wiley.

This book is a good source that provides step-by-step guidelines on preparing and running usability tests.

Further Reading

A List Apart (http://alistapart.com).

A List Apart is a Web magazine for Web designers. It has a rich variety of topics, including such things as how to create a good navigation scheme, how to create good code, and how to publish effective content.

CNET Builder.com (http://builder.cnet.com).

This fairly comprehensive Web site has a host of resources on building Web sites, including graphics, programming, e-commerce, business strategy, and usability.

DUB, University of Washington (http://dub.washington.edu).

DUB is the research group jointly led by James Landay, one of the authors of the book you have in hand. DUB's research thrusts include tools for rapidly prototyping Web and speech user interfaces, novel uses of pen-based interfaces, and mobile computing. Research from DUB has been published in many premier conferences on human–computer interaction and on design.

HCI Bibliography: Human–Computer Interaction Resources (www.hcibib.org).

This is a great starting point that links to many, many resources on the Web.

Human-Computer Interaction Institute (HCII) (www.hcii.cs.cmu.edu).

The HCII is the premier place for doing research in human–computer interaction, of which Jason Hong, one of the authors of the book you have in hand, is a member. The HCII combines technology, design, and behavioral psychology in its research and educational programs.

Human–Computer Interaction Resource Network (www.hcirn.com).

The goal of the Human–Computer Interaction Resource Network is to advance human–computer interaction practices and resources.

IBM. (No date) *Web Design Guidelines* (www.ibm.com/ibm/easy/eou_ext.nsf/publish/572).

IBM's Web design guide provides good tips on the Web design process.

Usable Web (www.usableweb.com).

Usable Web is another collection of links about Web site design, including information architecture and human factors. The site also provides short descriptions of links and a search engine that finds things quickly.

Usability.gov (www.usability.gov).

The U.S. Department of Health and Human Services hosts Usability.gov, an online resource for "developing usable & useful Web sites." Although its primary mission is to improve the communication of cancer research, you will also find guidelines, case studies, and statistics to help guide the development process.

Professional Groups

ACM SIGCHI (Special Interest Group on Computer–Human Interaction)
(www.acm.org/sigchi).

> The Special Interest Group on Computer–Human Interaction (SIGCHI) holds an annual conference called CHI, the premier forum for research on people and computer systems. SIGCHI's Web site highlights issues such as accessibility, education, and intercultural issues. Finally, SIGCHI maintains a useful mailing list called CHI-WEB that discusses ongoing issues of designing for the Web, at http://sigchi.org/web.

American Institute of Graphic Arts (www.aiga.org).

> The American Institute of Graphic Arts is a national organization promoting excellence in graphic design. Its site includes links to membership information, events, publications, and local chapters.

American Society for Information Science and Technology (ASIS&T)
(www.asis.org).

> The American Society for Information Science and Technology is a national organization that is "leading the search for new and better theories, techniques, and technologies to improve access to information." The society also holds an annual conference called IA Summit (www.iasummit.org).

Human Factors and Ergonomics Society (www.hfes.org).

> The Human Factors and Ergonomics Society is an international organization with many special interest groups that are relevant to interface design and evaluation. The society also holds an annual conference.

Usability Professionals' Association (www.upassoc.org).

> The Usability Professionals' Association (UPA) promotes usability concepts and techniques. In contrast to ACM SIGCHI, the UPA is targeted more at practitioners than at researchers. The UPA holds an annual conference.

CREDITS

Figure G1.1
© 2006 800-Flowers. Reprinted by permission.

Figures H13.2, K16.5, L6.1, L6.2
© Amazon.com, Inc. All rights reserved.

Figure F3.5
© 2000 Amazon.com, Inc. All rights reserved.

Figures 2.5, D1.3, E2.4, E6.4, F1.3, F6.3, F9.2, F9.3, F9.4, F9.5, G4.3, G4.4, G5.3, G5.4, G7.3, K3.3, K4.3. © 2001 Amazon.com, Inc. All rights reserved.

Figure J3.4
© 2001 Amazon.com, Inc. All rights reserved. *Crossing the Quality Chasm,* National Academy Press, 2001.

Figures E6.5, H4.3, H4.4, J3.2
© 2002 Amazon.com, Inc. All rights reserved.

Figures A1.2, B1.1, F1.1, F3.1, F3.2, F5.2, F7.1, F8.3, G2.5, G2.6, G3.2, G4.1, G6.3, J1.1, K3.5
© 2006 Amazon.com, Inc. All rights reserved.

Figure H13.1
© American Airlines. Reprinted by permission.

Figure H13.3
© American Honda Motor Co. Reprinted by permission.

Figure H1.1
© 2006 American Honda Motor Co. Reprinted by permission.

Figure G1.4
© 2006 Ann Taylor. Reprinted by permission.

Figures H13.4, K17.3
© Apple Computer, Inc. Reprinted by permission.

Figure A6.1
Reprinted by permission of the Association of Online Cancer Resources, Inc.

Figure M3.6
Reproduced by permission of AT&T Corporation.

Figure L3.2
BabyCenter, LLC. © 1997–2002.

Figure D1.4
© 2006 Banana Republic. Reprinted by permission.

Figure J1.2
© 2002 Barnes & Noble, Inc. Reprinted by permission.

Figures F3.3, G1.3
© 2006 Barnes & Noble, Inc. Reprinted by permission.

Figures A3.1, I6.1
© Beliefnet, Inc. Reprinted by permission.

Figure E2.1
© 2006 Big Brothers Big Sisters of America. Reprinted by permission.

Figure B6.1
Reprinted from www.bmrc.berkeley.edu.

Figure B7.1
© 2006 BPI Communications, Inc. Used with permission.

Figure G1.2
© 2006 Brooks Brothers. Reprinted by permission.

Figure F9.1
© 2006 Buy.com, Inc. Reprinted by permission.

Figure A8.2
© 2001 Carnegie Mellon University. All rights reserved.

Figure M3.7
© CDA International Ltd. All rights reserved.

Figure G2.3
© 2006 CD Universe. Reprinted by permission.

Figure H7.3
Courtesy of Lanny Chambers, author/designer.

Figure D3.4
© The Children's Place. All rights reserved.

Figure K10.3
The Chopping Block, Inc. Web designer: Thomas Romer; Illustration: Thomas Romer, Jaylo (www.tmbg.com).

935

Figure C2.3
The CIENA logo and the CIENA.com Web site have been reprinted with permission from CIENA Corporation. CIENA is a trademark or registered trademark of CIENA Corporation in the United States and other countries and is being used with the permission of CIENA Corporation.

Figure H12.4
© Cisco Systems, Inc. All rights reserved.

Figure K12.6
© Citigroup, Inc. Reprinted by permission.

Figure D7.3
© CNET Networks, Inc. All rights reserved.

Figures I5.1, K9.1, K10.2
Used with permission from CNET Networks, Inc. Copyright © 2001. All rights reserved.

Figure D7.1
Used with permission from CNET Networks, Inc. Copyright © 2006. All rights reserved.

Figure K16.2
© CollectableDiecast. All rights reserved.

Figures C2.1, J2.1, K2.1
Epicurious.com © 2006 CondeNet. All rights reserved. Reprinted by permission.

Figure H5.1
© Cookie Central. All rights reserved.

Figure F2.4
Courtesy of Cooking.com.

Figures A2.1, A2.3, D7.2, I6.2
The News Story/Interview supplied hereunder is protected by the copyright laws of the United States and other countries.

Figure M1.5
The News Story/Interview supplied hereunder is protected by the copyright laws of the United States and other countries.

Figures A3.2, D5.1, E5.2, E8.4, L4.1
© craigslist 2006, all rights reserved.

Figure K4.1
© Crate and Barrel. Reprinted by permission.

Figures H8.1, K13.1
Reprinted by permission of Dell Computer Corporation.

Figure A12.3
© digg. All rights reserved.

Figures E4.2(b), H4.5
© Eastman Kodak Company. Reprinted by permission.

Figures 2.4, A1.3, E6.1, E9.1, E9.2, F1.2, F4.1, F6.1, G4.5, H1.2, H2.2, H2.4
These materials have been reproduced with the permission of eBay, Inc. Copyright © eBay, Inc. All rights reserved.

Figure K6.1
© 2006 Eddie Bauer, Inc. All rights reserved. Eddiebauer.com © is a registered trademark of Eddie Bauer, Inc.

Figure K11.1
Screen shot courtesy of Edmunds.com, Inc.

Figures D6.1, K16.3
© E-Loan, Inc. All rights reserved.

Figure I1.1
Reprinted from www.epa.gov, February 13, 2002.

Figure A9.2
© 2006 ESPN. Reprinted by permission.

Figure L6.4
© Expedia, Inc. All rights reserved.

Figure E4.3
© 2001 Exploratorium (www.exploratorium.edu).

Figure E3.1
Reprinted from www.export.gov/safeharbor, September 26, 2001.

Figure A6.3
© FCC-GC. Reprinted by permission.

Figure B3.2
© 2006 Findlaw, a Thomson business.

Figure A10.2
First Internet Bank of Indiana (www.firstib.com) is the first state-chartered, FDIC-insured institution to operate solely via the Internet. Services include checking and savings accounts, CDs, credit cards, and personal loans. First IB also offers online bill payment, real-time transfers between accounts, and the ability to display checking, savings, and loan information on a single screen.

Figure E8.1
© Friendster, Inc. All rights reserved.

Figures H3.3, I2.1
© Fry's Electronics, Inc. All rights reserved. Fry's Electronics and Outpost.com are registered trademarks of Fry's Electronics, Inc.

Figure M1.4
Reprinted by permission of Fuji-Xerox Palo Alto Laboratories (FXPAL).

Figures F5.3, H6.2
© Gap, Inc. Reprinted by permission.

Figure M1.2
Reprinted by permission of Geneva Lab.

Figures L2.1, M3.9
Reprinted with permission from Geo-caching.com.

Figure M3.3
Reprinted by permission of the Georgia Institute of Technology.

Figure F3.4
© 2006 Godiva Chocolatier, Inc. All rights reserved.

Figures A10.4, E5.1, H9.5, H9.6, H11.3, J3.5, K15.3, K15.4, K17.2, L6.7, M1.1, M1.8, M2.1
© Google. Reprinted by permission.

Figure D9.4
Google, Inc. Harry Potter, characters, names and all related indicia are trademarks of Warner Bros. © 2001.

Figure A3.3
Greenpeace.

Figures A7.2, A12.1, M1.2
Copyright © 2006 Hewlett-Packard Company, L.P. Reproduced with permission.

Figures A7.1, J3.3
Courtesy of IBM Corporation.

Figure I5.2
© IFILM Corp. All rights reserved.

Figure E2.2
© iVillage, Inc. All rights reserved.

Figure I4.1
© iWon, Inc. 1999–2001. All rights reserved.

Figures H11.1, L6.6
© Kayak.com. Reprinted by permission.

Figure K8.1
© Keynote Systems, Inc. All rights reserved.

Figure A5.3
© 2006 Kiwanis International. All rights reserved.

Figures B2.2, G2.1
© The Knot Inc. All rights reserved.

Figures H4.5, K3.1
The Knot (www.theknot.com. AOL keyword: weddings.).

Figures D4.6, G3.4
© Lands' End, Inc. Used with permission.

Figure E5.3
LEGO and the LEGO logo are trademarks of LEGO Group. © 2001 The LEGO Group. This page from the LEGO® website is used here with permission. The LEGO Group does not sponsor or endorse *The Design of Sites*.

Figure E5.4
Reprinted with the permission of LexisNexis. LexisNexis and the Knowledge Burst logo are registered trademarks of Reed Elsevier Properties, Inc., used with the permission of LexisNexis.

Figure L4.2
Courtesy of James Lin.

Figures E8.3, H4.1, K3.2
© 2006 LinkedIn Corporation. All rights reserved.

Figures A1.1, E6.6
Reprinted by permission of L.L.Bean, Inc.

Figure L5.2
Lowestfare.com & Globe Design is a trademark of Lowestfare.com, LLC, which owns all copyright in the Flight Page. Use of this material is pursuant to a license from Lowestfare.com and is strictly limited under the trademark and copyright laws of the United States.

Figure K10.1
Reprinted by permission of Suzanne Rich and Todd Lehman, founders of LUGNET, www.lugnet.com.

Figure B7.4
© 2006 Lycos, Inc. Lycos® is a registered trademark of Lycos, Inc. All rights reserved.

Figures AE.1, AE.4
Reprinted by permission of MarketTools, Inc.

Figures A2.2, D7.4
Copyright © 2006 MarketWatch.com, Inc.

Figure B8.1
© 2002 Martha Stewart Living Omnimedia, Inc. All rights reserved.

Figures D8.1, G6.1
© 2002 Martha Stewart Living Omnimedia, Inc. All rights reserved. Photographer: Simon Watson.

Figure A8.3
Reprinted with permission of The Math Forum © Drexel, an online community for mathematics education <http://mathforum.org/>. © 2006 The Math Forum @ Drexel.

Figure H6.3
Reprinted from businessweek.com, December 12, 2005. © 2005 by The McGraw-Hill Companies, Inc.

Figure A12.5
© MetaFilter Network LLC. Reprinted by permission.

Figures A7.3, A10.3, B9.7, E1.1, H2.1, H8.2, K2.2, K12.1, K14.1
Microsoft screen shots reprinted with permission from Microsoft Corporation.

Figures D2.1, D4.5, H8.3
Courtesy of Monster.com.

Figures D5.2, D5.3, D5.4, D5.6
The Motley Fool, Inc. (www.fool.com).

Figure E9.3
Mountain America Financial Services, LLC. Reprinted by permission.

Figures C1.1, D4.7
Screen shots of MSNBC used by permission from MSNBC. MSNBC is not a sponsor of and does not endorse *The Design of Sites* and/or Addison-Wesley.

Figures D9.1, D9.2, D9.3
Screen shots of MSNBC used by permission from MSNBC. MSNBC is not a sponsor of and does not endorse *The Design of Sites* and/or Addison-Wesley. Harry Potter, characters, names, and all related indicia are trademarks of Warner Bros. © 2001. Harry Potter story courtesy of NewHouse News Service.

Figure L5.1
© 2006 Napster. Reprinted by permission.

Figure J3.4
Reprinted with permission from National Academy Press.

Figure D6.2
Courtesy of the United States' National Cancer Institute.

Figures E4.4, G2.4, G3.3, H6.1
© Netflix, Inc. All rights reserved.

Figure A5.4
© 2006 Network for Good. All rights reserved.

Figure A9.4
The Apartment is a 2000 commission of New Radio and Performing Arts, Inc. for its Turbulence web site with funds from the Jerome Foundation. Artists Marek Walczak and Martin Wattenberg.

Figure K16.1
Copyright © 2005 by The New York Times Co. Reprinted with permission.

Figures D11.1(a), D11.1(b), K15.1
Copyright © 2006 by The New York Times Co. Reprinted with permission.

Figures M3.6, M3.7
Reprinted by permission of Nokia Corporation.

Figures F2.3, F4.2, F5.1, F7.2, F8.2, G7.1, K5.1
© Nordstrom, Inc. Reprinted by permission.

Figure A12.4
Reprinted by permission of Northfield Citizens Online, www.northfield.org.

Figure M3.1
© NTT DoCoMo, Inc. All rights reserved.

Figures D11.5(a) and D11.5(b)
Copyright Opera Software ASA. All rights reserved.

Figure B1.3
© Overstock.com. All rights reserved.

Figure M2.2
© Palm, Inc. All rights reserved.

Figure L3.1
Reprinted by permission of the People for Ethical Treatment of Animals.

Figure D3.3
pewinternet.org, June 16, 2006. Reprinted by permission.

Figure A8.1
Phillips Academy Andover, Mass. Photographer: Lionel Delevinge.

Figure M2.3
© PMC-Sierra, Inc. All rights reserved.

Figures H3.1, H4.5
Courtesy of Pottery Barn Kids, www.potterybarnkids.com.

Figure E4.2(a)
© 2006 Proctor & Gamble. Reprinted by permission.

Figure A9.1
The screen shot taken from http://www.pbs.org contains copyrighted material of the Public Broadcasting Service.

Figure K3.4
Used by permission of Dack Ragus (www.dack.com).

Figure A9.3
Reprinted by permission of Random Art.

Figures G1.3, G2.2
© RedEnvelope, Inc. All rights reserved. The RedEnvelope mark and logo are trademarks of RedEnvelope, Inc.

Figure B8.2
© 1996–2006 REI. Reprinted by permission.

Figure M2.4
© Research in Motion Limited. Reprinted by permission.

Figure F2.1
© 2006 roomandboard.com. Reprinted by permission.

Figure A5.2
Copyright © 2002 Rotary International. All rights reserved. Rotary International is a registered trademark of Rotary International. Used with permission.

Figures A10.1, B4.2, F6.2
© salesforce.com, Inc. All rights reserved.

Figure A3.4
Reprinted with permission of Salon.com.

Figures A4.2, A4.3
Courtesy of City of San Jose, California. www.ci.san-jose.ca.us.

Figure A11.1
SAP and mySAP.com are trademarks of SAPAktiengesellschaft Systems, Applications and Products in Data Processing, Neurottstrasse 16, Walldorf, Germany. The publisher gratefully acknowledges SAP's kind permission to use its trademark in this publication. SAP AG is not the publisher of this book and is not responsible for it under any aspect of press law. Copyright © 2001 SAP AG. All rights reserved.

Figure A12.2
© 2006 SCI FI. All rights reserved.

Figure G7.2
© Copyright 2001 Shutterfly 2001. All rights reserved. (www.shutterfly.com).

Figures C2.2, F1.4, F4.4, F7.3, F8.1, H7.1
© snapfish.com. Reprinted by permission.

Figure M1.6
© Spiegel Online. Reprinted with permission.

Figure F3.6
© Staples, Inc. All rights reserved.

Figure K17.1
© State Farm Insurance. Reprinted by permission.

Figure B5.1
Copyright © 2001 Sun Microsystems, Inc. All rights reserved. Reproduced subject to terms of authorization from Sun Microsystems Inc.

Figure H7.2
Copyright © 2006 Sun Microsystems, Inc. All rights reserved. Reproduced subject to terms of authorization from Sun Microsystems Inc.

Figure A7.4
© 2006 SurveyMonkey.com. All rights reserved.

Figure A4.1
Courtesy of City of Sydney (www.cityofsydney.new.go.au).

Figure H3.4
Steve Brendish: Taxpayers Australia.

Figure AE.2
Reprinted by permission of TechSmith Corporation.

Figure D2.5
© Third Currency, LLC. All rights reserved.

Figure G3.1
© TiVo Inc. All rights reserved.

Figure M3.2
Courtesy of TomTom One.

Figure A1.4
© 2001 Trilegiant Corporation (www.netmarket.com).

Figure A6.2
Tsunami Help Blogspot.com. Reprinted with permission.

Figure E2.5
From www.tveyes.com. Reprinted by permission.

Figures H3.2, H4.2
© The United States Mint. All rights reserved.

Figure B9.1
Copyright © 2000 www.universalusability.org. Permission granted for reprinting.

Figure M3.4
Courtesy of the University of California at San Diego.

Figures E7.3, H4.5
© Virgin Mobile USA, LLC 2002–2005. All rights reserved.

Figure A5.1
Used with permisson of Volunteer Match.

Figures B2.1, G5.1, G5.2, G6.2
Images courtesy of Wal-Mart.com, Inc. Copyright 2000–2002 Wal-Mart.com, Inc. and Wal-Mart Stores, Inc.

Figures B9.2, B9.3
Reprinted by permission of The Weather Channel Enterprises, Inc.

Figure K15.2
© Weblogs, Inc. Reprinted by permission.

Figure K16.4
Reprinted by permission of Wells Fargo.

Figure K7.1
Reprinted by permission of Whatis.com.

Figure M3.8
© Wherify Wireless, Inc. Reprinted by permission.

Figures A7.5, I3.2
Courtesy of Williams-Sonoma, Inc.

Figure H2.3
Reprinted by permission of Wine and Spirits Magazine.

Figure D3.1
© 2006 WN Network. Reprinted by permission.

Figures B3.1, B4.1, B7.2, B7.3, C1.2, D1.1, D2.4, D4.1, D4.4, D5.5, D6.3, D8.2, D10.1, E2.3, E8.2(a), E8.2(b), G4.2, H9.1, H9.2, H9.3, H9.4, H11.2, H12.1, H13.5, K1.1, K2.3, K15.5, L1.1, L6.3, M1.7
Reproduced with permission of Yahoo! Inc. © Yahoo! Inc. Yahoo! and the Yahoo! logo are trademarks of Yahoo! Inc.

Figure J3.1
© 2001 Zagat Survey, LLC. Zagat Survey are registered trademarks of Zagat Survey, LLC, and zagat.com is a service mark of Zagat Survey, LLC.

Figure L6.5
Reprinted by permission of Zazzle.com.

Douglas K. van Duyne, entrepreneur and inventor, is cofounder and a principal of Naviscent, a Web research and design firm, and Dune Design Group, a strategic digital product design firm. He was a cofounder and CEO of NetRaker Corporation, a pioneer in online usability and market research. His teams have developed innovations for companies including MBNA, Yahoo, Intel, Safeway, Agilent, and other Global 2000 companies. With more than twenty years of experience in product design and development at companies like GO Corporation and KidSoft, he has been an innovator in online shopping, e-commerce, and software and multimedia development. He holds a degree in computer science from the University of California at Berkeley. He lives in San Francisco, New York, and London.

James A. Landay is a professor of computer science at the University of Washington. Previously, he served as the director of Intel Research Seattle, which focuses on the emerging world of ubiquitous computing, as the chief technical officer and cofounder of NetRaker, and as an associate professor of computer science at the University of California, Berkeley. He received his B.S. in electrical engineering and computer science from Berkeley in 1990 and his M.S. and Ph.D. from Carnegie Mellon University in 1993 and 1996, respectively. His Ph.D. dissertation was the first to demonstrate the use of sketching in user interface design tools. He has published extensively in the area of human-computer interaction, including articles on user interface design and evaluation tools, Web design, gesture recognition, pen-based user interfaces, mobile computing, ubiquitous computing, and visual languages. He has also consulted for a number of Silicon Valley companies. Landay lives with his wife, Eileen, sons, Andrew and Timothy, and their dog in Seattle.

Jason I. Hong is a professor of computer science in the Human-Computer Interaction Institute at Carnegie Mellon University. Jason received his B.S. from Georgia Tech and his Ph.D. in computer science from University of California at Berkeley. His dissertation work investigated privacy in ubiquitous computing environments. Jason has worked at IBM Research, Fuji Xerox Palo Alto Laboratories, and Xerox Research, where he investigated topics such as collaborative Java applications, paper-based user interfaces, and techniques for viewing and navigating Web pages on cell phones. His current work is in usable privacy and security, anit-phishing, and location-based services. Jason is a voracious informavore, consuming vast quantities of Web, print, television, film, and musical media, with an emphasis on world history, technology, social impact of technology, and facts that are just plain weird. Jason currently lives with his wife in Pennsylvania.

Note: The letter f *denotes a reference to a figure.*

process funnel, 548, 551
product details, 442
reusable images, 780, 781
separate tables, 773, 774
shopping cart, 451
site branding, 370, 371
site map, 756, 757, 758
style sheets, 360, 364
unified browsing hierarchy, 681
Navigation design, 79, 884
Navigation methods, 217, 220f
customers' intentions impulses, 217, 218f
redundant links, accessibility options, 255–256
styles of navigation, 217, 219t
tools, placement of, 218–220
Navigation rules, 273
Navigator. *See* Netscape
Naviscent, usability research, 849
NDA. *See* Nondisclosure agreement (NDA)
Netflix
above the fold product details example, 446f
privacy policy example, 385, 386f
Netmarket
e-commerce example, 125f
example, 124
Netscape, 884
Network effect, 155, 884
Network for Good, site example, 158
Network of help, 155
Networks, value of, 175n
The New York Times, style sheets, 356f, 357f
Newman, Mark, 83
NEWS MOSAICS (A2), 128–135
account management, 564, 565
advanced, 135
basic, 134
blogs, 201, 204, 206
clear forms, 601
educational sites, 174
fast-loading content, 782
headlines blurbs, 297
intranets, 195
nonprofit sites, 154
online shopping, 120
permalinks, 735, 737, 743
personalized content, 303
privacy preferences, 410
subscription only, 135

News site
archives, 133
audience, 131
basic capability, 128
differences from other media, 129–133
form, 129–131
time access issues, 129
Newsletters, 373, 884
Next-step navigation style, 217
Nielsen-Hayden, Teresa, 144
Nielsen, Jakob, ten heuristics, 77
Nolo Press, Web page examples, 25
Nondisclosure agreement (NDA), 884
Nonprofit site, 154–155, 155
advanced, 159–160
basic, 159, 159f
examples, 157f
network of help, 155
specific solutions, 156t
NONPROFITS AS NETWORKS OF HELP (A5), 154–160
blogs, 207
educational sites, 175
message boards, 314
nytimes.com, archives, 133

O

OBVIOUS LINKS (K10), 714–718. *See also* Links, obvious
accessibility options, 253, 255, 257, 261, 265
descriptive, longer link names, 173
embedded links, 701, 704
familiar language, 722
floating windows, 578
high-visibility action buttons, 695
homepages, 276
jump menus, 745, 749, 751
location bread crumbs, 700
navigation bar, 685
preventing phishing scams, 428
progress bar, 629
shopping cart, 450
sign-ins new accounts, 555, 558
site map, 754, 756, 758
style sheets, 360, 364
Ogilvy, David, effective advertising strategy, 278
Online shopping. *See also* E-commerce
PERSONAL E-COMMERCE (A1), 120